Family Tree of GEORGE III

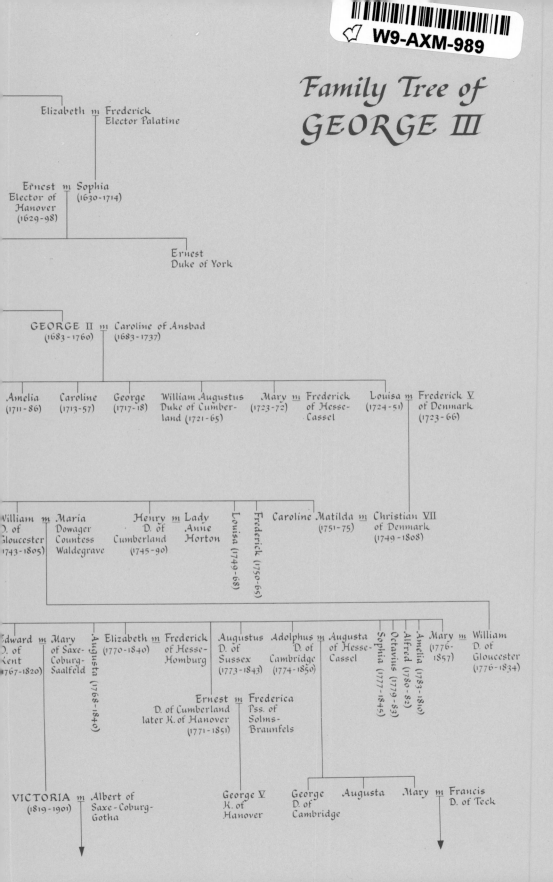

Elizabeth m Frederick
Elector Palatine

Ernest m Sophia
Elector of (1630-1714)
Hanover
(1629-98)

Ernest
Duke of York

GEORGE II m Caroline of Ansbad
(1683-1760)   (1683-1737)

Amelia   Caroline   George   William Augustus   Mary m Frederick   Louisa m Frederick V
(1711-86)   (1713-57)   (1717-18)   Duke of Cumber-   (1723-72) of Hesse-   (1724-51) of Denmark
                                            land (1721-65)   Cassel   (1723-66)

William m Maria   Henry m Lady   Louisa (1749-68)   Frederick (1750-65)   Caroline Matilda m Christian VII
D. of   Dowager   D. of Anne   (1751-75)   of Denmark
Gloucester Countess   Cumberland Horton   (1749-1808)
(1743-1805) Waldegrave (1745-90)

Edward m Mary   Augusta (1768-1840)   Elizabeth m Frederick   Augustus   Adolphus m Augusta   Sophia (1777-1845)   Octavius (1779-83)   Alfred (1780-82)   Amelia (1783-1810)   Mary m William
D. of   of Saxe-   (1770-1840) of Hesse- D. of   D. of   of Hesse-   (1776- D. of
Kent   Coburg-   Homburg   Sussex   Cambridge Cassel   1857)   Gloucester
(1767-1820) Saalfeld   (1773-1843) (1774-1850)   (1776-1834)

Ernest m Frederica
D. of Cumberland Pss. of
later K. of Hanover Solms-
(1771-1851)   Braunfels

VICTORIA m Albert of   George V   George   Augusta   Mary m Francis
(1819-1901) Saxe-Coburg-   K. of   D. of   D. of Teck
           Gotha   Hanover   Cambridge

GEORGE THE THIRD

GEORGE THE THIRD

STANLEY AYLING

ALFRED·A·KNOPF

NEW YORK

1972

THIS IS A BORZOI BOOK
PUBLISHED BY ALFRED A. KNOPF, INC.

Copyright © 1972 by Stanley Ayling

Library of Congress Cataloging in Publication Data:

Ayling, Stanley Edward.   George the Third.

Bibliography: p.
1. George III, King of Great Britain, 1738-1820.
DA506.A2A9   1972   942.07′3′0924 [B]   72–2325
ISBN 0–394–48169–0

Manufactured in the United States of America

FIRST AMERICAN EDITION

TO
JANE, SALLY, JONATHAN,
AND ELIZABETH

CONTENTS

PART FOUR

DEFEATS AND A RECOVERY

PART FIVE

SHOCKS AND SHADOWS

ILLUSTRATIONS

PREFACE

It is now over forty years since Sir Lewis Namier revolutionised accepted views of eighteenth-century political history. It is twenty since Richard Pares delivered his memorable Ford Lectures, *King George III and the Politicians*. Over the past decade or so, the already immense store of printed documents has been enriched by Professor Aspinall's publication of thirteen more packed volumes of George III's correspondence and that of the Prince of Wales. Recently too, illumination of a quite different kind has come from the investigations by Drs Ida Macalpine and Richard Hunter into the nature of the 'royal malady'. During these forty years an enormous amount of detailed work has been done on the reign's constitutional battles, the structure of its politics, its parliamentary personnel, the development of the cabinet, the rôle of the prime minister, the emergence of parties, the influence of the Crown. There have been social and economic studies in plenty; one or two excellent general histories of the reign, notably Steven Watson's in the Oxford History of England; and Sir Herbert Butterfield's study of the historiography of George III, *George III and the Historians*, a corrective to hasty judgments. Only a biography of the King himself seems to be wanting.

A non-specialist, I am aware of the snares that lie in the path of any writer rash enough to venture into this notoriously controversial field. George III without the Constitution would certainly be Hamlet without the Prince; but this book is not a work of constitutional history, still less an original contribution to it. I have tried instead to write a narrative biography of a man of very decided stamp who was also a monarch of unusual importance – though I am conscious that this in itself will seem to some an enterprise of such culpable recklessness as to require some precautionary sub-title concerning fools and angels.

My chief sources have been the almost inexhaustible contemporary memoirs, letters, diaries, and printed documents of every kind; and above all the correspondence of the King himself, of his ministers, and of his family. By gracious permission of Her Majesty The Queen I have been allowed to quote extensively from all the published volumes of these letters.

As scholars will know, among the more distinguished casualties of Namier's fire was the reputation of Sir John Fortescue as the editor of

George III's earlier letters; and I must acknowledge here the kind assistance I have received from Her Majesty's Librarian at Windsor, and
from the Deputy Registrar of the Archives, Mrs de Bellaigue, in clarify-
ing certain difficulties in Fortescue's text. I have plundered the wisdom
of too many academic historians to enumerate them in full, but a
special obligation is due to those editors of the royal correspondence
who succeeded Fortescue – Romney Sedgwick and Professor Aspinall.

I wish also to thank Mr Oliver Millar, Deputy Surveyor of the
Queen's Pictures, and the staff of the National Portrait Gallery for their
help with the illustrations; Mr John Howe and Mr Alan Bartlett for
reading drafts of the text; and in particular Mr Philip Ziegler, of Collins,
for invaluable assistance of many kinds.

Occasionally, for ease of understanding, I have relegated initial capi-
tals to lower case and have taken the liberty of modernising punctu-
ation, but in general I have left original spelling unaltered.

S. A.

PART ONE

THREE GENERATIONS OF THE HOUSE OF HANOVER

CHAPTER ONE

Frederick, Prince of Wales

FREDERICK LOUIS, Prince of Wales (1707-51), George II's son and George III's father, who did not live to mount the throne himself, is generally, and almost exclusively, known as that 'poor Fred' who

> *. . . was alive and is dead.*
> *There's no more to be said.*

If the son is to be understood, however, a little more has to be said of the father. For a considerable time he was the focus of the opposition to George II and his governments; and he it was in the first instance who was to be the Patriot King that 'gloried in the name of Britain'. Partly because of his own conduct, but partly too because he earned the enmity or contempt of two brilliantly readable memoir-writers, Lord Hervey and Horace Walpole, Poor Fred has come down chiefly as a caricature Prince of Wales, the son who was hated with a fanatical but (one is asked to assume) deserved hatred by his own parents George II and Caroline of Ansbach; who nearly killed his wife in labour by rushing her off in a coach from Hampton Court to St James's; the 'patriot' and dilettante who patronised Handel's rival because the King patronised Handel; who gave Lord Bute his first leg-up on the ladder of fame by asking him to make a fourth at cards on a rainy afternoon at Egham races; an insignificant figure who fortunately died early, worth in general only a light-hearted footnote.

To Horace Walpole's father, Sir Robert, for nearly fifteen years George II's principal minister, the Prince of Wales was an obvious and dangerous enemy, for the simple reason that within the conventions of Hanoverian politics the King's heir was always the centre of opposition to the King's governments. Walpole was afraid that, when Frederick succeeded to the throne 'he would tear the flesh off [Queen Caroline's] bones with hot irons'; but of course it was his own flesh he was afraid for too. Robert Walpole's judgment on Frederick, therefore, should not necessarily be taken as gospel:

A poor, weak, irresolute, false, lying, dishonest, contemptible wretch, that nobody loves, that nobody believes, that nobody will trust, and that will trust everybody by turns, and that everybody by turns will impose upon, betray, mislead, and plunder.[1]

Henry Fox was shorter but as damning: 'worthless.' As for Hervey, our richest, spiciest, spitefullest source of fact and gossip upon George II's court, he had once been the Prince's political adviser but had been ousted by Dodington. Moreover, Hervey had a mistress who had subsequently been taken over by Frederick and set up in Soho Square on an allowance of £1,600 a year. Charity therefore is hardly to be expected in his judgment or objectivity in his selection of facts; and Frederick was not in a position to hit back, as Pope was when stung by the same fly.*

Hervey's hostile view of the Prince was mild compared with that of the rest of the royal family. His sisters all disliked and fell out with him. Queen Caroline had come to despise and detest him, and solemnly declared she had seen through him since he was six months old. 'An ávaricious sordid monster,' she called him; if the Pretender offered him half a million for the throne she was convinced he would pocket it. 'Look, there he goes – that wretch! – that villain! – I wish the ground would open this moment and sink the monster to the lowest hole in hell.' 'My dear first-born is the greatest ass and the greatest liar and the greatest *canaille* and the greatest beast in the whole world, and I heartily wish he were out of it.' These and many more such outbursts[2] were made by the Queen either to Hervey or to Robert Walpole. As for the King, once a brief period of tolerant contempt had passed, when he had first brought the Prince over in December, 1728, from Hanover (where George I had directed that he was to be educated), mortification and hatred possessed him at the mere sound of his eldest son's name. He would have preferred to dismiss him entirely from his conscious-ness, and did in fact customarily cut him dead. 'Wherever the Prince stood, though the King passed him ever so often or ever so near, it always seemed as if the King thought the place the Prince filled a void space.'[3]

Yet it must be obvious that Frederick had some arguments on his side of the question. For instance, whereas George II when he had been Prince of Wales had received an allowance of £100,000 a year, he set aside for his own son only £24,000, which with the additional £14,000 as Duke of Cornwall George considered ample for so detest-able a son. When the Prince married, his allowance was raised to

---

* See Pope, *Epistle to Dr Arbuthnot*, lines 309-33:

    Yet let me flap this bug with gilded wings
    This painted child of dirt that stinks and stings . . .
    A Cherub's face, a reptile all the rest . . .

£50,000, a sum George professed to find 'very competent' in view of his own numerous and expensive progeny; but the following year Frederick persuaded his parliamentary friends to move an address requesting the King to settle the full £100,000 upon him. Domestic bitterness, always present, was at this point extreme; but the King was able to gain some satisfaction when the 'rascally puppy' was defeated by a comfortable majority: 234 votes to 204.

Hostility of ruling monarchs to their heirs was of course nothing new or strange. At this time, among the great and famous alone, Peter of Russia put his heir to death, and Frederick William of Prussia, George II's cousin, threatened his (the future Frederick the Great) with the same fate. That the Prince of Wales's party should be regarded as the main focus of opposition to the King and his government was so taken for granted that when in 1760 George III succeeded to the throne as a young bachelor of twenty-two, the absence of a Prince of Wales and of the 'reversionary interest' that went with him was to seem like the suspension of the natural political order, and prove a principal factor in the constitutional battle of George III's early years. (Nature was soon to re-establish itself as George III's own eldest son continued the old tradition.) In George I's day all the aspiring politicians who were not among the 'ins', and all those who, looking towards a royal demise, preferred to invest in the future, had at one time or another been seen at the Prince of Wales's court at Leicester House, Walpole and his brother-in-law Townshend among them until brighter opportunities had beckoned them back to the King's service. That earlier Prince of Wales, however, was now George II, a choleric German in his early fifties; and his Princess of Wales, Caroline of Ansbach, the woman that George perpetually slighted, insulted, nagged, depended on, and after his fashion loved, was not only Queen, but also Regent during the King's frequent and prolonged excursions to his beloved Herrenhausen, in pursuit of Hanoverian relaxations.

Caroline 'looked, spake, and breathed', wrote Hervey, 'but for him, was a weathercock to every capricious blast of his uncertain temper, and governed him (if influence so gained can bear the name of government) by being as great a slave to him, thus ruled, as any other wife could be to a man who ruled her.' The Queen had some pretensions to learning, and in most matters was a woman of judgment and pungent political sense; not, however, in matters relating to her 'monster' son. As Queen and Regent, as mother, and as a wife who was obliged to be philosophical, she was in constant consultation both with the chief minister Walpole and the courtier Vice-Chamberlain Hervey.* Walpole

* The relationship between Hervey and the Queen became very close. He

too admired Caroline, as well as to a degree depending on her. But all three of them, Walpole, Hervey, and the Queen, ultimately of course depended on the will of the Sovereign himself, and they became fertile in devices for humouring his follies and diverting his lightnings. A ballad of the day, imputed to Gay* perhaps only because of the notoriously anti-governmental edge of *The Beggar's Opera* and *Polly*, sang of these royal outbursts, which Hervey more charitably attributed to piles:

> *. . . In his head he loves a drum*
> *As children love a rattle.*
> *If not in field, in drawing room,*
> *He daily sounds to battle.*

But the influence of the Queen, 'his consort plump and dear,' was popularly recognised:

> *God prosper long our gracious King*
> *Now sitting on the throne,*
> *Who leads this nation in a String,*
> *And governs all but One.*

The ill will of the ballad-writer cannot however resist scurrilously turning her undoubted political and personal intimacy with Robert Walpole into intimacy of another sort:

> *O may she always meet success*
> *In every scheme and job,*
> *And still continue to caress*
> *That honest statesman, Bob.*

It was Walpole who persuaded the Queen, who was past fifty and putting on weight, to invite the King, in order the more firmly to anchor him in England, to bring over from Hanover his latest fancy, the dark-eyed, shapely Mme Walmoden – whereupon George II, who was capable of surprising everybody, penned to his wife from Hanover a love letter thirty pages long, and on his belated return paid her the most devoted, if short-lived, attention. (Mme Walmoden did in fact come to England, but not until after Caroline's death in 1737. She was created Lady Yarmouth and survived in the King's favour until his

---

admired and was genuinely devoted to her; she relied much on his sympathy and intellectual companionship. Indeed she declared he should have been her son.

* See *Ode for the New Year*, printed in Gay's *Collected Poems*, Oxford ed., 653, wickedly ascribed by the unknown author to 'Colley Cibber Esq., Poet Laureate'.

death.) Both Hervey and Walpole tried tactfully to suggest that a certain moderation in the royal attitude towards the Prince, whom many thought poorly treated, would prevent him from being able to steal popularity and stir up more resentment against George II and his government. 'My God,' declared the Queen, 'popularity always makes me sick; but Fritz's popularity makes me vomit.' The Prince had been courting it among the 'Patriot' opposition to Walpole, supporting toasts at a dinner in Pall Mall: 'The Trade of this Country,' 'The Naval Strength of England,' and so forth[4]. And, as Walpole was well aware, George II's was still a very foreign régime. He was not a popular King; he certainly did not 'glory in the name of Britain' as George III, when he first acceded, was justly to proclaim that *he* did. When during the foul weather in December, 1736, the King was thought to be in grave danger at sea during his return from Hanover, sympathetic anxiety was far from being the only popular sentiment. To the question, 'How is the wind to-day for the King?' the wag's answer was, 'Like the people, against him.' A few weeks earlier the Queen had been hissed at the Opera.* According to the King, writes Hervey,

> No English or even French cook could dress a dinner; no English confectioner set out a dessert; no English player could act; no English coachman could drive, or English jockey ride, nor were any English horses fit to be drove or fit to be ridden; no Englishman knew how to come into a room, nor any Englishwoman how to dress herself, nor were there any diversions in England, public or private, nor any man or woman in England whose conversation was to be borne – the one, as he said, talked of nothing but their dull politics, and the others of nothing but their ugly clothes. Whereas at Hanover all these things were in the utmost perfection.

English was still a foreign tongue to George II – he had, after all, already passed the age of thirty in 1714, when his father had acceded to the British throne. Although his command of the language became adequate for most purposes, French remained the *lingua franca* of the Court, as of most European courts; and when George or Caroline wished to communicate privately before company or to vituperate with especial vehemence, they would relapse into German. The King once said to Lady Sundon that in England 'he was obliged to enrich people for being rascals and buy them not to cut his throat'. The House of Commons and all the English 'were king-killers or republicans'.[5]

* Egmont, *Diary*, ii, 308. He does add – 'upon which others clapped'; but he notes how the unpopularity of the Crown was reflected in the growing popularity of the Prince of Wales.

And the Queen, although she was more restrained than the King and would on occasions praise British love of freedom, did not differ so entirely from him:

> I have heard her at different times speak with great indignation against assertors of the people's rights; have heard her call the King, not without some despite, the humble servant of Parliament, the pensioner of his people and a puppet of sovereignty, that was forced to go to them for every shilling he wanted, that he was obliged to court those who were always abusing him, and could do nothing of himself.[6]

The Prince of Wales's best hope of escaping the domination of his father and mother was marriage and an independent establishment – a not unreasonable ambition in a man of twenty-seven. In George I's time a Prusso-Hanoverian double marriage had been mooted, between Frederick and the Princess Royal of Prussia, and between Frederick's sister Amelia and the future Frederick the Great. On George I's death, his successor's quarrel with his cousin Frederick William I brought all this to nothing, though at one time the Prince of Wales almost attempted the Prussian match as a runaway affair of his own. Next he entered a conspiracy with the old Dowager Duchess of Marlborough secretly to marry her granddaughter, Lady Diana Spencer; the date and the place, Windsor, were fixed, but when Walpole got wind of the affair that was the end of it. The Prince himself rejected his father's next candidate, a Danish royal princess, on the grounds of her deformities and mental shortcomings; perhaps the King's suggestion had been deliberately intended as an insult. Finally on his 1735 visit to Hanover, George determined upon what he considered a suitable wife for his son. He contrived a meeting at Herrenhausen with the young Princess Augusta of Saxe-Gotha, arranged the match, and on his return informed Frederick of the marriage proposal. On the not wholly unfavourable report of an emissary that the Prince sent out to reconnoitre, he accepted, in humble duty rather than with enthusiasm. As the King remarked later, with his usual mixture of horse sense and wild exaggeration, in the matter of eligible Protestant princesses there was no great choice: 'The Princess of Denmark he would not have. The Princesses of Prussia have a madman for their father, and I did not think ingrafting my half-witted coxcomb upon a madwoman would mend the breed.' The Princess of Saxe-Gotha accordingly arrived at Greenwich on 25th April, 1736. At seventeen years of age, speaking not a word of English and few of French, a tall girl 'with a very modest and good-natured face to make her countenance not disagreeable', she was married to the Prince in the chapel of St James's Palace two days later. The ceremony did not therefore impede the King's departure for Hanover in May; indeed he declared he would not have let it. At the wedding, Hervey's cool malice was there to record every insinuation against the Prince's behaviour or non-behaviour:

> At supper nothing remarkable happened but the Prince's eating several glasses of jelly, and every time he took one turning about, laughing, and winking on some of his servants.
>
> The King went after supper to the Princess's apartment whilst the Queen undressed the Princess, and when they were in bed everybody passed through their bed-chamber to see them, where there was nothing remarkable but the Prince's nightcap, which was some inches higher than any grenadier's cap in the whole army.
>
> There were various reports on what did and did not pass this night after the company retired. The Queen and Lord Hervey agreed that the bride looked extremely tired with the fatigues of the day, and so well refreshed next morning, that they concluded she had slept very sound.[7]

This idea that the Prince was too peculiar or too incompetent to consummate his marriage persisted with the Queen to the point of obsession. His failings and unnaturalness as a son must surely argue unnaturalness and failings as a husband too; could Hervey kindly ascertain first-hand evidence from the Prince's former mistress? It was more than likely, the Queen was ready to believe, that Miss Vane's little Fitzfrederick was no Fitzfrederick at all, but very possibly a Fitzhervey. The lady's retailed report on the Prince's sexual performance was not enthusiastic;* neither was it wholly damning. But Queen Caroline's absurd and vindictive suspicions persisted even after the Prince of Wales reported his wife pregnant. Caroline seemed determined to convince herself that her son would procure a spurious child, another warming-pan changeling like that supposed to have been smuggled between the Stuart sheets in 1688. There had even been talk of Frederick himself (who was physically unlike both his parents) being another such – a theory to which George II added some apparent weight by his constant denunciations of his son as a *Wechselbalg* (changeling), 'no true

---

* Frederick over the years had kept various mistresses apart from Anne Vane: the daughter of an oboist at the Playhouse, a prima donna at the Opera, a Kingston apothecary's daughter. Yet there is good evidence that he was no Don Juan. Colonel Schutz, his Privy Purse, told Lord Egmont that 'he talks more of his feats in this way than he acts', and despite the well-advertised record of his earlier escapades, Anne Vane told Hervey that the Prince came to her 'incredibly ignorant' in sexual matters (Egmont, *Diary*, i. 92-93 and 350).

son of mine'. But he was surely calling him a bastard in a modern metaphorical rather than a literal sense. Some slight colour was given to this peculiar theory of Queen Caroline's by the Prince's determination to have the Princess lie-in at St James's, not under the eye of the King and Queen at Hampton Court where the Court was in residence and the King had commanded the confinement to be. 'Sir Robert, we shall be catched,' Caroline pronounced. 'At her labour I positively will be . . . I will be sure it is her child.' The ludicrous pantomime culminated in July, 1737, when, the Princess's labour coming on unexpectedly, the Prince whisked her off secretly and riskily, *in medias res*, in a coach from Hampton Court to St James's. They had earlier made two other secret bolts for it, but returned on the alarms of labour proving false. Now the baby was all but born *en route*; and the next day, reported Hervey, anxious as ever to make the Prince appear ridiculous, 'with holding her pillows in the coach, he . . . got such pains in his back he could hardly stir.' Certainly the Prince's combination of foolhardiness, farce, and lèse-majesté provided ammunition for his detractors, the more so as he humbly apologised to the King afterwards. At St James's the Princess had been 'delivered of a little rat of a girl, about the bigness of a large toothpick case', only two Lords of the Council having been able to arrive in time. The Queen, foiled of her surveillance and furious at these evidences of her son's folly and contrariety, was nevertheless prepared to admit that the child, being such a 'poor, little, ugly, she-mouse', instead of a 'brave, large, fat, jolly boy', was truly Frederick's. The baby was to be known as the Lady Augusta. She was the first of the Prince of Wales's nine children; the future George III was to be the second.

Before he was born in 1738, the rift between King and Prince had become open and total. In a letter which Hervey had the honour and gratification of drafting and Walpole of approving, George signified his pleasure that 'you and all your family remove from St James's as soon as ever the safety and convenience of the Princess will permit'. The Prince and all his supporters – that 'faction that acts with no other view than to weaken my authority in every particular' – were not to be suffered 'into any part of any of my palaces'. When Frederick drove away from St James's at this peremptory behest of his well-hated father, many of the onlookers, wrote Lord Egmont,[8] were in tears. There was little doubt on which side popular sympathies, of high or low, in general lay. When the Prince attended a performance of Addison's *Cato*, the whole audience rose and applauded him at the line: 'When vice prevails and impious men hold sway.' Eventually he set up his rival court and formed his 'shadow cabinet' at that old home of princely opposition, Leicester House. Carlton House and Savile House* (used as a children's nursery) were his subsidiary town houses, and Cliveden in Buckinghamshire his country establishment; Kew was added as a second rural retreat; but for the moment in 1737 he was homeless, and found temporary refuge in St James's Square, where he rented the Duke of Norfolk's house. It was here, on 4th June, 1738 (24th May, Old Style), in a Georgian brick mansion much like its neighbours – one of which housed William Pitt – that George William Frederick, later George III, was to be born.

From the close of 1717, when George I had expelled *his* Prince of Wales, the future George II, from his court of St James's, the house in Leicester Fields where George and Caroline set up their rival court had become a lively rendezvous for writers and men of fashion as well as for politicians, a milieu in which they could exercise their wit and social talents and air their resentments against the ruling régime. Gay, Pope, Swift, and Arbuthnot had been of that company; so in their opposition days had Walpole and Townshend. Leicester House had for a space been an altogether smarter place than George I's St James's. Then during the early days of the new reign, George II had been careful to keep his own son in leading strings under his royal roof. The opposition running was made in Parliament by an alliance of Tories (such as William Wyndham) and dissident Whigs (like Pulteney), and in the world outside by Bolingbroke and his supporters in *The Craftsman*.

When Bolingbroke retired once more to France, to a voluntary, second exile, the opposition was to prove no less virulent in the hands of such men as Cobham of Stowe and the ambitious young men round him – Cobham's Cubs, the Patriots, or 'the Boys' as Walpole contemptuously called them: Cobham's nephews Richard, George, and James Grenville, Lyttelton and the rest, including their brightest star, young William Pitt. Already by 1733, Frederick Prince of Wales was in contact with these men, and as the 1730's progressed each year had taken him more openly into the rôle of their patron and taken away from Walpole a little more of that unquestioned authority he had wielded in earlier days. It was the Patriots who led Frederick on to demand a doubled allowance and to break with his parents. Then in 1737 came Frederick's expulsion from George II's court, and soon afterwards the death of Walpole's firmest ally there, Queen Caroline.

By 1738 the Walpole sun was beginning to set. His policy of entente

* Leicester House stood at the north-eastern corner of what became Leicester Square, and Savile House, which during the later 1750's was Prince George's town house, adjoined it on the west. Carlton House, in Pall Mall, was bought by Frederick from the Earl of Chesterfield.

with France, his patient attempts to improve relations with Spain by negotiation, his determination not to be dragged into a European war at Austria's side, though they helped to keep down the land tax, were increasingly not to the national taste, which began to demand a more martial posture. British sea-captains attempting to trade on Spanish American coasts – simply smugglers in the Spanish view – had been roughly handled, and sometimes in return given as good as they got. Incidents were frequent, and there had been nothing particularly out of the way in the misfortunes of Captain Robert Jenkins of the *Rebecca* in 1731. This subsequently notorious hero was caught by the Spaniards, who removed from his ship all its instruments and a good deal of its equipment, including the captain's left ear. This, reported the *Daily Advertiser*, was slit down by the cutlass of a Spanish officer, 'and then another of the Spaniards took hold of it and tore it off, but gave him the Piece of his Ear again, bidding him carry it to his Majesty, King George.' Then they left him, as he later told an outraged House of Commons in 1738, drifting and helpless, but nevertheless remembering to commit his soul to God and his cause to his country. The authentic ear was produced, prudently preserved and bottled, and together with the story of Jenkins's sufferings, it caused an immense hubbub of patriotic indignation, led by the Prince of Wales's party. The previous year the Spanish coastguard patrols had seized five British ships and their crews were still languishing in Spanish jails. 'Seventy of our brave sailors,' declared Alderman Wilmot of the City of London, 'are now in chains in Spain. Our countrymen in chains, and slaves to Spaniards! Is not this enough to fire the coldest?' An unconvinced Walpole, lambasted by Pitt, the Patriots, and the popular press, was eventually pushed (he saw no obligation to resign) into a war with Spain which was gradually to expand into the major European and colonial struggle known as the War of Austrian Succession. For once George II and his hated son were briefly and broadly in agreement: they were both of the war party – the Prince of Wales so fervidly that he kissed Pitt after his eloquent House of Commons speech condemning Walpole's appeasement policy as 'a stipulation for national ignominy'. When war was finally declared in October, 1739, the bells pealed, the stocks rose, and the mob rejoicing in the streets were toasted by the Prince of Wales from the steps of the Rose Tavern at Temple Bar. The following year it was before Frederick too that a masque was performed that included among its items one destined for longevity; the music was by Arne, the lyrics by Thomson, the title *Rule Britannia*!

Once more Leicester House (and also Cliveden by the Thames)

under a Prince and Princess of Wales now provided a rival court, a
rallying ground for the disappointed expectations or hopeful calculations of politicians, and a setting for men of fashion or of letters. The
best George II and Walpole had managed to do for poetry was to
appoint the actor-manager Colley Cibber* to the laureateship. Frederick
could number among 'his' poets Pope†, Swift, and Thomson; Pulteney,
Carteret, and the Patriots among his politicians; and among the ladies
the Duchess of Queensberry (that fashionable law unto herself who
had openly insulted George II and had been expelled from Court) and
the Duchess of Marlborough, still trenchant and formidable at nearly
eighty. Until 1736, since George II had patronised Handel's Italian
operas at the Haymarket or Covent Garden, Frederick had naturally to
take under his wing Handel's rival, Bononcini, at Lincoln's Inn Fields,
but the situation changed somewhat in that year when Handel composed an anthem for Frederick's wedding; his rehabilitation with
George had to wait for the *Dettingen Te Deum* and London performance
of *Messiah* in 1743. Frederick himself played the 'cello, as his Prussian
cousin Frederick played the flute; whereas the fathers of both Fredericks
maintained a military and militant hostility to such artistic airs and
graces. Everyone knows George II's failure to appreciate 'bainting
and boetry'; the Prince of Wales, on the other hand, loved to play
Maecenas in 'Cliveden's proud alcove' among his friends and political
followers of the moment.

Like his cousin Frederick the Great, the Prince wrote mediocre
French poetry and songs for masques. He was a generous patron of
painters English and French – George Knapton, Charles Philips, John
Wootton, Jean-Baptiste Vanloo, Barthélemy du Pan, Philippe Mercier;
the most discriminating royal art-collector, in fact, between Charles I
and George IV. When Reynolds heard of his death, he lamented the
loss of one who 'would certainly have been a great patron'. He was an
amateur, too (in both senses) of the theatre, and had once collaborated
with Hervey in the authorship of a comedy whose opening performance at Drury Lane was so noisily received that the audience
had their money returned. He wrote – or at least took part in writing
– an anonymous autobiographical novel, expressing his grievances
against his parents. In the gardens of Kew House, which, like those of

---

* Of whom Dr Johnson wrote the double-edged lines:
> *Great George's acts let tuneful Cibber sing;*
> *For nature formed the Poet for the King.*

† 'The Prince showed uncommon deference for Pope, whom he visited at
Twickenham . . . It is, however, related that Pope fell asleep at table on one occasion
when the Prince was discoursing of poetry' (Wraxall, *Memoirs*, i, 311).

Carlton House, he employed William Kent to reconstruct, he developed the botanical collection begun earlier by Queen Caroline, and had a modish summer-house decorated with *chinoiseries*. At Cliveden he played the country gentleman in fishing and shooting, in village cricket and rowing races on the Thames. Frederick was a cricket enthusiast. He not only played it with his sons, but expected guests at Kew and Cliveden to join in, even a heavyweight as unathletic as Dodington. That over several seasons he captained the Surrey team, however, could doubtless have been a tribute to rank rather than proficiency. At Cliveden too he would call in to drink his ale at The Chequers and The Three Feathers, for was he not the People's Prince? 'He would enter,' wrote Dr John Doran,[9] 'the cottages of the poor, listen with patience to their thrice told tales and partake with relish of their humble fare . . . He was a man to be loved in spite of all his vices.' He 'would walk the streets unattended to the great delight of the people', or would make more ceremonious public appearances as at Bartholomew Fair by torchlight, with a party of Yeomen of the Guard clearing the way; then several more bearing flambeaux and flanking the procession, and in the midst, 'dressed in a ruby coloured frock coat very richly guarded with gold lace, and having his long, flowing hair curiously curled over his forehead and at the sides with a very large bag and courtly queue behind . . . the amiable Frederick, Prince of Wales.'

Some of the *raison d'être* of the Prince's opposition temporarily disappeared during the events of 1742-45: the fall of Walpole, the acceptance of the Prince's full £100,000 allowance at last, the vigorous prosecution of the war (even by George II personally at Dettingen), the employment of some of the Prince's supporters in the Newcastle-Pelham-Carteret coalition, and the Jacobite revolt of 1745. But again by 1747, still half afraid of Queen Caroline's old project of promoting his brother Cumberland above him as heir apparent (George II had chosen him and rejected Frederick to lead the anti-Jacobite army in 1745-6), Frederick was writing to his associates in the old terms: 'I hope with my friends' assistance to rescue a second time this kingdom out of wicked hands.'[10] Again the Leicester House 'Court' attracted much attention; 'the refuse of every party,' commented Horace Walpole. 'The Prince of Wales gains strength in Parliament,' wrote Chesterfield, 'in proportion as the King grows older.'[11] As a counter to this, Newcastle was suggesting to Lord Chancellor Hardwicke the possibility that Frederick might be threatened with the deprivation of his right to educate his son, as George I had done earlier.

CHAPTER TWO

The Education of a Prince

NOT much is to be told of the future George III's infancy. A small detail or two singles itself out, such as the identity of his wet-nurse and his subsequent, very characteristic, loyalty to her and her family. Thirty-five years later, George wrote to Lord Bristol, of his Household (who was as it happens a son of Lord Hervey):

> I have learnt that my Laundress Mary Smith died on Monday. She suckled me, and to her great attention my having been reared is greatly owing; this ought to make me anxious for the welfare of her children, who by her great imprudence are left destitute of support. I therefore desire you will appoint her youngest daughter Augusta Hicks to succeed her as Laundress.

Frederick, it appears, was a conscientious enough parent, severe though the condemnation of historians has been on his frivolity and unreliability. In his letters to the two eldest of his sons, George and Edward (there were in all five sons and four daughters) there are unmistakable signs of benevolence and concern: 'That none of you, my dear George, may ever forget your duty but always be a blessing to your family and country is the prayer of your friend and father . . . Pray God that you may grow in every respect above me . . . good night, my dear children.' 'The Prince's family,' wrote Lady Hervey in 1748,

> is an example of innocent and cheerful amusement. All this last summer they played abroad, and now in the winter in a large room they divert themselves at baseball, a play all who are or have been schoolboys are well acquainted with. The ladies as well as the gentlemen join in the amusement, and the latter return the compliment in the evening by playing for an hour at the old and innocent game of push-pin.[1]

The Prince may have thought it amusing to patronise charlatan fortune-tellers in company with the Princess or Lady Middlesex, or when tipsy to break the windows of the Duchess of Buckingham's and Lord Berkshire's houses, or with Lords Middlesex and John Sackville to attend Clerkenwell bull-baitings in disguise; but the domestic

atmosphere was far from frivolous. A visiting French marquis, expecting 'faro or scandal', was asked to choose his entertainment between
playing rounders ('baseball') and listening to a reading from Addison.
Amateur theatricals were much to the taste of the dilettante Prince,
who encouraged his children to take part in them, believing that it
taught them deportment and speech. One of the first appearances of
George upon the stage of history was as a ten-year-old Portius in
Addison's *Cato*, and it happened that the future Lord North* was
alongside him in the cast playing Syphax – his father was for a short
time the children's Governor. For the occasion a prologue had been
specially written to link 'great Cato's name' with those who defended
liberty and patriotism in their own day. It was young George who
spoke the lines; among them the following, lest he should be thought
to be speaking 'superior to his years':

> *What, tho' a boy! It may with truth be said,*
> *A boy in* England *born, in* England *bred,*
> *Where freedom best becomes the earliest state,*
> *For there the love of liberty's innate.*
> *Yet more – before my eyes those heroes stand*
> *Whom the great William brought to bless this land,*
> *To guard with care that gen'rous plan*
> *Of power well bounded, which he first began.*[3]

Quin the actor, Garrick's rival, was employed to supervise some of
these royal rehearsals, and helped the young Prince to speak well. Later,
on George's first speech from the throne being universally praised for
the grace and clarity of its delivery, Quin commented 'Ay, it was I who
taught the boy to speak.' Bubb Dodington, that weather-vane politician
who had been in and out of Frederick's service as present calculations
and future prospects determined, reports on 11th January, 1750:
'Went to Leicester House, to see Jane Grey† acted by the Prince's
children,' and again a year later, 'Spent the week at Kew, where we
had plays every day.'

If George learned to speak and carry himself well, his reading, like
his emotional development, was backward, and both these handicaps
were to be deepened after his father's death, when his mother ring-

---

* The personal resemblance between the two boys 'was thought so striking as to
excite much pleasantry on the part of Frederick himself, who often jested on the
subject with Lord Guildford [i.e. Lord North senior] observing that the world
would think one of their wives had played her husband false, though it might be
doubtful which of them lay under the imputation' (Wraxall, *Memoirs*, i. 310).

† Rowe's tragedy, *Lady Jane Grey*.

fenced her children from their 'corrupting' contemporaries. But Frederick had clear views on how his children should be educated, and set out the regimen for their Governor, Lord North, from 'Clifden, Octbr the 14th, 1750'. It comprised Latin, music, fencing, dancing, history, mathematics, and religion:

The Hours for the Two Eldest Princes

To get up at 7 o'clock.

At 8 to read with Mr *Scot* till 9, and he to stay with 'em till the Doctor [Preceptor] comes.

The *Doctor* to stay from 9 till Eleven.

From Eleven to Twelve, Mr *Fung*.

From Twelve to half an hour past Twelve, *Ruperti*; but Mr *Fung* to remain there.

Then to their Play hour till 3 o'clock.

At 3 Dinner.

Three times a week at half an hour past four, *Denoyer* [the dancing-master] comes.

At 5, Mr *Fung* till half an hour past 6.

At half an hour past 6 till 8 Mr *Scot*.

At 8, Supper.

Between 9 and 10 in Bed.

On Sundays, Prayers exactly at half an hour past 9 above stairs. Then the two eldest Princes, and the two eldest Princesses, are to go to Prince George's apartment, to be instructed by Dr Ayscough in the Principles of Religion till 11 o'clock.[2]

And in Frederick's 'Instructions for my son George, drawn by my-self, for his good, that of my family, and for that of his people, according to the ideas of my grand-father, and best friend, George I', there is certainly a great absence of frivolity. Here, in this political testament of some thousand words, is something of Frederick's, if not Bolingbroke's, 'Idea of the Patriot King', and just a hint, towards the end, of 'George, be a King', that famous piece of advice which – so it always used to be held, on flimsy evidence – was dinned into the ear of the adolescent Prince by his mother after Frederick's death.

To my son George,

As I always have had the tenderest paternal affection for you, I cannot give you a stronger proof of it, than in leaving this paper for you in your mother's hands, who will read it to you from time to time and will give it to you when you come of age or when you get the Crown . . . It is for your good, for that of my family, and of the

good people you are to govern, that I leave this to you. I entertain
no doubt of your good heart, nor of your honour; things I trust, you
will never loose out of sight. The perverseness and bad examples of
the times, I am sure, will never make you forget them . . .

I know that you will have allways the greatest respect for your
good mother, as I have already exhorted you in my will; and all you
can do, consistently with your own interest, for your brothers and
sisters, you certainly will do . . .

There follows earnest advice on avoiding wars, reducing the National
Debt, and separating Britain from Hanover as that 'wise and good
Prince' George I had advocated in the will his son had suppressed.
'Unsteady measures' had sullied the reign of George II, and if it should
outlast the life of his son the testator, let it be a future George III's
ambition to 'retrieve the glory of the Throne. I shall have no regret
never to have wore the Crown, if you but fill it worthily. Convince the
nation that you are not only an Englishman born and bred, but that
you are also this by inclination'.

By the end of the War of Austrian Succession in 1748, George II
was already nearly sixty-five – a good old age for those days – and it
was generally assumed that he would not live much longer. The Prince
of Wales was well prepared for his father's death. Some earlier supporters of the Prince, Pitt, Lyttelton, and Chesterfield among them,
had left him; Pulteney (Lord Bath now) had retired from politics; but
there was no shortage of hopeful men at Leicester House or Carlton
House – Egmont, Talbot, Henley (the future Lord Chancellor Northington), Dodington, Dashwood, Furnese among them. (Dodington
had abandoned the Pelham ship and reverted to Frederick during
1747.*) Frederick formed his own 'shadow cabinet', which gathered
periodically at Carlton House to meet contingencies and formulate
policies. Hanover was to be detached, a large militia raised – more
popular than an expensive standing army – and, above all, the Augean
stables of the Whigs were to be cleaned, their manipulation of the
parliamentary system ended, and their power over local Justices of the
Peace thwarted by the simple device of enabling *all* gentlemen paying
over £300 a year in land tax to be Justices. The credibility of this high-
sounding attack on 'abuses in offices' is more than a little tainted by
reading of the arrangements that were made to ensure the winning of

---

* The year before, Horace Walpole, describing in a letter to Sir Horace Mann the
fireworks and illuminations to celebrate the Pretender's defeat at Culloden, observed
with tart amusement, 'Mr Dodington, on the first report, came out with a very
pretty illumination; so pretty, that I believe he had it by him, ready for *any* occasion.'

the election that would follow the King's death, and also by the inclusion in the Prince's shadow cabinet of some pretty unreforming characters, including that rather bloated blowfly Bubb Dodington, buzzing hopefully at this time towards the smell of meat.

Although Pelham, First Lord of the Treasury, was noting every month 'the increasing strength of the Prince's Opposition' and the dissolution of his own parliamentary forces, so that it seemed probable to him that Newcastle and he would not be able to subsist through the session of 1750-51, Dodington was cheated of his Secretaryship of State and the Pelhams succeeded in surviving. At Kew on 5th March, 1751, the Prince of Wales caught a cold which turned to pleurisy. On the 15th, Dodington reported him out of all danger, but five days later he was seized with an uncontrollable 'fit of coughing and spitting'. When the attendant supporting him called to the Princess 'the Prince is going', she 'caught up a candle and came to him, but he was dead before she reached him'. Because of the suddenness of his death after an apparently complete recovery, a post-mortem was carried out, which ascribed his death to an abscess or 'imposthume in his breast' that broke and suffocated him. There was a second abscess 'supposed to have been of long standing and imputed to a blow' – which again was understood to have come from a cricket ball at Cliveden.* Dodington writes that the King 'ordered the bowels to be put in a box covered in red velvet . . . and buried in Henry the VII's chapel'. They interred the remains unceremoniously – disgracefully so, considered Dodington, 'without anthem or organ', and with merely the Duke of Somerset as chief mourner.

To Prince George, the new Prince of Wales, aged twelve, his father's sudden death was a shock. He felt, he said, as he did when he saw a workman fall from some scaffolding at Kew. Moreover, it meant, to begin with, that he was required to go and live under George II's eye at Hampton Court. An on the whole unloving eye it was too; the boy, said George, 'lacked the desire to please'. Many years later the Duke of Sussex, sixth son of George III, walking through the apartments once used by the young Prince, remarked 'I wonder in which of these rooms it was that George II struck my father. The blow so disgusted him that he could never after think of it as a residence'.[4] Luckily the Hampton Court interlude was not long-lived. The King permitted his daughter-in-law to continue living at Kew with her children, and had the common sense to look with scepticism upon the

* Fox to Hanbury Williams 22.3.1751 and Coxe's Pelham, ii. 164. Horace Walpole says 'the blow of a tennis-ball three years before' (*Memoirs . . . of the Reign of George II*, i. 72).

alarums that were being raised concerning the Prince's 'Jacobite' education.

Since 1745, the men in charge of George's schooling had been the Preceptor, Dr Ayscough, Frederick's Clerk to the Closet and later Dean of Bristol, and George Scott, sub-Preceptor, the only person round the young Prince, apart from his brother, with whom he succeeded in making any contact.[5] There was also a Governor, who at the time of Frederick's death was the elder Lord North. The Pelham Whigs, unable to control the education of the two eldest princes while Frederick lived, were determined to exert some surveillance after his death. They advised the King to dismiss North and Ayscough, and installed in their respective places harmless and largely fainéant nominees, Lord Harcourt and Dr Hayter, Bishop of Norwich, who was generally considered to be the bastard of an earlier Archbishop of York. Harcourt, said Lord Mansfield, was a cipher; Horace Walpole called him 'a civil, sheepish peer' who was 'in need of a governor himself'. As for Hayter, a careerist, he impressed nobody. The Dowager Princess of Wales reported to Dodington that he lacked 'that clearness that she thought necessary'. 'She supposed he was a mighty learned man, but he did not seem very proper to convey knowledge to children.'[6] George's own later verdict on him was that he was 'an intriguing, unworthy man more fitted to be a Jesuit than an English bishop'.[7]

Ructions soon followed these appointments. Hayter accused sub-Preceptor Scott of insulting language and personal violence; being also a mathematician and Fellow of the Royal Society he was naturally suspect as an atheist.[8] Harcourt then smeared *his* deputy, Stone, and also the Princess's private secretary, Cresset, with being Jacobites. There was some hoary old evidence that years ago Stone, in company with Murray (the future Lord Mansfield) had toasted the King over the water. Young George had even had 'Jacobite' books discovered in his room, the most heinous one being an English translation of Père d'Orléans' *Révolutions d'Angleterre*, a work defending the conduct of James II – though considering that George could not read at all fluently till he was eleven, we may well wonder how his mind could have been very seriously contaminated by the Father's work. Nevertheless, the brouhaha was sufficiently loud to persuade George II to appoint a committee of inquiry, whose verdict, briefly, was that there had been much ado about nothing.

Harcourt and Hayter now resigned and a new Governor and Preceptor were appointed, Earl Waldegrave and the Bishop of Peterborough. Again, George's own retrospective judgment on his Governor, Waldegrave, was disapproving – 'a depraved worthless man'[9] – though the Dowager Princess Augusta told Dodington that the children liked him. It is hardly surprising that by this time the education of George and Edward was seriously in arrears. It seems that Scott had managed to get through to George a little, for when it had been suggested that he might have to be dismissed along with Stone, the boy threatened to burn his books; but undoubtedly not much had been taught to either Prince, and they were both backward. Several times their mother admitted as much to Dodington.[10] Scott, she allowed, was 'a very proper preceptor', but Stone hardly earned his keep. When Dodington inquired what his duties were exactly, she replied that 'she did not know, unless it were to walk before the Prince upstairs, to walk with him sometimes, seldom to ride with him, and now and then to dine with him – but when they did walk together, the Prince generally took that time to think of his own affairs and say nothing'. She herself, if she were to live forty years in the same house as Stone, 'should never be better acquainted with him than she was'.[11] The lack of communication was mutual, indeed multilateral. Those about the Prince, said Augusta, 'knew him no more than if they never saw him'. He cared, it seemed, for nobody but his brother. She 'did not observe the Prince to take very particularly to anybody but him'.[12] A few years later George, at twenty, was himself commenting to Bute that 'through the negligence, if not wickedness' of those around him in earlier days he had not 'that degree of knowledge and experience' one of his age might be expected to have acquired.

His mother's own attitude made things much worse. Suspicious, prim, conscientious, censorious, she was terrified of her children coming into contact with the 'bad examples' of their contemporaries. Over and again she deplored the corrupt manners and morals of the young people of the day – and she was determined to be the mother of a virtuous and uncontaminated King. Hence the shy, rather lazy, luckless George grew up emotionally starved, corralled away from the big wicked world. It is not to be wondered at, that his mental and emotional age lagged far behind his calendar years. As late as 1759, when George was twenty-one, Pitt, while extolling the 'innocence' of his conduct was still lamenting 'the very recluse manner in which he lived'.

His new Governor, Waldegrave, found him both 'uncommonly indolent' and 'full of princely prejudices contracted in the nursery and improved by Bedchamber women and Pages of the Back Stairs'.[13] He himself set about, so he claimed, giving George 'true notions of common things'; and he later left a discerning judgment of his royal charge, delineating the boy and to a large extent foreshadowing the man:

His parts, though not excellent, will be found very tolerable, if ever they are properly exercised. He is strictly honest, but wants that frank and open behaviour which makes honesty appear amiable . . .

His religion is free from all hypocrisy, but is not of the most charitable sort; he has rather too much attention to the sins of his neighbours. He . . . does not want resolution, but it is mixed with too much obstinacy.

He has great command of his passions, and will seldom do wrong, except when he mistakes wrong for right . . .

He has a kind of unhappiness in his temper, which, if it not be conquered before it has taken too deep a root will be a source of frequent anxiety. When ever he is displeased, his anger does not break out with heat and violence; but he becomes sullen and silent and retires to his closet . . . Even when the fit is ended, unfavourable symptoms very frequently return, which indicate that on certain occasions his Royal Highness has too correct a memory.*

George II, no hypocrite, admitted that he was glad his son was dead, but he treated Augusta and her children very fairly, even with a certain grudging kindness. Waldegrave declared that he behaved to Augusta 'not only with politeness but with the appearance of affection'. It was a considerable concession that she should have been allowed to keep jurisdiction over the education of her son, the heir to the throne and therefore soon inevitably to be the focus of a new opposition. And when the question arose of who was to be Regent in the event of the King's absence, incapacity, or death, George was persuaded to accept Augusta rather than her brother-in-law the Duke of Cumberland.

William Augustus, Duke of Cumberland, Commander-in-Chief, the young victor of Culloden and subsequently 'the Butcher', had come to be an important political figure, feared and mistrusted by Whigs, Tories, and Leicester House alike. George II had thought him the natural choice for Regent-presumptive, but it was widely felt that he was far too dangerous and immoderate a man. His atrocities in the Highlands after the Forty-Five had been well publicised, his introduction of 'Prussian' discipline in the army much criticised, and an anonymous pamphlet of 1751, attributed to Frederick's adviser Egmont, had likened his ambitions to those of Richard III. The suggestion that he be appointed Regent aroused fears that Horace Walpole compared with the panic when the Jacobite army was at Derby. The King told Newcastle that the resentment felt towards his son was all based on lies;

---

* Waldegrave, *Memoirs*, 8-10. The passage was written in 1758 when George was twenty. Waldegrave was Governor from 1752-56.

nevertheless it was strong enough to incline George to prefer the little-liked Princess Dowager to the much-feared Duke.[14]

Augusta rightly or wrongly saw Cumberland as an intriguer against her son and his succession. The King, she told Dodington in October, 1752, was 'very respectful' to her, but Cumberland had not vouchsafed one visit to her, or asked after her, all summer; 'she could not help wondering what views were at the bottom of it'. It was partly this sharing of the popular suspicion and hatred of Cumberland that persuaded the Princess the more readily 'to keep well with the King and consequently countenance those ministers he employed'[15] – that is to say in particular the Duke of Newcastle and (until his death in 1754) his brother Henry Pelham. This acceptance of the lesser of two evils, although it did not preclude Augusta from inveighing against the incompetence of the Government, carried with it acceptance too of the Pelhams' nominees to oversee the Prince's education; hence those ministerial minions Harcourt and Hayter. Later, in June, 1756, by which time Prince George, just eighteen years and of age, had found his first great friend and prop in Lord Bute, we find him writing (to Bute): 'I had almost forgot to say that Lord W[aldegrave] dropp'd that he feared in granting my staying with Mama, the K[ing] would expect compliance in me naming the family' – that is, those who were to be appointed to the Prince's household. In other words, if the King was being so kind as to let the Prince stay on at Leicester House and Kew instead of coming to Kensington or St James's, at least he proposed to exact a price, and that chiefly meant the exclusion of Bute, whom, as Waldegrave tried tactfully to explain, the King did not consider 'a proper person to be put about his Royal Highness'. He was persuaded finally to relent on this point, but made it clear that as a reward for his 'indulgence and condescension' he expected 'perfect union and harmony in the royal family'.

Augusta not unnaturally saw all personalities and policies in terms of her eldest son's future fortunes. The international struggle in a Europe whose balance of power had been revolutionised by the rise of Prussia; the colonial and naval struggle between France and Britain; the re-emergence of active hostilities in both these respects from 1755 in the Seven Years War; the rivalries of the parliamentary factions at home, those constantly shifting patterns of manœuvre; the running war, over-lapping these rivalries, of the royal 'parties' – the King's managed by the Duke of Newcastle, the Duke of Cumberland's managed by Henry Fox, and the Dowager Princess's managed by Lord Bute; all these were in Augusta's eyes seen in terms of her eldest son and the throne which he was one day soon to hold. If there was to be war again with France, let it be soon, she argued to Dodington, before the new reign began. 'She saw the terrible consequences [of being soft with the French] and of a patched-up peace, which must break out, when the French perfected their naval plan, and fall upon her son, young and inexperienced, at the beginning of his reign . . . She was solicitous to push the war, and wished Hanover into the sea, as the cause of all our misfortunes.'[16]

Then there was the question of the Prince's marriage. The royal houses of Britain and Prussia were already of intermingled blood; Frederick the Great's brother-in-law was Duke of Brunswick-Wolfen-büttel; what more suitable, therefore, than that the Prince of Wales should be married to one of his daughters? There was a shortage of Protestant princesses of proper status and nubility, and in any case the elder Brunswick princess, Caroline, was sufficiently attractive to provoke George II into telling Waldegrave that if he had been twenty years younger he would himself have made her Queen of England.[17] But Augusta, suspicious, possessive, afraid that her son was to be snatched from her, and indignant that the negotiations seemed to be proceeding over her head, pronounced them premature. The Prince was only seventeen. He ought, so she told Dodington, 'to mix with the world – the marriage would prevent it – he was shy and backward, the match would shut him up for ever'. Further, she violently objected to the Princess's mother, the Duchess of Brunswick, Frederick the Great's sister, 'a most intriguing, meddling, and also the most sarcastical person in the world, and will always make mischief'.[18] The young Prince of Wales was not apparently loath to accept his mother's matrimonial arguments. He was in any case outstandingly immature; by no means lacking the ordinary passions, but sexually timid and still mother-dominated. George Scott reported on this aspect of his charge whom he knew and understood better perhaps than anyone else during these adolescent years:

> He has no tendency to vice, and has as yet very virtuous principles; has the greatest temptation to gallant with the ladies who lay themselves out in the most shameful manner to draw him, but to no purpose. He says if he were not what he is they would not mind him. Prince Edward is of a more amorous complexion . . .*

So, as Horace Walpole reported, 'the young Prince declared violently

---

* See B. Willson, *George III as Man, Monarch, and Statesman*, 28. But the account by this author and many others of the 'almost forgotten romance' between the Prince and the Quakeress Hannah Lightfoot is probably best forgotten altogether.

against being "bewolfenbuttled" ', and that particular marriage project
was eventually closed, though not finally until 1759. When in that year
the Duke of Brunswick wrote pressing for a final decision, his letter so
incensed the young Prince that he declared that 'tho' there should not
be another Princess in Germany likely to make me happy, I would
never consent to take one out of that House'.[19] But the British royal
family still had a Brunswick wedding. Augusta's eldest child, also
named Augusta, the baby that had so nearly been born in the coach on
the road from Hampton Court to St James's, was in due course married to the Duke of Brunswick's son, Charles William, the 'enlightened'
despot-Duke of 1780-1806 who was destined to confront the French
Revolution at the cannonade of Valmy and fall on the field of Auer-
städt.

For the three or four years following his father's death, then, there
is no doubt that the young Prince of Wales was protected by his
mother from those influences, physical, social, and intellectual, which
enable a boy to grow up. There was nothing to stir him out of that
natural indolence of mind to which most boys are subject until they are
either pricked by the spur of imagination or urged by the pressures of
discipline. George had neither. He was ill-educated, under-stimulated,
intellectually blinkered, and subjected to a surfeit of convention and
virtue, so that his horizons failed to expand and he became as censorious as his mother. 'No boys,' remarked much later the King's
youngest brother to Hannah More, 'were ever brought up in a greater
ignorance of evil than the King and myself . . . We retained all our
native innocence.'[20] He made the comment in an approving sense, but
ignorant innocence is a condition in a healthy adolescent that we would
be inclined nowadays to approve less enthusiastically than Hannah
More – even if we did not travel to the other extreme with Henry Fox,
who at this same time was educating his sons with unlimited indulgence,
having decided two hundred years before modern progressives that
'young people are always in the right, and old people in the wrong'.

The Princess Dowager was a woman with a grievance and many
fears. Her enemies were either in control, like the Pelhams, or threatening (so she thought) to cheat and forestall her, like the Duke of Cumberland. Many of the friends who had been numerous until Frederick's
death had drifted away, or gone over to the enemy, or were at best suspect, as Dodington was. By her own lights she was a good mother, full
of maternal solicitude, jealously guarding the welfare of her children

It seems almost certainly not to have happened. See L. Melville, *Farmer George*,
Chapter 5, and Jesse, *George III*, i. 31-36.

and above all the rights of her eldest son. She was vaguely aware that it was not good for him to be so cocooned from the world, but did not see how she could remedy matters without inviting direr evils. So he grew up, in a sense 'deprived'; a far from stupid boy (Augusta herself reckoned him, though not quick, reasonably 'applicable and intelligent'), but except for his brother Edward friendless; shy, somewhat lazy, more than a little priggish, and though usually good-natured and cheerful, tending towards unhealthy introspection. As his mother put it to Dodington, 'his mind has a serious cast on the whole'. [21] 'Bigoted, young, and chaste,' wrote Walpole – rather as though the three adjectives carried equal censure. [22]

When her husband died in 1751, the Princess Dowager, although she had borne eight children and was carrying a ninth, was a woman of only thirty-two. She was neither brilliant nor beautiful; tall, ungracious, and long-nosed; of very ordinary, even commonplace, personality. 'Decent', 'civil', 'prudent' are the descriptions most commonly used of her by her contemporaries before 1751; as Chesterfield put it, she was 'without parts'. Waldegrave pays her a left-handed compliment: she 'was represented a woman of excellent sense by those who knew her very imperfectly'. She could, he adds, 'act with tolerable propriety' so long as she had wise and prudent counsellors. Her counsellor-in-chief, however, after Frederick's death was a man whom political leaders and the public agreed first to write off as of no importance and then to unite in mistrusting: the Earl of Bute.

CHAPTER THREE

The Rise of Bute

JOHN STUART, third Earl of Bute, was on his father's side descended from a bastard branch of the Scottish royal family and on his mother's from the first Duke of Argyll. His father, supporting the Hanoverian succession, had been a representative peer of Scotland under the terms of the Act of Union, and his two maternal uncles, successively second and third Dukes of Argyll, had been pillars of the Hanoverian establishment in Scotland. Born in Scotland in 1713, he had been brought up in England from the age of ten, gone to school at Eton, and for four years, when still in his twenties, himself sat at Westminster as a representative Scots peer, though he does not seem to have taken part in debates. But, following the second Duke into opposition in 1739, he had lost his seat in the election of 1741, and from that moment he was an unemployed gentleman at large. The following five years he spent back in Scotland, much of them in the Isle of Bute, 'with as much pomp and as much uncomfortableness in his little domestic circle as if he had been king of the island'. So wrote Shelburne, who saw this affectation of living in the wilds as 'a gloomy sort of madness'. But Shelburne, like Dr Johnson, was a pre-Wordsworthian. To be a Scot was itself bad enough; actually to 'affect living alone' on a remote Scottish island reading 'out of the way books of science and pompous poetry', with 'a very false taste in everything', made a man a curiosity indeed. 'He excell'd most in writing, of which he appear'd to have a great habit', continues Shelburne. The 'out of the way books of science' whose study he found eccentric chiefly seem to have concerned agriculture, architecture, and botany: studies not perhaps so bizarre as Shelburne implies, and at least the last of them not altogether wasted, for Bute later came to be closely concerned with Princess Augusta in the planting of the Royal Gardens in the grounds of Kew.

In the mid-1740's, however, exiled from politics, proud, ambitious, and for a man of his birth impoverished, Bute naturally looked southwards. He had been married young, to the daughter of Edward and Lady Mary Wortley Montagu. In time, since Wortley Montagu disinherited his son, the daughter was to bring Bute vast wealth, but at this juncture it was a large family, not a fortune, that was arriving, and in 1746 Bute came south to try his luck in the great world for the second time. He had splendid assets, if no money. Charming and vigorous at thirty-three, he was strikingly handsome, with 'the best leg in London'. He shone in private theatricals, then so fashionable; he moved elegantly among the salons and assemblies and routs. Then his chance summons by Frederick Prince of Wales to the card-table at Egham races led to an invitation to Cliveden and more theatricals. Soon he was one of the leaders of Leicester House society and had plainly won the friendship of the Prince and conquered the heart of the Princess. He had also acquired a useful pension, and by 1750 was appointed Lord of the Bedchamber in Frederick's household.

Whether Bute and Princess Augusta were lovers is a matter that cannot be certainly known, though the probabilities are against it. Their association over many years was undoubtedly intimate; there is no evidence that it was adulterous. The important thing, however, was that the world in general, high and low, was convinced that it was. Some, such as Chesterfield, who had once been of the Prince's party, were prepared to keep an open mind, but more were of the same opinion as Horace Walpole, who was 'as convinced of amorous relations as if I had seen them together'. Already before Frederick's death people had been talking. There was a much-repeated story emanating from the glamorous and scandalous Elizabeth Chudleigh, one of Augusta's maids of honour, who, after being reproved by her mistress for immodesty, was able to slip back the pert reply: 'Votre Altesse Royale sait que chacune a son But.' Lord Waldegrave wrote knowingly: 'the sagacity of the Princess Dowager had discovered other accomplishments [in Bute] of which the Prince her husband may not perhaps have been the most competent judge.'[1] Augusta certainly spent long hours in seclusion with her sage and handsome Scotsman. She was in many ways a lonely woman who felt in constant danger of being put upon by a hostile world, and Bute after Frederick's death was a great moral support to her and an adviser who was always at hand to proffer what seemed wisdom. Anxious to silence scandalous gossip, they took to an arrangement by which he visited her secretly by the back stairs, thereby merely making the whispers more excited. As Wraxall mildly commented, 'it cannot be denied that Lord Bute enjoyed a higher place in the favour of the Princess than seemed compatible with strict propriety.'[2] Not all those long hours, people concluded, could have been spent in improving conversation, even with one so everlastingly ready to improve others by his conversation as Lord Bute; and since the Princess was always pointing the finger of accusation against the depravity of the age (an attitude her son was soon to acquire from her),

her enemies had the pleasure of adding the charge of hypocrisy to that of immorality.

The importance of Bute, a Scotsman without fortune or standing among the grander ruling families, was for a time underestimated by the Whigs. The Pelhams thought a Dodington worth buying back to their interest, because Dodington had negotiable parliamentary assets. But Bute had no boroughs to bargain with. He did not even have a seat in Parliament himself – nor did he have over the full twenty years from 1741 to 1761. Pelham and Newcastle to begin with, therefore, did not think him worth their trouble. His uncle Argyll said in 1756, when it was too late, that he had been 'extreamly well dispos'd' towards the administration and yet had been 'slighted and passed over'. [3]

By that time, however, the surprising Bute had made a second personal conquest, more complete, more improbable, and a great deal more far-reaching in its effect, than his first over the Princess Dowager. He had become the total master of the young Prince's mind and heart – guide, philosopher, friend, paragon, seat of all wisdom and virtue. The future King had become infatuated with the man the world took to be his mother's lover. It was a mawkish sort of infatuation, involving complete self-abnegation. For years the Prince, both before and after his majority, had no thoughts that were not Bute's – or if they were not Bute's, then he sought correction of them, for then indeed they must be improper. The unwisdom of cutting the adolescent Prince off from the corrupting world now yielded its strange reward. A few wild oats would have brought a happier harvest and a better-balanced man – for here eventually it was a *man*, of twenty-one and over, who was still in thrall to a mentor of charm and sensibility who was also an ambitious and calculating politician – inclining to his motions like a puppet, echoing Bute's own original opinions with the vehemence added by his own assent, dutifully hating Bute's political rivals, thirsting for guidance, bursting with implanted virtue, putting aside all thoughts and desires that were not consonant with Bute's interests and opinions.

Until 1755, Bute may be regarded merely as the Princess Dowager's adviser and confidant; it was in that year that he was seen to be emerging as a political factor. It was he who then negotiated a marriage of convenience between Pitt and the Grenvilles on one side and Leicester House on the other. Circumstances had given them common enemies in the persons of the Duke of Cumberland and his parliamentary manager Fox,* both of whom had – alarmingly from Leicester House's

* Suspicion of their supposedly malevolent designs had been so well-sown in the Prince's mind that by 1757 he was writing to Bute of the serious danger of losing 'the greatest of stakes, my Crown'; an invader, he wrote, 'with a handful of

point of view – been promoted to the Regency Council. Fox too had been preferred to Pitt for leadership of the Commons. The outrageous Pitt was still *persona non grata* with the King, who effectively blackballed him from the commanding heights of office; and any elevation for Fox was gall and wormwood for Pitt, his clear rival – as in the next generation the triumphs of the younger Pitt were to provide such a long and bitter draught for Fox's son Charles. Thus Pitt and the Princess were temporarily united by common antipathies and fears, and Bute was the man to negotiate the alliance between them.

In the early summer of this same year, 1755, the Princess appointed Bute personal tutor to the Prince, then approaching seventeen, regardless of the fact that Waldegrave and the preceptors were still officially in charge. Bute was immediately able to make contact with George in a manner that no one, not even George Scott, had previously been able to. The Princess could 'not express the joy she felt' to see that Bute had gained her son's confidence and friendship. 'Imprint your great sentiments in him,' she begged, and so make mother and son happy – this, incidentally, in a note written much more in the style of a grateful friend than of a guilty lover. Nothing if not conscientious, the new tutor began his educational offensive with a long, high-flown epistle, very 'literary', upon the education of princes, with a brief history of the world thrown in by way of prolegomena:

> And now my Prince, let a friend who most sincerely loves you, be happy enough to think that you will give attention to these short abstracts . . . Next to your own family you have condescended to take me into your friendship, don't think it arrogance if I say I will deserve it. The prospect of forming your young mind is exquisitely pleasing to a heart like mine.

But he sees 'rocks and quicksands' ahead and the mutterings of 'many enemys'.

> Then comes the most fatal mine of all (my dear Prince I do beseech you to attend to this) it will sooner or later be whispered in your ear, don't you know Lord Bute was your father's friend and is strongly attached to the Princess, he only means to bring you under your mother's government, sure you are too much a man to bear that; now should this ever happen, and I am convinced one day it will . . . hear, Sir, what Lord Bute will say – I glory in my attachment to the Princess, in being called your father's friend, but I glory in being

---

men might place himself on the throne and establish despotism there' – and he meant of course the Duke of Cumberland with troops from Germany.

yours too, I have not a wish, a thought but what points to your happiness alone.[4]

For a year, then, before George came of age he had been in Bute's charge, and Bute had been the political ally of Pitt. Matters other than their common dislike of Cumberland and Fox tended to hold them together for a while. The Princess Dowager had, so said Dodington, 'wished Hanover into the sea'. This sentiment was that of a sizeable body of public opinion, and it was of course the subject upon which Pitt had first made his parliamentary reputation during the thirties and early forties in his attacks on the 'despicable electorate'* and the policies of Walpole and Carteret. George II had never forgiven him. More recently Pitt had been attacking the foreign policy of the Government in which he himself was Paymaster-General. Still, now, at the opening of the Seven Years War, Britain's involvement in the affairs of the German states through her Hanoverian connection remained one of the chief obstacles blocking Pitt's leadership of the Commons and acceptance in the royal Closet. In November, 1755, he had at last been dismissed from the Pay Office, which he had occupied for nine years. It was to need a succession of disasters in America and at sea, including the loss of Minorca, to enable popular opinion to force the minister upon the monarch – or upon the other politicians whom he treated at best with such scant courtesy, at worst with such arrogant disdain. And then, although for George II it was a retreat to have to accept Pitt, for Pitt too it was a step back from earlier attitudes to have to conform to the implications of a 'Hanoverian' policy – continental entanglements and expensive armies in Europe to protect the Electorate from the French. Unlike Pitt, Bute and Leicester House remained opposed to active British participation in a German war. Writing to Bute in July, 1758, George voiced his fears (which were of course Bute's fears too) that, if British forces were not sent quickly back into action in raids upon the French coast

I am certain that the K[ing] will make a push to have them sent to G[ermany], and I can't help feeling that your wavering friend [Pitt] would not be against it; if this unhappy measure should be taken we shall be drawn deeper in a Continent War than ever; and when I mount the Thr[one] I shall not be able to form a M[inistry] who can have the opinion of the people.[5]

* The phrase is echoed in one of Prince George's letters to Bute in August 1759: 'that horrid Electorate which has always liv'd upon the very vitals of this poor country.'

This remained a constant fear at Leicester House, that the new reign would begin with the country bogged down in a costly and unpopular war.

In 1756, a year after his appointment as tutor, Bute had been the central figure in a dispute concerning the arrangements surrounding the Prince of Wales's attainment of his majority at eighteen. George II at first insisted that this man must be refused the post of Groom of the Stole that the Prince proposed for him; the King, wrote Newcastle to Hardwicke, 'looked upon my Lord Bute as closely connected with the Opposition'. Waldegrave was the man for the post, said the King, but the Prince personally pressed Waldegrave to excuse himself.[6] Alternative offers were made to Bute; a pension was mooted; but Bute was not to be bought off, and at last after much negotiation and persuasion, George II relented, though he declined to bestow the gold key of office personally,

> as was usual, but sent it by the Duke of Grafton, who slipped it into his pocket, and advised him to take no notice of the manner. The Earl, on being wished joy, was said to reply, he felt none, while the Duke of Newcastle was Minister.[7]

Mention of the intrusive Scotsman and his influence at Leicester House remained liable to send the old King into one of his cholers. 'What has he to do with it?' he demanded of Newcastle, when Bute put in his oar in the matter of an Excise appointment – it was a request for a place for the Prince's old sub-preceptor Scott; 'and I am sorry to say,' continued Newcastle, 'I hear'd a language, which I have not hear'd before, since I came in last.'[8]

By the spring of 1756, the conquest of the Prince's heart and mind was so complete that among the letters which he now poured out to Bute can be found the sort of language that a lover might use to his mistress. 'I will with the greatest affection and tenderness be yours till death separates us.' 'While my dearest is near to me . . .' 'I long for tomorrow or at farthest for Friday to see you again, without you Kew even tires me.' This correspondence, whose very survival was long unknown,* contains some of the most revealing documents that George ever committed to paper – jumbled in composition, erratic in syntax and spelling, passionate in prejudice, pathetic in self-abasement and consciousness of inadequacy, even moving in the writer's deeply felt determination to improve and so become a monarch worthy of

---

* L. B. Namier (as he then was) first tracked it down and began bringing it to light in his *England in the Age of the American Revolution* (1930). Romney Sedgwick completed the task in his edition of the letters (1939).

England's 'antient state of lustre'. The sincerity of their dog-like devotion is patent, their evidence of immaturity and inner turmoil often painful. One of the earliest of them sets the tone:

My dear Lord,

I have had the pleasure of your friendship during the space of a year, by which I have reap'd great advantage, but not the improvement I should if I had follow'd your advice; but you shall find me make such a progress in this summer, that shall give you hopes, that with the continuation of your advice, I may turn out as you wish.

It is very true that the Ministers have done everything they can to provoke me, that they have called me a harmless boy, and have not even deign'd to give me an answer when I so earnestly wish to see my friend about me. They have also treated my mother in a cruel manner (which I will neither forget nor forgive to the day of my death) because she is so good as to come forward and preserve her son, from the many snares that surround him. My friend is also attack'd in the most cruel and horrid manner, not for anything he has done against them, but because he is my friend, and wants to see me come to the throne with honor and not with disgrace and because he is a friend to the bless'd liberties of his country and not to arbitrary notions. I look upon myself as engag'd in honor and justice to defend these my two friends as long as I draw breath.

I do therefore here in the presence of Our Almighty Lord promise that I will ever remember the insults done to my mother,* and never will forgive anyone who shall offer to speak disrespectfully of her.

I do in the same solemn manner declare, that I will defend my friend and will never use evasive answers, but will always tell him whatever is said against him, and will more and more show to the world the great friendship I have for him, and all the malice that can be invented against him shall only bind me the stronger to him.

I do further promiss, that all the allurements my enemies can think of, or the threats that they may make pour out upon me, shall never make me in the least change from what I so solemnly promiss in this paper.

I will take upon me the man in every thing, and will not shew that indefference which I have as yet too often done.

As I have chosen the vigorous part, I will throw off that indolence which if I don't soon get the better of will be my ruin, and

---

* Concerning her alleged improper relations with Bute.

will never grow weary of this, tho' ————* should live many years.

I hope my dear Lord you will conduct me through this difficult road and will bring me to the gole. I will exactly follow your advice, without which I shall inevitably sink.

I am young and unexperienc'd and want advice. I trust in your friendship which will assist me in all difficulties.

I know few things I ought to be more thankfull for to the Great Power above, than for its having pleas'd Him to send you to help and advise me in these difficult times.

I do hope you will from this instant banish all thoughts of leaving me, and will resolve, if not for my sake for the good of your country to remain with me. I have often heard you say, that you don't think I shall have the same friendship for you when I am married as I now have. I shall never change in that, nor will I bear to be in the least depriv'd of your company. And I shall expect that all my relations shall show you that regard which is due to the friend of the whole family.[9]

The Prince's contrite self-examination and resolve to mend his ways, presumably after some lecture by Bute on the dangers of laziness and irresolution (including, perhaps, being too spineless in his attitude to Fox) are embarrassingly illustrated in a subsequent letter, written when he was only ten weeks or so from his twentieth birthday. It was not only the juvenile Victoria – if it *was* Victoria – who said, 'I will be good':

My dear Lord,

I have had your conversation of Wednesday night ever since in my mind; it greatly hurts me that I cannot make an excuse for myself. I am conscious of my own indolence which none but so sincere a friend as you, could so long have boren with. I do here in the most solemn manner declare, that I will entirely throw aside this my greatest enemy and that you shall instantly find a change; my negligence which I reckon as belonging to indolence is very great but shall absolutely be for ever laid away.

I will employ all my time upon business, and will be able for the future to give you an account of everything I read.

As to what you mention'd in your note of last night concerning F—x it has made me strictly examine myself; and I do now here tell you that I am resolved in myself to take the resolute part, to act the man in everything, to repeat whatever I am to say with spirit and not blushing and afraid as I have hitherto; I will also never shew the

* George II.

least irresolution and will not from being warm on any subject, by degrees grow quite indifferent about it, in short my conduct shall convince you that I am mortified at what I have done and that I despise myself as everybody else must, that knows how I have acted; I hope that by altering now I shall be able to regain your opinion which I value above everything in this world.

I beg you will be persuaded that I will constantly reflect whether what I am doing is worthy of one who is to mount the Throne, and who owes everything to his friend.

I will by my behaviour shew that I know if I in the least deviate from what here I promise and declare, I shall loose the greatest of stakes my Crown, and what I esteem far beyond that, my friend. I hope this will persuade you not to leave me when all is at stake, when nobody but you can stear me thro' this difficult, tho' glorious path. I am, my dear Lord, with great sincerity

Your most oblig'd friend,
George P.[10]

On a dozen occasions in these letters George belabours himself for his inadequacies and above all his indolence – 'my natural indolence', 'my own indolence of temper', 'that incomprehensible indolence, inattention and heedlessness that reigns within me'. 'I act wrong perhaps in most things', he confesses ruefully; and after each wigging from Bute he comes up, dutiful and penitent, for more:

> You were perhaps surpriz'd at my silence last night when you spoke so strongly to me; do not think me too indulgent to myself, when I aledge that this was entir'ly owing to my being extrem'ly hurt at the many truths you told me . . . I am deeply afflicted at the many things you told me . . . They have set me in a dreadful light before my own eyes. I now see plainly that I have been my own greatest enemy.[11]

He was spurred on yet at the same time weighed down by conscience and the voice of duty – 'duty to my Creator, to my country, to my friend and to myself'; duty to restore 'my much loved country to her antient state of liberty . . . free from her present load of debts and again famous for being the residence of true piety and virtue'. Otherwise, he added, with a not very credible and uncharacteristically literary touch of 'period' sentiment, it would be better for him to renounce the throne and retire to some 'uninhabited cavern'. Until that improbable day, 'the thoughts of what I ought to do shall be ever in my mind'. It was a depraved, dissolute age – had he not been told so a thousand times by those around him, particularly by his mother who had bent her energies to isolating him from it? All around were vice, dissipation, and irreligion, and although he discovered that he himself had 'such an unhappy nature', and that he could not 'in good measure alter that', perhaps he could alter the even unhappier condition of his deeply loved country, whose morals were astray, whose religion was lacking, whose finances were in disorder, whose government was in the hands of evil men 'intent on their own private interests instead of that of the public'. His mission, therefore, he wrote to Bute in August, 1758, when the old king's reign had still just over two years to run, must be to 'attempt with vigour to restore religion and virtue when I mount the throne'.

The *sine qua non* for this idealist enterprise was Bute himself, the kind but stern taskmaster, the indulgent demigod, the bland expositor of the universal mysteries; Bute, who was both rash in ambition and, as time was to show, timid at the point of crisis; into whose lap luck, or fate, had poured so challenging a windfall, yet who already felt what Namier described as 'the sentimental charm of dying ahead . . . his eyes fixed all the time on the grand, the moving scene of his future resignation'.[12] ('Why am I doomed to climb ambition's steep and rocky height?' he pondered as early as January, 1759.)

Bute the politician hungry for power was not visible to George. To him he was not a politician at all but a species distinct; 'A friend and an able man, whose integrity and ability I should do a great injustice if I did not look on them as greatly superior to any of the politicians.' 'I find daily what a valuable treasure you are to me, and in what a pretty pickle I should be in a future day if I had not your sagacious counsels.' If only Bute stood firm he had 'no fears with regard to a future day'. 'With my friend at my side,' wrote George, fumbling for the right words from *Macbeth*, 'I say *come what come may, time and tide runs in the roughest day.*'

> Let my dear friend be assur'd of this, that in all events I will keep
> most steadily to the part so often talk'd of between us, and will with
> the greatest affection and tenderness be yours till death separates us.

Although he had examined, on Bute's exhorting him to do so, how far he could trust his own courage, and was 'as sure as he could be of anything' that, 'let things go ever so ill', he *could* still trust it, yet the mere thought of Bute deserting him put him 'on the rack . . . tis too much for mortal man to bear'. The prospect of facing the future bereft of his prop filled him with something like panic. And when, towards the end of 1758, the alliance between Bute and Pitt broke down and it seemed possible that Bute's enemies would be strong enough to keep

him out of the highest office at the next King's accession, the note of
alarm was loud at the prospect of having another as prime minister and
having to do without Bute's 'holsome advice that alone can enable me
to make this great nation happy':

> I have pretty much turned over in my thoughts the idea you had the
> other night, of not accepting the Treasury in a future day; the more
> I reflect upon it, the more I with horror see the inevitable mis-
> chiefs that would arise from your taking such a step, to this poor
> country, and consequently to myself.[13]

Bute's health was in the end the main cause he was to give for his retirement from office, an 'old inveterate illness', 'a great relaxation of my
bowels of many years standing',[14] and in these letters both before and
after accession it is the cause of repeated royal solicitude. George hopes
that staying by the fire will have done Bute good; he trusts that the
night air has not harmed his bad throat; his mother and he 'are very
desirous to know how dear Ld. Bute does after his bleeding'; 'I hope
my friend's rhubarb will be a cure for the pain he has felt some days in
his bowels'; 'I am sorry my dearest friend is so thoroughly rummag'd
by his medicine', and so on. But if only Bute's health and spirits remained good, what might they not achieve between them? The Prince
had been reading that soliloquy of Shakespeare's Henry V, spoken the
night before Agincourt ('*What infinite heart's ease must kings neglect that
private men enjoy?*'), and the more he thought upon it, the more, so he
told Bute, he admired it. 'If you are but well,' he wrote, 'and Providence assists us, England may yet be free and happy.'

The break with Pitt and the three Grenvilles (George and James,
and Pitt's brother-in-law Temple*) evoked cries of indignant outrage
from George. 'I could write you volumes,' he wrote, 'if I attempted
enumerating the many insolencys we have received from that faithless
band'. He was already, as Waldegrave had noted, quick to assign
blame to others, and was constantly 'provoked' or 'incensed' by
the behaviour of all those whose deeds and attitudes did not fall in
with the wishes of Bute and himself. But Pitt's 'betrayal' brought forth
an especial invective. In 1757, he had joined forces with the Duke of
Newcastle, taken charge of the prosecution of the war while Newcastle
continued, as First Lord of the Treasury, to run the day-to-day parliamentary business, and begun to preside over that impressive succession
of military and naval triumphs that set the seal upon his reputation as a
statesman – the capture of Louisbourg and of Guadeloupe, the victory
at Minden in Germany, the naval victories of Lagos Bay and Quiberon

* Richard Temple-Grenville (1711-79), 1st Earl Temple.

Bay, the taking of Quebec. George was nothing if not a patriot and he rejoiced keenly in his country's successes; 'heaven be praised', he wrote off to Bute in October, 1759, on learning of Wolfe's capture of Quebec. But the fly in the ointment was that all these splendid events were triumphs for Pitt and therefore conversely setbacks for Bute, so that 1759, Pitt's *annus mirabilis*, brought less joy to Leicester House than to the nation at large. Pitt was a hawk and Bute a dove, and over those months, until the death of George II in October, 1760, Pitt was playing from strength and Bute from weakness. None of the patronage that might have been expected came the way of Leicester House. Bute plainly feared that even on George III's accession, the combination of Pitt, the national hero, and Newcastle, the old firm, might be strong enough to exclude him from the power he coveted. His overtures to Pitt, conducted through an intermediary, Sir Gilbert Elliot, M.P.,* were strongly and resentfully rebuffed. When, therefore, a few weeks before the old King's death, dispatches reached London of the capture of Montreal – in effect the final conquest of Canada – they were two-edged tidings for his grandson:

> I wish my dearest friend joy of this success; but at the same time I can't help feeling that every such thing raises those I have no reason to love. [*He has heard of plans for a new continental expedition.*] I myself imagine 'tis intended sooner or later for Germany; if that should be the case I hope this nation will open her eyes and see who are her true friends, and that her popular man is a true snake in the grass. I flatter myself my dearest friend is better this morning . . .[15]

A second slap in the face from Pitt and the King concerned Lord George Sackville, a protégé of Leicester House and the general who, after the battle of Minden in August, 1759, was publicly blamed by his commander Prince Ferdinand of Brunswick for failing, despite repeated orders, to bring his cavalry into action, and thereby preventing the annihilation of the enemy. Sackville was brought home by the King's orders, court-martialled, found guilty and unfit to serve, struck off the Privy Council, and forbidden not only the King's Court but the Prince's too. This humiliation of one of the Prince's party, who 'would have been a very useful man', was hurtful enough. That it should have

---

* Pitt's rough notes for Elliot are printed in Namier, *England in the Age of the American Revolution*, 105-107, complaining of his treatment by Leicester House. 'To be ground between two courts is too much . . . everyone is more at home at Leicester House than I . . . I will not be rid with a check rein . . . it is impossible for me to act in a responsible ministerial office with Lord Bute. He . . . gives hourly indications of an imperious nature, I can't bear a touch of command, my sentiments in politics like my religion are my own, I can't change them . . .'

been occasioned by a 'little German prince' acting without consultation, was 'pretty pert'. But that the King should deny Sackville access to the *Prince*'s court was both a calculated insult and 'contrary to our constitution'. 'I am not under the King's roof and therefore undoubtedly have the right of admitting whom I please without H. M.'s leave . . . my dear friend I don't doubt sees the necessity of my taking a bolder and more resolute part, nothing but that can draw men to follow my banner.'*

He expected hostility from 'this old K——'; but it seemed to him that Pitt had gone out of his way to prove his enmity, though it is true that Pitt was to some extent caught between the opposing fire of the King and the Prince; as he expressed it, 'ground between two courts'. When for instance in July, 1759, the Prince, feeling that he could not 'remain immur'd at home like a girl' and wishing to play some part in the war befitting his age and station, wrote formally to the King requesting an Army appointment, the King took it to mean that he wished to be appointed nominal Commander-in-Chief as Cumberland had been in 1745. Indeed it is very likely that persistent fear of Uncle Cumberland prompted this application of the Prince's in 1759. The King would have none of it; '*il veut monter un pas*', he growled; and he accepted the advice of Newcastle and Hardwicke to return a non-committal answer. Bute meanwhile had been pressing Pitt to use his influence on the Prince's behalf, and did in fact succeed in obtaining some trifling concessions in the draft of the royal reply. But the Prince was incensed by the vagueness of it, amounting to a rejection; and was convinced that both Newcastle and Pitt had worked against him. It was yet one more of those 'slights and indignitys' of which he was obsessively complaining:

> You will see by H.M. letters how shuffling it is and unworthy of a British monarch; the conduct of this old K makes me asham'd of being his grandson; he treats me in the same manner his knave and counsellor the Duke of Newcastle does all people, for this answer by some may be look'd upon as agreeing to my petition, by those who think further, as an absolute refusal.
>
> I am going to carry a copy of this unworthy letter to my mother.[16]

He regarded Pitt's failure to make a strong case for him in Cabinet simply as a treachery. Henceforth Pitt was 'the blackest of hearts', 'the

---

* Sackville under the terms of a will adopted the name Germain. He struggled for years to rehabilitate his reputation, and as Third (or American) Secretary was eventually to play an energetic and important, however disastrous, part in the direction of the war with the colonists.

most ungrateful and in my mind most dishonorable of men. I can never bear to see him in any future ministry'. 'Indeed my dearest friend he treats both you and me with no more regard than he would do a parcel of children, he seems to forget that the day will come when he must expect to be treated according to his deserts.' Pitt, in short, from being Bute's ally, had gone over to the enemy and joined the ranks of those evil men of whom the political world seemed so lamentably full – Fox, Newcastle, the Grenvilles (or Greenvilles as he persisted in writing, one of his few quite consistent spellings at this time), Temple, 'that proud overbearing man', and the rest. 'My dearest friend,' he wrote, 'we must look out for new tools our old one's having all deserted us,' but – with belligerent relish for what yet might be 'in a future day', with the grace of God and the continuance of Lord Bute's strength – 'we may make them all smart for their ingratitude.' 'I would rather die ten thousand deaths than truckle at their impious feet,' he exploded, when in 1759 his fears persuaded his reason that a projected Cumberland-Fox administration supported by Newcastle would actually refuse to accept him as King.

George's idolisation of his mentor by no means indicated any lack of normal sexual susceptibility. On the contrary, he noticed that he had a 'daily encreasing admiration for the fair sex'. This propensity, however, worried his conscience, not so much from any puritanical revulsion as from an acute sense of duty. The unfortunate young man had been so instructed in virtue, so indoctrinated with talk of the obligations resting upon a future King, that he could neither have his fling as most young men of his station managed to, nor court the girl he had fallen in love with, like any ordinary citizen. He was, he declared to Bute, all too conscious of the harm that could be wrought to empires by the wrong women in positions of influence. The French monarchs sprang readily to his mind; inevitably, also, his own grandfather. So, though he was in love, the native hue of his *resolution*, so constantly insisted upon, had become 'sicklied o'er with the pale cast of thought'. 'You have often accused me of becoming grave and thoughtful,' he wrote to Bute some time* during the winter of 1759-60. He wished to explain, to 'lay my whole breast naked before you'.

The girl was the very young Lady Sarah Lennox, newly arrived at Court from Ireland, the sister of the third Duke of Richmond, and sister-in-law of Henry Fox (though he was more than old enough to be her father). 'If you remember,' she wrote to a lifelong friend forty-five years later, 'I was not near 15 when my poor head began to be turned

* He did not date these early letters, though he usually timed them – 'near Seven', 'past Twelve', etc.

by adulation in consequence of my suposed favor. In the year 1759, on the late Princess of Wales birthday, 30 of November, I ought to have been in my nursery, and I shall ever think it was unfair to bring me into the world while a *child*.'[17] The best-known of Reynolds' portraits of her does not appear to disclose any superlative beauty; 'Lady Sarah Lennox Sacrificing to the Muses' shows her posing in a conventionally sublime attitude and looking rather foolish – which last she certainly was not. Many contemporaries, however, convey a quite different impression. Horace Walpole, seeing her in private theatricals, thought 'no Magdalen by Correggio half so lovely and expressive' and declared her to be 'a very young lady of the most blooming beauty, and shining with the graces of unaffected, but animated nature'.[18]

Certainly her effect upon the Prince of Wales was potent:

> I most sincerely thank you for your kind letter [he wrote to Bute], it encourages me to write without disguise; if I say things you think improper, impute them to the violence of my love. I did not write this morning expecting any aleviation to my present misery except that of opening my soul to a sincere friend; but finding my melancholy increases and feeling culpable in having kept you so long in the dark, I resolv'd to acquaint you with it, who I am sure will pity me. What I now lay before you I never intend to communicate to any one; the truth is the D. of Richmond's sister ariv'd from Ireland towards the middle of Novr., I was struck with her first appearance at St James's, my passion has been encreas'd every time I have since beheld her; her voice is sweet she seems sensible . . . in short she is every thing I can form to myself lovely. I am daily grown unhappy, sleep had left me, which never was before interrupted by any reverse of fortune; I protest before God I have never had any improper thought with regard to her; I don't deny having often flatter'd myself with hopes that one day or other you would consent to my raising her to a Throne.[19]

Thus Bute's consent must be gained before this young man of twenty-one could think of marriage or even make love. 'I submit my happiness to you who are the best of friends.' If Bute said no, then he would 'grieve in silence, and never trouble you more with this unhappy tale', even though he burned with jealousy when he heard that the Duke of Marlborough 'made up to her', and was so worried and torn that he could not sleep at night. Yet the abyss of his devotion to Bute was so bottomless that 'if I must lose my friend or my love, I will give up the latter, for I esteme your friendship above all earthly joy'.

Bute's reply to this baring of the princely breast attempted to sound sympathetic while turning the whole idea down flat. He would go away to the country and weigh every circumstance, but meanwhile – 'Think, Sir, . . . who you are . . . and prepare your mind with a resolution' – that word again – 'to hear the voice of truth'. The voice of truth was of course to be the voice of Bute. Lady Sarah Lennox came from the Fox stable. That alone was enough to disqualify her, apart from all other considerations.

George was quick to pronounce himself 'thoroughly convinced . . . of the impropriety of marrying a country woman' – a description which the Duke of Richmond's sister might well have found odd. 'The interest of my country,' he vowed,

> ever shall be my first care . . . I am born for the happiness or misery of a great nation, and consequently must often act contrary to my passions . . . I thought the just setting down my resolution never to marry an English woman would please my dearest friend, and convince him his honest intentions the other night have not been without effect.

It would be safer as well as more conventional to resume in the Almanach the hunt for German princesses broken off at the rejection of the Brunswick girls. Bute took it that the Prince's reference in his letter to the difficulty he was having, despite all his 'phylosophy and resolution', in subduing his 'boiling youth' meant that he wished to marry soon. But no; George assured him that so long as 'this Old Man' lived, he would stay unmarried; in an affair of such delicacy he wanted no interference from his lewd old grandfather. However, searches among the marriageable Protestant princesses of Germany continued. These, wrote the Prince, would bind him to nothing, and meanwhile he would 'by every method attempt to render the thoughts of marriage less disagreeable'.

CHAPTER FOUR

The Whigs and the Monarchy

GEORGE II's death, whose assumed imminence had been a factor in every politician's calculations for more than a decade, occurred suddenly at Kensington Palace from a heart attack in October, 1760.

> He rose as usual at six, and drank his chocolate; for all his actions were invariably methodic. A quarter after seven he went into a little closet; the German *valet de chambre* in waiting heard a noise, and running in found the King dead on the floor. In falling, he had cut his face against the corner of a bureau. He was laid on a bed and blooded, but not a drop flowed: the ventricle of his heart had burst.[1]

The reign had ended in a blaze of victory. On the whole George II had been an unloved monarch – even the anonymous author of the little 'Poor Fred' doggerel had admitted 'We had rather it had been his father' – but the resplendent successes of the last year or two of the reign had naturally rubbed off somewhat upon the King himself, who after all was a soldier at heart. John Wesley who in 1755, seeing King George in the robing-chamber of the House of Lords, could only moralise about the insignificant-looking little man being dressed up in a 'blanket of ermine' and a 'huge heap of borrowed hair' – 'Is this all the world can give, even to a King?' – was five years later prompted to ask a surprisingly different sort of question: 'When will England ever have a better prince?'[2] This mellowing was partly of course the consequence of royal longevity; the same process was at work in the later years of Elizabeth I, Victoria, and George III himself. George II died within sixteen days of his seventy-seventh birthday, at an age to which no previous British sovereign survived, and only George III and Victoria after him. On the whole, too, his reign, though it had seen riots in plenty, one rebellion, and two major wars, had been one of gently rising living standards, if we except some important sections of the community such as Irish peasants, Scottish Highlanders, and the gin-soaking poor of London. George's resource and valour on the field of Dettingen had brought approval and applause for a while, but in general his subjects regarded him as tight-fisted, short-tempered, coarse-fibred, mean-spirited, undignified, and above all foreign. Like his father he had plainly cared more for Hanover than for England; not only his wife, but the only one of his mistresses who stayed the course (the Walmoden, Lady Yarmouth), had been German. Yet George II had virtues too. Pitt, who had attacked his policies and one might think had no particular reason for loving him, declared that he 'had something of humanity, and amongst many other royal and manly virtues, he possessed justice, truth, and sincerity'. 'He always was what he appeared to be,' wrote Lord Charlemont. 'He might offend but he never deceived.'

The legend was put about after his death, largely by the enemies of the dominant politicians of his reign, that he had abdicated from the exercise of his kingly powers and allowed himself to become putty in the hands of the leading Whigs. Thus in 1761, a pamphlet by Lord Bath (that is, Walpole's and Hervey's old enemy Pulteney), published anonymously and entitled *Seasonable Hints from an Honest Man*, spoke of a 'set of undertakers' who had 'made use of the legal prerogatives of their master to establish the illegal claims of a factious oligarchy'. A 'cabal of ministers had been allowed to erect themselves into a fourth estate' to enslave the other three and put the sovereign in leading strings. Bath hoped that George III would put an end to all this and make ministers 'depend on the Crown and not the Crown on the ministers'.

George II was never anybody's putty, but this over-simplification of what had been happening since 1714, and many other similar commentaries, contained sufficient elements of truth to become for more than a century part of the accepted canon of British constitutional history: the theory that the first two Georges, their hearts and often their persons abroad in Hanover, abandoned power, patronage, and even policy to their Whig factotums and subsided into a kind of Dogeship while the 'Venetian oligarchy' of the Stanhopes and Walpoles and Pelhams and Russells and the rest ruled the roost unhindered except by their own internal divisions. The corollary of this theory was that George III, by attempting to overthrow the Whigs and rule through arbitrarily chosen ministers, was aiming at personal power and hence an anti-constitutional revolution.

The truth is rather more complicated. It was indeed true that between 1714 and 1760 the monarch was incapable of ruling except with the support of Parliament and that he was unable to command this support except by the employment of those ministers that Parliament would trust. This had been the secret of the power wielded by Walpole and the Pelhams; they had been the King's men in Parliament and

Parliament's men in the royal Closet. The rub came when public and parliamentary opinion demanded actions or men that the Crown disliked. The king might hold out against them for a long time. It was he after all, as everyone assumed must be, who was still at the centre of government; and men of whom he disapproved – whether great like Pitt or small like Dodington – he might exclude so long as he could maintain in office an administration capable of carrying parliament along with it. He needed in effect a set of executive ministers who could conduct a foreign policy of which he could approve, who would secure the taxes, obtain the parliamentary majorities, make the right appointments (in which they would look after the interests of his friends and their own) – in short manage his affairs and the country's with the minimum of friction. Thus the Duke of Newcastle did become in time George II's political agent or 'undertaker' – the supremely painstaking and chronically harassed managing director of the national firm. The King, however, remained the firm's chairman, and by no means a fainéant chairman, although frequently persuaded against his will; as George II succinctly complained, either 'forced or wheedled'. Both George II and George III reigned through an age of transition without comprehending the powerful historical processes which were progressively transforming the constitution. The hour hand of the clock is not seen to move; and the British constitution was (and is) susceptible to variable and subjective interpretations. George II growled and grumbled, but had to make the best of situations as they arose. George III, unwilling like his grandfather to abrogate power that was, so he had been taught, rightfully his, was to make a strong bid to retain this historic authority. To a degree he was to be successful, in the longer term to fail. During the next century his granddaughter Victoria was to make a not dissimilar, though weaker and more spasmodic, attempt; she was of course very far from the impartial 'constitutional' monarch that the historians of her age, contrasting her with George III, liked to imagine. (Her ministers knew better.) She had, it is true, less scope for personal initiative than George II or George III, since the rise of organised political parties largely dictated her choice of ministers. Largely, but even then by no means entirely; and she too, obstinate and conservative as her grandfather, failed similarly to halt the long-term decline of royal power.

If too much used to be made, in pre-Namier days, of the subjection of the Crown before 1760 to the tyranny of the Whig magnates, George III's struggle to regain his royal rights may since have been too easily written off. Some historians have been at pains to show that *nothing* was essentially different in 1760, except for the single and simple fact that there was suddenly no heir round whom an opposition could organise itself. 'There is now no reversionary resource,' wrote Hardwicke. 'Instead of an old King and a young successor, a young healthy King and no successor in view.'[3] And upon this Romney Sedgwick comments: 'There is nothing to add to this explanation';[4] the rest of the story of George's attempt to recover the powers of the Crown and to make the Cabinet 'King's servants in fact as well as in name' was a 'legend' grounded in the fictions invented by opposition politicians. Both George II as Prince of Wales, and then Frederick in his turn, it is argued, had signified an intention, similar to George III's, to liberate the Crown upon their accession from the domination of ministers.

But in fact if nothing really was different in 1760, then in 1760 a remarkable number of people were deceiving themselves, both among those who approved and those who disapproved of George's style of monarchy. It may indeed be true – it probably is – that George III had never read Bolingbroke, but he had certainly been brought up to believe in the idea of a Patriot King, and the propaganda papers of the Court, such as the *Auditor*, were soon to be hailing him in those very terms. Undoubtedly it is true that George II had by no means been entirely ruled by his ministers; but George III, like his mother and Bute, was convinced that he *had* been; and George III (as Bute told Newcastle) did have 'a notion of not being governed by his Minister or Ministers, as the late King had been'; and he did aim at destroying the factions and at uniting politicians behind the Court. Although in fact he had a greater respect for Parliament than either of his predecessors, he did intend to rule as well as reign. *Le roi règne et ne gouverne pas* was not for him. There were significant differences between 1760 and 1727 in addition to the absence of a 'reversionary resource – a young healthy king and no successor in view'. George II had taken over an already established Walpole in command of the House of Commons; George III brought with him an unpopular favourite to be chief minister without a seat in Parliament. George II in 1727 was middle-aged, pragmatical, and Hanoverian; George III in 1760 was young, patriotic, and deeply committed; resolute, idealistic, and opinionated. He meant business in a way that George II never had. It will not do to be too dismissive of his bid to recover royal power. As Sir Herbert Butterfield once drily observed, 'it might seem that George III, with his talk of "destroying corruption" and "annihilating the distinction between Whig and Tory", had not sufficiently soaked himself in Namier.'[5]

The question over which George II had grumbled to Newcastle that he was being 'forced or wheedled' was essentially trivial. It was merely whether Lord Temple, Pitt's proud and turbulent brother-in-

law, should or should not be awarded the Garter. The King hated
Temple and objected. Pitt was using his power to force Newcastle to
make the King yield – which at last, after Newcastle had been driven
nearly to distraction, he eventually did. This storm in a teacup constituted the political 'crisis' of September-October, 1759. Yet its very
triviality perfectly illustrates a point, important to be understood,
concerning the politics of this era. This dispute which so wrung poor
Newcastle's withers occurred, after all, at the height of the Seven Years
War – in a real sense the first world war – when empires were being
lost and won in India and Canada and the Caribbean; when the founda-
tions of Britain's commercial strength and imperial greatness were
being established, and her naval supremacy was being won; at a time
too when the first steps were being taken in Lancashire and Yorkshire
and the Midlands along the road of industrialisation; at the precise
moment, in fact, that one of the less political dukes, Bridgewater, was
setting James Brindley about building his canal from the Worsley
collieries to. the fast-growing town of Manchester, with that most
celebrated of all the symbols of the new age, Barton Aqueduct, a
waterway striding over a river. Within the next few years Watt would
have perfected his steam engine that was to revolutionise the world.

The politicians *were* concerned of course with the war – wars were
a legitimate theatre of political contention – but with little else of these
great events. The argument that set Newcastle rushing off anxious
pitiable screeds to Hardwicke, pleading for support and advice, was
over the question whether Pitt and Temple should be allowed to succeed in a piece of private political blackmail. And if they did not get
their way, then there would be resignations and another complicated
pother over who was to cabal with whom to carry on the King's
government. Yet this far from world-shaking matter was highly
characteristic of the Georgian political scene, at least until the 1780's.
Politics until George III's accession and to a large extent afterwards,
though it had its landed interests, its East India interests and its West
Indian sugar interests, was not much concerned with issues,* and not
at all with -isms or -ocracies or incipient economic revolutions. Much
more frequently it was about peerages and 'places', deaneries and
pensions; petitions to contest a disputed election or irregular appointment; personal antagonisms; who was to be 'in' and who 'out'. Legislation did not yet have the dominant function that it later acquired, and

* With the single important exception of the 'Hanoverian question'. Cf. Pares,
George III and the Politicians, 112: 'I know of no deliberate attempts to make acceptance of office conditional upon stipulations as to policy earlier than the beginning
of George III's reign.' Ideology had disappeared with the Stuarts.

even in the field of legislation the great majority of statutes were of a private or local nature, many of them in a national context trivial.

No one had yet thought of the state as a great engine to control men's affairs in the national interest, and far the greater part of the population had little connection with government or politics at all. It is as true to say that parliament and government ignored the mass of the people as to say that the people, most of them lacking a vote or a stake in the country, ignored parliament and government – except perhaps when an election gave occasion for temporary excitements, or sometimes when government impinged upon individual freedom in the person of the excise man, or when some sudden economic pinch provoked riots, like those of the London weavers in 1765. Local government was a rather different matter – the magistrate-squire was a living reality, powerful flesh and blood. But there was general agreement, as Lord Shelburne remarked, that 'Providence has so ordered the world that very little government is necessary'. The civil service was minute. The giant modern apparatus of local authority and state would have amazed the men of two hundred years ago; the multifariousness of modern government would have both astonished and distressed them. Political parties, in any modern sense of the term, were likewise unknown to them. And such expressions as 'the public' or 'public opinion' conveyed to them a meaning essentially limited and exclusive. The 'public' which could have an 'opinion' was at most a few hundred thousand, and the inner political world itself was infinitely smaller even than that. The great ruling families numbered only a hundred or two, where everybody knew, or at least knew of, everybody else and was very likely related to them. The grand world was a very small world indeed, and, in the manner of a club or family, intensely concerned with personalities, rivalries, scandals, antagonisms, rights of seniority, rules of behaviour, marks of respect, snobberies, trivialities of every kind. Nobody was aware that 'a new age was struggling to be born'; nobody, except perhaps in one sense George III himself. He, indeed, in his raw, amiable, naïvety, had set himself the task of renewing the springs of governmental purity and social virtue, of slaying the dragons of corruption and vice. When his old grandfather finally perished, with him should perish also the bad old days, and a new Britain, with the help of God and Lord Bute, should be born.

PART TWO

THE CROWN
AND THE FACTIONS
1760-1770

CHAPTER FIVE

The Young King

WHEN on 25th October, 1760, a message from the old King's *valet de chambre*, giving news of George II's sudden death, was relayed to Prince George while he was out riding at Kew, he immediately turned back, pretending that his horse had gone lame, pledged everyone to silence, returned to Kew House, and set off straightway for London, meeting on the road a coach-and-six with the blue and silver liveries of Pitt, one of the two Secretaries of State, which had come to give the news officially. The day so long awaited having at last arrived, George's first moves were of course to get in touch with the key man, Bute, and ask for his advice – indeed, his instructions:

> I thought I had no time to lose in acquainting my dearest friend of this: I have order'd all the servants that were out to be silent about what had passed as they value their employments, and shall wait till I hear from you to know what further must be done.[1]

And a later note just before setting out for Carlton House:

> I am coming the back way to your house, I have received a letter from my Aunt [Amelia] with an account of the late King's my grandfather's death; the coach will soon be ready.[2]

Bute had to be consulted before the Privy Council could meet. There followed shorter interviews with the Duke of Newcastle and Pitt, since, for the present at least, Bute and the King had agreed that it would be convenient and necessary to retain these leaders in office. All this took some hours, so that when the Duke of Cumberland, arriving post-haste from Windsor, went first to Kensington and was thence sent on to Savile House, he still had to kick his heels for two or three hours before 'excuses were made that they did not know he was there', and finally he was informed that the Council meeting would be after all at Carlton House. Here they all – Cumberland himself, the Archbishop of Canterbury, the Secretaries of State and the rest – waited a further hour before 'at six o'clock the Archbishop (ridiculously enough) acquainted us with the King's death, of which we informed the King'.[3]

Newcastle had arrived at Carlton House trembling for his position, but was very civilly received, being informed by the King that 'he had always had a very good opinion of me; he knew my constant zeal for his family and my duty to his Grandfather'. After further mutual politenesses, 'His Majesty said these remarkable words – "My Lord Bute is your good friend; he will tell you my thoughts at large".'[4] Newcastle, it seemed, 'my grandfather's knave and counsellor', was not – or not immediately – to be cast into outer darkness after his long lease of influence. However, he was to find his sudden presence in limbo chilling and nerve-wracking. More in sorrow than in anger he reproached Hardwicke for not rushing up to town to guide and console him. 'My fate, or at least my resolution, probably must be taken before to-morrow evening; and therefore I most ardently beseech your Lordship to dine with me to-morrow.' Hardwicke obliged, but advised his friend to quit, and Newcastle did indeed offer his resignation on 27th October.[5] But many persons and considerations persuaded him to think again: Bute, first of all; the King, who 'desired' it – 'nobody can do me so much service at the Treasury as you'; Lady Yarmouth; the Archbishop of Canterbury; many of the Whig leaders; Newcastle's own 'friends' and dependants, a numerous band; Pitt, who told Hardwicke that the First Lord was 'indispensably necessary'; and finally the powerful forces of habit and inertia, the old man's inability to put aside the strings of power. So, as Horace Walpole contemptuously put it, 'this veteran, so busy, so selfish, and still so fond of power,' decided to 'take a new court lease of folly' and make the best of the new situation despite its anomalies.[6] 'Strange,' commented the no less harsh Fox, 'that unless a worthless and a silly and an ignorant man is at the head of state it cannot flourish.'[7] But of course Fox knew as well as everyone else that Newcastle would not be at the head of affairs. Bute was the leader, even though he declared his intention to continue as a 'private man'. What did that mean, Pitt asked Hardwicke, a 'private man'? Was it not clear that Bute intended to be '*the* minister behind the curtain'?[8] Powerful as he would be, Bute could at least be foiled by the old guard in one of his ambitions – to become an English peer, an aim in which he was supported by George. The House of Lords had already ruled in 1711 that this was for a Scottish peer illegal, and Newcastle declared the thing unthinkable. 'His people' would not stand for it.

Pitt was a harder nut to crack than Newcastle. *His* people were not merely a group of politicians but the British people themselves; he was a national idol. But he had weaknesses too, apart from his chronic ill-health – his gout, his 'gout in the bowels', and worst of all his 'gout in the head', those recurrent bouts of paralysing depression. He had an inordinate talent for making enemies, by his egoism, his disdainful airs of superiority, the severity of his rectitude, his obsessive sense of mission. He could command awe, but never, outside his family circle, love or friendship. He could have no colleagues, but only admirers and subordinates. Apart from his brother-in-law Temple, he had no friends among the ministers. Moreover, his wish to prosecute the war with vigour and glory until the utmost advantage could be squeezed out of British successes conflicted with a growing desire, shared by Bute and the King with many others, to disengage from hostilities as soon as possible, taking what could be taken.

Like Newcastle, Pitt (though the 'blackest of hearts') was received amicably by the King before the first full Cabinet meeting, but certain passages read to that assembly a few hours later infuriated him. The speech began innocuously enough with conventional references to the late melancholy event. George's authentic voice is heard in much of what followed: '. . . the weight now falling upon me . . . I feel my own insufficiency to support it as I wish but . . . I shall make it the business of my life to promote in everything the glory and happiness of these Kingdoms . . .' Then came the politics: 'As I mount the throne in the midst of a bloody and expensive war, I shall endeavour to prosecute it in the manner most likely to bring an honourable peace . . .' Pitt, the architect of victory, and with so many worlds to conquer, could not, without protest, accept 'bloody and expensive' and the emphasis laid on seeking peace. That evening he had a two-hour session with Bute, the man whose road to the top he had done more than any other to block, but with whose status as king's favourite he must now try to accommodate. In the end, the published text of the King's speech contained significant differences from the spoken version. The war was no longer 'bloody and expensive'; it was 'expensive, but just and necessary'; and although the King still expressed a wish for peace, it was peace 'in concert with my allies'. During his conversation with Bute, Pitt had agreed with him on the necessity of keeping Newcastle at the Treasury, but insisted that 'if the system of the war was to undergo the least change', he, Pitt, would resign from its direction. As for Bute wishing to be a 'private man, if he could see his country out of the present plunge', said Pitt, 'the only difference between them was that his Lordship would practice his philosophy in a Court, he in a village.'[9]

Relations between Pitt and Bute, and therefore also between Pitt and the new King, continued prickly. 'Lord Bute and Pitt had warm words at Court,' the Duke of Devonshire entered into his diary on 17th November. 'Pitt attacked him very roughly upon the treatment he met with' as chief minister in the House of Commons* yet as one

* Newcastle of course being in the Lords and Bute merely 'behind the curtain'.

kept in ignorance of what was going on (in particular about the new
King's Civil List); 'he would serve on tho' ill used but the world should
know it.'[10] As for the King, he was impatient of having to placate this
arrogant and formidable minister: 'I plainly see if every ill humour of a
certain man is to be sooth'd, that in less than a couple of months I shall
be irretrevably in his fetters; a state of bondage that an old man of
seventy odd groan'd [under] and that twenty two ought to risk everything rather than submit.' This man of 'ambition, pride, and im-
practibility' meant, it seemed to George, to disturb both the royal
repose and that of his subjects, and 'if I do not show them', as he wrote
bravely enough to Bute, 'that I will not permit ministers to trample
on me . . . my subjects will in time come to esteem me unworthy of the
Crown I wear.'[11]

At least the Duke of Newcastle was not trampling on him. On the
contrary, the Duke lamented bitterly that the boot was on the other
foot:

> Every day produces something less promising than the former . . .
> For myself, I am the greatest cipher that ever appeared at Court.
> The young King is hardly civil to me; talks to me of *nothing*, and
> scarce answers me upon my own Treasury affairs . . . Is this giving
> me the countenance and support which is necessary for me to carry
> on his Majesty's business, much less what is sufficient to make me
> happy and easy?[12]

As Hardwicke replied – and it may well have been so – something of
the King's seeming slights perhaps came from his reserve. He lacked
confidence and *savoir faire*, however mettlesome he could sound on
paper. But that he was striving to be gracious, at the Levees and Drawing Rooms for instance, is borne out by Horace Walpole's comment
made less than a week after Newcastle's plaint: 'The levee room has lost
so entirely the air of the lion's den. The young man don't stand in one
spot with his eyes fixed royally upon the ground and dropping bits of
German news. He walks about and speaks freely to everybody.'[13]
And of course the difference between Walpole's impressions and Newcastle's is easily accounted for. Polite small talk was one thing, even if
it cost some effort and took some learning; political consultation was
another. Newcastle had been used to expecting it, with very few gaps,
since 1724; his deprivation was traumatic.

The impression the new monarch made during these first few weeks
was in fact almost universally favourable. He had great advantages.
First, as Dr Johnson remarked, much of his popularity arose from the

fact that he was *not* his grandfather.* He was young, and England had not seen a young monarch mount the throne since 1558; the average age of accession from 1603 had been forty. Above all he was English – at least by inclination and upbringing, so that one might disregard his ancestry. Certainly there had been no such enthusiasm to greet a new ruler since the restoration of Charles II just a hundred years before. The day the King went to the House, wrote Walpole to George Montagu, 'I was three-quarters of an hour getting through Whitehall: there were subjects enough to set up a dozen petty kings: the Pretender would be proud to reign over the footmen only; and indeed, unless he acquires some of them, he will have no subjects left; all their masters flocked to St James's.' 'One hears nothing of the King,' wrote the poet Gray to Wharton, 'but what gives one the best opinion of him imaginable.' Laurence Sterne wrote to his friend Croft, 'The King seems resolved to stop the torrent of corruption and laziness. He rises every morning at six to do business, rides out at eight to a minute, returns at nine to give himself up to his people.' Mrs Montagu, the bluestocking, found dignity and decency; 'mildness and firmness mixed; religious sentiments and a moral court unblemished; application to business' – there was no more talk of indolence now; George's reformation in this respect was spectacular – 'affability to everyone; no bias to any particular party or faction . . . Thank Heaven that our King is not like his brother of Prussia [Frederick the Great], a hero, a wit, and a freethinker, for in the disposition of the present times we should soon have seen the whole nation roaring blasphemy, firing cannon, and jesting away all that is serious, good, and great.'[14] Henry Fox, however, was quick to note that he was 'capable of great resentment where his dignity is trenched upon'. Fox's own brother-in-law, the young Duke of Richmond (Sarah Lennox's brother) soon discovered the truth of this. After having taken umbrage at Court appointments that had brushed aside the claims of his brother and cousin, he took part in what George called a 'very offensive' interview, flinging back in the King's face the Bedchamber appointment he had only just received. 'I think this is the first time in my life I have been thoroughly in a passion,' George wrote to Bute; 'I thank heaven for being rid of him.'[15]

What all noted with interest was George's tact towards his uncle Cumberland, the man he had been brought up to regard as the prime menace to his position. The bogy had always been somewhat unreal,

* – though Johnson could not resist airing a characteristic prejudice and some reasonable doubts. The young man had unfortunately 'long been in the hands of the Scots'; and people 'were so much inclined to hope great things that most of them begin already to believe them'.

the more so after Cumberland fell out of George II's favour for concluding in 1757, after his defeat at Hastenbeck, the Convention of Klosterzeven by which he agreed to disband his army and evacuate Hanover. Resigning all his military appointments, he had retired into private life, and then suffered a stroke which left him, though still only in his late thirties, partially paralysed. Cumberland himself was wary of the new monarch's professions of kindness; according to Fox he thought 'all his My's civility to him grimace; that HM has no sincerity'.[16] However there is no reason to doubt George's declared intention 'to live well with all his family'. Had things happened so, they would certainly have made a Hanoverian novelty. The King even forbade the name of his brother the Duke of York to be mentioned in the prayers for the royal family, for if included it would have had to take precedence of Cumberland's. Fair and honourable treatment was accorded too to Lady Yarmouth, the once desirable Mme Walmoden, whose status with the widower George II had gradually matured to that of trusted old companion and confidante. She never quite managed him as Caroline had, but had become a far from negligible intermediary in the King's business. He had left behind for her, among a confusion of wills, a small cabinet, with a signed declaration. With whatever distaste, George III saw that she reaped the reward of the contents, £9,000 in bank bills and 1,100 guineas in cash.*

The age was irreligious and depraved; this had been the Leicester House canon during the fifties. It is not surprising therefore that one of George's first acts was to issue a Proclamation for the Encouragement of Piety and Virtue, and for the Preventing and Punishing of Vice, Profaneness, and Immorality – altogether, it might be thought, a tall order, but to some extent in tune with the reviving religion and renascent puritanism of an age that had already produced Wesley, Whitefield, and the Countess of Huntingdon, and was soon to feel the moral impetus of the Clapham Sect and the humanitarian and sabbatarian earnestness of the Evangelicals. Indeed George's proclamation anticipated the sentiments and much even of the language of Wilberforce's Society for the Reformation of Manners and Suppression of vice:

> We . . . do hereby declare our royal purpose and resolution to discountenance and punish all manner of vice, profaneness, and immorality . . . particularly in such as are employed near our royal

* Holland, *Memoir*, 11. Others quote the respective sums as £6,000 and 2,000 guineas. According to *The Court and City Kalendar* for 1764, Lady Yarmouth was still in 1763 drawing a pension of £4,000 from the Irish list.

person . . . and . . . we will upon all occasions, distinguish persons of piety and virtue, by marks of our royal favour . . . And we do hereby enjoin and prohibit all our loving subjects, of what degree or quality soever, from playing on the Lord's day at dice, cards, or any other game whatsoever; and we do hereby command and require them . . . decently and reverently to attend the worship of God on every Lord's-day on pain of our highest displeasure, and being proceeded against with the utmost rigour that may be by law . . .[17]

All this might merely produce sceptical smiles among the sophistic-ated,* though most of these, it may be remembered, considered free thought and pagan morality the rights and luxuries of above-stairs only, and were strongly in favour of religion for servants and the lower orders in general. Many of the aristocracy and gentry endured divine service only to set an example to villagers and domestics.

The King's piety was at least honest and serious, and he soon showed it in many directions. When a preacher sang his praises from the pulpit of the Chapel Royal, he remarked sharply to the chaplain Dr Wilson that he attended church to hear God's praises, not his own. He soon got rid of Sunday Levees at St James's and frowned with increasing severity on gambling at Court, first reducing the number of hazard tables, then limiting the hours of play and finally outlawing it alto-gether.† Card-playing for stakes was in turn forbidden, and *all* card-playing among Court servants. His own attendance at religious services was regular and his manner there reverential. At his coronation his laying aside the Crown while receiving the sacraments brought much favourable comment from the godly. He ate and drank sparingly, and kept no mistress either at this or any future time – behaviour strict to the point of eccentricity in an eighteenth-century monarch. Simple, regular, and abstemious, he was a pattern of respectability and decorum. In this respect at least the Princess Dowager had not laboured in vain.

Of the King's opening of the new reign's first parliamentary session, with much dignity, and a speech delivered in accents of purest English, everybody spoke well. Fox agreed with the rest that his

* Much like those among the Austrian aristocracy of this time, when Maria Theresa set up a Chastity Commission for improving the morals of the upper classes.

† The advantages of a public lottery, however, appealed to him: 'The idea of opposing the Lottery yesterday seems rather extraordinary, unless mankind could be entirely prevented from gaming. I am certain it is right for the public to avail itself of that vice rather than lay taxes on the necessaries of life.' (King to Lord North, 8.3.1781).

Majesty 'was much admired', but plainly thought that he had been over-coached by that one-time amateur actor Bute: the King 'was thought to have too much studied action, and it was observed that he laid the accent on the first syllable of allys and revenues, which is after the Scotch pronunciation' – an interesting linguistic point, and an indication of how narrowly he and 'the Favourite' were being observed. To discuss the speech itself, prior meetings had of course been held, first of the inner group or 'conciliabulum' of Bute, Pitt, Newcastle and Hardwicke (though the last was no more a minister than Bute – one might regard him as Newcastle's 'favourite'). Then a wider circle of ministers and notables discussed its contents; and finally the full Cabinet heard it. Parliament was to open on Tuesday, 18th November; the full Cabinet met the day before; but on Sunday, 16th, Newcastle, down at Claremont in Surrey, was astonished to receive a draft of the already agreed speech with an insertion made the previous day in the King's own hand, of a paragraph on whose inclusion George strongly insisted. 'I made no observation,' wrote Newcastle immediately to Hardwicke, 'but that this method of proceeding can't last. We must now (I suppose) submit.' The next day, Monday, 'before the whole Cabinet Council who were in the inward room of St James's [Fox recorded] Pitt took Lord Bute and talked to him as one gentn. should not talk to another, not letting him go to the King, though in waiting and rung for, and his Majesty was left alone above half an hour employed by Pitt in scolding Bute.'[18]

The speech, whose text again referred to the war as 'both just and necessary' – Pitt's version, rather than Bute's – was duly delivered, and delivered well, Scots accentuation or no. The war was to be vigorously prosecuted, and Frederick of Prussia and the other allies fully supported, but only 'to bring our enemies to equitable terms of accommodation'. Much the best remembered part of the speech was the insertion that had so rattled Newcastle, including the famous words, 'Born and educated in this country, I glory in the name of Britain.'* In fact, there was nothing very new or extraordinary in this. Insistence on sustaining the rôle of a patriot king was something that had been hammered into George by his father from the tenderest age. The genuine truth of the interpolated words constituted indeed the strongest card in George's early popularity. But for Newcastle and his friends there were two things about them that they did not like. First, the leading Whigs had come to assume that King's Speeches

* – or *Briton*, which sounds precisely the same and was the version that came to be accepted, though *Britain* in the King's supremely legible handwriting is there to prove the error.

were written exclusively by politicans not kings; and secondly, they took 'Britain' to imply that *Scotland* was receiving too much emphasis.* The King, it was noted, had not gloried in being English, and once more the hand of Bute was seen. 'I suppose you will think Britain remarkable,' wrote Newcastle. 'It denotes the author to all the world.' 'Scotchman' at this time had become little less than a synonym for undesirable immigrant. Bute was to be unpopular in any case, as royal favourite, as reputed lover of the Princess Dowager, as supposed author of an unpopular tax on cider, and as the political enemy of Pitt the conquering hero. That he was a Scot made bad much worse.

It was already six years since the last general election in 1754; and now a new reign in any case necessarily meant another. In view of the new dispensation, there was much speculation how the thing would be 'managed'. That it would and must be managed was never in question. All the general elections of the eighteenth and early nineteenth centuries were; and throughout the entire period, until 1830, no government in power was ever careless enough to 'lose' one – even if that word may be properly used of those days before the existence of organised parties. Governments occasionally lost parliamentary divisions and were forced to trim or abandon measures; but with a judicious expenditure of favours, and of a little secret service money, it was regularly possible to ensure continuity in the king's government. This meant neither that all constituencies were rigged nor that vast sums were spent on bribery. But under all the Georges the sitting government had control of sufficient patronage and local influence to retain majorities in the House of Commons; and during the reigns of the first two Georges, Walpole, Henry Pelham, and his brother Newcastle had perfected a system of management which at least always ensured the king a stable government and a House of Commons which, while not servile, was in general prepared to give support to the Crown and its ministers. The chief critics of the system had not been reformers, still less democrats, but those like Bolingbroke or Pulteney or Dodington who had played the game of influence and jobbery, and lost.

In this art of parliamentary management Newcastle in particular had made himself so peculiar a specialist that George was obliged to regard him, temporarily at least, as indispensable. He had at his fingertips the delicate balance of this constituency, the vulnerability of that, the

---

* This was still rankling nearly a decade later with Junius: 'When you affectedly renounced the name of Englishman, believe me, Sir, you were persuaded to pay a very ill-judged compliment to one part of your subjects, at the expense of another' (*Letters*, 19.12.1769).

likely outlay necessary to secure the other. He was master of the nice intricacies of rewards for services rendered or to be rendered – a court appointment here, a pension or an Irish peerage there, a deanery for a candidate's cousin, an Admiralty clerkship for his nephew, an annual allowance to some local landowner who had brought a factious part of the country over to his Majesty's interest. All these payments and *douceurs* Newcastle adjusted to the rank, standing, and services of the beneficiary; he had become the supreme prize-distributor and seat-broker. His control of Crown, Treasury, and Admiralty boroughs, together with his bargaining to contrive the support of a large proportion of the 200-odd boroughs under the control of private patrons, was what gave this querulous and widely despised politician his undeniable power.

George III would dearly have liked to throw him overboard and put Bute in his place. This, however, Pitt had vetoed, preferring Newcastle as the devil he knew. So Bute had to be for the time being 'a private man'. Between the three of them, Bute, Pitt, Newcastle, there developed for a time an unstable equilibrium. Pitt wanted Newcastle at the Treasury because he would find money for the war. Bute, since Pitt would not have him at the Treasury, preferred Newcastle there to Pitt himself. Pitt could of course, perfectly properly and 'constitutionally', have been dismissed by George III, but who save Pitt could command the support of the House of Commons, without which no king of Britain could govern? Bute could command the ear and mind of the King, and he could also dispense offices and favours; but so long as Pitt commanded the Commons and Bute was not a Minister of the Crown, Bute could not dictate policy. Thus each of the members of this trio had to accommodate with the other two, and a very uneasy accommodation it was. As for George, his 'resolution' was obliged to dwindle into compromise. The simple hopes cherished at Leicester House soon turned into complicated frustrations. In the Leicester House days 'politicians' had been a synonym for 'evil men'. Now he was forced to become one of them himself and painfully learn about the 'art of the possible'.*

Although there is no doubt that with George III's accession men were convinced that a new style of monarchy had arrived, more active, more prepared to stand by its rights, there is equally no doubt that many of the old accounts of a sharp break in 1760 in the continuity of constitutional development, of royal interference in parliamentary elections, with bribery used on an unprecedented scale to secure seats

---

* Not without cries of pain. He once declared: '*Ce métier de politique est un très vilain métier; c'est le métier d'un faquin; ce n'est pas le métier d'un gentilhomme.*'

for the King's friends, cannot be borne out. Upon the election of 1761 itself, here for instance is Lecky, stating the old legend:

> Notwithstanding the professions of purity that were made by the King's friends, it was noticed that the general election which now took place was one of the most corrupt ever known in England, that large sums were issued by the Treasury, that the King took an active part in naming the candidates, and that the boroughs attached to the Duchy of Cornwall, which had hitherto been at the disposal of the ministry, were now treated as solely at the disposal of the Crown.[19]

This account of things was demolished by Sir Lewis Namier forty years ago.[20] It is true that Newcastle himself was at first very nervous, 'cipher' as he now felt himself to be, of being no longer allowed to manage the election. He anxiously awaited the list of men that the King might insist on, and feared it might be lengthy. At last, to his huge relief, *three* names were put forward by George – all three moreover, commented Newcastle, 'very unexceptionable' and he would be delighted to 'take care of them, on very easy and certain conditions'. As for Bute, he did not find it easy to absorb himself in election business; in any case, even if Bute had wished to, he could not have managed the election except through Newcastle or by first removing him, since the whole apparatus, with its local agents, worked through the Treasury and to a lesser extent the Admiralty – and while Newcastle controlled the Treasury, the son-in-law of his ally Hardwicke (Lord Anson) controlled the Admiralty. Namier reckoned 'Bute's friends' newly elected in English constituencies in 1761 to amount to only eleven or twelve. The truth is that the March, 1761 election turned out after all to be much like elections held under the first two Georges, with a similar assortment of placemen or Court nominees of one sort or another (about one-third of the whole), of the 'connexions', and of independent country gentlemen. As Bute himself had said to Dodington, 'the new Parliament would be the King's, let who will chuse it'; and it *was* Newcastle after all who had the choosing, for the last time. Totting up the tally of his 'friends' after the results, he reckoned 292 members, 144 of them new. His 'doubtfuls' came to 113, including Pitt; 'others' 108. Very soon, however, all these classifications were to become meaningless. New circumstances brought new loyalties, and as Newcastle's power continued to dwindle, his 'friends' were steadily to drift away.

Certainly, then, there was a 'Court' party in the new Parliament – but then there always had been in earlier Parliaments. Certainly too, the designation 'Tory' (if seldom employed) was no longer a smear or a recipe for political oblivion.* 'Prerogative' may even have 'become a fashionable word', as Horace Walpole asserted. With a new King, a young and vigorous King known to have strong opinions; with no Prince of Wales, but instead a King's favourite not in the administration, there was a new feeling in the political air. The sense of new directions was not entirely a fiction sired by Whig historians out of disgruntled politicians. But the old story that George III, 'his head stuffed full of obsolete ideas of the prerogatives of the Crown'[21] set about instituting a constitutional revolution, systematically and corruptly filling the House of Commons with his minions, 'a confederacy of renegades from every political section of the state . . . afterwards known by the appellation of "King's Friends" ' – all this will not stand up, and since it has long been discarded, hardly now requires to be lengthily considered. For one thing, though one might say that there was a vague sort of 'Tory party' in 1760 (numerically small), there was certainly no 'Whig Party', but instead a collection of sparring groups (or factions, as George preferred to call them) of whom the Duke of Newcastle's friends, soon to be known as the Rockinghams, were the most numerous and important.† As for 'renegades', in the shifting alliances and allegiances of eighteenth-century political manœuvre, all politicians were renegades of a sort – not least Pitt himself, who had renegued from Leicester House to St James's.

The idea of a firm, universally accepted constitution is as false as the idea of two firmly established parties, Whig and Tory. Far from 'overturning the constitution', George III would, as Lord North once said, have 'lived on bread and water' for it, *as he understood it*. And it is a nice question who was being more 'unconstitutional' in the context of 1760 – George for seeking to govern through a favourite who was not in the Cabinet, or Pitt for denying to the King his right to appoint the minister of his choice.[22] The right of the Crown to choose its own principal minister was at this time incontestable. As Fox wrote: 'The H. of Commons has a right, and has sometimes exerted it, to accuse a Minister, and make it very inadvisable for a Prince to retain him in his

* After the failure of the Jacobite movement, the terms 'Whig' and 'Tory' had become largely meaningless, by 1760 almost entirely so.

† 'There are four parties, Butes, Bedfords, Rockinghams, and Chathams' – Lord Northington in 1767. In the same year Rockingham himself reckoned there were nine main groups in the Commons, five of these being the principal 'connexions'. By 1783, however, Lord North was referring to 'three great parties' only – his own; the followers of Fox and Portland (the old Rockinghams); and the followers of Shelburne and Pitt. By 1804 there were again four main parties, Pittites, Grenvilles, Foxites, and the group round Addington.

favour. But I do not remember they ever undertook to say who should succeed him.'[23] The really critical point was the distinction between right and advisability. George's 'constitutional' right to employ Bute seems incontrovertible; whether it was advisable to rule through a personal friend with no standing either in Parliament or the country is an entirely different matter.

Historians continue to argue, as politicians did two centuries ago, over the constitutional propriety of George's choice of Bute as minister, and eventually as chief minister. Sir Lewis Namier had no doubts: 'the executive was the King's as truly as it is now of the President of the United States.'[24] For Richard Pares too 'the King had a constitutional right to choose Bute', though in using it in a 'somewhat unacceptable way' he was affronting 'the political class'.[25] Sir Herbert Butterfield, while acknowledging the King's 'undoubted constitutional right', found a good case for the opposition too. The British constitution was not standing still, and the opposition were anticipating the future. Yet, argued Butterfield, George also might have been anticipating the future if he had 'pulled it off'.[26] W. R. Fryer cannot accept this last, and suggests that Butterfield may sometimes confuse 'constitutional' with 'legal': an action may be legal but unconstitutional in the sense that it disturbs well-established and respected custom.[27] Since it seems that no one can pin down what the constitution was at any precise moment, but merely describe what it *had been* and what it *became*, all this makes an absorbing and subtle game which has, no doubt, long years yet to run. I. R. Christie even doubts whether the constitution in mid-Georgian times was doing anything so 'determinate' as drifting; it would be 'more apt to think of oscillations . . . within the confines of an unchanging and fairly elastic framework', with royal power expanding as divisions among politicians grew sharper, and contracting as they lessened.[28]

One thing at least is unquestionable: nobody at that time saw any other way of conducting elections but through management, or of running Parliament but through influence. The Treasury and the King (from the Civil List) were always prepared to spend money to get into Parliament the men they wanted, and certainly in 1761, as before and since, ambitious individuals were ready to lay out considerable sums themselves in order to get into Parliament. 'The expense is incredible,' chattered Horace Walpole to Sir Horace Mann in that year. 'Venality is grosser than ever. We have been as victorious as the Romans and are as corrupt.' But these remarks bear more resemblance to conventional comment on the English weather, which is always getting worse, than to factual assessment. In fact there was about as much and as little corruption in 1761 as at any other election in the century. The venality of 1761 was not grosser than the venality of Horace's father Robert (whose reputation he venerated); and as for the Romans, Horace Walpole could never resist a stylistic felicity. The one thing about the 1761 election that was slightly out-of-the-way was the rather larger than usual proportion of sinecurists and Court officials among the placemen,* partly because of the amalgamation of the old and new Courts on George's accession, and partly because Newcastle was trying everything he knew to find 'pasture for all the beasts he had to feed'. Like Walpole, those long in opposition – as Bath and Dodington had been, or Burke and Charles Fox were to be – always exaggerated the corruption of government. In office, they seldom considered changing the system, unless to their own party's advantage.

Indeed, thoroughgoing parliamentary reform was not yet being suggested by anyone, and, as for ideas of democracy and equality, they hardly surfaced at any point in British political thought between the Levellers and Tom Paine. Horace Walpole, in the course of defending his own inherited advantages and sinecure posts, expressed his age's acceptance of the necessity of inequality. 'While there are distinctions of rank and unequal divisions of property, not acquired by personal merit, but by birth or favour, some will be more fortunate than others.'[29] The King could not have put it better – indeed, of course, not nearly so well. In his assumptions about the principle of Subordination – one of his favourite words, like Resolution – George III was in no way out of step with the overwhelming majority of his subjects, high or low.

All through the early months of 1761 wary negotiations continued (largely through the mediation of that experienced go-between Count Viry, the Sardinian) to regularise the governmental situation and permit Bute to be appointed Minister. If not acceptable at the Treasury, Newcastle's preserve, perhaps he might be given one of the two Secretaryships of State.† After much beating about the bush, Newcastle himself at last proposed this to the King, if only the thing could be done without 'disobliging Mr Pitt . . . In all events, Mr Pitt must not be

* The term 'placemen' includes members of the administration, Court officials, civil servants, and sinecurists – in all something between 200 and 250 members.

† Until 1768 there were two Secretaries, one for the Northern and one for the Southern Department. From 1768 to 1782 a third Secretary was added for American affairs. From 1782 there were again two only, one for home affairs and one for foreign.

offended'. Perhaps the Duke of Devonshire might be approached to approach in turn the terrible Mr Pitt, since Newcastle would not. But in the end it was Bute himself who faced Pitt. After venting his usual grievances Pitt 'coldly acquiesced'. So Lord Holdernesse was persuaded to resign by the offer of a pension of £4,000 a year for life and Bute had his place as Secretary. It was one more step up the ladder; only one yet remained. Simultaneously the Chancellor of the Exchequer, Legge, who refused to resign, was dismissed and replaced by Lord Barrington, the perfect example of the non-party career politician, servant of King and administration – any administration, regardless of political complexion.

Bute made his appointment the occasion for a letter to his pupil and monarch – another of his great word-mountains down whose sides flow the lava streams of self-approval, self-deception, and sententiousness:

> In this universal satisfaction [with the King] I meet with a little flattery that I do not blush to own I am sensible to . . . While they justly praise my King, some think I have a little merit in his education . . . I may want talent for business, faction may overwhelm me and Court intrigues destroy me . . . but . . . I know and feel I have in serving you done my duty to my God, my Country and my King . . . To tread an unknown path I sacrifice peace, quiet, and all my little happiness to your commands . . .[30]

and so on, for some 1,600 words. And then again, in the midst of all the self-congratulation and self-doubt, comes that most tell-tale of all Bute's touches. Twice in the same letter he foresees betrayal by the inadequacy of his faculties, the weakness of his bowels, or the malice of his enemies, and he wishes to take out an insurance policy against failure:

> As I now launch out into a stormy sea in hopes that I may in some measure answer your expectations that I may do some little good, here suffer me, Sir, to desire in the most solemn manner that I may have your Royal promise to ensure me a safe retreat again near your person, in case I find myself unable to do what I wish, let it proceed from what honest cause it may; whether from the storm of faction bearing me down, from my talents not being calculated for the business I enter on, from the independency of my mind not being able to undergo the drudgery of public business, or lastly from finding my health and constitution impaired by it, or events of private life rendering it insupportable to me, in any of these cases

suffer me once more to entreat you Sir as my King, my Master and
my Friend, to retire again next your person, or if that suit not your
convenience, remember I this day enter my protest that you must
not be displeased if I at a sudden warning retire from courts and
business at one and the same minute. [31]

Bute's entry into the administration did little to sweeten the political
atmosphere or lessen the intrigues among the ruling group, where
the grand and protracted argument of 1761-62 was brewing: whether,
or on what terms, to extricate Britain from the 'bloody and expensive'
war with France, and what attitude to adopt towards Spain, whose
alliance with France was soon to be sealed in another Bourbon Family
Compact. However, in the months immediately following his 'd.
friend's' admittance to office the King, though he was heavily involved
in the political wrangling and industriously learning the trade of
monarch, had his head full of personal problems. A King must marry;
'matrimony,' as he stiffly put it, 'must sooner or later come to pass.'

CHAPTER SIX

Sarah Lennox and Charlotte
of Mecklenburg

GEORGE continued privately to hanker after his English bride, for the German prospects, being assiduously followed up by emissaries and Hanoverian contacts such as Schulenburg and the brothers Münchausen, were not exciting. It was a sellers' market; Protestant princesses who were amiable of disposition, tolerable of appearance, and unencumbered by impossible or even insane relations were very hard to come by. The Hanoverian prospectors reported adversely on the Princess of Schwedt and the Princess of Darmstadt, both of whom were said to be 'stubborn and ill-tempered to the greatest degree' – though, *faute de mieux*, in April, 1761, George was confessing to Bute, that if *he* was satisfied, it should be the Princess of Darmstadt; 'I should be for settling this as soon as possible the worst thing to my liking is her size.' She was, however *bien faite*, undeniably *grande*. There remained, however, the '[P——ss] of Strelitz' (Charlotte of Mecklenburg-Strelitz) who it seemed had a 'very amiable character' and 'very good sense', and if that was the case, George considered, 'a little England's air will soon give her the deportment necessary for a British Queen.' Admittedly Schulenburg reported, *'ce n'est pas justement une beauté,'* but though the accounts of her were not 'in every particular as I could wish, but yet I am resolv'd to fix here; the family of the Princess of Darmstadt has given me such melancholy thoughts of what may perhaps be in the blood'.[1] This was written in May, 1761.

However, that he was not *quite* resolved is clear from various other sources, and in particular from the correspondence of the Fox and Lennox families. Sarah Lennox in a postscript to a letter to Fox's niece Susan Fox-Strangways, written on 25th February from her brother the Duke of Richmond's at Goodwood, says: 'My brother begs you'll go to Court, and let me know what *he* says to you' – *he* clearly meaning the King.[2] Next month she broke her leg in a fall from her horse, and a few weeks later Fox was telling his wife (Sarah's elder sister) that 'the King ask'd Connolly yesterday a hundred questions about Lady Sarah, wonder'd and was concern'd she should be left to the care of a country surgeon . . . inquired very tenderly . . .' Lady Susan wrote later: 'A fall from her horse at Redlynch prevented Ly S. dancing; she was therefore very near His Majesty's chair, who had neither eyes nor ears for any other object. I almost thought *myself Prime Minister.*'³ So, too, perhaps did Fox, her uncle, a deeply interested party. Himself of relatively humble origins, he had, seventeen years previously, made a runaway match with Charles II's great-grand-daughter (by Louise de Kéroualle); now there was the heady possibility of becoming brother-in-law to the Queen of England. In March, while Sarah Lennox was down in Somerset and the German bride-prospecting was showing no sign of a lucky strike, it seems that a conversation took place at Court between the King and Susan Fox-Strangways, and, according to the account of it retailed in the *Memoir* of her uncle Henry Fox, it ran as follows:

K[ing]. You are going into Somersetshire; when do you return?

L[ady] S[usan]. Not before winter, Sir, and I don't know how soon in winter.

K. Is there nothing will bring you back to town before winter?

L.S. I don't know of anything.

K. Would not you like to see a Coronation?

L.S. Yes, Sir. I hope I should come to see that.

K. I hear it's very popular my having put it off.

L.S. *Nothing.*

K. Won't it be a much finer sight when there is a Queen?

L.S. To be sure, Sir.

K. I have had a great many applications from abroad but I don't like them. I have had none at home, I should like that better.

L.S. *Nothing* (frightened).

K. What do you think of your friend? you know who I mean; don't you think her fittest? . . . I think none so fit.

At this time Lady Sarah was setting her cap at Lord Newbattle, the future Marquis of Lothian. She was certainly not in love with the King, and apparently rebuffed him. When he approached her at Court a week or two later he asked, 'Have you seen your friend lately? Has she told you what I said to her? Do you approve?' Lady Sarah according to Fox made no answer. In an only slightly differing version of the story written by Lady Sarah's son Henry Napier from notes taken down much later from his mother's conversation, the King, having taken Lady Sarah 'into a recess in one of the large windows, asked her what she thought of his proposal. "Tell me, for my happiness depends on it!" "*Nothing, Sir,*" was my mother's reply, upon which he left her abruptly, exclaiming pettishly *"Nothing comes of nothing."* Thus ended his first offer.'[4]

Henry Fox was agog, though he was aware well enough of the difficulties and opposition, and much put out when the royal family, including his own patron Cumberland, all agreed upon one thing at least, that Lady Sarah Lennox was no suitable candidate for Queen. George persisted in his tentative and awkward approaches, on one occasion protesting his strongest attachment 'loud enough for Lady Kildare [an aunt of Sarah Lennox's] to hear'. When reports were abroad of Lady Sarah's flirtation with Lord Newbattle, they seemed to confirm what the elders and wise men said of her skittishness and unsuitability. Thirty-two years later, writing of her lasting joy in her second marriage, she admitted her 'thoughtless, wild, and giddy spirits' when she was sixteen.[5] Indeed, said Lord Bute's friends after- wards – though they were patently inventing the story – the King intended Sarah Lennox only for a mistress, not a wife.[6]

According to Henry Napier there was in fact a second, briefly more successful, offer of marriage from the King:

> After her recovery [from the broken leg] and subsequent appearance in London the King's joy was palpable; his conversations were renewed, his hopes revived, and once again he ventured to say, in allusion to the former conversation, 'I hope you will think of it.' She did so, and accepted him.[7]

However this may be, the King appears to have been easily talked out of his only flickeringly romantic intentions and left Sarah Lennox to conclude – temporarily at least – that he had 'neither *sense, good nature,* nor *honesty*'. Happily she was not of an ambitious disposition and was soon more concerned with other misfortunes and their consolations. 'To many a girl' (wrote Henry Fox) 'H.M.'s behaviour had been very vexatious, but Lady Sarah's temper and affections are happily so flexible and light, that the sickness of her squirrel im- mediately took up all her attention, and when it, in spite of her nursing it, dy'd, I believe it gave her more concern than H.M. ever did.'[8] She herself was writing, 'I have almost forgiven him; luckily for me I did not love him, and only liked him; I did not cry I assure you ... The thing I am most angry at, is looking so like a fool.' She continued to attend Court, where, she wrote, the King appeared frightened when he saw her, and she claimed to have managed to fire an angry look in return. When he came to speak to her, there followed a short exchange of small talk about horse-riding and the weather, and George III's brief unequal struggle between prudence and passion, between duty and desire, was concluded. This last half-hearted dash by the 'boiling youth' had occurred in June, 1761; by 8th July his forth-coming marriage to Charlotte of Mecklenburg-Strelitz was announced, to Fox's chagrin. Fox's niece, Lady Susan, wrote much later:

> When the Princess of Mecklinburg was named in Council the sur-prise was great to all who were not in the secret. He had better have given up his *favourite* than his *Berenice*; an *English* beauty, queen, wd have pleas'd his people as much as a Scotch Minister disgusted them. [9]

The English beauty was not too proud to accept the invitation to be-come a bridesmaid:

> Dear Pussy – I have only time to tell you that I have been asked to be a brides-maid, and I have accepted of it . . . I was always of opinion that the less fuss or talk there is about it the better, and to let it drop to the world. But to him and his sisters, I was and always will be as high and grave as possible; for I think the least flirting would ruin my character quite. But this is not his doing; he only sees the list, for others to make it. [10]

As the years passed, she became a steadily more consistent champion of her monarch's virtues. 'I am delighted to hear the King is well,' she was writing in September, 1804, 'for I am excessively *partial* to him. I always consider him as an old friend that has been in the wrong; but does one love one's friends less for being in the wrong even towards oneself? I *don't*, and I would not value the friendship of those who measure their friendship by my *deserving*.' [11] Happy in the love and achievements of her sons (who she could not help feeling were 'better annimals' than the royal brood), she expressed sorrow that Courts were 'not the soil where family affection and cordiality flourishes', and she pitied Kings 'for being robbed of that blessing by their situation, for they have all the tender feelings of the heart as warm as their subjects'. [12] When later in 1804 her second husband died, leaving her poorly provided for, the King granted an annual pension of £800 for the education of her daughters and for herself *as the widow of a valued officer*. After years of failing sight, she soon, like George himself, had blindness to add to her afflictions; but she survived to the age of eighty-one, outliving George III by six years.

With Lady Sarah at last put behind him in July, 1761, George wished to lose no time in the wedding preparations. The Coronation of the royal pair was fixed for 22nd September. George fretted with impatience when news of the death of the Duchess of Mecklenburg-Strelitz, Charlotte's mother, arrived only four days after the official announcement of the marriage intentions, and he begged Bute to 'consider how long we must delay my marriage for this untoward accident'. Not overlong as it proved. Lord Harcourt, newly dignified with the Mastership of the Horse, was forthwith appointed to supervise the Princess's coming over, and was already busy with arrangements for the journey, providing for German servants and cooks to be routed ahead of the Queen-designate and her notably small retinue; 'he has also bespoke the livery lace for 25 liverys.' When Harcourt sailed for Strelitz early in August, Walpole expressed the astringent hope that he would succeed in finding a duchy so inconsiderable. (It was not so small as all that – roughly the size of Sussex.) Harcourt, on arrival, concluded a proxy marriage in mid-August; embarked from Cuxhaven a week later with his nervous seventeen-year-old charge, who, after a rough and delayed crossing, arrived 'off Leosstoff in Suffolk' on 5th September. Ahead of her person, George had been sent a lock of her hair, 'which seems at candle of a very fine dark colour, and very soft,' and also a request that she should be permitted to import her own male hairdresser – which surprised the King, the orders having been 'so very positive that only two women were to come'. From Harwich the bridal party proceeded through Romford and down the Mile-end turnpike, by Shoreditch and Islington and Hyde Park to St James's, where her bridegroom received her. As a private man, he returned 'sincere and humble acknowledgments' to his Creator 'for this greatest blessing that he has been pleased to point out'; and as a public man he prayed that God would make her fruitful.[13]

Having as yet little or no evidence of her character, everyone was busy assessing her physical appearance. This was in general judged to be unremarkable. Her nose had an upward tilt, and undoubtedly her mouth, though it housed fine teeth, was too large. Her colouring was dark, and some discovered a hint of the mulatto in her looks. There seems no reason, however, either from the judgment of those who quizzed her so narrowly in 1761, or from portraits of her at that time, why her bodily attributes should be described in the derogatory terms some recent historians have indulged in.* Horace Walpole, always ready to damn amusingly with faint praise, declared in later years that as she grew older 'her want of personal charms became of course, less observable . . . I said one day something to this effect to Colonel

* For example, J. H. Plumb in *The First Four Georges* (p. 95) describes her as 'formidable ugly' and Richard Pares in *George III and the Politicians* (p. 65) simply as 'hideous'.

Desbrowe [Disbrowe], her Chamberlain. "Yes," he replied, "I do think
the *bloom* of her ugliness is going off." '14 But Walpole on her arrival in
England granted her fine hair and a 'pleasing' countenance. The many
representations of her by artists of the seventeen-sixties, including
Allan Ramsay and Zoffany, show admittedly no stunning beauty,
but a young woman of pleasant and alert appearance. Lord Harcourt
allowed her a good figure, pretty eyes, and a fine complexion, while
Mrs Papendiek, the daughter of one of her German gentleman-pages,
wrote that 'her countenance was expressive, and intelligent. She was
not tall, but of slight, pretty figure; her eyes bright and sparkling with
good humour and vivacity . . . and her hair really beautiful'. Gainsborough's fine later portrait painted in 1782, together with others of
the King and thirteen of their children, shows a woman of dignified
distinction. So too does Benjamin West's of 1779. All this seems rather
a long way from the story of the ogress who was sexually so repulsive
that sleeping with her helped to drive poor George III out of his mind.

The new Queen, somewhat overawed, nevertheless seemed civil
and anxious to please. A certain nervousness, to begin with, became
her. Faced with the procession of those to be presented to her at the
private nuptials, including her ten bridesmaids (the Ladies Sarah
Lennox and Susan Fox-Strangways among them), she exclaimed '*Mon
Dieu, il y en a tant!*' Fifty-six years later Lady Susan was to recall in her
Journal the Queen's 'distressing situation on arriving, that the Princess
of Wales could not be at St James's, and that the King himself told her
what she must put on to be married in, that she was quite oppress'd
with the weight of her dress . . . Never was any body more loaded.
Later the Queen often mentioned her agitation, and her hand trembling
as the Duke of York led her, and his comforting her by saying, "Courage, Princess, courage!" '15 By comparison however with modern
royal occasions, the wedding, which took place after dinner on the
evening of her arrival – direct from a stormy and protracted sea
crossing – was quiet, brisk, and informal. The Queen played the
harpsichord and sang some songs while the guests in the drawing-
room awaited supper. She spoke a little French to the guests and
German to her bridegroom, before protesting some fatigue, retiring
to a private supper with the King, and so to bed. There, certainly, over
the coming years, she was to assist to some purpose in the answering
of her husband's prayer 'as a public man' to his Creator.

To begin with, George proved a strict husband; indeed many
agreed with Walpole that he deliberately deprived his young wife of
company and kept her practically prisoner, in order to prevent her
from becoming corrupted by the poisons of the age. It is true that at

first she mixed but little, except with her two German ladies-in-waiting and apart from the English lessons which she took daily with Dr Majendie, and often with George himself. (She learned eventually to speak the language 'with surprising elegance and little or nothing of a foreign manner'.*) The young King and Queen shared a taste for music; Charlotte had a pleasant singing voice, and both of them possessed some proficiency on the harpsichord – George played the flute and violin as well. There were sober domestic amusements, such as backgammon and picquet, and more frequently as time progressed visits to the theatre (the Queen's first appearance at Drury Lane caused such excited curiosity that a girl was killed in the crush of sightseers). But there was little public display and so few social excitements involving the 'imprisoned' Queen that some of the *beau monde* soon began to turn up their noses. The Queen had no contact with society, sniffed Horace Walpole, 'except for the Ladies of the Bedchamber for half an hour a week in a funereal circle, or a ceremonious Drawing Room.'

This relative isolation imposed upon Charlotte to begin with was reinforced by the vigilance of the formidable Mademoiselle Schwellenberg, who had been with her from her infancy and set herself up as a sort of guardian she-dragon. 'She was to be styled Madame, as a distinction from her companion; her apartments were close to the Queen, and no one was to be admitted to her Majesty's presence without first having been introduced to Madame.' So overbearing did this Madame become that George proposed to send her back to Strelitz. However, 'finding that this intention made the Queen uneasy,' he contented himself with giving Mademoiselle Schwellenberg a dressing-down *in the presence of the Princess Dowager*, 'which hurt the Queen very sensibly.'[16] In her old age, Queen Charlotte herself confirmed that her husband's care for her had been at first rather severe and constricting; yet in retrospect approved 'the dear King's great strictness, at my arrival in England, to prevent my making many acquaintances'. His motives, she said, had simply been to prevent her getting caught up among the factions and intrigues of the political world. Whatever his reasons, which were doubtless complicated, the King was soon looking for a house away from St James's where the Queen and he could remove themselves somewhat from the grandeur and formalities of the Court. The King took a fancy to Wanstead House, which was remarkably fine

* Forbes, *Life of Beattie*, i. 351. Fanny Burney bears this out. The Queen, she writes, preserved slight traces of a German accent and certain German idioms, but her command of English expression and vocabulary was 'copious' (D'Arblay, *Diary*, ii, 337). Mrs Siddons, on the other hand, refers to the Queen's 'gracious broken English' (*Reminiscences*, 12-13).

and elegant, but it was thought to be rather too far from St James's, and eventually he bought from Sir Charles Sheffield, a natural son of the late Duke of Buckingham (whose title was now extinct), the house only a few hundred yards distant from St James's which soon became known as the Queen's House and was enlarged and virtually rebuilt from 1825 as Buckingham Palace. 'Buckingham House was purchased and bestowed on her Majesty,' wrote Walpole, 'St James's not seeming a prison strait enough.'[17]

It was in the acquisition and adaptation of the Queen's House that George III, that unostentatious prince, came as near as he ever came to extravagance. Built in the first decade of the century for John Sheffield, Duke of Buckingham, it was a red-brick mansion, not vast but palatial enough for a Duke's town residence, with a forecourt that became eventually the *inner* courtyard of Buckingham Palace, and a bow-fronted iron 'palisade' whose imposing central gates led out towards the wide Mall that ran between 'the Canal', still at that time a long narrow rectangle, and the palace of St James's. This Mall was flanked by handsome avenues, then 'of goodly elms on the one hand and gay flourishing limes on the other, that for coaches, this for walking'.[18] Along its vista, from the house, the eye commanded an imposing view of the cities of Westminster and London at a respectful distance, with St Paul's towering over all. Nearer, all around, were the parks and gardens of St James's and its neighbouring great houses, and meadows still grazed by cattle (soon to be joined by Queen Charlotte's tame zebra*); and away to the north the heights of rural Hampstead and beyond.

For this desirable property the King, in 1762, paid £28,000, and already by 1764 he had spent considerably more than that sum on structural alteration, extensions and redecorations. Of the new buildings the most important – important too for countering the ill-based legend of George III as a dull-witted philistine – was the fine octagonal Library, itself soon enlarged by the addition of the King's Upper Library, and later of the Queen's Library. The Queen's new apartments also included a fine music room, a modish new 'Japan Room' and a large Saloon Room, where later in the reign she was to hold her Drawing Rooms. All was furnished and redecorated in the currently fashionable styles, and everything from furniture to the 'Genoa'

---

* The young Queen seems to have loved animals of all kinds, from little lap-dogs, several of whom peep from her portraits, to elephants, two of whom were kept near the Queen's House. Presumably these were the same two which having 'died near Pimlico' had the posthumous honour of being dissected by the great John Hunter.

damask for the hangings was of English manufacture. Some of the finest mid-Georgian furniture surviving to-day went into these Queen's Apartments, much of it from the firm of Vile and Cobb, Chippendale's neighbours in St Martin's Lane; for example, an 'exceedingly fine mahogany secretary' and a 'very handsome jewel cabinet' on 'a mahogany frame richly carved' – the latter presumably to house the jewels that the King presented to the Queen at their marriage. The seven cartoons painted by Raphael for the Sistine Chapel tapestries, first bought by Charles I, were removed on the King's orders from Hampton Court to adorn the walls of the Saloon Room.* Windsor Castle and Kensington Palace too, the latter's associations with George II, like Hampton Court's, rendering it unlovely to his grandson, were denuded of some of their treasures to beautify the Queen's House.

It became very much the King's House too. The royal pair lived there, in at least relative privacy and simplicity – given that the severe and ossified demands of Court etiquette always forbade real informality – and went to St James's in general for Drawing Rooms or Levees only, though it was at St James's that the future George IV, the first of Charlotte's fifteen children, was born in August, 1762. Continuing to shun Hampton Court, George favoured as rural retreats Richmond Lodge and the neighbouring parental mansion of Kew, where Sir William Chambers, whom Bute introduced to George, had for years been busy improving the gardens with a wealth of trees and plants as rich or exotic as his architectural improvements – his Orangery, for instance, or the Pagoda. Chambers's renovations and alterations at Windsor were to follow later in the reign.

If the King saw to it that his young consort's contacts with society were restricted, the pair became mutually devoted, and he certainly did not neglect her. In a letter to Bute soon after his marriage, he wrote: 'I cannot finish without again telling [my dear friend] how really happy I am, and how I now see more than ever the great advantage of the various advices he has given me. Indeed I find myself if possible now more sensible of his friendship than ever.'[19] Nevertheless, what Bute himself had years before forecast was beginning to come true. In the King's letters 'Dearest' was declining towards 'Dear', or simply 'D'. Marriage, experience of the world, and eventually his sense of Bute's own shortcomings, would in time wean the young King from his dependence upon his favourite, however slow the process.

* They remained there till 1788, when they were removed to Windsor. In 1814 the Prince Regent, acting true to Hanoverian form, had them taken back to Hampton Court.

CHAPTER SEVEN

The Peace and the Politicians

THE inclusion of Bute in the ministry coincided with the first serious overtures to end the Seven Years War, a move with which George III was strongly in sympathy. Surprisingly, a rumour in that same month (March, 1761) that even Pitt was now prepared to listen to talk of peace sent government funds soaring four full points on the Stock Exchange; surprisingly, that is, in view of the passionate support lent to Pitt and the war by the City of London. Things, however, were not altogether simple and clear-cut. Pitt in fact was *not* inclined for serious peace talks until his expedition to capture Belle Ile, off the Brittany coast, had succeeded, and a strong party among both City merchants and the general public did still long for the tide of victory to run for ever. The King, on the other hand, agreed with those politicians and taxpayers who, as the contemporary historian Adolphus wrote, argued that 'France could prosecute the war in Germany for ten years without increasing her debt five millions sterling, while we could not carry on for the same period without increasing ours upward of 50 millions'.[1] George, like these men, 'treated the popular enthusiasm for the war as a dangerous delusion,' and he certainly shared his subjects' resentment at paying Frederick the Great – no longer the 'Protestant hero' – £670,000 a year to fight for his own private and Prussian ends.

In fact Pitt wanted a good deal more than Belle Ile. He told George that Britain should, and could, totally destroy French power in the East Indies, round off the West Indian operations by taking Martinique, and insist on the exclusive rights to fish off Newfoundland. He would settle for peace on no lower terms. 'Madder than ever,' had been Bute's comment on Pitt just before he became a fellow-minister; and voices against a continuance of the war were powerful. Great victories had been won, naval supremacy established, Canada taken, much of the French West Indies, great areas of India. Enough was enough. Country gentlemen were for peace, if only to get the land tax down. Inside the administration Pitt was beset by ministers unanimously agreed, apart from Temple, on one matter and one only – the domineering intransigence of their great colleague. Strongest among ministers for ending the war was the Duke of Bedford, but the rest of them were broadly in favour of opening peace parleys on a not too take-it-or-leave-it basis. And now there was a King on the throne notably less martial-minded than his predecessor, and caring as little as most of his subjects for spending British blood for the defence of Hanover or lavishing British guineas for the rescue of Prussia.

While peace negotiations dragged haltingly on throughout 1761-62, the domestic arguments concerning peace and war brought down first Pitt and Temple, and then at last Newcastle. Yet though George III, to put it mildly, was not sorry to see these men go, he was not himself responsible for their going. In each case it was internal Cabinet disagreements and resentments that precipitated the resignations. Pitt departed for reasons both personal and political: personal, because his fellow-ministers could not stomach his arrogance and united at last to stand up to him; political, in that the rest of the Cabinet, Temple excepted, were not prepared to swallow his demand for a pre-emptive strike at Spain. Since he claimed to know positively from intercepted letters that Spain intended to engage in the war on the side of France, Pitt proposed to attack first, both in the Philippines and the Americas, and to seize the Spanish treasure fleet while it was still *en route* from the River Plate. These bold moves were what a majority of the Cabinet would not accept, and the way these men felt about Pitt is heard clearly in the elegantly acid tones of the senior member, old Lord Granville: 'Though he may have convinced himself of his infallibility, still it remains that *we* should be equally convinced before we can resign our understandings to his directions and join with him in the measures he proposes.' The King, singling out Bute for congratulation for having in the Cabinet resisted Pitt's 'black scheme', maintaining thereby 'the honour of the British Crown', underestimated the resistance of other ministers; for, he wrote, if only they were as spirited as his dearest friend, he (George) would there and then say 'let that mad Pitt be dismissed'. As things were, he calculated – Pitt having at this point not yet resigned – 'we must get rid of him in a happier minute.'[2] A fortnight later Pitt had got rid of himself, disdaining to serve where he could not direct. He took Temple with him out of office, but his other brother-in-law in the Cabinet, George Grenville, remained as Navy Treasurer, and from this time increased in importance as an advocate of retrenchment, and therefore of peace. *His* brother-in-law, Lord Egremont, succeeded Pitt as Secretary of State.

So, through no active intervention of the Crown (though, as Newcastle said, the King 'plainly wanted to get rid of him at all events'[3]), the great minister went, temporarily losing some popularity by accepting, for his wife and her issue, the barony of Chatham, and for himself a pension of £3,000 a year for the duration of three lives. 'Oh, that foolishest of great men,' exclaimed Gray, 'that sold his inestimable diamond for a paltry peerage and a pension.'

The painful scene when 'that mad Pitt' attended upon the King to surrender his seals and hear George's proffered rewards has been often recounted. 'Mr Pitt,' reported the *Annual Register* of 1761, 'was sensibly touched with the grandeur and condescension of this proceeding. "I confess, Sire," he said, "I had but too much reason to expect your Majesty's displeasure. I did not come prepared for this exceeding goodness – pardon me, Sire, it overpowers – it oppresses me." He burst into tears.' There was perhaps less insincerity and play-acting in all this than would seem, skilled actor though Pitt undoubtedly was. In the abstract at least, he deeply venerated monarchy and he admitted being affected by George's 'gracious marks of approbation . . . They are unmerited, and unsolicited; and I shall ever be proud to have received them from the best of sovereigns'. If there was play-acting, it was rather on George's side, in his gentlemanly disguise of his feelings of intense relief.

He was able to give some vent to his truer feelings a month later, after the deplorable events of Lord Mayor's Day (9th November, 1761). Pitt, against his own better judgment, but persuaded by his friend the Lord Mayor Elect, William Beckford, and by Lord Temple, accepted an invitation to appear at a Guildhall banquet to which the King and Queen drove in state. There seemed little enough remaining, at least in the City of London, of the burst of popularity that had welcomed the new King on his accession just over a year before. The streets were grudging and silent. Poor Bute would have been happy enough to settle for silence, however sullen; but instead his coach was set upon by mobs engaged for the purpose, and he was saved from serious mischief only by his own prudently hired bodyguards. When, however, the chariot bearing Pitt and Temple arrived, there was tumultuous acclaim; the speeches at the banquet were all in honour of Pitt's triumphs; and the King of England, surrounded by the other members of the Royal Family, was in effect snubbed and humiliated on a grand public occasion. Horace Walpole permitted himself to go further in criticism of Pitt and his henchmen over this incident than anywhere else in his voluminous commentaries:

Sir Samuel Fludyer, the Lord Mayor, caused diligent inquiry to be made into the proceedings of the day, and learned that Beckford himself had visited several public-houses over night, and had appointed ringleaders to different stations, and had been the first to raise the huzza in the hall on the entrance of Mr Pitt. *His* joining himself to a pomp, dedicated to a Court he had just quitted, that was not decent. The ambition of drawing to himself the homage of the people was not modest. To offer himself as an incentive to civil tumult, and to how dangerous consequences he could not tell, was not a symptom of very innocent intentions.[4]

However, only seven weeks later, Pitt's predicted war with Spain arrived, and he was in a position to consider himself more than justified. Military and naval plans completed before his resignation were put into execution, and the almost embarrassing catalogue of victories, begun in 1758, resumed: in the Caribbean theatre, Martinique, Grenada, St Lucia, St Vincent, Tobago, and Havana; in the Philippines, Manila. Naturally none of this displeased either King or public. The problem, as ever, was British participation in the German war, and there George's sentiments were unequivocal: 'I cannot help wishing that an end was put to that enormous expense by ordering our troops home . . . I think that if the D. of N[ewcastle] will not hear reason concerning the German war that it would be better to let him quit than to go on with that and have myself and those that differ from him made unpopular.' Frederick of Prussia, having earlier appeared to be beaten, had just had a stroke of extraordinary luck and now looked like fighting on for ever; on the accession of the new Tsar Peter III, Russia had withdrawn from the Franco-Austrian alliance. Our business, wrote George, was to bring that '*too ambitious monarch*' Frederick to his senses, 'to oblige that *proud overbearing Prince* to see he has no safety but in peace.'[5] Newcastle also would have liked, eventually, to ditch Frederick. He favoured a full reversal of the diplomatic revolution of the 1750's and a return by Britain to her old Austrian alliance. But until that major diplomatic turnabout could be managed, he tried to convince his colleagues and the King that they must continue to support Prussia with a subsidy, as an essential bulwark against French might. He failed to convince the King, and in the Cabinet only Devonshire was on his side, Grenville leading the opposition.

In April, 1762, the King had written to Bute: 'The more I see of this fellow [Newcastle] the more I wish to see him out of employment'. And again:

The more I consider the Prussian subsidy the more objections arise in my mind against it, and as to the German war I am clear that if France is not willing for peace, we must instantly nock it in the head, and if men leave my service because I love this preferably to any other it will be they that will be run at and not me; the successor I have long had in my eye to the D. of N—— is a man void of his filthy arts who will think of mine and his country's good, not of jobs; if my friend does not know him by this character, I will add that he now holds the seals, and lives in S[outh] Audley Street [Bute's address].

Through May the Duke was consulting his friends, his conscience, and his future prospects. What finally determined him was the desertion of his principal officers within the Treasury itself; only Barrington, the Chancellor of the Exchequer, sided with him. By 26th May, Newcastle had at last resigned. According to Fox, 'the King made the Duke of Newcastle an offer of what might make his old age easy and comfortable, and us'd such kind words that his Grace burst into tears.'[6] For the second time George's graciousness when his most disliked ministers resigned had produced this lachrymose effect. Fox was as unimpressed as doubtless the King himself was: 'the Pelhams can cry when they please, and their tears are regarded accordingly.' Newcastle declined the pension.

Everything now pointed to Bute's heading the ministry officially as well as in fact; 'there wanted but the office of Prime Minister,' wrote Walpole, 'to glut the Favourite's ambition.' Yet it would not have been like Bute to be without doubts and qualms, as the near-certainty of Newcastle's departure impended. He could not persuade Grenville to take the Chancellorship of the Exchequer, which upset his plans. His bowels were troubling him again, and the rhubarb was both ineffic-acious and all too efficacious; in short, he was 'rummag'd'. His nerves were not strong. He spoke once more of his own 'ignorance of busi-ness' (one point at least upon which his many enemies agreed with him) and again spoke of retiring, words which the King declared 'chilled his blood'. The mutual relationship of the two men was in process of significant change. Although it was another two or three years before the King finally shook himself free from dependence upon Bute's judgment, it was already George who was trying to instil more *resolution* into the man who had earlier reproached him for lacking it: 'Is this a moment for despondency? No, for vigour and the day is ours.'[7] He even rallied his friend's flagging spirits with a little royal playful-ness, as Bute was about to be admitted to the most noble Order of the Bath: 'The proprietor of Windsor Castle can't help inquiring how the Junior Knight Elect finds himself . . .' By 29th May, three days after Newcastle's resignation, he found himself in fact First Lord of the Treasury and Prime Minister. The peak so long gazed at with longing from below, the summit so coveted yet dreaded, had been scaled at last. Bute's good fortune had been extraordinary and deeply resented; his misfortune was that he was a mountaineer with no head for heights.

Five more months proved to be necessary before Bedford was able to agree with the French upon the complicated details of the peace pre-liminaries, and a further five before the Peace of Paris could be finally proclaimed in March, 1763. They were months of persistent intrigue; of anxiety for Bute, of humiliation for Newcastle, of aloofness for Pitt, of opportunity for Fox, of belligerence yet frustration for George III. At first Newcastle would not go into open opposition, partly because to do so ran counter to the habits and attitudes of a lifetime (and to the advice of Hardwicke), but principally because he yet hoped that if he played his cards right and kept his 'friends' around him he would be taken back into the administration. Then there was the Duke of Cumberland, still prominently in the political picture and mistrusted by Bute and the King. In May, 1762, George was noting his 'rather sulky conduct', and Bute's fear was that, under the aegis of Cumber-land, Pitt and Newcastle would be reconciled and together oust him. George Grenville too, now Secretary of State, was suspected of being privy to this move, but Pitt's preference for lordly isolation and his contempt for Newcastle brought it to nothing.

However, the Paris negotiations were proving thorny and stubborn, and peace an elusive rainbow; ministers were divided, and uneasily conscious that any settlement deemed over-conciliatory would have to be steered through the Scylla of public opinion and the Charybdis of Pitt's scathing eloquence in the Commons, where he was continuing to claim that 'England can raise 13, 14, nay 15 millions a year with ease, and France is on her last legs and can go on no longer'. Henry Fox, the Paymaster, drawing constantly nearer to Bute, took an opposite view: 'France is not in such haste, I fear, to make peace as we must wish her to be and must be ourselves.'[8] The King, like Bute, was torn and frus-trated. He resisted any projects, such as a suggested attack on Ferrol, which might prolong hostilities; but he protested that people must not think that he was 'mad for peace . . . No, quite otherwise if it can't be honourable'. What he feared was that his ministers were losing the peace by rejecting better terms than they might obtain in two years' time, and he cited the Utrecht parallel of 1711-13.[9] By July, 1762, George was bewailing to Bute the 'sophistry, timidity, and weakness' of the administration. Mansfield and Egremont both irritated him; even more, perhaps, 'the great Secretary Greenville,' formerly so hot for economy, whom he told that he ought to abandon some of the minor haggling with the French; 'I insisted no stress should be laid on trifles.'[10] As for Germany, where Bute discontinued Frederick's subsidy and thereby incurred wrath from Pitt, George considered that 'the K. of Prussia had no one but himself to blame for not being a party to the Peace'.[11] 'To be brief peace is the thing that is absolutely necessary for the well-being of the country.'[12]

Indecisions had to be ended, so a decisive Cabinet meeting was called for 6th October. Now the only important member of the 'Duke of Newcastle's Friends' remaining in the Cabinet was the Duke of Devonshire. Newcastle and his allies were anxious to avoid seeming to be a party to an unpopular peace. Devonshire, therefore, who was in Bath, declined to attend Cabinets. Specifically summoned by Egremont in the King's name 'as the final decision of the peace was now to be taken', he wrote excusing himself as being somewhat ignorant of the proposals. At this the King exploded:

> I have just received the D. of Devonshire's refusal to attend Council, this I believe is an unheard of step, except when men have meant open opposition to the Crown; this is a personal affront to my person, and seems to call for the breaking of his wand [of office as Lord Chamberlain]; I enclose a copy I have taken of his letter, and send it to Kew that my d. friend may instantly see the sentiments of the D. of Newcastle for I have no doubt that the D. of Devonshire is too timid to have taken such a step had not he known the Ds. of C[umberland] and Newcastle would approve it, we must therefore turn our eyes some other way . . .[13]

The following day the King sent for Fox. This was a step which Bute had been contemplating for some time, and he had had some talk with Fox in September. For five years Fox had been happily amassing a large fortune as Paymaster.* But, however lucrative, it was a minor office, like the Chancellorship of the Exchequer; and the holders of these posts were not in the Cabinet. Fox was now fifty-seven; his health was not good; and he had recently shown an inclination to indulge his pleasures, including the newly fashionable and supposedly therapeutic sea-bathing, at his recently acquired mansion at Kingsgate near the North Foreland. He looked forward to a civilised semi-retirement, though so inveterate a politician was hardly likely to have kept his finger out of the pie. Now the King suddenly offered him the

---

* Under the system then accepted, not only was there a percentage rake-off on contracts, but also the balance of the very large sums of public money passing through the Paymaster's hands might be invested to his private profit.

post of Secretary of State, in place of Grenville, and with the leadership of the House of Commons. His task was to be the piloting of the Peace through the Commons, acting in effect as political manager of the Court party. Fox being Fox, he expected reward in the shape of a peerage. He accepted the Commons leadership but declined the Secretaryship, offering to the King reasons of health, but admitting to Bute that to accept the Secretaryship 'would be adding unpopularity to unpopularity'.[14] Except for Bute himself, no leading politician of the day could have had more enemies than Fox.

For George III all this was like calling upon the Devil to cast out sin. Fox ranked very high in wickedness among those evil politicians against whom the virtuous Prince of Wales had animadverted. To the outgoing Grenville, who expressed his surprise and protest at the unwisdom of calling in 'so unpopular a man as Mr Fox', the King explained that it was necessary to 'call in bad men to govern bad men', but he assured Grenville that it was 'but for a time, the expedient of the moment only'.[15] Thus the prince of virtue and principle was by now quite as deeply immersed in expediency as the despised politicians. George had certainly taken an extreme and drastic step in employing Fox, this 'man void of principles'. Whenever he heard him named, the King avowed, 'bad character comes strongly into my thoughts,' and there is no doubt that he intended to rid himself of him as soon as conveniently possible. But the ends, he judged, justified the means; and the ends were primarily three: the conclusion of peace; maintaining the 'independancy' of the Crown, threatened by the insolence of the Whig factions, especially Newcastle's; and, above all, the maintenance of Bute at the head of affairs. Fox was to be Bute's hatchet man; he could never be the King's friend.

The King indeed, in the autumn of 1762, looked more than ready to be his own hatchet man. He swore that if the Duke of Devonshire should come to see him, he would not leave the closet as Chamberlain, and when in fact he did appear, George would not even receive him, but sent a message that he should leave his wand of office with the page. In November he ordered Devonshire's name to be struck off the Privy Council. All this was more than Devonshire himself, or his allies Newcastle and Hardwicke, had bargained for, though Devonshire was probably intending to resign in any case. It was the manner of his going that shocked; Fox himself deprecated the roughness of it. But George was spoiling for a fight. He had been determined to dismiss Devonshire, he told Bute, before Devonshire *dismissed him*.[16] 'Are his brothers the Cavendishes gone out, so much the better. Will more great men follow, let them. I prefer six open enemys to two secret ones, to one false friend.' When George Cavendish came to surrender his staff, George brusquely showed him the door. He shed no tears when Lord Rockingham followed. The heat was to be put on Newcastle's Friends, and the reality of that friendship tested, as against loyalty to the Crown and the King's Government. 'Force and steadiness will undoubtedly overturn this faction,'[17] that combination of 'soi-disant great men', as Bute described it, that 'had been formed against the lawful right and liberty of the King'. The 'proud Dukes' had behaved long enough as if the country belonged to them.

Fox began to wonder whether the King was not being a little *too* warlike on behalf of his rights and his dignity, and tactfully tried to counsel caution, while still forecasting victory in the showdown over the Peace. To George this was provoking and pusillanimous. 'The sword is drawn,' he told Bute, 'vigour and violence are the only means of ending this audacious faction.'[18] Did the Duke of Cumberland intend to oppose? Let him; 'if he does he shall be treated as he deserves.' 'Courage, my d. friend, go on as you have begun and they will soon see that their disgrace is the sole fruit of the[ir] impious conduct.'[19] 'Impious' is a revealing word; the assault of these men upon the King's dignity was an assault on monarchy and the constitution of the land. The same frame of mind is evidenced in another of George's choleric outbursts at this time, on this occasion against Frederick of Prussia, who, though seldom unready to desert his own allies, was naturally indignant at his desertion by Britain. Frederick had written that he would rather trust the veracity of the late Russian ambassador in London than the British version of words that had been spoken. 'In plain English,' George wrote, 'he gives me the lie; no private man of any spirit would bear such treatment one moment, and I have a still stronger call on me, the character of a King makes it necessary not to suffer this ill usage, my country is attack'd through me, for as our interest is inseparable, when my veracity is doubted that is not only giving me an affront but tis affronting Britain.' This identification of the Crown with the nation's honour, of slights upon his own authority and dignity with attacks on the national interests, and therefore 'factious' or 'impious' or even treasonable, reflected what he had been brought up to believe. He had high notions of the obligations of a monarch, but also of the deference due to him. They led him to an over-sensitivity to criticism. Very soon now the first damaging Wilkes episode was to originate in just this tendency of George's to take political attack as an affront to his person as monarch; and affronting the King 'tis affronting Britain'.[20]

Despite the last-minute complications produced by Albemarle's

capture of Havana, the Preliminaries of the Peace had been agreed at
Fontainebleau in good time for George III to announce the fact at the
State opening of the new parliamentary session on 25th November. It
was likely to be a crucial and ill-tempered session, and in the Commons
Fox was about to do the job expected of him, before being rewarded
by translation to the Lords. He was an experienced tactician, educated
in the school of Sir Robert Walpole, and it was soon obvious that
Newcastle had worked himself into an impossibly exposed and contradictory position. The man of moderation who had recently been
instrumental in ousting Pitt and had purred, if not crowed, with
pleasure at the event, could hardly now pose credibly as the champion
of a tough peace. His many-times-counted 'friends', when faced with
the prospect of choosing between Newcastle on the one hand, and
King and Government on the other, first wavered and then broke.
Worst blow of all, Hardwicke's own sons, together with their followers,
deserted; so did 'my Lord Mansfield and his friends'; the Duke of
Rutland and his son the Marquis of Granby, commander-in-chief of
British forces in Germany; and Newcastle's ewe lambs, the hitherto
most loyal Shropshire group of Pelhamite M.P.'s. Those remaining
faithful into the voting lobby were a sadly depleted band, soon to be
victimised by Fox and the Court for their constancy. Before that happened, a pallid and emaciated Pitt, theatrical in black velvet, with his
legs and thighs wrapped in flannel and his hands thickly gloved, had
been borne by his servants to the House to make his famous three-and-
a-half hour onslaught (but in tones low and quavering) on a peace,
which, he claimed, left us 'nothing, though we have conquered everything'. The desertion of Prussia was base, the cession of conquered
territory craven and inept.

Pitt, however, could command more awe than support. Pitt's
'nothing' did, after all, include Canada, Cape Breton Island, all Louis-
iana east of the Mississippi, Florida, Minorca, Senegal, Dominica,
Grenada, Tobago, St Vincent, all Clive's conquests in Bengal, timber-
cutting rights in Honduras, and freedom to navigate the Mississippi
River. Major restorations of territory had certainly been made to France
and Spain, but Britain had had her bellyful of victories and high taxes,
and most Members were prepared to settle for this sizeable nothing.
Fox in any case was making doubly sure of the forthcoming vote,
attaching Newcastle's 'doubtfuls' to the King's interest by bribes,
irritations, or menaces. Ever since Newcastle lost control of the
Treasury in May, 1762, his position had been slippery, and one could
hardly expect owners or managers of boroughs to continue in loyalty
to a master who had lost control of the purse-strings. Most of them

transferred, under Fox's pressure, to the Court, and when the time came
in December for the Commons to vote on the Preliminaries, the
Government won an easy victory by 319 votes to 65. Now Fox, never
the man to let a good opportunity, financial or political, slip through
his fingers, declared for a 'thorough rout'.

Those who had been unwise or honourable enough to keep their
money on a plainly outmanœuvred Newcastle and had voted against
the King's Government, and those too who were helplessly committed
to his patronage, 'in Sussex down to officers of £50 per annum only,'
were ruthlessly removed from their places. In the course of a great
wail of woe to Hardwicke, Newcastle bemoaned the misfortunes now
assailing his friends:

> I never expected any regard would be paid to myself for having
> spent all my time and all my fortune in support of this royal family;
> *that* I suppose is my *crime* . . . My heart is almost broke for the cruel-
> ties with which they are treating poor innocent men, in order to be
> revenged on me . . . Mr Fox declares he will not spare one single
> man. To-morrow is the day of execution. My cousin Harry Pelham
> is to be turned out of the customs. Poor Jack Shelley to have his
> custom house place (which my brother gave him in trust) taken from
> him; poor Jack Butler to lose his employment held in the same
> manner . . . I am to be removed from my three lieutenancies . . .
> There is to be quite a new admiralty . . . and my Lord Villiers and
> Tom Pelham turned out . . . Poor Wilkinson, the only one in the
> ordnance, turned out . . . The Duke of Devonshire, the Duke of
> Grafton, and the Marquess of Rockingham are also to be removed
> from their respective lieutenancies . . . I intend to wait upon your
> Lordship in the evening of Tuesday next. Pray receive me kindly
> and pity me, for I ought to be an object of your Lordship's pity and
> compassion . . .
> If we are all removed from our lieutenancies and this persecution
> of all my friends in the under offices is pursued, against persons to
> whose charge no ill-conduct can be laid, might it not be made a
> proper cause of complaint in the House of Commons? . . . Is not
> such an extent or ill use of power, as *cognizable* and as much to be
> blamed, as the exerting a power which does not belong to the
> Crown or those acting under it?[21]

Other such purges were not unknown to the eighteenth century;
the Whigs had done far worse to the Tories and their dependants, for
instance, following the accession of George I in 1714; but there had

been nothing like this massacre of Newcastle's innocents for a long time. It marked the end of the Pelham empire, though it was not, of course, the end of the 'system'. It was not even quite the end of Newcastle himself, who was to return in diminished shape as Lord Privy Seal in Rockingham's 1765 ministry. But the substance of his power ended in January, 1763. He had had, though still not quite seventy, a very long innings, and enjoyed – it is the wrong verb for him – a career paradoxically rich in its combination of industry, self-pity, shrewdness, helplessness, and the exercise of political power.

George III, who had not forgotten but had certainly abandoned for the time being his intentions to purify British politics, concurred strongly with Bute and Fox over this purge of the Pelhamites. Any office-holder who had voted against the Government 'at a time like this ought to be made an example of'. [22] But the King was deeply concerned during these months by the swelling violence of the campaign outside Parliament against Bute, with whose unpopularity he himself, and more particularly and offensively still, his mother the Princess Dowager, were so intimately connected. Bute was not even safe on the streets; on his way to the opening of Parliament on 25th November, he was again assaulted by a mob and had to be rescued by the soldiery. Inside Parliament the King and he had won their victory and, through Fox, were mopping up the remnants of the defeated enemy. It may or may not be true that when the Peace Preliminaries were finally carried in Parliament, the Princess Dowager exclaimed 'Now my son *is* King of England', [23] but it is certainly true that the decline in his own popularity was connected with an obstinate conviction among the populace that the King's 'Scotch favourite' was, or at the least had been, the Princess's fancy man. Cartoonists, with their Boot for Bute and their Petticoat for Augusta, and writers of lampoons were busy with the old rumour. The anti-government press made play with every kind of suggestive insinuation, so much livelier and fuller of reader-interest than the loyal counterblasts of Bute's own hack propagandists – among whom was Smollett, editor of the *Briton*. One of the scurrilous weeklies, the *Monitor*, was prosecuted. Another, the *North Briton* – its very title a jibe at Bute and the Scots – edited by John Wilkes and circumspectly supported by his friend and patron Earl Temple,

unawed by the prosecution of the *Monitor* . . . and though combated by two Court papers called the *Briton* and the *Auditor* . . . proceeded with an acrimony, a spirit, and a licentiousness unheard of before even in this country. The highest names, whether statesmen or magistrates, were printed at length, and the insinuations went still higher. In general, favouritism was the topic, with the partiality of the Court to the Scots.[24]

Wilkes started the *North Briton* in June, 1762, and one of its earliest numbers was on the subject of the young Edward III, who, he wrote, 'was held in the most absolute slavery by his mother and his minister; the first nobles of England were excluded from the king's councils, and the minion disposed of all places of profit and trust.' The crudely suggested parallel between George, Augusta and Bute on the one hand, and on the other Edward III, Isabella, and Roger Mortimer (her presumed lover, co-ruler and fellow-murderer) was so outrageous that prosecution might well have followed, but for the sounding-board that it would have provided. In Paris the following month on private business, Wilkes was asked by Mme de Pompadour how far the liberty of the press extended in England. 'I do not know, but I am trying to find out,' he replied. The *North Briton*, therefore, continued to chance its arm, sometimes to the alarm of Temple, who had already advised Wilkes to 'avoid that sort of personality which regards any of the Royal Family',[25] and also to cease libelling the Scottish nation in general. He had of course no objection to attacks on Bute in particular. Even inside Parliament the George-Augusta-Bute trio were not safe from such impudent *jeux d'esprit* as Nicholson Calvert perpetrated about a fictitious family called Steady. He described two old Steadys and a young one. Young Steady had a mother who was on terms of improper intimacy with her Scotch gardener, and Calvert expressed the hope that young Steady would recall his true friends and sack his gardener. A man with the toughness of a Walpole, a Carteret, or a Fox would have weathered such attacks and given as good as he got. Bute had neither the necessary thickness of skin nor quickness of riposte. In debate he discoursed rather vapidly, with what Horace Walpole (who hated him) described as 'lofty ignorance';[26] haughty and distant, he 'dropped but now and then from a cloud an oracular sentence'.[27]

The supposed 'plan for absolute power' which the King's reputation, the popular prejudice against Bute, and Fox's extinction of the parliamentary opposition had between them lent some credence to, was given further support in the public mind by the new taxation proposed by Bute and his Chancellor of the Exchequer, Dashwood.* This was a proposal for a cider excise of 4s. per hogshead, to add to the existing

---

* A notorious libertine whose employment in the King's service, like Fox's, or later the Earl of Sandwich's, did little to convince men of their monarch's desire to clean up politics. Dashwood, moreover, was universally considered to be incapable of mastering the details of his own cider tax.

beer excise – while the land tax was still to stand at its top rate of 4s.
The war had indeed proved unprecedentedly expensive, a point that
speeches from the throne had continued to insist on, and not all the
costs could be met from loans. But there were three major objections
to Bute's cider tax; it fell especially heavily on some counties only
(there were riots in the west country): it was ill understood and in-
competently handled by Dashwood; worst of all it was an *excise*, and
the very word, as Walpole had found in 1733, was a red rag to the
English bull. With its implications of tyrannical officialdom – the
Englishman's home being no more his castle when the exciseman had
right of entry and inspection – it was a word as emotive to the
eighteenth century as 'prerogative' to the seventeenth, or 'bureaucracy'
to the twentieth.

In the middle of the cider rumpus Bute threw in his hand. 'A fortnight's opposition has demolished that scandalous but vast majority
which a fortnight had purchased; and in five months a plan of absolute
power had been demolished by a panic. He pleads to the world bad
health; to his friends more truly, that the nation was set at him.'[28] As
usual Walpole was being a little too neat and literary. Although Bute
rejoiced that the King had now indeed 'the sceptre in his hand', there
was no 'plan of absolute power', and Bute's retirement was not quite
such a sudden panic decision as most people immediately concluded.
His recurrent illness was genuine enough, though probably it would
not of itself have occasioned resignation. He wrote at the end of
January to a Dr Campbell, an old friend: 'a great relaxation of my
bowells of many years standing is increasing on me continually.' He
was also suffering from insomnia and nervous strain. He felt, he said,
like a man on the edge of a precipice. As we know, he had always kept
open the option of resignation, and frequently frightened George III
by reminding him of it. Even in Parliament he had hinted that he would
retire when the peace was achieved, 'which had rather confirmed men,'
says Walpole, 'in the opinion that he had no thoughts of it.' But now
the Peace of Paris was concluded at last, by a treaty which, whatever
was said against it by Pitt and his supporters, marked the greatest
single leap forward in British territorial expansion in the nation's entire
history.

In his letter to Dr Campbell, Bute tried to find reasons for resignation outside himself and his own sickness, but he failed to notice that
the two non-medical reasons he offered were self-cancelling: one, that
his work for the King was done, so that after the Peace the kingdom's
helm might 'be manag'd by a child'; and the other, that Britain was so
factious and unmanageable that 'the Angel Gabriel could not at pre-

sent govern this country, but by means too long practic'd and such as
my soul abhors.' [29] It is clear that Bute was sick of abuse and calumny,
and had discovered the truth of what he had always feared, that he
would not have the stomach or stamina necessary for the political game
at the top level. It was a game, perhaps, for professionals and Bute was
an amateur – an amateur, moreover, privately admitted by the back
stairs. The Pelhams and Cavendishes and Russells and Stanhopes and
the rest of the 1688 club had always felt quite simply that Bute had no
right to be where he was. Others not of their rank had earned the
privilege by one means or another; Hardwicke, for instance, by outstanding pre-eminence as lawyer and judge; Pitt by his genius – a
tiresome quality but unmistakable. Even of Fox, another generally
detested outsider, it was conceded that he had ability. This 'Scotchman', however, never had anything but the Princess's friendship and
the King's loving trust. He lacked, so they agreed, 'parts'. And now,
at the very moment when, with the King's backing and the ruthless
tactics of Fox to help him, he had chastised and apparently confounded
the greatest in the land, at the very moment of victory he was throwing
in his hand – an unaccountable man. Let one of the Stanhopes express
with his own fastidiousness the verdict of the 'old families' upon this
Scottish gate-crasher:

> Lord Bute, who had hitherto appeared a presumptuous, now ap-
> peared to be a very timorous Minister, characters by no means in-
> consistent . . . He had honour, honesty, and good intentions. He
> was too proud to be respectable or respected; too cold and silent to
> be amiable; too cunning to have great abilities; and his inexperience
> made him too precipitately undertake what it disabled him from
> executing. [30]

As early as November, 1762, Bute had warned the King that he
wished to retire. George had then pleaded with him. The rest of the
ministry were 'abandoned' and 'vicious' men, so how could a king
determined to root out irreligion and reform public morals work with
them? Talk of Bute's retirement gave him the greatest concern:

> I own I had flattered myself when peace was once established my
> d. friend would have assisted me in purging out corruption, and in
> those measures that no man but he that has the Prince's real affection
> can go through with; then when we were both dead our memories
> would have been respected and esteemed to the end of time. [31]

George was informed of his friend's final decision at least a month
before the actual resignation on 8th April. On the whole, he now took

Bute's departure remarkably calmly, while still calling it the cruellest blow he could have received. He could easily credit, he wrote, how Bute was 'heartily sick of his situation'. Since 1761, when Lady Bute had succeeded to her share of the Wortley Montagu fortune, her husband had been a very rich man; there could be no financial obstacle to his retirement. The King hoped, however, that Bute would 'accept the Chamberlain's staff and become again a Court officer'. But such matters were insignificant against what Bute himself was proposing, that *Fox* should succeed him. This at first George absolutely vetoed. The 'scene of corruption' that they had witnessed all that winter, though he had countenanced it, had not been a pretty sight. He had 'an aversion', so he claimed, 'to Fox's whole mode of government' and had no intention of letting it become permanent. He remembered what Fox had said earlier: 'We will give Lord B. a Garter and a Court appointment and then we may do what we please.'[32] The very judges, said the King, would become instruments of corruption under such a man.

Yet by 14th March, the King had come round to the idea of accepting Fox, *faute de mieux*. 'I know the soundness of my d. friend's judgment' – Bute had frankly told George that nobody but Fox would be able to control the Commons. And indeed the alternatives to Fox seemed to the King depressing or even nightmarish. Newcastle's friends were not to be thought of – Devonshire, Hardwicke, and the rest. The Duke of Bedford was 'never tir'd of dirty demands that he presses'.[33] Pitt and Legge were 'more obnoxious to me than any men, no misfortune could drive me to act with them'.[34] Grenville, Egremont – he disliked them both. Halifax he thought 'the worst man that could be in the place except Ch[arles] Townshend',[35] whom George on another occasion wrote down as 'the worst man who lives'.[36] It was the old story: 'though young I see but too much that there are very few honest men in this world.'[37]

Fox, however, was himself having complicated arguments and quarrels with Bute, just before the latter's resignation, over the composition of a future ministry and the conditions attaching to Fox's leadership of it. The fact was, he only half desired that leadership. His wife was pressing him to refuse it for the sake of his health and her own. 'He cannot refuse it,' George had said; but refuse it Fox indeed did, assuming that he would go to the Lords and keep the Pay Office with its handsome salary and perquisites. Having later half withdrawn his refusal, he was suddenly faced with a bombshell: the King and Bute did not intend him to have the Pay Office after all. Wranglings, accusations and counter-accusations and every kind of nastiness (both between Fox and his enemies, and Fox and his 'friends') ended at last with his hanging on to the Paymastership for two more years, parting with the King after the sourest of interviews, and being created Baron Holland of Foxley. Straightening out his private pickings from the Paymaster's public accounts long outlived Fox himself, and occupied in all a few months short of twenty years. He was certainly to have need of all the money he could lay hands upon, having eventually to set aside £140,000 of it to settle his sons' gambling debts alone.

Unlike Fox, Bute, when he resigned, showed after all no inclination to retire. A short stay at Harrogate appeared to have done wonders for his health. It seemed that Bute, even though the honey had come to taste of wormwood, could by no means resist the prospect of another mouthful. His numerous enemies kept close watch on him; very soon Hardwicke was relaying to Newcastle – still writing and writing away, the pair of them – a report that 'Lord Bute comes frequently to his own house at Kew in a morning and the talk of the place is that he frequently sees the King there'.[38] And in fact the King was still protesting to Bute that he would love him 'till death'. There was still nobody else 'whom I or this nation can depend on',[39] and the thought of what lay ahead gave him what he sometimes called his 'black devils'. The very contemplation of his new ministry, headed by the triumvirate of George 'Greenville' and Lords Halifax and Egremont, made him glum; glum, and as usual self-righteous, ever ready to strike up his old tune about the degeneracy and vice of the age, so much more like a mumbling octogenarian than a hale young man in his middle twenties.

CHAPTER EIGHT

Grenville, Wilkes, and America

GRENVILLE had been left in no doubt of the King's cool attitude towards him, and had every reason to suspect Bute. His suspicions would not have been allayed if he could have read a letter written by George[1] – plainly agreeing to an earlier counsel of Bute – that it would be an advantage to have a somewhat uncohesive cabinet, 'having men not too much ally'd in the active posts of Government,' so that the royal 'independency' might be preserved.[2] The editor of his letters comments that his independency was in fact no independency, but still a dependency upon Bute, and this is of course in a sense true. But George did understand by 'independency' something real: briefly, that the Crown, not politicians, must control the nation's executive. This was the British constitution as he understood it, though the first two Georges had been in danger of losing that control and their politicians in danger of upsetting that constitution. George's wish was to *restore* the constitution and to keep the politicians in their place – in which, as Bute could now safely concur, a little inter-ministerial rivalry and jealousy might well assist.

From the beginning Grenville felt his own status as the King's first minister insecure. He knew that he had been put in as second or third best. He had not had the choice of his own colleagues, the King's selection having been guided chiefly by the advice of the outgoing ministers Bute and Fox. He knew that he was regarded merely as a stopgap, and that through the summer of 1763 intricate parleys were being conducted and bargains struck among his rivals and enemies – Pitt, Hardwicke, Newcastle, Devonshire, Bute, the Bedfords – for the formation of a new ministry. The King himself, his idealism shaken but not yet quenched by three years on the throne, continued to hanker after some more broadly based government which would unite the factions and extinguish the idea of 'opposition', which was such anathema to him – even if this meant coming soberly to terms with politicians that he had impulsively cried out against and sworn he would have no truck with. Several times during 1763 he made overtures through Egremont to Hardwicke, offering him the Lord Presidency,[3] which Hardwicke turned down, not wishing to isolate himself

from his allies. But what would have been a significant coalition between Pitt and the big guns of the Newcastle Whigs almost came off at
the end of August, 1763; and if it had been accepted, then the Grenville-
Egremont-Halifax triumvirate would have proved a very temporary
stopgap indeed.

On Saturday, 27th August, Pitt, having already consulted both Bute
and the Newcastle Whigs, had a three-hour interview with the King;
the following day, Sunday, he went down to Claremont to see Newcastle; messages were sent to those Whig lords who might expect to be
in a new cabinet, and their replies exhaled a happy expectancy.[4] Commanded by the King to appear at Buckingham House on Monday, Pitt
found that the temperature had dropped sharply, and that his terms
were not after all acceptable. Of the reasons for the King's week-end
change of attitude much mystery was made, and it was not lessened by
Pitt's own deliberately opaque comment – that if he were examined
upon oath, he could not say at what point the negotiation broke off,
but that if the King were to assign any particular reason for it, he would
never *contradict* it. Horace Walpole remained sure that the stumbling
block had been Pitt's insistence on Temple as First Lord.[5] On the other
hand, both Pitt and Hardwicke affirmed that at one point the King
actually suggested Temple for that office – which does, in view of the
violence of George's distaste for the man, reinforced by Temple's
current association with Wilkes, seem on the face of it improbable,
though George's plight made him capable of many turnabouts and
contradictions. Some said that Pitt had stepped up his demands over
the week-end, pushing the King past the limit; or that Bute, to save
himself and in cowardly fear of Pitt's revenge – a Parliamentary inquiry
or even impeachment – persuaded, or condemned, George to go
on enduring Grenville's triumvirate.[6]

There seems, however, no good reason for doubting Grenville's
own account of the affair, written from Downing Street to Lord
Strange a few days later:

> Mr Pitt insisted upon excluding all that had had any hand in the
> Peace, which he represented as dishonourable, dangerous, and
> criminal . . . With regard to persons, he proposed to turn out almost
> every civil officer of rank in the King's service, and to introduce all
> those who had engaged in the Opposition in their stead . . . The
> great extent and the violence of these propositions, and of many
> others . . . determined the King to reject such terms . . .[7]

This broadly conforms with Hardwicke's report of the King's remark
to Pitt at the Monday interview: 'Well, Mr Pitt, I see (or I fear) this

won't do. My honour is concerned, and I must support it.'[8] In other words, the King had been ready to allow Fox to purge the Pelhamites who voted against the Peace, but he would have no counter-purge of those who had stood by the Government. Twice during the week-end, between the two Pitt interviews, he had received Grenville; more important, he had seen Bute. Each time Grenville saw his master he reported him as 'a good deal confused and flustered', or 'in the greatest agitation',[9] and this is not surprising. The King spent these days, as he was to spend so many more, between the devil and the deep – on the one hand, Pitt and the Newcastle Whigs, on the other Grenville. By choosing to keep Grenville he thought he could at least save his friends and his 'honour'. But the very fact that he had come close to accepting a ministry the names of whose likely members read like a roll-call of all those whom he had sworn never to employ again shows the straits he was now in.

Almost at the same moment that Pitt was failing to get acceptance of his terms, Lord Egremont died, and Grenville was obliged to strengthen his ministry by allying with the 'Bloomsbury Gang' – the Duke of Bedford and Earl of Sandwich in particular. The King's lack of faith in his chief minister having been so publicly demonstrated, Grenville was in a rather paradoxical situation: weak and exposed, because slighted, yet able to make strong demands, since the King's efforts to get rid of him had failed. George Grenville was a far from negligible man, a good thrifty administrator, conscientious and industrious. Certainly lacking imagination and vision, he nevertheless had an excellent head for business – which is a kinder way of saying what the King said of him, that he had 'the mind of a clerk in a counting-house'. Conscious of his own rights, he ran into difficulties both with his colleagues and the King. Conscious of the nation's rights, he stumbled into terrible trouble in America. Stiff and arrogant-sounding, he was a difficult man to love. Yet it is impossible not to have some sympathy for him. Not only was he faced by a monarch who at best tolerated him – in his Diary, Grenville's sense of insecurity is vividly, and indeed ludicrously, illustrated by the scores of entries in which he tells himself how civil the King had been to him that day and had expressed the greatest respect for him and admiration for his handling of affairs, and so forth – but he also had to contend with colleagues who bickered among themselves and with him, and who in some instances felt themselves superior to him.*

* Note Albemarle, *Rockingham Memoirs*, i, 175: 'Soon after the failure of the negotiation with Mr Pitt in 1763, the Duke of Bedford became President of the Council, and the ostensible head of the Government.'

As Leader of the House of Commons for a time under Bute, Grenville had chafed at his lack of say in patronage and appointments. Now as Prime Minister, he was determined to assert his rights both against the King and his colleagues. Sandwich, Bedford, and Halifax, in particular, considered they had the right to a share in the dispensing of patronage. Grenville stubbornly insisted that it must be his; it must be *all* his, and the world must so understand, 'or the whole must break.'[10] He insisted too to the King in his dogged, pedantic, but single-minded manner, that he must be the sole channel through which royal business passed. On one occasion when the King informed the Surveyor General that he proposed to 'curtail' the office of Painter, Grenville, in the King's own words, 'had the insolence to say that if people presum'd to speak to me on business without his previous consent, he would not serve an hour.' For this, had he given way to his feelings, added George, he would have dismissed him there and then; 'but I thought it detrimental to the business of the nation to make any alteration during the sitting of Parliament.'[11] These arrogant demands of Grenville were aimed against Bedford, Halifax and Sandwich; against the King; but equally against the unseen hand of Bute, still known to be in constant communication with his master.

Bedford in particular loathed Bute, and pressed the more 'correct' Grenville (who indeed did not need much pressing) to insist that Bute remove himself from London. So the man who had so often professed his anxiety to retreat from the hurly-burly (and half meant it) accordingly had to agree to retire 'from all business whatsoever' and 'absent himself from the King for a time, till an Administration, firmly established, should leave no room for jealousy against him'. Hardwicke, hearing of this, in fact wrongly hearing that Bute was 'to go beyond sea for a twelvemonth or more', was still sceptical of the efficacy of this banishment. 'You know,' he wrote to his son Lord Royston, 'Cardinal Mazarin was twice exiled out of France and governed France as absolutely while he was absent, as when he was present.'[12] Grenville, when Bute was obliged to resign his post of Keeper of the Privy Purse, even sought to veto the King's appointment in his place of Sir William Breton, an old Leicester House man, who, Grenville claimed, 'was so nearly connected with Lord Bute that it would stand as strong to the public, as if it was Lord Bute's Private Secretary.' In this matter, however, George refused to yield, and with some heat: 'Good God, Mr Grenville, am I to be suspected after all I have done?' 'Not by me, Sir,' answered Grenville . . . 'after all you have said to me, it would not become me to do so; but such is the present language and suspicion of the world.'[13]

Fears of Bute's hidden influence lingered for a long time to come. It is significant that the letters, hitherto so full and frequent, from George to his Dear Friend, appear almost to cease from September, 1763. Only four are extant for 1764, only one for 1765. Then came three long ones in 1766, leading to the final break. Fears of the 'minister behind the curtain' were very strong – much stronger than any evidence justifies – but it is practically certain that many more letters passed between the two men during 1764-65, and that they were destroyed for reasons of political prudence. Bute's friend Jenkinson owned to Grenville in November, 1765, that, although Bute's influence had not affected the King in the dismissal of Grenville's ministry, 'the intercourse in writing . . . always continued . . . The King wrote him a journal every day of what passed.'[14] In particular, the Duke of Bedford let it be known that he regarded Bute's return to London in March, 1764, after a winter of 'exile' at Luton Hoo, as 'an entire infraction of the bond on which he had consented to take office'.[15] Bedford protested loudest, but all the Whigs remained intensely suspicious of Bute's presence anywhere within royal reach. 'Lord Bute makes many hugger-mugger visits at Richmond,' wrote Lord Royston* to his brother, 'in a way neither creditable to his master nor himself.'[16]

Far and away the most portentous developments during Grenville's stewardship of the King's business concerned an issue remote, or seeming so at first, from this kaleidoscope of domestic political intrigue – namely the new policy towards American taxation and trade regulation. Undoubtedly, however, the greatest public excitement and parliamentary fury arose from the first big Wilkes episode. In fact, between the publication of Number 45 of the *North Briton* on 23rd April, 1763, and the sentence of outlawry passed on Wilkes by the Court of King's Bench on 1st November, 1764, there was hardly a dull moment. With the Wilkes affair we are not of course removed from the politicking and faction-battles. It is still the same world of magnates and manœuvre, of Westminster and St James's, of Claremont, Woburn, and Stowe. But with Wilkes there are other worlds as well; the canvas is broader. It involves out-of-work artisans and Thames-side mobs; pagan rituals in Buckinghamshire and pornography in the House of Lords; affairs of honour at fourteen paces, and (perhaps) attempted murder in Hyde Park; intercepted letters and outwitted government spies; riot, suicide, and sudden flight over the Channel. The Wilkes story provided a mixture highly and variously coloured, and brilliantly

---

* Soon to be the second Earl of Hardwicke. Both the first Earl and the Duke of Devonshire, co-leaders with Newcastle of the main body of the Whigs, died in 1764. Their death, and Newcastle's age, signalled a vacancy in the leadership.

news-worthy: a potpourri of melodrama, scandal, slapstick, wit; high politics, the majesty of the law, the authority of Parliament, the reputation of the King. It proved a beanfeast for the lawyers, a *cause célèbre* for the scribblers and politicians, a constant threat both to the regal dignity and metabolic stability of George III.

Compared with the Stamp Act and its consequences, this first of the Wilkes rough-and-tumbles was of minor significance. What Grenville tried to do in America raised a storm that blew for twenty years, and at the end left an irreparable trail of ruin – or so it seemed at least on this side of the Atlantic. General warrants and issues of parliamentary privilege or seditious libel stirred up, by comparison, little more than a teacup tornado. Yet this in its way was important too; the Wilkes affair of 1763-64 gave a focus to the multiple complaints that had built up in the first few years of the new reign: industrial hardships accompanying the post-war falling-off in business as well as social and political discontents associated with the King's method of government and Parliament's own behaviour. It both dramatised and increased the unpopularity of George III. But Wilkes, though he sometimes claimed to be, was not seriously concerned with great issues of political or social reform, any more than was his turbulent and arrogant patron Lord Temple, who was driven forward by his own pugnacity and what Shelburne called 'a most sovereign contempt for the Royal closet . . . which he never wished to conceal even at his own table'. Wilkes was a *frondeur*, not a revolutionary; a *franc-tireur*, not a campaigner; a spark, and a very lively one, but not a flame. His talent was to give his followers, whether of the 'middling' or 'inferior' sort, both of whom he claimed to champion, a bold and often entertaining object lesson in how to thumb the nose at the 'establishment', both parliamentary and royal. His speciality was to combine impudence with wit. His reputation arose from the public's pleasure in watching a middle-weight exchanging blows with a ringful of heavy-weights, one of them actually the King himself, and even on occasions flooring them.

Wilkes in the *North Briton* had once or twice before proceeded on the principle of *denying* the possibility of some mischief or scandal as the best way of suggesting its existence – for instance, in his Isabella and Mortimer squib. So when issue Number 45, in its attack on the King's Speech proroguing Parliament just after Bute's resignation, went out of its way to insist that there could be no question of insulting George III, since everyone knew the King's speech was written for him by his ministers, George's anger was in no measure lessened by Wilkes's disclaimer. Wilkes, echoing the views of Pitt and Temple, lamented that 'a prince of so many great and amiable qualities' could be 'brought to give the sanction of his sacred name to the most odious measures, and to the most unjustified public declarations, from a throne ever renowned for truth, honour, and unsullied virtue'. The Royal Speech had declared the Peace to have been honourable to the Crown and beneficial to the people. This, wrote Wilkes, was a lie. As for the 'happy effects' which several allies of the Crown had derived, that assertion too was false; we had abandoned Prussia. Only by bribery had the Treaty been ratified at all. Moreover, continued Number 45, the Scotch favourite was still exercising a hidden influence, and the existing ministers (Grenville, Egremont, Halifax and the rest) were 'a weak, disjointed, incapable set', 'tools of despotism and corruption.'

George might not have disagreed with the expression 'tools'. As it happens, it was the very term he allowed himself to use in a letter to Bute concerning his ministers' proper relationship to the Crown.[17] Even so, Wilkes's words could hardly write the King down as less than a liar and a corrupt despot. It was not simply that George was outraged by Number 45. He had not forgotten Isabella and Mortimer, or the earlier sniping and smears. What was more, Number 45 plainly showed Grenville and his colleagues that the journalistic minions of Pitt and Temple proposed to treat them no more kindly than they had Bute. So on the question of whether or not to prosecute Wilkes there was no difference of opinion between the King, the prime minister, and the two Secretaries. They were all for slapping hard down upon such flagrant opposition before it got further above itself. Had they singled out Wilkes alone and issued a warrant for his arrest, this in itself might not have prevented a 'Wilkes affair', for Wilkes as an M.P. would still have claimed privilege; but Lord Halifax compounded the trouble awaiting King and ministers by issuing, on 30th April, a general warrant for the arrest of 'the authors, printers and publishers of the North Briton, No. 45', on a charge of seditious libel.

Wilkes, who had feared arrest months before No. 45 appeared, was well prepared for the event when it happened. When the Secretaries' messengers first appeared at his house armed with a general warrant, he refused to accompany them and dispatched some of his friends to the Court of Common Pleas to secure a writ of habeas corpus on the grounds that he was being detained illegally in his own house. Persuaded by constables and the threat of main force, he later agreed to proceed up the road to talk to his neighbour Lord Halifax, but only if they summoned a chair to convey him in proper style. At Halifax's house he confronted the two Secretaries with a combination of witty insult and flat refusal to answer questions. His first writ of habeas corpus being deemed insufficient on a technicality, the Secretaries had him conveyed to the Tower of London, where his light-hearted insolence was in no way impaired by the surroundings. He would rather not have a room where a Scotchman had been, for fear of the pox; he would prefer the accommodation enjoyed by Secretary Lord Egremont's father – Sir William Wyndham, a *Jacobite* Tory. Temple now secured for him a second and watertight writ, and the Court of Common Pleas ordered a relaxation of Wilkes's confinement. Things were plainly going wrong for the King and his ministers, although they had many shots in their armoury yet.

Wilkes, M.P. for Aylesbury, was also a Colonel of the Buckinghamshire militia, and George lost no time in commanding Lord Temple, as Lord Lieutenant of the county, to have his friend and dependant relieved of his colonelcy. This Temple had no option but to do, but phrased his letter of dismissal in terms of such sympathy for Wilkes as further to anger the King. Temple had written that he could not help expressing concern 'at the loss of an officer . . . endeared to the whole corps', whereupon George commanded Temple's own dismissal from the post of Lord Lieutenant, and an ostentatiously curt note written by a clerk, and merely signed by Halifax, informed Temple: 'His Majesty has no further occasion for your service as Lord-Lieutenant and Custos Rotulorum for the County of Buckingham.'

On the legality of general warrants there were conflicting judicial opinions. Some precedents suggested that they were not legal, but many more that they were. Hardwicke admitted that he had personally signed many. Pitt, who was prominent in the attack on them, had himself in earlier days issued three. Halifax had made use of one as recently as 1762, and there had been no protest. Whether the validity of general warrants was upheld was likely to depend entirely on the opinions of the judge before whom they were challenged. In theory, of course, the judiciary was above the political battle, but, in a day when judges were also politicians, practice and theory were markedly at variance. Lord Mansfield, who presided over the King's Bench, was a supporter of Government and Court; Pratt, Chief Justice of the Common Pleas, was a close friend of Pitt. If, therefore, Wilkes and his supporters took their cases against the Secretaries to the Common Pleas, the Secretaries were careful to have theirs tried in the King's Bench. Pratt, in fact, soon ordered Wilkes's release on the grounds that a Member of Parliament could be arrested only for treason, felony, or a breach of the peace; not for libel, which at most could only *tend* to a breach of the peace. This judgment not only emboldened Wilkes to ignore a subpoena to appear before the King's Bench, but released a flood of summonses against the Secretaries both from Wilkes himself and the many others,

especially printers, whose houses had been searched and property confiscated under the authority of the general warrant. London juries,
largely merchants and in general supporters of Pitt, then proceeded to
bring in verdict after verdict granting substantial damages against the
King's agents. Wilkes was eventually awarded £1,000 against Mr
Under-Secretary Wood; Leach, a master-printer, £400; the composi-
tors who were dragged from their beds, £200 to £300 each; while
most of the journeymen printers were happy to settle for £100, with
costs against the Government. Every decision, culminating in Wilkes's
£1,000, was greeted with keen enjoyment by the London merchant and
artisan classes and with riotous shouts of 'Wilkes and Liberty!' from
the mob.

So far there had been much bloodier noses on the King's side than
on Wilkes's. The contest, however, was only beginning, and when
Parliament resumed business in November, 1763 – Egremont by now
having died and Sandwich taken his place, George and Pitt having
failed to come to terms, and Grenville having allied with Bedford and
rusticated Bute – the royal hand was much more cleverly played and
Wilkes's correspondingly overplayed. Against the advice of Temple,
whose funds he depended on, Wilkes set up a press in his own house in
aptly named Great George Street, reprinted the *North Briton* entire,
including No. 45, and began running off twelve copies of a bawdy and
libellous parody of Pope's *Essay on Man*, entitled *Essay on Woman*. This
was not originally or mainly written by Wilkes but by his one-time
friend, now dead, Thomas Potter, the dissipated son of an Archbishop
of Canterbury. Wilkes, however, did update it with topical allusions of
his own. While Wilkes was thus chancing his arm, Grenville, Halifax,
and Sandwich prepared their tactics, this time with care and deliberation. Among the evidence which by bribery they spirited out of
Wilkes's house without his knowledge was a copy of the *Essay on
Woman*.* As for the King, he was absolutely determined to make an
example of Wilkes and to win this battle with the forces of insubordination. 'I hear from all hands,' wrote Wilkes to Temple on 9th July,[18]
'that the King is enraged at my insolence, as he terms it'; and he heard
right. 'I regard not his frowns nor his smiles,' added Wilkes. 'I will
ever be his faithful subject, not his servant' – and then, as though immediately to withdraw this protestation of half-loyalty, 'hypocrisy,
meanness, ignorance, and insolence characterise the King I obey. My
independent spirit will never take a favour from such a man.' He was
hardly in danger of being offered one.

* The foreman who was held to have betrayed Wilkes here was so execrated by
popular opinion that he was unable to find work and committed suicide.

From Temple the favours he was receiving were substantial; however, and luckily, it was 'an honour' to ask for money from such a 'steady friend to Liberty'. Wilkes was reluctant to go to France to see his daughter Polly, who was being convent-educated there, for fear of incurring his patron's disapproval. However, he did go, staying in Paris for two months and returning very nervous on reports that Temple was displeased with some of his recent actions. Directly Wilkes was back in Great George Street, his every movement was watched by Government spies, and a plan of campaign was worked out between Grenville, the Secretaries, and the King, ready for the opening of Parliament on 15th November. Grenville, by agreement with Speaker Cust, rose immediately, forestalling the opposition, to announce that he had a message from the King, asking the House to take into consideration that Wilkes had evaded trial for libel by pleading privilege as a member.

There followed in the Commons several days of tense debate on the limits of parliamentary privilege and on the cognate subjects of the *North Briton*, the liberty of the subject, and general warrants, while in the streets outside the populace vented its anger and high spirits in a jamboree of rowdy demonstrations for 'Wilkes and Liberty!'. George followed every move with the minutest attention, as Grenville faithfully supplied him with accounts of the debates and detailed lists of every Commons division.[19] Opposition from Pitt and the Newcastle Whigs was to be expected, particularly in defence of the sacred liberty of the subject; but any back-sliding by Government supporters, and especially by any office-holder, was flintily noted by the King. On 24th November (at '36 minutes past 9') he could hardly wait to hear how things were going. 'The great consequence of this day's debate to the very being of the Constitution' made him 'most anxious for a line'; and then again half apologetically, 'I wish but for a line.'[20] At the end of the debates a weary but, as ever, conscientious Grenville, at four in the morning, sat down humbly to beg leave to congratulate his master upon 'the transactions, which upon the whole have been as advantageous as is possible. The division was 258 to 133 . . . In the division Mr FitzMaurice, Col. Barré and Lieut. Col. Calcraft all voted in the minority, as did Genl. Conway'.[21] And only a few hours later George was writing back to propose without more ado the dismissal of Conway 'both for his civil and military commissions . . . and any others who have . . . gone steadily against us', and giving it out that the rest would have the same fate if 'they do not amend their conduct'. These 'others' eventually included Barré and the young Lord Shelburne; but it was Conway who more than any other roused the indignation of the

King, who had in fact already proposed after the first day of the debate that he should be dismissed 'instantly, for in this matter I am personally concerned'. [22] Conway was Groom of the Bedchamber; he commanded a regiment of dragoons; and his brother Lord Hertford represented the Court of St James's in Paris. Open opposition from such a one George regarded as unpardonable defiance.

Horace Walpole fought long and hard to save his friend Conway; Grenville himself advised the King at least to delay, but, as Walpole reported, 'Mr Grenville said twice, *the King cannot trust his army in the hands of those that are against his measures*' [23] – a royal attitude that for Walpole, for Pitt, and for most of the Whigs represented an unpardonably vindictive use of prerogative power and a denial of the rights of conscience. But Conway held posts in two of the three spheres where George always assumed that appointments and dismissals were matters for him, and ultimately (though he might take advice) for him alone: the army, the royal household, and senior preferments in the Church. After the close shave that the Government was soon to have in the division following the general warrants debate in February, 1764, the King was rather more willing to listen to Grenville's advice that they should avoid any sweeping dismissals; and even Conway, the prime offender, was maintained in his posts for another two months, until well after the Wilkes affair had subsided. It therefore occasioned the more shock – and to Walpole outrage – when his dismissal was eventually announced in April, 1764.

On 16th November, 1763, Wilkes had been 'called out' by Samuel Martin, one of Bute's followers and an old enemy of Wilkes. Martin, it transpired, before making his challenge had been practising pistol-shooting in systematic if ungentlemanly fashion, proposing to make no mistake about hitting his opponent and, according to Walpole at any rate, intending to murder him. As it was, he wounded him painfully in the groin, an incident which caused the Commons to adjourn and Wilkes to be immobilised for over five weeks in bed. During this time it was the House of Lords' turn to get its teeth into him. They were asked to declare the *Essay on Woman* 'a most scandalous, impious and obscene libel', and Sandwich in particular was able to indulge himself by quoting to the House, with histrionic moral indignation, the poem's indecencies. Dedicated to Fanny Murray, a well-known daughter of joy and mistress among others of Beau Nash, it was not a very witty piece of bawdry. The piquancy of the situation lay in two circumstances: one, that the editor of Pope's *Essay on Man*, Warburton, Bishop of Gloucester, present in the House, was made in the *Essay on Woman* to provide the blasphemous and lubricious commentary being quoted with such affected horror by Sandwich; the other, in the very fact that it was Sandwich who was handling the attack on Wilkes – 'Satan preaching against sin,' as Lord Despenser commented. Sandwich, Lord March, and Despenser himself (formerly Dashwood, Bute's Chancellor of Exchequer) had been fellow-members with Wilkes of the Hell-Fire Club, fellow-amateurs of the rites of Venus and devotees of the Bona Dea among the whimsically phallic groves of Medmenham. But these former 'monks of Medmenham' signally lacked a sense of sodality, and Sandwich had thrown himself enthusiastically into the preparations to destroy his one-time companion in stylish lechery. (Hence he became derided as 'Jemmy Twitcher', who 'peached' on Macheath in *The Beggar's Opera*;* it was pretty generally agreed that there should have been loyalty among rakes as among thieves.)

The two-pronged attack on Wilkes from each house of Parliament, with this time no Chief Justice Pratt to shield him, left him in serious danger. He still had a few exhilarating moments, as when on 3rd December the attempted execution of the parliamentary instruction to the common hangman publicly to burn the *North Briton No.* 45 before the Royal Exchange was overwhelmed by a mob that rescued the paper and burned instead the old Bute-Augusta symbols of a boot and a petticoat. They pelted the constables, injured the presiding Sheriff, and yelled for Wilkes, Temple and Cumberland – the last presumably on the grounds that he had been among the thirty-odd peers voting against the Government.† The King, 'disturbed and exasperated' by the riot, was still further 'hurt and offended' by the refusal of the Common Council of the City of London to take sides over the incident, and thus 'prejudge' Wilkes's cause. It was also in December that Pratt, awarding Wilkes his £1,000 against the Under-Secretary, pronounced firmly on the illegality of general warrants. But Wilkes had given too many hostages to fortune. On 24th December he eluded the Government's 'eyes' and fled to France. On 20th January he was expelled from the Commons. After the full-scale parliamentary debate on general warrants in February, 1764, in which the opposition mustered their full forces and ran the Government to a mere ten votes,

---

* 'That Jemmy Twitcher should peach I own surprised me. 'Tis a proof that the world is all alike, and that even our gang can no more trust one another than other people' (Act 3, Scene 4).

† Grenville's Diary, two months later, February 9, 1764: 'the King told Mr Grenville that he was informed that the Duke of Cumberland had had an apoplexy, and that he believed him to be very ill; but that he did not send to inquire after him, because, after the Duke's behaviour to him, nobody would suppose he could inquire out of regard for him.' Cumberland recovered, and the King was to have need of his services yet.

Lord Chief Justice Mansfield in the King's Bench found John Wilkes to be the author of both Number 45 and the *Essay on Woman*, pronounced judgment against him, and issued a writ for his arrest. When by 1st November Wilkes still had not returned to England, the Court declared him an outlaw. The *Annual Register* announced this as completing 'the ruin of that unfortunate gentleman', a premature judgment; yet the Court, though it had lost the early rounds against Wilkes, and though it was run close in the Commons over general warrants, did appear to have swept the field by 1764.

By 12th July, Grenville's diary was reporting:

> The King continues more than usually cheerful; seems pleased with the conduct and success of his affairs; and gives not the least reason to suppose that there could be any foundation for the report of an intended change of Ministry; but, on the contrary, speaks with great slight and disregard of the most considerable people of the Opposition.

There was a certain element here, as with much that Grenville wrote, of whistling in the dark – he always needed to assure himself that the King thought well of him, and that things were going well; yet it was true that 1764 proceeded without the crises that marked 1763 and 1765-66, to say nothing of the greater disasters to come. The very fact that King and ministers, in the same boat, had together negotiated some turbulent water reduced the tension between them. The King had his own way of putting this: 'Whenever Opposition allarm'd them they were very attentive to me; but whenever releas'd from that their sole ideas were how to get the mastery of the Closet.'[24] George III, though he respected Grenville's capability and gladly co-operated with him in his measures of economy, would never entirely trust him as a man. And Grenville could never feel secure, never be quite sure that the King was not listening too much to others, perhaps to those 'inferior persons who get about His Majesty and seemingly indisposed him to his principal servants',[25] or, worse, to Bute again. There was no evidence that George was not keeping his word. Although he was obstinate and strong-willed, he was honester than most men, and he assured Grenville that he had no *political* conversation with Bute since the end of August, 1763.[26] Suspicion of secret influence, however, refused to subside. It was noted, too, that the group of members in the Commons who passed by the name of 'Lord Bute's friends' often stood on the sidelines when ministers were attacked.

In one respect at least the King could generally approve of Grenville's doings. They were both men who looked hard at the cost of things.* What Grenville did for the nation at large, George had to a large extent done among the accounts of the Court household. 'Every stratagem was invented to curtail the common expense of the palace,' wrote Walpole; 'nothing was heard of but cooks cashiered, and kitchens shut up. Even the Maids of Honour . . . were reduced to complain of the abridgement of their allowance for breakfast.'[27] Henry Fox, who appreciated the value of money, showed a better understanding of the King's desire to prevent waste, while noting the part it played, after the early short-lived enthusiasm, in his unpopularity: 'Now,' he wrote, 'because Lord Talbot [the Lord Steward] has prevented him from being cheated in the shameful degree that has been usual in his kitchen, they make prints treating his Majesty as they would a notorious old miser . . . To this pass are we brought by newspapers and libels, and the encouragement given to the mob to think themselves the Government.'[28] And indeed for the next two or three decades there circulated many prints and doggerel verses, caricaturing the royal miserliness and supposed stupidity.

Grenville's economies involved greater matters, but he too had an eye for candle-ends. Winding up the war brought the supply vote down from £13½ m. to £7¾ m., though this did not permit him, as he would have wished, to lower the land tax. The army, to Pitt's horror, was reduced from 120,000 to 30,000. Naval upkeep was so skimped that not only the followers of Pitt but the First Lord of the Admiralty also, Lord Egmont, considered the French would hold superiority at sea in the new war they seemed to be preparing for; and in a dozen years' time, off the coasts of America, these fears were to be proved reasonable. But trifles did not escape Grenville's scrutiny – the expenses allowed to ambassadors; the excessive cost of a horse-police patrol suggested by Sir John Fielding; the claim of the King's two brothers, Edward of York and Prince William, to increased allowances. When the Duke of York came to argue this last matter out, he got very little change out of Grenville, who coldly denied his charge that everybody else seemed to be getting pensions out of the King. 'The list of pensions and gratuities,' replied Grenville, 'has never been so low for many years as it was last year.' And when the Duke grumbled that George III paid less from the Civil List to his own relatives than had George II, Grenville again contradicted him, and showed him it was £38,000 more. Characteristically he then asked the King if he

---

* Grenville looked too hard for the King's liking in one respect, refusing a grant for £20,000 which would have enabled him, in order to preserve the privacy of the gardens of Buckingham House, to acquire land in what became Grosvenor Place and its by-roads.

might examine the Civil List accounts. He suggested practical economies. The King, wishing to do the right thing by his family, *from the Irish establishment* contrived an extra £3,000 a year for the Duke of York, but when he proposed to do likewise for Prince William, Grenville persuaded him that this should be deferred. Another *six* thousand a year out of Ireland, might, he thought, be difficult to justify.[29]

Avoidance of wasteful expenditure was only one aspect of securing economies. Grenville's methodical eye looked in two other directions – towards prevention of tax evasion and towards alternative or supplementary sources of revenue. Both these fixed his attention on the American colonies. He saw there a military establishment paid entirely from British taxes, and widespread neglect of the laws regulating trade. Smuggling and illegal trading, in fact, were so open and long-established that Americans had ceased to think of them as illegal at all. He noted too that many of the revenue officers were absentees in England, enjoying their salaries, often as a political reward, while employing American deputies to perform their duties.

Prosecutions for illicit trading were infrequent and convictions more infrequent still, since trials were usually before juries sympathetic to the accused. Large fortunes had been made, even during the Seven Years War, by trading with the French. For thirty years, the difficulties of enforcing, in particular, Walpole's old Sugar Act of 1733, which had placed a duty of sixpence a gallon on foreign-imported molasses, had meant that it had been generally ignored. The illegal foreign trade had come to be officially 'indulged'. Customs officers would generally settle for a halfpenny a gallon or less – which they then frequently pocketed as a perquisite of office; and the economy of the northern states had come substantially to depend on trading their lumber, fish, and farm produce for cheap French or Dutch molasses from Guadeloupe and Martinique, Haiti, and Guiana.

To Grenville's legalistic, accountant's mind, these were anomalous abuses. In his view, the colonists, whose trade bases enjoyed the protection of British ships and of British, or British-paid, troops, were providing no contribution to their own defence, and they were making nonsense of laws of trade that were of a kind generally accepted by all colonising nations. He accordingly proceeded along various lines of action. He tightened up the anti-smuggling machinery and system of trade regulation. Customs officers were henceforth required to go personally to America instead of hiring deputies, and they were armed with general search warrants, instead of having to seek a separate warrant for every building they entered. Alleged smugglers were to be tried (though in the event few were) in the Admiralty court at Halifax,

which did not offer trial by jury, and British men-of-war were dispatched to assist the revenue men. Next, in 1764, Grenville lowered
the duty on molasses from sixpence to threepence, but proposed to
ensure that the threepence was in fact collected. Twopence had been
considered the highest practicable limit, but Grenville was under
pressure from a British West India lobby whose votes were valuable
to him. Also in 1764 he imposed new restrictions on colonial trade and
currency, and new customs duties for the purpose, not as hitherto of
regulating trade, but specifically *of raising imperial revenue*. Finally, in
February, 1765, he introduced into the Commons a bill to levy a stamp
duty, of the sort already existing in Britain, on certain articles and
documents, including wills, mortgages, licences, pamphlets, newspapers, almanacs, playing-cards, dice, and college diplomas.

It was not a new idea; Treasury officials had been discussing its
possibilities for a decade or more. And now this Stamp Act slipped
quickly through Parliament with negligible opposition. Nobody
understood that the Americans would see this apparently equitable and
reasonable tax as a monstrous and unconstitutional innovation, denying the principle of 'no taxation without representation'. Nobody
appreciated the depth of the resentment the colonists would feel at
being made to pay towards the upkeep of an army in whose composition they had no say, which they were convinced was maintained
principally with a view to keeping *them* in subordination, and which
had signally failed to protect them from the Indians. Earlier colonial
grievances had usually been local – the Virginians' complaint, for
instance, when the Crown overruled their legislature's bill to commute
their Anglican clergy's 'tobacco stipend' into cash, or the anger of the
Connecticut lumbermen at the harsh interpretation of the old law
regulating the cutting of white pine for naval timber. The effects of
the Sugar Act and the tightened customs control were more generally
resented; but Grenville's new duties of 1764, and his Stamp Act of
the following year, were the first steps towards uniting all the mainland
colonies with a sense of shared outrage. The immediate hullabaloo
that was raised by the Stamp Act took everybody in Britain by surprise – even Pitt, who had said he was against it but had been too
gouty, or had not bothered, to come to Parliament to say so.

Ministers come and go – and seldom did they come and go so fast
as in the 1760's. Kings go on, to the grave. Grenville was a figure soon
more or less forgotten by Americans, and his successors who tried
their hand at the American problem, Rockingham, Townshend, even
North who lasted longer than most, were but transient agents of
wrongdoing. Men need a single, stable, permanently recognisable

personification of their enemy, a 'Boney', Tsar Nicholas, Kaiser William, Hitler; and George III was to do very well in American eyes for this rôle. He proved an easy man to hate, a ready-made tyrant, with his old-fashioned ideas and his obduracy; even his physiognomy was a gift for cartoonists, with the receding forehead, and the prominent Hanoverian eyes. He was a very identifiable dragon, there for the slaying, and in Washington the colonists were to find their St George. But all that George III did, at least in these early stages of the quarrel, was to act the part of a constitutional monarch. He supported his ministers. It was their initiative and none of his.

CHAPTER NINE

The King's Illness
and the Fall of Grenville

In fact, while the Stamp Act was passing swiftly through an un-concerned Parliament, the King, whose day by day attentiveness to political matters was usually intense, was in little condition to influence events. For three months intermittently, from January, 1765, he was ill, and his illness was something of a mystery. All that was positively known of it at the time was that it originated in what seemed to be a chesty cold, and that it was serious. Until recently the mystery of the royal malady and the derangement that it ultimately produced has remained, a challenge to the amateur physician and psychologist inside every historian. It was one of the Namier school who once wrote, 'It has become fashionable for the historian to present his characters in terms drawn from psycho-analysis; he had better not do so unless he is quite sure of his ground,'[1] and Namier himself said, 'the unqualified practitioner must not be let loose, not even on the dead.' However, Namier did not always heed his own severe canon; and while he simply followed the psychiatrists who retrospectively diagnosed George's malady as manic-depressive psychosis,* others developed more extravagant fancies – as, for instance, that his dogged faithfulness in the marriage bed with a repellent wife toppled his unstable nature into madness.

Since 1966, when the *British Medical Journal* first published the results of the researches of Dr Ida Macalpine and Dr Richard Hunter, it has really looked as if we might write of George's physical and mental sufferings in terms of something better than guesswork or fantasy. Approaching the formidably detailed record of the several doctors who attended the King during the illnesses of his middle and later years – forty-seven volumes of Dr Willis alone, for the 1788-89 attack – these modern investigators were physicians seeking a diagnosis; they had no Freudian preconceptions. And they discovered what they called 'a classic case of porphyria'.† This is a rare inborn metabolic disorder,

* In particular M. Guttmacher, in *America's Last King: an Interpretation of the Madness of George III* (New York, 1941).

† They later extended their inquiries to George's ancestors, relations, and

typically making its first onset during the patient's adolescence and very likely ushered in by what seems to be merely a persistent cold and cough. Then may follow many symptoms varying with the severity of the attack; among others, colic, constipation, and nausea; acute chest or stomach pains and cramps; affections and lesions of the skin; a very fast pulse, with fever, profuse sweating and sometimes delirium; gabbling speech followed by hoarseness or loss of voice; severe insomnia (George III once went entirely without sleep for seventy-two hours); polyneuritis, with weakness and sometimes swelling of limbs and joints; inability to taste, or to bear objects touching the skin; gross irritability; and in the worst cases mental aberration; hallucinations and delusions. Almost all these at one time or another George III suffered from, and showed, too, the further symptoms characteristic of the disease (and also witnessed to in the cases of James I and Frederick the Great), the final clinching piece of evidence for Drs Macalpine and Hunter – the passing of urine variously described as blood-red, purple, or the colour of port wine: hence the name 'porphyria'.

The diagnosis, then, is 'acute intermittent porphyria'; and in all, George was its victim on five main occasions before the final twilight; more if we count slight attacks or 'periods of flurry'. Not all of them produced mental symptoms, and always when the malady receded the King was left fully sane. This is true even for 1810 and after, but in the last decade remissions of the disease left him senile, blind, and at last deaf too. Indeed, until that year 1810, when he was seventy-two, the total time during which his mind was wholly deranged was only about six months,[2] though from 1801 onwards there were longer periods when his behaviour was 'hurried', moody, or unpredictable. Whether the word 'mad' should be used seems merely to be a matter of definitions; since the publication of the work of Drs Macalpine and Hunter there has been a distinct tendency to cloak the expression in inverted commas. But many forms of mental disturbance seem likely to have as biochemical a genesis as porphyria, and how should any clear line be drawn between 'hereditary metabolic imbalance producing mental derangement' and what our forefathers reasonably enough called madness? In 1788-89, and on occasions afterwards, George, according to his doctors' reports, 'baffled all attempts to fix his attention', lived 'in a

descendants, and suggested a much longer list of victims and possible victims, including Mary Stuart, James I, Frederick the Great, four or five of George's children including George IV, and his granddaughter Princess Charlotte. See *Porphyria – a Royal Malady* (British Medical Journal, 1968) and *George III and the Mad-Business* (1969).

world of his own', 'continually addressed people dead or alive as if they were present', his speech being 'like the details of a dream in its extravagant confusion'. Whether one speaks of 'madness,' however, or merely of 'delirium,' the significant facts are that for the great majority of his days till 1810 his mind was unclouded, and that his periods of mental derangement arose from physical disease.

The first bout of porphyria occurred in June, 1762, when a 'feverish cold' failed to clear up normally. Though it was a relatively mild attack, Fox for one took it seriously:

> H.M. was very, very ill. It is amazing and very lucky that H.M.'s illness gave no alarm, considering that the Queen is big with child and the law of England has made no provision for government when no King or a minor King exists.[3]

The King suffered from a violent cough accompanied by an 'oppression on his breast', sometimes described as a 'stitch'. He was blooded seven times and had three blisters applied – such rough treatment, thought Hardwicke, that the doctors must fear something serious; and it is plain that they did. The 'manna' they prescribed, which George referred to in his letter to Bute of 7th June, was merely a laxative, but the asses' milk they proposed to put him on next day shows that they, like others, feared that the symptoms might be a prelude to consumption. The Queen, reported Dr Duncan, 'never quitted his bed.' But in a few days he was up, albeit warned by his doctors to take care of himself for some time to come; he attended no Levee or Drawing Room for a period of three weeks. Walpole gave thanks to God that he was recovered, 'and we have escaped a confusion beyond that was ever known, but on the accession of the Queen of Scots – nay, we have not even the successor born.'[4]

In 1765, the King suffered a second attack, or more accurately series of attacks, more protracted and alarming. They began in mid-January with troubles and treatments similar to those of 1762, and developed severely enough to remind him sharply of mortality. From January to March he was frequently cupped to reduce his fever and kept very quiet. He was, however, far from bedridden and continued as far as possible to conduct business punctually, and even to attend most of the Privy Council meetings, either at St James's or, for the convenience of a sick man, at the Queen's House. There was renewed fear of consumption; the symptoms included a rapid pulse, sharp pains in the chest, hoarseness, and severe fits of coughing. On 26th February, Grenville wrote: 'The King all this time continues ill, and sees none of his ministers'; and again on 5th March: 'The King sees nobody whatever, not even his

brothers. Lord Bute saw him on Monday for a quarter of an hour.'
When twelve days later Grenville was again at Buckingham House, the
Queen tried to dissuade him from troubling the King so much, 'nor
talk so much upon business,' and when nevertheless the following day
Grenville again attended, he noted that George's 'countenance and
manner were a good deal estranged', though he was 'civil, and talked
on several different subjects'. Clearly Grenville was somewhat mystified
by the King's malady; not unreasonably, for the doctors were themselves mystified, and had little to offer beyond the frequent countings
of the pulse, purgings, and bleedings. (Even if they had not been confronted with so rare a disease as porphyria, then of course quite un-
recognised, they had none of the materials, practical or theoretical, to
make an accurate diagnosis, let alone effect a cure; they were still
proceeding in learned ignorance from age-old theories of the 'four
humours'.) Grenville could neither make out what was wrong, nor
decide how serious it was. It made 'a great deal of talk', he said, and
thought 'few people believe him to be as ill as is given out by Lord
Bute's friends'.[5] Horace Walpole, however, who was very far from
being Lord Bute's friend, wrote that the King's illness had occasioned
a general alarm, and he was 'apprehended to be in much danger'. And
the King himself was sufficiently disturbed by what he had been
through to propose to his ministers, immediately on his recovery in
April, the passing of an Act to provide for a Regency in the event of
his early death.

Had there been confidence between King and ministers, the nomin-
ating of a Regent and a Regency Council in 1765 might have proved a
less exasperating business. As things were, their mutual suspicion and
resentments occasioned the maximum public unpleasantness, and was
the direct cause of an open breach between the King on one side, and
Grenville, Bedford, Halifax and Sandwich on the other. The trouble
began when George, instead of straightforwardly appointing the
Queen as Regent (as Caroline had been under George II and as Grenville now suggested) declared that the appointment should be left to
the royal discretion when the time came. Suspicion was immediately
aroused; was the King thinking of some deathbed nomination of
Bute? And when this fear was removed by George's consenting to
limit possible Regents to a short-listed Regency Council consisting of
members of the royal family, a new difficulty arose: who exactly constituted the royal family? Legal opinion agreed that the Queen must be
included; the King's four brothers and his uncle Cumberland were
named; and foreign connections were eliminated by inserting into the
Regency Bill the phrase 'usually resident in this country'. But then

came the rub. Was the Princess Dowager of the royal family? And if she was, would the gate be open for the rule of Princess and Favourite – Bute all over again?

Consultations and debates in both Houses were no less embittered for being conducted in terms necessarily veiled and disingenuous. Raw wounds were scraped over publicly and privately. The Cabinet was disunited within itself, the Lord Chancellor (Lord Northington) and Lord Egmont being the two most inclined to fall in with the King's wishes; and at one point Northington flatly refused to attend further Cabinet meetings – he had, so he said, already given his views. The House of Lords, having first rejected the Duke of Richmond's motion to name 'the Princess Dowager and others descended from the late King now resident in England', were then informed by Halifax to their astonishment that the King would accept the re-committing of the motion *omitting the Princess's name*. The full story of this manœuvre is not known, but George, after a short interview for which he was inadequately prepared, does seem to have been 'bounced' into accepting this extraordinary insult to his mother; tricked, so Walpole guessed, by Halifax and Sandwich persuading him that the Commons would in any case strike out Augusta's name. Immediately repenting of what he had consented to, and 'colouring' as he remonstrated to his prime minister 'with great emotion',[6] he tried to get undone the damage that had been done. But wounds were in no way healed, or dignity restored, by the Commons' *re-insertion* of Augusta's name into the list of Regency Councillors, on the motion of some of 'Bute's friends'. Bute himself gave out that the motion was none of his making; and indeed it is likely that it was contrived by Northington rather than Bute, acting with the King's approval. In the House of Lords, the King wrote later, 'every iron was in the fire to thwart [the Bill]; and in the H. of C. things were brought back in some degree not by the Ministers but independent men.'[7] As things turned out, the greatest possible affront was occasioned all round. Nothing could have been more clumsily handled. Ministers had been made to look devious, and in the end sheepish, 'servilely revoking what they had insolently and unjustifiably done . . . Obnoxious as the Princess was,' wrote Walpole, 'the heinousness of the insult to her, and of the treachery to the King, shocked all mankind, and seemed doubly offensive in men from whom the King had a right to expect defence . . . It was not by *their* hands that the nation wished to see Princess and Favourite humbled.'[8]

The Regency Act was finally passed in mid-May, 1765. The second half of that month brought the King no respite. Instead, further political humiliation, and the frustrations and tensions that went with it, brought back his illness for a short period. Everything suddenly seemed to be happening at once. The King decided to rid himself of his ministers. The political world entered a period of flux, where it was felt that anything *might* happen, and something *must*. And in the middle of it all, the House of Lords, and then Bedford House, were besieged by a large mob of rioting silk weavers from Spitalfields.

Severely hit by French imports coming through Italian ports, encouraged by a Commons bill to prevent this evasion of duty, and outraged when the Duke of Bedford persuaded the Lords to reject it, these men, many of them hungry and half-destitute, had first marched peacefully enough to Richmond, intending to petition the King. The following day they pelted Bedford as he came from the House, injured him with a paving stone thrown into his chariot, followed him home, and there laid siege to him. 'His Grace's house would have very soon been levell'd with the ground,' reported Halifax to the King, if troops had not protected it. The Riot Act was read, more troops called in, and at last a cavalry charge cleared Bedford Square. While Bedford, ludicrously enough, complained to George that the riots had been instigated by Bute, the King himself, unwell down at Richmond Lodge,* showed the utmost concern. Any kind of mob violence, any overturning of the principles of order and proper subordination, always roused in him the strongest reactions.

On 21st May, he returned to St James's and consulted with the Duke of Cumberland and Lord Northington. Only then did he send for Grenville, who knew well enough that moves were afoot to find a fresh ministry, and had complained only the day before that 'with a mob at our doors, there is no Government within to repress it'. On this subject of the riots (reports Grenville) George showed 'great disorder and agitation. Hurt with people thinking he had kept out of the way through fear, he said he would put himself at the head of his army, or do anything to save his country'.[9]

He did not in fact take command of the army. Instead, in his exasperation and anxiety, he threw himself upon the support and kind offices of the Duke of Cumberland; no action could better demonstrate his sense of isolation and extremity. He proposed to make use of Cumberland in two respects: first, to attempt again to establish a ministry led by Pitt – who still remained aloof down at Hayes, wrapped in his virtue and his gout-flannel; and second, to get Cumberland to take up the post of Commander-in-Chief, or Captain General, in face of the civil emergency. Whigs like Horace Walpole thought this latter move a recipe for civil war; their man, and Grenville's too, would have

* The King's retreat in the Old Deer Park between Kew and Richmond.

been the Marquis of Granby, 'the most popular man in England.' Fortunately, however, the civil commotion soon abated. As Cumberland commented: 'I don't imagine these reports ought to break a moment of Your Majesties rest I wish to God you had no more formidable enemies than these poor wretches.'[10]

In his other rôle as royal negotiator-in-chief – where he proved a more benevolent uncle and more loyal subject than George had earlier given him credit for – Cumberland journeyed down to Hayes and brought back Pitt's terms, which, though they remained stiff, seemed to offer the King an escape. At the very moment, however, when the King, Cumberland, and Egmont were trying to build a new ministry, with some hopes of Pitt but rebuffs from the Newcastle Whigs, Grenville showed everybody that he too had cards up his sleeve. In fact he redealt the pack, by arranging a reconciliation, to everyone's astonishment, with his brother Lord Temple, which meant in effect detaching Temple from their joint brother-in-law Pitt. The Pitt-Temple alliance was to have been crucial in the King's new ministry. So again Pitt withdrew. The King was defeated, and it was the sitting ministers who now seemed to hold the trumps.

Determined to teach their ungrateful monarch a lesson, fearful still of hidden influences upon him, and vindictively thumping their cards upon the table, they commissioned Grenville to interview George and tell him the five points he must consent to: Bute 'to have no share whatever in any shape in the King's councils'; Bute's brother, Stuart Mackenzie, to be removed from office and from his control of the Scottish patronage; Granby to be made Commander-in-Chief instead of Cumberland; Holland to be dismissed from the Paymastership; Lord Weymouth (Bedford's man, whom the King considered an improper person*) to be made Lord Lieutenant of Ireland. On one of these points only, Cumberland's replacement by Granby, could George gain any concession, and that only by personally persuading Granby to hold back. The dismissal of Mackenzie hurt the King most; he had given his royal word to Bute's brother that even if he had to remove the patronage from him, his appointment as Lord Privy Seal for Scotland, a sinecure, should be regarded as permanent. Grenville's Diary reports the King as falling 'into great agitation upon the article relating to Mr Mackenzie . . . "he should disgrace himself if he did it" ';[11] but the emotional temperature at that moment in the Closet is perhaps better gauged from the rough notes Egmont made on the back

* Briefly Lord Lieutenant, he never visited Ireland. In youth a heavy drinker and gambler, he won his way into the King's regard and was twice Secretary of State. In 1789 George created him first Marquis of Bath and stayed with him at Longleat.

of the King's letter of 23rd May, than from Grenville's own smoother account:

> The King came into the Queen's drawing room as usual of Thursdays wc. he made shorter than usual – and whispered me going out to follow him – He asked me whether the duke of Cumberland had told me what had passed – he then began to tell me himself in great agitation – that he had submitted to all their terms but that of giving the command of the Army to Granby . . . That as to Mackenzie, he had treated Grenville with great indignation – That he told him he saw evidently that they were not satisfied with his parting with his power, but that nothing wd. content him, but parting with his honour too – Bid him take notice what he told him – and earnestly and in great anger bid him take notice of this – more than once – That he had forced him to part with his honour . . .[12]

The King's health, so recently recovered, was threatened again by these emotional disturbances. On Friday, 24th May, the day following the events narrated by Egmont, Grenville recorded finding the King 'very gloomy, with an air of great dissatisfaction'. When Grenville passed on from one of the new appointees thanks for the King's 'intended goodness', he snapped back, 'It's your goodness, Mr Grenville, not mine.' Doctors were already waiting in the ante-room. 'He gave Sir William Duncan his hand to feel his pulse, which was quick,' but, he explained, 'he had eaten very little and had no fever. He inquired earnestly . . . how the Duke of Cumberland did after all his fatigue, and if he stood it well' – Cumberland, half-blind, asthmatic, and very fat, had already suffered two or three heart attacks – 'and that, for his part, he never slept above two hours for several days past.'[13] The 'agitation' remained, and it was in fact to get worse before he was rid of this set of ministers, who continued unwisely to ram home their temporary advantage. On Sunday, 26th May, the King was still at Richmond, 'his mind so agitated that he did not choose to take the Sacrament that day' (a rare omission); 'nor was there any drawing-room.'[14]

It must have been about this time that in an undated letter to Bute, he cried out against his tormentors. His reference to his 'ulcered' mind is of course not proof of recent mental lapses, but certainly he writes like a man who has felt himself stumbling on the edge of a chasm:

> . . . I wish sometimes I were a private man that I might with my own arm defend my honour and freedom, against men whose families have formerly acted with more duty to the Crown than these wretches their successors; Lord Granby is so weak that the last man

that sees him has him, I don't doubt but the opposition and Lord Holland will try their arts to carry him off; I would rather have that than things remain on the present footing; every day I meet with some insult from these people; I have been for near a week as it were in a feaver my very sleep is not free from thinking of the men I daily see; patience cannot last I encline much to putting everything to a quick upshot, that I may know who are my friends, and who secret foes; indecision is the ruin of all things; excuse the incoherency of my letter; but a mind ulcer'd by the treatment it meets from all around is the true cause of it.[15]

Icy hostility continued for another six weeks, during which there was what amounted to a ministerial interregnum. The King for a time did not speak to Grenville until spoken to. He employed 'a kind of sneer' to Halifax, referring to Grenville's making the most of his influence (while it lasted) on behalf of his relations. He asked for the young Duke of Devonshire to be presented to Court and made a fuss of him, knowing this would displease his ministers. He refused Grenville's nomination of a new member of the Queen's household to replace Lord Weymouth. This was no office of state, he said. The Queen would please herself. Indeed she already had. 'Mr Grenville bowed and said no more.' George made no secret that it was still his aim to rid himself of these men. To Grenville he offered the reason that they could not agree among themselves, which was at least not untrue. In a private memorandum he alleged their lack of 'weight, abilitys, and dutiful deportment', and their 'insolence'.[16]

By 12th June, the Duke of Bedford felt that he had had enough, and having prepared a 'remonstrance', asked the King's permission to read it to him. This occasioned the notorious interview, somewhat written up and 'improved' by Walpole and subsequent histories (which have all four hostile ministers present and the King sweating and almost choking with indignation). George's own account, in a letter written the same day from Richmond Lodge to Northington, is soberer but revealing enough:

So very extraordinary an affair has happen'd this day that I cannot help troubling you with it; the D. of Bedford came to ask leave to go for some time to Wooburn and then began a harangue complaining that tho I supported him and his colleagues, yet that I appear'd not to like them, consequently that he and they were resolv'd when he came again to Town to resign if they did not meet with a kind reception, and those they thought their enemys were not frown'd upon; you will my dear Lord easily conceive what indignation I felt at so very offensive a declaration, yet I master'd my temper and we parted with cool civility . . .[17]

'Nothing but stone,' he wrote, 'could have bore this fresh insolence.'[18] Hence, five days later, Cumberland on the King's behalf was again driven down to Hayes to treat with Pitt. George had no great hopes of this visit, but somehow or other a means must be found of preventing the Crown being 'dictated to by low men . . . so that the world might see that this country is not at that low ebb that no administration can be formed without the Grenville family'.[19]

Pitt, it transpired, had no particular prejudice against Bute and was willing to reinstate his brother Mackenzie, but insisted on Pratt as Lord Chancellor; on a statutory condemnation of general warrants; and most emphatically of all on an alliance with Prussia and Russia as a counterbalance to the hostile power of France and Spain. The King much disliked this last proposal as 'ramming Austria deeper with France and kindling a new war by unnecessary alliances', but it is probable he would have swallowed his objection if Pitt had made acceptance an absolute condition.[20] After further meetings, both between Cumberland and Pitt, and between Pitt and the King, everything once more seemed to point to an understanding being reached. The 'blackest of hearts' had by 25th June become 'my friend' – for so, declared George, the part Pitt had acted, or seemed ready to act, had earned him the right to be called. 'Think it not strange if in my present distress I wish to see you again,' he wrote; and the same day Pitt, 'with the most profound veneration' professed his heart 'over-flowing with duty and gratitude to the most gracious of sovereigns'. But for the third time full and open negotiations with Pitt broke down when they looked set to succeed. He himself was intending to be Secretary of State and chief minister in the Commons, with Temple as First Lord. Pitt however was a sick man, and hence, as Temple knew, must often be an enforced absentee. Temple therefore did not see how the administration's business could be carried on in the Commons in face of the likely opposition of the main body of the Whigs, who were not to be among Pitt's ministers. This, then, was what Temple gave out as his 'publick reason' for refusing to co-operate; there were at least two further private reasons. He could not agree with Pitt on the men they were to engage with; and, above all, Temple was frightened of being expected to play second fiddle to his brother-in-law. He had a highly developed sense of his own status, and told the King he would not 'come in as a child and go out as a fool'.[21] For George, this was a setback but no tragedy. He had never hoped for much from Temple, and was under no illusions about a man he regarded as arrogant and unreliable. Without Temple, Pitt declared himself unable to proceed. So, as Cumberland put it, they were 'all afloat again'.

By now, however, the King had gone so far towards ditching Grenville, Bedford, and his two Secretaries that he could hardly turn back and toe their line again. What he would have liked, and still dreamed of, was 'to dissolve all factions and to see the best of all partys in employment'. [22] But if this was not to be, then he must once more put the past behind him, wipe the slate clean as might be, and make the best of things with the chief of the factions, the main body of the Whigs: that is, the friends of the Duke of Newcastle (older generation) and of the Marquis of Rockingham (the younger brigade); generally from this time forward collectively known as 'the Rockinghams'. Once more, therefore, Cumberland was pressed into service. He did more than profess his 'utmost duty zeall and respect'; he demonstrated it by producing, in very short time, a new administration, predominantly but not exclusively Whig – the old Leicester House faithfuls Lords Egmont and Northington kept their posts, and also the rain-or-shine Lord Barrington.

So once more the Duke of Newcastle was among the King's servants, for positively the last time; now Privy Seal. So too was Conway, whose 'instant' dismissal George had so recently pressed for; he became a Secretary of State and led the Commons. At the head, as First Lord, was the young Rockingham, who had been among the Lords Lieutenant so unceremoniously thrown out only two and a half years earlier for opposing the Peace. And Pratt, who had so 'infamously' upheld Wilkes in the Common Pleas, was to be raised to the peerage as Lord Camden. One might expect the King to have been depressed and labouring under a sense of defeat, but it was not so. Even the prospect of Newcastle appeared tolerable after Grenville and Bedford, and George seemed positively delighted when Hardwicke's lawyer son, Charles Yorke, accepted office as Attorney General. The truth was that the word 'never' had been uttered so often and impetuously over the past decade that George was obliged to make several meals of eating it. He had numbered so many enemies among the great of the land that it had become impossible, for a time at least, to rely entirely on friends. At twenty-seven the King was no longer the naïve retarded adolescent he had been at twenty-two. He had grasped that politics, like so much else, was a choice less between good and bad than between bad and worse. At least Rockingham seemed to him gentlemanly and honourable, even if his claims to leadership on grounds of ability or intellect were slender. His private reputation was tolerably blameless; he was not a 'low' man; he meant well; and for George all this was a relief after the pedagogical nagging of Grenville and the suspicious belligerence of Bedford. When a still self-justifying Grenville came to surrender the Seals, he insisted that the King should concede he had been both efficient and respectful – since the malice of his enemies was putting about the contrary. This was the well-known occasion when Grenville, tediously demanding to hear 'by what means, either omission or commission, he had drawn down his master's displeasure', was made to 'start' at George's reply and protest he did not know how such a thing might be repeated: 'The King said in general that he had found himself too much constrained, and that when he had anything proposed to him, it was no longer as counsel, but what he was to *obey*.'[23]

CHAPTER TEN

The Rockinghams
and the Break with Bute

ROCKINGHAM was thirty-five when he became prime minister for the first time. He had inherited with his wide estates and immense wealth the orthodox Whig attitudes that had taken his father, under Robert Walpole, from a mere barony to a marquisate. His natural inclinations, until the Duke of Cumberland promoted his elevation to the Treasury, had tended more towards the turf than politics. He was certainly more in his element on the gallops of Newmarket Heath than on the Government benches in the Lords, where he sat attentive but dumb. Aware of his limitations, he apologised to the King for his failure to speak, and when at last he plucked up courage George wrote: 'I am much pleased that opposition has forced you to hear your own voice, which I hope will encourage you to stand forth in other debates' – curious but not unfriendly words from a King to a chief minister. Four months later Horace Walpole was still commenting, 'The Duke of Bedford forced Lord Rockingham to rise and say a few words'; but with Rockingham it was noticeable that his appetite for power grew with tasting, and eventually he was to cling stubbornly to office.

For the first few months of its existence Rockingham's youthful and inexperienced ministry was given some semblance of solidity by the presence at its councils, almost as a kind of viceroy, of the Duke of Cumberland. Chesterfield described the administration as an arch without a keystone, 'and that keystone will and must necessarily be Mr Pitt.' For a time Cumberland did very well as a substitute, but at the end of October (just two months before the death of the Old Pretender whose cause he had destroyed at Culloden) his heart finally gave out, as it had been threatening to do for a decade. His death left the Rockinghams very shaky; for the next six months or so of their tenure of office they were 'waiting for Pitt', and when he finally threw them over they were living posthumously.

One of the charges made against George III is that he failed to give full support to his Whig ministers, and that he was always looking beyond Rockingham towards Pitt. That he wished to gain Pitt for the administration and so strengthen it is true, but so of course did Rockingham himself; and indeed much the larger part of public opinion wished to see the most famous statesman of the age associated with the nation's government. The young Duke of Grafton had joined the ministry as Secretary of State solely on the understanding that Pitt, his political god, would be invited to join too. As for the King, his principal concern was to get a stable government, willing to respect his rights and dignities – one that would prevent 'those constant changes of administration that have enervated the executive power, and that if not stop'd now will soon anihilate it'.[1] There was no concealment between the King and Rockingham over the adherence of Pitt. When the question arose whether, yet once more, as Grafton proposed, a 'treaty' should be attempted between George and Pitt, the King readily agreed with Rockingham that 'if it should miscarry all public opinion of this ministry would be destroyed by such an attempt'.[2] And when this provoked Grafton to threaten resignation, the King reminded him: 'As I had invariably supported them [the ministers] I had a right to expect they should continue; that if private honour prompted him to try to get Mr P. into office it ought also to remind him that he was not at liberty to displace the D. of N. and Lord R.'

However, George would not risk another interview with Pitt, which could not possibly remain secret, merely on a hint that this most unpredictable man might be pleased to unbend. He wrote to Egmont, 'It would be *both below me and impolitick to see* [Pitt] *alone when he comes to Town*';[3] and finally, in January, 1766, he told Rockingham, 'You have very properly put an end to the idea of writing to Mr Pitt. I don't doubt of [your ministry's] success, but if you in the least seem to hesitate, inferiors will fly off.'[4] He was careful therefore to court Pitt only through Rockingham and Grafton, but that intransigent man's response when they met him in mid-January was so hedged about with provisos about Newcastle (to go out) and Temple (to come in) and so full of the 'many removals' that would be imperative, that it soon became clear Pitt would join the ministry only if he could take it over and do what he liked with it. Even Newcastle's very creditable and patriotic offer to resign if he were the sole obstacle – which the King called handsome – cut no ice.* Pitt must have full power and be nobody's mere ally. He specifically refused to work under anyone who

* Newcastle, his health failing, and finally losing office when the Rockingham ministry fell in 1766, died in 1768. 'My old kinsman and contemporary,' wrote Chesterfield, 'is at last dead, and for the first time quiet . . . I knew him to be very good-natured, and his hands to be extremely clean, even too clean if that were possible. For after all the great offices that he held for fifty years, he died £300,000 poorer than he was when he first came into them; a very unministerial proceeding.' (*Letters*, iv, 391.)

had previously been chief minister. As the second Lord Hardwicke put it, 'the Great Commoner always expects implicit acquiescence. He will save everybody the trouble of *thinking*.'[5]

The other main charge of royal intrigue and disloyalty arose out of the American situation, which produced much the most critical issue to concern Rockingham, Parliament, and the nation. Walpole spoke here of the 'notorious treachery of the Court'.[6] The eloquent propaganda of Edmund Burke, Rockingham's private secretary from 1765, did much to furnish this undistinguished magnate and his following with an artificial halo that lasted many years, and correspondingly to implant in George's brow horns that grew wickedly for a century and a half. Macaulay in 1844 could see the Rockinghams as

> men worthy to have charged by the side of Hampden at Chalgrove, or to have exchanged the last embrace with Russell on the scaffold in Lincoln's Inn Fields. They carried into politics the same high principles of virtue which regulated their private dealings, nor would they stoop to promote even the noblest and most salutary ends by means which honour and probity condemn. Such men . . . we hold in honour as the second founders of the Whig party.[7]

From the inception of this 'wisest, purest, and most progressive administration of the eighteenth century' the King was held to have plotted and intrigued against it and at last brought it to an abrupt and premature conclusion.

Criticism centred round George's conduct over the repeal of the Stamp Act in January-February, 1766. This unlucky measure of Grenville's had brought forth defiance and disturbance in America on a large scale, and occasioned a boycott of imported goods so damaging to British mercantile and manufacturing interests that a powerful lobby for repeal soon sprang up at home to reinforce the urgency of dealing with the threat of rebellion across the Atlantic. 'Nottingham,' wrote Walpole, 'dismissed a thousand hands; Leicester, Leeds, and other towns in proportion. Three in ten of the labourers of Manchester were discharged.'[8] Rockingham's Government, therefore, among whose leading members only Conway had opposed the Stamp Act originally, decided by a majority, when they saw its effects on both sides of the Atlantic, to repeal it, but simultaneously to introduce a Declaratory Act asserting the Westminster Parliament's full sovereignty over colonial affairs. George made no moves to oppose these steps, though inside the Cabinet Northington and Egmont resisted the repeal of the Stamp Act, and Yorke, the Attorney General, even wanted the Declaratory Act to be made stronger, specifically asserting Britain's right to tax.[9] George's own initial reaction to any talk of rebellion or violence was of course for firmness rather than conciliation.

When the debates on the Stamp Act began, Grenville made a sharp speech defending what he had done. If they surrendered to violence there would be revolution. 'Great Britain protects America: America is bound to yield obedience. If not, tell me when the Americans were emancipated . . . The nation has run itself into an immense debt to give them protection; and now they are called upon to contribute a small share . . .' But it was Pitt, making one of his rare appearances, that the crowded benches wished to hear, and in a performance to rival his great onslaught on the Peace of Paris he did not disappoint them. Admitting first that he 'stood up for this kingdom', that he was no 'courtier of America', that the British legislative power over the colonies was 'sovereign and supreme', still, he said, there was a plain distinction between taxes levied for the purpose of raising a revenue, and duties imposed for the regulation of trade. 'The gentleman asks when were the colonies emancipated? I desire to know when they were made slaves.' Taxation was 'no part of the governing or legislative power'. The Americans were 'the sons, not the bastards of England'. She could 'not take money out of their pockets without their consent . . . The gentleman tells us America is obstinate. America is in almost open rebellion. I rejoice that America has resisted'.

This last was the kind of language that made Sir Fletcher Norton, ex-Attorney-General and future Speaker, rise to accuse Pitt of sounding 'the trumpet to rebellion' – a metaphor very close to George's later condemnation of him as the 'trumpet of sedition'. But there is no evidence that in January, 1766, the King reacted strongly against Pitt's attitude. True, he talked of 'wild men' on both sides, and Pitt may well in his view have come within the category; but at least it made no difference to his continuing efforts to attract Pitt into the Government ranks.

During the period of the crucial vote, the lobbies of the House were besieged by excited merchants who cheered Pitt and the pro-repeal men as they came from the chamber and hissed Grenville, who was so incensed at his reception that he could not resist gripping hold of the nearest man to him by the collar. The majority for repeal was 275 to 167, and Americans for a time jubilantly celebrated their relief. As well as one statue to their champion Pitt, the citizens of New York raised another to George III, in gilded lead before long to be melted down to serve more hostile uses. The substance of the charge against the King at home was that he had encouraged his friends to vote against repeal. During its passage two divisions were in fact lost by the Government in the Lords, and among the opposition in both Lords and Commons there were certainly pensioners, placemen, and prominent members of the Royal Household, none of whom was punished for his vote. Men remembered what had happened to 'Newcastle's innocents' or to those (notably Conway himself) who had voted against the Government over privilege and general warrants. The King, it appeared, had double standards. He was twice pressed, in particular, to dismiss one Dyson, a Lord of Trade, especially detested by the Whigs; but he asked for time to consider, and Dyson stayed.

'As to my friends differing from Ministers where they think their honour and conscience requires it, that I not only think right but am of the opinion it is their duty to act so.'[10] Plainly the King did not regard a vote against repealing the Stamp Act in the same light as a vote against the Peace or general warrants. In that sense he did employ double standards; but it is not true that he intrigued against his ministers. When he was pressed by an understandably nettled Rockingham for allowing Lord Strange to give out that the King was against repeal, he was at such pains to make his position clear and 'exculpate' his conduct 'in this unpleasant affair . . . this very arduous transaction' that he took the trouble to write it down five times in varying words of similar substance:[11]

> I told [Lord Rockingham] I had on Friday given him permission to say I prefer'd repealing to enforcing the Stamp Act; but that modification I had ever thought both more consistent with the honour of this country, and all the Americans would with any degree of justice hope for.

If the different parties were 'too wild' to come to modification, however, he emphasised several times that he was for repeal rather than enforcement. Few believed him. Most thought with Chesterfield that the repeal 'was carried in both houses by the ministers against the king's declared intentions'.

George always considered that he had every right to maintain his own supporters in the Cabinet and Government to leaven the Whig lump, and at all times refused to consider a homogeneous one-party administration. If Rockingham sought to broaden the base of his ministry, the King wrote to Bute, 'without my friends being also made part of it,' then he himself and his parliamentary supporters (to say nothing of Bute and his) 'would be irretrievably capotted'. He would never 'take a whole party' without his friends 'being comprehended'. It never occurred to George that any disloyalty to his Whig ministers was involved by his treating such men as Northington and Egmont as intimates to be trusted with confidence and rewarded with affection, while with the other ministers he was merely businesslike and correct. It was a case of 'them' and 'us', and he saw nothing wrong in that. From the Whigs' point of view it was inconvenient that some Cabinet discussions could not be kept secret from the King, but there was no 'double Cabinet' or secret cabal either then or later, as the Rockingham and other Whig writers were constantly and obsessively to complain. Conway, less of a party man than the others, later affirmed that he 'neither knew, saw, or felt a secret influence'. At different times, Wedderburn, Jenkinson and North all went on record to the same effect.* And the royal honour, as George time and again insisted, meant that so long as Rockingham and his team could 'subsist with credit', it was part of the contract that they should be maintained. 'I promis'd them ample support, this I am as a man of honour oblig'd and will punctually act up to.'[12] As individuals he declared that he wished them well;[13] but inevitably they came lower in his scheme of things than those who 'had no predilection for this or that set of men', as Egmont put it, but whose first duty and obligation was to the Crown and the Crown alone. It would in any case have been presumptuous for the Rockinghams to demand Cabinet solidarity and unanimity when they were very far from commanding a parliamentary majority of their own.

In the spring and summer of 1766, the breach between King and ministers once again grew wide. George was prepared to swallow their making general warrants illegal ('tho the most able of my servants were against the measure') and laid no objections to their repealing the cider tax, although he considered both these moves aimed chiefly at gaining popularity. What finally raised his royal hackles was their attempt to use his family's finances as a bargaining counter. On Cumberland's death £25,000 per annum had been set free, and it was agreed that £24,000 of this should be divided equally between the King's three younger brothers, Edward Duke of York, William Duke of Gloucester, and Henry, for whom the Dukedom of Cumberland was re-created after his uncle's death. (A fourth brother Frederick had died in 1765 – and in fact the Duke of York was to survive only until 1767.) However, with the Duke of Grafton's resignation† and increasing fears among ministers that the King would dismiss them, they tried

* Grafton, *Autobiography*, 177-78; Wraxall, *Memoirs*, iii, 39-41. For a discussion of the Rockinghams' obsession with the 'hidden influence' and 'double cabinet', see I. R. Christie, *Myth and Reality . . .* , 36-54.

† On finally abandoning hope of Pitt's joining the Government. He was succeeded, on Rockingham's insistence and to the King's strong displeasure, by that other natural descendant of Charles II, the Duke of Richmond, Sarah Lennox's brother and the first man George had quarrelled with on mounting the throne.

to make their retention in office a condition of passing the grants through Parliament before the session ended. Otherwise the money would have to wait, and since in those days Parliament normally met for only about half the year, the new session was unlikely to begin before January. The King wrote to Egmont, 'He [Rockingham] wants me now to break my word, which I cannot do . . . My brothers have been with me and are sensible I mean to stand by them.' And then to this willing listener once more he burst forth with the old self-pitying tale of injuries done: 'See what treatment I receive from every set of ministers . . . Because a few weak boys are unwilling this session to pass the provision for my brothers my word is to be set at naught; *my prudence is now exhausted I am enclin'd to take any step that will preserve my honour.*'[14]

At least it set him free, so he considered, from any residual obligation to maintain Rockingham and his 'weak boys' in office. He no longer felt bound to accede to their requests on routine matters – the creation of peers for instance. 'As to Peerage,' he wrote sharply to Rockingham, 'I thought I had yesterday as well as on many former occasions ex-press'd an intention of not at least for the present encreasing the Peerage.'[15] No doubt he savoured such gestures, but a return of his 'flurries' and the tone of his more private letters show well enough that he was worried how best to act. Back in February, during the American debates, he had been briefly confined, and blooded for a fever. Now again, he told Bute, he could neither eat nor sleep. 'Nothing pleases me but musing on my cruel situation . . . Indeed if I am to continue the life of agitation I have these three years, the next year there will be a Council [of] Regency to assist in that undertaking.'[16] Fully primed by Egmont of the dissensions within the Cabinet, convinced (especially after Grafton abandoned it) that it was cracking up, and knowing that Rockingham and Newcastle refused to have it reinforced from the ranks of the King's or Bute's friends, he was by midsummer determined to settle for yet another change, yet one more attempt to recruit Pitt. This time it was Northington who was given Cumberland's old task of taking soundings – the King always preferring to initiate any such delicate negotiations through an intermediary.

So the lobster quadrille began once more, while the King poured out his troubles to Bute in one of three last long letters that escaped destruction, begging that his words 'must be trusted to no living soul; . . . pity your unhappy friend for indeed he deserves it'. How-ever, Northington's indirect approaches to Pitt via Lord Camden proved sufficiently encouraging for the great man to be summoned from Bath to town, whence however fresh illness soon compelled his retreat to the country airs of Hampstead. From there on 15th July, 1766, he wrote:

> Your Majesty's most gracious commands find me still with a fever upon me, but I hope with the bleeding and other remedies I am under I may soon be able to lay myself at your royal feet. If the fever leaves me, I will not fail to be at yr Queen's House at Eleven on Thursday to receive your royal commands.[17]

This time the jealous truculence of Lord Temple was not allowed to stand in the way. He turned down the Treasury once more, after 'haranguing' the King and breaking angrily with Pitt, who, since he was determined not himself to take over so arduous a post, persuaded the young Duke of Grafton somewhat reluctantly to accept. Grafton, though far from the incompetent debauchee that 'Junius' was soon to be lashing, was too fond of gentlemanly leisure and pleasure to be fully committed to political ambition; more comfortable at the Jockey Club than the Treasury Board. But he was a Duke; his status was incontestable (never an irrelevant consideration with the King); he revered Pitt and since it was assumed by everybody that it was Pitt who would be the real prime minister, objections to Grafton's appointment, later all too obvious, did not seem to carry great weight.

George III was always convinced that it was the spirit of party, that same spirit Burke was soon to endow with respectability and even sanctity, which lay at the root of the nation's troubles, and hence of his own. He was not alone in this. It was a common cry among non-party members, that large company of independent country gentlemen who constituted about a third of the Commons, and who were traditionally willing to support the King's government whatever its make-up, so long as their basic interests were not too violently disregarded. These men, almost as much as the placemen, were natural King's Friends. It was these who in 1762 had supported the Peace against Pitt, their natural patriotism being at that time exceeded by their not less natural desire for relief from land tax. In normal times their instinctive propensity was for King George rather than King Rockingham, and it was towards these men that Pitt and the King now looked to sustain a new and reformed style of government, a 'great and conciliatory plan'. The King wished passionately 'to try to form an administration of the best of all partys and an exclusion to no descriptions' – though closer consideration did in fact exclude 'Greenville and the late Secretarys', men he would never again tolerate near his person; 'private feelings makes that impossible.' (He was still rashly free with his use of the word 'never'.) If Pitt were prepared, as he now promised, to head a ministry of men devoted to King and country and ready to turn their backs on party – perhaps even with Rockingham and some of his followers in the 'more subaltern offices' their talents were suited to – *that* would be the sort of government he had dreamed of. 'I hope now,' he wrote to Bute, 'God is giving me this line to extricate this country out of faction.'[18] It was a sincere cry; no British monarch was ever more ardently committed to the national well-being or prepared to work for it more single-mindedly; but neither was any more surely convinced that that well-being demanded on the one side firmness, and on the other a due subordination. The sort of unpleasantness he had received from 'insolent' or 'unprincipled' ministers had, he claimed, merely served to increase his 'natural firmness',[19] and as for 'subordination to government', it was that alone, he told Pitt, which could 'preserve that inestimable blessing liberty from degenerating into licentiousness'.[20] By the end of July, 1766, Pitt had received the Privy Seal and, since this office could be held only by a peer, had been created Earl of Chatham.

When the Chatham ministry was formed the King was twenty-eight. He had reigned through six years of political turmoil, working incessantly and gaining steadily in experience, though a great deal of it had been painful. Losing nothing of that desperate persistence that he liked to call firmness, he had learned the lesson that to avoid breaking one must often bend. His nature was stubborn, but his behaviour was very far from the rigid obduracy that has often been pictured. While he had not abandoned his youthful ambition of silencing factious intrigue and uniting politicians behind the throne, at twenty-eight he understood better than before that nothing is simple, least of all in politics, which is to say in human nature. In both senses of the word he had learned some of the *craft* of kingship.

One of the casualties of this process had been the career of Bute. His subterranean friendship with the King appeared to have survived the imposed limitations of the three years following his fall in 1763; all too well in the suspicious eyes of most observers. Yet long before the final break Bute had ceased to be the sole confidential adviser that he had once been. The King had learned to lean on others' shoulders as well, Cumberland's, Egmont's, Northington's – and in a different sense, altogether non-political, the Queen's. Bute was still a respected confidant and a sympathetic recipient of the royal woes, but he was no longer needed as imperatively and pathetically as in the old days.

It was in January, 1766, during the Stamp Act debates, that the earliest signs of a rift appeared. At that time the King declined Bute's offer of a meeting, on the grounds that it would inevitably leak out and 'ministers might have pretended schemes were hatching for their dismission' – and he had pledged himself to support them so long as they could effectively continue. But he plainly saw that he had offended Bute: 'I think my d. friend seems hurt I did not see him.' Bute's private advice by letter, when the Rockinghams looked groggy, was that George must come to terms with Grenville or Pitt, and when Pitt was eventually given *carte blanche* to form his 'national' non-party administration, Bute had good hopes that this would include himself and some of his friends, and moreover assumed that the King would press for their inclusion. Nothing of the sort happened. Pitt would have no truck with Bute, and the King observed no distinction between Bute's party and the others. He and Chatham were out to *break* parties, not to coalesce them. Horrified, Bute poured out simultaneously his loyal devotion and bitter reproaches in another of his long *cris de coeur*, self-justifying and self-pitying:

> . . . Alass my dear Sovereign, what view or selfish purpose can I have; I have for ever done with this bad public, my heart is half broke and my health ruined with the unmerited barbarous treatment I have received, the warmest wish remaining is to see you happy, respected and adored . . . Is it possible you should not see the total difference between men setting up to be leaders of a party, for seditious or ambitious purposes, and me? . . . O my Prince, I won't repeat my thoughts, they wound me . . . but I for your sake as well as my own will never be thus importunate again . . . But however 'tis over [his humiliation at the hands of Chatham] and I shall never name it more; as for my party, as it is termed, that also is at an end, I have too much delicacy to desire men to follow me when I know the doing it is a barr to their preferment; leaders keep party together by plan and future hopes, I never had any but your service . . . and thus I end as I began, entreating my dear Prince to forgive me troubling him with so tedious a letter; my own justification made it necessary, and I hope when read his good heart will not blame me, and that tho' committed to the flames, it will induce him to believe me what I always was, devoted to him in another manner than any other man is or ever was in this country.[21]

Even so, rebuffed and bruised, Bute earlier in this same letter had asked permission to continue his special relationship: 'I say, Sir, suffer me in this most humiliated position to possess your friendship independent of your power; I have never merited being deprived of that.' Things, however, could never be the same again, though it was to take years yet before the Rockinghams and the public at large were cured of their suspicions. At the very moment (July, 1766) that Bute was writing to the second Lord Hardwicke, 'I know as little, save from newspapers, of the present busy scene as I do of transactions in Persia,' an incurably suspicious Duke of Richmond was confiding to his journal:

I was told that Lord Bute went this day about noon to his own house at Kew. He did not go to the common road over the bridge, but came by the river side in his coach; from his own garden he crossed alone to that of the Princess of Wales's at Kew. The King also about the same time went to the Princess of Wales's at Kew and stayed there two hours. 'Tis remarkable, that 'tis said that the Princess was not herself then at Kew, so that this was not accidental. [22]

Twelve years later Bute felt obliged to issue a statement 'upon his solemn word of honour' that, ever since 1765, he had never 'presumed to offer an advice or opinion [to the King] concerning the disposition of offices, or the conduct of measures either directly or indirectly'. [23] What he said was, for him, all too sadly true. From 1766 Lord Bute became for the King merely one more politician, and for a few more years, as such, he still played a small part in affairs. Before long, however, he was nothing, a has-been, a memory. Like the ageing Lord Holland, he went abroad to Italy in search of health, but failed to find it. 'I have tried philosophy in vain, my dear Home,' he wrote; 'I cannot acquire callosity.' He complained that he was 'grown such a stripling, or rather a withered old man'. [24] He could forget neither the malice of opponents nor the ingratitude of the King, and wished, he said, 'to retire from the world before it retires from me.' He could hardly be said to be wrong about the King's ingratitude, at least insofar as George succeeded very soon in persuading himself that Lord Bute had always been 'insufficiently firm'. He took rather longer to fancy that he had never at any time wished to see Bute in office at all, but the time was one day to come when he could convince himself even of that. [25]

CHAPTER ELEVEN

The Chatham Fiasco

CHATHAM'S earldom had two consequences. It lost him a great deal of his popularity, even in such places as the City of London, where he had been accustomed to the status of a demigod, and it deprived him of his established forum and centre of power, the House of Commons, where his ministry was to be left deprived of any solid talent.* Conway as Leader of the House was honest and conscientious, but as Secretary for the Northern Department enjoyed little power of management, and Chatham seldom deigned to consult him; Charles Townshend, although brilliant, was erratic and unpredictable. Of the Government's leading members among the Peers, Grafton was the new First Lord; Camden took the Woolsack from Northington, who became (with suitable financial compensation) the new Lord President. Granby similarly replaced old Lord Ligonier as Commander-in-Chief; Ligonier, at ninety, being 'quieted with an earldom'.[1] The new Secretary for the Southern Department was one of Pitt's cleverer young men, the Earl of Shelburne. Nearly as arrogant as his master, he was generally considered sharper than was altogether decent in a nobleman. Lord Gower, of the Bedfords, was offered the Admiralty (Egmont having resigned), but the Bedford clan put such a high price on their favours, in the way of peerages and places, that the King was quick to make up Chatham's mind for him to reject their 'extravagant proposal . . . This hour demands due firmness, 'tis that has dismade all the hopes of those just retir'd, and will I am confident shew the Bedfords of what little consequence they also are . . . for to root out the present method of banding together can only be obtain'd by withstanding their unjust demands, as well as engaging able men, be their private connections where they will'.[2]

This last was the nub of the matter. Unluckily for George III, 'due firmness' was not enough, and would not have been even if Chatham had played the part expected of him. Both human nature and the trend

---

* 'The silence of the [House of Lords], and the decency of the debate there, were not suited to that inflammatory eloquence by which Lord Chatham had been accustomed to raise huzzas from a more numerous auditory' (Walpole, *Memoirs*, ii, 291).

of history were in motion against the King. 'The present method of banding together,' in the developed form of the party system, with all its advantages for stability and its now increasingly apparent blemishes, was destined to prevail; and short of an unthinkable royal tyranny (unthinkable to the King too) nothing was going to prevent ambitious groups and individuals setting a price on their support for the administration of the day. The government of patriotic renewal, of independents associated under the banner of Chatham, King, and Country, was always fragile and soon tattered. One of its essential weaknesses was its total *dependence* on Chatham. He was to be a sort of *roi soleil* in himself, in whose gravitational system the inferior ministers would move as well-ordered satellites. When the centre grew weak, as it soon did, planetary eccentricity soon became apparent – or, to put it in Chatham's metaphor, the 'infelicity which ferments and sours the councils of his Majesty's servants grew more bitter'. And when the centre lost all substance, and Chatham became simply a void, only the anxious energies of the King averted administrative chaos, or what for him personally at least had become as great an evil, the return of the triumphant factions.

For a little while Chatham, excited by the prospect of power again at last, was all resolve and high intentions. His dictatorial temper had once more both policies and people to work upon, and he attacked both with energy. 'Lord Chatham,' Charles Townshend once remarked on coming from a meeting of ministers, 'has just shown us what inferior animals we were.' As for the new policies, a northern alliance with Prussia and Russia was at the heart of them, but it very soon appeared that the ruler of neither of these powers was interested. Their ambitions were drawn more towards the invitingly defenceless condition of Poland, and in Russia's case the weakness of the Ottoman Empire. This rebuff did not worry the King greatly; the very thought of Frederick the Great was enough to bring him quickly to the boil, and he favoured, if possible, a rapprochement with Austria rather than Prussia. Chatham's aims in the New World prospered little better; the advent to power of this recent champion of the colonists did nothing to prevent the presentation of new grievances and of demands that so emphatic an imperialist could not dream of accepting. At home it was apparent very soon, well before the end of 1766, that the 'great and conciliating plan' was dead. Rockinghams, Bedfords, Grenvilles, all three of the chief political clans, were arrayed against him, and only their own mutual jealousies prevented the administration's overthrow. All that seemed to be left among the governmental wreckage was the reciprocal loyalty and respect of Chatham and George III. George clung tight to Chatham for obvious reasons; without him he was once more likely to be 'capotted'. Chatham too depended absolutely now upon the King; gone were the days when the wind of popular favour could help him storm the Closet.

However, for one whose career had so often flouted the wishes and claims of royalty, Chatham's expressions of the intensity of his devotion to the monarch, even making due allowance for the conventional floridity of Georgian letter-writing, touch an extreme of fulsome obsequiousness. That he should usually begin his communications by begging to be permitted to lay himself with all duty and submission at the King's feet reflects a not unusual formality in writing to royalty, but no other of the King's servants managed to sound so frequently like some eighteenth-century Uriah Heep. For ever Chatham is entreating, with the deepest veneration, most humbly to renew the tender of his devoted services, or he is wanting words to offer his ardent acknowledgments of the King's boundless goodness. If Disraeli, where royalty was concerned, believed in 'laying it on with a trowel', Chatham must be allowed a shovel; and when such language is set beside the intransigent arrogance of his genius, his Olympian hauteur (everywhere at least outside the happy circle of his own immediate family), the contrast at first seems so extraordinary as to be absurd or even repellent. But Chatham was an astonishing tangle of contradictions, and his devotion to the *idea* of monarchy had always been intense, even when his conduct had signally failed to convey any such impression to either of the monarchs he served under. What his actions and effusions show is not that he was being consciously cynical or insincere, but that the almost religious respect for the principle of monarchy, and even for the person of the monarch, was universally embedded very deep, and sometimes especially deep in the minds of those who so often opposed the exercise of kingly authority; Burke, for instance, equally with Chatham.

George III, only too anxious now to let bygones be bygones, had as yet no reason to doubt the genuineness of his minister's perfervid protestations. Even when, in face of mounting difficulties and returning gout, Chatham went back to Bath, George continued to rally and encourage him in the friendliest terms. The obstinate fact remained, the Government was falling apart, and Chatham's 'unfeigned veneration for the King's truely royal determination' was hardly enough. Early in 1767, Gilly Williams was writing from Bath to George Selwyn: 'Lord Chatham is here, with more equipage, household, and retinue, than most of the old patriarchs used to travel with in ancient days. He comes nowhere but to the Pump Room. Then he makes a short essay

and retires.'[3] George's sympathy began to be mingled with some impatience and exasperation. By January, 1767, he was 'mortified' that
Chatham's gout would prevent his coming to town.[4] (He had set out
from Bath, got stuck at Marlborough, and returned to Bath.) And in
February George was complimenting Northington, who was also unable to walk because of gout, on his 'resolution being superior to that
of others'.[5] Conway and Grafton were doing their best, but the
Government was so weak that a vote to reduce the land tax by a shilling
in the pound was carried against it in the Commons, as a consequence
(as the King rightly pointed out) of the Rockinghams' and Grenvilles'
irresponsibly hunting for popularity among the back benches. It was
a heavy rebuff, but the King was busy assuming a cheerfulness he
could hardly feel, and encouraging his rather downcast servants; these
things would happen, and would merely stimulate him, so he assured
them, to act with greater vigour.[6] They helped to stimulate Chatham
too, and by 3rd March, to the royal and general relief, he managed to
get himself back to London. On the same day, however, a dictated note
in Lady Chatham's hand arrived to express the customary overflow of
reverence, but also the depressing news that the chief minister was still
'out of a condition to attend his Majesty's most gracious presence'.
After unsuccessful attempts to patch up differences that had arisen
among ministers over the policy of taxing the profits of the East India
Company, and to replace Townshend by Lord North, Chatham re-
lapsed into passivity. Some slight indications of improvement in April
prompted George to hope that 'the moment this unfavourable wind
changes' a move could be made to North End, with horse-riding to
speed the patient's convalescence. The King always had more faith in
horse-riding than doctors. Chatham did go to North End, but only to
sink there into a condition almost of coma.

By the end of May the King's Government, such as it was, could
hobble along only by George in effect taking upon his own back a fair
proportion of the burdens of prime minister. Grafton and Conway
were both held in office only by his earnest adjurations, while Northington, who was ill, and Camden, who was disgruntled, would both have
liked to resign. Would the Earl of Chatham see the King? The mountain was ready to go to Mahomet, but Chatham professed himself too
weak to receive so heavy a load. Would he then consent to see Grafton?
'Five minutes' conversation with you would raise the Duke of Grafton's spirits, for his heart is good.' Chatham did agree to see Grafton,
and Grafton consented to soldier on, strongly as he must have been
drawn towards devoting less distracted attention to his personal affairs
and enjoyments. Grafton, unlike his hero Chatham, had never sought

to be cast for the lead – but through these difficult months he did his duty according to his lights, and the King appreciated the fact: 'his heart is good.'

When majorities in the Lords threatened to be very low, the King even 'whipped' his two surviving brothers into attending and voting.[7] He clung desperately to the hope that Chatham would recover and resurrect their common project. He practically commanded him not to consider resignation, 'for tho confined to your house your name has been sufficient to enable my administration to proceed.' He even tried to get him to change his doctor for one of his own recommending, but without success. Chatham's power to hold a pen disappeared with his power to think, and letters to the King arrived regularly in Lady Chatham's hand, imploring indulgence; protesting duty, submission, ardour; but recording total uselessness, unspeakable affliction, utter inability. Sceptical Horace Walpole wondered 'how much the mounte-bank had concurred to form the great man', and like many others sus-pected that the 'master dissembler' was now, if not actually malinger-ing, being 'extravagant by design'; but when through Lord Camden in August the King received an up-to-date account of the true condition of the patient, the news was so disturbing, 'such an abasement of human nature,' that he asked Camden to keep its details private. Camden had had a letter from Chatham's solicitor, who had visited him and re-ported a 'visible alteration for the worse, his hands tremble more . . . paler and thinner in the face . . . much emaciated in his body . . . more than once bewildered . . . head so much confused he scarcely knew what subject he was speaking on . . . miserable beyond conception . . . very much worse, and in my opinion dangerously ill'.[8] Chatham, in fact, while not considering resignation, had abdicated.

He had almost abdicated life itself. In his morass of depression he spent day after day shut away alone in a darkened top-floor room at North End, gazing out sometimes over the Middlesex fields, or sunk over the table leaning his head on his hands. Even when his wife came in, he had hardly a word to utter. His meals were passed to him through a double-doored hatch, so that the servants should not see him or he them. Chatham had never been one to do anything by halves. His one style, as Walpole said, had always been the epic – the 'multi-plication table' was not for him. Even his gout had always been more a kind of drama than mere gout; and now he had become the abject victim of what his uncomprehending contemporaries called 'gout in the head', an airy designation indicating that the maleficent humours had been driven from the legs through the abdomen to the brain. 'Manic-depressive psychosis' is a more modern hypothesis. Whatever the diagnosis, the undoubted facts are that this mysterious man, who in good times could command such immense vigour and transcendent abilities, was the victim of an alarming variety of afflictions, among which were gout, dyspepsia, insomnia, recurrent nervous and physical prostration, and, at his worst, mental confusion, with severe melancholia. Some part of his failure in 1766 may reasonably be put down to his incompetence in handling men and a tendency to run away from uncomfortable facts; but there can be no doubts about the depth of the trough into which, by the summer of 1767, his mind and body had sunk.

It is clear that already by the end of 1766, the attempt by the King and Chatham to break the factions had come to grief, and probably this failure was not so much a result of Chatham's illness and withdrawal as a contributory cause of them. It is improbable that a hale and vigorous Chatham would have done much to alter the course of British party politics. Many, however, have suggested that he might have avoided the disasters that were brewing in America. How, is seldom pursued in much detail. Already before his collapse Chatham was talking of the Americans as 'irritable and umbrageous people quite out of their senses'. Certainly George III himself was not a bitterer opponent of American independence, and on the face of it it does seem unlikely that a Chatham in full possession of his powers, however willing to be conciliatory, could have done much to change the direction of history. Concession and firmness vie closely as harbingers of revolution. It would be fascinating to play out something akin to one of those sophisticated modern war games, and watch the flow of events with the moves on this side of the Atlantic being made by Chatham, Shelburne, Rockingham, Burke, and Charles Fox, instead of Grenville, Townshend, Hillsborough, North and the King – but of course the King would have had to be playing in either game, and what then? And what changes would have to be made among the players on the other side of the Atlantic?

It is true that while Chatham was either at Bath sulking like Achilles in his tent, or plumbing the depths of melancholia at North End, Burton Pynsent, or Hayes, his colleagues made another ill-starred attack on the problem of American taxation that a Chatham in control would not have consented to. By May, 1767, Charles Townshend and his Treasury officials had hatched an ingenious scheme, supported by Cabinet, Parliament, and Crown, for circumventing the colonists' objections to direct taxation. Instead, Townshend imposed indirect taxes – duties on paper, lead, glass, painters' colours, and tea – which, though aimed equally with the Stamp Act at producing revenue, could arguably be passed off as commercial regulation, which so far neither the Americans nor Chatham had in theory objected to. Indeed Chatham had vehemently asserted the mother country's undoubted right to regulate trade. But he had also put colonial conciliation, along with the Russo-Prussian alliance, at the head of his priorities, and would undoubtedly have avoided this particular new provocation of Townshend's, which succeeded only in producing fresh American anger and rioting, new boycotts of British manufactures, and agitation for an end to *all* British taxation of the Colonies.

Charles Townshend, witty, eloquent, reckless, and unpredictable, died, also somewhat unpredictably, soon after his taxes were through Parliament; but in January, 1768, the accession, at last, of the Bedfords* to the Government served only to stiffen the line taken towards the Americans. So also did the creation of a third Secretaryship of State, for America, an 'empire' carved out of Shelburne's Southern Department and given to the 'hard liner' Hillsborough. Shelburne, emphatically a Chathamite, found his position suddenly very weak, with his department split up and the Bedfords calling for his blood. In the vital matter of American policy his natural allies in the administration were Camden, Conway, Granby – and one might have added Grafton if only he had not detested Shelburne personally. Moreover, Grafton's 'perplexity', as he himself wrote, 'was not a little encreased by the instigations to remove Lord Shelburne which fell daily from his Majesty.'[9]

When it became clear that Shelburne was to be dismissed, and also that another of Chatham's protégés, Sir Jeffrey Amherst, was to be pensioned off from his position as absentee Governor of Virginia,† Chatham, still 'weak and broken', but not so torpid as to be unable to see which way the wind was blowing, and how 'his' Government was busy reversing his policies and sacking his supporters, finally used the pretext of his ill-health (which was if anything rather better than worse) to inform Grafton of his intended resignation. To the King this came as a shock. As he wrote to Grafton, 'tho' I have within these years met with enough to prevent my being much surprized at any thing that may happen,' yet he must stigmatise Chatham's action as 'singular' and

* Lords Gower and Weymouth were given Cabinet office, and Rigby became Paymaster. On Weymouth's appointment as Secretary of State, the King finally consented to Conway's stepping down to a lesser post, though he continued to attend Cabinets, and lead the Commons. Townshend's death brought Lord North to the Chancellorship of the Exchequer, an appointment the King was delighted to make.

† To remove the patent abuse of the Virginians having to find the salary for a non-resident Governor.

'improper' – 'shutting himself up from the knowledge of the motives on which Administration act, and yet chusing without being called upon to express a disapprobation at the resignation of Sir Jeffrey Amherst and of the intended removal of Lord Shelburne.' It was an 'unfriendly part'; it was desertion. To Chatham himself he protested that he had a 'right to insist' that he should remain in service and concentrate on the job of getting better, but the only consolation George could extract from the reply was what he called 'an open avowal that his illness alone is the cause of his retiring', which at least he considered would remove from Camden any pretext for his deserting the ship too.[10] Chatham's letter – he was no longer dependent on Lady Chatham as amanuensis – was as fulsomely loyal and floridly abject as ever, but the suspicion of calculation and insincerity beneath the surface pathos, and a consideration of the hostility of Chatham's past and future behaviour, may temper the reader's natural sympathy with more than a dash of revulsion:

> Sir – Penetrated with the high honour of your Majesty's gracious commands, my affliction is infinite to be constrained . . . to lay myself again at your Majesty's feet for compassion. My health is so broken that I feel all chance of recovery will be entirely procluded by continuing to hold the Privy Seal . . . Under this load of unhappiness, I will not despair of your Majesty's pardon, while I again supplicate on my knees your Majesty's mercy . . .
>
> Shou'd it please God to restore me to health, every moment of my life will be at your Majesty's devotion . . .
>
> I am, Sir, with all submission and profound veneration your Majesty's most dutifull and devoted servant.[11]

Both Grafton and Camden decided to remain, as much out of a sense of duty as from any desire to cling to office; and Grafton, who had already been acting as prime minister for so many uneasy months, was to endure another two mortifying years as prime minister proper. These two leaders, as the chief ministerial supporters of a sympathetic policy towards America, found themselves outnumbered in the Cabinet, and unable to secure the total repeal of Townshend's duties; the tea tax was to stay, against their vote; and they regarded Lord Hillsborough's subsequent dispatch, laying down Government policy for the guidance of colonial governors, as unfaithful to the 'kind and lenient words' they had managed to get Cabinet approval for.[12] Thus Junius's attack on Grafton as going forward to 'blood and compulsion' in America was as ill-informed as it was vicious.[13] But the Cabinet majority, with Hillsborough and the Bedfords in the lead, did go forward on their collision course, and it must be allowed that on the whole the King was on their side – the side of that 'firmness' that he eternally talked of. He certainly viewed Lord Chancellor Camden with growing disfavour, and went out of his way to congratulate Hillsborough upon his editing (Camden said distortion) of the instructions to the colonial governors, 'without greatly deviating from the words of the minute.' Hillsborough, he said, had restored the *original* intention of the Cabinet majority![14]

Yet even in this matter of American policy George was several shades more prudent than Hillsborough and the Bedford group. To Hillsborough's proposals to punish or overawe the insubordination of Massachusetts and the other fractious areas, to provide for compulsory billeting of troops and so forth, true, he gave general assent in his accustomed phrases, 'highly proper', 'very right', 'not much objectionable'. Inevitably too the governors were to be recommended to use 'a moderate yet firm language', but it was the moderation that he stressed: 'they ought to be instructed to avoid as much as possible giving occasion to the Assemblies again coming on the apple of discord.' And when he came to consider Hillsborough's proposals for confiscating the powers of the Council of Massachusetts Bay into the hands of the Crown, such an extreme action, he wrote, might indeed 'from a continuance of their conduct become necessary; but till then ought to be avoided as the altering Charters is at all times an odious measure'; and Hillsborough's plan to gag all criticism from the people of Massachusetts by the threat of complete forfeiture of their Charter seemed to the King 'of so strong a nature that it rather seems calculated to increase the unhappy feudes that subsist than to asswage them'.[15] These sober opinions consort strangely with the traditional image of the bolt-eyed, addle-witted royal bully of Whig caricature and American legend.

A prime minister in Grafton's situation to-day would of course either replace the ministers who disagreed with him or himself resign; and indeed Grafton would have liked to resign, and resolved that if further measures likely to worsen the American situation were approved in Cabinet, he would. But they were not, 'and there was no alteration in His Majesty's condescending goodness' to him.[16] It would have been better for his historical reputation if he had departed with Chatham and Shelburne, but there was a further reason why he did not. It would have been interpreted, by the King and the public, as running away from Wilkes.

CHAPTER TWELVE

'Whereon Almost My Crown Depends'

FOR Wilkes was back from exile, and once more 'the chieftain of riot and disturbance'. After two earlier brief sorties to London which had been rebuffed, the first by Rockingham and the next by Grafton and Chatham, he had decided in February, 1768, to risk everything, defy his outlawry, and challenge authority by standing for the parliamentary constituency of the City of London. To begin with, playing it *piano*, on 4th March he sent his footman to the Queen's House with a letter full of the most loyal and respectful protestations, requesting a royal pardon. There was no answer. George III on his side was anxious not to repeat the mistakes of 1763; and neither Grafton nor the Secretaries wished to imitate the impulsiveness or invite the humiliations then suffered by Egremont and Halifax. In the City election Wilkes came bottom of a poll of seven candidates, but this victory for the Court party proved the merest preliminary skirmish. Wilkes immediately proceeded to stand for the semi-urbanised county of Middlesex, which extended then right in to the boundaries of Westminster and the City, and where his popularity was high among the numerous owners of small businesses, shopkeepers, and such craftsmen as qualified for the forty-shilling franchise: the 'middling sort.' Even in the more rural areas and among the gentry he was not without friends. As for the 'inferior sort', though they lacked votes, they were well supplied with grievances. As it happened, the election, and the subsequent months of the Wilkes disturbances, coincided with a period of high food prices, heavy unemployment, and widespread strikes; and although the violent disorders that accompanied these strikes were in origin economic, not political, in such hard times there was never likely to be a shortage of disgruntled or desperate Londoners predisposed for a riot and ready to wear the blue cockade of Wilkes. The London apprentices in any case, hard times or no, were always within shouting distance of a little teenage violence, and 'Wilkes and Liberty!' made as good a shout as any. The silk weavers of Spitalfields were, during 1768-69, deep in all kinds of internecine outrage that originated from bad times and price-cutting. Sailors were refusing to sail til wages were raised. Among the coal-heavers there was a vicious dispute in progress arising from low earnings and a war between two rival trade organisations. It did not take much to turn 'Wilkes and Liberty!' into 'Wilkes and the coal-heavers for ever!', and from one of the ensuing affrays seven coal-heavers were subsequently hanged in Stepney before a crowd of some tens of thousands.

The Middlesex election of 28th March, held at Brentford Butts, proved very noisy but relatively peaceful. Trouble of course had been expected, and in view of the utter inadequacy of the police, Barrington, the War Minister, acting closely with the King himself, had seen to it that plenty of troops were available. George wrote to him, 'I shall not stir from home so that you may come or send to me if any thing arises that requires my immediate decision.'[1] Troops, however, could not be everywhere, and that night (Wilkes being well ahead in the poll) and the following night (after his victory had been declared) the hooliganism of the mob, triumphantly returned from Brentford to London, was irrepressible. Windows that were not lit up in celebration were smashed, special damage being done at the Mansion House (the Lord Mayor was a strong anti-Wilkite) and at the town houses of such well-known Court supporters as Bute and Egmont. The Duke of Northumberland avoided similar trouble by lighting up on demand, submitting to drink Wilkes's health, and diverting the rowdies into an adjoining tavern. The Austrian ambassador, 'the most stately and ceremonious of men,' was taken from his coach and had '45' chalked on his shoe-soles.

The self-appointed tribune of the people now further humiliated the forces of law and order by ordering his own committee to patrol the streets the following night, and so preserve the peace, and he ostentatiously instructed his supporters, as they proceeded from Brentford to the town, not to pass by St James's Palace, 'that no insult or indecency might be offered to the King.'[2] Apart from attempting, and failing, to keep order, the Government was at a loss to know how best to proceed. They were well aware that if they grasped the danger too firmly it might explode in their hand. It was left to Wilkes, therefore, to retain the initiative. Even when he surrendered for arrest in April intending to answer for his outlawry and appeal against it, Lord Chief Justice Mansfield first found a good legal reason for delay, and later set it aside on a technicality. At last Wilkes was obliged to send for the sheriff's officer, asked him to be so kind as to make the arrest, and then had the Attorney General informed. A further delightful embarrassment then supervened: the prison marshal taking him discreetly (it was hoped) over the river to the King's Bench prison was overpowered by a mob who unshafted the horses and themselves drew the coach in noisy exuberance along the Strand and past Temple Bar, eventually depositing a rather exhausted Wilkes in the Three Tuns Tavern at Spitalfields, whence he was obliged to escape from his admirers by night and personally apply at the prison for admittance.

Both in the streets of the City and outside the prison in St George's Fields, Southwark, Wilkes's supporters maintained for some weeks riotous demonstrations that became closely entangled with the industrial grievances, and turbulence continued for some weeks. The boundary between a strike demonstration and a Wilkite riot became hard to draw. As Secretary Weymouth reported to the King, the Thames seamen, having said that they would allow no ship to sail until their wages were raised,

> came this day [6th May] at two o'clock thro' Great George Street towards the Queen's House, finding the King at Richmond they proposed going there . . . They cry for redress and seem to disclaim Wilkes, however as Wilkes's affair is now before the King's Bench, there are several of the Mob there.[3]

The King, hearing that the seamen had in fact crossed Kew Bridge, ordered the gates to be shut against them and the servants to say that he was not at home, and in any case had no power to act in such a wages dispute – 'not liking by giving any answers to encourage these acts of licentiousness.' On 9th May, he was ready, so he wrote to Secretary Weymouth,[4] to come to London 'at the shortest notice and at any hour' if the emergency should worsen. The following day it did, and the King set off straightway for London: 'bloodshed is not what I delight in, but it seems to me the only way of restoring a due obedience to the laws.'

The bloodshed that day, 10th May, arose when a very large crowd of some 15,000 to 20,000 persons assembled outside the prison in St George's Fields – apprentices, Wilkites, casual and curious spectators, a motley and soon unruly assembly. As the Riot Act was being read stones were thrown, and one of them hit the Justice, who thereupon (acting in the spirit of Weymouth's recommendation, itself reinforced by the King's approval[5]) activated the waiting troops. Some of these from a Scots regiment – their being Scots made bad inevitably worse – in pursuit of presumed rioters mistook their quarry and killed a publican's son in a cow-house. The Riot Act being read a second time, other troops opened fire in the Fields; five more persons were killed and more wounded. This became known as the 'St George's Fields Massacre'; its circumstances present some similarities with the bigger

'Peterloo Massacre' of half a century later. From south of the river the sparks of violence set going sporadic outbreaks all over Westminster and the City. Two of the Southwark justices had their houses smashed up; the Mansion House was again attacked; yet again a Boot and a Petticoat were paraded, this time on a gibbet through Cornhill; and outside the House of Lords, while some of the yells were for 'Wilkes and Liberty!', others were for cheaper bread and beer, for 'it was as well to be hanged as starved'.[6] 'We are glad,' wrote Walpole to Mann on 12th May, 'if we can keep our windows whole, or pass and repass unmolested. I call it reading history as one goes along the streets . . . I do not love to think what the second volume must be of a flourishing nation running riot.'

The King had the same fears, or worse. By 15th May, he was happy to note that the seamen had 'come to their senses',[7] but the prevalent spirit of licence and insubordination, and its prime instigator, the personification of all mischief, Wilkes, must somehow be extinguished. George was still wary, however. He closely followed the disposition of troops, and incidentally deplored that the necessary concentration round London denuded a restive west country. In April, he had been 'averse to making any show of troops on the day of opening the [legal] term, for that naturally would draw a concourse of people together'. He was well aware that there were legal and tactical diffi-culties in the way of excluding Wilkes from Parliament, now that he had been properly and constitutionally elected, but somehow a way must be found, and then proceeded upon 'with vigour'. He had been industrious to hunt for possible precedents; and confident as he was in Lord North's loyalty and energy, he felt obliged to emphasise to him that he considered it

> highly proper to apprize you that the expulsion of Mr Wilkes appears to be very essential and must be effected . . . The case of Mr Ward* in the reign of my great grand father seems to point out the best method of proceeding on this occasion, as it will equally answer whether the Court should by that time have given sentence; or should he be attempting to obtain a writ of error. If there is any man capable of forgetting his criminal writings, I think his speech in the Court of King's Bench on Wednesday last reason enough to go as far as possible to expell him; for he declared number 45 a paper that the author ought to *glory in*, and the blasphemous poem, a mere *ludicrous production*, but I will detain you no longer on this subject; and desire you will send me word when the meeting is over . . .[8]

* John Ward, expelled the House in 1727 after conviction for forgery.

In June, 1767, the Court of King's Bench at last pronounced sentence on Wilkes in respect of his offences of five years before; for the *North Briton No.* 45 and the *Essay on Woman* together he was to be fined £1,000 and go to prison for 22 months. He was spared the addition of the pillory, customary for libel and blasphemy. 'He affected ease and indifference by picking his teeth and talking to those near him while Mr Justice Yates was animadverting upon the nature of his crimes,' and was 'by a little management' got safely back to prison, 'notwithstanding great pains by his friends to stir up and prepare the mob.'[9]

Never did prisoner serve a term more comfortable or exhilarating. His first-floor rooms overlooked St George's Fields, and visitors of either sex could come at any time. He was glutted with presents from his admirers on both sides of the Atlantic – hams, pheasants, salmon, turtles, cases of wine, butts of ale, *forty-five* hogsheads of tobacco from Maryland, commemorative medallions, gifts of money, everything. A succession of feminine devotees, one of them the young wife of a Wilkite City alderman, liberally supplied his sexual wants. His political allies could freely use the King's Bench prison as a campaign headquarters, and the campaign prospered. One of its chief organisers was Serjeant Glynn, as austere and level-headed as Wilkes was licentious and provocative, and on the death of Wilkes's fellow-member for Middlesex, a by-election returned Glynn with a comfortable majority. John Horne, the radical Brentford parson later known as Horne Tooke (and also later to break with Wilkes) was meanwhile busy promoting the Society of the Supporters of the Bill of Rights, which included several members of Parliament and enough wealthy backing to raise £20,000 towards paying Wilkes's very considerable debts. Keeping up the political pressure and his reputation for impudent bravura, Wilkes in December published a copy, with his own commentary, of Lord Weymouth's letter to the magistrates before the St George's Fields 'massacre', urging them not to be backward in asking for the use of troops; and he included with this publication a calculatedly offensive comment on Lord Barrington, who had written to congratulate the magistrates on their zeal. Surely, asked Wilkes, the 'Lord B——n' who had signed that strong letter could not be Lord *Barrington*, who was known to be *sola libidine fortis*, strong in lust alone? A few weeks later Wilkes scored yet another success, managing to get himself elected as an alderman of the City, though unhappily prevented from taking up his duties for the time being by his place of residence and the hostility of his fellow aldermen and councillors.

The hope of the moderates in the Government had been that if they did not react over-rashly, the Wilkes problem might melt away. 'As times are,' wrote Camden to Grafton, 'I had rather pardon W. than punish him,' despite the fact that he found his behaviour 'audacious beyond description'.[10] Grafton, having first consulted Temple (by now lukewarm for Wilkes), even made a private but in the event abortive approach through the bookseller Almon, for a bargain: no more legal challenges from Wilkes, no more talk of expulsion from Parliament.[11] There were so many other pressing problems to concern ministers: the resignation of Chatham and Shelburne; the Boston rioting; the affairs of the East India Company and of Ireland; the French seizure of Corsica (which Lord Shelburne would have made a *casus belli*); and in Grafton's own case the form at Newmarket and the matter of his own divorce, which finally passed through Parliament early in 1769.* Wilkes, however, snugly entrenched among the amenities of the King's Bench prison, had no intention of allowing the Government, or the City, or his own followers, or the nation at large to forget him.

George III on his side equally had no intention of forgetting Wilkes, or of allowing his preoccupied or over-cautious ministers to do so. When Conway, Granby, and Sir Edward Hawke argued against the wisdom of expelling Wilkes from Parliament the King indicated his displeasure. He anxiously watched and encouraged the committee under Lord North inquiring into the best mode of proceeding, and when Lord Hertford protested to the King on behalf of his brother Conway when the latter was not invited to attend one of North's committee meetings, George replied tartly that since Conway was against expelling Wilkes he could hardly expect to be consulted on the best tactics to secure his expulsion. Further, he hoped Hertford would see to it that his own sons would support the expulsion, 'for I should be sorry that any one could say that in a measure whereon almost my Crown depends, his family should not have taken an active part.'[12] *Whereon almost my Crown depends*; that was how seriously George viewed the Wilkes affair. He followed the Commons debates of February, 1769, with anxious interest, studied and copied out the lists of speakers for and against, expressed 'some surprise' at the inconsistent voting of a number of members, but was reasonably satisfied with the majority of 82 in favour of Barrington's motion declaring that the member for Middlesex 'be expelled this House'.

Grenville, one of the Noes, had warned members that Wilkes would only get himself elected again, and what would they do then? This was of course to happen, to happen again, and yet again; and each time they

---

* The first Duchess of Grafton thereupon married the Earl of Upper Ossory, and afterwards became the regular recipient of some of the ageing Horace Walpole's sprightliest letters.

would expel him afresh. But before the final show-down of the fourth Middlesex election, other related events occurred to rouse the King's wrath. Some loyal aldermen of the City decided in March, 1769, to present his Majesty with a petition to counter the Wilkite agitation, and 130 gentlemen set out from the city on 22nd March to proceed to St James's. They were so 'insulted, pelted, and maltreated' on the way that 'several coaches were obliged to withdraw, some to return back, others to proceed by bye-ways, and those who arrived at St James's were so daubed with dirt, and shattered, that both masters and drivers were in the utmost peril of their lives'.[13] Only a dozen or so coaches made the distance. The Duke of Northumberland was 'severely pelted outside St James's. Some of the mob, declared one witness, were shouting "Wilkes and No King!"'[14] The Riot Act, though it was read, produced little effect. Only seventeen arrests were made, and only five prosecutions followed. What, however, most infuriated the King was that a grand jury refused to find a true bill against even these. His feelings overflowed in sharp notes to Lord North: 'This seems to me so extraordinary that I hope you will inquire into it and send me a full account of what passed.' The grand jury had manifestly been 'factious and partial . . . If there is no means by law to quell riots, and if juries forget they are on their oath to be guided by fact not faction, this constitution must be overthrown, and anarchy (the most terrible of all evils) must ensue; it therefore behoves every honest man with vigour to stand forth'.[15]

Wilkes's first and second re-elections for Middlesex were unopposed, but on the third occasion in April, 1769, the Court party persuaded Colonel Henry Luttrell to resign his Cornish pocket borough seat in order to make a contest. Like the first, this fourth election proved a noisy and colourful affair, with plenty of cheap beer, bands of music, processions, banners, as many constables as could be mustered, a little mild pelting of Luttrell, and even a little huzza-ing outside St James's, alarming the Guards, who fixed bayonets as a precaution. But again the election itself was orderly, and again Wilkes won easily, by 1,143 votes to Luttrell's 296. Only two days later, by 197 votes to 143, the Commons resolved that 'Henry Lawes Luttrell, Esq., ought to have been returned a member for Middlesex and not John Wilkes, Esq.'. Thus for the first time, and rather by accident than design, Wilkes had managed to raise an issue of real constitutional significance. How far did the Commons' privileges extend in the determination of its own membership? 'A question touching the seat of a member, in the Lower House, could only be determined by that House'; such was Mansfield's judgment. And Grafton wrote: 'The two Houses must separately be sole judges of the seats of their members. Destroy that right, and their independance is gone: for where else can it be placed?'[16] In 1763, Wilkes had himself pleaded parliamentary privilege against the law. Now privilege succeeded, if only temporarily, in maintaining the Commons' right, in such exceptional circumstances, to set aside the repeated and emphatic judgment of the electors. In Stuart times this same issue had been fought and won by Parliament in a different context. Then it was Parliament against the King; now it was King and Parliament against the People – or at least the People as represented by the freeholders of Middlesex. The exceptional circumstances which Parliament pleaded against Wilkes were that his election had been procured by an undue pressure of mobs: it had been tantamount to coercing Parliament; hence based on a malpractice and void. Grafton, North, the Bedfords, the placemen, a majority of the independent members, even the young Charles Fox, and of course the King himself, were prepared to accept this argument, against a minority derived mainly from Rockinghams, Grenvillites and Chathamites.

George was relieved and delighted at the vote, and the next day let North know how pleased he was with him personally. With Conway under suspicion of softness and with most of the other principal ministers in the Lords, North was fast emerging as the King's right-hand man; in fact if not in name Leader of the House:*

The House of Commons having in so spirited a manner felt what they owe to their own privileges as well as to the good order of this Country and Metropolis, gives me great satisfaction, and must greatly tend to destroy that outrageous licentiousness that has been so successfully raised by wicked and disappointed men; but whilst I commend this, I cannot omit expressing my thorough conviction that this was chiefly owing to the spirit and good conduct you have shewn during the whole of this unpleasant business.[17]

Grafton was well aware which way the wind was blowing. The King, he wrote, 'was more sensible to dictate his will to me than first enquire my opinion . . . as had been his usual practice. My tame submission to be overruled in Cabinet might give the king's friends an idea that I might be more pliant, and rest my favour on their support.'[18] Chief of these King's Friends was now undoubtedly Lord North, once George's childhood companion, Syphax to his juvenile Portius in Addison's *Cato*; the boy whose physical resemblance to the young Prince had once caused facetious comment at Leicester House.

* North's being merely a courtesy title, he of course was a House of Commons man. He did not succeed to the earldom of Guilford until 1790.

Wilkes and the Wilkites were not yet done with, and a fortnight after the Commons vote on Luttrell, the King was still on the war-path, making sure that Secretary Lord Rochford would have 'every meeting at the London Tavern and Mile End watched', and at the same time assuring him, and no doubt trying to assure himself, that 'if firmness be now shewn this affair will soon vanish into smoke'. Wilkes was not one readily to vanish into smoke, and for a few years yet, in prison or out, in the King's or upon the Aldermanic Bench, he was able to provide a continuance of trouble. In the long run he did not so much vanish into smoke as dwindle into respectability, but before this minor Mephistopheles was metamorphosed into a likeable conservative old gentleman he managed to stay in the thick of various noisy discontents.

First, the Commons' acceptance of Luttrell brought a spate of petitions from widely scattered English counties and towns condemning the corruption of Parliament and begging the King to dissolve it and dismiss his ministers. So strong were the terms in which the City of London couched its 'loyal' protest against ministerial misgovernment and defiance of the Constitution that the King went out of his way to indicate his displeasure on receiving at his Levee the Lord Mayor, Beckford,* and City officers. Having first kept them waiting in an ante-chamber, he took their petition without any of the customary polite condescension, handed it straight to the lord-in-waiting, and turned immediately to speak to the Danish minister.[19] He then rejected a second City remonstrance, which in March, 1770, was condemned in both Houses as factious and insubordinate. When the Lord Mayor and his henchmen, attended to St James's by a vociferous crowd of supporters, presented to the King yet a third petition which was formally rejected as 'inconsistent with the interest and dangerous to the constitution of the Kingdom', Beckford had the temerity to answer back – which (considered Rigby) was 'the first attempt ever made to hold a colloquy with the King by any subject, and is indecent in the highest degree'.[20] George, as much taken aback as those in attendance, made no further reply. Salt was rubbed into the wound when Beckford's supporters blew up his outburst into a 'speech', which was printed verbatim in the newspapers. 'Since the fall of Chatham,' wrote Burke in April, 1768, 'there has been no hero of the Mob but Wilkes.' For a time in 1770, Beckford threatened to run him close, at least in London. But

* William Beckford, Pitt's old ally; a very rich and assertive West India merchant, Lord Mayor in 1762 and 1769; father of the William Beckford who wrote *Vathek* and constructed at Fonthill the most grandiose of all English 'follies'. In 1769 Lord Mayor Beckford, proprietor of the earlier Fonthill, was also busy organising the Wiltshire petition.

a month after committing his bold little outrage at the King's Levee he died. The City Fathers proceeded to erect a statue to his memory in the Guildhall, the pedestal defiantly engraved with the legend of his 'speech'. Wilkes remained very much alive, and for a space did indeed enjoy something like the place of honour in the City of London that Pitt had once enjoyed before he misguidedly became Lord Chatham – the hero simultaneously of the mob and the wealthy merchants. Wilkes, however, habitually made enemies as fast as friends, and in the City their numbers soon became pretty equal.

The petitioners, 60,000 of them in all, were a mixed company of malcontents; city radicals, Chathamites and Grenvillites, Whig land-owners of the Rockingham persuasion, and the county freeholders they influenced. Chatham himself, restored to health and belligerence,* strongly encouraged them; small use as he had for Wilkes, he had even less for the administration. In the other direction, the Duke of Bedford, Lord Lieutenant of Devonshire, making a personal appearance there to discourage the raising of a petition, was dealt with so roughly that he had to be spirited away, secretly, by the Bishop from a crowd besieging Exeter Cathedral, while at Honiton he was nearly murdered. Naturally the petitions produced a fair crop of loyal counter-petitions. Not that even the protesting petitions were overtly disloyal, though many who signed, and many more not represented in the petitions – voteless but literate and increasingly critical of the old order that excluded them from a share of the nation's management – thought they saw behind the Luttrell affair not only a corrupt set of ministers and M.P.s but also the insidious growth, since 1760, of the exercise of royal prerog-ative, and they still suspected the lurking Favourite and the Princess Dowager. The commonest convention of the petitions, however, was that the King should be prevailed upon to deliver his people from bad politicians. A letter in the *Bristol Journal* in March, 1769, urging the preparation of a petition to emulate London's, sets the ambivalent tone nicely. After damning the 'abandoned' administration of Grafton, and the rotten foundation of 'Bribery and Corruption', it proceeds to assert that 'the Iron Hand of Arbitrary Power has been stretched out to crush you', yet manages to conclude in an ecstasy of loyalty with 'Rouse, my countrymen! rouse! lay your grievance at the foot of the

---

* 'Lord Chatham appeared at the King's levee [of 7th July, 1769] when it was thought he would never produce himself again . . . He was perfectly well and had grown fat . . . The King was very gracious and whispered him to come in the closet after the levee, which he did and stayed there twenty minutes.' (Walpole, *Memoirs of the Reign of George III*, iii, 248.) But there was no thought of reinviting him to be prime minister.

Throne. You have a King who is the Father of his People, who wants only to *know* in order to *redress* your complaints'. These petitions, though the Luttrell affair sparked them off, were both more and less than a Wilkite phenomenon; more, in that they represented a general feeling that something was rotten in the state of the country; less, in that the signatories were of such diverse persuasions that there was never much chance of any cohesive reform movement emerging from them. Very soon the serious radical reformers were to break with Wilkes altogether.

Interthreaded with Wilkes and the petitions, and with the 'present discontents' that Burke was already penning his thoughts upon, ran the letters of Junius in the *Public Advertiser*, 'dedicate to the English Nation.' There have been many solutions put forward for the identity of this hard-hating, elegant polemicist, and Disraeli once included in his choice of bores all those holding opinions on the subject. At different times Wilkes, Burke, and Temple were all fancied to be the author; Philip Francis emerged in time as clear favourite, but Shelburne still has backers. For the refinement of its savagery the style of Junius has never been surpassed. His periods roll with controlled venom. No political writer ever thundered more tellingly, or more unfairly, in the high Olympian manner; none steered a rapier more suavely through the ribs of his victims, among whom Grafton, Bedford, and Mansfield were especially singled out. At first the King was not directly attacked, though in such a passage as the following, in the famous diatribe addressed to Grafton on 8th July, 1769, it would be hard to say that this 'best of princes' was not taking almost as many of the thrusts as the unlucky Grafton, that 'libertine by profession';

> It is not, indeed, the least of the thousand contradictions which attend you, that a man, marked to the world by the grossest violation of all ceremony and decorum, should be the first servant of a court, in which prayers are morality, and kneeling is religion. Trust not too far to appearances, by which your predecessors have been deceived, though they have not been injured. Even the best of princes may at last discover, that this is a contention, in which everything may be lost, but nothing can be gained; and as you become minister by accident, were adopted without choice, trusted without confidence, and continued without favour, be assured that, whenever an occasion presses, you will be discarded without the forms of regret . . .

While attacks on ministers were couched sometimes in cruel irony, sometimes in the directest invective, reference to the King, until December, 1769, remained in language conventionally loyal even when hostility was discernible through the polished disguise. When the Duke of Bedford and his dependants ('whose characters, I think, cannot be less respected than they are') were being flayed and minced in the letter of 19th September, George III was still 'this gracious monarch', 'a discerning judicious prince'. But on 19th December, in what Walpole described as 'the most daring insult ever offered to a prince but in times of open rebellion, and aggravated by the many truths it contained',[21] Junius turned directly to criticise the King, to attack the whole drift of political affairs since his accession, and finally threaten the possibility of revolution. The language of this Letter 35 was more moderate, the tone less vituperative than in the onslaughts upon the politicians, but the matter was dynamite. After the flimsiest formal pretence that this was only the sort of letter he *would* write, were he asked for his advice by a 'gracious, well-intentioned Prince', he begins:

> Sir, – It is the misfortune of your life, and originally the cause of reproach and distress which has attended your government, that you should never have been acquainted with the language of truth, until you heard it in the complaints of your people. It is not, however, too late to correct the error of your education . . . We are far from thinking you capable of a direct, deliberate, purpose to invade those original rights of your subjects, on which all their civil and political liberties depend . . . At your accession to the throne, the whole system of government was altered . . . A little personal motive of pique and resentment was sufficient to remove the ablest servants of the crown; but it is not in this country, Sir, that such men can be dishonoured by the frowns of a king . . . On *your* part we are satisfied that everything was honourable and sincere, and if England was sold to France, we doubt not that your Majesty was equally betrayed. The conditions of the peace were matter of grief and surprise to your subjects, but not the immediate cause of their present discontents. [Wilkes is then praised], though in the earnestness of his zeal he suffered some unwarrantable insinuations to escape him. He said more than moderate men would justify, but not enough to entitle him to the honour of your Majesty's personal resentment . . . Is this a contention worthy of a king? . . . The destruction of one man has been now, for many years, the sole object of your government . . . From one false step you have been betrayed into another. [Your ministers] have reduced you to the necessity of chusing out of a variety of difficulties; – to a situation so unhappy that you can neither do wrong without ruin, nor right without affliction . . .

Taking it for granted, as I do very sincerely, that you have personally no design against the constitution, nor any views inconsistent with the good of your subjects, I think you cannot hesitate long upon your choice between ministers and people . . . If an English king be hated or despised, he *must* be unhappy . . . but if the English people should no longer confine their resentment to a submissive representation of their wrongs . . . let me ask you, Sir, upon what part of your subjects would you rely for assistance? [Colonial and Irish policies are then condemned.] It is not then from the alienated affections of Ireland and America that you can reasonably look for assistance; still less from the people of England, who . . . are parties against you.

The Scotch are then attacked (this was routine in popular polemics of the day), and the King menacingly reminded of how they betrayed Charles I, when he ran to throw himself on their help. Junius proceeds to warn George not to expect all the army to be as loyal as the Guards: 'your marching regiments, Sir, will not make the guards their example either as soldiers or subjects.'

You have still an honourable part to act. The affections of your subjects may still be recovered. But before you subdue their hearts, you must gain a noble victory over your own. Discard those little, personal resentments, which have too long directed your public conduct. Pardon this man [Wilkes] the remainder of his punishment; and if resentment still prevails, make it, what it should have been long since, an act, not of mercy, but contempt. He will soon fall back into his natural station . . . It is only the tempest, that lifts him from his place.

. . . Let it appear to your people that you can determine and act for yourself. Come forward to your people. Lay aside the wretched formalities of a king, and speak to your subjects with the spirit of a man, and in the language of a gentleman. Tell them you have been fatally deceived . . .

The people of England are loyal to the house of Hanover . . . The name of Stuart, of itself, is only contemptible; armed with the sovereign authority, their principles are formidable. The prince who imitates their conduct, should be warned by their example; and while he plumes himself upon the security of his title to the crown, should remember that, as it was acquired by one revolution, it may be lost by another. [22]

Much of this ringing advice, if acted upon, would undoubtedly have brought down on the King's head the fiercest calumny, and probably from Junius first of all, for he seems to be inviting him to stand forth as Patriot King and leader of the people against Parliament and constitution. One can hear the cries of 'arbitrary government' and 'prerogative power' that would have gone up had the King really done that. Some of the letter contains sober sense, the advice for instance to let the Wilkes affair die a natural death; but in this matter the King, as we shall discover, was arriving independently at a similar conclusion. Further, the same tactics might well be, and in fact were, applied to Junius himself. Of course George considered Letter 35 monstrous, and, since the author could not be identified, the printer and publisher, Woodfall, was prosecuted on the Attorney General's initiative, for uttering a false and seditious libel. But when the law, as with Wilkes, threw up technical obstacles the case was dropped. Junius, like Wilkes, was allowed to 'fall back into his natural station'.

Until overtaken by other excitements, the Junius furore, and public approval of his attacks, were considerable. Chatham was further encouraged to re-enter the mêlée. There was no more talk of helping the King to quell the factions. Instead Chatham made approaches (which were coldly received) to the chief of them, Rockingham's. In any case, a faction ceased to be a faction when it was led by Chatham. 'I am resolved to be in earnest for the public,' he wrote, 'and shall be a *scarecrow of violence* to the gentle warblers of the grove.' He was soon busy bringing strong pressure to resign upon all those ministers he could still influence – Camden and Granby in particular.[23] As for Grafton, he struggled on with the King's support until the opening of Parliament in January, 1770. Then, when Chatham threw himself into a full-scale attack on the King's Government, with veiled hostile references to the Crown's personal influence, Camden, who had so long trembled on the brink of resignation (and of course the Lord Chancellorship was worth in all about £20,000 a year), at last took the plunge and admitted how he 'had for some time beheld with silent indignation the arbitrary measures' of the ministry and how he 'had often dropped and hung his head in Council'.[24] He knew of course that the King was bound to dismiss him – he refused to resign – and of course the King did, promptly and unceremoniously. Granby resigned on the same day. Grafton, with only Conway inside the Cabinet left standing by him, at last gave up at the end of January, while promising his 'full desire to give all assistance to His Majesty's Government' in the future.[25]

It is impossible not to feel sympathy with Grafton, one of the most unsuccessful, but also unlucky, of prime ministers. Circumstances had lifted him up and betrayed him; a more unscrupulous or less loyal minister would have resigned long before. His attitudes were civilised and his views moderate, notably on American issues. The King respected him and to the last tried to persuade him to remain, though he had Lord North ready to fill his place. He was not discarded, as Junius said he would be, 'without the forms of regret.' When, before his resignation, the King conferred the Garter upon him, he remarked that it gave him the greater pleasure in that he was 'one of the very few who had received it unsolicited'.[26] Harried by Wilkes, mauled by Junius, mistrusted by the Bedfords and Court men who had come to dominate his Cabinet, first abandoned and then destroyed by his former hero Chatham, Grafton was the victim of his own good nature (not allied to great abilities), of his enemies' malice, and above all of those discontents which, as the first decade of the reign ran to a close, were multiplying so alarmingly.*

The end of that decade was marked by the firm grasp on government assumed in 1770 by North and the King, but the Wilkes story had some little way yet to run.

After the petitioners of 1769 came the printers of 1771. Well before this Grafton had resigned, North become prime minister, and Wilkes, having served his full twenty-two months, been released and taken up his aldermanic duties in the City. With his keen nose for scenting useful trouble, he had immediately become involved in the battle then getting under way between the House of Commons and the printers and journalists who reported its debates. Such reporting had always been resisted by the House, and in 1728 had been specifically banned as a breach of Commons' privileges. Yet by 1771 over a dozen papers were issuing regular, and often sharply slanted, accounts of Commons' business.

Both Lord North and the King would have preferred to keep out of Wilkes's way, if possible; there had been 'Wilkes trouble' pretty continuously now for three years. When the printers' case first looked serious, the King was all for playing it down, and avoiding another clash between the Commons and 'the vulgar'. On 21st February, 1771, he wrote to North:

> I have very much considered the affair of the printers that is now coming before the House, I do in the strongest manner recommend that every caution may be used to prevent its becoming a serious affair . . . It is highly necessary that this strange and lawless method of publishing debates in the papers should be put a stop to; but is not the House of Lords as a Court of Record the best court to bring

---

* He was to survive another forty years or more and die in the odour of sanctity, a dedicated Unitarian.

such miscreants before, as they can fine as well as imprison, and as the Lords have broader shoulders to support any schism that this salutary measure may occasion in the mind of the vulgar.[27]

However, as the City's behaviour grew more brazen, the Cabinet thought things could not be allowed to drift, and on 9th March, George agreed to sign a proclamation for the arrest of two of the printers, with the offer of a £50 reward. One of them caused himself to be arrested in the City by his own servant (who claimed the reward); he was next brought before Alderman Wilkes, who of course released him forthwith. When, the same day, the House's messenger, one Whittam, armed with the Speaker's warrant, arrived to arrest a third printer, John Miller, the biter was bit and Whittam himself arrested for assault. Aldermen Wilkes and Oliver, as magistrates, made the deputy serjeant go bail for him, and committed Whittam for trial at the next quarter sessions.

This was now war between the Commons and the City of London, and the King sadly agreed that 'as things are come to this pass there is no means of retracting', and therefore 'the honour of the Commons must be supported'. He reminded North that originally he had been 'averse to meddling', but now

> the authority of the House is totally anihilated unless it in an exemplary manner shews its rights are not unpunished to be infringed. I am therefore of the opinion that the Lord Mayor and Alderman Oliver ought to be committed to the Tower, and then a Secret Committee may be appointed to examine further into the affair; it will be necessary to consider if they refuse to obey how they are to be forced . . .[28]

He offered the further practical suggestion that the Lord Mayor might be escorted to the Tower by water, 'that no rescue might ensue.'

The burned child fears the fire. Wilkes's name significantly does not appear alongside those of the Lord Mayor and Oliver. 'As to Wilkes,' wrote George, 'he is below the notice of the House.'[29] 'Have nothing more to do with that devil Wilkes.' And when the Commons ordered all three to answer the charge of breach of the Commons' privilege, the King again wrote to North:

> I owne I could have wished that Wilkes had not been ordered before the House; for he must be in a jail for the next term if not given new life for some punishment inflicted on him . . . and I do not doubt he will hold such a language that will oblige some notice to be taken of him.[30]

Wilkes would accept his summons only if it was made out to him as member for Middlesex; he intended to use the printers' case as a lever to reopen the expulsion issue. The King, however, and the resourceful North, were on this occasion craftier tacticians than he. The summons for him to appear at the Bar was indeed dispatched, but for a day when the House would not be sitting! The various attendances of the Lord Mayor and Oliver, before they were eventually (though only briefly) confined in the Tower, were all accompanied by noisy and mildly riotous demonstrations, mostly by 'respectable tradesmen and the better sort', though the mob as usual was ready to join in. On one occasion North had his carriage's windows shattered, and the following day the King was insulted by shouts as his state coach drove down Parliament Street. Wilkes came no nearer to the Bar of the House than Palace Yard. By 21st March, the King was writing that 'this unpleasant affair seems now to promise an issue that will tend to restore due authority to the injured privileges of Parliament';[31] and, in fact, despite the challenge of Wilkes, the printers, and the City, the House of Commons under North continued to exercise its authority on occasions to exclude strangers and thus restrict the Press's reporting of debates. There were, however, no more prosecutions, and the privacy of parliamentary business became increasingly difficult to sustain. In this year, 1771, a nineteen-year-old compositor from Norwich joined the staff of the official Commons printing house; his name was Luke Hansard.

When, three years later, Middlesex yet again elected Wilkes to Parliament, he was allowed quietly to take his seat; and the same year, at the third attempt, he became Lord Mayor of London. In the Commons he did introduce a parliamentary reform bill, but did not press it to a division, and never cut a great figure there. By the time of the Gordon Riots of 1780, he had become sufficiently a pillar of law and order to take a musket and shoot down the drunken mob – someone said the two most active men in London during that terrifying week were the King and John Wilkes; and unless too cynical a view should be taken of Wilkes's change of posture towards his old allies of the inferior sort, credit should be allowed for his honest hatred of religious bigotry. A delicate irony dictated that Alderman Wilkes should, following the riots, have to commit to prison one Moore for printing 'seditious and treasonable papers', and for setting fire to *Lord Mansfield*'s house. He lived long enough – another seventeen years – to become, if not exactly a Tory, at least politically a quietist; when an old woman once shouted 'Wilkes and Liberty!' as he passed, he said, 'Be quiet, you old fool, that was all over long ago.' He was even on various occasions received at Court, where the King was surprised to discover so civilised a man and Wilkes is reported once to have declared that he was never a Wilkite. Perhaps by this he merely meant that he was never deeply involved with the serious programme of reforms which some of his fellow radicals proposed. Or perhaps it was simply that 'old men forget'.

PART THREE

THE KING
AND HIS FAMILY

CHAPTER THIRTEEN

Man and Monarch

For a boy generally condemned, and repeatedly self-condemned, as indolent, George III grew into a man of quite exceptional industry; it is difficult to think of a British monarch who worked harder. His days were filled with the routine business of monarchy: the formal and social duties of state occasions, of Levees and 'Drawing Rooms';* interviews and consultations with ministers; the minutiae of appointments and preferments, which had his indefatigable attention for fifty years; endless letter-writing, in that pre-telephonic pre-mechanical era when all communication other than by private meeting or message was perforce by longhand (the King never employed a personal secretary until his eyes finally failed in 1805); laborious composition or writing out of memoranda on matters of public concern or private interest (or of a nice mingling of both, as in his copying 'Anecdotes of the Court of France by Mr Ainslie' in 1772, an essay of several thousand words on the influence of the Du Barry family and the reputed sexual impotence of Louis XV's grandsons[1]); abstracts of reports from subjects who had special knowledge of affairs abroad, in India, in Canada, in some area of special interest or brewing trouble in Europe – 'A Short State of Saxony' in the King's handwriting in 1771, for example, occupies some four to five thousand words[2]; details of 'Artillery in North America' carefully itemised, 'Effective strength of the infantry,' 'Reflections on the present state of the Navy and the reasons why the Fleet is not in greater forwardness than it is'; Commons division lists, copied laboriously from ministers' reports, each Member's voting record narrowly scrutinised and recorded – no comment for those of settled opposition, emphatic disapproval where support had been reckoned on but failed to materialise, expressions of satisfaction when the Government majority was higher than expected; attention to pleas for mercy from capitally convicted criminals, with summaries of evidence and judicial reports conscientiously weighed; consideration of a never-ending stream of begging letters from viscounts aspiring to become earls, earls to become marquises, marquises to become dukes,

* The Queen's Drawing Rooms were for both sexes, the King's Levees for men only.

dukes to obtain Garters; and from all sorts of men of influence seeking preferment in the Church or promotion in the armed services or appointment to a place or pension, either for themselves or for a relative or dependant; lists and memoranda pertaining to 'Knights of the Garter according to the date of their installations', and to peerages and honours of all kinds, an enormously complicated subject whose niceties he took with the utmost seriousness and upon which – the propriety of this, the impropriety of that – he held views of almost religious intensity; these and a host of other miscellaneous matters of public and personal business filled his days. It was noted that when he visited Portsmouth in 1773, for the naval review, he was not satisfied until he had 'examined many ships of war personally, and investigated every thing both in the dock-yard and ordnance wharf with the greatest precision. His Majesty was always an early riser and one morning he rose before five o'clock to take an accurate survey of the ramparts, bastions, platforms, outworks, etc. which defend the garrison'. Again when he inspected the Dockyard in 1778, he wrote to his sons from Portsmouth: 'After giving the gentlemen a little time for the bad custom of toasting, I sent them word five [a.m.] was a good hour to visit the Yard.'[3] Thackeray, while intending it as a belittlement, was in fact not far wrong when he wrote that George

> knew all about the family histories and genealogies of his gentry, and pretty histories he must have known. He knew the whole *Army List*; and all the facings and the exact number of buttons, and all the tags and laces, and the cut of all the cocked hats, pigtails and gaiters in his army. He knew the *personnel* of the Universities; what doctors were inclined to Socinianism, and who were sound Churchmen; he knew the etiquette of his own and his grandfather's Courts to a nicety, and the smallest particulars regarding the routine of ministers, secretaries, embassies, audiences; the smallest page in the ante-room or the meanest helper in the kitchen or stables. These parts of the Royal business he was capable of learning, and he learned.[4]

A dunce well-suited to such trivia, which marked the limits of his capabilities; that was Thackeray's verdict. For him the King was less King than cabbage: 'the cleverest tutors in the world could have done little probably to expand that small intellect, though they might have improved his taste and taught his perceptions some generosity.' Well before Thackeray, Sir Nathaniel Wraxall (1751-1831), though in general crediting George III with considerable virtues, had similarly a much-quoted passage about the King never delighting in study or passing his time in occupations likely to improve the mind, his reading being confined to an after-dinner newspaper over which he usually fell asleep in half an hour.[5] Much of all this runs flat against evidence. George III was not of course an intellectual. He was not given to spinning epigrams. Early in life he developed instead his own proprietary brands of cliché. His views on most subjects were as conventional as those of the great majority of his subjects; his imagination was circumscribed by rigid social assumptions. His writing had more fluency than style or correctness, though it was often pungent and vigorous. George III was very far from a blockhead; he was never an easy man to fool. Neither was he an ignoramus. He had always spoken and written fluent, if far from flawless, German and French, and (*pace* Wraxall) he taught himself to be knowledgeable over a wide range of subjects. Until old age he never lacked willingness and determination to learn.* And he was certainly not a philistine; he viewed the arts and sciences with gentlemanly regard.

Brougham, though he too wrote of the King's 'narrow understanding', was one of those who, being nearer to the centre of things than the school of Thackeray, and having been one of the first to study, and publish, a little of the vast royal correspondence, knew better than to consider George a dunce:

He made himself thoroughly master of all the ordinary details of business . . . His attention was ever awake to all the occurrences of government. Not a step was taken in foreign, colonial or domestic affairs, that he did not form his own opinions upon it, and exercise his influence over it. The instructions to ambassadors, the orders to governors, the movement of forces, down to the marching of a single battalion . . .; not only the giving away of judgeships, bishoprics, regiments, but the subordinate promotions, lay or clerical; all these form the topics of his letters; on all, his opinion is pronounced decisively; on all his will is declared peremptorily. In one letter he decides the appointment of a Scotch puisne judge; in another the march of a troop from Buckinghamshire into Yorkshire; in a third the nomination of a Deanery of Worcester; in a fourth he says that if Adam, the architect, succeeds Worsley at the Board of Works, he shall think Chambers ill-used.[6]

Georgiana, Duchess of Devonshire, not one who by birth or circum-

---

* In the first brief visit he was allowed to have from his two sons in 1789 after his recovery from porphyria, politics being barred, there were two things at least we know he spoke of. First, he could beat Hawkins at picquet; second, *he had been brushing up his Latin.*

stances was likely to be over-generous in favour of her monarch, once observed how *quick* he was, like the Prince of Wales. They both had 'a wonderful way of knowing what is going forward'.[7]

The King's sense of humour was sometimes on the heavy side, with especially as he grew older a 'Hey? hey?' or a 'What? What? What?' to stab the point home.* Yet though lacking lightness of touch he did not lack quick wits, and was more than capable of the sharp riposte or quirk of wry humour. When, for instance, during his tortured confinement during the autumn of 1788, he had damned doctors in general and rebuked the Rev. Dr Willis in particular because he had abandoned the Church, an honourable calling, for medicine, and Willis had replied 'Sir, our Saviour himself went about healing the sick,' the King came back smartly with 'Yes, yes, but he had not £700 a year for it.'[8] And a fortnight before this, aware that he had been gabbling immoderately from the effects of his illness, he suddenly pulled himself up and remarked to the equerry by the bedside that he was 'getting into Mr Burke's eloquence, saying too much on little things'.[9] George III, wrote Brougham, was 'far from deficient in natural quickness', and few of those who had most to do with him found so. 'I believe your Grace has a large family – better than a dozen?' he once asked Archbishop Sutton. 'No, Sir,' replied Sutton, 'only eleven.' 'Well,' said the King, 'is not that better than a dozen?'

His manner on formal occasions was usually affable but dignified; once, however, Eldon, entering upon a ceremonious speech in the full regalia of a Lord Chancellor, was surprised to be suddenly interrupted. The King had remembered that it was the fourth of June, Eldon's birthday as well as his own; and it tickled his fancy to wish him many happy returns; 'now you may go on,' he said.[10] He once expressed surprise to the Groom in Waiting to see George Selwyn leave a Levee during which a knight was to be made, before the ceremony took place. Its resemblance to an *execution*, said the King, was remarkable, and he knew as well as Horace Walpole how Selwyn loved 'nothing upon earth so well as a criminal, except the execution of him'. When Watson, Bishop of Llandaff and politically no friend of the King, published his *Apology for Christianity*, George observed that he was never before aware that Christianity stood in any need of apology. Surprisingly, this same Dr Watson was the author also of an improved method of manu-

---

* It seems very possible that this famous mannerism began as an unconscious device for filling the inevitable gaps between the King's condescending to make a conversational opening and the doubtless often hesitant replies of those condescended to. The first time the very friendly King spoke to Fanny Burney he reduced her to total silence.

facturing gunpowder, and when, as a Christian bishop, he was embarking on an *apology* for this too in conversation with the King, 'Do not let that distress you,' he was reassured, 'for the quicker the conflict, the less the slaughter.' 'I mention this,' writes Watson, 'to do justice to the King, whose understanding it was the fashion to decry.'[11]

Hard work, attention to duty, moderation in the pursuit of pleasure, firmness and courage in the face of adversity; these were the qualities he stood by. How constantly, and with what uneven success, he preached them to his own children! 'I have settled certain hours in the day for studying,' wrote seventeen-year-old Prince Augustus to him from the south of France; 'from 7 in the morning till eleven. Those are four good hours, and as I have had the honour of hearing your Majesty say, are inestimable. Those hours of work are more worth than any in the day.'[12] The King's reply to these filial overtures epitomises a fair part of his working philosophy:

> I have received very regularly letters from you . . . and I trust that the passing the succeeding winter in the same fine climate . . . will completely restore your health. I am happy you are able to resume part of your studies, which employment will make you with more pleasure enjoy those of relaxation; there is no greater wisdom than so to economise amusements that they shall continue so during life, which, if too much sought after, naturally must sooner or later become irksome; besides, if the mind be not constantly in the habit of serious employment it will lose its energy, and those powers a man may have been blessed with will entirely vanish.[13]

As for courage, for George III it represented the most important of all virtues. We can catch the dutiful and prudent echo of the father's precepts in the letters of another of his sons. Prince Ernest, eighteen years old, at Göttingen in Hanover (whose King he was one day to be), knew as well as the Duke of York or Prince Augustus the sentiments his father liked to hear, whereas (as with William and Edward too) what they were so often obliged to write – requests for money to pay off debts – was bound to displease him. 'I am at present very busy studying tactics . . .' wrote Prince Ernest hopefully. A German general had given him a reading list of military authors, 'but at the same time recommends strictly religion, for without that no man can live . . . Gustavus [Adolphus] said that the Christian was the best soldier, and this is a very true remark, for nothing can give us true courage as religion.'[14]

Ernest, the future Duke of Cumberland, though he grew up to be the most unpopular man in England, passed the parental test in this

respect at least, and so did *almost* all the King's other children. Only
one of them, he thanked God, lacked this most essential of all virtues.
This the King once ventured 'with some warmth' to George Rose
when out riding with him; and added, 'He is to succeed me.' At least
part of the reason for his insistence during the early eighties on the
Prince of Wales's taking a full part in the Windsor stag-hunts was his
conviction that his morally and physically flabby son must benefit from
the challenges and dangers of these strenuous pursuits. (They would
also help to keep him away from Charles Fox.) The Princesses were to
be spoiled no more than the Princes by luxury and easy living. Even
the delicate Amelia, the darling of his later years, was not to be pam-
pered when – then aged twenty-one – she had been shaken by being
thrown from her horse. The King insisted that either 'she should, if at
all hurt, get into one of the carriages and return to Cuffnells [George
Rose's seat in Hampshire] to be bled, or otherwise mount another
horse and ride on'. Rose's humane and polite suggestion that she
should go on by carriage was 'not well received'; the King could not
bear to think that a child of his should *lack courage*.[15]

It would be fair to grant that he did not himself lack it, or the
capacity for resolute initiative in a crisis. It is, of course, common
practice for political and military leaders to profess a confidence they
do not always feel before the battle, like boxers before the big fight;
but when in July, 1779, sixty-six French and Spanish ships of the line
threatened the Channel coast, the King was not simply making conventional noises or whistling to keep up his spirits when he professed
'not the smallest anxiety' if the British ships, even if there were fewer of
them, could only 'bring the combined fleet of the enemies to a close
action'. He had 'the fullest confidence in Divine Providence; and that
the officers and men of my fleet will act with the ardour the times require'.[16] He only wished Lord North could 'view it in the same light
for the ease of his mind'. Never would he doubt that 'whenever it shall
please the Almighty to permit an English fleet fairly to engage any
other, a most comfortable issue will arise'.[17] George's John Bull pugnacity and tenacity showed one side of the medal;* the reverse was
always a Colonel Blimp's slowness to bow to unpleasant realities, a
tendency to huff and puff. But until latter days, when mental and physical infirmities gradually destroyed him, the readiness to stand and

---

* 'The English people,' wrote Leigh Hunt, 'were pleased to see in him a crown-
ing specimen of themselves – a royal John Bull.' But George, long before, had
recognised the same figure in himself, and critically at that. 'I owne I rather encline
too much to John Bull, and am apt to despise what I am not accustom'd to' (Sedgwick, *Letters of George III to Lord Bute*, 106).

fight was strong. When a quarter of a century later the French, now under Bonaparte, were again poised to invade, George, at sixty-six, was nevertheless making contingency plans to send the Queen and the Princesses off to the west of the Severn while he personally took charge of the nation's front-line defence.

His conduct in a very different sort of crisis in 1780, more local but more immediately alarming – the Gordon Riots – demonstrates the King's impatience with inaction in the face of danger. It was a very real and indeed horrifying danger; the No Popery fanatics and the drunken London rabble had already caused worse destruction than any seen in Britain since the Great Fire of 1666. All hell was loose in the City, and the civil powers seemed to have abdicated, paralysed by legal niceties concerning the Riot Act and the use of troops. So at least it appeared to the King, who complained of 'the great supineness of the civil magistrates'.

> The tumult must be got the better of or it will encourage designing men to use it as a precedent for assembling the people on other occasions. If possible, we must get to the bottom of it, and examples must be made.[18]

It was on the fifth day of rioting that an anxious and exasperated George took personal charge in the Privy Council, extracted an on-the-spot opinion from the Attorney-General, Wedderburn, on the propriety of calling in the military under common law *as citizens combating a felony*, and had them sent forthwith into action – necessarily bloody action – which succeeded promptly in quelling the riots. For some days and nights, several thousand troops were quartered in the gardens of Buckingham House, with their officers lodged in the Riding House.

While nagging political or personal worries, working on his metabolic idiosyncrasies, were always liable to produce the 'flurries', the two attempts made upon the King's life were met with cool self-possession. Both would-be assassins were deranged and later committed to Bedlam. The first was Margaret Nicholson, a domestic servant who attempted to knife the King in 1786, as he stepped from his carriage outside St James's; the second was James Hadfield, a paranoid psychotic whose brain had been damaged by sabre wounds incurred in the Duke of York's Flanders campaign, and who shot twice at the King from close range as he was entering his box at Drury Lane in 1800. An hour or two after this second attempt (he was then sixty-two) he did not fail to indulge himself in the short nap to which he had become accustomed between the conclusion of the main piece – on this occasion Cibber's *She Would and She Would Not*, with Mrs Jordan and

Michael Kelly – and the farce or 'burletta' or musical entertainment that fashion then demanded should follow.* Kelly himself described how, immediately after the shots had narrowly missed their target, 'the King, on hearing the report of the pistol, retired a pace or two, stopped, and stood firmly for an instant; then came forward to the front of the box, put his opera-glass to his eye, and looked round the house without the smallest appearance of alarm or discomposure.'[19]

George's personal regimen was strict, and for the first fifty years of his life he was active and healthy. (The illnesses of 1762 and 1765 were exceptional interludes, together covering a period of only a few months.) It is said that early in his reign he was warned by his uncle Cumberland, that 'fleshy Cyclops', that a tendency to corpulence resided constitutionally in the family, and 'I am much mistaken if your Majesty will not become as large as myself before you attain to my age'. However that may be, and whether or not the King replied that it all came from insufficient exercise, he certainly observed a manner of life, in diet so frugal and abstemious, in physical activity so regular and vigorous, that was calculated to avoid corpulence and promote longevity. There was 'no virtue' in it, he told Mrs Delany; 'I only prefer eating plain and little, to growing diseased and infirm.'[20] He rose early, at six usually, and worked for an hour or two before breakfast. At Kew his prayers were private, upon rising; at Windsor he waited for the Queen and 8 o'clock, when together they attended the service of morning prayer in St George's Chapel. Between breakfast and dinner, which might be taken with the Queen at four o'clock, or sometimes an hour or two earlier very frugally on his own, he would again be working on official papers, or interviews, or public and ceremonial duties. At some time on most days he would ride out, and he took his riding seriously. Sometimes in his Kew days he would combine business with pleasure and ride up the five or six miles to the Queen's House, in whatever weather. Then, having gone on in a sedan to St James's and dressed, he would hold a Levee, which might well be

---

* Sheridan's quick wits were equal to the situation. The audience patriotically demanded the National Anthem three times over, and already by the second time Sheridan had composed *ad hoc* an extra stanza, 'which was received with the most rapturous approbation':

> *From every latent foe,*
> *From the assassin's blow,*
>   *God save the King!*
> *O'er him thine arm extend;*
> *For Britain's sake defend*
> *Our father, Prince, and friend.*
>   *God save the King!*

long and tedious, give audiences until five or six, all perhaps on a few slices of bread, butter and a dish of tea, 'which he sometimes swallowed as he walked up and down previous to getting into his carriage in order to return to the country.'[21]

At Richmond or Windsor he delighted, usually once and sometimes twice a week, in hunting, where he took 'the most dangerous leaps with the utmost indifference'.[22] Until 1788, the royal chase included both the stag and the hare, but not fox-hunting, which had to wait until the nineteenth century before it became generally accepted in the south of England. From 1789 the demands of stag-hunting proved too severe for a physique weakened by illness and advancing years, but the King continued to ride with the harriers until his afflictions absolutely forbade it. This 'utmost indifference' to physical challenge, at least until his fiftieth year, did not, apparently, always extend to his servants. Colonel Goldsworthy, one of his equerries, reflected ruefully in 1786, at a safe distance among fellow-sufferers in the Household, upon the trials of serving so arduous a King. After 'fagging away like mad' in the field all day,

> being wet over head, soused through under feet, and popped into ditches, and jerked over gates, what lives we do lead! Well, it's all honour, that's my only comfort . . . Home we come, like so many drowned rats . . . sore to the very bone, and forced to smile all the time! And then after that what do you think follows? 'Here, Goldsworthy,' cries His Majesty: so up I come to him, bowing profoundly, and my hair dripping down to my shoes: 'Goldsworthy,' cries His Majesty. 'Sir,' says I, smiling agreeably, with the rheumatism just creeping all over me! but still expecting something a little more comfortable. I wait patiently to know his gracious pleasure, and then, 'Here, Goldsworthy, I say!' he cries, 'will you have a little barley water . . .?' Barley water after a whole day's hard hunting![23]

Every morning, summer and winter (wrote Mrs Papendiek), Mr Montagu, royal riding attendant and riding master to the Princes, had to be in his riding house ready for the King. In the hunt, 'many a time the stag was taken after a run of thirty miles or even forty, with the same number of miles to return. This the King often did on horseback, but he sometimes returned in his carriage.'[24] There were no royal racing stables yet, and he left Newmarket to the Rockinghams and Graftons, and later to the smart young men of Brooks's. Already, however, it was becoming customary for the King, with his family, to attend the meeting at Ascot Heath, where on the first day, for a prize of a hundred guineas presented by the King, there was always a race open to those hunters that had regularly followed his hounds the preceding winter.

When George was at Cheltenham in June, 1788, hoping to recuperate after what was still thought only a 'bilious fever', everyone noted his passion for physical activity. This had previously been exercised largely in the semi-privacy of the great parks adjoining Windsor or Kew. Now, when he was as it were on holiday in the full public gaze, there was surprised comment not only on how early in the morning he rose, taking the waters 'at so early an hour that few of his subjects were to be found there', but on how far he walked and rode, often without even an attendant equerry, talking unaffectedly on the way with farmers about sheep and cattle prices,* and upon anything or everything to whomever else he chanced to meet. The King 'eats cherries like other men', reported William Eden, 'but walks further than most.'[25] And although Sir George Baker, his physician, was then advising him for some arcane reason against strong exercise 'during the use of Cheltenham-water', he was 'constantly on horseback, when the weather permitted, from eleven to three'.[26] He expected, so he wrote, benefit from the waters, from the change of air, and from the respite from work, but above all he rested his hopes for recovery in none of these things so much as 'the exercise of riding and good mutton'.[27]

He was altogether a plain good-mutton man. 'I am just returned from Kew,' wrote Addington in December, 1804, 'where I passed an hour and a half with his Majesty, and partook of his dinner, which consisted of mutton chops and pudding.'[28] In diet 'the only luxury in which he indulged was in fruit, which was cultivated in the royal gardens to high perfection, and served at table in great abundance'.[29] The notorious frugality of the royal fare seemed to many of his aristocratic contemporaries demeaning or ridiculous, while for the cartoonists and satirists of the hostile press, and for the Peter Pindars and doggerel-mongers in general, it provided heaven-sent material with which to build up a picture of a skinflint royal couple with small-yeoman or petty-bourgeois tastes. It was a time when even a modest country parson like James Woodforde reckoned to follow up his first course of roast mutton and baked pudding (or perhaps 'a roasted pike with a pudding in its belly') with a second course of 'pig's face' or

* He had failed back in London to see why his own sheep sold at Smithfield for 4½d. a pound when the Queen's House butcher sold the mutton back to him at a shilling – and he had had the butcher in to tell him so (Huish, *Public and Private Life . . .* , 343-44).

roast duck, and then a meat pie or neck of pork and gooseberry sauce
for third, followed by a final topping-up of plum pudding, fruit tarts,
syllabubs, or jellies. And such meals as Woodforde's, even when they
rose to roast swan ('good eating with sweet sauce'), or fare such as
Dr Johnson's – 'veal pye with plums and sugar,' and drinking-
chocolate laced with 'large quantities of cream or even melted butter' –
hardly stood comparison for variety or bulk with the lordly dishes that
the aristocracy sat down to. The King's plain bread and butter, and
plain beef and mutton, and strict limits of four glasses of wine at
dinner, and at supper one glass of wine and water,* and *barley water*
after hunting indicated a self-denial that approached the eccentric.
Queen Charlotte followed his example in matters of diet as in so much
else: she was 'what many private gentlewomen would call whimsically
abstemious, for at a table covered with dainties she prefers the plainest
and the simplest dish, and seldom eats of more than two things at a
meal'.[30] When in the mid-nineties, war brought rising prices and hard
times, the homely country virtues practised at Court might even have
served as a patriotic example. 'I take the liberty of sending you a
receipt for potato bread,' wrote the Queen to the Prince of Wales,
whom one cannot easily imagine being converted, 'which proves to be
remarkably good, and we have had it baked with great success at
Windsor. The Kg. also has given orders . . . to have no other bread
served to the Household and even to his own table *than brown bread*,
and it is to be hoped that this will encourage others to do the same.'[31]

Neither would the King and Queen keep late hours, one of the
times' 'silly dissipations' which Horace Walpole joined in deprecating.
It was the fashion (he was writing in 1777) to go to Ranelagh 'two
hours after it was over'. The music stopped at ten, the company arrived
at twelve and, so he added, Lord Derby's cook 'said he should be
killed by dressing suppers at three in the morning'. By that time, after
evening prayers, some music perhaps, and a game of backgammon or
picquet with an equerry,† George and Charlotte had usually been abed
for four hours or so (though not infrequently he was up late working,
timing letters meticulously '¼ before midnight', '½ after midnight'). A
country life was best, so the Queen wrote to her son Augustus. In 1790

* Huish, 350. He had also, it appears, another beverage that he kept by him,
called simply 'cup', a concoction whose chief ingredients seem to have been lemon
and water.

† Fanny Burney suggested that a new post should be created for one of them,
Backgammon Player to His Majesty; and writes later in 1787: 'The following evening
. . . the King sent for Colonel Ramsden to play at backgammon. "Happy, happy
man!" exclaimed Colonel Goldsworthy exultingly, but scarce had he uttered the
words ere he was summoned to follow himself' (D'Arblay, *Diary*, iii, 222, 259).

she bought Frogmore, on the edge of Windsor Home Park, to gratify her rural tastes, hoping in time to make it 'a perfect *bijou*'.* True, a King and Queen must mix with the world. Levees and Drawing Rooms were not to be avoided; and theatres and concerts were positively enjoyable. So was the company of 'a few select friends whose cheerfulness of temper and instructive conversation will pass the time away without leaving any remorse for what is passed'. An occasional royal ball at Windsor or St James's might demand a midnight supper and sitting up until three, but nothing could be more foolish or distasteful than 'the extremes of the present fashion where night is turned into day and day into night, where people go everywhere and enjoy nothing, and where amusement is pursued and never found'.

This was one of many respects in which the royal family's habits lay much closer to those of the great majority of their subjects than to those of the rich and fashionable. In the short run, the fact that the King and Queen were out of sympathy with the manners of the *beau monde* increased a certain sense of royal isolation, a feeling the King had that he, with too few friends of dependable honesty and loyalty, was embattled against powerful forces of evil in times that were out of joint. In the long run the King's very ordinariness and 'decency' provided a bond between him and the people. 'The people,' moreover, in this sense was to include not only the middling sort, so many of whose attitudes of sobriety and industrious solidity he shared, but also, to the despair of Painite republicans and radical reformers generally, a considerable majority of the labouring classes too. The growing popularity of the King, especially from the mid-eighties onwards, despite all the earlier grumbles concerning his obduracy and the incompetence of his ministers, despite prolonged domestic crises and American disasters, was not merely the natural consequence of a long reign and the acceptance of George III as an institution in himself; nor did it spring chiefly from the focusing of patriotism upon a figurehead in time of war and foreign menace. Years before the great war with France, the outbursts of national pleasure at the King's escape from assassination

---

* By the time Great Frogmore had been added to Little Frogmore (1792) and the larger Dutch-style house entirely remodelled by Wyatt, Frogmore had become a very handsome and sizable *bijou*. The grounds soon had their own farm, with barn and corn-mill, and the inevitable Gothic ruin, and a 'temple' and 'hermitage'. The last two were designed by the most artistic of George III's daughters, Elizabeth, who, thwarted in her ardent desire to be suitably married, found consolation in the rural retreat of her 'prettiest little tiny cottage' at Frogmore. A book for which she did the illustrations (in another's name) was, ironically enough, entitled *The Birth and Triumph of Cupid*. She wrote verses, made watercolours, mezzotints, and engravings, and on the Frogmore farm bred pigs 'of the Chinese breed'.

in 1786, and then at the recovery from his mental derangement in 1789, were to indicate beyond doubt that he was already in middle age achieving the status of the 'good old King'. This was at least partly a tribute to character and integrity, and a recognition of affinity which might well have been less willingly accorded to a more brilliant or even to a more successful king.

Religion's place was central. The King was unable to conceive of either a good or a happy man who lacked faith*; and atheistical scoffing represented to him the most destructive and socially dangerous tendency of the times. At no period in his life did he question either the practical necessity or the theological rightness of the Established Church of England; nor could he forget that it was in its defence that his predecessors had arrived upon the throne. He clung as tightly to its traditions as to those of the monarchy itself. With only the rarest breaks for illness he attended its services and took its sacraments with meticulous and earnest regularity. Fanny Burney for one found the compulsory attendance at his early morning prayers a discipline on winter mornings hard to bear – and the draughts at Windsor were exceeded only by those at Kew. He was very far, moreover, from regarding the Church's celebrations as a matter of mere routine. Before the 1805 Garter Installation he was asked whether the new Knights would be required to take Communion. 'No, my Lord,' he replied; 'the Holy Sacrament is not to be profaned by our Gothic institutions. Even at my coronation I was unwilling to take it, but they told me it was indispensable.'[32] Queen Charlotte's piety surpassed even the King's. He was merely a good critical judge of sermons; she was a connoisseur, devouring them volumes at a time and begging her sons on the Continent to send her well-recommended tomes. Her reading of a sermon aloud was included, of routine, together with prayers and Bible stories, in her after-Sunday-dinner sessions with the young Princesses.

The King paid, of course, the closest attention to the Church's hierarchy in its upper ranges; and possessing as he did decided views on the relative suitability of aspirants for preferment, would not be deterred in the making of appointments by ministers or other influential men wishing to suit their political convenience or canvassing for their relatives and dependants. His three prime desiderata in a bishop he made clear to Lord North: 'I wish to confer the bishoprick on the

* He would have fervently approved of the Queen's sentiments expressed to her son Augustus: 'Without religion none can be happy . . . In prosperity it keeps us within bounds and it tells us that the hand who gave it can also take it from us; and in adversity it supports us in our distress, and strengthens our trust in the Almighty'.

clergyman who for private character, as well as orthodoxy and learning, may seem best qualified to sit on the bench.' Even in the King's later years, when he did not always get his own way with ministers on political issues, in the matter of Church appointments it was his decision that carried the day. When, for instance, the Archbishop of Canterbury died in 1805, Pitt wished to appoint Dr Tomline (*né* Pretyman) to succeed; he had earlier been Pitt's tutor, then his secretary, and as his eventual biographer he was to write a book which Macaulay pronounced 'the worst of its size in the world'. The King's man, however, was the Dean of Windsor and Bishop of Norwich, Dr Manners Sutton. Knowing that Pitt wished to discuss the appointment on the following day, the King, nearly blind then but still active, immediately rode over from the Castle to see the Dean, who was dining with friends; had him brought to the door; shook him by the hand; and exclaimed, 'My Lord Archbishop of Canterbury, I wish you joy. Not a word. Go back to your guests.' Pitt's displeasure had to be swallowed gracefully but, as the King said, 'if a Private Secretary of a First Minister is to be put at the head of the Church, I shall have all my Bishops party-men and politicians.'[33]

Strictly Anglican, he was not as intolerant as his implacably anti-Catholic stance would suggest. When Pitt was preparing his Canada Bill in 1790, the King stressed to him that the people whose welfare must first be considered were the original French-Catholic inhabitants.[34] And when in 1787, a new Lord Lieutenant of Ireland had to be found, the King was emphatic that Pitt must look for 'the person most likely to conduct himself with temper, judgment and an avowed resolution to avoid partiality'. He must have 'no predelection but to advance the public good'. George III's hostility to Catholic Emancipation, though here as in so much else he did reflect the popular view of the 'average Englishman', was certainly obdurate and in the illumination of hindsight ill-advised, but it arose rather from political conservatism than religious intolerance. The Hanoverian settlement, the British Constitution itself, was based on Protestant ascendancy, which he had sworn to maintain. Apart from his practical objection to enfranchising Irishmen who had recently been in a state of revolution, he vetoed Catholic emancipation during the last decade of his active reign for much the same reasons as he had earlier resisted parliamentary reform; both must overturn the constitution, that 'most beautiful combination that ever was framed'.[35] There was too the matter of his conscientious scruples: 'Tell me who took the coronation oath, did you or did I? Dundas, let me have no more of your Scotch metaphysics.' As for the legal position of nonconformists, his view is well expressed in some of his letters during 1772, one of the several years when petitions were advanced for ridding them of the disabilities they suffered under the Test and Corporation Acts. The Presbyterians of the day, he told North, seemed 'so much more resembling Socinians than Christians that I think a test was never so necessary as at present for obliging them to prove themselves Christians'.

With George, if a thing had existed for a long time the case for abolishing or reforming it needed to be very powerful indeed. 'I owne myself a sincere friend to our Constitution both ecclesiastical and civil and as such a great enemy of innovations, for in this mixed government it is highly necessary to avoid all novelties. We know that all wise nations have stuck scrupulously to their antient customs . . .' Hence to Lord Bristol he wrote, 'At the Revolution of 1688, the Toleration Act was established, the Dissenters have not been molested therefore why now must an alteration be made?'[36] His advice to his prime minister (concerning an attempt to remove the disabilities of Dissenters) makes the same point, and reveals at the same time the electoral calculations of the political manager that the King had by that time become:

> I think you ought not to press those gentlemen who are brought on that interest into Parliament to oppose this measure, as that would be driving them out of those seats in a new Parliament, but I think you ought to oppose it personally through every stage, which will gain you the applause of the Established Church and every real friend of the Constitution, if you should be beat it will be in doing your duty and the House of Lords will prevent any evil; indeed it is the duty of Ministers as much as possible to prevent any alterations in so essential a part of the Constitution as everything that relates to religion, and there is no shadow for this petition as the Crown regularly grants a Noli prosequi if any over nice Justice of the Peace encourages prosecutions.[37]

The Church of England was an essential part of the Constitution, but that did not prevent the King from advising one of his bishops to 'imitate the zeal' of the nonconformists. Nor did he have any sympathy for those sectarian-minded Anglicans who jealously attacked (though they soon copied) the educational innovations of Joseph Lancaster in his 'monitorial' schools for the poor. The King in fact subscribed to them and allowed Lancaster, a Quaker, to boast his patronage. Quakers indeed usually earned his respect, and he by no means joined with the generality of the higher ranks in the Church and society in despising the enthusiasm of the Methodists, whom he found 'a quiet good kind of people who will disturb nobody'. When the King and Queen in 1772 received the rather special and dissident Methodist the Countess of Huntingdon, they were impressed by her piety, and the King once declared he wished there was a Lady Huntingdon in every diocese in the kingdom. Her object in seeking an audience had been to protest to him over the 'routs' that Dr Cornwallis, Archbishop of Canterbury, was said to be permitting under his roof, and George promptly wrote to the Primate to give 'notification of the grief and concern' he felt over 'these levities and vain dissipations.' 'I trust you will suppress them immediately,' the King's note concluded, 'so that I may not have occasion to show any further marks of my displeasure, or to interpose in a different manner. May God take your Grace into his Almighty protection . . .'[38]

For all his plain living and quiet domesticity, George III seldom allowed either himself or others to forget that a King was a unique person, or that the kingship of Britain, the burden of whose majesty he bore, was a venerable and awesome thing. Nobody spoke to the King until first spoken to. Nobody *sat* in the intimacy of the King's presence, except as a very unusual mark of condescension. The younger Pitt while prime minister once stood for three and three-quarter hours in continuous consultation with his monarch. (Fanny Burney and Mrs Siddons used to stand at a desk when reading to Queen Charlotte.) Some men still thought it proper to kneel on entering the royal Closet, as the elder Pitt had done, gout or no. Lord Wellesley attested that it was his own never-failing practice. For the King, decorum and protocol were of the utmost significance. There was always the correct and well-established manner in which a thing was to be done. Grand occasions must be grandly celebrated, private occasions graced in their own proper manner. Forms and traditions were always to be observed, orders of precedence never to be disregarded. Even such informal unbending as the royal family's walks upon the Terrace at Windsor or the Promenade at Weymouth gradually acquired a formality of their own. Affability in Levee or Drawing Room by no means implied any improper camaraderie. Divinity still hedged the king, and subjects who bruised his dignity, whether they were 'low men' like George Grenville or Alderman Beckford, or 'soi-disant great men' like the Dukes of Richmond, Devonshire, or Bedford, offended not merely the King personally, but the natural order itself. The very existence of such men as Wilkes or Charles Fox was a kind of *lèse-majesté*. Even a royal duke was still a subject, and one has only to remark the awed and often abject tone of the letters his sons wrote him – whatever they said about him in private among themselves – to appreciate the height of the royal pedestal and the necessity of ritual self-abasement in approaching it.

Nature, the will of God, and the boon of British tradition together imposed the need of respect not only for kingship but for rank and social status. In 1795, following a successful minor engagement in the Mediterranean, the King wrote to Lord Spencer at the Admiralty: 'As the second Lieutenant Mr Maitland conducted himself very well I trust he will soon meet with the same favour [promotion]; being a man of good family will I hope also be of advantage in the consideration, as it is certainly wise as much as possible to give encouragement, if they personally deserve it, to gentlemen.'[39] At the very time when in America and France revolutionaries were proclaiming the equality of mankind – whatever that might be interpreted to mean – George III was intent to observe the nicest distinctions of inequality. A duke was very different from a marquis, and there was a very sensible gulf between an earl and a viscount. Again, an *Irish* viscount was of a totally different order of creation. It did not do to blur these entirely proper distinctions. The very idea of an Irish *marquis*, a novelty suggested by Lord Harcourt, caused him pain and irritation. 'I desire I may hear no more of Irish marquises, I feel for the English earls and do not choose to disgust them.'[40] When in 1788 the Prince of Wales was pressing his mother to take a very deserving case into her Household – a West India merchant's daughter whose husband, faced by card debts, had just committed suicide – he received this very revealing reply: 'The King from the beginning of my coming to England having desired me to keep every place in my Family as near to the rank in which I found it, must of course preclude the person in question.'[41]

Among commoners and laymen, the distinctions made by the King were no less sharp than among peers, soldiers, sailors, or clergy, but perhaps more difficult and subtle; certainly they did not necessarily correspond to degrees of wealth. 'Nabobs, planters, and other volunteers' might be able to buy out the Bank of England, but as loyal members of Parliament, George reminded North, they were no substitute for well-established 'gentlemen of landed property'. When in 1784, he found himself obliged to raise a private loan of £24,000, it was to the banker Henry Drummond that he applied, 'chusing to deal with a gentleman rather than addressing myself through others to the common sort of moneyed men.' Yet no mere gentleman, however honourable in acres, was to be accorded the same respect or opportunity of advancement as one born to the nobility: 'Ld. North cannot seriously think that a private gentleman like Mr Penton is to stand in the way of the eldest son of an earl . . . it is diametrically opposite to what I have known all my life.' Expressed thus flatly, so outmoded a view raises the modern eyebrow. But he was saying no more than a Chesterfield or Horace Walpole or any Georgian aristocrat felt in his bones; or than Burke was implying in his hesitation to intrude 'such a crawling existence' as his own into the august company of the Duke of Devonshire; or than was taken for granted by such contemporary experts in the subtleties of class gradation as Miss Burney or Miss Austen, who like their King knew so perfectly their own place and everybody else's.

CHAPTER FOURTEEN

Patron and Amateur

ALTHOUGH the King's inclinations forbade lavish expenditure, he took his obligations as royal patron seriously and conscientiously. In painting, he had his reservations concerning the excessively fashionable and expensive Joshua Reynolds, already established as prince of the London art world; it seems probable that the young King thought him too big for his boots. At least it was clear that he stood in no need of royal patronage. The King's favourite artist at this time was the Pennsylvania-born Benjamin West, who arrived in England in 1763 and was introduced at Court by an admiring Archbishop of York. Soon George too was all admiration for the dramatic 'history painting' of this young American, whose large canvases like 'Regulus', in the high Roman fashion, or 'The Death of General Wolfe', celebrating contemporary heroic tragedy, were to have an enormous vogue, which 'history painting' in general continued to enjoy for another half-century or so. When in 1776 William Woollett made a print of the 'Death of Wolfe', he was created Engraver to His Majesty – a new post and a double compliment, to the original artist and to the high crafts-manship of the engraver. Public taste endorsed the King's to the tune of earning Woollett £15,000 during the next fourteen years for this engraving alone.

The world of art in 1760, like that of politics, was full of factions and rival groupings. The chief of these, the Society of Artists, had in April of that year, begun giving public exhibitions of its works, but internal quarrels abounded, and both West and Reynolds for a time left the Society. By 1765, however, it had received a royal charter of incorpora-tion. It was mainly on the initiative of Benjamin West and the royal architect Sir William Chambers that the King was persuaded to support the foundation of a new and more ambitious society. The King would have liked West to become its first President, but West himself was in no doubt about the name that ought to grace the office. Joshua Reynolds, being then approached, intimated that he would accept if he were granted the honour of a commission to paint the King and Queen. So the Royal Academy 'for the purpose of cultivating and improving the arts of painting, sculpture, and architecture' was inaugurated in December, 1768. Reynolds eventually (but only after long delay) executed his two portraits, was knighted, and remained President of the Academy until his death in 1792, when West succeeded him. Between them the two men presided for over fifty years. During the first twelve of these there was an annual financial deficit to reckon with, amounting in all to £5,120, and this sum the King personally made up. In this same initial period the Academy had also to make shift for premises with Dalton's print-shop and auction-room in Pall Mall, but in 1780 George manifested his continued interest and favour by presenting 'a noble suite of rooms' in Somerset House, newly rebuilt by Chambers. Here on 1st May, according to the *Morning Post*, 'the concourse of the people of fashion who attended the opening . . . was incredible; the carriages filled the whole wide space from the New Church to Exeter Change.' The paper added, however, a little sourly, 'At the end of one of the lower rooms are the portraits of their Majesties by Sir Joshua Reynolds, which, if it were not likely to be deemed high treason against the prince of painters, we should like to criticize pretty freely.' The King had at last given Reynolds three sittings in the previous year, and found his company as uncongenial as his style. It was only grudgingly that he appointed him 'principal portrait painter in ordinary' on Allan Ramsay's death in 1784. On his side Reynolds took little joy in the dignity, and grumbled privately at the remuneration.

In 1772, the King made Benjamin West 'historical painter to the Court' at the handsome annual salary of £1,000. Another American who shone in the same *genre*, J. S. Copley, was also patronised by the King. His son, as Lord Lyndhurst, was in the course of time to rise to the Woolsack; he himself, taking the tide of history-painting at the flood, scored a big success with his 'Death of Chatham' in 1781. For the Court he painted George III's three youngest daughters playing with a tambourine among their spaniels, one of his best works, though it did not have the *réclame* of his 'Death of Chatham'. During the early years of his reign the King's favourite portraitist was undoubtedly Allan Ramsay, who having already enjoyed one successful career in Scotland, took the high road south, was appointed to the Court in 1767, and with a staff of assistants to keep the output flowing, did many fine canvases of the King, the Queen, and their rapidly increasing family, until an accident to his right arm ended his career.

The German-born Zoffany was another who enjoyed Court favour. He had come to England from Rome at the close of George II's reign and already by 1760 had made his name as a painter of portraits and conversation-pieces. Together with the younger George Dance, he was one of those nominated to membership of the Academy by the King in 1769. Then, armed with George's recommendation, he was employed during the seventies by the Duke of Tuscany in Florence, and later travelled and painted in India. Returning to England in 1790, he worked here for twenty more years as a naturalised British citizen, and is buried, as Gainsborough also is, in the churchyard of royal Kew. Francis Cotes and Nathaniel Dance in the sixties, and later in the reign Sir William Beechey, Gainsborough's nephew Dupont, Peter Stroehling, and John Hoppner (another of German extraction*) were among other painters commissioned by the King. Upon Reynolds's death in 1792, Thomas Lawrence was appointed principal portrait painter, having three years previously, when only twenty, done the fine portrait of Queen Charlotte that is now in the National Gallery. Gainsborough, an original member of the Academy, was another of those who like Reynolds had no particular need to seek royal patronage. Society, fame, and fortune had flowed into his Bath studio as they had to Reynolds's in Leicester Square. But after he moved to Pall Mall in the seventies he was commissioned several times to do portraits of George III (though he admitted to him he preferred landscapes and only wished they sold as well). He made besides numerous paintings of Queen Charlotte and her children, and became, according to Mrs Papendiek, the Queen's favourite portrait painter.[1]

As a collector of paintings George III can hardly stand on a level with Charles I, or as a connoisseur with George IV. Even so his keepers of pictures collected abroad to some purpose. Among many, two outstanding purchases were Vermeer's 'Lady at the Virginals', and a fine collection belonging to the British Consul in Venice, including several Canalettos and Zuccarellis, which used to hang on the grand staircase of the Queen's House until the Prince Regent removed them. It was, however, as a collector of books that George III was outstanding.

It would be true to say that George respected, rather than loved, literature. There was at one time a royal suggestion that he should

---

* However, according to Mrs Papendiek, an intimate of the Hoppners, 'Mr West, the friend of no one who might possibly interfere with his success, pronounced poor Hoppner as the possessor of a talent too inferior for royal notice, and he left Windsor with blighted hopes' (Papendiek, *Court and Private Life* . . . , i, 232). Hoppner's mother was one of the German attendants at Court, and the interest shown by George III in the boy's education had given rise to a foolish rumour that he was the King's natural son. After he left Windsor he became one of the leading and most fashionable painters patronised by the Prince of Wales.

establish a new literary order of knighthood, with numbers limited to twenty-four, taking precedence immediately beneath the Knights of the Bath. It even acquired a name, the Order of Minerva, but never an existence. The King's collection of books, however, assembled for the new library in the Queen's House, soon became one of the finest in the country, and many scholars were given free access to its, eventually, 63,000 volumes. That the King too made frequent use of it should surprise only those who cling to the legend that he was too incurious to wish, or even too dunderheaded to be able, to read a book. It would be more relevant to say that he was frequently too busy; of the vast quantity of printed or written material that came before him, the overwhelming proportion must have been letters, reports, and official papers. And of the rest the greater part concerned the practical arts and sciences where his interests principally lay. 'George the Third,' observed Walter Scott, 'might be termed a bibliographer rather than a student; yet he read a good deal also, and rather for improvement than amusement.' He was not a bookish man; nevertheless he had respect for scholarship. His orders to those collecting on his behalf were 'never to bid against a scholar, a professor, or any person of moderate means who desired a particular book for his own use'. By his own account, the only book he ever thought it important to *steal* was James Beattie's *Essay on Truth* (controverting Hume's 'atheism'); 'I stole it from the Queen, to give it to Lord Halifax to read.' Presumably his detestation of Voltaire stemmed conversely from the same religious reasons. He considered him, so he told Miss Burney, 'a monster'. But at least it is reasonable to suppose that he had read some Voltaire; and also some Rousseau, whom he 'thought of with more favour' – indeed, granted a pension to. He had certainly read quite extensively in English and European history – Hume on the early Stuarts for instance; Bishop Burnet; Paul de Rapin's *Histoire d'Angleterre* and Nathaniel Bacon's *Historical and Political Observations*. Intensively too; when a book seemed to him of serious importance, he would often take pains to make a synopsis of it – Blackstone's *Commentaries* for example – as he habitually did with arguments upon vital political topics.

He felt strongly that such seats of learning as Eton College and the Universities of Oxford and Cambridge ought not merely to command, but to deserve, respect. Provostships of Eton or Regius professorships ought not to be viewed as havens for undistinguished or lazy divines with powerful political friends. 'I desire Lord North,' he wrote in October, 1781, 'will direct the instrument to be prepared appointing Dr Joseph Jowett of Trinity Hall Regius Professor of Civil Law; but I expect the gentleman is to engage to read lectures, and not to turn this which was founded for the improvement of the young gentlemen at Cambridge into a sinecure which has of late rather disgraced those appointments.' And two months later he had to insist that the new Provost of Eton in place of Dr Sleech (who 'was certainly not adequate to the situation') must be a man 'eminent in letters . . . At Eton I must not have any but an able man'.

In literary matters the King's opinions tended to be those of the honest outsider not overmuch impressed by conventional canons of taste. Hence his well-known rhetorical question to Fanny Burney (whose own novels he read and admired, in a wondering kind of way) upon the subject of Shakespeare's plays: ' "Was there ever," cried he, "such stuff as great part of Shakespeare? Only one must not say so! But what think you? – what? – Is there not sad stuff? what? – what? . . . But one should be stoned for saying so!" ' At least George knew his Shakespeare well enough to enumerate 'many of the characters and parts of the plays he objected to'. And when in 1788 he knew that his illness had affected his mind, but, being then lucid, sought a book to read, it was *King Lear* that he asked for. The doctors saying no to this, he circumvented their veto by asking for the works of the elder George Colman, which he knew contained an acting edition of *Lear*.[2] 'Very beautiful,' he said, 'very affecting, and very awful . . . I am like poor Lear, but thank God I have no Regan, no Goneril, only three Cordelias.'*

If what the King liked in literature and the arts was not always what pundits said one ought to like, the greatest of all the pundits, the Great Cham himself, Dr Johnson, was surprised and impressed when he once had conversation with the young King in the library. The librarian was a certain Barnard, a friend of Johnson and fellow-member of 'The Club', who had earlier consulted Johnson over the purchase of some of the royal books and had offered him the run of the library. The King's permission had had to be obtained, so that he knew Johnson was in the habit of occasionally reading there, and one day in February, 1767, he asked Barnard to let him know the next time the great man was present. According to Boswell, Johnson never tired of relating to his friends every circumstance of the meeting that followed, and Boswell himself went to unusual and extraordinary pains to recount every detail, even obtaining royal approval of their authenticity before publication. His account[3] tells much of Johnson and his deep-rooted true-blue royalism, but also something of the King's civilised respect

* Meaning the elder trio of his daughters, Charlotte, Augusta, and Elizabeth. Charlotte, Princess Royal and later Queen of Württemberg, 'wept in relating this' many years later to Mrs William Wynn' (D. M. Stuart, *Daughters of George III*, 13).

and willingness to remain in *statu pupillari* before the prestige and powers of so learned a professional. As soon as George had been apprised by Barnard of Johnson's presence

> Mr Barnard took one of the candles that stood on the King's table, and lighted his Majesty through a suite of rooms, till they came to a private door into the library, of which his Majesty had the key. Being entered, Mr Barnard stepped forward hastily to Dr Johnson, who was still in a profound study, and whispered him, 'Sir, here is the King.' Johnson started up, and stood still. His Majesty approached him, and at once was courteously easy.

They talked of the relative size of the Oxford and Cambridge libraries, Lord Lyttelton's newly published History of England, 'the controversy between Warburton and Lowth, which the King seemed to have read,' the *Journal des Savans* and the Monthly and Critical Reviews, the *Philosophical Transactions*, and various such weighty matters. When the King expressed a hope that Johnson would execute 'a literary biography of this country', and Johnson remarked that he considered 'he had already done his part as a writer', the King delighted him by replying that he 'should have thought so too if he had not written so well' – a compliment, declared Johnson to Boswell, 'fit for a King to pay. It was decisive.' Had Johnson capped the King's remark? he was asked. 'No, Sir,' replied Johnson, 'it was not for me to bandy civilities with my Sovereign.' He rated George III's manners 'those of as fine a gentleman as we may suppose Lewis the Fourteenth or Charles the Second'. 'Sir,' he said to Barnard when the King had gone from the library, 'they may talk of the King as they will; but he is the finest gentleman I have ever seen.'

Joseph Priestley was another of the many outstanding men who were allowed the run of the royal library, but the welcome he received contrasted strongly with Johnson's: 'If Dr Priestley applies to my librarian, he will have permission to see the library as other men of science have had; but I cannot think that the Doctor's character as a politician [he was a radical] or divine [he was a Unitarian] deserves my appearing in it at all.'[4]

This King's Library remained at Buckingham House until 1823, when George IV, planning the new Buckingham Palace, and with a filial devotion as moving as it was belated, donated the collection to the nation 'as a just tribute to the memory of a parent whose life was adorned with every public and private virtue'. It was to house the King's library that the building of the present British Museum was begun in that year.

When in town George and Charlotte used to attend the playhouse with fair regularity; the Queen, indeed, once declared to Fanny Burney that she preferred plays to all other amusements. During the 1786 season, for instance, Mrs Papendiek reported, 'their Majesties gave every encouragement to [the theatre] by appearing every week at one or the other house' – that is, at Drury Lane or Covent Garden, where, at both establishments, theatrical performances alternated with a season of oratorios. It was at the Covent Garden oratorios that 'the Linleys, father and son, conducted and led the orchestra on the stage, and the three Miss Linleys sang' – the eldest and most beautiful of whom had been since 1772 (secretly) and 1773 (publicly) Mrs Richard Brinsley Sheridan. Sheridan, in fact, though *persona non grata* at Court from the time of his entering Parliament as an ally of Charles Fox (1780), wrote during the seventies the choicest of all examples of the type of play the King was most disposed to enjoy – what he called 'good modern comedies', of which he declared there was a sad want. He infinitely preferred these polite comedies – 'genteel' or 'sentimental' comedies as Mrs Papendiek called them – either to tragedies, which lay heavily upon him, or to the older comedies, which he found immoral. Sheridan may hardly be thought excessively proper, and indeed only his personal friendship with the Lord Chamberlain secured a licence for the *School for Scandal*'s first performance in 1777. But his *Trip to Scarborough*, first seen in the same year, illustrates well the difference between what was acceptable at that time compared with eighty or a hundred years earlier – for the *Trip to Scarborough* was not strictly by Sheridan at all, but merely a rehash of Vanbrugh's *The Relapse*, with the improprieties removed. George III's views on this tinkering with the old comedies were conveyed once to Fanny Burney: ' "And they pretend," cried he, "to mend them; but it is not possible. Do you think it is? – what? . . . They might mend the speeches; – but the characters are all bad from the beginning to the end." '[5] Even Mrs Siddons, the queen of tragedy, whom George admired ('I think there was never any player in my time so excellent – not Garrick himself') usually performed 'genteel comedy' when the King or Queen was to be present.* Mrs Siddons also had the honour of giving play-readings before George and Charlotte at the Queen's House, and taught elocution to two of the young Princesses, as Quin had once to their father. Among the men, in the decade following Garrick's retirement, John Henderson was regarded by the King as the greatest of stage players. Perhaps Miss

---

* Fanny Burney, when she first saw her, performing before the King and Queen at Weymouth, thought her ill-suited to it. 'What pity thus to throw away her talents. But the Queen dislikes tragedy . . .'

Burney, for whom admittedly the King could do little wrong, but who after all was not wholly a simpleton in matters literary or dramatic, was not far out, not just being obsequiously over-generous, when she assessed the King's judgment on plays and players as 'almost always good, because constantly his own, natural, and unbiassed, and resulting from common sense, unadulterated by rules'.[6]

In music, both the King and Queen maintained their own orchestras; the Queen's Chamber Band in particular numbered among its members several of the outstanding musicians of the day. Both George and Charlotte were knowledgeably musical; both were enthusiastic listeners and tolerable performers. The Queen sang and played the harpsichord (and later the newly introduced pianoforte); the King played the flute and harpsichord, and sometimes too amused himself upon the violin. His devotion to Handel was almost religious, and in the Queen's Japan room at Buckingham House the master's bust by Roubiliac always stood in the position of honour upon the chamber organ. Handel had died in 1759, but (Dr Burney had once told Fanny) the aged composer had forecast, 'While that boy lives my music will never want a protector.'

Among the living, Thomas Arne did not write much of consequence after the early seventeen-sixties; William Boyce was Master of the King's Musick and principal organist of the Chapel Royal during the sixties and seventies, but he too had passed the best of his composing days. Undoubtedly the most illustrious 'English' composer of these decades was John Christian Bach, youngest son of the great John Sebastian (whose own compositions were almost unknown here). Coming with credentials from Strelitz and a high reputation already won at Naples and Turin, John Christian Bach was taken under the wing of the English Court in 1762, settled in London (so that among the numerous family he is often known as the 'London' or 'English' Bach), and remained there for most of the remaining twenty years of his life. He was soon appointed Music Master to Queen Charlotte, to whom his first two sets of keyboard concertos are dedicated. He gave lessons too to the royal Princesses and sometimes, of an evening by appointment, played the keyboard accompaniments for the King's flute.

It was Bach who in 1764 was in charge of the arrangements when the eight-year-old Mozart, already a veteran of the concert platforms of Vienna and Paris, appeared by command before the King and Queen and astonished them by his preternatural powers. Chancing upon him, with his father Leopold, a week later near St James's, the King let down the window-sash of his carriage, waving and nodding his head in the most friendly and enthusiastic manner. Indeed, Leopold reported home, the graciousness of the royal reception was *unbeschreiblich*. A second summons to Buckingham House followed, when the incredible child played the organ, improvised a melody on a Handel *continuo*, accompanied the Queen in an aria, and rattled off at sight anything the King cared to put before him at the harpsichord.

The concerts promoted by J. C. Bach and his fellow-German C. F. Abel at the Hanover Square rooms soon became the most distinguished and fashionable in England, and for a time – especially between 1763 and 1767 – Bach's Italian operas at the King's Theatre in Haymarket (later His Majesty's) proved as popular as Handel's had a generation before. It would surely be safe to assert that no British monarch since George III has graced with his attendance both the first and second nights of a new operatic performance, but, as Burney wrote,

> Mr Bach's first opera in England, called *Orione* . . . was honoured with the presence of their Majesties on the first night, February the 19th 1763, and extremely applauded by a numerous audience . . . Their Majesties honoured the second representation likewise with their presence, and no other serious opera was wanting for near three months.[7]

Thirteen years later, Lord March was writing to George Selwyn, 'The King was at the Opera, which he scarce ever misses.' Operatic fashions, however, were fickle. Bach's popularity declined, and he died debt-laden in 1782. It was J. P. Salomon who took over the management of the Hanover Square concerts, and in 1791 first introduced Haydn there to the London musical world, which he was to enrich with his last twelve symphonies.

This was the new music. The King preferred the old. When Salomon first arrived upon the London scene, wrote Mrs Papendiek, 'at the Queen's House the fondness for the ancient masters kept him aloof.' It was the fashionable Prince of Wales rather than the staid King who for a time took Haydn under his wing. At an all-Haydn chamber concert at the Duke of York's country seat, the Prince of Wales, wrote Haydn, 'played with us on his violoncello, quite tolerably.' Better still, he commanded a portrait of Haydn to be done by Hoppner. Haydn was flattered and entranced by this dazzling, delightful young man. Not only was the Prince 'the handsomest man on God's earth'; he had 'an extraordinary love of music and a lot of feeling'. It was largely true; George III had an eldest son more sensitive to the arts than he could ever be himself; more brilliantly endowed; with greater flair and panache and the desire to do things on the grand scale. In music, the theatre, painting, and architecture, the Prince's patronage was rivalling and soon outshining George III's. Unfortunately, however, as Haydn found, the rewards were more immediate in prestige than in hard cash; five years later the composer was having to apply to Parliament for payment of his teacupful of the Prince's oceanic debts.[8]

The King had become closely involved with the 'Concerts of Ancient Music', which were given regularly from 1776 – twelve every winter plus an annual *Messiah* – and where the royal attendance became after a time so regular that they became known also as 'The King's Concerts'. One of their odder features was that applause was permitted or encores solicited only from the royal box. Committee members, of whom George III was one, chose the programme in turn – the last to do so was the Duke of Wellington in 1848. From 1784-87 and again in 1791 these concerts included grand celebrations of the music of Handel; nothing delighted the King better. Purcell too was honoured, and other such old masters, wrote Burney, 'as an intemperate rage for novelty had too soon laid aside as superannuated.' Their works were performed 'by a select and powerful band, with such correctness and energy, as the authors themselves never had the happiness to hear'. Those who think of eighteenth-century musical performances as essentially small-scale would be surprised to read that in 1787 'the band of vocal and instrumental performers amounted to eight hundred and six musicians, exclusive of the principal singers, consisting of twenty-two.'[9] It was from the King's Concerts, and from the profits of the sale of Dr Burney's account of them, that a fund was established to create the Royal Society of Musicians.

Burney was the chief musical historian of the day and the King took a close personal interest in him, in his work, and incidentally in his daughter Fanny – at last identified to the general astonishment as the secret author of the vastly successful *Evelina*. The King was sorry that they had been able to find for the excellent Dr Burney only that rather miserable little £50-a-year place at Chelsea Hospital (he had been overlooked for the post of Master of the King's Musick) and felt that some recompense had been made when it became possible for the Queen to offer Fanny the post of assistant to Mme Schwellenberg, Queen Charlotte's Keeper of the Robes, at £200 a year. Burney overflowed with gratitude and gratification at so signal a mark of royal benevolence and approval. Fanny entered, and endured, her five-year imprisonment in the royal 'monastery' with more mixed emotions; unalloyed devotion and loyalty to her father, and to the King and Queen, who were both kind to her, mingled with not a little sense of personal deprivation, and curtailment of social intercourse. When her father was writing his accounts of the King's Concerts, George could not resist proffering him written suggestions and additions, which Burney naturally adopted. Similarly, when Burney's *General History of Music* was nearing its final stages, the King was not content to wait for the finished work. He requested to see it, read it through with his accustomed thoroughness, and volunteered from his own pen further material, one item of which was a tribute to Fischer the oboe player. These additions also were of course incorporated by Burney.

Dr Burney was a man of many parts, and among his sidelines was the study of astronomy. (His very first publication had been *An Abridged History of Comets*.) Among his musical friends was the Hanover-born William Herschel, who was the son of an oboist in the band of the Foot Guards there and had come to England in 1757, and thereafter earned his living as an organist and music-teacher. Herschel, too, with his brother and sister, made a hobby, which grew to be a passion, of studying the stars. Constructing for himself a six-foot Newtonian telescope, he conceived the sizable notion of 'surveying the entire heavens and if possible ascertaining the plan of their general structure'. While by night he investigated the nature of sunspots, the climate of Mars, or the general 'behaviour of the variable stars', still by day he plied his trade of musician, until in 1781 he discovered the hitherto unknown planet Uranus; was made, with his friend Burney, a Fellow of the Royal Society; and obtained the patronage of the King. (Only second thoughts dictated 'Uranus'; the new planet had originally been named by Herschel 'Georgium Sidus'.) Herschel could make strong claims upon royal respect and admiration, for George too had considered the heavens and probed among the stars from the Observatory that he had built in the grounds of Kew in 1760. Kew was also where Joseph Banks the astronomer and Joseph Banks the botanist could most happily and fruitfully co-exist. And when Sir Joseph, by now President of the Royal Society, proposed Herschel's name for the post of astronomer-in-charge of Kew Observatory the King was sympathetic. Unfortunately, however, the ageing holder of the post had a son to whom it was as good as promised. George therefore did the next best thing, awarding Herschel a pension of £200 a year, which allowed him to abandon music-teaching, if not to live in affluence. (Marriage to a wealthy widow eventually effected that too.) When George later went over to Datchet from Windsor to spend an evening pottering among the now famous astronomer's instruments, Herschel reported to his sister that 'the King has very good eyes and enjoys observations with telescopes exceedingly'; and when some years after-

wards Herschel was busy constructing his forty-foot telescope, then the
world's biggest, George III contributed the substantial sum of £2,947
towards the cost, and followed this with an annual maintenance alloca-
tion.[10] This was in the 1780's and the Court by then had removed from
Kew to Windsor, where 'Dr Herschel was begged to go over whenever
any appearance in the heavens was likely to interest the King . . . A ten-
foot telescope was placed so as to be always ready', but whenever something special was to be visible, Herschel 'would send down a twenty
feet telescope without making the slightest trouble'.[11]

At Kew also was housed the splendid royal collection of mathematical and 'philosophical' instruments and models, eventually about
two thousand of them in all, which witness to the King's interest in
mechanical and scientific matters and leave one wishing that Joseph
Wright of Derby had happened to be among his Court painters. There
were – indeed *are*, for they are now handsomely displayed at the
Kensington Science Museum – beautifully fashioned terrestrial and
celestial globes; orreries, and every kind of device then known for
simulating the motions of planets and comets; microscopes, from the
simple to the very ornate – one of silver has its base decorated with
delicate statuettes; working models of atmospheric and pneumatic
engines (machinae pneumaticae) and of compression and exhaustion
pumps – one of the steam pumps a close cousin to Glasgow University's
historic Newcomen model whose repair first launched James Watt
upon his momentous improvements; an apparatus to illustrate the
utility of the Archimedean screw; 'philosophical tables' of elegant
workmanship, complete with such accessories as parallel cycloidal
grooves to demonstrate the truths of Newtonian dynamics; a variety
of serious toys to show the powers of magnetism; every kind of
mechanical plaything, in short, to fascinate the amateur and instruct the
student. Many of them were the work of George Adams the younger
(1750-1795), of 'Tycho Brahe's Head' in London, Mathematical
Instrument Maker to his Majesty. Adams not only dedicated his own
Treatise of Celestial and Terrestrial Globes to George III, but engaged
Dr Johnson himself to compose the dedication. Hence, declared
Boswell, 'it could not fail to be very grateful to a Monarch distinguished
for his love of the sciences.'

For all this love, there are no indications that George III ever paid
more than distant attention to the revolutionary new discoveries that
were already in the early decades of the reign beginning to transform
the northern and midland counties of his realm. He admired Josiah
Wedgwood's pottery, and even influenced (in the direction of greater
plainness) the design of the famous green and gold service of 'Queen's

ware' that Wedgwood made for Charlotte. Wedgwood was appointed, first Potter to the Queen and then Potter to the King. When, on the several occasions that he and his partner Bentley came to the Queen's House to present their latest products, the King, as Bentley wrote, always 'entered very freely into conversation' and seemed 'to have the success of all our manufactures much at heart'; but he never thought of returning their visit by going to Etruria – still less Manchester or Bradford or any other of those infant monsters whose development was the most portentous of all the signs of the times. Once as Prince of Wales he may have toured Scotland incognito but, as King, Oxford (or more precisely Blenheim Palace) remained his Ultima Thule. Portsmouth to the south and Plymouth and Worcester to the west set the other limits of his journeyings. Never was a king of recent centuries less travelled. Not once did he see a coal mine or an iron foundry, and when the accident of a convalescing holiday took him in the summer of 1788 to the textile country round Stroud, his delight was enhanced by the sheer novelty of the experience. Agriculture was the only industry where he could talk with the innovators and improvers of his day on the knowledgeable terms born of experience and contact.

Yet if he admired Brindley's canals and Watt's steam engines and Crompton's 'mules' only by report and from afar, mechanical contrivances and fastidious workmanship never ceased to fascinate him. As telescopes and the remote wonders of the sky, and George Adams's intricate demonstrations of the marvels of science, so clocks, watches, chronometers, barometers, hygrometers,* and the delicate skills of the craftsmen who made them, engaged him both as patron and amateur dabbler. It was to the King, at Kew, that the great horologist John Harrison presented the fifth and last of his epoch-making chronometers; it remained accurate to within $4\frac{1}{2}$ seconds over a period of ten weeks. His fourth, on a journey to the West Indies and back in 1761-62, had demonstrated beyond argument that it could determine longitude to within a maximum error of eighteen miles. An Act of 1713 had promised a prize of £20,000 to any such timepiece proving accurate to within thirty miles, yet in 1773, Harrison, past eighty years old, was still short of his full reward. It was only after the King's personal intervention that the last £8,750 was wrung out of the Board of Longitude, and Parliament, in June, 1773.

At Windsor there is an undated memorandum in the royal hand setting out in meticulous detail the stages for mounting and un-

---

* For example, 'an hygrometer, upon an improved construction, applicable to the management of the moisture and temperature of the hot and green houses of the botanical establishment at Kew' (Huish, *Public and Private Life* . . . , 353-54).

mounting a watch, with an explanation of the motion. The King may merely have been copying from a handbook, but the pages could be read as an answer to a self-set examination for testing his knowledge of the processes in their correct order. Such an exercise would have been characteristic. He certainly collected the work of the master clockmakers and watchmakers of his day, and spent, for him, lavishly upon it. In 1764, for instance, he paid the Cornishman John Arnold 500 guineas for 'the smallest repeating watch ever attempted', set in a finger ring, and the following year he bought two exceptionally fine and sophisticated 'astronomical' and 'barometric' clocks, one from Alexander Cumming for £1,178 (he threw in £150 a year for maintaining it), and from Eardley Norton, for £1,042, another which stood on the centre table of the Octagon Room in the King's Library at Buckingham House. These expensive masterpieces absorbed him.[12] When a year or two later he bought another of them, this time from Christopher Pinchbeck, he even took some small part, together with Sir William Chambers, in planning the design.[13] We establish some standard by which to estimate the value of these elaborate clocks by noticing that the King reckoned to pay up to ten or twenty times as much for them as for his portrait by Reynolds (though Reynolds did get the bonus of a knighthood); and even the enormously ornate and luxurious state coach, the 'Coronation Coach', built in 1762 – designed by Chambers, built by Butler the coachmaker, its Tritons and palm-trees sculpted by Joseph Wilton, its allegorical panels painted by Cipriani, the whole 'a very beautiful object,' judged Walpole, though crowded with 'improprieties' – cost only £7,588.[14]

In the middle decades of the reign at Windsor, earning himself the nickname of Farmer George, the King took his modest place alongside Turnip Townshend and Coke of Holkham and the other notable improving landlords of the century; and upon the death in 1790 of his brother the Duke of Cumberland, Ranger of Windsor Forest, George personally assumed control there, with the Duke of Gloucester's fourteen-year-old son William as merely nominal Ranger. At Richmond he had already turned over the Old Deer Park to sheep, and part of the New Park to arable; and now he 'disimparked' 1,222 Windsor acres to form three farms, improving the remaining land by draining, clearing, and planting. Through the agency of Sir Joseph Banks he first introduced merino sheep into England; 'a ram and two ewes procured from Bilboa' arrived at Kew in 1789. In the same year samples were brought back from Spain of what Banks declared to be the finest wool he had ever seen, and he was enthusiastic for pressing ahead with the King's 'truly patriotic plan' for improving British flocks.[15]

From their inception in 1784, George III had been assiduous in keeping up with Arthur Young's *Annals of Agriculture*, and in 1787 he contributed two letters to them above the pseudonym of Ralph Robinson – in fact the name of one of the Windsor shepherds.[16] He used to buy two copies of the *Annals*, one for himself and one for 'Mr Ducket, the able cultivator of Petersham', on the Richmond estates, for whom 'Ralph Robinson' had such regard that he made the Petersham farming methods the subject of his first letter to the *Annals*:

Mr Ducket's system of agriculture is a medium between the old and the drill husbandry . . . an employment of clover, turnips, and rye, as fallow-crops, and as intermediate ones between wheat, barley, oats, and rye, changing these occasionally according to the nature and state of the land. Of these intermediate crops, those which serve only to fill up the winter-interval are of the greatest use for winter and spring food, and what these take from the ground is amply re-supplied by the dung and treading of the cattle which feed on them; thus his ground, although never dormant, is continually replenished by a variety of manure, and thus unites the system of continued pasture with cultivation . . .

When Young, that pre-eminent propagandist of the new farming methods, was received on the Terrace at Windsor, he was intensely gratified by the King's first greeting: 'I consider myself as more obliged to you than to any other man in my dominions.' And later, when Young obtained permission through Sir Joseph Banks to be shown over the Windsor farm, he was conducted by the King in person on a long tour:

The King rode with me over his farm for two and half hours, talking farming, and reasoning upon points he differed in. Explained his system of crops . . .; inquired about the Board [of Agriculture] . . .; recommended me to compress the sense of quotations in short paragraphs, *'as there are many, Mr Young, who catch the sense of a short paragraph, that lose the meaning of a long one'* . . . He inquired about my grasses, sheep, etc.; he had himself only a hundred and sixty lambs from eight hundred ewes. His strong land farm is in admirable order, and the crops all clean and fine. He was very desirous that I should see all, and ordered Frost [the bailiff] to carry me to two or three other things next morning. I found fault with his hogs; he said I must not find fault with a present to him. The Queen was so kind as to give them from Germany . . . we must not examine them too critically – 'the value of the intention, Mr Young, is greater than a better breed' . . . Quoted particularly from the *Rural Economy*: Cattle give manure, and manure corn: '*Well understood now, Sir, but not so well before you wrote*' . . . He is the politest of men . . .[17]

Just as 'Farmer George' admired the realism and practicality of Young, he had perhaps more than he himself would have recognised in common with the William Cobbett of *Rural Rides* – a similar downrightness, similar obstinacy if for different prejudices, similar plain speaking if against a different sort of humbug. For all his insistence on protocol and correctness, and the rigidly prescribed confines of his social contacts, there was an unpretending directness in the King's judgments, even the most wrong-headed ones, that demanded respect. He was as much in favour of 'improvement' as Arthur Young or Josiah Wedgwood or Capability Brown himself, as long as it was not likely to disturb the natural order, moral or social. In these spheres, as in religion and politics, his attitudes were largely those of the age that was passing. Even in artistic or aesthetic matters; his passion for good old-fashioned Handel is mirrored by his rejection of new-fangled ideas about landscape. The countryside, like the country itself, ought to be obedient to a proper sense of order; anarchy was hateful there too. One autumn evening in 1804, the Pittite, George Rose, temporarily his host, was riding back with him from Lymington to Rose's home at Cuffnells on the edge of the New Forest, and

the King began the conversation again about the naked and dreary waste we rode over yesterday, abusing it as worse than any part of Bagshot heath; and said, on the whole he thought Windsor Forest incomparably a more beautiful one than this. To which I replied, it was fortunate in this as well as in other matters of taste, that all did not think alike. I suggested the disadvantage at which the King saw this country, but that in fine weather, even the part of the forest he had seen had its beauties, as the ground was finely thrown about; to which his Majesty replied, he had no taste for what was called the fine *wild* beauties of nature; he did not like mountains and other romantic scenes, of which he sometimes heard much.[18]

George III, we see, was as anti-romantic as he was anti-democratic, as remote from the spirit of Rousseau or the young Wordsworth as from the convictions of Dr Priestley or Tom Paine. We can catch echoes of the same attitude, both to art and to life, in a short note written from

St James's at '46 min. past 1 p.m., March 23, 1786' – a belief in precision, propriety, reticence:

> Lord Carmarthen's list of music for next Wednesday is very excellent . . .; his introducing Mrs Billington if he can get her to sing pathetic songs and not to over *grace* them will be doing an essential service to the concert.[19]

CHAPTER FIFTEEN

Paterfamilias
(1762-1788)

GEORGE III was himself one of nine children, and he fathered fifteen. With so scandal-gathering and unpopular a mother as Princess Augusta, so politically involved an uncle as William Duke of Cumberland, and so disagreeable an aunt as Princess Amelia, his parents' generation presented its own varying problems. Of his own, a sister and two brothers died between 1765 and 1768, and two more of his brothers contracted 'unsuitable' matches which moved him to promote the Royal Marriages Act. His elder sister Augusta, who had married the Duke of Brunswick in 1764, aroused George's strong annoyance when she revisited England eighteen months later and with her husband played blatantly to the opposition gallery. His youngest sister Caroline Matilda married the profligate and unstable Christian VII of Denmark the following year (she did not stop crying long enough, said Reynolds, for him to do justice to her pre-nuptial portrait). She, however, was not permitted by her husband to accompany him when he paid a similarly unwelcome visit in 1768, at the height of the Wilkes troubles. George had no grudge against this sister (little as he was soon to relish the reports he received of her rash public and private behaviour); but Christian, her intolerable yet pathetic little cock-sparrow of a husband, was flatly unwelcome. Unhappily George's known distaste for his Danish brother-in-law-cousin caused the visitor to be rapturously received by high and low. The Danish alliance was of political value, and George gave instructions that Christian's wishes should be fully ascertained and scrupulously followed, but he declared the whole thing 'very disagreeable' to him.[1] When the King of Denmark went home – at last – he slid rapidly downhill into insanity, while Caroline Matilda discovered the consolations and, for a Queen, the dangers of a true passion.

A little conventional profligacy, strongly as George III objected to it, might have been condoned among the royal brothers, and even later among the royal sons. The dissipations of Edward Duke of York, George's only close childhood companion, provoked no more than private frowns at Court. He, as it happened, was removed even from those by his death at Monaco in 1767, 'his immoderate pursuit of pleasure and unremitting fatigues in travelling' bringing on 'a putrid and irresistible fever' – which is Walpole's authoritative-sounding manner of saying that he was a gay dog and died from causes unknown. Even the conduct of York's two younger brothers Gloucester and Cumberland,* though the reverse of puritanical, might have been no worse than was to be expected from young men with good health, ducal allowances, and princely morals. In 1764, Lady Sarah Bunbury (Sarah Lennox) was writing to Lady Susan O'Brien: 'The Duke of Gloucester is following [the Duke of York's] steps . . . and trots about like anything.'[2] The most interesting and serious object of these trottings-about was Maria, Earl Waldegrave's young and strikingly handsome widow, who was busy turning down offers from the most acceptable suitors, including the Duke of Portland, widely considered the most eligible bachelor in the country. Maria was one of the three natural daughters (by a milliner) of Horace Walpole's brother Sir Edward, and the Duke of Gloucester's laying siege to her opened possibilities intriguing to society in general, but disturbing to George III who, with Lady Sarah safely put behind him, regarded royal blood as a commodity not to be intermingled with that of commoners however distinguished, and certainly not to be dissipated among the illegitimate granddaughters of former Whig prime ministers. 'The report of the week,' wrote Lady Sarah in March, 1766, 'is that the King has forbid the Duke of Gloucester to speak to his pretty widow . . . He has given her five pearl bracelets that cost £500 – that's not for nothing surely?'[3] Indeed it was not, but Lady Waldegrave, a woman of pride and principle, was not to be content with becoming merely the Duke of Gloucester's mistress. Her uncle Horace, fluttered and flattered though he was by the connection, advised her to give up seeing the Duke, but in September, 1766, she was secretly married to him by her private chaplain and before no other witnesses. For another five and a half years she continued to present herself to the world, though constantly with the Duke, as the Dowager Countess Waldegrave.

While the Duke of Gloucester was living in clandestine connubiality with Horace Walpole's niece, the King's youngest brother, The Duke of Cumberland, was venturing into deeper and murkier water. Henry, the fourth son of Frederick Prince of Wales, had emancipated himself promptly and radically from his mother's moral chains. By the time of his brother's secret wedding he was a thoroughgoing man-about-town of twenty-one. Had he merely gone 'rushing at once from the school-

* There were three Dukes of Cumberland, separate creations, during the lifetime of George III: his uncle William, victor of Culloden; his brother Henry; and his widely detested ultra-Tory son Ernest.

room to the stews and the night cellars',[4] things would have been bad but perhaps not irremediable. He did that, but also worse. Floundering into a passionately serious affair with Lady Grosvenor, he was accused by the Earl of criminal conspiracy, and had to find £13,000 in costs and damages.

George's observations to his prime minister North on this 'subject of a most private and delicate kind' were commendably realistic. He was of course disturbed, not so much at his brother's amorous follies, of which he was not ignorant, as at their impact upon the royal family in general. But first there was the question of the £13,000, and Cumberland, naturally not having it himself, had applied to the King, promising repayment in eighteen months. The money must be found within a week, wrote George to North; and if it were not, 'the prosecutor would certainly force the House [of Lords], which would at this licentious time occasion disagreeable reflections.' He would be seeing North the following Wednesday, but wished to prepare the ground: 'I am not fond of taking persons on delicate affairs unprepared.'[5]

The money was of course made available, but George's hopes that he had talked his brother Cumberland into adopting more prudent courses of conduct in future were not realised. The Duke, abandoning Lady Grosvenor, took up first with the attractive wife of a complaisant timber merchant, and then with Mrs Horton, 'a young widow of twenty-four, extremely pretty, not handsome, very well made, with the most amorous eyes in the world and eyelashes a yard long.'[6] Cumberland married her first, informed the King afterwards, and by this climax to his tale of recklessness brought down upon his head a ton of royal bricks. The King caused it to be known that visitors to Cumberland House would not be received at Court and asked representatives of foreign governments to have no contact with the Cumberlands. Until his death in 1790, however, the Duke managed to hold on to his comfortable Rangership of Windsor Park – and also to his alluring Duchess. The King never forgave him, and the Duke disappears into the footnotes of history.

The Grosvenor-Cumberland action was in 1770, Cumberland's marriage in 1771. The following year, 1772, brought a culmination of family crises and sorrows. It opened with a royal *coup d'état* in Copenhagen. A conspiracy of Danish nobles, with the connivance or agreement of Christian VII, forcibly detained Queen Caroline Matilda and seized the chief minister, Struensee, a German doctor who had also become the Queen's lover. Struensee and his chief associate were executed, while Queen Caroline, with her baby, was held in the fortress of Kronborg (Elsinore). These violent events, which coincided with the preparation of a Royal Marriages Act and the last weeks of the Princess Dowager, obliged George to bring gunboat diplomacy to Copenhagen to secure his sister's release and safe passage to Hanover. There, in the castle of Zell (Celle), Caroline, three years later, died suddenly and mysteriously. Her facial resemblance to George was strong; it seems that she must have shared other physical characteristics, for it now seems highly probable that she died of porphyria.[7]

By this time, the Princess Dowager had long occupied an unimportant back seat in affairs, though the suspicion and hatred with which the public regarded her lingered obstinately. The scurrilous press continued to harp upon the tired old theme of Bute. The merciless Junius wrote that 'it would indeed be happy for this country' if she were to die. By the end of 1771, still only fifty-two, she was on the way to obliging him, being in an advanced state of cancer, yet 'going out to take the air long after it was expected that she would die in her coach'.[8] There is some evidence that George III was not always on the most cordial terms with his mother in her last years, especially after his final rejection of Bute. His son Ernest passed on what he had heard from his elders (being only one year old at the time of his grandmother's death) that 'though exterior civility was kept up between my father and his mother, still there was very little intercourse during the last years between them'.[9] At least, however, George had remained a dutiful son and, regular in his domestic ways as he was, habitually visited her between six and eight o'clock of a Saturday evening. Now that she was visibly dying the King and Queen drove every evening to spend some time with her at Carlton House. A conventional and narrow-minded woman, but in many ways lonely and misjudged, she approached her end in severe pain borne with great fortitude, her last days embittered by the misalliance of her son Henry and saddened by the scandal and violence of the news from Denmark. On 7th February, the King wrote to North:

> I am sorry to acquaint you that my mother is grown so much worse that I cannot appear at Court this day; whenever this tragical scene is ended I shall give you notice of it that I may not from any personal affliction put the least delay to public business.

And the next day: 'What I yesterday expected has happened my mother is no more; I desire you will call here about one.'[10] The Princess's death was celebrated with few tears outside the small circle of those who knew her, and by crude rejoicing among the populace. At her funeral, wrote Walpole, some of the mob 'huzzaed for joy', and when it was disclosed that she had died intestate and left a mere £7,500, predictable conclusions were drawn concerning who had scooped the rest of it. In fact, though her parliamentary allowance had been £64,000 a year and her supposed parsimony had become legendary, her private charities had been widespread and generous. (She had also paid off her husband's very considerable debts.)

At the time of the Princess Dowager's death the King was planning a bill to prevent further marital imprudences among his relations. For the marriage of any member of the royal family below the age of twenty-five the King's assent was to be necessary, and for those over twenty-five, if his assent were withheld, a year's notice to the Privy Council and the approval of Parliament. Thus George hoped to guarantee the continued purity of the caste of royalty in general and the dignity of the British monarchy in particular. He expected, so he wrote to North,

> every nerve to be strained to carry the Bill through both Houses with a becoming firmness, for it is not a question that immediately relates to Administration but personally to myself, therefore I have a right to expect a hearty support from everyone in my service and shall remember defaulters.

A fortnight later, the opponents of the measure having somewhat shifted their ground: 'It is a known maxim of all military opperations that when the enemy change positions that is the right moment to push them with vigour.' (Among the enemy was now Charles Fox; the Royal Marriages Act marks his transition from friend to foe.) When the second reading passed the Commons by 200 votes to 164, too narrowly for comfort, the King hoped 'every engine' would be employed and asked for a list of deserters to be sent to him 'that would be a rule for my conduct in the Drawing Room to-morrow'. But by 24th March all the bill's stages were completed, and North was receiving royal compliments on the 'spirit of zeal' he had manifested throughout.[11]

Thus a law had been enacted whose paternalistic severity, coupled with the interpretation, long to be preserved, that Protestant royalty must wed none but Protestant royalty, was to make it impossible for George III's sons to marry the women of their choice (in effect to limit it to German princesses); to bastardise the children of Augustus, Duke of Sussex; to persuade the Prince of Wales into the most disastrous of marriages; intolerably to limit the marital field for the King's daughters, so that they were forced either into prolonged spinsterhood or into subterranean liaisons; and in general to exacerbate the quarrels and resentments that were in any case to be expected in so large and vulnerable a family.

It very soon appeared that two, not one, of the King's brothers had eluded the fiat. During the summer of 1772, Lady Waldegrave at last informed her family and the world that she had long been wedded to the Duke of Gloucester. In September the Duke notified the King of this fact, and in December, piling Pelion upon Ossa, he told him of the Duchess's pregnancy. In 1775, the King was still complaining of the 'extreme pride and vanity' of the Duchess and the 'highly disgraceful step' his brother had taken, all the more painful to him because he had 'ever loved him more with the fondness one bears to a child than a brother'.[12] In November, 1777, while assuring public provision for the Duke's children in the event of his death, he would provide nothing for the Duchess, 'a person who must always be odious' to him.[13] Even after he was formally reconciled to his two brothers in the summer of 1779, he specifically excluded any social reprieve for their wives, and although he would permit the Prince of Wales's attendance at his uncle's levees, he feared their evil influence – particularly Cumberland's – so profoundly that he forbade all other visits by the Prince to their private houses 'either in town or the country'.[14] Time however, at last, as is its habit, brought an odd reversal. In the same year, 1776, a son, William Frederick, had been born of the Gloucester marriage, and a daughter, Mary, their fourth, to George and Charlotte. Many years later this daughter Mary was to marry (at forty) the son of the 'odious' Duchess and herself become Duchess of Gloucester.

There was far from anything odious or sensational in George's own domestic story over this first quarter-century or so of his reign. Until his sons began to reach manhood and vex him with their wild oats and political associations, his domestic life, whatever the storms or gloom of the public scene, was sunny and relatively untroubled. Of the five Hanoverian kings, the first George shut his wife away in the castle of Ahlden; the second grumbled incessantly at his Queen Caroline, though in his cross-patch way respecting and depending on her; George, later the Fourth, was so disgusted by first contact with *his* Caroline that he very soon eschewed all further connection. These three all found need for a succession of mistresses, to whom however they sometimes remained by force of habit constant over long periods. William IV had lived long in comfortable and fertile union with Mrs Jordan before being at last pitchforked by dynastic necessity into matrimony with another. George III alone of the five was by inclination and conviction a family man. He had a wife who was faithful and amenable. If she was a shade *too* pious, so perhaps was he; there were no grounds for difference in that. She shared many of his attitudes and interests – music especially. At least until 1788, and generally afterwards, she kept entirely out of politics, and so was free from the opprobrium that dogged and blighted her mother-in-law. She was notably prolific. As wife, mother, companion, and consort, Queen Charlotte (at least during the first two-thirds of the reign) was in many ways a model. Lord Chesterfield called her 'a good woman, a good wife, a tender mother, and an unmeddling Queen'. Fanny Burney, who was in close attendance upon her for five years – and although on a few occasions, of course, things did happen to bring out in her a very rare flash of what she called her 'republican' mood – in general awarded her Queen and employer high marks:

> The Queen, indeed, is a most charming woman. She appears to me full of sense and graciousness, mingled with delicacy of mind and liveliness of temper . . . Her manners have an easy dignity, with a most engaging simplicity, and she has all the fine high breeding which the mind, not the station, gives, of carefully avoiding to distress those who converse with her, or studiously removing the embarrassment she cannot prevent.[15]

Now it is true that with Fanny Burney one must always 'add vinegar to taste'; her attitude to 'the royals' becomes at times unpleasantly flunkey-ish, and she certainly overworked some of her adulatory epithets. The Queen was 'sweet'; she was (in the nicest sense) 'condescending'; she was 'noble', 'kind', 'liberal', 'generous', 'benevolent'. Yet Miss Burney was not a best-selling novelist for nothing. She had a sharp eye and a lively narrative gift, and there is no reason to doubt the essential veracity either of her general view of the amicable nature of the relations between George and Charlotte over these years, or of the 'sweet' and revealing snapshot she offers of a moment of intimate affection between King and Queen after twenty-five years of marriage:

> Their behaviour to each other speaks the most cordial confidence and happiness. The King seems to admire as much as he enjoys her conversation, and to covet her participation in everything he either sees or hears. The Queen appears to feel the most grateful regard for him, and to make it her chief study to raise his consequence with others, by always marking that she considers herself, though Queen to the nation, only, to him, the first and most obedient of subjects.
>
> I cannot here help mentioning a very interesting little scene at which I was present, about this time. The Queen had nobody but myself with her, one morning, when the King hastily entered the room, with some letters in his hand, and addressing her in German, which he spoke very fast, and with much apparent interest in what

he said, he brought the letters up to her, and put them into her hands. She received them with much agitation, but evidently of a much pleased sort, and endeavoured to kiss his hand as he held them. He would not let her, but made an effort, with a countenance of the highest satisfaction, to kiss her. I saw instantly in her eyes a forgetfulness, at the moment, that any one was present, while, drawing away her hand, she presented him her cheek. He accepted her kindness with the same frank affection that she offered it; and the next moment they both spoke English, and talked upon common and general subjects.

What they said I am far enough from knowing; but the whole was too rapid to give me time to quit the room; and I could not but see with pleasure that the Queen had received some favour with which she was sensibly delighted, and that the King, in her acknowledgements, was happily and amply paid.[16]

If further evidence were wanting, the King himself supplies it in a letter to his eldest son written six years before, in August, 1780: 'I can with truth say that in nineteen years I have never had the smallest reason but to thank Heaven for having directed my choice among the Princesses then fit for me to marry, to her; indeed I could not bear up did I not find in her a feeling friend to whom I can unbosom my griefs.' And again three years later: 'Your mother, whose excellent qualities appear stronger to me every hour . . .'*

Biographers hungry for romance have laboured to find some shreds of evidence for a King hankering wistfully after his lost Lady Sarah, secretly enamoured of Lady Bridget Tollemache (Northington's daughter), or pining for Lady Pembroke, about whom he babbled – indeed thought he was married to – when his wits were crazed in later days; but the unexciting fact is that until his recurring illness imposed an accumulating strain on both of them, the King and Queen were well-suited and faithfully devoted to one another, and to their family, into which new members were received with a regularity that approached monotony: George Prince of Wales (later Prince Regent and George IV) in 1762, Frederick (later Duke of York and Commander-in-Chief) in 1763, William (later Duke of Clarence and William IV) in 1765, Charlotte (later Queen of Württemberg) in 1766, Edward (later Duke of Kent) in 1767, Augusta in 1768, Elizabeth (later Landgravine of Hesse-Homburg) in 1770, Ernest (later Duke of Cumberland and

* In 1791 the Prince of Wales added his own testimony in a letter to his brother Frederick: 'It was not everyone who could expect to be as lucky as his Majesty had been to meet with a person whose disposition suited so perfectly with his own as the Queen's did' (Aspinall, *Correspondence of George Prince of Wales*, ii, 599).

King of Hanover) in 1771, Augustus (later Duke of Sussex) in 1773, Adolphus (later Duke of Cambridge) in 1774, Mary (later Duchess of Gloucester) in 1776, Sophia in 1777, Octavius in 1779, Alfred in 1780, and Amelia in 1783. Only Octavius and Alfred succumbed in infancy, to their parents' great grief; for little Octavius in particular the King mourned long and bitterly; 'Heaven will be no Heaven to me,' he once said, 'if Octavius is not there.' In general, although his beloved Amelia died of consumption in her late twenties, and George, Frederick, Augustus, almost certainly Edward and possibly Sophia all suffered from the royal malady of porphyria,[17] these sons and daughters of George III were to prove, for their times, remarkably long-lived. Twelve passed fifty years of age and eight passed seventy, a record in pronounced contrast with that of George's own eight brothers and sisters, of whom five died between the ages of fifteen and twenty-eight.

During the sixties and seventies, and especially from mid-May onwards, the King and Queen would spend as much of their time as was possible in the country at Kew, where the older of the royal princes and princesses passed most of their childhood days – being, however, 'from their infancy . . . taken to St James's regularly on Thursdays' for the Drawing Rooms. From the age of ten they also attended the evening parties for cards and music at Buckingham House when the Court was in residence there, and when it was at Kew the smaller evening parties of the Queen. At Kew too 'there were birthday entertainments, dances, fireworks . . . and a constant variety of amusements adapted to their several tastes'.[18]

'Kew' in those mid-Georgian days was often taken broadly to include the whole stretch southwards and westwards from the village of Kew itself with its bridge over the Thames (Brentford on the farther bank, the scene of the Middlesex Elections, was opposed to Kew both politically and geographically) through Richmond to the park beyond. Kew Village and Green adjoined Kew House – or rather the two houses at different times so named.* Southwest of these royal residences were two expanses of ornamental ground – Kew Gardens, with

---

* To be strictly precise, *three* distinct houses have been known as Kew House or Kew Palace. In order of construction they were: (1) The red-brick 'Dutch' house built in 1631 for Samuel Fortrey, a merchant. This was used as a subsidiary residence from 1734 to 1801, and still stands. (2) The early Georgian 'White' house leased by the Capel family to Frederick, Prince of Wales; 'improved' by William Kent; the house of Princess Augusta, 1751-60; George III's country residence 1760-79 and occasionally thereafter until 1801; pulled down early in the nineteenth century. (3) A Gothic 'castle', crenellated and turreted, with a keep of four stories and cast-iron 'beams', designed by James Wyatt when George III decided upon a

Chambers's Temples, Pagoda, Orangery, and already a wealth of indigenous and exotic trees and shrubs, and (linked by just a footpath then, but now part of the Royal Botanic Gardens) Richmond Gardens, which lay opposite Syon House. Beyond these were the Old Deer Park, later turned over by the King to farmland, and Richmond Lodge, once the home of the rebel Duke of Ormonde but in the earlier part of the reign a favourite retreat of the King. Beyond this again was the little town of Richmond with its riverside promenade and terrace; and past Richmond Hill the much larger Deer Park, royal hunting ground since Charles I. Round Kew Green and at Richmond there were growing up houses and establishments of all kinds to provide accommodation for Court functionaries and officials of one sort or another: lords and ladies of the Bedchamber, wardrobe mistresses, pages and maids of honour, royal physicians and surgeons, governors and preceptors for the princes – the preceptors mostly bishops or bishops-to-be; governesses for the princesses, chaplains, musicians, gardeners, carpenters, riding-masters and stable staff, a whole 'class of assistants that increased in proportion as did the Royal Family'.[19]

Those royal princes junior to the Prince of Wales and Duke of York* were at one time 'boarded out' according to age-groups in the houses of their governors and preceptors on Kew Green. The future Dukes of Clarence and Kent made one pair, the future Cumberland and Sussex another, later joined by Adolphus (Cambridge). The ages of the princesses were less conveniently disposed. But all the children, of whatever age, 'were expected at the breakfast, which was at nine o'clock, from the eldest to the youngest, whom the wet-nurse herself took in.' Thus Mrs Papendiek (whose own severe smallpox attack at the age of eleven caused the King and Queen to have those of their sons who had been her playfellows inoculated – still, before Dr Jenner, a dangerous proceeding). Remembering from the eighteen-thirties the summer of 1776, she continues:

---

more ostentatious palace in 1801. Its interior was never completed, and George IV had it destroyed during 1827-28. Yet another palace had at one time been planned, by Sir William Chambers in 1769. This was to have been in Richmond Gardens, opposite Syon House, with vistas up and down the Thames. Work on this had begun, and reached ground-floor level, when the town of Richmond finally refused to give up a certain parcel of land, and the King ordered operations to stop. When the town learned in 1778 that he intended to remove to Windsor, it had second thoughts, but they came too late.

* These two elder sons had suites both at Buckingham House and Kew, where they occupied the Dutch House. Hence the Dutch House was often known as the Prince of Wales's House; Fanny Burney customarily refers to it thus.

Kew now became quite gay, the public being admitted to the Richmond Gardens on Sundays and to Kew Gardens on Thursdays. The Green on those days was covered with carriages, more than 300 *l.* being often taken at the bridge on Sundays. Their Majesties were to be seen at the windows speaking to their friends, and the royal children amusing themselves in their own gardens. Parties came up the water too, with bands of music, to the ait opposite the Prince of Wales's house. The whole was a scene of enchantment and delight; Royalty living amongst their subjects to give pleasure and to do good.[20]

There is doubtless some nostalgia in the remembrance of this idyll by an old lady of sixty-eight looking back over more than half a century. But increasingly to most Englishmen, and certainly to that small girl of eleven in the summer of 1776, among truths held to be self-evident was that George III was a gracious King whom God could be confidently relied upon to save.

The King was a fond, sometimes even a doting, father; but he would not have his children idle or mollycoddled. A strict régime of behaviour and study was prescribed for them, by himself for the Princes and by the Queen for the Princesses. 'The Queen saw her children bathed at six every morning, attended the schoolroom of her daughters, was present at their dinner, and directed their attire whenever not publicly engaged.'[21] The boys were to be up at six, whether at Kew or Buckingham House, and ready for lessons at seven. Until 1776, the elder Princes had as preceptor the Bishop of Chester, Dr Markham who, however, came to be regarded as too indulgent, and the King told Lord North that the boys 'would secretly feel a kind of victory' if Markham were allowed to stay on. Of the three older boys it was only the lively, industrious, and affectionate Frederick whose progress and conduct satisfied expectations; from the beginning things never went right between father and eldest son. The Prince of Wales did not apply himself to his work, the King complained to Lord Holdernesse, the Prince's Governor; moreover he showed 'duplicity' and had a 'bad habit . . . of not speaking the truth'. And it appeared that Prince William too was untruthful as well as wild and full of 'levity'. According to Walpole, the boys 'ridiculed Holdernesse to his face'. For whatever reason, he resigned in 1776, and the King took this opportunity of removing Dr Markham – and consoling him by elevation to the Archbishopric of York. His place as preceptor was taken by one of George's most trusted and respected divines, Dr Hurd, afterwards

Bishop of Worcester. Under his royally approved régime, the boys' programme of schooling ran from seven in the morning until three in the afternoon. It comprised religion and morals; history, government and laws; Latin; mathematics; natural philosophy or the 'liberal sciences'; French, German, Italian; and 'polite literature' – with the pursuit of such extra accomplishments as fencing, landscape-drawing, and music. 'Indeed my good Lord,' wrote the King to Dr Hurd, 'we live in unprincipled days, and no change can be expected but by an early attention to the rising generation.'[22]

Not surprisingly, however, other influences were at work with the Princes besides their father and their governors and preceptors. High-spirited boys would not remain content with the plain bread and butter of Dr Hurd's instruction and the thin soup of the amusements pater-nally approved for them – visits, suitably accompanied, to the theatre and to concerts; horse-riding with the equerries; hunting with the King; the Queen's card parties; afternoon calls upon Mrs Delany or others of those whom the Prince of Wales referred to as 'our old tabbies'; birthday parties for one of the brothers or sisters, like that in 1779 for the Princess Royal when, so Mrs Delany wrote,

> the King carried about in his arms by turns Princess Sophia and the last prince, Octavius. I never saw more lovely children, nor a more pleasing sight than the King's fondness for them, and the Queen's; for they seem to have but one mind, and that is to make everything easy and happy about them.

It was very pleasant for Mrs Papendiek at Kew to observe the King and Queen, 'after their early dinner at four o'clock' pursuing their domestic pleasures with 'their family around them, at full liberty, and enjoying themselves with their attendants',[23] or for Mrs Delany to watch the King, that devoted father, playing games on the floor with little Amelia, 'while in the next room is the band of music' playing Handel, or for Mr Gainsborough to be 'all but raving mad with ecstasy in beholding such a constellation of youthful beauty'[24] as was presented by the royal children when he was commissioned to paint them. They were indeed a more than ordinarily handsome brood, as Gainsborough's portraits themselves attest; and even allowing for the elements of feminine rhapsody in the panegyric of the 'old tabbies' it is true that much of the royal domestic scene at Kew in the seventies and at Windsor in the early eighties was calm and sunny – and seems the more so in the knowledge of the resentments and animosities to come.

These were days long before any hint of estrangement between

King and Queen. Most of the family were still too young for serious troubles; and whatever one or two of the elder Princes were beginning to feel about their father, all six of the Princesses grew up united in affection for him. So indeed they always remained; the depth and persistence of their love is all the more striking since he and the Queen between them, because of the shortage of prospective sons-in-law, turned Windsor for the Princesses into a sort of 'Nunnery'.* There were, it is true, muted protests against the stiffness of some of the royal requirements – all that 'terracing' at Windsor, for instance, being forced to show themselves to dutiful subjects with their parents on Sunday evenings (Princess Augusta was complaining of that at the age of twelve); or during the nineties, the Weymouth routines of sea-bathing and promenading, which meant being up with the lark and Father at five or six in the morning. But their passionate devotion to him through thick and thin was remarkable. 'My father,' wrote Princess Elizabeth, 'was the finest, purest, and most perfect of all characters. He was a man after God's own heart.'[25] Charlotte, the Princess Royal, described him in 1786 as 'the best of Kings and of fathers', and five years later again, 'It would do your heart as much good as it does mine to see how well our dearest father looks, to see him come home from a late day at St James's or a long hunt the least fatigued of the party, and always so good-humoured and cheerful.'[26]

By contrast, however, the King's relations with his sons, once they had passed childhood, were never easy, and with the eldest and hence, politically, most important of them they hardened into an ugly hostility. Of all objects in this life, he once wrote to the Prince of Wales, 'the one I have most at heart is to form my children that they may be useful examples and worthy of imitation.' But neither George's well-intentioned firmness nor the ministrations of Dr Hurd and his assistants and successors had any success in keeping the boys from the frivolities and vices common among young men of fashion. As Mrs Papendiek demurely lamented, 'Some about the young Prince swerved from principle, and introduced improper company when their Majesties supposed them to be at rest, and after the divines had closed the day with prayer.'[27] Already before he was seventeen the romantic and handsome Prince of Wales was self-confessed as 'rather too fond of wine and women'; he was certainly lavish with protestations of his unquenchable affection, though the objects of it changed with confusing rapidity. Among the first was Mary Robinson, who was playing under Garrick at Drury Lane, and who used for a time to be conducted with

* This was in fact the wry and rather forlorn description of the place with which they sometimes headed their intimate letters.

Frederick, Prince of Wales, with three of his sisters
(in the Dutch House at Kew).
(*Philippe Mercier*)

Augusta, Princess of Wales.
(*Charles Philips*)

Queen Charlotte in 1761.
(*The studio of Allan Ramsay*)

3rd Earl of Bute.
(*Sir Joshua Reynolds*)

Buckingham House.
(*William Westall*)

Kew House.
(*William Woollett*)

William Pitt the younger.
(*James Gillray*)

George Grenville.
(*After Reynolds*)

John Wilkes.
(*Richard Earlom*)

George the Third.
(*Thomas Gainsborough*)

Children of George III at Windsor in 1779.
(*Benjamin West*)

Lord Thurlow.
(*Thomas Phillips*)

Henry Dundas, 1st Viscount Melville.
(*Sir Thomas Lawrence*)

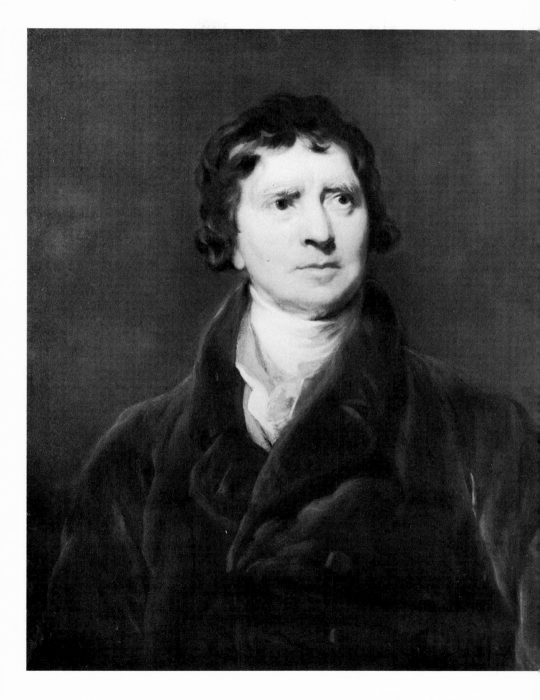

Henry Fox, 1st Lord Holland. (*Sir Joshua Reynolds*)

William Pitt, 1st Earl of Chatham. (*The studio of Richard Brompton*)

1st Duke of Newcastle. (*William Hoare*)

William, 1st Lord Grenville. (*John Hoppner*)

3rd Duke of Grafton. (*Pompeio Battoni*)

2nd Marquis of Rockingham. (*Sir Joshua Reynolds*)

Lord George Germain, 1st Viscount Sackville. (*George Romney*)

4th Earl of Sandwich. (*John Zoffany*)

Carlo Khan's triumphal Entry into Leadenhall Street.

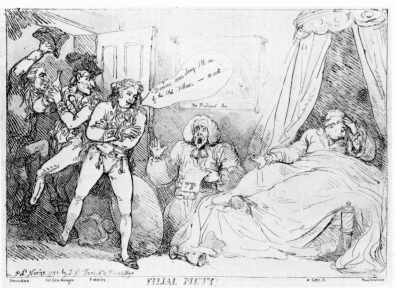

FILIAL PIETY.

Lord North.
(*George Dance*)

SAYERS CARTOON OF DECEMBER, 1783: Burke
blows the trumpet, and leads the elephant (North)
which bears the swollen potentate Fox to his triumph
over the East India Company.

ROWLANDSON CARTOON, 1788: The Prince of
Wales, in his cups, with his friends Colonel Hanger
and Sheridan, breaks into the King's bedroom, inter-
rupting the bishop praying for his recovery.

Queen Charlotte in 1790.
(*Sir Thomas Lawrence*)

Princesses Charlotte, Augusta and Elizabeth,
the three eldest daughters of George III.
(*Thomas Gainsborough*)

THE HOUSE OF COMMONS: Addington is in the Speaker's chair
to the right of the column nearest the window, with Can[...]
Speaker. (*Karl Anton Hickel*)

ssing the House. Wilberforce is in the second row behind him, slightly
ft. Fox (wearing hat) is on the opposition front bench, fourth from the

Charles James Fox.
(*Karl Anton Hickel*)

George, Prince of Wales, in 1807.
(*John Hoppner*)

George the Third, in Windsor uniform, 1807.
(*Peter Stroehling*)

the connivance of some of the Prince's entourage 'from the ait at Kew through the garden gate at the back of the house to the Prince of Wales's apartments'.[28] Mrs Robinson – 'Perdita' from her rôle in *A Winter's Tale* – was flooded with passionate love letters from her seventeen-year-old slave, and not only did she prudently keep them, but further managed to extract a promissory note for £20,000 payable on the Prince's attaining his legal majority and his own establishment. The King, learning of the existence of 'a multitude of letters' concerning the 'very improper connexion', agreed through Lieut.-Col. Hotham, the Prince's sub-Governor and later Secretary and Treasurer, to pay out £5,000 to get them back, and thought that that had ended the affair. What he did not know was that the annulling of the promissory note, eventually negotiated by Charles Fox, cost further annuities for life of £600 for 'Perdita' and £200 for her daughter.

As late as May, 1778, when the Prince of Wales was approaching sixteen and Prince Frederick fifteen, the King was still writing to them both in terms of earnest love:

> My dear sons, place ever your chief care on obeying the commands of your Creator. Every hour will shew you that no comfort can be attained without that. Act uprightly and shew the anxious care I have had of you has not been misspent, and you will ever find me not only an affectionate father but a sincere friend. May Heaven shower the choicest blessings on you both and on the rest of my children . . .[29]

Frederick did retain that love and his father's trust. But the antics and escapades of the Prince of Wales, his disregard of religious observance, his failure to make progress in his studies, his drinking, gambling, and 'love of dissipation' which had 'for some months been with enough ill nature trumpeted in the public papers'[30] were enough to dig a pit between father and son that only widened as the years passed. They were, of course, temperamentally incompatible – the King sober, orderly, pious, strict with himself and with others; the Prince, as his sister Elizabeth once put it, 'always in a dazzle'; impulsive, sensitive, unreliable, and as prodigal with his emotions as with his own and other people's money, yet generous-hearted and much loved – not only by that 'certain sort of ladies' which his chief equerry begged him to avoid corresponding with.[31] Almost every other member of his family except the King himself felt the spell of his charm and acknowledged his kindness and consideration. George's bewilderment at his heir's irresponsibility had at first an air of pathos:

The numberless trials and constant torments I meet with in public life must certainly affect any man, and more poignantly me, as I have no other wish but to fulfill my various duties . . . I have no reason to expect any diminution of my public anxiety. Where am I therefore to turn for comfort but into the bosom of my family?

This was written in August, 1780, in the middle of the struggle in America; with Britain at war too with France, Holland, and Spain; with crisis in Ireland and the Whigs hammering away at the King's government in debate after debate; with demands for parliamentary reform being taken up like beacon fires from county to county. The King was still appealing at that time to his son's 'own good sense'. 'God has bequeathed to you enough quickness of conception, when ever you will allow yourself calmly to reflect that . . . everyone in this world has his peculiar duties to perform . . . Believe me, I wish to make you happy . . .'[32]

However, the continuing manner of the Prince's behaviour, and the added menace of his association with the King's principal *bêtes noires*, from his brother of Cumberland to the leaders of the Whig opposition, soon increased the asperity of the royal admonitions. The Prince was now eighteen and of age, but he was not yet to be trusted with any but the most modest establishment of his own. He was to live at Buckingham House, under the parental eye. He was required to attend church on Sundays, and the St James's Levees and Drawing Rooms. When he went to plays or operas, it must be accompanied by his 'regular attendants'. He might attend balls or assemblies with the prior consent of either parent, but none at private houses, nor any masquerades ('you already know my disapprobation of them'). 'When I ride out in the morning I shall expect you to accompany me. On other days I shall not object to your doing it also, provided it is for exercise, not lounging about Hyde Park. Whenever you ride out or go in a carriage, one of your attendants must accompany you . . .' When towards the conclusion of so restrictive a set of instructions the Prince read, 'Be but open with me and you will ever find me desirous of making you as happy as I can,'[33] he might well have been allowed an exasperated smile. The regulations proved of course unenforceable, and the following three years were the most reckless and impassioned of the Prince of Wales's life.

One consequence was that Prince Frederick, bound closely to him by a common upbringing, was in 1781 sent away to Germany to be segregated from his brother's influence, and simultaneously to learn the trade of war. The third son, William, had already been at sea from the age of thirteen, and seen action in the siege of Gibraltar. Frederick was undoubtedly the favourite among George's elder sons, as Adolphus was to be among the younger; and from Hanover, at a conveniently neutral distance, he tried to avoid taking sides in the battle between his father and brother, and to do what he could to persuade the Prince of Wales to be reasonable. In this there is evidence that he was prompted by the King, who at the same time tried to use him to help separate the Prince of Wales from the company of the Duke of Cumberland.[34] 'Let me entreat you,' wrote Frederick, 'to do everything possible to set all right again as it only plagues both of you without answering the least end in the world' (Hanover, October, 1781); and two months later,

> For God's sake do everything which you can to keep well with him, at least upon decent terms; consider he is vexed enough in publick affairs. He may possibly be cross, but still it is your business not to take that too high. You know, my dearest brother, I hate *preaching* full as much as you do, but . . . I know you will excuse what I write because it comes from the heart.[35]

The preaching had predictably small effect, and in his replies the Prince continued to complain of the constraints to which he was subjected, while throwing out occasional discreet references ('I dare not express myself so openly in a letter') to the ways in which he was flouting them. In one respect the King had scored a small victory. Not only did the Prince of Wales hunt, as directed, twice a week with the King at Windsor; he positively enjoyed it – and indeed hunted on two other days in the week too, with the Duke of Cumberland, which must have pleased the King less. However, the Prince was writing to Frederick in October, 1781:

> I am sorry to tell you that the unkind behaviour of both their Majesties, but in particular of the Queen, is such that it is hardly bearable. She and I, under the protestations of the greatest friendship, had a long conversation together. She accused me of various high crimes and misdemeanours, all wh. I answered, and in the vulgar English phraze gave her as good as she brought. She spoke to me, she said, entirely without the King's knowledge. Now I am thoroughly convinced from the language she used and the style she spoke in she must previously have talked the subject over with the King, who wanted to try whether I could be intimidated or not, but when she found I was not so easily to be intimidated she was silent; after having tried various topicks in order to vex me . . . she

at last began talking about us both, and abused you monstrously, as
well as me . . .[36]

Frederick might perhaps be abused sometimes by the Queen, but
never by the King. Although he too was not slow to further the habits
of self-indulgence he had begun to acquire in England – Frederick's
capacity for wine and women, and his passion for gambling, were
hardly less than his brother's – nevertheless he was always being held
up by the King as a model to his other errant sons. The future William
IV, for instance, was seldom out of trouble. At the age of thirteen, as
Midshipman 'William Guelph', he had been accompanied afloat by
the young Rev. Henry Majendie, a future Bishop of Bangor. The restraining clerical hand, however, could not have been altogether
effective, for when in 1782 Prince William was transferred to the
Barfleur, his father took the precaution of writing to Rear-Admiral
Hood, requesting him to keep a specially strict eye on the Prince, who
was 'ever violent when controlled' and still insufficiently 'conscious of
his own levity'. Hood himself witnessed to William's 'volatile turn of
mind and his great flow of spirits'. A sojourn in Hanover merely increased his reputation, saddening to his father, for boisterousness,
extravagance, and dissipation. Frederick, more and more trusted *in
loco parentis* by the King, himself considered that his younger brother
was 'so excessively rough and rude that there is no bearing of it'.[37] In
reply to a direct query from the King, Frederick reported the following
year that William was 'rather improved with regard to swearing, but
unluckily he has taken an idea into his head that it does not signify in
what manner he behaves here'.[38] There followed, by the quarterly
messenger to Hanover, two kingly reprimands very typical of George
III's heavy manner: 'I cannot too strongly set before your eyes that if
you set yourself to indulge every foolish idea you must be wretched all
your life, for with thirteen children I can but with the greatest care
make both ends meet and am not in a situation to be paying their
debts.' He belaboured William for lacking common honesty, gentlemanly delicacy, civility and propriety – all those qualities that Frederick
was given out as possessing to so admirable a degree. William had persisted, the King wrote, 'in doing what you know would displease me,
and then thinking to get off like a child by saying you will not do the
like again. It is by a proper conduct, not by vague words that my
opinion of you is to be regained. You have in Frederick an excellent
example; follow it . . .' A return to naval discipline was thought desirable: 'When you return to sea you must be the Prince, the gentleman,
and the officer, which requires ideas I fear as yet you have not turned

your mind to.'[39] William, though 'most extremely hurt', was not disposed to take his father's lecturing too tragically, but he besought his eldest brother to 'speak to the Queen, for you know well we two are our mother's favourites'.[40] If this were indeed so, it had not prevented Charlotte reinforcing the King's earlier strictures, for in August, 1784, William wrote to the Prince of Wales, 'I yesterday morning received a set-down from the two persons that were concerned in begetting me. The female was more severe than the male' – and then, rather fatuously, 'I do not mention names for fear the letter should be opened.'[41]

Frederick did at least profit professionally from his stay in Hanover, and from his visits to the Courts and armies of Prussia and Austria. Like a dutiful son he sent his father long accounts of his doings, of the manœuvres, of the impressive Prussian training and discipline, of the political chitchat from Vienna and the dangerous ambitions of the Emperor Joseph II, of the relative merits of Göttingen and Luneburg for the education of Prince Edward, in his turn to be sent abroad and if possible to be preserved from moral corruption. Nevertheless, after some years he longed to be allowed to return home, and directly requested permission. George would not have it. Frederick must stay, and thus at least be kept at a safe distance from the Prince of Wales. As for Prince William, he frankly loathed Hanover. 'England, England for ever,' he shouted, 'and the pretty girls of Westminster.'[42] But when he was returned to the Navy, it was with one of the pretty girls of Portsmouth that he soon became more particularly involved. The naval commissioner there, one Henry Martin, had 'two daughters about my own age: we dance and amuse ourselves vastly well'. Indeed, Lieutenant Prince William of the *Hebe* developed so peremptory a passion for Sally Martin* that he was soon proposing marriage. He rushed to Windsor in an attempt to gain his parents' consent to the match, to be met first by an unsympathetic mother, and then by a father who lost no time in finding it 'indispensably necessary to remove him from the Commissioner's House at Portsmouth', and dispatching him first to Plymouth, and then across the Atlantic.

William ruminated glumly on the misfortune of being born a 'royal' and on the unreasonableness of parents: 'During the bloom of youth I am not allowed to enjoy myself like any other person of my age.' The Queen had given him some rare dressings-down, but at least, he judged, she was 'a tender mother and wished to keep peace among the chosen ones of Israel; I wish I could say as much for our worthy friend our near relation. What can be the use of his keeping us so close?

---

* Sarah Catherine Martin; she was destined to achieve a sort of anonymous immortality as the author of *Old Mother Hubbard*.

Does he imagine he will make his sons his friends by this mode of conduct?'[43] For two years William sweated it out in the West Indies, sometimes ill, contracting venereal disease,[44] often in the midst of complicated disciplinary squabbles, yet claiming that he 'gloried in the service'; running up debts; and complaining that he found his father's conduct 'inexplicable. It is near two years since I last saw him and I have on certain points asked his advice, but he never honours me with an answer . . .'[45] William's plaints were not done with, and there were vicissitudes to come. Returning to Plymouth, he was left in no doubt of his father's displeasure for having disobeyed the commands of a superior officer, but was pointedly visited and made much of by both his elder brothers (Frederick having at last been permitted by then to return from Germany). Predictably, William's amorous susceptibilities soon led him again into deep water. Now it was Sally Winne, a Plymouth merchant's daughter, so that a second time he was peremptorily posted abroad, which, so he wrote to his father from Nova Scotia, he took 'very hard'. He lived in 'hourly expectation of a thunderstorm' from his father, so he wrote to the Prince of Wales in February, 1788. 'Fatherly admonitions at our time of life are very unpleasant and of no use; it is a pity he should expend his breath or his time in such fruitless labour. I wonder which of us two he looks on with the least eyes of affection?'[46]

The King, who had once threateningly reminded young Prince William that of course, none of his Hanoverian scrapes would go unreported at St James's, seems by contrast to have been determined to hear nothing but good of his second son, Frederick. Certainly Frederick played his cards better than his brothers George or William, and on the whole had a superior talent for keeping his vices rather more private. These were nevertheless not inconsiderable, though it was not until after his realisation of Frederick's 'betrayal' during the crisis of 1788-89, that the King seemed to be aware of them. Until that time, being himself treated with much affection, Frederick found it not difficult to reciprocate. He was always careful to tell his father what he wanted to hear and to praise him from afar for his 'firmness and resolution' in dealing with those who wished to overturn the Constitution and 'render the Crown and Peers mere syphers'.[47] Already by 1784, he had been created Duke of York. Despite bouts of severe ill health he pursued his military studies with application, and when he was at last allowed to return home in 1787, he was still seen as brightly *en rose* by his father as Fanny Burney saw the pair of them, father and son:

I saw him alight from his carriage with an eagerness, a vivacity that assured me of the affectionate joy with which he returned to his country and family. But the joy of his excellent father! – Oh that there is no describing . . . It was indeed an affecting sight to view the general content, but that of the King went to my very heart, so delighted he looked – so proud of his son – so benevolently pleased that everyone should witness his satisfaction.[48]

Sir Gilbert Elliot saw the Duke of York with a difference: 'He is well-looking in point of feature . . . but has not an engaging countenance like the Prince of Wales, and he looks much more blackguard, dissolute and foolish than him.'[49] His losses at the faro table were soon rivalling those of Charles Fox and the Duchess of Devonshire;[50] neither did he neglect racehorses and women. Politically and socially he was soon to throw in his lot, temporarily at least, with the Prince of Wales against his father, and his behaviour during the King's coming breakdown was hardly to reward or justify all the paternal pride and benevolence of the preceding years.

Nine months after the Prince of Wales's eighteenth birthday, the King had written to him, 'I wish to live with you as a friend, but then by your behaviour you must deserve it.' There seemed little evidence that the Prince was making any great effort. He cut Levees to go hunting with Colonel St Leger. He neglected religious observance. He hob-nobbed with the Cumberlands, enjoyed masquerades, heavy drinking,* high play at the card-table, and every kind of fashionable, racy, and it should be added artistic and musical company. If among his friends were some notorious rakes and leading enemies of the King's government, so much the worse for the King. Among women, he flew from 'Perdita' Robinson to the wife of a Hanoverian diplomat, Madame Hardenberg. She, as he recounted the story in detail to Frederick, seduced him (an unreluctant victim) and soon had him so in thrall that he vowed he would sacrifice every earthly thing for her. 'Dearest brother, my heart is ready to burst.' He had already fainted confessing the whole truth to the Queen. 'Whether she [the Queen] was quite true to me I cannot say'; but of course the King soon knew of the scandal

* The Duchess of Devonshire was sure that it was drinking that caused his ill health; it certainly cannot have improved it. However, he suffered from the age of twenty, write Drs Macalpine and Hunter, from 'spasms in the chest, abdominal colic, pain and weakness in his limbs, insomnia, fast pulse, lowness of spirits, states of excitement and "shattered nerves",' and they quote Wraxall's assertion that he had been blooded over a hundred times before the age of thirty. These authors are in no doubt that the Prince had porphyria. He was certainly a sick man for much of his adult life.

and promptly expelled Hardenberg, 'who went off with my little angel
to Bruxelles' – which wrote finis to that particular episode except for
von Hardenberg, who was obliged on account of it to quit the Hanoverian service.* Frederick consoled his brother with an account of the
little angel's promiscuity, and more particularly of her earlier advances
to *him*. ('As for me, I desired no better fun, but unluckily the room was
full.') All in all, the Prince of Wales soon concluded 'il ne faut pas se
laisser mourrir de douleur'.[51] Instead he took up with Lady Melbourne.
'I have no gossip to tell you,' wrote Lady Sarah Napier in March, 1783,
with airy malice, 'but that the Prince of Wales is *desperately* in love with
Lady Melbourne . . . She dances with him, somewhat in the cow stile,
but he is *en extase* with admiration of it.'[52] Lady Melbourne's reign did
not last many months; her place had for some time been taken by Mrs
Hodges, until her brother 'said if her husband would not take her out
of town, *he* would, for he did not choose his sister should be talked of
in such a manner'.[53]

Worse than his sexual adventures in the King's eyes, and worse than
his conspicuous flouting of the royal instructions in general, was his
progressively deeper involvement with the King's principal enemies,
who were by that time and to his chagrin once more his ministers. He
bitterly observed that the Fox-North ꞁoalition was his son's ministry
rather than his own.[54] The wild young men of Brooks's Club, whose
brilliant idol was Charles Fox, were 'men who will not accept office
without making me a kind of slave',[55] and Lord North, that apostate,
had delivered him to Fox upon a plate. The King freely admitted
Fox's abilities – who did not? – but he could not but hate the man
whom he considered was at the same time bringing his system of
government to the point of collapse and completing the moral ruin of
his son and heir.

As chance had it, the Fox-North coalition, with the Duke of Portland as its nominal head, came into office a few months before the
Prince of Wales would be reaching his twenty-first birthday, when he
would have to be allowed a fully independent establishment. It was a
moment, with the American colonies finally lost, when George III
might well feel that his reign had been a failure. He was under heavy
stress and, as usual at such times, the effects on his health showed in
an attack of 'flurries'. He was so 'highly excited', said William Grenville, and he spoke with such 'inconceivable quickness' that one
could hardly get in a word of one's own. In this state he momentarily

---

* He prospered nevertheless. As Metternich was imported into the Austrian
service, so Hardenberg into the Prussian, where he rose to the rank of Prince and
the office of Chancellor.

considered abdication, as he had once when oppressed by the elder
Grenville; just before bowing to accept Fox and Portland as ministers
he sat down and wrote to his son of the 'cruel dilemma' he found himself in. It left him

> but one step to take without the destruction of my principles and
> honour; the resigning my Crown, my dear son, to you, quitting this
> my native country for ever and returning to the dominions of my
> forefathers . . . Your difficulties will not be the same . . . Your
> mother, whose excellent qualities appear stronger to me every hour,
> will certainly instantly prepare for joining me with the rest of my
> children . . .[56]

At Brooks's, Horace Walpole reported, 'they proposed wagers on the
duration of the reign.'[57] But there was, of course, no abdication; the
fighting mood returned.

Since the Prince was not on speaking terms with his father, he
approached the matter of his establishment at twenty-one indirectly
through the Queen – not surprisingly, George said, as the Prince's
conscience, 'if not entirely put to sleep, as well as his knowledge of my
sentiments, must have made him expect that on such an occasion I
should have utter'd very homefelt truths.'[58] Briefly, the King now
proposed £50,000 a year for his son, plus £12,000 from the Duchy of
Cornwall; Carlton House to be provided for him; and £29,000 to be
set aside by Parliament to pay his debts. This should give him £27,000 a
year more than the King had had himself when Prince of Wales and
should enable him 'to live handsomely but not with the shameful extravagance he has shewn till now . . . I must hope he will now think it
behoves him to take up a fresh line of conduct more worthy of his
station, that he may regain the good opinion of men of religion,
decency, and worth, and a continuation of levity may not shorten his
days'.[59]

Leading Whig ministers, however, had promised the Prince not
£50,000 but £100,000, and when through the Duke of Portland they
formally repeated an earlier request for this larger sum, the King took
the gloves off. Few prime ministers can have received from their
monarch a communication bristling with such scorn and outrage:

> It is impossible for me to find words expressive enough of my utter
> indignation and astonishment . . . When the Duke of Portland came
> into office I had at least hoped he would have thought himself
> obliged to have my interest and that of the public at heart and not
> have neglected both, to gratify the passions of an ill-advised young

man . . . If the Prince of Wales's Establishment is to fall on me, it is a weight I am unable to bear; if on the public I cannot in conscience give my acquiescence to what I deem a shameful squandering of public money.[60]

And to Lord North:

Believe me, no consideration can make me either forget or forgive what has passed, and the public shall know how well founded the principles of economy are in those who have so loudly preached them up.[61]

George moreover had copies of the correspondence sent to Hanover for the Duke of York to see; and Frederick, true to form, answered with two voices. One, to his father, gave him every support in his struggle against ministers 'who having forced themselves into power against the will of your Majesty have at last thrown off the mask'. The other, to his brother, merely referred to 'little differences and bicker-ings' which he hoped might now be over.[62]

So with his ministerial friends soon to be sent packing over Fox's India Bill, the Prince had to be content with the King's terms. Had he received treble the amount, it seems unlikely that he would have succeeded in living within his income. His debts continued to mount and he went on committing every kind of indiscretion and act hostile to the King. He rushed from taking his seat in the House of Lords to the Commons in order ostentatiously to hear Fox's speech after his dismissal. He did not actually campaign for Fox in the famous West-minster election of 1784 quite as publicly as the Duchess of Devonshire and her fellow-dazzlers, but he openly greeted the victory procession in the courtyard of Carlton House and provided an all-day celebration breakfast in the gardens, during the course of which he fell flat on his face in the middle of a quadrille and 'threw the load from his stomach into the midst of the circle'. All this was despite promises he had made the King that he would discontinue support for the Opposition; but he protested he could not desert Charles and his friends.

One of the closest of these friends was the Duchess of Devonshire herself, First Lady of the Whigs, queen of fashion, and a very empress of disastrous losers at the gaming-table – the lively-minded, weak-willed, warm-hearted Georgiana. But the supreme 'friend' that he could not contemplate deserting was Maria Fitzherbert, a Roman Catholic twice widowed by the age of twenty-four, with whom he had fallen in love all the more distractedly because being a woman of piety and principle she would not become his mistress. She fended him off until July, 1784, when one evening she was called upon by two of the Prince's gentlemen with the panic news that, mad for her love, he had stabbed himself with his sword; that he was threatening to tear off his bandages; that she must come to him immediately. Mrs Fitzherbert agreed under this severe emotional duress to go through some pledge of 'marriage' but, reasonably enough considering it null and void, fled abroad next day.

Undoubtedly this infatuation was of a different order from the Prince's earlier and more temporary involvements. He bombarded Mrs Fitzherbert with a barrage of impassioned letters. For many months she refused to return, knowing that even if the Prince renounced the throne to Frederick as he declared he would (thus getting round the anti-Catholic provisions of the Act of Settlement), still there remained the Royal Marriages Act of 1772. The Prince being under twenty-five, a marriage without his father's consent, even if made in heaven and sanctified by canon law, must remain invalid according to the laws of England.

At first the Prince decided to use the excuse of his disordered finances to go abroad and pursue his wooing to its conclusion there. He accordingly proposed this step to the King as 'a system of economy'. The King may not have known the whole Fitzherbert story at this stage, but he knew enough to penetrate the thin pretext. He wrote to Thurlow at the end of August, seeking legal confirmation of the view that 'the successor to the Crown cannot quit the realm without the permission of the Sovereign'. His son's plan, he informed the Chancellor, was 'to go without any of his gentlemen, accompanied by a French Catholic Officer, having concerted his scheme with the Duke of Chartres, who has found him a credit on Paris; though in the letter Brunswick is mentioned, that is only a blind, the other being the object'. When he saw Thurlow privately, he added, he would mention circumstances that would cause surprise – presumably these related to Mrs Fitzherbert.[63] Rebuffed, the Prince tried again, claiming to be shocked, misunderstood, and in the matter of money required to stint the 'magnificence' proper to an heir-apparent. Three times the King categorically commanded him not to go abroad. It was a project 'replete with mischief and disgrace' and one that the 'machinations of France' would 'know well how to take advantage of'.[64] 'If his improper plan was put into execution his character would be forever blasted in this country, and also in Europe. I therefore insist on his giving up a measure that would be a public breach with me.'[65] That such a public breach *would* be a disaster was acknowledged even in responsible opposition circles. Fox professed that 'no man saw more strongly the mischief of the K. and the Prince of Wales being at daggers drawn; it lower'd the country, lower'd the Royal Family, it gave foreign countrys hopes of seeing this sinking nation further distracted by partys and divisions'.[66]

Still threatening suicide, the Prince of Wales continued to spill oceans of frantic ink in letters to his 'dearest of wives, best and most adored of women'. He cried by the hour, struck his forehead, tore his hair, and generally demonstrated to his friends the intensity of his frustration and passion. At last in December, 1785, he succeeded in persuading Maria to return to London, where, at her house in Park Street in an atmosphere of the tensest conspiracy, he married her before an Anglican priest (paid £500 danger money) and two witnesses from her family. Various versions of the secret were soon flying round London and the King must have heard them. But he preferred simply to ignore Mrs Fitzherbert's existence.

Acrimonious negotiations proceeded for the next year or two concerning the Prince's debts, the proportion of them his father would be willing to pay, and the Prince's ability to cut down expenses in view of what he deemed his 'incompetent' income. The King demanded close and detailed accounts and narrowly scrutinised them, especially those private sums (were they political?) which the Prince refused to particularise, and the lavish projections for the embellishment of Carlton House. When the Prince's friends raised the matter in the Commons in April, 1787, the issue of his marriage at last came into the open. Was he, or was he not married? Fox, relying on the Prince's earlier disclaimer to him personally, flatly denied the marriage rumour as being 'a miserable calumny'; for which Mrs Fitzherbert never forgave him. Members smiled knowingly when Sheridan was put up to qualify the denial in a fog of ambiguous phrases. At last in May, 1787, a debt settlement was reached between Government, Commons, Prince, and King; the House voted £161,000 to pay outstanding monies owed, and another £60,000 for the Carlton House improvements. The King added a further £10,000 a year from the Civil List. 'But his Majesty thinks proper to add,' he wrote – third person to third person as throughout this stiff dispute – 'that while the Prince of Wales remains unmarried, he does not conceive any encrease of income can be necessary to enable him to support an establishment suitable to his rank and station.'[67]

Some sort of reconciliation followed, short-lived as it was to prove, and for a time the Prince of Wales again attended Court. In his letters to his son, the King had often signed himself *Your affectionate Father*, but it must be admitted that the sun of his affection glinted only rarely through the thundercloud of his reproofs. 'What can I do, my dear

Harris?' asked the Prince of the future Earl of Malmesbury one day in 1785. 'The King hates me . . . I have no hopes of him. He won't even let Parliament assist me till I marry . . . He hates me; he always did, from seven years old.' Irresponsibly, hysterically, impossibly as the Prince behaved, the reader of those parental letters may well incline to agree with Malmesbury: when the Prince first failed to convince him, he tried the effect of reading some of the correspondence to him, and Malmesbury had to admit that it was 'void of every expression of parental kindness or affection'. Even Queen Charlotte, who could be severe and never, over these years, failed to present a solid front with the King, managed sometimes to convey a loving warmth, however tinged with regret and remonstrance. But the King – 'Why, my dear Harris, will you force me to repeat to you that *the King hates me*? He will never be reconciled to me.' 'We are too wide asunder ever to meet.'[68]

PART FOUR

DEFEATS
AND A RECOVERY

CHAPTER SIXTEEN

'Blows Must Decide'

LORD NORTH's ministry, vulnerable in its early days, soon began to wear an air of durability, and by the time the Bostonians pitched their unwanted tea into the harbour, North seemed to be emerging as George III's Robert Walpole. Given the master-servant relationship which both assumed could never be forgotten, King and Minister saw current problems in a reassuringly similar light. North was a conservative-minded man of good connections, good parts, and good sense; an easy-going but efficient handler of the King's political and financial affairs; the very reverse of a hothead (with George's strong approval he had resisted the chauvinistic clamour that would have rushed into a war with Spain in a dispute over the Falkland Islands); an unopinionated man and a very tolerable scholar; civilised and likable, with a ready humour and swift ability in debate that belied his pose of studied inattention. His physical presence may have been unprepossessing, with his puffed cheeks and flabby dewlap, receding brow, and prominent heavy-lidded rolling eyes that gave him (in Horace Walpole's phrase) 'the air of a blind trumpeter'; but he was much sharper than he looked. He might have his feet up on the Treasury Bench while Burke or Barré, Savile or Sawbridge, fulminated from the benches opposite; but the command of his eventual reply, or some quietly puncturing interpolation, made him a considerable antagonist. After Grafton's 'desertion' – as the King rather unreasonably never ceased calling it – he undertook the government in what even Horace Walpole, a political enemy, described as 'manly style'. Compared with Grafton, he was 'more able, and more fitted to deal with mankind . . . Not very ambitious . . . not avaricious . . . what he did, he did without a mask'.[1] So judged Walpole, though George III would not in the end have named *resolution* as being North's outstanding quality. However, had North been granted a decade of calm, or even had he died in 1774, he would have gone into the history books as a competent and successful first minister. Even Chatham considered that North served the Crown 'more successfully and more efficiently upon the whole than any other man could be found to do'.

One of his virtues – as earlier of Robert Walpole's – was his skill in gauging the temper of the House of Commons. He took the trouble to understand men's motives and ambitions, strengths and weaknesses, including his own weaknesses, upon which – and increasingly as time progressed – he was never unready to expatiate. When he was hale of body and mind, and affairs were prospering, he was full of busyness and confidence; but when he was unwell – and he was never physically robust – or when he could not see his way through the maze, he was liable to retreat into professions of his own inadequacy. Nevertheless, for three or four years he enjoyed, on the whole, the confidence of the Commons, the King, and a considerable majority of the public. Moreover, as the months progressed, his administration gained important new adherents. On the deaths of George Grenville and the Duke of Bedford, favourable opportunities opened for him to exploit the desire of their followers for place; and among the recruits were men already, or soon to be, of first importance: the rival lawyers Alexander Wedderburn (a Grenvillite) and Edward Thurlow (a Bedford), and the Earl of Sandwich, another Bedford, who came to head the Admiralty at what was to be a critical decade. The Earl of Suffolk, the chief of the Grenvillites, also joined North; and even the Duke of Grafton returned to the ministerial fold.

When another of the older Whig leaders, Lord Halifax (who was North's uncle) lay mortally ill in June, 1771, the King did not wait for his death before intimating to the nephew the chance it would offer him to give tangible evidence of his esteem. Clearly George was more comfortably in accord with this prime minister than with any other since Bute:

> The sincere regard I have for you makes me, though much hurt at the certain loss of so amiable a man as Lord Halifax, yet with much pleasure acquaint you that whenever I shall receive an account of his death, I shall immediately appoint you Ranger of Bushey Park . . . I cannot conclude without assuring you that every opportunity of showing you the sincere regard I have for you is giving me the greatest pleasure.

The following year George's 'sincere regard' was further evinced; the first vacancy occurring among the Knights of the Garter went to North, a rare honour for a commoner. [2]

In the nursing of his Commons majority he had a solicitous ally and coadjutor in the King. 'The very handsome majority this day gives me infinite pleasure,' he would write; or 'I am sorry the House of Commons has yesterday been governed by a false love of popularity instead of reason, but as passion is a short madness, I trust upon matters that particularly regard the business of administration you will find them ever ready to give you the fullest support.'[3] When there was a general election in the late summer and autumn of 1774, George during its protracted progress followed the story of fillips and buffets for the Government with 'entire satisfaction' or indignant choler as the latest advices determined. Wilkes getting 'the upperhand' again in Middlesex gave the King no pleasure at all, though 'the poll for Westminster could not be more favourable'; and in general there was little cause to worry. 'If the plan for managing the election proposed by Mr Robinson be exactly followed it will undoubtedly be crowned with success,' the King wrote on 10th October, and a month later North's lists of prospective pros and cons for the forthcoming session caused George to be 'much pleased'.[4]

John Robinson, Secretary to the Treasury, was to be one of the most influential of royal servants and confidential advisers over a period of nearly twenty years. He was North's patronage secretary and political manager, expert and indefatigable as the Duke of Newcastle himself, the most trusted and discreet of trouble-sorters and wire-pullers. Indeed a brief extract from North's correspondence with him just before and during the 1774 election will give one the flavour of mid-Georgian political management in a nutshell. On 6th October, North was writing to him:

. . . I am heartily sorry that we cannot settle the Welsh dispute. You know that the seat at Plympton is at 3[000]. Lord H[ood] should be informed of that, as he said his son should pay 25[00] but that I leave to your discretion, as well as the whole arrangement and shall make but one or two observations upon it. Mr Legge can afford only 400*l.* If he comes in for Lostwithiel he will cost the public 2000 guineas. I promised Mr Butler that if we could find a seat for Sir Charles Whitworth even before the election, Mr Graves should come in for East Looe.

I think Gascoign should have the refusal of Tregony if he will pay 1000*l.*, but I do not see why we should bring him in cheaper than any other servant of the Crown. If he will not pay that price he must give way to Mr Best, if the latter will pay the money required; if he will not, but offers 2000*l.*, he may come in; but if he refused to pay that sum I would have the seat offered to Mr Peachy . . . The shortness of time will oblige you to take upon yourself to decide most of these smaller matters, and you may be certain that I shall be satisfied with your decisions.[5]

By the time the King's Government and Lord North were confirmed in power for a further statutory term of seven years, the danger that the long-simmering American discontents would boil over had already become apparent. The Townshend duties of 1767; the continuance of the tea tax after the other duties had been repealed; repeated instances of friction between state assemblies and royal governors, those agents of George III's prerogative; the posting of troops in Boston without the consent of the Massachusetts assembly and the bloodshed that followed; the intensive propaganda of the colonial extremists; the uncompromising insistence of the home government and colonial governors on their full constitutional rights and on the paramount demands of defence; the growing disregard by the Americans of the laws of trade and navigation, and the consequent running war with the revenue officers; above all the psychological chasm that was widening all the time between, on the one side, those Englishmen like the King himself who habitually spoke of 'the mother country' and implied 'parental' rights, and on the other, three thousand slow miles and an ocean of misunderstanding away, those two or three millions of Americans who expected recognition of their full civic adulthood, even if independent sovereignty was as yet the demand of a radical minority only.

In May, 1773, North's government attempted to kill two birds with one stone by a Tea Act which incorporated a simple but ingenious scheme for assisting the disordered finances of the East India Company and simultaneously undermining the illegal American tea imports from Holland and her West Indian entrepôt of St Eustatius. (There were Portuguese and other sources too.) The Company was to be allowed to export its large tea surpluses for the first time directly to America and sell there through its own agencies, being excused the shilling English customs duty while still paying the threepenny Townshend tax. Thus the right of taxation from Westminster would be maintained while the already cheap smuggled tea would be undercut. Unfortunately for British plans, this attractive-looking move underestimated the lengths to which American radicals would go to defend their principles, or American importers to protect their vested interests; and its consequence was that the merchant community was thrown into the arms of Boston extremists, and the tea into Boston harbour.

News of the Boston Tea Party reached London at the end of January, 1774. Its effect was immediately to harden opinion against the Americans. In the country at large there were very few, and in the Cabinet only two members, Bathurst and Dartmouth (North's half-brother), who did not give full support to measures for punishing the violent insubordination of the Bostonians. The King as usual stood with the majority. He interviewed General Gage, who had seen long service in America, had married an American, and was deemed to be one who knew what he was talking about. He proved to be one of the many bad advisers – 'local experts' and others – who told the King merely what he wanted to hear. Gage's language, said George,

> was very consonant to his character as an honest determined man; he says they will be lyons whilst we are lambs but if we take the resolute part they will be very meek . . . I wish you [North] would see him and hear his ideas of compelling Boston to submit to whatever may be thought necessary . . .[6]

What was thought immediately necessary was a statute which closed the port of Boston until such time as recompense was paid to the East India Company, and transferred the seat of government to Salem. This act raced through Parliament with few voices raised against it. 'The feebleness and futility of the opposition,' George considered, showed 'the rectitude of the measure,' and when ex-Governor Hutchinson, hot from Massachusetts, saw him privately in July, he easily convinced him – another 'expert' judgment – that 'they will soon submit . . . the people of Boston seem much dispirited'.[7] Further punitive acts affecting Massachusetts as a whole did receive stronger criticism from both Rockinghams and Chathamites, but passed easily enough. The powers of the provincial governor were reinforced and those of the assembly reduced. Town meetings were placed under restraint; billeting accommodation was to be provided for further troops; and many further curtailments were made in the rights under charter of the citizens of Massachusetts. None of these restricting measures was the work, as American radicals believed, of an unpopular home government serving a tyrannical royal master. Justified or unjustified, wise or unwise, they were strongly backed by such British public opinion as took any interest. Even Burke, the most imaginative and far-sighted of their opponents, was obliged to admit to the New York assembly that 'the popular current, both within doors and without, at present sets strongly against America'.[8] And North's Quebec Act, which followed, and came to be regarded by New Englanders as one more kick in the teeth, was neither intended as such nor in fact conceived in relation to the Massachusetts troubles at all. It was on the contrary an act of sound and liberal statesmanship for which both Lord North and General Carleton (later Governor of Quebec and first Governor of Canada) deserve some credit, and which the domination of French, Catholic Quebec by Protestant Britain had ever since 1763 cried out for. Since, however, Puritan New England chose to see it in a purely hostile light, as a slamming of the door against their future westward expansion,* a sop to Catholics and Indians, and an attempt to set up a disciplined autocracy to the north-west of them – the old French threat, with George III now taking the place of Louis XV – it came by the Americans to be included among the Coercive (or 'Intolerable') Acts of 1774.

Whig opposition to all these measures except the Boston Port Bill incensed the King. His views were simple, consistent, straightforward, and uncomprehending. 'Perhaps no one period of our history,' he wrote,[9] 'can produce so strange a circumstance as the gentlemen who pretend to be patriots, instead of acting agreable to such sentiments avowing the unnatural doctrine of encouraging the American colonies in their disputes with their mother country.' Numbered among these 'patriots' now was a formidable recruit, Charles James Fox. In February, Fox, in violent language, had held North to a promise to vote for the imprisonment of the journalist Woodfall for a libellous attack on Speaker Norton ('Sir Bull-face Double-fee'). North was obliged to march into the 'wrong' lobby. Fox continued to embarrass the Government by his rogue elephant behaviour, and soon North laconically dismissed him from his place on the Treasury Board: 'His Majesty has thought proper,' he wrote to him, 'to order a new Commission of the Treasury to be made out, in which I do not see your name.' Fox's presumption had greatly incensed the King, who told North, 'That young man has so thoroughly cast off every principle of common honour and honesty that he must become as contemptible as he is odious.'[10] It was a judgment he was never, until the very last few months of Fox's life, to vary.

Obsolete paternalism was at the heart of British errors of approach to the colonial problem. The 'mother country' – an expression which appears monotonously in George's observations on America, and perhaps one should write rather of 'maternalism' – was not with him merely a figure of speech. That is how he thought, and that was how most Englishmen thought: 'the just superiority of the mother country.' 'When [the Americans] are quiet and have respect for their mother country,' said North, 'the mother country will be good-natured to them.' The defenders of American actions spoke in no less parental tones; Chatham constantly so; Rockingham wrote that he 'would always consider that this country, as a parent, ought to be tender and

---

* Certainly the provisions relating to the Western territories, though specifically made temporary only, dimmed some lively prospects. Patrick Henry and George Washington, for instance, were only two Virginians among many who saw the value of their shares in the Pioneering Vandalia Company fall nearly to zero.

just; and that the colonies, as children, ought to be dutiful.'[11] To men of the calibre of Benjamin Franklin or John Adams such language was as ludicrous as it was offensive. What they made of Samuel Johnson's sort of attitude is not difficult to imagine: 'They are a race of convicts,' said that exasperated Tory, 'and ought to be content with anything we may allow them short of hanging.'

Gage was now sent back to America to combine the functions of commander-in-chief and Governor of Massachusetts, but on arrival he found a temper there which convinced him that with the number of troops at his command he would be unable to maintain order, still less enforce such law as the Coercive Acts had now introduced. It was 'an army of impotence' that Gage commanded, said Chatham, who was foremost among those pressing for its withdrawal and by his every speech storing up more royal resentment against him. The matter in America had now gone far beyond a mere boycott of British goods. There was widespread training of potential rebels. Arms were coming in from Holland and other European sources. A provincial congress was held in defiance of Gage's ban. And where Massachusetts led, Virginia and other states were following. Chatham likened the mood to 'the same spirit which called all England on its legs' against Charles I. It was not of course all England in 1641; neither was it all America in 1774; but it was enough. 'We shall be forced ultimately to retract,' said Chatham. 'Let us retract while we can, not when we must.' He would 'consent to be taken for an idiot' if the Coercive Acts were not in the end repealed. George did not take him for an idiot, but he did for 'a trumpet of sedition', and when in 1775 'the very bad situation of Lord Chatham's health and the great probability of his living but a little while longer' caused North to suggest raising the amount of his pension, the King replied that although on Chatham's death he would make the larger sum payable to 'the second son' (young William Pitt), Chatham's own political conduct during 1774-75 had been so 'abandoned' that it would be absurd for him to expect gratitude: 'I should chuse to know him totally unable to appear on the public stage before I agree to any offer of that kind, lest it should be wrongly construed a fear of him.'[12]

It was easy for Chatham to exercise his rhetoric on the folly and injustice that had driven the Americans to violence, but it is difficult to believe that, standing firmly as he did upon the necessity for maintaining laws to regulate trade and navigation and upon the paramount importance of defence, he would have made a much better fist of conciliation than Lord North. North's own mind was by no means closed against negotiation. Indeed one of the severest criticisms of his policy over the next year or two is that he simultaneously pursued mutually stultifying strategies of conciliation and punishment, peace and war. He certainly knew as well as Burke or Chatham that any prospect of raising effectual taxes in America was dead, and told the King so, though George still hankered after keeping the tea tax as a point of principle. He was not so blind that he failed to see that conciliatory gestures must come; but he was adamant that a successful assertion of authority must precede them. 'I do not wish to come to severer measures,' he wrote, 'but we must not retreat'; and on the whole, whatever the misgivings of some of the Cabinet, Lord Dartmouth in particular and North to some extent, ministers were with him on that issue. Once the coercive measures were passed, the King insisted,

> the dye is now cast, the Colonies must either submit or triumph . . . by coolness and an unremitted pursuit of the measures that have been adopted I trust they will come to submit; I have no objection afterwards to their seeing that there is no inclination for the present to lay fresh taxes on them . . .[13]

General Gage interviewed in the Closet was one thing; General Gage practically a prisoner with his troops in Boston quite another. He was now actually advocating a suspension of the Coercive Acts – an idea George declared to be 'absurd'. It would merely show the Bostonians that violence paid and that the British were scared. 'We must either master them,' he said, 'or totally leave them to themselves and treat them as aliens.' In this he may have been strictly correct; it may be that already it was too late for half-measures. He certainly did not like to think of North toying with ideas of negotiation. As for 'sending commissioners to examine into the disputes, this looks so like the mother country being more afraid of the continuance of the dispute than the Colonies and I cannot think it likely to make them reasonable'. He had no wish to drive them to despair, he said – he claimed to be 'a thorough friend to holding out the olive branch' – but a proper subordination must come first, and he therefore approved North's proposals for economic sanctions.[14]

Meanwhile in September, 1774, while Britain was electing its new Parliament, representatives of all the colonies except Georgia were meeting at Philadelphia to pledge support for Massachusetts and demand repeal of the Coercive Acts, in which they included the Quebec Act. From that time, as local associations and congresses began effectively to take over the powers of government, officers of the Crown grew more and more helpless. Revolutionary committees were widely established; guns and gunpowder were imported, manufactured, or stolen, while local volunteer armies organised themselves and began training. Loyalists among the colonials, though hardly less in numbers than the revolutionaries, naturally lacked their activism and enthusiasm – and where they did not, they were frequently set upon and victimised. By the end of 1774, unless either the British Government or the colonial leaders capitulated, the chance of avoiding a full-scale conflict looked slender, and to the King non-existent. He was 'sorry that the line of conduct now seems chalked out . . . The New England governments are in a state of rebellion, blows must decide whether they are to be subject to this country or independant'.[15]

Once war was seen to be unavoidable, many problems occupied anxious hours – how to muster sufficient troops, how to deploy them economically, how to ensure the readiness of the Navy. Urgent communications and painstaking memoranda in the royal handwriting proffer or summarise plans and advice concerning 'the proposed regts of infantry', lists of 'generals for the American campaign', which officers would be 'proper' for what tasks, what precedents unadvisable; 'effective strength of the infantry', 'artillery in North America', 'organisation of the army in America', 'foreign garrisons and reliefs, 1764-1775'. There was Gage's view of his likely needs to be considered – not less than 32,000 men, to include 'good irregulars such as hunters, Canadians, Indians, etc.'. (Major General Burgoyne was soon supplying an ancillary suggestion: 'supplies of arms for the Blacks to awe, in conjunction with regulars, the southern provinces.') Amherst ought to be consulted 'as to the quantity of artillery demanded for the detached war in New Yorke'. The King was not one to sit back and allow his politicians and generals to conduct the war on their own – or at least not without liberally proffered advice. He complained in August, 1775, that some of this had been rejected by the Cabinet. Had his suggestions been adopted 'the Army would have been at least 2 or 3000 men stronger at this hour'. There was also the serious problem of enlisting foreign forces, imperatively required in view of the small and scattered nature of the British army, 48,000 in all, one quarter of them in Ireland. The mercenaries would have to be mainly German, but an attempt was made during 1775 to hire Russians – which Empress Catherine rebuffed, 'and not in so genteel a manner as I should have thought might be expected. She has not had the civility to answer in her own hand and has thrown out some expressions that may be civil to a Russian but certainly not to more civilised ones.' As Elector of Hanover, George was not unnaturally foremost in supplying the King of England with men – five battalions for Minorca and Gibraltar to set free the British troops there for American service; and for this he claimed from the Treasury 'nothing but to be reimbursed all expenses', not failing to point out to Lord North that 'by these conditions Great Britain obtains a corps of 2355 men much cheaper than if raised at home'.[16]

'A few scalps taken by Indians and Canadians,' General James Grant considered, 'would operate more upon the minds of these deluded distracted people than any other loss they can sustain.'[17] The British engagement of mercenaries was in American eyes bad enough. The use made of Indians was a still bitterer source of resentment, and also of some very modern-sounding propaganda. No war, and especially no civil war, which this essentially was, fails to engender savagery, either in the deed itself, or the thought willing the deed. Germain would have liked to burn Boston and Philadelphia as a 'punishment'; and Silas Deane and Benjamin Franklin both expressed an anticipated pleasure at the thought, when the French landed, of their setting light to Liverpool and Glasgow as revenge for what the British had done in America. Undoubtedly there were British-inspired Indian atrocities, as there were also American atrocities committed against loyalists. But the accomplished exploitation of the Indian horror stories by Franklin in France illuminates an interesting facet of that many-sided man. The danger of French intervention in the colonial quarrel was well recognised in London; and France of course was fertile ground for American agents to cultivate. Franklin compiled a 'schoolbook' of atrocity incidents, true and fabricated; printed and circulated from his press at Passy what falsely purported to be a copy of a Boston newspaper relating how Indians under British orders had murdered men, women, and children, including unborn babes 'ript from their mothers' bellies'; and actually caused scalps to be dispatched to George III 'in order that he might regard them and be refreshed'. When challenged later over these tactics, Franklin justified them on the grounds that George loved blood and hated Americans.[18]

There were some soldiers and politicians in England who from the start thought it madness to undertake a war on the mainland of America. General Edward Harvey, the senior British staff officer, considered it 'as wild an idea as ever controverted common sense',[19] and he had a supporter in Lord Barrington, the Secretary at War, who argued that measures of naval blockade would be sufficient to bring about that submission which all, or very nearly all, agreed with the King was essential.[20] The condition of the Navy, however, was itself

far from shipshape. What Chatham had first forecast and then bemoaned was a fact. While the French had been busily rebuilding since
their defeats of fifteen years before, the British had concentrated upon
keeping down taxes. The Earl of Sandwich, at the Admiralty from
1771 – that same 'Jemmy Twitcher' who had once 'peached' on
Wilkes – was unfairly to be made the scapegoat when the Navy was
found to be inadequate, but he had fought North on the issue and inherited an unsound legacy. The chief reason for Sandwich's refusing
to let any ships of the line go to America in 1776, though he dared not
admit it, was that so few of them were fully fit for combat service. The
state of dockyards and the number and seaworthiness of ships, therefore, were further matters in 1774 and 1775 troubling the King's notes
and memoranda. He compiled careful lists of 'ships in ordinary', 'ships
building and repairing', and 'guardships'. He was concerned, as he had
cause to be, for stocks of seasoned oak and for replacing decayed
timbers. Under 'Sheerness' we find 'Mr Hunt's composition to prevent
the bite of the worm promises better than anything yet tried'; under
Portsmouth, 'Decay of the dead-eyes. Timber enough for a year's
construction. No worm of consequence in this port.' But at Chatham,
'The stock of timber insufficient . . . the depth of water not adequate
to the draught of the capital ships,' preceded by such interesting if
academic queries as 'Worming the rigging? and when introduced? . . .
How does ballast taken up in salt water come to be less damp than in
fresh water?'[21]

When in April, 1775, the first hard military blows were exchanged
at Lexington and on the road back from Concord to Boston, George
determinedly deprecated the expression, 'bad news'. It was Thomas
Pownall – once a colonial governor and now a junior to Lord Dartmouth, the American Secretary – who had used the phrase; and when
Dartmouth sent on to the King a newspaper report giving details of
the losses suffered by Gage's men, George replied that clearly the
account 'was drawn up with the intention of painting the skirmish at
Concord in as favourable a light as possible for the insurgents'. Gage's
object had been 'to spike cannon and destroy military stores', and it had
been achieved; casualties had been roughly equal on both sides. The
General in fact had no reason to feel displeased; 'I therefore hope you
will not see this in a stronger light than it deserves.'[22] The fight was
on. Loyal Englishmen must stiffen the sinews and summon up the
blood – and such forces as could be mustered. There can be no doubt
of the King's resolution and toughness; but equally no denying that
there were to be occasions when his 'action of the tiger' shared some of
the attributes of the ostrich's as well.

Lexington and Concord in April were followed in June by Bunker Hill, where General Howe, the new commander who had replaced Gage, suffered over a thousand killed and wounded and was subsequently besieged in Boston. The Duke of Grafton, Lord Privy Seal, alarmed by the drift of events in America and unconvinced by official optimism, told the King that he was being deluded by his ministers and resigned. His going enabled North to reconstruct his Cabinet with an eye to toughening it. It was in particular his half-brother, the pious Earl of Dartmouth, who was generally considered too mild and conciliatory for an American Secretary in the existing situation; and a reshuffle would offer North and the King the opportunity to bring to that office a vigorous hard liner who had long been pressing for office and the chance to rehabilitate his reputation, wrecked by the courtmartial after Minden, sixteen years before. His name had been Sackville, but as the legatee of Lady Elizabeth Germain, he had under the terms of the will adopted hers. Germain replaced Dartmouth in November, 1775, though not until Dartmouth's unexpectedly stubborn insistence on having the office of his choice, the Privy Seal, had caused a Cabinet crisis and brought North to the point of threatening, if only very gently, his own resignation. ('You shall find me ready to take any steps to extricate you from difficulty,' George reassured him. 'You are my sheet anchor and your ease and comfort I shall in the whole transaction try to secure.')

Lord George Germain, a stickler for the restitution of his honour, went out of his way from the moment of receiving the seals to underline his parity with the other two Secretaries. As minister for American affairs at such a time it was in any event likely that he would become the most important of the three, and he certainly began to behave as such. In a Cabinet presided over by a first minister who was at heart devoted to peace and retrenchment, Germain rushed in to fill the vacuum left by North's lack of strategic direction. If he was overbearing, he was energetic. No one might ever accuse him of fiddling while Rome burned; but he had no talent for working with others, and he never succeeded in overcoming the hostility of generals who disliked him and refused to forget his earlier military disgrace. With at least one of them, General Guy Carleton, he never tried, but instead constantly belittled and attempted to discredit him.

There were five principal British generals in North America between 1775 and 1781 – Howe, Carleton, Clinton, Burgoyne, and Cornwallis. Germain began bitterly at odds with the first two, and ended at daggers drawn with all but Cornwallis; and even Cornwallis was critical. Often assuming the direction of naval as well as military operations in

America, Germain was frequently at variance with Sandwich also, and more so than ever after France entered the war. Moreover, the Secretary at War, Barrington, had already asked, but had to wait three years, for permission to resign; not believing in the wisdom of a land war, he remained content to carry out instructions and rest upon his own impotence. Inevitably Germain became the director of campaigns which were always beyond his effective control, and whose geographical and tactical difficulties he was never in a fit position to estimate. He wished to be the 'supremo', and sometimes faced the Cabinet with *faits accomplis*, after first consulting the King. Doubtless the war demanded some such strategic overlord; but when General Howe, even at the moment of his success in taking New York, and specifically ruling himself out as a candidate, pointed out that 'a viceroy with unlimited powers' ought to be appointed *in America*, Germain brushed aside the suggestion. [23] The war would throughout continue to be directed from London, with an interval of three, and sometimes four, months between the receipt of consecutive instructions or dispatches.

He was over-confident too at the start, and proved another of those false prophets who encouraged the King to swallow the over-sanguine forecasts that were plentifully fed to him. In this respect the colonial governors were the prime offenders.

> Dunmore in his last letters seems confident [wrote Lord North] that he could restore order in Virginia, if he had the assistance of two or three hundred men . . . Martin [Governor of North Carolina] if he [be] properly supported and encouraged will probably be able in a short time to re-establish the authority of Great Britain in that colony. Lord William Campbell gives a very favourable account of the disposition of many of the back settlers in South Carolina and declares his opinion that two thousand men will be sufficient to set matters right within his Government . . . Georgia will return to her duty as soon as South Carolina is brought to a submission. [24]

As Jefferson was writing at this time, 'The ministry have been deceived by their officers on this side the water who (for what purpose I cannot tell) have considerably represented the American opposition as that of a small fraction, in which the body of the people took little part.' [25]

Encouraged by their Carolina advices, King and Cabinet had great hopes of a southern expedition in 1776. Clinton was to take two thousand men and a naval squadron to South Carolina, where it was hoped the loyalists would rise and help reassert the royal authority. George wrote to Sandwich with the utmost urgency: 'The English lion, when rouzed' must match the vigour of the rebels and show that it possessed also 'the swiftness of the race horse'. All official forms must be set aside in getting sufficient troop transports. To obtain crews he knew was difficult, but 'now a bounty is ordered, I trust things will be carried on with infinite dispatch'. [26] The southern expedition mounted its attack on Charleston, but failed for lack of local support. The attempt to defeat the bad Americans by enlisting the support of the good ones only served to demonstrate that what made men 'loyalists' was sometimes little more than a grievance against the ruling cliques of their own state. Readiness to die for King George was harder to enlist.

In New England, General Howe was forced to retire from Boston to Halifax in Nova Scotia, but then with his brother Lord Howe proceeded to preside over a strange phase of the hostilities, offering conciliation and peace with one hand while waging war with the other. With fears of French intervention growing, the idea of a peace commission appealed strongly to North, though many and perhaps most Americans would have agreed with Tom Paine that it represented 'a wooden horse which is to take those by stratagem whom twelve years of hostility could not reduce', and among the British Cabinet Germain, Suffolk, and Sandwich were all opposed to the project. The King saw little point in it either, and before confirming Admiral Lord Howe's mandate expressed scepticism to North: 'If Lord Howe should give up being a [peace] commissioner I should think it better for himself as well as the Service.' [27] The commissioners' first proclamation offering pardon to all Americans who renounced rebellion was issued in June, 1776; a second on 14th July. Despite the Declaration of Independence, however, and unremitting military operations, proclamations in similar terms continued fruitlessly until countermanded by Germain in the spring of 1777.

After Howe's forced retirement from Boston, British hopes rose when he captured Long Island and New York in August-September, 1776, and Clinton took Rhode Island in December. 'The health of G[eneral] Howe's army, the number of townsmen returning to New York, and the arrival of the Light Dragoons' the King considered 'very pleasant pieces of news'. He had seen, he was happy to inform Lord North on 1st January, 1777, a private letter from Howe claiming to be in control of the whole coastline from Rhode Island to the Delaware, so since British forces now commanded such extensive territory, it would matter less – however deplorable – that the contractors despite earlier warnings were still shipping them bad biscuits and flour.

Certainly in December, 1776, Washington's position looked distressed and bleak. New Jersey had been lost. Half Pennsylvania seemed ready to give up the fight, and the colonial army appeared to be disintegrating. Washington himself reckoned the game 'pretty near up', and his opinion was echoed from the other side by Lord Percy, who like many of his fellow-officers thought, 'This business is pretty near over.' No wonder that the King concluded that the accounts from America were 'most comfortable'.[28] Already, however, six days before George wrote his cheerful New Year's day letter to North, Washington in desperation had dealt a smart blow to an Anglo-Hessian force at Trenton, capturing nearly a thousand Hessians, and then whisked his own vulnerable forces safely out of Cornwallis's reach. It was the Hessian officers, the King considered, who had occasioned this setback at Trenton: 'I wish Sir W. Howe' – the General had been knighted for his successes – 'had placed none but British troops in the outposts.'[29] As it was, the Delaware was not crossed and Philadelphia not yet taken; the redcoats were rattled smartly back through New Jersey. It was a disappointment; but as the British retired to their winter quarters, and Sir William Howe to New York, his mistress, and civilisation, the generally held opinion was that it was no more than a postponement. The winter would give time for Howe and Germain, if they could only agree, to prepare the *coup de grâce*.

Not all the King's preoccupations over these anxious months concerned the war and its direction. Besides American, Irish and Indian affairs never stayed out of the picture for long; and the usual constant attention had to be paid to questions of the more exalted ecclesiastical preferments and of military and naval appointments. In addition applications for honours and claims for places and pensions had as always to receive the nice weighing in the scales of propriety and expediency which each case demanded. No adjustment in the administration could ever be made without scrupulous consideration of compensation for injured status, inducement for continuing support, or reward for services rendered – frequently for a combination of all three. It was proper that Lord Barrington, when he eventually retired, should be generously, but not too generously, treated. 'Lord Lyttelton has this morning agreed to give a constant support to administration upon condition that he may expect before the end of the session, a Privy Council office of the value of £1,500 a year.' Lord Rochford, being 'low' in November, 1775, was ready to resign but only upon a suitable arrangement, which among other favours should include the next available Garter and a pension proportionate to his rank. The King was too well conditioned to these long-established practices, too old a hand in this delicate game of status and cash, to question the general reasonableness of such demands, though he sometimes jibbed at impudence. Lord Rochford met no opposition, especially as his going facilitated a strengthening of the Cabinet. The King would merely remind North that the royal finances were 'in a very disgraceful condition'; still, he did not 'require one minutes time for consideration but most willingly consent to give Lord Rochford a pension of £2,500 per annum and to assure him that at the first Chapter of the Garter I will confer that order upon him'.[30]

These matters were of infinite importance even in the middle of a war that would determine two great nations' destinies. And during the weeks immediately preceding July, 1776, and the Declaration of Independence, one decision that seemed urgent to the King was that an Earldom of Montagu should *not* be conferred on Lady Beaulieu, whatever North had promised or half-promised. 'If you do wish an Earldom for Lady Beaulieu I will grant her one of any other name, to ease your mind, but fairly owne I think her conduct to me as well as that of all her family deserve none.' This Beaulieu demand annoyed him beyond measure. North's letter on the subject had, he confessed, thrown him *into the greatest state of uneasiness he ever felt.* (The words, spoken at that moment in the world's history, seem now to demand a second reading and even then to put the severest strain on credence.) The King's 'distress' continued for some days and caused Lord North to 'beg a thousand pardons' and Lord Suffolk to be 'grieved to the heart that your Majesty meets with so much vexation'.[31] Perhaps it was the desire to escape the vexation that turned his mind that particular week towards taking a first step to satisfy the Queen's wish that they should make a new home at Windsor,[32] with its fine park and its splendid scope for riding and hunting.

Physically North took much buffeting at this time, and George was often solicitous for him, inquiring after his condition, wondering if the hot atmosphere in the Chamber fatigued him, sympathetic when he had been kept late at the Commons by the persistence of the opposition. He knew of North's weak eyes* and his various ailments; but what he did not know, until one day John Robinson dropped a massive hint (and was then commanded by the King to tell the whole story), was that North, though not by the standard of his times an extravagant man, was heavily in debt; that this preyed on a mind already 'inervated' by the perplexities of the public situation, and 'that he was unable to bear the anxieties and distress brought upon him by these things'. Straightway the King put pen to paper, demanded to know of North whether £12,000 or £15,000 would set his affairs in order; 'Nay if

* Like the King's, North's last years were spent in blindness.

£20,000 is necessary I am resolved you shall have no other person concerned in freeing them but myself.' In his very seemly and grateful
acceptance of this offer North mentioned a figure of 'nearly £18,000',
whereupon the King made available to him an account of £20,000, of
which by 1782 North had drawn £17,000.[33] It was an honest gift,
emanating from a genuine desire to relieve North's dejected spirits,
though doubtless there was an element of self-interest in it too. North
had already mentioned resignation several times and George had no
desire to lose the minister he had described as his sheet anchor. It
turned out, however, that North paid a price for his financial relief.
From that day in 1777 onwards – only four weeks as it happened
before the disaster of Saratoga that marked the beginning of North's
end – he remained the moral prisoner of the King's generosity.

The master plan that was to end the American rebellion was worked
out by Germain, not with Howe but with General Burgoyne, who was
home on leave during the winter of 1776-77. There was little in it that
had not seemed obvious strategy for a long time. In brief, it envisaged
cutting simultaneously down the Hudson valley from Canada, and up
the Hudson valley from New York, making a junction at Albany, and
thus shearing off New England from the remainder of the colonies.
The severed fragments could then be reduced at leisure. General Howe
was informed of the proposals, which he said would necessitate a total
force of 35,000 men.

Germain discussed all this of course at the Queen's House, and often
had consultations there before going to meet his ministerial colleagues. The King, however, had his own ideas about Germain, and
should not be thought to have always collaborated with him in bull-
dozing projects through a squabbling or hostile Cabinet. Certainly the
Cabinet was far from united, but there were occasions when George
disapproved of Germain's opinions and of his methods, and he
might on such occasions warn other members of the Cabinet against
what Germain was about to propose. (On the other hand a view
unitedly represented to him by a Cabinet minute he would not resist,
though he might well have offered previous opinions against it.) He
appreciated that Germain was an overbearing man who bore grudges.
Of these the most deep-seated was against the Governor of Quebec,
General Carleton, yet in July, 1776, while Germain was busy intriguing
against him, Carleton was awarded a Knighthood of the Bath by the
King; and when the minister expressed a wish to recall him, George
refused to allow it and commented to North on Germain's 'great pre-

judice perhaps not unaccompanied with rancour'.[34] It was also clear to the King that Germain never missed an opportunity to criticise Howe or damn him with faint praise. 'It is surprising,' Germain wrote to the King at the very moment of fatal confusion in his own instructions, 'that the General should be so fond of concealing his operations.'[35] It was more than surprising – it has never since ceased to amaze – that the minister, having issued one coherent set of orders to Howe (the Hudson valley plan of campaign) should have airily approved of Howe's suggestions for a second and incompatible set.

The master plan was in consequence never put into operation. Perhaps when Howe did not get the total of 35,000 troops he had asked for, he merely washed his hands of the idea of a northward thrust up the Hudson. It seems inconceivable that he could have thought that he would have time *first* to move south and take Philadelphia and still be able to strike north and link up with Burgoyne coming down from Canada. The project of a junction at Albany had been approved by both King and Cabinet; yet Germain's dispatch to Howe of 3rd March (arriving on 8th May!) neither made specific mention of it nor countermanded Howe's known intention, also approved by Germain, to strike towards Philadelphia. The muddle was as complete as Germain's ignorance of the difficulties of climate and terrain that Burgoyne was bound to meet. Doggedly and ably Burgoyne slogged on, down the Hudson towards Albany, where his orders clearly stated he was to put himself under Howe's command. Howe was following what he took to be *his* instructions in capturing Philadelphia. The grand campaign, mismanaged on the grand scale by remote control, ended with Burgoyne's surrender at Saratoga on 17th October, 1777.

CHAPTER SEVENTEEN

After Saratoga

AFTER Saratoga, North presents a despondent and harassed figure. A man of less pride or less integrity would probably have cut and run, defaulting on the moral debt implicit in the promise he had made, on being rescued financially, never to desert his master and benefactor. A tougher man might have taken charge of the Cabinet and continued to earn the King's affectionate respect. A Chatham might have worked eighteen hours a day organising victory – or alternatively gone paralysed off to the country. But as North was miserably aware, he was no Chatham. He was paralysed with a difference. He was held fast in chains of obligation, weighted down with his own irresolution and incompetence. He could not go on, but he could not get out. Sometimes he did not even wish to get out but, loving power as much as most politicians, clung on to his position as on other days to his wretchedness. Scores of times he wrote to the King that he was unfit for his post, that he could not concentrate, that his nerve had gone, that 'his spirits, strength, memory, judgment and abilities' were 'sensibly and considerably impair'd'. The cries of woe and petitions for release in his letters over the rather more than four years between Saratoga and his eventual fall in March, 1782 – years when the Empire in America, the Caribbean, India, and Ireland was in jeopardy, when the fleets of France and Spain threatened to dominate the seas and launch an invasion, and when domestic government was in a state of chronic crisis – are repetitive almost beyond belief. His personal defects would 'probably grow upon' him and render him 'every day less and less fit'. His continuance in office was 'highly prejudicial to his Majesty's affairs'. He must request 'an immediate dismission'. His ministry could not last. It could not last the week. It could not last *the next twenty-four hours*.[1] Some 'broader bottom' must be found, some accommodation made with the opposition, above all some new First Lord of the Treasury appointed instead of his incompetent self: if not Lord Chatham (whom death soon removed from the discussion), then Lord Suffolk, or Lord Gower, or Lord Weymouth, or Lord Thurlow. (Thurlow himself once snorted *Lord Anybody*. Asked who would do to replace North, he suggested 'the first hackney coachman in the street'.)

But the King, too, if not yet in chains, was in constant fear of being put in them by a victorious opposition, and had so little room for manœuvre that he could find no way of letting North resign without, as he saw it, hazarding his whole system of government and having to accept as ministers men who would give away the dependence of the colonies (first America, and then inevitably the West Indies and Ireland) and so bring dishonour and defeat to King and country. As he showed in his treatment of those of his family whose behaviour displeased him, George could be tough and exacting. He could take a strong and self-righteous line, apply severe pressures, and impose unpleasant sanctions. He liked North. 'I love you as a man of worth,' he had written, 'as I esteem you as a minister.' To relieve him of debt had given him genuine pleasure, and it seems improbably out of character that in so doing he should have deliberately schemed to enmesh North in some sort of golden net of obligation. But why now had North's courage deserted him? Why could he not better deserve the trust and affection bestowed on him? George was in no doubt of his own vigour, his own manliness and resolution. Indeed it is true he had no need to be. It was well tested, and perhaps he did not need to remind himself, or his ministers and entourage, of its sterling quality quite so frequently as he did. But having fibre himself, he expected it of those who served him; and now North's seemed to have rotted. Once long ago, it was Bute who lost his nerve. Then Chatham had collapsed – worse, turned renegade. Grafton had 'deserted', and George still remembered North's conduct at that 'critical minute'. Indeed, he said, he would never forget it. Yet now here was North threatening to go the way of the others, and the King contrived for more than four long years to prevent him. He insisted that he should stay and see both battles through – with the rebels and enemies overseas, and at home with that 'set of men who certainly would make me a slave for the remainder of my days'.[2]

North's cries for mercy, relatively infrequent before the blow of Saratoga, became desperate and insistent after it. He was 'in such a situation that whatever he does must be attended with some disgrace, and much misery to himself, and, what is worse perhaps, with some detriment to the public'.[3] What the country needed in such critical times (as he rightly pointed out) was 'one directing Minister, who should plan the whole of the operations of government, and controul all the other departments of administration'; and he had never wished or claimed to be that. He refused to regard himself as *leader* of the Cabinet, and indeed often emphasised the point by failing properly to prepare any sort of agenda for its meetings – which, significantly, were held no more frequently at his home in Downing Street than at the residences of the other Cabinet ministers. These all ran their own departments, often in direct contact with the King, but they were frequently exasperated by North's vagueness and procrastination, his periods of uncommunicative depression, his fits of indolence, and his chronic indecision. None of these weaknesses needed to be pointed out to North; he himself lamented them willingly, abjectly, endlessly to his unrelenting master. George as constantly reminded him that he *was* his 'chief confidential minister', and in charge of the business of the House of Commons. He could not run away; he must pull himself together and exercise more resolution.* 'Your never quitting this subject and your avowed despondency,' the King wrote in March, 1778, 'obliges me to ask the three following questions, to which I expect explicit answers in writing.' One: could the Government be strengthened by taking in some of the opposition? Two: if not, would North try to exert himself? Three: if he would not, would he at least carry on until steps could be taken to put 'vigour into my service, the first of which will be my instantly putting the Great Seal into the hands of the Attorney-General'?[4] (This was Thurlow, whom the King was increasingly regarding as the strong man of his team; certainly as the next Lord Chancellor; possibly as the future leader of a broad-bottomed ministry.)

Challenged thus directly, North always capitulated; complained and cried woe, but capitulated. He was 'not capable' of exerting himself, but he would continue if the King insisted. A few weeks later he found himself

> so hurried and teazed on Thursday that I found it absolutely necessary to go into the country in order to endeavour to collect my scatter'd thoughts and to recover the use of my understanding.[5]

Exasperated but not heartless, the King agreed that a stay at Bushy might 'recruit' North's mind in readiness for the next session of Parliament but, when plaints persisted and backslidings threatened once more, 'you remember,' he reminded him, 'the last words you used were that you did not mean to resign.'[6]

* George, however, was himself not consistent. Did he really want North to be 'prime minister', or rather a sort of business manager and finance minister? We find him writing to John Robinson about North in August 1779: 'I fear his irresolution is only to be equalled by a certain vanity of wanting to ape the prime minister without any of the requisite qualities'. If he would 'get the Irish affairs in some train', see that offices were properly filled, 'and confine himself chiefly to the Finance branch, he may still be a very useful minister and gain much reputation' Add. MSS. 37834, f.133).

The King did on many occasions probe the possibilities of reorganising his Cabinet, either with or without North, and frequently progressed as far as tentative lists. As long as Chatham lived (until May, 1778), there was to be no question – if Chatham came into the administration, North *must* continue to head it. 'You must acquaint him that I shall never address myself to him but through you . . . I cannot consent to have any conversation with him untill the ministry is formed.' Then, if Chatham supported North, he would be received 'with open arms', but if he wished to come as a 'dictator' – and North pointed out that at the very least he would insist on 'appearing to form the ministry' – then 'I would rather lose the Crown I now wear than bear the ignominy of possessing it under their shackles. I might write volumes . . . I am shocked at the base arts all these men have used . . . Whilst any ten men in the kingdom will stand by me I will not give myself up to bondage . . . It is impossible that the nation shall not stand by me; if they will not, they shall have another King . . .'[7]

This was written in March, 1778. The national crisis was acute. There was near-certainty that France would declare war, a strong probability that Spain would follow, and the alarming possibility that the French and Spanish fleets would combine to dominate the Channel and prepare the way for an invasion. North forecast that if the load ('infinitely more than I can undertake') were not removed from his shoulders, 'national disgrace and ruin will be the consequence.' Still, he would not 'quit his place'. Seizing on this last assurance, George replied immediately to express his pleasure; he 'always thought' Lord North's sense of honour would prevail.[8] Indeed, it did. So too did the continuing winds of doubt, indecision, and intrigue. North's pleas to be disposed of arrived with undiminished frequency, and with them came also unwelcome, if realistic, advice. 'Peace with America and a change in the ministry are the only steps which can save this country,' he wrote to the King on 25th March. Even 'the most brilliant victories' over France, he was afraid, might bring ruin upon the country because of 'the enormous expence', and if Britain could only make 'an accommodation' with the rebels it would, he thought, prevent at least for some time a war with France.[9] Some of the rest of the Cabinet agreed with him; Weymouth, for instance, was strongly in favour of a settlement with America, but 'reserving a dependence'. George himself did not altogether reject this notion, and thought it worth 'keeping open the channel of intercourse' through the agency of Benjamin Franklin in Paris. (This did not prevent him considering Franklin an 'insidious man'.) He even brought himself to contemplate the possibility of eventual independence for the more intransigently hostile

American states, while a firm hold was maintained on Canada, Nova Scotia, and the Floridas, with strong garrisons 'to keep a certain awe over the abandoned colonies'.[10] Later, when France (and soon Spain too) had entered the war, he constantly recurred to this imperative necessity of holding strong military forces in the north and the south, even if it meant having to be content with a naval blockade, and long periods of military inaction, in the centre. But the King, in common with most of the public, did not often allow himself to think of conceding independence. It had been specifically excluded from the limits of discretion permitted to the exploratory but abortive commission sent to America under Lord Carlisle in the spring of 1778. In this matter of American independence, if in little else, the King stood with the dying Chatham, whose last faltering eloquent speech, ending with his dramatic collapse, was a passionate condemnation of any 'dismemberment of this ancient and most noble monarchy . . . Where is the man,' he demanded, 'that will dare to advise such a measure?'*

As the crisis grew more menacing – the 'Protestant nation' of Ireland was now also threatening to fight for its independence – George's obstinate energies gathered momentum. Come the four corners of the world in arms and we would shock them. 'The Old Lion will be roused,' he wrote to a desponding North when the 'faithless and insolent' French entered the war; and that formidable beast must 'deserve the respect of other nations'.[11] If Spain followed her Bourbon partner, Britain must still be ready to fight on every front; troops, however scarce and precious, must be spared to protect Gibraltar; and if Lord Howe was to replace Sandwich as First Lord of the Admiralty (in the event he did not, but joined the opposition†) it must be 'with the explicit declaration that he will zealously concurr in prosecuting the war in all quarters of the globe'.[12] There should be no more talk of independence for America. Everything asked for by the colonies as late as the summer of 1775 had now been conceded by North's Conciliation Bills; further concession would be 'a joke'. Could not the opposition – could not Lord North – see 'if any one branch of the Empire is alowed to cast off its dependency, that the others will infalably follow'? And that this same argument applied forcibly to Ireland?[13]

* George was 'rather surprised' that the House of Commons should unanimously vote for a public funeral in Westminster Abbey for the Earl of Chatham. If the compliment was to his part as war minister in the Seven Years War, that was acceptable; if 'to his general conduct', then it was 'an offensive measure' to the King personally (Fortescue, iv, 2336).

† However, he survived this aberration to become in old age one of the King's most highly esteemed friends.

There was no doubting the severity of the crisis. The French Toulon fleet under d'Estaing had been allowed to get through the Straits of Gibraltar and was at large off the American coast – though d'Estaing soon disgusted his allies by sailing off to the West Indies. The Brest fleet under d'Orvilliers meanwhile threatened the Channel. To signalise the urgency of the naval preparations and hasten the Royal Navy's departure, George, accompanied by the Queen, paid a strenuous official visit to Portsmouth. His memorandum on the subject was as detailed and meticulous as his inspection. (Characteristically, the journey down was measured to the minute: 'Left the Queen's House at 57 minutes past five, arrived at Portsmouth at 57 minutes past twelve.') Portsmouth Dockyard, however, afforded no refuge from the importunings of Downing Street. Another request arrived from North begging that he should be replaced by someone who could 'chuse decisively'. There had that day been heavy parliamentary criticism because the Fleet had not yet sailed. But everything possible was being done, the King assured him, 'and it is very absurd in gentlemen unacquainted with the immense detail of naval affairs to trouble the House of Commons with matters totally foreign to truth.' 'My good lord,' he replied to North's further lamentations, 'no mortal can withstand the will of Divine Providence; from the hour I arrived here, not an instant has been lost.'[14] When the Fleet did sail, the opposition Whig Admiral Keppel failed to defeat d'Orvilliers off Ushant, whereupon he was rashly accused of incompetence and misconduct by the pro-Government Rear-Admiral Palliser, his third in command. Such was the faction-ridden condition of the Navy's senior ranks, as far from Nelson's band of brothers as it was possible to be.

Keppel demanded a court-martial, was duly acquitted, and became as much a hero of the Whigs as if he had won a great naval victory; perhaps rather more so, since the victory was over the Government and the King. For two nights in February, 1779, London and Westminster were illuminated in Keppel's honour, and the City awarded him its freedom. Hooligans egged on, if not more positively assisted, by some of the young bloods of Almack's – *hired* by them, the King had no doubt – ransacked Palliser's house one night in Pall Mall, attacked the homes of Germain and North, and obliged Sandwich to make an undignified escape with his mistress through the Admiralty back garden. Keppel cockades became for a time almost as common as Wilkes's had once been, and Whig ladies could show their opinion of the Court and the Administration by wearing Keppel caps at the Opera. The King begged North to use care in going to the Commons: 'If possible come down whilst I am at the House as my guard will prevent any riot.' It would be necessary and sensible, he considered, to dismiss Palliser, notwithstanding the sympathy he deserved. He could not possibly stay in his post, and 'I owne I think it wiser to do it spontaneously than to be drove to it'. Sandwich disagreed. When Palliser (also court-martialled) was eventually obliged to 'resign', the King did not fail to point out that Sandwich in the end had had to come to 'a mean subterfuge to attain the same end'.[15]

There was now an acute shortage of senior admirals willing to take command and work under Sandwich's direction. Keppel and Howe both refused, and at one period George was reduced to wondering whether the Keppel-Palliser brouhaha (which continued noisily through the winter and spring of 1778-79) might not prove a blessing in disguise, since it might force Sandwich's replacement at the head of the Admiralty by a *sailor*, preferably Lord Howe. But Sandwich sailored on, about as unpopular with the admirals as Germain was with the generals, but not at all the negligent inefficient figure the opposition sought to paint him. He had worked hard to build up the Navy after the periods of neglect before and after the Seven Years War and George III at least recognised the fact. The King himself continued to pay very close attention to the condition of his armed forces, and the Navy in particular. His papers over these crisis months of 1778 and 1779 are full of detailed lists of ships in commission and building, references to naval dispositions and the movement of convoys, the recruitment – which mainly meant impressment – of sailors, and the raising of troops and militia companies. Among these last he at least did what he could to get competent leadership and refuse appointments sought purely on the principle of 'knowing the right people'. He wanted field officers who had seen service, colonels who had 'distinguished themselves in America',

> not men taken merely to oblige individuals; what Ld G. Germaine may have said I cannot answer for, but I ever objected to a corps entirely composed of men that had never been in the service, the captains of these companies must have been lieutenants, the lieutenants ensigns . . .[16]

While Sandwich was at loggerheads with the admirals, Germain had made such entrenched enemies of the generals that his leaving the Cabinet, the King was reckoning early in 1778, might be 'a most favourable event'. At least it was clear, he said, that either the Secretary (Germain) or the General (Sir William Howe) must retire.[17] As with Keppel, so with Generals Howe and Burgoyne (the latter a prisoner-of-war allowed home on parole); the opposition chose to see them as wickedly wronged men, and the independent members and placemen on whom North relied thought even less of Germain's handling of the Howe affair in the Commons than of his earlier management of the strategy that had ended at Saratoga. Charles Jenkinson, the King's second pair of eyes and ears (John Robinson provided a third) reported Germain as being 'indiscreet beyond description' when the matter came up for debate in the spring of 1779, and considered the turn-out of support for the Government 'disgraceful' – it might even lose its majority.[18] Sandwich too (though as a peer, of course, not present), was many times the target of Fox's merciless brilliance. One such attack came immediately after the brutal murder in Covent Garden of Sandwich's current mistress, Miss Ray the singer, for whom, libertine though he might be, Sandwich experienced shocked grief. Some disapproved of Fox's timing. But when he had his teeth in the prey, Fox never easily let go. Germain, *faute de mieux*, went on to the bitter end, like Sandwich. At least he was no defeatist, and certainly he was not of a resigning disposition. If he had to be *persuaded* out of the Cabinet, North advised George, he would want such a prohibitive douceur that it was difficult to see how the thing could be managed. A peerage, perhaps, and the Lord Wardenship of the Cinque Ports on the *full* salary of £4,000? Dangle no such baits, commanded the King; and later – 'I certainly have no intention to confer a peerage on Lord G'.*

This sinecure of the Cinque Ports was one of the favours George had bestowed on North, partly, as he admitted, to 'stimulate' him to continue at the head of the Treasury, though the reward was not made conditional. Even this plum proved a little sour, and North for a time felt himself 'mortified and humiliated' when he found that the appointment was to be 'during pleasure' and not for life, as had been the recent practice. George explained: 'I daily find the evil of having put so many employments out of the hands of the Crown' – he needed to husband his 'places'. No slight, he insisted, had been meant. But North, though he was more than ready to forgo most of the large salary (and did), still considered his honour somehow impugned; it was felt as a slur upon his reputation that he should 'have the office upon a less respectable footing than his immediate predecessor'. Worse, he thought he perceived 'some mistrust in his Majesty with respect to him'. Could this displeasure have had its occasion 'in my frequent and earnest applications for leave to retire?' If so, then 'dispose of me, Sir, as you will'.[19]

However, the King found it impossible to dispose of him. He was

* He did, of course, in the end (1782), when Lord George, upon his resignation, reassumed his ancient name of Sackville with a viscountcy.

constantly trying to piece together an acceptable alternative administration – and went on trying for years – but the pieces of the jigsaw
would never fit. 'I have seriously attempted to release you,' he reminded North; but always there was some bar. Lord Suffolk, at one
stage the most acceptable successor, died. Weymouth, Gower, and the
Bedfords were lukewarm and, all but Thurlow, they were to go over to
the opposition. The Shelburne group too (the former Chathamites)
were to prefer association with the Rockingham-Fox party to coming
into partnership with a Court administration. The King placed most
hope in Thurlow – rough-tongued, rugged, and able – and was
insistent that (at any rate as a first step) North should assent to his having the Lord Chancellorship. Thurlow's 'tallents and zeal' could be
depended on; 'a very firm and fair man,' George judged him.[20] But
North had secretly promised too much to his insatiable Solicitor-
General, Wedderburn, whose vitals were consumed with jealousy of
Thurlow; who yearned for the comforts and dignities of the Woolsack; and whose price for refraining from going into opposition was
extortionate.* George, exasperated by these mercenary intrigues,
grudgingly waited for North to extricate himself, temporarily at least;
but at long last managed to make Thurlow Chancellor – Wedderburn
for the time being having to content himself with succeeding Thurlow
as Attorney-General.

Perhaps 'the summer's repose' would enable North to regain some
vigour – George had expressed this hope in June, 1778 – 'and not let
every absurd idea be adopted as has too recently appeared.' The approaching new session of Parliament, however, found North's mind
still 'unrecruited', and Cabinet business as disorganised as ever. More
than once George wrote to the Treasury Secretary, the indefatigable
John Robinson, to get him to see that his master was prompter and
more 'exact' in answering his letters, and from North himself at the end
of October George demanded a plan to ensure a steadier attendance
of Government supporters. When after a week North had still done
nothing, the royal tone became peremptory: 'I must therefore insist
on your laying your thoughts on that subject before the Cabinet at
your meeting on Thursday.' North undertook to rally 'the placemen,
etc.', but had only a spasmodic effect on them. It was certainly difficult
to feel much enthusiasm for a Government with so little good to report,

---

* A peerage and chief-justiceship. Wedderburn was to become Lord Loughborough and Chief Justice of the Common Pleas in 1780. Thirteen years later, after
Pitt the younger enforced Thurlow's dismissal, he did at last attain the Woolsack,
and eventually the earldom of Rosslyn. Junius, admittedly not a generous critic of
anybody, described Wedderburn as one whom 'even treachery could not trust'.

and so obviously at sixes and sevens within itself. In February, 1779, a few hours before his windows were smashed during the Keppel riots, North was in fact defeated in the Commons on an opposition motion to bring in a bill to prohibit Members from gaining unadvertised Government contracts. Again three weeks later he was gloomily reporting a 'very bad attendance'. George suggested that a little more coaxing – 'a little civility' – towards Government supporters might help 'to bring things again into order'.[21] In any case, North must not take too tragically an occasional defeat in the lobbies; 'I am convinced,' he wrote, 'this country will never regain a proper tone unless ministers as in the reign of King William will not mind now and then being in a minority.'[22] This bracing advice had no tonic effect.

More bad experience in debate followed. Wedderburn, one of the ablest if most unlikable of his Front Bench colleagues, was back at his old intrigues, and seemed to have the sort of power over North that the stoat has over the rabbit. He was afraid North was going to resign, so he wanted his Chief Justiceship *immediately*; or failing that, something very handsome and tangible. Otherwise, he would cross the floor. North was worried into paralysis. Again the King tried to work through Robinson. 'Mr Robinson,' he told him, 'must to-day attempt his irksome part of rouzing Lord North.' Jenkinson wrote that it was clear that Wedderburn wanted something 'and that Lord North is not to be allow'd to do anything till that something is obtained'. Jenkinson considered that Wedderburn's bluff ought to be called. He should be told that he would in due course, *when one fell vacant*, have his Chief Justiceship, but only if he maintained his loyalty to Crown and Administration. Robinson agreed: 'Lord North's opinion is really the same as your Majesty's . . . His weak mind only wants *support* which your Majesty may give it.' He did give it; personally delivered the message to Wedderburn; and when Wedderburn announced later he never wished to see North again, gave it as his opinion that North would do well to be rid of him – a course North was still afraid to take. Apropos of this squalid bargaining, George wrote to Robinson:

> Lord North from wanting to get out of the evil of the day but too often falls into what may prove ruin in futurity; I own my mind always inclines to meet difficulties as they arise, and I would much rather have them soon fall on my head if not to be avoided . . .[23]

The war in America meanwhile, cause of North's tribulations and the prolonged ministerial uncertainties, did not take any very decided turn. Following Saratoga, the French alliance brought comfort to the rebels' spirits but less assistance to their military fortunes than might have been expected. In fact the Franco-American alliance soon turned rather sour. The British garrison was indeed obliged to abandon Philadelphia, in order to strengthen the forces in the West Indies. But d'Estaing's departure to the Caribbean left the redcoats still holding Rhode Island (with its naval base at Newport) and New York. The British fleet, although the French had outnumbered it, was once again in control of American coastal waters. In the centre Clinton, following his instructions, confined his activities to sporadic attacks upon the seaboard, but in the south British forces, with the help of local loyalists, succeeded in overrunning Georgia – 'a very good success', commented the King; and it happily coincided with the capture of St Lucia from the French, to compensate somewhat for the loss of Dominica. If the war was not being won, at least apparently it was not being lost; and George, like so many Englishmen, pinned his hopes, far too sanguinely as it proved, on loyalist assistance. Undoubtedly he was over-ready to believe the reports that were always coming to him (as for instance from Major-General Robinson in January, 1779)[24] that 'a majority of the people of America wish to be subjects of the King'. And when favourable papers reached him the following June, they seemed to show that the colonies 'had not been a gainer by the contest', and served to confirm him 'in an opinion long entertained that America unless this summer supported by a Bourbon fleet must sue for peace', when he would 'shew that the parent's heart is still affectionate to the penitent child'. He stressed, however, that 'propositions must come from them to us, no farther ones to be sent from hence; they ever tend only to encrease demands'.[25]

Lord North was of course engaged on a war he had done everything possible, short of ceding independence, to escape from. His misfortune was, when it was clear that the Americans would insist on independence or continue the fight, he really had no policy at all. All he could do was to plead incompetence, go on asking permission to quit, leave the war to the departmental ministers and the King himself, wear out his nerves trying to hold the ill-assorted Government together, exercise his debating talent and experience to defend it in the Commons, and employ his ingenuity in finding the taxes to finance a war that could never pay. Concerning this last, George III of course knew that in an immediate book-keeping sense he must be right; but what was involved, he insisted, was more than book-keeping:

I have heard Lord North frequently drop that the advantage to be gained by this contest could never repay the expence, I owne that let any war be ever so successful if persons will set down and weigh the expences they will find as in the last that it has impoverished the state, enriched individuals, and perhaps raised the name only of the conquerors, but this is only weighing such events in the scale of a tradesman behind his counter; it is necessary for those in the station it has pleased Divine Providence to place me to weigh whether expences though very great are not some times necessary to prevent what might be more ruinous to a country than the loss of money . . . Whether the laying a tax was deserving all the evils that have arisen from it, I should suppose no man could alledge that without being thought more fit for Bedlam than a seat in the Senate; but step by step the demands of America have risen – independence is their object, that certainly is one which every man not willing to sacrifice every object to a *momentary* and inglorious peace must con-curr with me in thinking that this country can never submit to . . . Consequently this country has but one sensible, one great line to follow, the being ever ready to make peace when to be obtained without submitting to terms that in their consequence must anihilate this Empire, and with firmness to make every effort to deserve success. [26]

And looking even at the book-keeping, in the longer term, the King foresaw ruin ahead if the home country conceded American independ-ence. The West Indies must soon become economically dependent on America. Merchants, he thought, would emigrate 'to climates more to their advantage, and shoals of manufacturers would leave this country for the New Empire'. 'This Island would be a poor island indeed.' [27]

As the British in 1779 faced the prospect of a Franco-Spanish fleet threatening to dominate the Channel and herald an invasion, Irish danger loomed as menacingly as the American, and rather more im-mediately. Ireland, without a militia of its own, and with most of its garrison employed across the Atlantic, was clearly vulnerable to an enemy expeditionary force which might expect to find support among the Catholic, and even possibly the Presbyterian, peasantry. The Irish Volunteers who now sprang into existence with such patriotic élan to meet this foreign threat were assisted in their raising of arms and uniforms, not only by local subscriptions, but also by Government funds. These Volunteers however were not only meeting, but making, a threat. Forty thousand armed patriots under such leaders as the Duke of Leinster and the Earl of Charlemont could hardly be ignored (they eventually numbered perhaps eighty thousand); and Grattan, Flood, and the parliamentary opposition in the Dublin parliament (a rather more corrupt shadow, or parody, of Westminster's) – as well as their Whig supporters in England, not a few of whom were absentee Irish landlords themselves – were ready to put the screw alike upon the Lord Lieutenant's government in Dublin and Lord North's in London in order to extract the maximum political and economic advantage from Britain's predicament. They demanded free trade. Like the Americans, they pledged themselves to wear only home-manufactured clothing. They limited their supply vote to six months. England had sown her laws, said Hussey Burgh, like dragon's teeth, and they had sprung up armed men.

George III's response to these menacing words and deeds was predictably negative and unyielding. Experience had convinced him, he said of Ireland in November, 1778, that 'this country gains nothing by granting to her dependencys indulgences, for opening the door encourages a demand for more'.[28] His Lord Lieutenant at this time was John Hobart, Earl of Buckinghamshire, a man of some realism and imagination, who was soon to warn that it would be as impossible to resist measures to free Irish trade 'as to stop the ocean with a hurdle'. This was not the kind of talk to recommend itself to George, who judged Buckinghamshire's conduct of affairs 'incomprehensible' and complained that he seemed 'alone to weigh his own personal difficulties and to forget what is owing to his native country'.[29] As for the Bishop of Derry,* who had warned North, from Paris, of French invasion plans, advocated the abolition of tithes and of all anti-Catholic laws and disabilities, and proposed a union of Catholic and Presbyterians in favour of a free constitution, the King considered him an alarmist and a crank. 'No man in his senses' could approve such dangerous democratical remedies.[30]

The French invasion did not materialise, but there was no relaxation in the Irish pressure on the governments of Lord Buckinghamshire and Lord North. North's attention to affairs being erratic and intermittent, it was, as so often, left to Charles Jenkinson and above all to John Robinson to evolve some kind of Irish policy; and Robinson, entirely with the King's approval, saw things much less Buckinghamshire's way than that of some of his hard-line ministers (Beresford, the Commissioner of Revenue, and Scott, the Attorney-General, in particular).[31] Doubtless Robinson's judgment reinforced the King's comments in November, 1779, that 'no dependence' could be placed on Buckinghamshire and that 'a more firm man' ought 'instantly' to be put in his place;[32] and on 14th November, the day before serious rioting began

* Augustus Hervey's brother Frederick, who succeeded him in 1779 as Earl of Bristol.

in Dublin, North wrote to him conceding nothing, and suggesting that the Irish Parliament should 'dare to be a little unpopular'. 'The mob,' North told the King (who thought his letter to the Lord Lieutenant 'very judicious'), 'are the masters of Parliament', and the politicians 'who have been stirring up the people have already raised the flame so high that it is too strong for them to manage'.[33]

The old remedy, firmness, was to be applied, and it was to have as little success in Dublin as earlier in Boston. Indeed it never *was* applied. Retreat towards conciliation came very quickly. By December, Grattan and Flood and the 'Protestant nation' in Ireland won at least part of what they had been struggling for, and North – beset by every kind of other difficulty – was obliged to concede free export of Irish wool and cloth, and complete freedom of trade between Ireland and the rest of the Empire.

Although George showed no more imaginative understanding of Irish than of American problems, at least he proved right in one respect. 'Opening the door' certainly did 'encourage a demand for more'. Given free, or almost free, trade, the Irish were never to rest until they gained political emancipation – though, for the next century or so, that was a concept much more difficult to be confident and unanimous about amid the social and religious divisions of Ireland than among the free settlements of America.

The likelihood of Spain joining France to attack Britain had long been assumed, and in April, 1779, the two Bourbon powers concluded their agreement for a combined descent upon the English coast. (Gosport or the Isle of Wight was to provide their initial beachhead, but knowledge of their plans being unknown here, all Irish and southern English coasts required guarding; Plymouth was considered a probable target.) The previous October, George had said that by the spring he expected the British Navy would be 'in a state to cope with both nations', but a bad six months had followed, with the Palliser-Keppel recriminations and disturbances, senior officers angrily divided into two camps, Admirals Keppel and Howe declining to take command, and Vice-Admiral Mann pleading bad health. The King was 'obliged to scan afresh the lists of Admirals', and eventually descried there the name of the elderly Sir Charles Hardy, who was accordingly, *faute de mieux*, invited to emerge from his retirement as Governor of Greenwich Hospital to take command of the Channel fleet at the hour when the nation faced what was probably its acutest invasion danger since the Armada of 1588. The King praised his ardour, stiffened him with the best Rear-Admirals he could find, and appointed Kempenfelt as

Admiral's Captain, he being 'much respected by all parties and one well qualified to heal all the little breaches'.[34]

When d'Orvilliers sailed from Brest early in June, 1779, aiming to make a junction with the Cadiz fleet, the British fleet was still in port, though being pressed urgently by Sandwich to sail (it got to sea on the 15th) and the King and North were as usual in the middle of an abortive attempt to reorganise the administration. (This particular new model would have involved Germain's going out, and Fox's coming in as Navy Treasurer.) North, though protesting – again as usual – that he felt 'his faculties of mind and body daily diminishing', was reported by Jenkinson as using

> yesterday in the House of Commons much firmer language with respect to America than I have known him, and Lord G. Germaine spoke with more spirit and more like a minister than usual, so that the cause of Government wore a better face than it has done for some time, and it is clear that what your Majesty thought proper to write and say had its effect.[35]

A day or two later North's son died; his spirits fell again; and he was again pressing to resign 'within two days of the prorogation of Parliament'. The King replied reprovingly before he knew of North's bereavement; wrote quickly again, when he heard, to express condolence; but still insisted on loyal perseverance and no deserting. As for the opposition's demand for a withdrawal of troops from America to concentrate resources at home,

> America cannot now be deserted without the loss of the [West Indian] Islands; therefore we must stretch every nerve to defend ourselves, and must run risks, if we are to play a cautious game ruin will inevitably ensue.[36]

As a move to avert that ruin, the King now did something which had not been done before in his reign, personally presiding on 21st June at an extraordinary meeting of the Cabinet at Buckingham House. For an hour, and eloquently, according to North, he recapitulated events from the Stamp Act onwards (declaring its repeal by Rockingham to have proved a disaster), defended his own actions, emphasised his respect for constitutional liberties, spoke up warmly for Sandwich and North, repeated his willingness to widen the basis of his administration, deplored departmental inefficiences and ministerial intrigues, urged firmness and solidarity in face of the external danger, and declared that he would rather 'part with his life than suffer his dominion to be dismembered'. There followed an hour and a half's discussion, during the course of which Thurlow's suggestion that a coalition with the opposition be considered went down as poorly with the King as might be expected. Later that day, writing to Sandwich, George wondered whether, 'in the kind of stupor of some departments, my idea of speaking out hath not given some degree of confidence.' If any minister wished to resign, he told Germain, he had better do so. As for Lord North, 'although there are many things about him I wish were changed, I don't know any who would do so well, and I have a great regard for him . . .' 'I will do all I can,' he declared, 'to push him on.'[37]

This emergency meeting of 21st June was one of the very few occasions on which George III 'acted as his own prime minister' in anything near a modern meaning of the expression.* That he did many things that a modern monarch cannot do hardly makes him his own prime minister. He expected to be consulted always, and was very ready to rap North over the knuckles if he promised an appointment without approaching him first. He kept up a constant dialogue, both with individual ministers and through them with the Cabinet as a body. He was the administration's ever-present partner, always at its elbow. He made suggestions, often sensible and shrewd, sometimes vociferous. Often enough he expressed dissent; and ministers, or the weekly Cabinet, sometimes did bow to his persuasion, and frequently did not. There are some significant words in one of those private memoranda he was in the habit of making on troublesome subjects – this one on America, written in 1779: '*I will interfere as little as possible with that great question*' – though that could never stop him pouring out advice. As he said self-justifyingly to North, 'I have accepted of persons highly disagreeable to me . . . and have yielded to measures my own opinion did not quite approve.' Sometimes of course his expressed opinion was made to sound like a very strong recommendation indeed, almost an order. (In July, 1779, for instance, he felt it imperative that Sandwich should make 'an alteration or rather addition' to the instructions being sent to the Channel fleet, and wrote: 'I cannot help stating my sentiments on paper and desiring Lord Sandwich to communicate it to the Cabinet.')[38] He did not normally interfere with major military or naval promotions, but sometimes he would overrule decisions concerning either an appointment or a dismissal.[39] In concert with his trusted confidants – at this time that meant Jenkinson and Robinson in particular –

* 'Indeed, one might well ask, who was Prime Minister at this time – George III or Lord North?' (Pares, King *George III and the Politicians*, 174). 'It was not the mere rumour of the streets that the King was his own minister.' (C. J. Fox, Parliamentary History, xx, 1120.) The King presided personally at two more such Cabinet meetings, in January, 1781, and January, 1784.

he regarded himself as a sort of standing ginger-group or stuffing-provider. He constantly acted as party overseer-cum-supernumerary chief whip. If a 'prime minister' felt unequal to the task of cutting another minister (like Wedderburn) down to size, the King would do it. If he was too diffident to dismiss a Chancellor (like Bathurst), the King would do that too. He was a sort of grand umpire and conciliator in ministerial disputes, and never allowed himself or others to forget that his constitutionally hallowed headship of the executive was no mere vestige, but a reality. And he was all these things in addition of course to being His Majesty the King, head of state, fount of honour, and defender of the Anglican faith.

Never did his energies seem more necessary than in the summer and autumn of 1779. There were those like North, and like many at the Admiralty, who counted ships, and finding the British outnumbered by the Franco-Spanish, advocated caution and a concentration on defence. There were others, like Lord Mulgrave (at the same time a Lord of the Admiralty and a serving sailor) and Captain Kempenfelt, who thought twenty-five or thirty in a line of battle was the optimum, and the enemy might well be encumbered by a superfluity of sail. The King was always on this second side. He assumed British seamanship would be superior. He had no patience at all with the jeremiahs of the opposition, like the Duke of Richmond, who set up a great cry of national crisis and then put obstacles in the way of vigorous preparation. (As Lord Lieutenant of Sussex, Richmond 'publicly and flagrantly' refused to co-operate in plans 'to drive cattle and remove or destroy haystacks, etc.' if the enemy should land, and he was therefore summarily deprived of his Lieutenancy. If this should prompt any other opposition Lords Lieutenant to resign in protest, well and good, said George; 'the sooner that office of dignity is in more friendly hands in every county the better.'[40]) He reminded Lord Sandwich of the part played by 'vigour of mind' in 1588, not forgetting the assistance of Divine Providence, of whose equally Anglophile beneficence in 1779 he entertained no doubts. And if Captain Kempenfelt's view of his commander-in-chief, Admiral Sir Charles Hardy, was fair – and there is reason to think it was – it was perhaps well that Divine Providence did between June and September, 1779, take a tolerant view of George III and the Britain whose name he gloried in. 'My God, what have your great people done by such an appointment!' cried Kempenfelt. In Hardy he could find 'a fund of good nature, but not one grain of the commander-in-chief'. Where, alas, was Lord Howe?[41]

The enemy fleet for a fortnight and more in August cruised un-molested in the Channel while Hardy stood away to the westward and avoided battle. His orders of 29th July, as specially toughened at George's request, had been to take every reasonable, but no unreasonable, risk to bring the enemy to action. The King did not credit the report that the French and Spanish ships numbered more than fifty;* however, 'be it as it will I owne I think an action highly desirable.' Hardy ought to 'avail himself of every contingency'. Instead he played a waiting game.[42]

Meanwhile there was frantic activity to improve the defences of Plymouth, with the military governor and Sandwich at cross purposes, and a general tendency for everybody to blame everybody else for the lack of previous preparation. North was down in Kent, feeling wretched and helpless, and several other ministers – not Sandwich – were out of town for August, leaving their departments to their juniors. By 2nd September Sandwich thought a battle 'inevitable', and wrote to remind the commander-in-chief that the eyes of all the world were on him. The very next day, however, Hardy, without prior permission, brought his fleet in to Portsmouth, officially to take on water, though some used the word 'retreat'. Mulgrave thought that if the enemy had had the enterprise at that moment they could have seized St Helen's. Of course Mulgrave did not know the extent of the sickness aboard the French and Spanish fleet, though there were indeed hopefully ghoulish rumours – it was said that corpses were so contaminating parts of the Channel that it was not safe to eat the fish.[43] The King, though anxious, and insisting that the British squadron, directly it was 'refreshed', should take promptly to sea again and give the enemy 'hard blows', would not listen to criticism of Hardy. He was a 'man of real resolution and not afraid of the murmurs' that coming back to port would occasion. 'None of the popular names would have dared to take such a part; but I am not surprised for the hand of Providence seems to be taking a part in our favour.'[44]

Providence, however, was being more inscrutable in the West Indies, whence news arrived of the loss of St Vincent and Grenada. These setbacks were followed by the return home of Admiral Barrington, another opposition Whig, who complained that Sandwich had left him with insufficient forces, and forecast total disaster in the Caribbean. Germain too was harshly criticised for his interference and lack of military understanding, both by General Grant from the West Indies and General Clinton from America: 'For God's sake, my lord . . .' wrote Clinton, 'leave me to myself and let me adapt my efforts to the hourly change of circumstances.' Privately the King was inclined to go at least half-way with some of these criticisms of his

* He was wrong: the figures, enemy to British, were 66 to 38.

ministers. 'The fleet in the West Indies is quite useless,' he told Sandwich, 'unless at least seven ships are relieved and men sent out sufficient to compleat those that remain . . . If we lose our sugar islands it will be impossible to raise money to continue the war,' and if we concentrated too many of our ships and troops on home defence, he argued, we would finish by having no Empire left. He would rather risk even the danger of an enemy landing in England; one must be ready (like Churchill in 1940) to fight them on the beaches and the hills and fields. 'I see the difficulties of the times,' he continued, 'but I know nothing advantageous can be obtained without some hazard . . . It is by bold and manly efforts nations have been preserved, not pursuing alone the line of home defence.'[45]

The King would stand by members of the Government if they would show some spirit and efficiency; but he saw no reason why they should be shielded from public scrutiny and criticism. When the parliamentary opposition in November, 1779, were pressing for an inquiry into the rottenness of Plymouth's defences at the height of the invasion danger, he did not see why the Master of the Ordnance, Lord Amherst, or others responsible should not face the music: 'If they can defend themselves, I do not see any evil can arise; if they have not done their duty it is right it should be known.'[46] Shortly before this, he had used some notably strong words to Sandwich:

If ministers will take a firm decided part and risk something to save the Empire I am ready to be the foremost on the occasion, as my stake is the deepest; but if nothing but measures of caution are pursued and further sacrifices are made from a want of boldness . . . I shall certainly not think myself obliged, after a conduct shall have been held so contrary to my opinion, to screen them from the violence of an enraged nation.[47]

By the end of 1779, though the invasion threat had receded, North's government had come very close to disintegration. If it had not been for the King it must have collapsed. First Gower, leader of the Bedfords, resigned, and he was soon followed by Weymouth, a fellow Bedford. Wedderburn announced that, though he would not give up his Attorney Generalship, he would have no further personal intercourse with North. As ever, North himself was requesting to be released. It appears he had caught sight of a letter from the King to Robinson, saying that if North would not treat his colleagues with civility and confidence, the 'mischief' would continue. 'Sir,' wrote North,

I have been miserable for ten years in obedience to your Majesty's commands, but since your Majesty has now form'd your opinion that I have been a great cause of this mischief, I hope that your Majesty has determined to permit me soon to retire . . . for really it is impossible to bear my misery and guilt at the same time . . . while the publick suffers and while nobody approves my conduct.[48]

The point sounds reasonable enough, and North had much to put up with. His crosses and alarms, he said, absolutely drove him to madness, and Robinson reported 'in the strongest and most alarming manner the distracted state of Lord North's mind'[49] – but the infuriating thing about him, apart from his erratic attention to business, was his day-to-day, or even morning-to-evening, vacillation. 'It would have been most desirable,' wrote George, 'if you had seen this morning the affair of Lord Hillsborough [who was at last to kiss hands as Secretary of State] in the same point of view as this night.'[50]

The key man, it seemed to George, must now be Thurlow (also a Bedford); and Jenkinson, Robinson, and the King between them exercised all the persuasion they knew to prevent him from joining his political friends in their attempt to force the King to oust North. When Thurlow decided not to abandon the Chancellorship, he was next approached as cabinet-maker extraordinary, intermediary and negotiator-in-chief with the now reinforced, though still much divided, opposition. But by Christmas it was clear that there would be no coalition and no compromise, and that North's ministry of the discredited (Germain, Sandwich, if unjustly, Amherst, North himself), the disgruntled (Thurlow,* Wedderburn, Rigby), and the newly imported or re-imported (Stormont, Bathurst, Hillsborough) would continue to hobble along. To Thurlow, when his parleys with opposition leaders had come to nothing, George wrote that as sovereign he considered he had done all he could 'to reclaim the factious, to form a coalition of the great and the virtuous', and to unite his subjects. This was the old will o' the wisp of the extinction of party, the government of national unity, the 'pristine lustre' of the constitution, that had led him towards Chatham nearly fourteen years earlier; but now he was experienced and realistic enough to know that this was no true light. He would continue to *consult* his ministers, he told Thurlow, 'and place in them as entire a confidence as the nature of this government can be supposed to require of me' – a chilly qualification; not so chilly, how-

---

* Thurlow expressed to Robinson in January, 1780, his exasperation with North; 'Damn him . . .' he said, 'nothing can goad him forward, he is the very clogg that loads everything.'

ever, as the 'disdain' he felt the opposition leaders had shown towards him:

> It is evident to me [he wrote] what treatment I am to expect from Opposition, if I was to call them now to my service. Nothing less will satisfy them than a total change of measures and men: to obtain their support I must deliver up my person, my principles and my dominion into their hands: I must also abandon every old meritorious and faithful servant I have, to be treated as their resentment or their mercy may incline them. These would be hard times indeed to be a sovereign in any situation. I trust to God that mine is not yet so bad as this. I will never make my inclinations alone, nor even my own opinions, the sole rule of my conduct in public measures; my first object shall be the good of my people.[51]

Parliament met on 25th November, and the opposition battered away at North, Sandwich, and Germain. For a time Irish affairs took the front of the Westminster stage, with the Whigs passionately supporting their counterparts in Dublin but having the ground somewhat cut from under them when in December North granted free trade and earned the temporary and surprised gratitude of the Irish opposition. Robinson and the King ought perhaps to have had some share of these kind feelings, for North's policy had emerged out of Robinson's work, and on 22nd November, Robinson had written to the King: 'Lord North [yesterday] adopted very much the ideas which you mentioned concerning Ireland.'[52]

From the beginning of the parliamentary session of 1779-80 there was a new tone about the opposition attacks. The Whigs – Bedfords, Shelburnites, and Rockinghams – had come very close, infuriatingly close, to overturning Lord North. That they had not succeeded was due partly perhaps to their own over-confidence, but chiefly to the stubborn persistence of the King. Now more and more it was against the King's conduct, the King's system of government, and even the King personally, that their onslaughts were directed. It was alone the corrupt influence of the Crown that maintained majorities in Parliament. It was the secret influence of Closet advisers outside the Cabinet (the old bogey of 'the minister behind the curtain' in a new guise) that determined the country's affairs. From the outset in his reply to the King's Speech Fox set the tone of parliamentary debate with language concerning the monarch that had not been heard in Parliament during the lifetime of living men, or been seen in print since the heyday of Junius. The same parallels that Junius had drawn with the House of Stuart were harshly driven home by Fox; and George was reminded that he should not forget that his 'claim to the throne of this country was founded only upon the delinquency of the Stuart family'. In what shining circumstances had the reign of George III, that 'grandson of a hero', begun; but now they 'had already seen the conquests of his grandfather wrested from him in the West Indies and his hereditary provinces of America erected into an empire that disclaimed all connection with him . . . How sadly was the scene reversed! his empire dismembered, his councils distracted, his people falling off in their fondness for his person!'[53]

The accusation of secret influence had now once again become one of the main themes of the Rockinghams' attacks. The Rockinghams had come to hold, as an article of faith, that the power of the Closet varied inversely with the cohesiveness of the administration; that the King always proceeded on the maxim of 'divide and rule'. By the time Burke published his *Present Discontents* in 1770 the doctrine of the secret influence was already a part of the Rockinghamite canon. It remained so throughout the seventies. North, wrote Burke, was 'an hireling, and the sheep are not his own'.[54] There was an 'interior Cabinet', a 'double Cabinet', a 'secret system', a 'hidden influence'. Suspicion of its existence and the resolve to destroy it lay at the root of Burke's insistence on the value of party and party solidarity. No group not cohering within commonly held principles would be strong enough to thwart the Court's divisive machinations.

It is certainly true that George relied much on Jenkinson and Robinson – and after the long-delayed interment of the Bute legend these were the two chief spiders the Whigs saw spinning their webs within the Closet. Neither of these men was a member of the Cabinet, though both were members of the administration: Jenkinson was Secretary at War and Robinson Treasury Secretary. It is true also that sometimes George went behind North's back to both of them. His motive, however, was not to undermine but to fortify him, to give him ballast, to get him to emerge from his 'dilatoryness'; to persuade him and encourage him and prod him. Robinson was North's man, and not till North fell in 1782 did any conflict arise between his loyalties to his chief and to his monarch. As for Jenkinson, he did frequently write to the King in tones that no one else presumed to use – rather like those of a tactful tutor helping his pupil along with advice and encouragement. 'I would be very civil to Lords Gower and Weymouth, and I would again and again press the Chancellor to be more explicite . . . I highly approve your Majesty's conduct . . .' 'I think it will be right to endeavour to keep [Lord North] in good humour.' 'Your Majesty should send for the Chancellour and put the business in the same train as it was before.'[55] On occasion too, Robinson and Jenkinson did use the almost conspiratorial language with him that 'insiders' might use about 'the others', and Jenkinson sometimes sounds more like the King's 'private eye' than his Secretary at War: 'I have heard nothing except that Lord Gower, Lord Weymouth, the Chancellour, and Mr Rigby dined alone together yesterday and that the Chancellour went in the evening to Lord North.' 'In all that the faction of the Bedfords are doing, there may be some plott; I half suspect it, but I cannot discover what it is.'[56] 'I will come to the Drawing Room, but do not mean to trouble your Majesty with an audience for fear of creating jealousies and suspicions.'

But Jenkinson was loyal to North even when most exasperated. 'Nothing,' he wrote in May, 1780, 'can be more proper or more forcible than your Majesty's answer to Lord North' – who had obviously shown him the royal letter – 'and cannot fail of making a great impression on him.' Jenkinson was undoubtedly a very special private adviser, but it is impossible to find in him a malign secret influence intriguing against the Cabinet. Indeed rather the reverse. A month after Yorktown he wrote to the King: 'Allow me as a faithful servant . . . to entreat your Majesty not to suffer any great question of policy to rest singly on discourses in your Closet between your Majesty and Lord North, or any one of your ministers, but to refer the same to our [Cabinet] Council for their deliberation, with orders for them to report to your Majesty their opinion thereon.'[57] In one respect the Rockinghams became the frustrated victims of their own propaganda. Fearing lest the King, in order to destroy them, would always secretly cabal with any other Whig connections which they might take as equal partners, they resisted the idea of a Whig coalition and came to think of themselves, though never able to command a parliamentary majority, as the only true Whigs.

CHAPTER EIGHTEEN

Towards Yorktown

THE combination of high war-time taxation with national humiliations was a sure prescription for domestic discontent; and now, alongside the Whigs' parliamentary offensive against a tottering Government there began to sound countrywide rumblings of popular protest. In Middlesex there was a revival of Wilkite agitation. In Yorkshire the Rev. Dr Wyvill built an organised movement out of the widespread indignation men felt at the high level of taxes, and their suspicious unease at the abuse of executive power and waste of public money. The fashion was suddenly for county committees and petitions to Parliament; and an inter-county committee was formed which went so far as to formulate a three-point national programme for cuts in Court expenditure ('economical' reform), annual general elections, and the creation of 100 new *county* seats at Westminster. Corruption was the petitions' universal target, the menace to the people's liberties their constant theme; and as the Yorkshire petition explicitly asserted, it was the Crown that was at the heart of the corruption, and the Crown's 'unconstitutional influence' which was the prime threat to liberty.

Most of Wyvill's support, and indeed the motive force of the petitioning movement as a whole, came from solid property-owning freeholders, many of them country gentlemen very remote from democratic views and attitudes. As Rockingham impressed upon the House of Lords, a total income of £800,000 a year was represented by the 600 gentlemen present at the meeting held in York Assembly Rooms on 30th December, 1779. Many of these squires and men of local substance, including Wyvill himself, had small liking for politicians, and there was even an attempt to exclude all members of Parliament from the movement's proposed general assembly. But from the beginning the parliamentary Whigs saw opportunities too good to neglect. Through Sir George Savile, a member for Yorkshire, Rockingham became closely associated with the movement in that county, and many of his fellow Whigs and some of the followers of Shelburne with those of the other counties that followed Yorkshire's example. Fox was active in Wiltshire, young William Pitt and Lord Mahon in Kent. The Dukes of Richmond, Manchester, and Rutland were enthusiastic local committee members. Shelburne, not to be outdone by the Rockinghams, employed his own academics – Drs Price, Priestley, and Jebb – to adumbrate a programme of peace abroad (but ruling out American independence) and reform at home.

Fox in particular was transformed by the petitioning movement into *Fox populi*, discovering that he could do more things than he previously knew. For years he had been impressing and astonishing friends and enemies alike upon the intimate benches of St Stephen's. Now he found that he could sway an open-air crowd in Wiltshire (the first uncorrupt assembly he had ever addressed, he said) or an audience of two thousand in Westminster Hall. 'You must be ministers of your own deliverance,' he cried, 'and the road to it is open. Your brethren in America and Ireland shew you how to act . . . Are we not possessed with equal veneration for our lives and liberties? . . . Did not our fathers fight and bleed for their rights?' To the King, Fox's villainy was now doubledyed; a friend to his country's enemies, he was now become also a democratical demagogue. Already close to treason, he now approached still closer to republicanism. When the story of his sexual dissipation and reckless gambling was added in, the King's picture of Fox was almost complete; it would need only his forthcoming friendship with the Prince of Wales to complete the detestable canvas. None even of Fox's many enemies could deny his brilliance, his power in debate, his resilience, his 'amazing quickness in seazing any subject' as the Duchess of Devonshire wrote.[1] Fox (or as she called him 'The Eyebrow') seemed, she said, 'to have the particular talent of knowing more about what he is saying and with less pains than anyone else. His conversation is like a brilliant player at billiards, the strokes follow one another piff puff . . .' But to the King every stroke, like the man himself, was anathema, 'unjust and indecent as everything that comes from that quarter must be expected.'[2]

The more radical among the petitioners soon fell foul of the run-of-the-mill aristocratic Whigs whose vested interest in private boroughs and the 'rotten' old system was hardly less than the Crown's own. No one would accuse the Marquis of Rockingham or the Duke of Portland of being democrats (even if there were doubts of the unaccountable Duke of Richmond – but then he was Fox's uncle). There was nevertheless one sector of the system which petitioners and parliamentary Whigs could unite in deploring. The King and his ministers maintained their majority by the manipulation of patronage; by jobbery. If therefore the numbers of jobs at the disposal of the Crown could be reduced; if the financial resources of the Crown could be cut back; if in brief the King's wings could be clipped, his power to keep the Whigs from office would vanish. All this harmonised well with the petitioners' complaints of taxpayers' money being wasted on Court sinecures.

During the session of 1780, therefore, the opposition's main assault on King and Government concentrated on 'economical' reform. In the Commons Burke, Barré, Fox, Savile, and the rest, and in the Lords Shelburne, hammered away day after day at a series of demands for the abolition of sinecure places, reforms of the Civil List, formation of a commission of accounts, publication of pension lists, and prohibition of parliamentary membership to government contractors. Debates were prolonged, often rancorous, and more than usually wearing; by March both Fox and Barré were 'hoarse and ill', and Burke 'wasted by fatigue and want of sleep'. North on his good days was more like his old self, alert in debate, all amiable reasonableness when that was the best defence, for instance in discussion of the petitions; belligerent in counter-attack when occasion presented – he had one notorious altercation with Speaker Norton on the subject of 'corruption', the pot calling the kettle black; despondent when he saw his Commons majority sinking to floor level or even below, but cheerful when debates went well, or when the news from abroad was good – and it was increasingly good as 1780 advanced. Did this baffling man really want to resign? By June, Jenkinson was writing to the King, 'Mr Robinson adds that he thinks I am a true prophet in having always said that Lord North never meant to treat or part with the smallest degree of power.'[3]

The nearest Burke and his economical reform came to success at this stage was when he managed to get a majority of eight in the Commons on a motion to abolish the Board of Trade, with its comfortably remunerated Lords of Trade. The Board of Trade lived on for a time nevertheless. An attempt to abolish the office of Third (or American) Secretary, on the grounds that America being *de facto* independent needed no Secretary, fell short by only seven votes. Why, asked Dundas, if the House was so dominated by corruption, did the Government have such close shaves? The King was pleasantly surprised to see a majority at all on this issue of the Third Secretary. There was, he knew, 'no small prejudice against its present possessor,' Germain. But when Burke turned to the Civil List and the King's Household the majorities for the Government increased notably. The explanation is plain. To attack ministers was reasonable; to abolish unpopular government departments would have been positively enjoyable; but to attack the King directly, through his private expenditure, was another matter. It affronted his dignity, and it offended the loyal susceptibilities of many of the independent members. Even Speaker Norton, appealed to by Fox, gave it as his opinion that the King ought to be *asked*, not obliged, to make economies in his Household. And that very odd and soon to be notorious member, Lord George Gordon, was one who objected to a reform 'which directed its attention to the King's very Bedchamber' – and noted by the by what many others had not failed to note, that Burke, while wishing to cut out some dead wood, had 'taken care of his friends' by allowing life sinecures to continue till the death of the existing holders.

The climax of the Whigs' 1780 attack on the Crown came after the Easter recess, when John Dunning, a Shelburnite lawyer and once Grafton's Solicitor General, moved as a rider to a consideration of the county petitions, *That the influence of the Crown has increased, is increasing, and ought to be diminished.* The motion was in general terms; it represented what many members, and many among the general public, genuinely felt, more or less strongly; and it passed by 233 votes to 215. North, informing the King at 2 a.m., was deep in depression and once more put in writing his need to retire. George responded with composure: Lord North must not take the vote as personal to him – it was all too clear against whom it was '*personally levelled*'. Yet it was not possible that a true majority wished 'to overturn the constitution; factious leaders and ruined men wish it [it was Fox the gambler who was "ruined"]; but the bulk of the nation cannot see it in that light'. He would remain 'temperate but at the same time firm'.[4] And in a week or two he had the satisfaction of seeing a further resolution of Dunning's, to prevent the House from being dissolved or prorogued until the petitions' grievances had been met and the balance of the constitution restored, handsomely defeated by a House very many of whom had no love for the Whig groups, little respect for their motives, and no desire to humiliate the King or revive the spirit of 1641. These were the independents who probably did better represent 'the bulk of the nation' than the Whigs, as the King claimed;* those who he was sure would not in a crisis 'stand neuter'; representatives of that public, as Jenkinson hopefully described them, 'not the interested and factious, who are always the most noisy, but the calm and dispassionate part of mankind'.

By the end of April, George was able to express 'satisfaction at the majorities on the rejection of the two questions relative to retrenchments in my Household'.[5] And steadily over the subsequent weeks, though distressed to find North still begging leave to resign, he was

---

* If we always remember that the term 'nation', by pretty general consent, implied perhaps one in twelve of the adult population. And even if we were to suppose it to include the other eleven, the Whig aristocracy would hardly have been likely to come off better.

given further pleasure to hear of defeats in Committee for Burke's Establishment Bill.

Indeed, governmental prospects at Westminster and military prospects in America both improved sufficiently between April and August, 1780, to convince the King that his hard-willed optimism had reason behind it; and this despite the worsening situation in Europe, where the Dutch* were soon to join the ranks of Britain's enemies. The north European powers too had leagued together in an 'armed neutrality' to resist the British navy's claims to search their vessels for contraband. In America, however, there was runaway inflation causing severe discontent, not least among the poorly clothed and fed colonial army. The number of loyalists grew rather than fell; and 'every account of the distresses', thought the King, 'shews that they must sue for peace this summer if no great disaster befalls us.'[6] More than compensating for the orderly British withdrawal from Rhode Island came news of more successes in the South, culminating in Clinton's taking of Charleston, with nearly 7,000 prisoners, in May, 1780; and in August, Cornwallis heavily defeated Gates, the victor of Saratoga, at Camden in South Carolina.

At home, too, the Gordon Riots of June, which painfully showed the alarming dangers which petitions and 'associations' and stirrings-up of popular discontent could lead to, assisted the appreciable improvement in the position of the Crown, the Government, and the party of order. To the King and all the Cabinet except Thurlow, the late summer of 1780 seemed a most favourable moment for a dissolution and general election, which was not due till the following year. Even Thurlow would not declare against it, only rumbling on about the 'damned nonsense' of shortening Parliaments and how 'Lord North ought to settle it'. The King thought 'it would be madness not to call a new parliament as soon as we have hobbled through the present session'.[7] As Sandwich put it,

> Our opponents are depressed, the nation is set against riots and rioters of all kinds, events have been favourable beyond conception; will you wait to give our enemies time to rally and re-unite, and for some blow in our military operations to turn the tide of popularity against us?[8]

Robinson, the Government's principal political manager and

* The Dutch had been freely supplying France with supplies, including war supplies, and had given facilities to the American privateer Paul Jones. The British began searching Dutch vessels in April, 1780, and declared war in the autumn.

Psephologist Royal, having computed and classified his *pros, hopefuls, doubtfuls, and cons*, forecast a successful issue. Strict secrecy was observed and deceptive manœuvres were contrived to lull the suspicious opposition, so that it was not until the very eve of dissolution on 1st September that Rockingham learned definitely of North's 'wicked intentions'. Then his excited comments to the Duke of Portland show clearly enough his vexation:

> The only idea on which the measure of dissolution can be adopted must be that his Majesty's advisers think that delay might risk the *influence of the Crown* getting out of their hands, and that *his Majesty* and they wish to secure as many tools to be elected as possible in order to have a large body of banditti to controul, thwart, and betray *any men* who venture to undertake administration when the present ministers perhaps *flye* their country. [9]

It turned out in fact that Robinson's electoral forecasts had been much too optimistic, even though to some extent his errors had been self-cancelling. But the election, though it proved to be far from a governmental triumph, did at least promise – or threaten – something like the *status quo* for a further seven years, and the Whigs had every reason to feel frustrated and depressed. Decisive success was so frequently to come nearly within their grasp, and yet so constantly to be dashed. Given 'no great disaster' in America, there now seemed no reason why the North ministry should not survive indefinitely. Equally, however, there seemed less and less prospect of their being able to bring the war to a victorious conclusion. And even if by perseverance and good fortune they did, how would they manage to govern the colonies even then?

Clinton and Cornwallis were strong enough to win battles, but always lacked the reserves to follow up successes or cope with guerrilla forces preying on their communications. Clinton himself, the King noted, was now 'of a very gloomy cast'. But 'the giving up the game', he insisted to North, 'would be total ruin'. A great state like Britain could not just 'subsist' as a small one might; 'a great one mouldering cannot get into an inferior situation but must be annihilated.' They *must* persevere. 'By giving up the game we are destroying ourselves to prevent being destroyed.'[10]

The American pattern for the first eleven months of 1781 did not differ markedly from that of 1780, except for the silent but eventually crucial factor of the growing dominance of the French at sea. With the welcome adherence to the royalist cause of the American renegade Benedict Arnold, Clinton felt himself strong enough to move north into Virginia; and Cornwallis, though he was successful in joining forces with Arnold and compelling the withdrawal of the forces under La Fayette, was constantly harried by American irregulars and unable to consolidate victories. To worsen matters, Clinton and Cornwallis were mutually at loggerheads. When in June, 1781, Fox brought forward once again in the Commons a proposal to inquire into the possibilities of peace, George characteristically described it as the impudence of a minority whose only wish seemed to be to put heart into rebels and Bourbons. It was a 'hacknied' suggestion in any case and he praised the 'manly fortitude' of the majority who rejected it.[11] William Pitt, the newly elected Shelburnite member for Appleby, just twenty-two, expressed the feelings of this impudent minority as well as any – indeed eloquently enough to win the enthusiastic praise of Fox:

> It was a most accursed, wicked, barbarous, cruel, unnatural, unjust, and diabolical war . . . The expense of it has been enormous, far beyond any former experience, and yet what has the British nation received in return? Nothing but a series of ineffective victories or severe defeats – victories only celebrated with temporary triumph over our brethren . . . or defeats which fill the land with mourning for the loss of dear and valuable relations slain in the impious cause of enforcing unconditional submission . . .[12]

Unfortunately, it was becoming a 'hacknied' war, which had now lasted more than six years. The King, like Germain, remained doggedly optimistic; certain as ever of the justice of his cause; and continued to express 'the greatest confidence in [the] valour of both Army and Navy and above all in the assistance of Divine Providence'. Still, in November, 1781, a few days before the news arrived from Yorktown, he was hoping Clinton would 'soon have somewhat decisive to communicate'. The new session of Parliament was then almost due, but the opposition groups felt in general cheated and dispirited. 'Our opposition is scattered,' Lord Camden considered, 'and runs wild in both Houses under no leader'; and Rockingham himself had 'no doubt that his Majesty and his ministers will hold out and encourage various idle hopes' with a majority 'composed of some credulous fools and many corrupt knaves'.[13]

Two days before Parliament reassembled, 'somewhat decisive' news did at last arrive from America, and it was black news. Hemmed in by French and Americans to the landward, and seaward by the French navy, Cornwallis had capitulated at Yorktown. Lord North, Germain

said, received the tidings 'like a ball in the breast'. Germain himself
recognised the general hostility to continuing the war, even 'among the
real friends of Government', and within a fortnight the Cabinet had
decided 'not to send to North America any more force than what is
necessary to recruit the regiments there'.[14] Yet the King's Speech,
though it baldly referred to the 'loss of my forces' in Virginia, gave no
hint that operations were to be wound up. 'A good end may yet be
made to this war,' George once more insisted to North, 'but if we de-
spond certain ruin ensues.' When men had recovered from the shock,
things would go on not so differently, though the 'mode' of the war
would require alteration.[15] Clinton having resigned his command,
Carleton would be the right man to succeed him, and if Germain would
not work with him Germain must go – even though 'on one point I
shall ever coincide with Lord G. Germain, this is against a separation
from America'. The viscountcy of Sackville served somewhat to
sweeten the Third Secretary's departure at the end of January. He was
not to be disgraced.

The opposition was, of course, encouraged by the news from Yorktown. Some were exultant. Even from the ministerial side Dundas's
behaviour showed clearly that the Government was tottering; it was
he who had pressed hard for the removal of Germain, and of Sandwich
too. As for Fox, he made no bones of laying responsibility for the continuing folly of the American war squarely upon the King:

There was one grand domestic evil, from which all our other evils,
foreign and domestic, had sprung. The influence of the Crown. To
the influence of the Crown we must attribute the loss of the army in
Virginia; to the influence of the Crown we must attribute the loss
of the thirteen provinces of America; for it was the influence of the
Crown in the two Houses of Parliament that enabled his Majesty's
ministers to persevere against the voice of reason, the voice of truth,
the voice of the people.[16]

What North envisaged was a partial running-down of the American
war, while holding on to New York, Nova Scotia, and Charleston as
bases from which to continue operations against the French, Spanish,
and Dutch. In February, 1782, however, the elderly ex-Secretary of
State, General Conway, brought forward two motions to end all
offensive warfare in America. As Conway explained when pressed, he did
not mean immediate military surrender but he did mean the abandonment of any idea of subduing the colonies. His first motion failed by
one vote; his second was passed, with a rider that the King be in-

formed of the decision of the Commons. The Government did survive a few more precarious votes of confidence while the King yet once again struggled, through Thurlow, to magic forth a broad-based administration that would not leave him at the mercy of Rockingham and Fox. But as Robinson reported, the Rats were 'very bad'. A delegation of independent members warned North of the withdrawal of their backing, and North in his turn warned the King that this time the game was really up: 'Your Majesty is well apprized that, in this country, the Prince on the throne cannot, with prudence, oppose the deliberate resolution of the House of Commons . . . Your Majesty's affairs grow worse by every hour that my removal is delay'd.'[17] The first of those two statements the King two years later was successfully to challenge, with the aid of the younger Pitt. But a discredited and defeated North was no younger Pitt, with the prospect of a successful general election in his pocket; any more, as he had so often lamented, than he was an elder Pitt, moving mountains and compelling glory out of the air.

Now at last in his own phrase 'drove to the wall', George for the first time seriously considered abdication in favour of his eldest son. He drafted a message in contemplation of the step. He told Thurlow he valued his principles and honour above his Crown, and was 'resolved' – how often did he serve himself up that word which he must eat so soon – *resolved* not to become the slave of an opposition pledged to American independence. The new administration, however, was in being before the end of the month. Only Thurlow remained from the North Cabinet; Dundas also retained his post of Lord Advocate. When the day of parting came at last, George was bitter. There was a 'more general removal . . . than I believe was ever known before. I have to the last fought for individuals, but the number I have saved except my Bedchamber is incredibly few . . .' 'The agitation of my mind,' he wrote to the Duke of Montagu (who though 'strongly run at' had been retained), 'you may discover by the badness of my writing'; and after he had harshly reprimanded North for his delays in submitting accounts, he at least half-apologised by attributing his expressions to 'a mind truely tore to pieces'.[18] North nevertheless was rewarded for his long tenure of office by at last getting what he had always wanted, tenure *for life* of his Wardenship of the Cinque Ports, and now with the full salary of £4,000 of which he had previously accepted less than half. We can hardly know whether it was a sense of failure or of relief that predominated at the end. At least his facility for the apt pleasantry remained with him. On the night of his resignation, a biting snowy night of late March, opposition members, expecting protracted exchanges, commanded their conveyances for midnight. North cut matters very short, ordered his own coach early, and as he moved through a crowd of shivering members waiting for theirs, remarked genially, 'Good night, gentlemen; you see what it is to be in the secret.'

CHAPTER NINETEEN

'The Contest Is Become Personal'

IN the new Government, a coalition of the followers of Rockingham and of Shelburne, with Rockingham First Lord and Shelburne and Fox Secretaries of State, the King preserved ideas of withstanding the Rockinghams' blast by clinging closely to the relative shelter provided by Shelburne and his friends, who were loath to accept American independence. Whether or not in his first ministry of 1765-66 Rockingham had had the full royal support he felt entitled to, there can be no doubt that he did not have it in his second of March-June, 1782. Whether 'divide and rule' was a fixed royal maxim earlier, as the Whigs believed, there can be no doubt that the King now found the ready-made dissensions between Shelburne on one side and Rockingham and Fox on the other far from unwelcome. Rockingham, like Grenville in 1763, fought to gain for himself exclusive rights of patronage, and although the balance of forces within the Cabinet itself was fairly even, the Rockinghams predominated among junior ministers. Shelburne, however, was not to be brushed aside; and knowing the King's hatred of the Fox-Rockingham party, he was eager to insinuate himself in the Closet and do his best simultaneously to soothe the royal apprehensions and become the most trusted and therefore somewhat especial minister. Fox, hating Shelburne and ever ready to identify the people at large with the Rockingham interest, soon concluded that the new ministry 'was to consist of two parts – one belonging to the King, one to the public'.[1] He also began to see in Pitt, the young member he had so recently praised, 'the man that the old system, revived in the person of Lord Shelburne, will attempt to bring forward to its support.' In the eventual truth of that shrewd prophecy was to lie the whole history of his future frustrations and defeats.

Not surprisingly, the most important domestic actions of the new government were aimed at the King and his influence. Crewe's Act disfranchised Crown revenue officers on the grounds that they were too susceptible to political pressure. Clerke's Act prevented Government contractors from sitting in Parliament; this affected as many as seventeen members. Burke, now Paymaster, attempted much in a little time. He went some way to reforming the system of public accounts, which had hitherto managed to unite the characteristics of the Augean stables and the Cretan labyrinth. He did now succeed in abolishing the office of American Secretary, the eight Lord Commissionerships at the Board of Trade (at £1,000 a year each), three places at the Board of Works, and six more at the Board of Green Cloth (worth £1,018 a year each). His reform of the King's Civil List, however, intended as the centrepiece of economical reform, only succeeded in combining the maximum of irritation to the King and his household with a minimum of practical benefit to the public. It was founded on the Rockingham doctrine that George III spent vast sums from the Civil List on maintaining a vicious plan of political corruption. There was indeed an old-established system of both governmental and private expenditure on the management of elections. George himself had recently protested to North, when belatedly faced with the accounts, at 'the immense cost' of the election of 1780. It had in fact cost the public £62,000, and there were in all perhaps two hundred place-holders of various kinds in the Commons – about fifty fewer than in 1761, and many of them by no means lobby-fodder, as North latterly knew too well.[2] The 'independence' of eighteenth-century placemen certainly far exceeded that of present-day servants of the party whip. The great mountain of corruption that Burke and his friends had thundered against and now sought to flatten had been built up in their imagination much beyond its actual size.

The basic idea of Burke's reform of the Civil List was simple; as it turned out much too simple. From the £900,000 to be annually allotted to the monarch, payments were to be made according to categories of priority, and the lowest of the priorities was to be the payment of the salaries of the ministers concerned with the finances. Their own pockets were thus to provide the most urgent of incentives to the avoidance of waste and bribery. Unfortunately Burke had refused to allow for an essential item in the Civil List accounts, the miscellaneous payments, sometimes nearly a sixth of the whole. Since in fact these charges had to be paid as they arose, and no minister thirsted to sacrifice his own emolument, the Civil List soon ran into deficit, and much of Burke's Establishment Act had eventually to be treated as a dead letter. 'It is impossible to describe to you,' Shelburne wrote to Grafton after Burke's resignation, 'how provokingly my time is taken up with the nonsense of Mr Burke's bill. It was both framed and carried through without the least regard to *facts*.'[3] An effective reform of the Civil List had to wait for the younger Pitt. Not, however, before some exacting, and the King considered insulting and demeaning, economies had been forced on a royal household often ridiculed for its abstinence and parsimony – and this at a time when the Queen's cornucopia of baby princes and princesses had not yet ceased pouring out its store. If it was the name of Fox that rang most distastefully of all in the King's ears, it was Burke's that long continued to rankle most with his family and household.

Economical reform was usually calculated to unite the Whigs. The reform of Parliament itself always divided them. When Pitt brought the subject up in May, 1782, arguing with perhaps a calculated imprecision for 'a more equal representation', he found plenty of opposition from his own side of the House, however warily he trod on the delicate subject of rotten boroughs. Fox, Sheridan, and Savile were among those who spoke for him; Burke, acknowledged to be hostile, had to be persuaded by Fox to absent himself. Among the peers Richmond was an apostle of reform, but Rockingham was hardly less conservative on the subject than Thurlow or the King himself. (Thurlow, though Lord Chancellor, even spoke against his Cabinet's economical reform, which further raised his stock with George.)

This brief second Rockingham ministry was united indeed on very little. Ireland provided a somewhat enforced exception. Renewed agitation there, with Grattan in April moving the ringing resolution in the Dublin Parliament that no power on earth but the King, Lords, and Commons in Ireland had authority there, and with the Volunteers in full cry for Irish legislative independence, made swift response inevitable. Grudgingly Fox made the best of it. 'Unwilling subjects were no better than enemies,' he said – the intended parallel with America was clear – and the British Government swiftly conceded independence to the Irish Parliament. Undeniably it became independently Irish; unhappily it was wholly Protestant, unrepentantly corrupt, and born moribund. Its executive was still dominated by Westminster. As for the King's Irish sovereignty, it was not threatened by the events of 1782; nor was the standing of the Church of England by whose supremacy he set such store, and the threat to which was later to cause his adrenalin to surge so dangerously. He admitted vaguely in 1782 that 'some arrangement' had to be made with the Irish; in the main left it to his ministers; but showed his general dislike of their conduct by grumbling, 'If the same spirit which seems to direct the foreign negotiators is adopted in that business, this island will be the poorer.'

On the broad question of the war and its continuance, he was convinced that France was close to bankruptcy and would crack before Britain, if only men would not be craven or mischievous. The Dutch had already had the worst of the exchanges, and lost St Eustatius in the West Indies to Rodney. Britain had again lost Minorca; but Gibraltar held out, and (though ready in a general peace to abandon it in exchange for Minorca or Porto Rico) George pressed hard on Rockingham's First Lord of the Admiralty, Keppel – a reluctant Keppel, he complained – to speed plans for its relief. Soon, giving some overdue vindication to Sandwich and belated joy to the Northites, came tidings of the important triumph won by Rodney and Hood over the French fleet at Les Saintes; 'glorious news', sang Shelburne; 'the most compleat victory,' echoed the King, 'that has occurred this war.'[4] De Grasse, the French admiral, was captured with his flagship; nine French battleships had been destroyed; Britain again ruled the waves of the Caribbean and the waters off America's Atlantic coast; and the Navy now felt confident of taking on all three of the European navies opposed to them and of relieving Gibraltar into the bargain. The victory, George was quick to point out, had 'so far roused the nation that the peace which would have been acquiesced in three months ago would now be a matter of complaint'.[5]

Before news of Les Saintes had had time to arrive in England, George had written to Shelburne in a mood of bitterly ironical resignation at the Whigs' decision to recall the non-Whig Rodney from his command: 'As it is the unanimous recommendation of the Cabinet . . . I shall not object to it; but I hope Lord Keppel has a proper admiral in his eye to succeed him.' Fox and Keppel were now in something of a fix; George was 'not surprised' that they gained unpopularity by appearing to disgrace the new naval hero. If they would not countermand his recall at least they dared not object to a peerage for him. But an *Irish* viscountcy would be enough, George considered, always ready to smell a rat where the Rockinghams were concerned and suspecting that they intended to propose an English barony only because that would cause a by-election for the Westminster constituency. An English barony, however, it was to be, with the thanks of Parliament and a pension of £2,000. The Irish peerage went to Hood, who had played a major part in the victorious campaign.[6]

Looked at as a whole, the war was very far from lost, the King insisted; and he was resentful that peace negotiations were partly in the hands of men whom he regarded as defeatists; *partly*, since the Cabinet being divided between Fox and Shelburne, so too were the peace negotiations. Shelburne stood for bargaining American independence against a general peace, Fox for unconditional American independence. While Shelburne held out for a price – 'a dreadful price' too, George commented – Fox was giving everything away by his 'precipitancy', and allowing the subtle and 'insincere' Benjamin Franklin to make rings round him.[7]

On 1st July, Rockingham died. Fox's position, difficult before his death, now became in his own view impossible. He had already been outvoted in the Cabinet on the issue of unconditional independence. He considered Shelburne a pompous hypocrite and detested him. He knew that the King detested *him*, and would always incline towards Shelburne. But as the surviving head of a major element in the coalition, he now claimed what no one had ever claimed before, the right to nominate the incoming prime minister. Lacking any more appropriate intermediary, he and his friends asked Shelburne therefore to request that his Majesty make the Duke of Portland his First Lord of the Treasury. (Fox had neither the rank nor the wealth to command the nominal leadership, but he would of course have been the effective leader.) It was hardly surprising that the King, faced with a constitutional claim which was certainly novel and to him outrageous – and brought by such a messenger from such a quarter – proceeded without delay to appoint Shelburne. Fox had a five-minute interview in the Closet, and there and then surrendered his seals of office. The King pretended to no one that he was sorry to see Fox go. He wrote to Robinson: 'Every honest man' and everyone who loved the British constitution 'must wish to the utmost to keep him out of power'; and to North (asking him to support Shelburne in Parliament and use his influence with the country gentlemen): 'The present contest . . . is no less than whether the sole direction of my Kingdoms shall be trusted in the hands of Mr Fox . . . The contest is become personal and he indeed sees it also in that point of view.'[8]

Many of Fox's friends, and his uncle the Duke of Richmond, considered his resignation an act of personal pique against Shelburne and judged it a piece of outstanding political unwisdom. Only Cavendish followed him out of the Cabinet, though Burke, Sheridan, and Fitzpatrick resigned their non-Cabinet posts in solidarity with him. He had not frequented the faro table at all during the strenuous hundred days of his Secretaryship, but soon now he was back again at Brooks's with his heavy-drinking, high-playing young cronies and admirers, who paid the arrears of his subscription to renew the delights of his company. He took a new mistress in 'Perdita' Robinson, who two years earlier had enslaved the Prince of Wales. From her rooms, said Fox, you could see Lansdowne House, and he owed it to the public to keep a strict eye on Lord Shelburne who lived there. 'Perdita' did not last; before the year was out he had begun to find lasting comfort in Elizabeth Armistead, the 'dear Liz' of the rest of his days and at long last his wife.* But worst of all, in the King's eyes, this dangerous and destruc-

* As Christopher Hobhouse put it, 'Mrs Armistead's origins were wrapped in

tive politician – who was at the same time to his friends the most brilliant and lovable of men – now became the close companion of the Prince of Wales.

Separate negotiations continued through the summer and autumn of 1782 between Britain and the Americans, and between Britain and the Bourbon powers, from their side the Americans mistrusting the French and Spaniards hardly less than they did the British. John Adams was convinced that British proposals came 'piping hot from Versailles', and over the question of who was to have the Floridas, the Americans seemed to prefer that it should be Britain rather than Spain. The two main issues that delayed the conclusion of terms were the right to fish off Newfoundland and Nova Scotia, and the treatment to be accorded to those Americans who had remained loyal to the King. At last, in November, 1782, compromises were agreed. 'Thanks be to God,' Adams exclaimed,'. . . our Tom Cod are safe in spite of the malice of enemies, the finesse of allies, and the mistakes of Congress.' In Westminster, Shelburne's new Chancellor of the Exchequer, Pitt, was preparing a bill to make possible new trading agreements with the Americans. As for the loyalists, Congress agreed eventually to 'earnestly recommend' to the separate states that confiscated estates should be restored and their owners allowed to return, a gesture of theoretical goodwill that had predictably small effect. From their side the British recompensed the loyalists for at least part of their losses and facilitated the movement into Canada and Nova Scotia of those who wished to go. The prime issue of independence had not for some months been seriously in question. Slowly and grudgingly George edged towards accepting the inevitable. In November, 1782, when preliminaries were at last agreed (though ratification was to await a general peace), his comments to Shelburne were still stubbornly un-self-critical, and the touch of sour grapes in the final sentence was unworthy of him:

> I cannot conclude without mentioning how sensibly I feel the dismemberment of America from this Empire, and that I should be miserable indeed if I did not feel that no blame on that account can be laid at my door, and did I not also know that knavery seems to be so much the striking feature of its inhabitants that it may not in the end be an evil that they become aliens to this Kingdom. [9]

It is fair to say that his thoughts on what had happened in America,

---

obscurity: as for Mr Armistead, he is generally supposed to have been a figure of speech.' Once poor, she had had the Earl of Derby, the Duke of Dorset, and the Prince of Wales among her lovers before she came to Fox and proved his salvation.

while never ceasing to cause him pain and melancholy, grew more philosophical as the years passed, and even came to include a measure of self-reproach – but always more for losing than having been at all in the wrong.

From the general settlement concluded at Versailles early in 1783, the British Empire (the major disaster in America apart) emerged less scarred than might have been expected at the black moments of the war. Except for Tobago the British West Indies of 1763 remained intact. France gained nothing of consequence in India, a slave-trading post in Senegal, much resentment in America, and, as it proved, a stimulus towards bankruptcy and revolution at home. Britain, ceding Minorca and the Floridas to Spain, in the end retained Gibraltar, after a tussle within the Cabinet over the desirability of exchanging it for further West Indian territory, or some other *quid pro quo*.* The Dutch came empty away – or rather worse.

The terms of peace at least did not reverse the verdict of 1763, which had been the aim of the Bourbon powers, and they were probably as good as any British government could have obtained in 1783. Inevitably however – as in 1763 with Bute – they provided a focus round which general dislike of Shelburne could fester. In the tradition of his master Chatham, he kept his colleagues at a chilly distance; maintaining unity in the Cabinet, William Grenville said, by the simple method of never meeting it. One by one, members of his administration found reasons for leaving. Keppel condemned the peace terms and departed. Richmond, Grafton and Carlisle followed. From the opposition benches Charles Fox, commanding now the support of about ninety members, watched with reviving hope the failing fortunes of the man he reckoned the *second* villain in the land.[10] (It was very obvious whom he meant as the first.) Shelburne, feeling his foothold slipping, could not fail to see the alternatives before him. As Gibbon calculated it, the state of the three main parties was now 'Ministers, 140; Reynard, 90; Boreas, 120'. A plus B made 230 to 120. A plus C made 260 to 90. But B *plus* C, Fox plus North, the craziest of all ideas if men had ever meant what they said, made 210 to 140, in which case Shelburne was finished. Shelburne first tried Fox, sending Pitt to sound out the prospects of a rapprochement; but when Fox hinted at an accommodation only if Shelburne were prepared to stand down as premier, Pitt

---

* The King was a West Indies man: 'I would wish if possible to be rid of Gibraltar, and to have as much possession in the West Indies as possible' (December 11th, 1782); and eight days later, 'I should have liked Minorca, the two Floridas, and [or?] Guadaloupe better than this proud *Fortress*, and in my opinion source of another war, or at least a constant lurking enmity' (Fortescue, vi, 4021, 4034).

snubbed him in his iciest manner: he had not come there, he said, to betray Lord Shelburne. There remained North and the 120 Northites. These were divided between those advised by Jenkinson and Robinson, who were for the King and Shelburne, and those led by Eden and Wedderburn (now Lord Loughborough) who saw the potential of an arrangement with Fox. They did not have long to argue the pros and cons. In the midst of the clangour of the debate over the peace (which Fox condemned root and branch), and less than a week after Pitt's abortive parley with Fox, Lord North, the erstwhile King's 'tool' – the premier recently in danger of impeachment – that formerly so inde- cisive and dilatory man – had made a pact with his most savage critic. The Fox-North coalition was a going concern on the opposition benches in time for the assault on the peace terms in particular and the Shelburne government in general.*

In view of Fox's earlier tirades against North and his recent, explicit, and contemptuous rejection of the very idea of such a union, a Fox- North coalition appeared to most of the politically aware public, and to the Press, as cynical and contemptible. Like the Hitler-Stalin pact of 1939, it made a cartoonists' bonanza. Even North himself was soon stricken (North-like, on and off) at what he had done. 'I am perfectly miserable,' he wrote to his father, 'and tremble at the vexations and troubles that are hanging over me';[11] and it was soon obvious that the dominant personality in the new alliance was not to be his, but Fox's. Yet Fox, the gambler, had made what was to prove the most reckless and damaging throw of his career. Certainly it is true that much of the indignation worked up against 'the infamous coalition' was 'synthetic and theoretical, designed to appeal to the political innocents';[12] and no doubt tergiversation has always been common enough practice among politicians. And so long as politics was a sophisticated game, with no holds barred, for aristocrats only, any trick which worked might be justified. But Burke and Fox had invested heavily in *principles*, and Fox in particular had stood forth mightily as man of the people – or at least of a good many of the people. These might be excused a degree of political innocence and been forgiven for supposing he had meant

* It is a plausible but unprovable thesis that North would have been less inclined to turn away from the King and towards Fox if he had not been nursing a grievance concerning the repayment of a large debt incurred to Drummonds the bankers for secret service and election expenses in 1780. In law it was strictly North's debt, though the King bore at least an equal moral responsibility for it. After North's resignation, despite (or even perhaps because of) earlier generosity to him, George tried to insist that North should bear the burden of repayment. When North reasonably protested that this was 'out of his power', the King alleged that he had been defrauded, but grudgingly repaid Drummonds by instalments.

what he said. But now Fox, the people's emperor, was suddenly seen to have no clothes. He would be able to command temporary voting strength, and soon give Shelburne his *coup de pied*, but he had jerked the sympathies of 'the people' appreciably towards the King, and gone some way towards justifying the King's own prejudices against him. At the time of its formation, the Fox-North coalition seemed to George to mark the blackest moment of his reign, coming as it did alongside the bitter tension over the Prince of Wales. In the long run it can be seen as an important stage in the turn-round of public opinion in his favour.

Even though George's hide had toughened greatly since his accession, and he had worked comfortably with many ministers whom in the early days he would have revolted against as 'bad men', he did not now propose voluntarily to clutch vipers to his bosom; in particular such a viper as Charles James Fox, whose venom was to the King unique even in that 'most profligate age' in which he lamented he had the misfortune to reign.[13] With Shelburne outmanœuvred and resigning on 24th February, the clearly prescribed next step for a modern monarch would be to send for the leader of the Opposition and invite him to form a government. In February, 1783, that would have brought the Duke of Portland to the First Lordship of the Treasury, Fox to the Foreign Office, and North (or possibly Lord Carlisle, a Northite acceptable to Fox and his friends) to the Home Office. George was very far from a modern monarch; when he had a royal model in his head at all, it was usually William III, who figured frequently in his self-justifications and searches for precedents. He had no intention of allowing himself to become the prisoner of the Commons' nominees. Through thick and thin he clung to certain doctrines and convictions: that the Crown's right to choose its ministers was indisputable; that in the mixed British constitution the House of Commons must, no more than the King, pretend to be a dictator; that all parties were essentially odious, and the Fox faction supremely so; and that the only worthy government was a union of 'the best and ablest men the Kingdom might produce'.[14] Hence there now followed an extraordinary five weeks during which, in anger, frustration, and sometimes desperation, he explored every conceivable alternative to a Portland-Fox-North ministry, while the country did without a government and in the end administrative business came near to breaking down totally. One effect of this was unrest and several minor mutinies among soldiers and sailors waiting for pay or discharge, or both.

The King turned first, quite hopefully, to Pitt who, George thought, received his invitation 'with a spirit and inclination that makes me think he will not decline';[15] and Pitt did nearly, but not quite, accept – being deterred by the prospect of North's tipping the scales against him. Jenkinson then suggested Lord Gower, that veteran in the premier stakes who had so often before withdrawn before the starting post, or pulled up lame. This time, while professing himself *'almost* determined *at any hazard'* to run, he again proved a non-starter. Gower, however, mooted to the King the idea that Mr Thomas Pitt (William Pitt's cousin, later Lord Camelford) might be prepared to lead the Commons. 'Mr Thomas Pitt or Mr Thomas Anybody,' George is said to have answered. Thomas Pitt sent the King his reply at length, protesting his hatred of the unnatural coalition and his unswerving loyalty; but also his own indolence and incompetence; at the same time, however, shrewdly proposing that Fox and his friends should be accepted as ministers and given enough rope to hang themselves. The people, he thought, would 'execrate them' and their projects of reform.[16] Lord North himself was several times desired to report at Buckingham House and pressed to lend his weight to a broad-bottomed coalition, without result. The second Earl Temple was a further possible candidate; he was another who was profuse in sympathy and encouragement to the King to stand up to the 'unprincipled' men leagued against him.*

At first George refused to see Portland at all, and only slowly retreated from this extreme position, attempting next to negotiate with him through North. At last on 19th March, Portland was granted an audience, but was himself embarrassed by his inability to put forward names for a coalition ministry, its factions already quarrelling among themselves. When Portland suggested a ministry wholly of his own supporters, George rejected it out of hand. Later when Portland was able to submit for royal approval the names of seven principal members of a projected coalition government, the King declined to look at them. He wanted to see the list complete. At a subsequent meeting he glanced cursorily at the names, gave the paper back without comment, and when Portland remonstrated that surely the King could trust those seven men not to introduce further 'improper' persons, George

---

* George Nugent-Temple-Grenville (1753-1813) nephew of the first Earl Temple and the eldest of George Grenville's three surviving sons, all of course cousins of Pitt. Earl Temple's brothers were Thomas and William (later Lord) Grenville. Temple became eventually Marquis of Buckingham, and is not to be confused with John Hobart, second Earl of Buckinghamshire. Such confusion is made more possible since both men served as Lord Lieutenant of Ireland (Temple twice) during the period 1777-89, and the Earl of Buckinghamshire was often referred to as Lord Buckingham.

replied tartly that that was 'asking more than any man above forty could engage to do', and broke off the negotiations.[17]

He now turned again to William Pitt, his best hope of rescue. A second time, however, Pitt declined. 'I am clear Mr Pitt means to play false,' George wrote to Lord Weymouth, 'and wants I should again negotiate with the coalition.' He would rather abdicate, he vowed; 'yield the game to them and let my son be the puppet which Mr Pitt's letter seems to indicate the House of Commons [is] not disinclined to see their sovereign.'[18] This talk of stepping down in favour of his son – going in fact to Hanover – was more than mere talk. He drafted, but never of course dispatched, a solemn letter to the Prince of Wales* and two long messages, one to the Commons and one to the Houses of Parliament jointly, announcing his abdication and presenting an apologia for his conduct over the previous twenty-three years. Pitt's second refusal made the royal position seem hopeless. The King had explored all routes of escape and found them all blind alleys. On 1st April he bowed to the inevitable. He had withstood, he said, this infamous coalition

> till not a single man is willing to come to my assistance and till the House of Commons has taken every step but insisting on this faction by name being elected ministers. To end a conflict which stops every wheel of government and which would affect the public credit if it continued much longer I intend this night to acquaint that *grateful* man Ld. North that the seven Cabinet counsellors the Coalition has named shall kiss hands to-morrow and then form their arrangements . . .[19]

This was written in a letter to Temple, who was soon to play a vital part in the scheme by which George eventually rid himself of his 'captors'. A later passage in the same letter seems to dispose of any notion that this time he considered himself under any obligation to be loyal to his ministers. He had had to retreat, but was already thinking in terms of *reculer pour mieux sauter*:

> A ministry which I have avowedly attempted to avoid by calling on every other description of men, cannot be supposed to have either my favour or my confidence and as such I shall most certainly refuse any honours that may be asked by them . . .† I trust you will be steady in your attachment to me and ready to join other honest

* See p. 231.

† This was much more than merely a hostile gesture. The creation of peers could assist majorities in the Lords; the lack of them was to prove crucial. Moreover, the

men in watching the conduct of this unnatural combination, and I hope many months will not elapse before the Grenvilles, the Pitts and other men of abilities and character will relieve me of a situation that nothing but the supposition that no other means remained of preventing the public finances from being materially affected would have compelled me to submit to . . .[20]

When, in replying, Temple wished that nothing might 'delay the hour of your Majesty's deliverance from that thraldom that bears so heavily upon you', George held on to his consolatory phrases with gratitude, pleased that Temple viewed 'the strange phrensy of the times in the same light as it has struck me; perhaps you may be surprised how that shaddow, popularity, has already deserted those whom reason too clearly reprobated'.[21]

During the eight and a half months of the Coalition's tenure of office, relations were at best curt and business-like, usually sullen or frigid, at worst explosive. Between George III and his Foreign Minister, Mr Fox, the epistolatory proprieties were observed, and Fox did his best to assure his 'first of villains' of his loyalty:

> He begs leave humbly to implore Your Majesty to believe that both the Duke of Portland and he have nothing so much at heart as to conduct Your Majesty's affairs . . . in the manner that may give Your Majesty the most satisfaction, and that . . . it will be the study of Your Majesty's Ministers to show how truly sensible they are of Your Majesty's goodness.

Filing these protestations among his papers, the King endorsed them, 'No answer.' And when Fox submitted to him the last alterations proposed in the definitive treaties of peace with France and Spain, George, who regarded his Foreign Secretary as a principal cause of earlier British weakness in the negotiations and hence imperfections now in the treaties, replied bad-temperedly: 'I do not mean to call on Mr Fox for further explanations on this subject: unnecessary discussions are not to my taste, and the Cabinet having by a minute approved of the projects, I do not propose to give myself any additional trouble with regard to them.'[22] But when the blow of Prince Octavius's death struck the Palace, and Fox and Portland were obliged to apologise for intruding public business upon private grief, George, acknowledging their condolences, replied to Portland at least – he would not write so to Fox – in more civil and human terms:

---

award of lesser honours was an essential part of eighteenth-century parliamentary management.

The D. of Portland's reluctance at sending me the commission for passing the bills, I look upon as an instance of his delicacy. I believe he has been in the situation it has pleased the Almighty to place me now, therefore can judge the state of my mind; but the real trust I have in Divine Providence, and the balm I feel in religion so far supports me that I am fully able to sign any warrants . . .[23]

Such civilities did not prevail one morning six weeks later, when George sat down 'at 59 minutes past 10' – exact even under outrage – to express in the most blistering terms his 'utter indignation and astonishment' at Portland's conduct over the matter of the Prince of Wales's establishment.*

For George, the Coalition's mere existence was an offence. Its wish to be generous, lavish even, with the Prince of Wales, after all the indignation over royal expenditure, stoked up the fires of resentment. It was however the ministry's one projected measure of first-class importance, their India Bill, which precipitated the final confrontation between King and Government, and gave George his chance to bring off his own version of a palace revolution.

Nearly everybody agreed that the governing of British India, with its political and military implications, had grown to be too big an undertaking for a commercial company – one moreover whose finances were in confusion. Earlier schemes, such as that of John Robinson's whereby half the Company's directors were to be appointed by the Government, had run up against the opposition not only of the Company itself – well entrenched in Parliament – but of the obsessive Whig fear of increased executive power and royal influence. Burke's India Bill – for in fact it was Burke's rather than Fox's – was ingeniously contrived to remove power from the 'corrupt' hands of the Company without putting it into the equally 'corrupt' hands of the Crown; to deal with the sort of abuses that Burke had seen writ large – larger than life, no doubt – in the régime of Warren Hastings, without adding to the abuses of power which, according to Fox and Burke, so disfigured that of George III. The bill however was itself vulnerable to the charge that one of its chief aims seemed to be to transfer power to the 'corrupt' hands of the Whigs themselves. That Burke wished fervently to do good to India and Indians is not to be disputed, but even he did not deny the party advantages to be gained from his measure. And Fox also was of course well aware that he was dealing with an explosive issue:

They are endeavouring to make a great cry against us [he told Mrs

* See p. 231-2.

Armistead], and will I am afraid succeed in making us very unpopular in the City. However, I know I am right and must bear the
consequences . . . If I had considered nothing but keeping my
power, it was the safest thing to leave things as they are . . . and I am
not at all ignorant of the political danger which I run by this bold
measure . . . I write very gravely, because the amazing abuse that is
heaped upon me makes me feel so. [24]

Both Burke and Fox knew that by awarding themselves the privilege of appointing commissioners and assistant commissioners – there
were to be sixteen in all, with their tenure not dependent on a change
of government – the Whigs would be accused in effect of stealing the
patronage of the East India Company for their own ends. Sir Gilbert
Elliot, one of the proposed sixteen, seems to have assessed both the
public and partisan advantages of the India Bill (at least in its intentions) as fairly and realistically as anyone: 'There never was a measure
taken,' he wrote, 'so beneficial to so many millions of unhappy people
as this one. This is one good reason for my liking a part in it. There are
many lesser ones, amongst which a great deal of patronage and probably a handsome salary are two . . .' [25] North was one who was less
happy about the bill, but its case was ably argued in the Commons;
many independents voted for it; and it received majorities varying
between 106 and 114.

The House of Commons was not yet, however, the nation's dictator.
There were three counterpoises to it to be weighed in the scales. There
was the public; there was the House of Lords; and there was the King.
The public, which Fox had not recently been much in favour with, was
more than ready to see in him (as in James Sayers's famous cartoon)
'Carlo Khan', the swollen potentate of Indostan, riding on North as an
elephant led by Burke as a lackey. As for the Lords, the bill's fate there
was unpredictable; passage probably, but the issue might hang on the
bishops' votes. The King's attitude at the outset had not been hostile;
he was as aware as most of the deficiencies of the East India Company;
had been critical of Hastings; and was certainly not committed, as he
was in so many matters, to the *status quo*.

In the measure's unpopularity among the public and the opposition
he and those close to him could see, however, a patch of blue sky no
bigger than a man's hand. After eight months he remained convinced
that in the spring he had been roughly and unconstitutionally handled,
and betrayed into hostile hands. He was now prepared in return to use
rough tactics of his own, which, though they were to be sensationally
successful, were of themselves of very dubious propriety. 'Rough' is

perhaps the wrong word; the finesse employed was considerable. There was to be nothing crude, like a royal veto – it would have been the first for three-quarters of a century. Neither did he intend to let the bill take its chance in the Lords and then, if it was passed there, dismiss his ministers, dissolve, and risk an election. In those circumstances he might well have lost it. But if he could be sure that the Lords would reject the bill, he would then stand on firmer ground for expelling the Coalition. It was the means he adopted for bringing pressure on the House of Lords which render him vulnerable to criticism. With George III there was no British nonsense of being a good loser. He proposed to win. His political conscience was 'a good girl' in an honest cause, and did what she was told; and no man could have been more unshakably convinced than the King in 1783 – or for that matter at any other time – that what he as monarch wished and demanded was what the good of the nation cried out for.

It was Temple and Thurlow who made the first moves encouraging George to take strong action. Thurlow was a dismissed Lord Chancellor anxious to return to his great and lucrative office. Temple had resigned the Irish Lord Lieutenancy and had, together with his Pitt-Grenville relations, been regarded for some time by the King as a potential agent of rescue. These men had a ready listener as they stressed to him that the India Bill was a device to steal his patronage.[26] The fact that Thurlow had an audience with the King did not long remain secret, and other members of the opposition soon began to co-ordinate their plans. Of these men Jenkinson was naturally one. 'I have talked with Lord Thurlow on all this,' he wrote to Robinson, 'and have settled with him what ought to be done . . . You may be assured that the King sees the bill in all the horrors that you and I do.'[27] Jenkinson and Robinson were joined by Richard Atkinson, a proprietor of the East India Company; by Dundas and Pitt; and by the maverick Duke of Richmond. All these were eventually privy to the plot that was being hatched. 'Everything stands prepared for the blow,' wrote Atkinson to Robinson, 'if a certain person has the courage to strike it.'

Careful precautions were taken to preserve secrecy. Lord Clarendon, who had held the Duchy of Lancaster until the Whigs removed him in 1782 and was anxious to have it back again, was employed to act (through the Hanoverian minister in London, for double safety) as intermediary between the King and Pitt, both of them rightly assuming that they were being well watched and neither fully trusting the other yet. George as well as Pitt wanted to look very carefully before he leaped. There was to be 'no dismission till a strong succession was secured'; and, through Dundas, Robinson was set to work to prepare another of his electoral forecasts – notwithstanding the signal in-accuracy of those he had made in 1780. This time his prognosis, though not over-optimistic, offered, as Atkinson put it, 'no *manly* ground for apprehension.'

On 11th December, Temple had an audience with the King, and took from him a written statement that

His Majesty allowed Earl Temple to say that whoever voted for the India Bill was not only not his friend, but would be considered by him as an enemy; and if these words were not strong enough, Earl Temple might use whatever words he might deem stronger and more to the purpose.[28]

Since a favourable issue for the opposition in the Lords was still not wholly certain, the King summoned the Archbishop of Canterbury also for an audience. The Archbishop held the Bishop of London's proxy, so a 'swing' of four votes was directly involved, quite apart from the likely effect of his example; and although he remained a doubtful quantity till nearly the end, he finally voted against the bill, as did eleven others of the twenty bishops who cast votes. George's by now carefully publicised intervention was decisive. Two divisions in the Lords gave majorities against the bill of eight and nineteen. In the Commons there were angry remonstrances, and Fox declared privately that the Government was beaten by the King's treachery. Ministers would not resign, however. On 18th December, therefore, the day following the final Lords division, Fox and North, who were con-ferring together with Portland, were required at midnight by a royal messenger to surrender their seals. The King's brief message to North was written; that to Fox was merely to be passed on by North. He chose, he said, not to receive the seals from them personally 'as audiences on such occasions must be unpleasant'.[29] The following morning Pitt kissed hands as First Lord of the Treasury and Chancel-lor of the Exchequer.

CHAPTER TWENTY

Recovery and Retrenchment
(1783-1788)

'WE are so strong,' Fox wrote just before his dismissal, 'that nobody can undertake without madness; and if they do, I think we shall destroy them almost as soon as they are formed.'[1] It was a calculation that had failed to take sufficient account of the King's obstinate determination to be rid of his enemies or to foresee his acumen in seizing the moment to strike. Fox did not recognise the extent to which the ground was loosening under his feet. His optimism omitted to provide for a situation where George would be able successfully to stand forth as the champion of the constitution against a faction-dominated House of Commons. Above all, and not unnaturally, it did not envisage the emergence of a new chief minister who would represent the royal interest so tellingly in the Commons that he would succeed in winning over enough independents and wavering followers of Lord North to whittle away the Whig majority inside the House and persuade enough borough patrons outside it to switch their allegiance to the party of the King.

When George invited Pitt to be his new chief minister, no conditions were laid down on either side. The King could hardly afford to exact any; he was prepared to accept any prime minister who would deliver him from the toils. And Pitt did not need to. When he had previously refused the premiership it was chiefly because he saw himself being too dependent on North's support. He could now head a ministry with a reasonable hope of running matters in his own way. Naturally he needed the King's backing, but he was very far from coming into office as a royal puppet. Not at all an unqualified supporter of the King's prerogative, he had on several earlier occasions spoken against its abuse, and was on record as declaring that he expected its early decay. He was, after all, son of the man whose funeral in Westminster Abbey had been boycotted by the Court;[2] his suspicion of his king was not less than that of most of the Whig magnates; but then his mistrust of *them* was not inconsiderable either.[3]

The King needed Pitt and Pitt needed the King; but they also needed an administration, and it proved difficult to find men of substance to man it. Eventually, however, Pitt contrived to assemble his coalition; and of course it *was* as much a coalition as that of Fox and North.* Among his following at the close of 1783 were Thurlow and Gower, once of the Bedfords; Jenkinson, Robinson, and the King's men in general (though Jenkinson and Robinson were not offered posts); Dundas, a deserter from the camp of Lord North; the Duke of Richmond, a former Rockinghamite, though always a law unto himself; William Grenville, Pitt's cousin, and others of the old Chatham-Shelburne connection, such as Lord Sydney (Thomas Townshend), Lord Camden, and the Duke of Rutland. Shelburne himself was given no office; he was prickly and unpopular, and his exclusion emphasised the point that 'Shelburnites' in fact no longer existed.† They were *Pittites* once again. 'This young man,' as Dundas said, 'does not choose to suffer it to be doubtful who is the effectual Minister.'

When Parliament reassembled after the Christmas recess, Pitt, the only member of his not very distinguished Cabinet in the Commons, had to face the music, with the assistance of his auxiliaries Dundas and William Grenville. Opposition was sometimes derisive, on account of his extreme youth; usually acrimonious; and always numerically superior. Fox carried the first motion against him by 39 votes, and a few days later another, condemning as unconstitutional the continuance of this minority government, by 21 votes. These were 'intemperate resolutions of desperate men', wrote George to Pitt; but he was prepared to take any steps that might be proposed 'to oppose this faction and to struggle to the last period of my life . . .' If in the end he should lose, his line was 'a clear one'[4] – a plain reference to abdication. At Versailles, according to the Duchess of Clermont, they were at this time 'sure there will be a revolution and that Fox will be King'.[5] But George had no intention of losing. He was buttressed, as usual, by his stubborn certainty that *he was right*. He was totally convinced of the constitutional propriety of his position; it was Fox and the Commons who were asserting novel and dangerous doctrines. In the King's version of the constitution, which was essentially that given almost the status of holy writ by Blackstone's *Commentaries*, legislative authority

* What had made Fox's alliance with North seem specially preposterous was the violence of his earlier philippics against his partner; but in essence the coalition of Fox and North was hardly more outrageous than that of the elder Pitt and Newcastle in the later fifties, or even of Bute and Henry Fox in 1762-63.

† Lansdowne MSS., quoted in Ehrman, *The Younger Pitt; the Years of Acclaim*, 133. Wraxall, however (iii, 22), was 'assured that Pitt . . . did offer Lord Shelburne a seat in the Cabinet, a proposition which was declined . . .' Shelburne was rewarded, or consoled, with the *Marquisate* of Lansdowne, George having decreed that *dukedoms* were, for the time being at least, to be reserved for his own sons.

was delicately balanced upon the powers of three elements: the monarch, with his ancient prerogatives; the lords spiritual and temporal, 'chosen for their piety, their birth, their wisdom, their valour, or their property'; and the commons, 'freely chosen by the people from among themselves, which makes it a kind of democracy.' The balance was perfect – as indeed was the entire constitution, according to the theories, or fictions, of Blackstone. There could, he maintained, be 'no inconvenience attempted by either of the three branches, but will be withstood by one of the other two, each branch being armed with a negative power, sufficient to repel any innovation which it shall think inexpedient or dangerous'. According to Blackstone, *nothing* could endanger so 'admirably tempered and compounded' a constitution but 'destroying the equilibrium of power between one branch of the legislature and the rest'. The influence of this vastly respectable establishment lawyer upon the founding fathers of the American constitution is sufficiently obvious. But the devil can quote scripture too, and Blackstone gave George III perfect theoretical authority for his conduct in 1783 and 1784. Quite clearly to George, the Commons were taking it upon themselves to assert a tyranny over the other two elements in the constitution. And when the leader of that Commons majority asked rhetorically, 'Had not a majority of the House of Commons almost from time immemorial governed this country?'[6] George could reasonably comment that Mr Fox was as unhistorical as he was 'democratical'. The answer to the question was No; though it would be necessary at the same time to admit that for a long time it had been impossible to govern the country for any length of time *against* the wishes of the House.

> Though I have too much principle [the King claimed] ever to infringe the rights of others, yet that must ever equally prevent my submitting to the executive power being in any hands than where the Constitution has placed it . . . My cause . . . is that of the Constitution as fixed at the Revolution [of 1688] and to the support of which my family was invited to mount the throne.[7]

Standing pat on the constitution as fixed at the Revolution the King could hardly be faulted. But what must, of course, be said for the Fox doctrines of 1783-84 – ministerial responsibility to the majority in the House of Commons and the effective ending of royal prerogative – is that they were prophetic. Their sense of the future was surer than their sense of the present or authority from the past.

As for the House of Lords, 'if they were confounded,' wrote Blackstone, 'with the mass of the people . . . their privilege would soon be borne down and overwhelmed by the popular torrent, which would effectually level all distinctions.' A body of nobility was necessary 'in order to support the rights of both Crown and people, by forming a barrier to withstand the encroachment of both'. George III's letters to Pitt of 3rd and 4th February, when the Commons majority was attempting to force the resignation of the government, are perfect Blackstone. On 3rd February he felt that 'it would highly become the House of Lords to throw off their lethargy, and also vote an address that shall show they feel every branch of the legislature has its fixed bounds and that the executive power is vested in the Crown';[8] and on 4th February:

I trust that the House of Lords will this day feel that the hour is come for which the wisdom of our ancestors established that respectable corps in the State, to prevent either the Crown or the Commons from encroaching upon the rights of the other. Indeed, should not the Lords stand boldly forth this Constitution must soon be changed, for if the two only remaining privileges of the Crown are infringed, that of negativing Bills that have passed both Houses of Parliament, or that of naming the Ministers to be employed, I cannot but feel . . . that I can no longer be of utility to this country, nor can with honour continue in this stand.[9]

Once Pitt and his administration were installed and had recovered from the shock of Lord Temple's immediate defection, the King was impatient to dissolve Parliament and go to the polls. He was not inhibited by the fact that the 1780 Parliament had run less than half its course, and customarily since the Septennial Act of 1717 Parliaments had expected to run their full, or almost full, course. Here it was not Fox or Burke but the King – and eventually of course Pitt too – who was in tune with accepted constitutional practices of the future. If 1780 gives a precedent for the 'snap' election to take advantage of a favourable turn of events, 1784 anticipates the ploy of 'going to the country' upon a major issue. In two letters of 24th January, 1784, the King pressed his point. Indecision, he wrote the next day, was 'the most painful of all situations to a firm mind'. Of course it was proper for Mr Pitt to consult his colleagues first, but 'we must be men: if we mean to save the country, we must cut those threads that cannot be unravelled. Half-measures are ever puerile, and often destructive.'[10] Pitt chose instead to wait; and he waited altogether for three months. This was partly for technical parliamentary reasons – he had to ensure the voting of supplies and get the annual Mutiny Bill passed before the old one expired on 25th March; and after mid-January practical objections to a dissolution followed by a hurried election were overwhelming. Pitt also needed time to complete the customary 'arrangements' to ensure his success in the controlled seats. And as for the more open seats, he judged that time was likely to be on his side there too.

Inside Parliament, in their fight for the vital support of independent members, it was clear that Pitt and the King were gaining upon Portland and Fox. What many of these uncommitted men would have most liked to see was another and broader-based coalition, again under Portland perhaps, and including both Fox and Pitt – a proposition alarming to the King, to whom it would have seemed a sell-out to the enemy. But Pitt had no intention of selling out, and Fox none of giving in. Each, while professing willingness to co-operate, set terms he knew the other must refuse. In brief, while each would serve *with*, neither would serve *under* the other. This suited George well enough, as he watched opinion drifting steadily away from Fox and his supporters. These nevertheless showed their strength in the Commons and their resentment towards Pitt and the King by forcing a postponement of the vote on supplies; and twice they carried addresses requesting the King to dismiss his ministers. The first, carried at 5.30 a.m. on 21st February after a stormy debate, caused George to comment that at any other period of his reign such proceedings would have caused him astonishment, but by now he was beyond astonishment; and

> as the Opposition seem so fond of bringing King William forward on all occasions, I should think his exact words in 1701, with such additional ones as the peculiar moment may call for, would not be improper to be uttered from the Chair of State when the whole House bring up this strange and . . . unconstitutional address.[11]

He further reminded Pitt that there were other addresses, 'loyal' ones, coming in in increasing numbers from all parts of the kingdom, demonstrating that royal rights were 'essential to the people's liberties'. Pitt's response, therefore, which George on 25th February was to deliver to the Speaker and a large representative concourse of members, should be 'civil' but firm. 'I trust my faithful Commons will not wish,' it ran, 'that the essential offices of executive government should be vacated until I see a prospect that such a plan of union as I have called for . . . may be carried into effect.'[12] By this time both he and Pitt were pretty confident that such a union would be unnecessary, and was indeed out of court; but the fiction of its desirability was to be maintained.

Three days later, Pitt, who had already been awarded the freedom of the City of London, attended a ceremonial presentation (with gold box worth a hundred guineas), and dined with the City Fathers at Grocers' Hall, where he was lavishly praised – among others by the City Chamberlain, John Wilkes. On his way home he was assaulted by an opposition mob, armed with bludgeons and broken-off sedan chair-poles, outside Brooks's Club. Pitt himself was unhurt, escaping into some adjacent houses, and thence to nearby White's; his brother-in-law Lord Mahon, his brother Lord Chatham, and more particularly his coachmen and his carriage took the main brunt of the violence. But the 'outrage', as George described it, did the Whigs no good. Every means, the King trusted, 'would be employed to find out the abettors of this, which I should hope may be got at.'[13] When it was put about that Fox himself was not merely an abettor but an instigator, he virtuously refuted the allegation by offering to bring forward Mrs Armistead to testify that he had been at the time in bed with her.

The last cards the Opposition could have played were to refuse to grant supplies and to limit the application of the Mutiny Bill to a cur-tailed period. On these issues they were divided. Sir Gilbert Elliot 'was sorry to observe a sort of boggle' over taking these drastic steps; but he was still hoping on 20th February that they would be taken all the same.[14] The tide, however, was ebbing away from Fox, slowly in the Commons, more rapidly in the country; and it was significant that, though he pressed for Pitt's dismissal, he said nothing of the need for an election. Finally, on 8th-9th March, a sort of Grand Remonstrance against the King's conduct of public affairs – a 'kind of manifesto', George called it – was carried, but by one vote only, 191-190. The narrowness of this division showed Fox and Portland that further tactics of obstruction must be counter-productive. It was clear that the long constitutional crisis was over, and that the King had won. On 9th March, Fox allowed the Mutiny Bill to go through for its full annual period. His supporter Lord Palmerston *père* noted 'an epi-demical kind of spirit that has gone about the country in favour of the King's prerogative and against the House of Commons';[15] and inside the House itself during the debates of 8th and 9th March, while one member (Mr Powys) lamented that whereas in 1688 'a vote of the Commons could bestow a Crown', now it could not 'even procure the dismissal of a minister', another (Sir Matthew Ridley) regretfully con-ceded that 'the House was now defeated, and defeated by those who ought to be its natural supporters and defenders – the people'. He alleged of course that it was Pitt's misrepresentations that had done it. 'The people had not only abandoned them, but turned against them . . . No wonder that with such auxiliaries prerogative should triumph over the privileges of the Commons. But whether it was wonderful or not, it was a melancholy truth that the House of Commons had been defeated, and that prerogative now reigned triumphant.'[16] Fox, who had earlier championed the people against the Commons,* was now, it seemed, forced into an embarrassing reversal of faith, and it was the Commons who were to be regarded as the only palladium of popular liberties.

The King gave thanks for the victory in his own misleadingly sedate manner – he must have been elated – and gratefully associated Pitt's own conduct with the happy turn of events:

> Mr Pitt's letter is undoubtedly the most satisfactory I have received for many months . . . This faction will by degrees be deserted by many, and at length be forgot. I shall ever with pleasure consider that by the prudence as well as rectitude of one person in the House of Commons this great change has been effected, and that he will be ever able to reflect with satisfaction that in supporting me he has saved the Constitution, the most perfect of human formations.[17]

Now at last Pitt was ready for a general election; and the results, as they built up during April, 1784, showed that 'the people' did undeniably support Pitt and the King, despite Fox's personal triumph in the Westminster constituency. Of course it was an election managed like all others of the era. There was no declaration of *vox populi* uncontaminated by lucre or the lure of place, preferment, or a step up the ladder of honours.† But the sweeping nature of the victory meant that much more than the management of patronage had been at work.[18] Nothing demonstrates better than the 1784 election that, even within the limitations imposed by the corruptions of the system, it was possible for decisive movements of national opinion to declare themselves. Free voters as well as borough patrons and managers gave a thumbs-down for Fox and North, and the memory of their notorious coalition. For Pitt it was the sweetest of successes, and doubly so because most emphatic in the more genuinely representative constituencies. In the counties, for instance, where Robinson had forecast an even balance, supporters of Pitt won 48 seats against his opponent's 29; in the open boroughs the figures were 125 to 96; while success was relatively less

---

* 'When the representative body does not speak the sense of the constituent, the voice of the latter is constitutional and conclusive' (Fox, April, 1780).

† Two typical election 'jobs' were to make a baron of Edward Eliot, who could answer for seven Cornish seats, and to give an extra barony (with remainder to his second son) to the already grossly be-titled and wealthy Duke of Northumberland, who was reckoned to control six seats and influence a seventh. 'They are crying peerages about the streets in barrows', wrote Horace Walpole to the Countess of Upper Ossory. In the course of the next seventeen years of Pitt's tenure of office 140 peers were to be created.

in the close boroughs, where Robinson had over-optimistically reckoned on the Government's influence pulling in 131 out of 177 seats.

In the new House, meeting in May, 1784, Pitt could count on a majority of about 150. The King was delighted to have so clear a demonstration of what he had always maintained, that the inclination of the country was against 'faction', and loyal to Crown and Constitution. For the first time for nearly a decade he had the backing of a firmly led and apparently cohesive ministry, however mediocre and disparate its members. Once more the resounding name of Pitt stood at the head of his Treasury, and this time it was a healthy and confident veteran of just twenty-five, not an imperious unaccountable invalid of fifty-eight. For the first time for more than twenty years, since the short honeymoon with the public in the earliest days of the reign, George might in 1784 be reckoned a popular monarch, as the general demonstrations of affection following his escape from assassination in 1786 and mental derangement in 1789 were soon to emphasise. The American disasters of so short a time ago, and the long constitutional crisis of the early seventeen-eighties, were receding quickly into the unhappy past. There were the usual mutterings and rumblings coming out of Ireland, and the old demands for parliamentary and civic reforms from dissenters and others, but nothing that 'firmness' could not cure. The Wilkes and even the Gordon disturbances seemed a long time ago; indeed Wilkes himself was now a King George's man like most others. Happily, the country's industry and trade – even her trade with the American ex-colonies – were expanding as never before. 'These prodigious accumulations of commerce, power, and wealth,' wrote Wraxall, 'have obliterated almost the recollections of the American struggle, and have closed all the wounds caused by that unfortunate war.'[19] George certainly found grounds for thinking his tenacity had been vindicated, and could pause, as he did not infrequently during the course of a long life, to give due praise to his own unyielding rectitude.

'If others will not be active, I must drive,' George had written to Lord Sandwich in 1779. Five years on, the situation was very different, and if from 1784 the King appears to take a rather smaller part in active politics than previously, it betokens neither a decline in his political interest nor (at least before his illness of 1788-89) a waning of his faculties. Since he now had a minister with whom on the great majority of matters he saw eye to eye, he was confident and content enough to leave most business in his hands. Politically speaking, he could relax to a degree that had not been possible before. By the early 'eighties the

King had settled in at Windsor, and he saw no reason why he should not enjoy there, as far as was possible, the life of a country gentleman devoted to his family, his domestic interests, and his outdoor pursuits. He was still meticulous in his attention to public business, but never made the mistake of staying in town when he could be out. In July, 1785, the Home Secretary on one occasion sent on to him at Buckingham House the box containing the minutes of the preceding day's debate in the Lords. Two hours later he had to dispatch again, this time to Windsor, 'upon hearing that his Majesty was gone thither.' The King, as usual, replied immediately with his comment on the political matter, but with an additional advice for Lord Sydney's benefit: 'In summer a box sent to the Queen's House is less likely to meet [me] than at any other place, for I certainly see as little of London as I possibly can, and am never a volunteer there.'[20] Once he had decided to phase out Kew as his principal country residence, he became more and more absorbed in Windsor plans and developments, and came much to prefer his new country home to his old. Charlotte, though she was as happy as he to escape from town, did retain an affection for the old surroundings in which her children had for the most part grown up. 'We go next Tuesday to Kew,' she wrote to Prince Augustus in the summer of 1786, 'in order to have one more day at that delicious place, which to be sure has lost something of its pleasure by you and your brothers not being there, yet still it has its charms.'[21] Kew had its charms, yet she agreed with her husband: 'Windsor is just the place for us.'

It was back in 1778 that the King had suddenly cancelled operations on Sir William Chambers' new palace being built in Richmond Gardens, and decided to concentrate on the potentialities of Windsor. As early as June 1776, the Queen had taken a fancy to the little house there that Queen Anne had lived in before her accession, and asked if she might have it. 'This,' wrote George to North, 'will give us the means of some pleasant jaunts to that beautiful Park.' He followed up this purchase by buying, in the following year, Nell Gwyn's old house from her descendant the Duke of St Albans. Much taken by the beauty of the old Castle's situation, the space of its parks,* and the opportunities they offered for field sports, yet not wishing to disturb the existing tenants, he decided not to occupy the Castle itself – more than a little ruinous by now in any case – but instead to renovate and extend some of its more peripheral buildings and to buy such extra housing and stabling outside as he needed. Kew, even with the Dutch House and the neighbouring accommodation round the Green, had proved too small for

* These he further enlarged in 1781 by the purchase of the extensive manors of Winkfield and Sandhurst.

the needs of the now very large royal family, with the small armies of attendants that even a Court as thriftily conducted as that of George and Charlotte demanded. To Windsor therefore they gravitated gradually between 1778 and 1781, at first for short stays only, to view the improvements as they developed. But although part of the place's attraction had originally lain in its seeming so excellent a site for the residence of the Princes, these were soon scattered abroad or at Carlton House, and Windsor was to become the home primarily of George, Charlotte, and their six daughters. The Upper (or Queen's) Lodge eventually housed the King, Queen, and three elder Princesses; the Lower (late Burford) Lodge the three younger.

As the 'eighties advanced, George spent more and more of both time and money in his new surroundings. He became deeply involved in the management of his Windsor farms. He followed closely Chambers's architectural plans. Over a decade he spent £12,000 on 'improvements' to St George's Chapel; one of them was a new east window with a transparency of the Resurrection by Benjamin West. Altogether, within a dozen years of first coming, he laid out £70,000 – not a vast sum by the standards of that age of great projects, but for him more than a trifle:

> As is common enough [he] was led on from little to more, having begun the building with no other design than occasionally for him and the Queen to sleep at whenever he might hunt in the neighbourhood or make an excursion and find it too late for them conveniently to return to Kew or the Queen's Palace in the evening. The King told Dr Fisher if he could have foreseen that Windsor would be their chosen residence he would have prepared the Castle and resided in it.[22]

Eventually he did; but it was not until 1804 that the Castle proper was to become the royal family's regular residence[23] – by that time a family whose harmony was sadly jangled.

Fanny Burney wrote in 1786: 'The Royal family are here always in so very retired a way, that they live as the simplest country gentlefolks.' Remembering some of the details of life at Windsor that she herself describes, one must find *some* exaggeration here; nevertheless her meaning is clear. At St James's there were still the formal Levees and Drawing Rooms; Court dress was *de rigueur*; foreign ambassadors were presented; here, or at Buckingham House, ministers were received in the Closet, one at a time, for consultation, or came to kiss hands on taking up or surrendering office; from St James's the King drove in state to Parliament for its great formal occasions. But at Windsor, 'the

King has not even an equerry with him, nor the Queen any lady to attend her when she goes for her airings.'[24] The Windsor life, for all the divinity that hedged it, was in many respects simple. The King wished it so; but those around him, whether of the family or the Household, did find some of his more Spartan requirements difficult to live up to. For him, at least, early morning prayers were as strictly to be observed as the traditional protocol of Westminster or St James's; but his fellow-worshippers found the Chapel temperature in wintertime – which he appeared to find spiritually bracing – more than flesh could bear. As General Goldsworthy grumbled genially to Fanny Burney:

> When the Princesses, used to it as they are, get regularly knocked up . . . off they drop, one by one:—first the Queen deserts us; then Princess Elizabeth is done for; then the Princess Royal begins coughing; then Princess Augusta gets the snuffles . . . till at last, dwindle, dwindle, dwindle – not a soul goes to the chapel but the King, the parson and myself; and there we three freeze it out together.[25]

Windsor began to develop its own institutions. There was, for instance, the Terrace promenade, devised by the King to afford an opportunity for him and his family to 'show themselves to the people', and for the people – which in practice meant mainly the geographically available nobility and gentry – to pay their respects in return. The proceedings had a formalised informality. First would come the Princesses, two by two, with their nurses or governesses and their ladies ('*dragged for two hot hours* on the Terrace,' fumed Miss Goldsworthy); then such of the Princes who chanced to be in residence; finally, arm-in-arm with the Queen, the King himself, in the dark blue 'Windsor' uniform that he had taken a fancy to adopt from the livery of Lady Pembroke's servants at Wilton. From time to time the royal party would stop to exchange civilities; or they would simply perambulate up and down, bestowing the general largesse of their notice and acknowledging the bobbing of curtsies and doffing of hats. At first a novel exercise in public relations, soon successfully institutionalised, 'terracing' seems to have been regarded by the King as both a pleasure and a duty – a pleasure, no doubt, partly *because* a duty; it certainly, for him, symbolised a bond between monarch and people which he never ceased insisting upon, and which increasingly from the early 'eighties became a reality.

'Never a volunteer' in London, he was necessarily a regular conscript there, and even in the country was never long away from state business. He was clearly relieved, after long years of difficulty, to have so able an instrument of government as Pitt. 'I cannot conclude,' he wrote to him in May, 1784, 'without expressing my fullest approbation of the conduct of Mr Pitt on Monday; in particular his employing only a razor against his antagonists, and never condescending to run into that rudeness which, though common in the House, certainly never becomes a gentleman.'[26] On many different occasions George's observations betray this distaste for the *ungentlemanly* element in the Commons. When Lord Stormont, in 1786, introduced an unwelcome 'dish of foreign politicks' in the Peers' debate on the King's Speech, the King himself commented that that was the sort of thing one expected from the Commons but hardly from the Lords.[27] He was sure in March, 1788, that the opposition were speaking at excessive length in order 'to oblige the old and infirm Members to give up their attendance' – ungentlemanly behaviour again – 'which is reason sufficient for the friends of Government to speak merely to the point, and try to shorten debates.'[28] There was always a feeling in George's mind that opposition, though a cross that had to be borne, was essentially obstructive and disreputable. 'It is very unpleasant to me to observe,' he wrote in February, 1786, 'by Mr Pitt's note that he has been detained at the House of Commons by the fertile imagination of Mr Burke.' Measures once decided in Cabinet should be pushed through briskly: 'A good division after a pretty general call for the question [to be put] is the only means of counteracting those who only stir up debate for the purpose of delay.'[29]

The King's communications to his premier blend advice, sympathy, and – with one important exception – approval. Pitt's grasp of complicated issues, his mastery of financial intricacies, his thrift in expenditure, his cool authority in debate, his unfailing administrative efficiency, could hardly fail to command respect. The King, besides communicating his own, was very ready to pass on that of others: 'I understand,' he wrote, 'that Lord Camden, who never before heard Mr Pitt in Parliament, expressed at the Ancient Concert last night great commendation of his masterly performance.'[30] Once when Pitt had apologised for an unusual hitch in sending papers, George begged him not to worry. He knew very well it was Thurlow's fault. Pitt's 'punctuality' was 'too well known to give any room for suspicion and the good Chancellor is rather famous for loving delay'.[31] These middle years of the 'eighties, too, were those of the Prince of Wales's Fitzherbert follies and of the first parliamentary effort to regularise his parlous finances. The King and Pitt rowed the same boat: 'The proposed answer to the ill-advised letter of the Prince of Wales so thoroughly meets with my sentiments,' wrote George in July, 1786, 'that I have copied it with the alteration of a single word'; and again in the same month, 'The draft of a message which Mr Pitt sent to me on Saturday evening met so thoroughly with my ideas that I have verbatim copied it.'[32] At this same time the Whigs were first pressing their charges against Warren Hastings, and George was clearly a little pained to find Pitt voting with 'the adverse party' in condemnation of the exorbitant fine extracted from the Rajah of Benares. 'As to myself,' George told Pitt, 'I own I do not think it possible in that country to carry on business with the same moderation that is suitable to an European civilised nation' – a sentiment not far removed from the substance of Hastings' own case and Clive's before him, though Hastings at least would have jibbed at the assumptions behind the word 'civilised'. However, the King went out of his way to avoid being critical: 'Mr Pitt would have conducted himself yesterday very unlike what my mind ever expects of him if . . . he had not taken the part he did.'*

The one matter on which George III and his chief minister emphatically disagreed concerned the reform of Parliament – not the Rockinghams' economical reform, which was purely anti-monarchical, but a modernisation of the archaic parliamentary system itself. Here Pitt was a committed man. He could hardly be expected to throw overboard his convictions and promises simply because he was now prime minister. In May, 1782, as a young private member, he had in very moderate and general terms moved for a select committee to be set up to consider the existing state of the representation. A year later, by now an ex-minister and a convert in broad terms to the Wyvill proposals, he introduced a second motion, lost like its predecessor, to prevent bribery and improve the representation of counties and metropolitan boroughs – that is, what were thought the 'purer' parts of the system. All this was in line with his father's views and in no way democratic in intention. He rejected the extension of the right to vote as unpractical and dangerous, and he did not at this stage favour disfranchising the rotten boroughs because, as Chatham had once said, the limb might be mortified, but amputation might mean death – a view which, if generally extended, would approximate very closely to that of the King, who wrote of Alderman Sawbridge's reform proposal

---

* Back in 1779, when George first read Philip Francis's damaging revelations concerning Hastings, his attitude had been very different. 'The Company is ruined and Parliament turned into ridicule unless Mr Hastings is instantly removed from his situation' (The King to North, Fortescue, iv, 2634).

of June, 1784, that 'without the greatest caution it may give birth to greater evils than those attempted to be cured'.[33]

In March, 1784, a premier without a majority, Pitt still bravely assured Wyvill that his zeal for reform was unabated, and the following December '*as a man* and *as a minister honestly and boldly*' promised him that he intended going ahead with 'a meliorated system of representation'.[34] A delighted Wyvill could not resist sending his friends a circular letter telling them the good news, which soon found its way into the papers and so to the King. He was of course displeased. So to a degree was Pitt himself, who wished Wyvill had not made quite such public use of his name. George told the Home Secretary, Sydney, that he had been much hurt by reading 'a certain letter in the public papers' and had thought better of Pitt 'than that he would have allowed a known demagogue to take advantage of a private conversation'. Did not everybody want a quiet session after all the storm and stress of war and constitutional crisis, and was this the way to get the nation out of its 'despicable situation in the opinion of all other countries'?[35] Nevertheless, Pitt persevered, and hoped to make his forthcoming bill a fully ministerial measure. Its terms were far from democratic, and seen from two centuries' distance – or even from 1832 – Pitt's bill certainly appears rather a puny baby. The proposals were, first, that in small boroughs *where electors gave their consent* they could be bought out and the seats, 72 of them, re-allocated to London and the counties; and, second, that forty-shilling copyholders and certain leaseholders should be added to the electoral roll. By March, 1785, he was ready to submit the gist of this to the King, with more than a hint in his covering letter that he expected support, or at least no royal encouragement of opposition from 'those who are supposed to be connected with Government' – which might include ministers but meant particularly the Court placemen in Parliament, the 'Household Brigade'.[36]

The King was in a delicate predicament. He had absolutely no desire to lose Pitt or precipitate a new crisis. Equally he had every desire to see the bill rejected. His manner of proceeding to assist the bill's defeat with the minimum of fuss or loss of dignity to its author, showed the sort of circumspect skill that a quarter of a century of political battle had taught him. First, in confidence, he let Lord Sydney look through the reply he proposed sending to Pitt, inquiring if he perceived anything objectionable in it.[37] In itself this was a silent move against the measure's becoming ministerial. The letter was in fact tactful and studiously polite; it assured Pitt that 'out of personal regard' George would not dream of influencing anyone against the measure. (He had of course no need to; everybody knew his attitude.) He would, so he assured Pitt, 'think ill of any man who took part on either side without the maturest consideration' or voted 'contrary to his own opinion'.[38] We notice, of course, that this was not quite how he had expressed himself to the Peers over Fox's India Bill, but then Pitt was not Fox, and circumstances alter cases.

What Pitt gained, for what it was worth, was the Court's non-intervention. He did not press his demand for full ministerial or royal support. No more than George did he wish to create a crisis, and one more parliamentary defeat would not constitute a disaster. He had already, since his election triumph of 1784, suffered three: on refortifying Plymouth and Portsmouth, on Irish trade, and on his vindictive-looking insistence on a scrutiny into the election of Fox at Westminster. The reform bill was now thrown out by 74 votes. He had demonstrated to his reformer friends and perhaps to himself that he had done what he could; and to suggest that he was content to escape from his commitments with no worse accidents is not to question his sincerity. That he was no crusader hardly needs proving. From his side, the King was content to regard his premier's 'unfortunate' attachment to the reformers' cause as a youthful folly that he had now worked out of his system, and in the least harmful manner. Fortunately for him, less fortunately for the nation, he was right. Pitt never again tackled parliamentary reform. Nearly half a century had to elapse, and a revolution come close to erupting, before *the system* – Cobbett's *The Thing* – suffered any significant alteration.

The Emperor Joseph II had declared in 1783 that England had fallen to the status of a second class power, but George needed no one to tell him that a nation's strength in the world depended first on its internal prosperity and stability. The lost American war had cost 115 millions sterling, and nearly doubled the National Debt. This was the uncomfortable context in which Pitt's fiscal and administrative reforms were set. This was what demanded the paring away of wasteful public expenditure, pruning of sinecure offices, reorganising of the civil service, taking the profit out of smuggling, tireless searching for new sources of revenue.

The reform of the Civil List had its place in this search for retrenchment and efficiency – but Pitt's approach to the royal finances was notably less hostile and more constructive than that of Burke and the Rockinghams. No more was heard of economical reform; waste and muddle were eradicated in a process of quiet administrative rationalisation, not by anti-monarchical vendetta. Retrenchment being much in the public mind (however delightfully private affluence luxuriated), George III was sensitive on the subject of his own financial situation. The Civil List until the late 1780's remained a tangle of complication; it was by no means regarded, as it is now, as a sum solely to support the necessary expenses and due dignities of the sovereign and his household. Quite apart from the sums allocated from the Privy Purse towards election management (George was setting aside a regular £1,000 a month for this between 1777 and 1781), the Civil List was then expected to sustain such additional items as the secret service; the salaries of ambassadors, judges, the Speaker, the Lord Chancellor, the Commissioners of the Treasury and other government servants; a long list of bounties and pensions; miscellaneous items regularly exceeding £100,000 a year; and occasional substantial advances to support policies which it was inconvenient for Parliament to vote supplies for.

In March, 1786, George wrote to Pitt: 'Without the smallest affectation I am much concerned when obliged to be the cause of any expense to the country, yet . . . it is not occasioned by any extravagance of mine but the natural cause of things in general being dearer and Heaven having blessed me with a numerous progeny.'[39] Until Pitt began the complicated task of separating the King's private from his public and political accounts, the Crown was always liable to be accused of extravagance when it had to come to Parliament to pay its inevitable debts. As to George's strictly personal expenditure, it was not seriously challenged. He thought, however, that there were limits to the thriftiness that ought to be expected of him, and more particularly of the Queen. He resented the shifts the Court was reduced to by what he thought the malice of the Rockinghamite 'economisers', and one day in 1785 told one of the Maids of Honour 'that she could not be allowed to have dinner in her own apartments; that Burke's Economical Bill had made it impossible that her rooms should be decorated, and she must not allow her apothecary to prescribe medicines to her servants.'[40] He 'meant not to have spoken to Mr Pitt till he was less hurried', he wrote in July, 1786; but since the matter had now been raised, he wished to remind him – and Parliament – that the Queen, on no more than was allowed her with *one* child in 1763, had kept 'all my sons and daughters till they came out of the hands of women'. By now three already of his daughters were of an age to appear at Court, which necessitated further expense, and although 'every oeconomy is in the most rigid manner attended to', the Queen was having to draw heavily on capital to 'maintain six daughters for less than [George II's] four were forty nine years ago when every article of life was cheaper than now'.[41]

Pitt incorporated the royal income into the consolidated accounts, and managed to meet the King's reasonable demands on the Civil List at an annual cost of rather over £900,000. Future grumbles were to centre not round the King, but the Prince of Wales and his brothers. George III and Pitt hardly needed to tell one another about the need for 'every oeconomy'. When, for instance, the Duke of Richmond was soliciting on behalf of Sir Guy Carleton for his services in North America, and was suggesting the creation of a new post – 'Inspector of Troops', with a pension and a Dragoons regiment thrown in for good measure – George's comments were caustic: 'Mr Pitt must easily see' this would not do. The regiment of Dragoons seemed to the King, that keen rider, especially inappropriate, 'Sir Guy being little used to get on horseback.'[42] Mr Pitt did indeed easily see. And, on a bigger matter, when in 1786 Pitt put forward his ambitious version of the old Sinking Fund idea, to slim down by steady stages the swollen bulk of the National Debt, there were not likely to be differences between King and minister. Characteristically George related the fiscal steps to overseas policies past and future:

> Considering Mr Pitt has had the unpleasant office of providing for the expense incurred by the last war, it is but just he should have the full merit he deserves of having the public know and feel that he has now proposed a measure that will render the nation again respectable, if she has the sense to remain quiet some years, and not by wanting to take a showy part in the transactions of Europe again become the dupe of other Powers, and from ideal greatness draw herself into lasting distress. The old English saying is applicable to our situation: 'England must cut her coat according to her cloth.'[43]

Indeed at times during the decade 1783-1793 George III in foreign affairs was almost an isolationist, though *as Elector of Hanover* he was a willing member of the *Fürstenbund* formed to resist the ambitions of the Emperor Joseph II. In general from the very beginning of his reign he had been on the side of pacific policies. Now more than ever it was necessary for retrenchment at home to be accompanied by peace abroad. In July, 1784, he wrote to the Foreign Secretary, Carmarthen: 'Till I see this country in a situation more respectable as to army, navy, and finance, I cannot think anything that may draw us into troubled waters either safe or rational.'[44] Two years later he was underlining with his approval – and a characteristic dash of self-approval – Pitt's refusal to fish among the waters of Creole discontent in Spanish America: 'As I ever thought the conduct of France in North America unjustifiable, I certainly can never copy so faithless an example.'[45]

The King once told Thurlow he would never rest his head on his last pillow in peace when he remembered the loss of his American colonies. The national shame; the expense; the 'wrongs' done to him, particularly by the French, during what he never ceased to maintain had been a just war; not least, the lessons to be drawn; all these formed the background to his generally realistic and cautious views on foreign politics between the peace of 1783 and the French Revolutionary war of 1793. As for the position to be taken towards the infant United States themselves, there too he had to acquire realism, though it was a painful process. When in August, 1783, Fox had asked him, when defeat was still ringing in his ears, if he would receive an American ambassador, his refusal was predictable: 'I shall ever,' he answered, 'have a bad opinion of any Englishman who would accept of being an accredited Minister for that revolted State.'[46] When, however, two years later the first United States envoy was admitted to present his credentials at St James's – it was John Adams, later President, who had not so long before helped Jefferson, Franklin, and the rest to draft the Declaration of Independence – the atmosphere had a certain understandable tension, but the exchanges a dignified moderation. (Happily Adams had almost as poor a view of the French as George III.) The envoy observed the reverences laid down by usage, and pronounced a few diplomatically conciliatory sentences, which George found 'extremely proper'. Adams was not without what he feared was 'visible' agitation, but the King's reply came in a voice the shakier of the two. Everything he had done in the late contest, he said, he had done from the duty he owed his people. 'I will be very free with you,' he added. 'I was the last to consent to the separation; but the separation having been made and having become inevitable, I have always said, as I say now, that I would be the first to meet the friendship of the United States as an independent power.'[47]

When Pitt faced criticism in 1785, as Joseph II and the French pursued their ambitions in the Netherlands, George's support for him was emphatic. After the American war the only sane policy was one of moving towards a position of strength by first pursuing economic recovery, even if the French were seeking aggrandisement by intervening in Holland. Britain should be 'taking advantage of the blessings of peace by improving the revenue and making treaties of commerce . . . No system of foreign alliance can be devised that will not within the year bring us into a war which I am certain no man of sense can wish; and the other line of conduct will in a few years put us in a situation to be courted; now I fear if we move it must be by courting'.[48] And when in September, 1786, the British envoy at the Hague, seeing the French apparently carrying all before them in the struggle between the 'Patriots' and the House of Orange, agitated for a more active British policy and in particular asked for funds to support the latter cause, George showed peremptory concern lest Pitt should be persuaded by the Foreign Secretary or the ambassador into abandoning his policies of thrift, caution, and non-intervention:

> The accounts from Holland yesterday have much affected me as the great activity of Sir James Harris and his inclination to commit this country must draw us into great difficulties if great caution and sane temper is not shown in answer to him. I therefore wish to see Mr Pitt at St James's a little before one . . . It would be unjustifiable when this country if she remains some years in peace will regain former wealth and consideration by being too meddling should be drawn into a fresh war which must bring on ruin be it ever so prosperous.[49]

As things turned out fortune went against the French in Holland. In the more favourable circumstances that followed the deaths of Vergennes and Frederick the Great; with the prospect therefore of more co-operation from Prussia; and with the diplomacy of France hampered by her growing financial crisis, George did consent eventually to advance £70,000 towards the Stadtholder's cause from the Civil List (after Pitt had given his word that Parliament would repay him next session). Prussian troops then came to the aid of the Orange party, and in concert with them George finally acquiesced in a show of force from Hanover and the Royal Navy. French influence in the Netherlands collapsed; the alliance of Prussia, Britain, and Holland followed; and by 1788 George III and Pitt could be reckoned to have scored a considerable diplomatic victory – even though the imminent French Revolution and its repercussions were very soon to throw everything back into the melting-pot.

Still the royal advice continued to be for peace, and still Pitt never omitted 'receiving your Majesty's commands before any answer is prepared'. It was the Baltic theatre where danger was most acute in 1788, Sweden having rashly embarked upon war with Russia and appearing to be in immediate danger of attack also from Denmark. The Baltic was a sea whose freedom of navigation was vital to Britain's commerce and particularly to her naval supplies, and Pitt's Cabinet were alarmed at the prospect of the destruction of the balance of power there. They therefore proposed to join Prussia in threatening the Danes with war. In the event some distinctly unauthorised and 'Palmerstonian' personal diplomacy by the British minister in Copenhagen did

result in the Danes being restrained. The crisis was at its height,
however, and still unresolved, over the very weeks when George's own
alarming medical crisis was approaching. Pitt needed to consult the
King before sending the British proposals to Berlin, but was 'almost
afraid to mention the circumstance' in view of George's unhappy state
of health. The King knew that illness was already affecting the lucidity
of his expression; but a few days before his collapse in early November
he tried to convey to Pitt, who hesitated to act without royal approval,
his anxiety lest Britain should be dragged into an avoidable war. He
had been on the throne 'within a few days of twenty-eight years,
having been not on a bed of roses'. It was not just because he was now
ill and weakened; but every time he thought back to the American
business – 'the most justifiable war any country ever waged' – he must
be 'a second Don Quixote' if he were to consider getting into a general
war again.

> I think it fairer to speak out thus early than by silence be supposed
> to have changed my opinion, if things should bear a more warlike
> appearance than I now expect, and if I should then object to a general
> war.
>
> I am afraid Mr Pitt will perceive I am not quite in a situation to
> write at present, but I thought it better even to write as loosely as I
> have here than to let the box return without an answer to his letter.[50]

PART FIVE

SHOCKS
AND SHADOWS

CHAPTER TWENTY-ONE

Royal Malady
and the Regency Crisis

ON 11th June, 1788, the King had suffered a series of severe abdominal 'spasms' lasting from three in the morning until eight in the evening, and remained for two or three days ill of a disorder described either as 'bilious' or as 'gouty' – those two blanket epithets that served to cover so much nakedness in Georgian medicine. When one of the Lords of the Bedchamber, Fauconberg, offered his house at Cheltenham for royal recuperation, George accepted; and after Parliament's prorogation in July he proceeded there with the Queen and the Princesses Charlotte, Augusta, and Elizabeth, to take the medicinal waters and try the restorative virtues of this small but genteel resort. The waters, the King persuaded himself, proved 'salutary'. He found a pint and a half 'the proper quantity to give him two openings', so he reported to Sir George Baker, his physician, and he had 'never been obliged to take the rhubarb pills'.[1]

'Never did schoolboys enjoy their holydays equal to what we have done our little excursion,' wrote the Queen to Prince Augustus. The Princesses, who had never before been so far from home, were reported by Miss Burney as being in high health and spirits. The King went about everywhere almost like a plain country gentleman, with no guards and often unaccompanied by equerries. Wraxall told how he delighted 'to enter into conversation with persons who accidentally fell in his way'. He chatted with farmers about crops and prices. He considered the textile country around Stroud, then mightily prosperous, the most beautiful sight he had ever seen. The royal party visited the Gloucester Infirmary and the new half-built County Jail, the King leaving £300 for the relief of its debtor inmates. At the Cheltenham playhouse, renamed Theatre Royal, Mrs Jordan played Roxalana in *The Sultan* by royal invitation. At the King's request the Three Choirs Festival at Worcester was advanced by three weeks so that his party might attend, and every moment they spent in Worcester was 'one holiday and jubilee'. 'This, I suppose, is Worcester New Bridge?' the King inquired of some bystanders. When told yes, it was, he invited them there and then to give a 'huzza' for it. He had the Duke of

York down to visit him, getting a timber construction up in five days to house him and his party, Lord Fauconberg's house being already overcrowded. He had a new well sunk in the grounds to facilitate the taking of mineral waters, and had the local apothecary in to 'annalise' them, as well as treat Miss Burney's influenza. Wherever they went, as the Queen wrote, 'immense crowds of people' welcomed them everywhere. The King's popularity was plain for all to see, and he returned to Windsor delighted with his five weeks holiday and apparently quite restored in health.[2]

At Kew, however, on 17th October, there occurred another 'spasmodic byleous attack' and Baker found his patient in severe abdominal pain and respiratory difficulty, having for some time, it appeared, been suffering nocturnal cramps and 'rheumatick' pains in all his limbs, as well as a skin affection. Next day Baker noted the urine to be discoloured, though he was of course in no position to ascribe this to anything but the effects of the 'bile', and no physician anywhere would for another century and a half have been able by looking at the combination of all the various symptoms to have diagnosed porphyria.* For the ensuing two or three weeks George's condition fluctuated, but in general deteriorated. He was able to keep in touch with Pitt. Indeed on 24th October, he made a great effort and appeared at a Levee specially to quieten alarmist talk and to stop, as he put it, 'further lies and any fall in the stocks'; and he journeyed the following day to Windsor with the intention, never realised, of coming back to St James's again on 29th October. Meanwhile he rode out in the grounds, despite lameness and intermittent fever, until 5th November. He endured the usual bleedings, cuppings, and purgings – the whole debilitating hit-or-miss routine of current medical practice. But no one knew better than the patient himself – not even the Queen, whose desperate anxiety was manifest – that the cause for alarm was acute. There were all the old signs of 'agitation and flurry of spirits'. He slept 'hardly . . . one minute all night', he told Fanny Burney. He could *hear* himself talking too fast and excitedly, yet was sometimes powerless to check himself; 'a rapidity,' as Miss Burney described it, 'a hoarseness of voice, a volubility, an earnestness – a vehemence, rather – it startled me inexpressibly.'[3] He caught himself out in his own mental confusions; having for instance selected one prayer for morning service, he unaccountably found himself repeating another quite different one. The public was fed with the story that he had gout (or sometimes the trouble was described as dropsy); but if he had gout, the King argued,

* And very few even then. J. Waldenström first 'defined acute intermittent porphyria as a clinical entity in 1937' (*Porphyria – a Royal Malady*, 21).

kicking his heel against his other foot, how could he do *that* without causing pain? He found his vision worsening, his head throbbing, giddiness suddenly attacking him, his legs failing him. He could not manage without a walking stick. 'I was present,' wrote Fanny Burney, 'at his first seeing Lady Effingham on his return to Windsor this last time. "My dear Effy," he cried, "you see me, all at once, an old man!" ' He continued to attend the evening concerts in the Palace; but music, he confided to Dr Ayrton, master of the choristers, seemed now to affect his head. He feared he would 'not be able long to hear it'. And his compulsive fidgetiness at the concerts was apparent to all present. They took place in the evening, and it was in particular towards evening that this nervous excitement took command of him. Often he would gabble uncontrollably or repeat the same thing many times over. In bed, when sleep did come, it was disturbed and sometimes delirious. All too well he was aware that he was treading near an abyss. Once, when the Queen said something conventional about everyone having to bear up under afflictions, he put his arm round her waist and said, 'Then you are prepared for the worst.'[4]

On 3rd November – the same day that the King was writing a determinedly optimistic letter to Pitt, his last for sixteen weeks – Fanny Burney reported the Queen, though struggling to appear serene, as being 'almost overpowered with some secret terror'. It was now that George at last consented to seek a second medical opinion, and Baker called in old Dr William Heberden (who had a house in Windsor and in his time had attended William Cowper and Dr Johnson*). By November it was obvious that 'the worst' had indeed come. At noon Miss Burney watched the King going out in the chaise with his eldest daughter 'for an airing; he was all smiling benignity, but gave so many orders to the postillions, and got in and out of the carriage twice, with such agitation' that her apprehension was heavy. At dinner a few hours later, the King suddenly became delirious and violent. The Prince of Wales had just arrived from Brighton, and according to his own account later told at Lord Jersey's, his father seized him by the collar and thrust him against the wall.† Fanny Burney's version of this unpleasant family scene (she was of course not present at it) tells of

* His eminence was unquestioned. His *Commentaries on the History and Cure of Diseases* ran through many editions, and it was his account of angina pectoris that led to its first being recognised by the profession as a distinct disease entity.

† Not surprisingly, there is no corroboration of these details from elsewhere. Similarly, the accounts of how the Prince soon afterwards 'introduced Lord Lothian into the King's room when it was darkened, in order that he might hear his ravings at the time when they were at the worst' can be traced to one source, W. W. Grenville, strongly hostile of course to the Prince's party – though Grenville did

the Prince being in tears, the Princesses in misery, and the Queen in
'violent hysterics'.[5]

Sir George Baker found the King 'under an intire alienation of
mind', unable to keep still enough to have his pulse taken; next
morning it was 'at least 120'. He had chattered deliriously for most of
the night, and next morning Miss Burney, up early, and seeing only
horror on every face she met, could still through the door hear his
voice 'talking unceasingly . . . lost in hoarseness and weakness . . .
almost inarticulate'. She heard him endlessly repeating that Baker told
him lies, and saying, 'I am nervous. I am not ill, but I am nervous. If
you would know what is the matter with me, I am nervous.' The in-
fection of her tears spread to the Queen, who thanked her for it: 'It is
a great relief to me – I had not been able to cry before, all this night
long.' In the early hours, candle in hand, the distraught man, worried
by his wife's absence from his room, had come to hers; drawn the bed-
curtains to reassure himself of her presence; 'stayed a full half hour;
and the depth of terror during that time no words can paint.'[6]

The next night, while the ante-room to the King's bedroom was
full of equerries and pages wearily keeping watch with Sir George
Baker and the two Princes, they were suddenly disturbed by the appearance among them of the King who, 'amazed and in consternation,
demanded what they did there'. When Baker tried to explain to him,
he penned him in a corner and told him he was an old woman. Then
'the Prince of Wales, by signs and whispers, would have urged others
to have drawn him away', but he would not go. He rambled on about
Frederick being his friend. When the Queen's Chamberlain, Colonel
Digby (Fanny Burney's 'Mr Fairly') tried to lead him back, again he
resisted, and demanded 'Who are you?' 'I am Colonel Digby, sir, and
your Majesty has been very good to me often, and now I am going to
be very good to you, for you must come to bed, sir. It is necessary for
your life'; and the patient allowed himself to be taken back quietly,
'like a child.' From this time, wrote Fanny Burney,

> as the poor King grew worse, general hope seemed universally to
> abate; and the Prince of Wales took the government of the house
> into his own hands. Nothing was done but by his orders, and he was
> applied to in every difficulty. The Queen interfered not in anything;
> she lived entirely in her two new rooms, and spent the whole day in
> patient sorrow and retirement with her daughters.[7]

---

claim that the incident 'begins to be pretty well known here' (23.11.1788, Buckingham, *Memoirs*, ii, 12).

It was over five weeks after taking the first shock of her husband's derangement before she saw him again. In part this may have arisen from her own attitude to the shape taken by events, for according to Lord Ailesbury, when the Lord Chancellor wanted her 'to take charge of the King's person she desired to decline it, which he said it would be cruelty to do'.[8] She was undoubtedly in a state of high resentment against her two eldest sons and the manner in which the Prince of Wales had taken charge not merely of the King's person and medical treatment but also of his official and even private property as though he were already dead or judged incurable. Fanny Burney leaves no doubt just how shaken and ill her mistress was, and the Queen's own agitation was doubtless a factor in the doctors' ruling that her being allowed into the sickroom would only increase the King's own agitation and make him worse.

The Prince of Wales now called in his own physician, the fashionable Dr Richard Warren, whom the King had never been able to abide even when fully sane. (There were soon to be four more doctors on the scene too, making seven in all.) Everybody, Baker and Heberden included, deferred to Warren when he arrived, but the King utterly refused to be seen by him. His diagnosis was therefore obtained by stealth, with Baker sending 'intelligence concerning his pulse, etc.' through the door, close to which Warren's ear was cocked to listen to the royal conversation. Avoiding the Queen, he then made straight off to the Prince's quarters. He had heard enough to conclude that George was mad; *Rex noster insanit.* 'Warren is strongly inclined to think the disorder permanent,' wrote William Grenville to his brother, and it was likely, Grenville considered, that the Prince of Wales must be appointed Regent, with kingly power; likely too that he would 'dismiss Pitt without hesitation'.[9] Certainly the Prince was already in communication with Sheridan, and he in turn was parleying with Thurlow, who was considered a possible 'catch' and known to be hostile to Pitt. Fox was in Italy with Mrs Armistead, and could not possibly be home for some time. Pitt at first was pessimistic: 'The disorder might either be one locally fixed on the brain' or it might be of a more peripatetic nature, in which case 'it might be dangerous to life'. On the whole, he noted, 'there was more ground to fear than to hope, and more reason to apprehend durable insanity than death.'[10]

The King's condition fluctuated all through November, during which month he remained at Windsor. Sometimes he seemed better, and conversed lucidly with his attendants, often describing to them his recently experienced hallucinations and 'sensible of having been much out of order'. His talk then was much to the point, wry sometimes, even sharp-witted. But soon he would be worse again, in his delirium seeing Hanover through Herschel's telescope, composing dispatches on imagined issues to foreign courts, capriciously bestowing exalted honours upon attendants temporarily in favour, striving to save precious documents from the flood which he conceived to be submerging London. There were times when, if crossed, he would be vehement and noisy, or even violent – then lapse into melancholic or despairing rumination. 'Yesterday se'nnight,' so Lord Sheffield heard, 'he talked incessantly for sixteen hours, to divert him from which they endeavoured to turn him to writing; at length he began to compose notes on Don Quixote.'[11] As for the nature of the royal malady, William Grenville knew nothing more or less than the doctors, which was little indeed:

> The cause to which they all agree to ascribe it, is the force of a humour which was beginning to show itself in the legs, when the King's imprudence drove it from thence into the bowels; and the medicines they were obliged to use for the preservation of his life have repelled it upon the brain . . . The physicians are now endeavouring, by warm baths, and by great warmth of covering, to bring it down again into the legs, which nature had originally pointed out as the best mode of discharge.[12]

Hence repeated blistering of his feet with plasters of cantharides and mustard, which left them sore and suppurating, and materially aggravated his many bad nights*; and hence the hot baths which, when he came to resist taking them, he had to be 'managed' into. Not surprisingly, all the doctors at different times came in for his scorn or anger. He objected to the gentlemen pages' constant shadowing. He resented not being allowed to shave himself. He demanded the return of his drawer keys, which the Prince of Wales had taken charge of; and when the doctors refused him, Warren, the particular object of his rage, had to be protected by the two pages in attendance. The King's mirrors were removed too; it was considered that the shock of seeing his own emaciated face, with its swollen veins and eyes 'like blackcurrant jelly', would be too severe. On 12th-13th November, he again experienced delirium, violent agitation and loquacity, and sleeplessness for twenty-nine hours. On 18th-19th November, recorded Colonel Greville (Fanny Burney's 'Colonel Welbred', one of the equerries that sat with him), after only two hours' sleep he 'talked for nineteen hours

---

* He often writhed and thrashed about in agitation and pain, and tore off his dressings. Attempts were also made to take off the evil humour by applying leeches to his temples.

with scarce any intermission'. On the 23rd he 'talked with great rapidity on strange subjects, and sorry was I to hear that these were not free from indecencies'. Several times Greville comments on the indecencies, 'much unlike himself.' On more than one occasion during November he was in immediate danger of death, but each time lapsed into coma after convulsions.

The expectant Whigs, scenting sweet herbage on the breezes from Windsor, told one another confidently that his recovery was impossible, though there were some like Sir Gilbert Elliot who did not 'much relish . . . this triumphant sort of conversation, especially before the battle is won'.[13] The reports however that Captain Payne, the Prince of Wales's Comptroller, was sending from Windsor to Sheridan and Loughborough back in town were splendidly optimistic. The Duke of York, 'just come out of the King's room,' had said that 'every moment' his father was becoming worse. 'His pulse is weaker and weaker,' wrote Payne complacently; 'and the doctors say it is impossible to survive it long.' Payne obtained his information largely from the pages and then tended to improve on it, having a strong personal interest in the prospective new dispensation – the Prince had promised him a Lordship of the Admiralty. On one occasion he reported the King 'howling like a dog' in his ravings, and in general his intelligences concerning the Windsor situation were little more reliable than those of the Duchess of Devonshire, who committed to her diary rumours picked up from various sources, such as 'showing his backside to his attendants, saying that he had not the gout', jumping naked out of bed, and (back in the summer at Cheltenham) running a race against a horse.*

In Fox's absence, and to the annoyance of the Duke of Portland, who was by general consent the party's titular leader and the prospective First Lord of the Treasury, it was Sheridan who, with the Prince's apparent approval, was playing the part of ministry-maker. Loughborough too, who had high hopes of the Lord Chancellorship, was very busy; his chief fear lay in the possibility – sometimes it seemed the likelihood – of Thurlow's weathering the storm, on the grounds that the Chancellor was above party and might reasonably retain his office. On 11th November the *Morning Chronicle* had to con-

---

* *Georgiana's Diary*, in W. Sichel, *Sheridan*, ii, 403-05. *A History of the Royal Malady by a Page of the Presence* was the source of other notorious tales, for instance of the King just before his collapse stopping his carriage in Windsor Park, shouting 'Ah, there he is!' – meaning the King of Prussia – and shaking hands with the lower branches of an oak tree 'with the most apparent cordiality and regard'. This kind of thing sold well in 1789.

tradict a report that George III was already dead – Fox, hurrying back
from Italy, heard the same rumour as he passed through Lyons. It was
not long before the papers were beginning to print lists of ministers and
posts in the coming Whig administration. The *Morning Post* did so on
28th November; *The Times* waited until 10th December. So long as the
Prince of Wales remained at Windsor – which meant until the King
and Queen moved to Kew on 29th November – the obligation upon
him to keep up the appearance of a long filial face, despite his being
bitterly at odds with the Queen, prevented him from 'breaking out into
any unseasonable indulgence of his spirits before the public',[14] but no
such demand upon the proprieties lay upon his supporters in London.
At Brooks's the atmosphere was buoyant – in sharp contrast with the
City, where the fear of Pitt's coming dismissal caused a two-point fall
in the stocks.

Ministerial pessimism, however, began to lift after the crisis had run
for three weeks or so. On 24th November, Pitt went to Windsor and
suggested that fresh medical advice should be sought from a Dr
Anthony Addington, one-time family consultant of the Pitts, father of
the country's next prime minister, and keeper twenty years earlier of a
madhouse. He was the only physician thus far consulted to have had
special experience of treating the mentally deranged. His first suggestion, which was vetoed, was that the patient should be allowed to
see his wife – which 'occasioned much confusion, as the King immediately begun to prepare his room for her reception'.[15] But his principal contribution, which had vital political effects, was to encourage
Pitt to think that a complete recovery might well occur – a very
different prognosis from Warren's. Addington also recommended a
move away from Windsor, where there was no outdoor privacy from
spectators on the Terrace, to Kew, which had extensive secluded
gardens where the King might get air and exercise. This was a view
the other doctors could more easily concur in, as Kew was in much
handier range of their London practices. It was nearer to Westminster
too, and both Pitt and Thurlow favoured the change. The only obstacles were the King himself, who point blank refused to budge, and
the Queen, who knew well how strongly George preferred Windsor
to Kew and feared the effect on him of a forced removal. As for
amenities, there was perhaps little to choose. Both houses suffered
wickedly from cold and draughts, and 1788-89 was to be one of the
bitterest of winters. (For the King this was immaterial, since the doctors prescribed that his room ought to stay cold, but the sufferings of
his attendants and the Queen's, especially at freezing Kew, shiver
through Fanny Burney's pages.)

The Queen finally consented that the King should be moved, but only on condition that she went too. Persuasion having failed with the King, the ruse was eventually adopted of facing him with the news that the Queen and Princesses had already gone, and then luring him to follow them in order to be among them. On the day fixed, he put up a long losing struggle. At about ten the Queen, the Princesses, and two ladies-in-waiting, left – the Queen, wrote Miss Burney, 'drowned in tears'. Then doctors, equerries, pages, the prime minister, all tried their persuasions upon the King unavailingly. Twice he took refuge from everything and everybody behind drawn bed-curtains. At one stage Pitt tried writing him a formal letter from the ante-room, and George even attempted to pen an answer to it, but had not the power. Only the threat of force and the promise that the three trusted attendants, Goldsworthy, Harcourt, and Greville, would travel with him at last succeeded in getting him dressed and led to his waiting carriage and escort of cavalry; and so the tormented man came to his palace of Kew, to be bolted and barred inside his allotted quarters, where the Prince of Wales had already done the rounds in person, chalking names on each door, and seeing that the Queen, the Princesses, and their ladies were allocated quarters where not even the noise of their feet over-head could remind the King of their nearness.[16] Most foolishly and unforgivably, permission was not given, after all, for him to see his wife and daughters.* Perceiving thence that he had been tricked, he planned to escape at night; grew sullen and turbulent by turns; refused food and threw his medicine away; became once more delirious and deranged; until by 3rd December, Colonel Greville was recording in his diary 'the worst day H.M. has experienced'.[17]

The fifth of December was a day of two important landmarks. It saw the opening of Parliament with the prospect of debates on the nature of the Regency that was to be set up, and also the arrival at Kew of the Reverend Dr Francis Willis, thought by some to be a quack mad-doctor but recommended by the Queen, who had received favourable reports of him from Lady Harcourt. Willis kept a private asylum at Gretford in Lincolnshire and claimed a remarkably high proportion of cures among his patients. He professed no doubt of his ability to add the King to his tally of successes, and his optimism, coming on top of what Dr Addington had said, brought new heart both to the Queen and to the Administration.

In the parliamentary debates of December and January, Pitt's policy

* 'I could not sleep all night – I thought I heard the poor King . . . His indignant disappointment haunted me. The Queen too was very angry at having promises made in her name which could not be kept.' (D'Arblay, *Diary*, iv, 195-96).

was to accept the necessity of the Prince of Wales's Regency, but to place certain restrictions on it and play for time in the hope that the King would recover. If the King were not to, then Pitt's future would seem to lie back in his barrister's chambers. In the Commons therefore, on 10th December, he moved the appointment of a committee 'to examine into, search for, and report precedents'. Fox, impatient of the delay such a committee must entail, and thirsting for office, asserted – rashly as it soon appeared – that 'there existed no precedent whatever that could bear on the present case . . . It behoved them, therefore . . . to restore the sovereign power and the exercise of the royal authority'; the Prince should be given full powers to act as sovereign immediately. Pitt saw and seized the chance this gave him, as he put it, to 'unwhig the gentleman' and expose Fox, of all men, as the champion of royal powers irrespective of Parliament's wishes. Against Fox, made to appear the protagonist of inherent right, Pitt could stand forth as the defender of parliamentary privilege. Pitt, who in 1783-84 would have been helpless without George III's support, could now show that the hopes of Fox and the Whigs depended on the very principle Fox had been foremost in denying – unfettered royal authority to choose ministers. None of Fox's subsequent attempts to extricate himself, by claiming for instance that the Regency was to be merely 'a trust for the people', could do much for his line of argument; and one must remember that in 1788 parliamentary votes were still to be swayed by such triumphs in debate as this of Pitt's. There were many country gentlemen uncommitted to parties and with minds still to be made up. In Parliament as well as around the royal sick chamber there were many waiting to see which way the cat would jump – and if the cat jumped the wrong way for them, the 'rats' would be in trouble. Even among committed Whigs Fox was seen to have blundered, for, at the very least, his tactics produced just the delays which were Pitt's best hope. Moreover, the Whigs, so cockahoop a month before, were now at sixes and sevens. Fox mistrusted Sheridan, and Sheridan Grey. Loughborough was disgruntled at being asked by Fox to give Thurlow the right to remain Chancellor if he wished. Portland, the ostensible head of the party, did not think Thurlow worth the wooing. Elliot too, thought him 'a treacherous and dangerous character' – as did Pitt from the other side of the fence. As things were going, the hope that Sheridan, Fox, and the Prince of Wales might be able to detach the Chancellor from Pitt dimmed as Thurlow contemplated the hole he would fall into if he threw in his lot with the Whigs and then the King recovered. On 8th December he had agreed with Lord Carmarthen that 'there was no probability of the K's recovery';[18] but only one week later, on 15th December, impressed by the new Willis atmosphere of confidence, he made his notorious descent from the fence and, with that fluent accompaniment of well-timed tears which so many public men then seemed able to command, he declared, 'When I forget my Sovereign, may my God forget me.'

But the King in fact had not yet recovered; and Fox, though ill and 'fatigued to death', wrote with obstinate optimism to Mrs Armistead that same day that he and his party would be in office 'in about a fortnight'. The King, he told her, 'notwithstanding the reports,' was 'certainly worse and perfectly mad', and 'the Prince must be regent'.[19] The Prince of Wales, though he too was worried, himself sometimes gave the impression of a man celebrating victory in advance. He was back among his companions of Carlton House and Brooks's, bibulous in public at the Opera and uninhibited at private parties, doing nothing to discourage the scurrilous attacks on the Queen in the opposition press, although in mid-December he had given a written promise, in response to her agitated request, that neither he nor the Duke of York would make use of her name 'in any shape or upon any occasion whatever'. (Both 'Peter Pindar' and the *Morning Herald* insinuated that Pitt was repaying her for her support with presents of diamonds.) In this hostile attitude towards their mother and in their private writing-off of the King as 'a complete lunatick' the two brothers were at one.[20] 'You will see in the Opposition papers that they are beginning to abuse the Queen in the most open and scandalous manner,' wrote William Grenville to his brother on 21st December. 'If we were together, I could tell you some particulars of the Prince of Wales's behaviour towards the King and her, within these few days, which would make your blood run cold.'[21] And there was a story coming from the Duchess of Gordon, who claimed she heard it from the Prince's own mouth: when he and the Duke were upbraided by the Queen for going through the King's drawers at Kew, the Duke said to her, 'Madam, I believe you are as much deranged as the King.'[22]

The King was quite clear-headed enough to understand the implications of the arrival of Dr Willis, *the keeper of a madhouse*, but he received him calmly at first, told him he was sorry he had given up the Church (an honourable profession) for medicine ('one I heartily detest'), and suggested that he should make a good beginning by removing *Dr Warren* to the madhouse. Willis brought his own special brands of physic, tried in the experience of twenty-nine years, and was in general very full of himself and the virtues of his treatment. But when he produced one of the basic tools of his trade, a strait-waistcoat, and appeared to have three 'physical assistants' (apart from his son Dr John

Willis) by whose aid he *broke in* troublesome patients, George became violently enraged. Over the next weeks terrible battles ensued whenever he became disobedient or turbulent, and the humiliating punishment of the strait-waistcoat was many times inflicted. Sometimes too, he was tied down to the bed.[23] However, though George inevitably came to fear and resent the Willises and their men, it did soon appear that though plagued by many setbacks he was on the whole showing a trend towards improvement. And the Willises combined the harshness of the strait-waistcoat with an imaginative measure of trust. They granted occasional privileges to the patient which scandalised the other doctors, letting him for instance handle his own knife and fork, his own razor to help Mr Papendiek shave him, his penknife to trim his nails with. From 11th December they allowed him to walk in the gardens, with the Willis team and other attendants at hand. On 13th December they let him at last see the Queen again, together with Princess Amelia – an emotional occasion, and it was unfortunate that that night he had another relapse into delirium and waistcoat treatment. (Warren and the anti-Willis faction loudly represented this as justification of their own earlier wisdom in isolating him from the family.)

Above all Dr Willis exhaled an infectious confidence. The Queen, who had become 'so dreadfully reduced that her stays would wrap twice over', though she was horrified by some of his methods, clung to his opinion as to a life-raft. Fanny Burney was 'extremely struck' by him, 'a man of ten thousand' – and hardly less so by his 'extremely handsome' son John.[24] And of course for Pitt and the Government, Willis was a godsend. His evidence to the Privy Council inquiry was full of assurance, well-founded or no; 'all but decisive as to the certainty of the King's recovery in a short time,' wrote Grenville.[25] Willis became quite openly the doctor who stood for Pitt, the King, and the Queen; a sort of Crown witness-in-chief, just as Warren became the prime expert and principal prop of the Whigs, the Prince, and the Duke of York.* The rival doctors' diagnoses and prognoses were exchanged across the floor of the two Chambers during the debates of December and January like musket fire; attacks on the other side's favourite physician, his political bias, his incompetence, his charlatanry, flew like poisoned darts. It was ironical that at the very moment in mid-December when administration supporters were most generously using up their Willis ammunition; when Thurlow, the suspected renegade-in-

---

* It was about this time that the King picked out a knave from a pack of cards he was playing with and wrote on the back, 'Sir Richard Warren Bart First Physician to the King' (R. F. Greville, *Diaries*, 164).

chief, was falling tearfully back into line; when the Prince of Wales's regiments were looking a little ragged, the King was again going through a very bad phase – one of his worst, with delirium, abuse, rebellion, confinement, torture from his blistered feet, sleep so scarce and fitful that it was measured by the quarter-hour, the wildest derangement and irrationality, the most disturbing pathos. There was one occasion for instance that Colonel Greville tells of, when the hapless man 'got a pillow case round his head, and the pillow in bed with him, which he called Prince Octavius, who he said was to be new born this day'.[26]

When the Commons resumed business on 6th January, there was a further interrogation of the doctors, which the Whigs were hopeful would this time refute Willis's optimism, yet by involving more delay it further retarded their cause. The medical prognoses were of course again contradictory; once more it was Willis and Warren in flat opposition and at daggers drawn, with their other colleagues in varying postures between them. Willis and Warren could not agree even on simple *facts* like pulse rates. The Opposition gained little from the exercise; and worse quickly followed for them. By 10th January, Fox's afflicted bowels had put him out of action again. At much the same time the Duchess of Devonshire was noting: 'Sheridan hears Grey has abused him. Grey is abused by others . . . Great private treachery . . . [Talk of] Sheridan courting the Prince and encouraging the praise of him where Fox is abused.'[27] The Opposition was torn by internal jealousies, private intrigues, and policy differences.

Battle was now joined, not only at the King's bedside and on the parliamentary benches, but throughout the country. Addresses flowed in to both camps from nationwide political meetings, but generally the weight of popular sympathy leant against the Prince's party. In the City of London, in particular, they even guaranteed the wherewithal to present Pitt with an annuity of £3,000 a year if he should be forced out of office; and the prospect of having Sheridan as Chancellor of the Exchequer caused them great misgiving. In the country, Pitt's championing of Parliament's privilege against Prince's prerogative had given his supporters a strong slogan and a polemical advantage. The Prince's personal reputation was a millstone round the Whigs' neck, over which there always hung too the threat of a Mrs Fitzherbert revelation – a sword of Damocles whose thread Mr Rolle, one of the members for Devonshire, made a speciality of threatening to cut. This Fitzherbert weapon was one which Pitt would not employ. If the Prince of Wales was to be Regent – and everything still pointed to it – the country would be in a sad situation if he came to that office a discredited liar.

The Government's tactics were to use their majority to impose such severe parliamentary restrictions on the prospective Regent that he would be unable to make a clean sweep, and his new ministers would be hard put to it to wield their power without concessions to Pitt and his supporters. In proposing his Regency Bill, therefore, Pitt advocated four checks: the Regent was to have no power to create peers; his right to grant offices, salaries, or pensions was to be strictly limited; he was to have no jurisdiction over the King's lands and property; and the care of the royal patient and management of his Household were to be in the hands of the Queen.

While the debates of January were proceeding, the King continued in his course of violent ups and downs. In his confused periods 'he talked much of Lady Pembroke' as he had begun to do in December, and 'much against the Queen, and dwelt upon a variety of subjects with great inconsistency and incoherence'. In clear intervals he would half remember the 'many improper things' he had been saying, especially concerning Lady Pembroke, an old friend of many years' standing; and then he experienced 'a sense of shame'.[28] He spent long hours in the strait-waistcoat, and after 24th January in the 'restraining chair' – his coronation chair, as he sometimes called it. This expression should not be taken as implying any humorous philosophical acceptance on his part. On the contrary, violent restraint bred violent resentment and rage, until exhaustion supervened. But the Willises were convinced that in 'controul' lay the key to their successes. To us it seems more probable that these came in spite of the treatment, or at least of this part of it; but for them, and for most contemporary mad-doctors, the strait-waistcoat offered three advantages. It replaced the older more barbarous practice of *beating* lunatics into submission; it meant that violent patients could hurt neither themselves nor others; and it inculcated 'salutary fear', so that the mere threat of it would tend towards subsequent self-control. 'By working on it,' they said, 'one removes their thoughts from the phantasms occupying them and brings them back to reality.'[29] Fanny Burney, never observing the means employed, but only hearing of the improvement gained, saw the Willises through rose-tinted spectacles, miracle men 'surely sent by Heaven to restore peace and health, and prosperity to this miserable house'.[30] It could hardly be quite like that that their patient viewed them, even when lucid. And the Queen, inclined though she was towards Dr Willis, was deeply outraged by the employment of such humiliating devices as strait-waistcoats and restraining chairs upon the King of England. 'I gave great offence to the Queen,' Willis said later, but 'when my gracious sovereign became violent, I felt it my duty to subject him to the same system of restraint as I should have adopted with one of his gardeners at Kew'. He went further, and suggested that it was the Queen's resentment that helped persuade Pitt to break the promise that Willis claimed had originally been made to him, of a baronetcy and a pension of £1,500 a year.[31]

Walks in Kew and Richmond Gardens continued, though once, when George asked to go up the Pagoda and was refused, he lay down on the grass and had to be carried back. On 16th January, he knelt on a chair and prayed that he might recover his sanity or die. The following day he remembered that 18th January was the Queen's birthday and asked for a new coat to receive her in. He did see her, and the three Princesses as well, but as Fanny Burney commented, 'it was not a good day.' Another part of the Willis treatment was now being regularly applied, a course of tartar emetic 'cunningly . . . and variously masked' in his food and drink – which, though it made him feel desperately wretched, the great inherent strength of his constitution enabled him to weather also.

With Fox retired sick to Bath, three months gone by since the King's wits went astray, the Whigs in disarray, and the battle of the medical bulletins now running strongly in favour of Willis, it was 5th February before Pitt needed to move the first reading of the Regency Bill; just the time when George's health began to take decisive steps forward, with no repetition of the earlier relapses. His walks in the Gardens were now made regularly, and it was during one of these, on 2nd February, that Fanny Burney had the fright and excitement of her life. Strict instructions had been given for all the staff to keep completely out of the way of the King and his little group of attendants. Her panic therefore was considerable when, taking the air herself, she suddenly realised that the King had seen her, recognised her, was calling out to her. 'Heavens, how I ran! I do not think I should have felt the hot lava of Vesuvius.' But the King began to give chase. 'Still, therefore, on I flew' – until at last an attendant caught her up, told her she must stop, since it hurt the King to run. When he came up, apparently quite clear-headed, he inquired innocently why she had run away so.

Shocked at a question impossible to answer, yet a little assured by the mild tone of his voice, I instantly forced myself forward, to meet him . . . I looked up, and met all his wonted benignity of countenance, though something still of wildness in his eyes. Think, however, of my surprise, to feel him put both his hands round my two shoulders, and then kiss my cheek! . . . I believe . . . it was the joy of a heart unbridled, now, by the forms and proprieties of

established custom and sober reason . . . What a conversation
followed! When he saw me fearless, he grew more and more alive,
and made me walk close by his side, away from the attendants . . .
He assured me he was quite well – as well as he had ever been in his
life; and then inquired how I did, and how I went on? and whether
I was comfortable?

He ran on animatedly for a long time on many subjects; about his
pages, particularly one Ernst whom he resented; and about Dr Burney;
and he tried to sing 'the subjects of several airs and choruses' of Handel,
but so hoarsely that it was painful to hear him. Eventually he became
a little too voluble, said some rash things about Lord Salisbury and
Mme Schwellenberg (Fanny Burney's particular cross; 'never mind
her,' he said, 'I will be your friend as long as you live') – and then the
Willises intervened to steer him away.

The medical bulletin next morning read as uninformatively as on
most mornings: 'His Majesty passed yesterday quietly, he had a good
night, and is much as usual this morning.' More and more the reports
referred to his Majesty's composed manner, and the satisfactory
number of hours' sleep. By mid-February he was walking seven or
eight miles a day in Kew and Richmond Gardens. On 10th February
he told Dr Willis he would like to see the Lord Chancellor, saying he
had been ill seventeen weeks and had much to inquire about.[32] It was
not a happy time for the Whigs to be attacking the Regency Bill,
particularly as their chief Commons spokesman, Burke, chose the
occasion to make some of the most violent but least effective parliamentary speeches of his career. The nub of his argument was to turn
the old Whig mythology inside out, convincing himself but few others
that the essence of the Whig principle was respect for the 'splendour'
of the Crown, and what the Bill violated was the sacredness of the right
of hereditary succession, that most precious of safeguards against the
insatiable ambition and power-lust of such men as William Pitt.[33] In
the medical sphere he followed upon the cue of Dr Warren, who had
pronounced that even if the King did recover sanity, it would be at
least a year before he could be regarded as cured. In Committee, Burke
told of his own researches into the mad-business, and of his visits to
'those dreadful mansions where these unfortunate beings are confined'. Of those who had 'recovered', some 'had butchered their sons' –
that seemed a little near the knuckle – 'others had done violence to
themselves by hanging, shooting, drowning, throwing themselves out
of windows . . .' This was altogether too much for the House. Whatever his reputation as a political philosopher, Burke's reputation as a

parliamentarian was at its lowest after these Regency debates. By 16th February the Bill was ready to go to the Lords; but only three days later the Lord Chancellor was in a position to inform them that the King was in a state of convalescence. The Bill was dead; Fox and the Whigs were once more frustrated; and the 'rats' had little cover to run to.

CHAPTER TWENTY-TWO

'Good Order and Our Excellent Constitution'

By 17th February, and again three days later, the King had been deemed well enough to see Thurlow, who on the second occasion began, though tactfully, to acquaint him with some of the business transacted during the long nightmare of his illness. Three days later again it was the turn of the Prince of Wales and Duke of York, who were allowed to see him for half an hour, but only in the presence of the Queen and on the understanding that, however anxious they were to make an early bid to justify their conduct to him, there was to be no talk of politics. By that time, 23rd February, the King must have known of the storm that had been raging, for on the same day he wrote to Pitt – it was the first time since 3rd November – informing him that 'care was taken for the conversation to be general and cordial'.[1] The following day Pitt travelled down to Kew, found the King composed, dignified, and clear as a bell – though near to tears as he expressed his gratitude to those who had stood by him in his illness.[2] Had the Regency Bill gone through before he recovered, he subsequently told his brother Gloucester, it would have been like 'taking out a Statute of Lunacy' against him, and 'no power on earth should have prevailed on him to resume the Government';[3] he would have retired to Hanover.*

Instead, here he was on 6th March, writing off to Göttingen to thank Adolphus, just fifteen, for the filial feeling that at least one son had recently shown, and to declare he was 'truely in perfect health' though avoiding all bustle and fatigue. Now that the doctors had departed, this last point was specially stressed by the Queen, who must have persuaded him that same day to adopt an extraordinary little artifice of hers, by which he actually wrote her a *letter* 'desiring her to acquaint' their two eldest sons that the King must decline to discuss subjects that might agitate him.[4]

The Duke of York did nevertheless come promptly to see him, on these terms, and reported to Sir Gilbert Elliot that his father's con-

---

* But of course he had also said more than once that a King who had had to submit to a strait-waistcoat could never resume his royal functions. Saying and doing were inclined to be different things.

versation in general was affectionate and rational, though 'with one or two instances of singularity' – as though he and the Whigs were determined to discover the King not yet quite reliably sane. ('Frederick only voted against us *once*, did he?' George asked Chief Justice Kenyon the following day.[5]) Charles Fox was writing to Mrs Armistead as late as May, 'As to the poor man, he is mad.'[6] The Prince of Wales's friend Lord Rawdon, later Lord Moira, suggested more gently that there were perhaps still strings which when touched might produce 'false music'.[7] Reports of this Whig reluctance to acknowledge defeat provoked Thurlow to snarl that whenever *he* went to Kew he supposed they *wound the King up*, for *he* could never see anything wrong with him. The fact that ministers now had daily access to the monarch, while the royal brothers were denied any opportunity to exculpate themselves, caused the Prince of Wales much indignation; it was neither 'decent nor just', and his mother 'had much to answer for'. With Elliot's assistance, he began to prepare a long apologia for his conduct, and in fact was falling over himself in prolix protestations of past innocence and present loyalty to such an extent that Fox advised him to proceed more cautiously, 'there were so many delicate points to be touched on.' The apologia was never sent.[8]

Charlotte was certainly not yet in a forgiving mood. At her first Drawing Room following the crisis, with the Prince present, she made herself conspicuously pleasant to the 'loyal' and cold-shouldered the 'disloyal' among the company. She had invitations to the Buckingham House parties sent to the Prince and the Duke, but also wrote explaining that their friends must not expect to be asked. (This scandalised the Duke of Portland.) She even discriminated among her own Maids of Honour according to the supposed record of their recent attitudes – which caused them to band together in a letter of protest.[9] When in May the Duke of York fought a duel on Wimbledon Common with the Duke of Richmond's nephew and heir Colonel Lennox, she showed no concern for her son's condition (according to Fox he had 'one of his curls shot off') and soon afterwards at a ball showed Lennox the utmost courtesy.

The Prince and Duke did nothing to improve matters by their public behaviour. On St George's Day the King attended a Grand Thanksgiving at St Paul's – a five-hour marathon culminating in a *feu de joie* from the Guards under the windows of Buckingham House – all of which he survived well, only being overcome by emotion once in St Paul's, when he covered his face briefly with a handkerchief.[10] Naturally the brothers were obliged to attend, but chatted throughout the ceremony to one another and to their uncles of Cumberland and

Gloucester, laughed privately between one another, and according to one hostile source ate biscuits during the sermon. And when White's Club held a thanksgiving fête at the Pantheon, they allowed their complimentary tickets to be offered for sale in Bond Street.[11]

The Queen, in her resentment against the Opposition and her anxiety to protect the King, appeared for a time to be liable to disprove the substance of what Chesterfield had written of her – 'tender mother and unmeddling queen'. She did now sometimes appear to be meddling, under Thurlow's guidance. The Prince and Elliot were sure of it; 'She has acquired the same sort of authority over him that Willis and his men have,' wrote Elliot.[12] Equally sure from the other side was Lord Hawkesbury (once Charles Jenkinson, soon to be Earl of Liverpool). But Pitt's position was now very strong; and the King, though he declared that in future he must 'decline entering into a pressure of business', and indeed for the rest of his life would 'only keep that superintending eye which can be effected without labour or fatigue',[13] was soon sufficiently back in control for suspicions regarding Charlotte to die a natural death.*

The King's health was not of course quite as 'perfect' as he proclaimed it to Adolphus. His voice was still hoarse; he was painfully thin; 'three stones lighter than he was,' estimated Sidney Smith. The flesh of his cheeks had fallen away so that his eyes seemed to protrude more than ever; and the vision of those eyes began now to give the trouble that blinded him fifteen years later. For months to come, he found too that he tired quickly. A succession of audiences at Windsor on 17th May had 'thoroughly fatigued him', he confessed to Lord Sydney. 'Little ruffles' still upset him unduly, 'and still more so' when they related to Lord Buckingham,† to whom he was determined not

---

* There is, however, an interesting phrase in Malmesbury's *Diaries* (ii, 460) for June, 1792: 'Pitt said he did not come with the King's command to propose a coalition, but that he would be responsible that it would please the King *and the Queen* . . . [my italics]. William Elliot too, writing to Sir Gilbert, quotes Pitt as saying 'he had reason to believe that the coalition would be very acceptable both to the King and the Queen' (Minto, ii, 42-43).

† The second Earl Temple and first Marquis of Buckingham. The King had never forgiven him for deserting the ship in December, 1783. In an interval between the onsets of his derangement in November, 1788, he once avowed that he hated nobody – why should anybody hate him? Then suddenly his scrupulous honesty, and perhaps lurking sense of humour, flashed through. 'I beg pardon,' he corrected himself, 'I do hate the Marquis of Buckingham' (Auckland, *Journal*, ii, 244). His sanity recovered, the King was now able to indulge his feelings, at least to the extent of refusing to grant the Marquis the Dukedom the Grenvilles considered due to him (Buckingham, *Memoirs*, ii, 167-72). Over the military appointments there was a compromise.

to knuckle under in a trial of strength over senior military appointments. To Pitt he admitted feeling 'a certain lassitude and want of energy both of mind and body, which must require time, relaxation, and change of scene to restore'.[14] However, an early sign that the King and Pitt were again in business together was the dismissal of those office-holders and others – even four of the royal pages – who had miscalculated by putting their eggs into the Prince's basket during the winter. Lord Lothian lost his regiment of Horse Guards. The Duke of Queensberry, who had been a Lord of the Bedchamber for twenty-eight years, suddenly found himself removed from employment. Dr Watson was obliged to *remain* Bishop of Llandaff though he dearly coveted the vacant see of St Asaph; he had been the only bishop to vote for the Regency Bill, and was now much put out by being treated with the rest of the 'rats'. (Lord Camden's nephew Hardinge, the Queen's Attorney General, on a visit to Windsor found the King going 'slap-dash into politics, Queen and all', and 'laughing heartily at the *Rats* by that name'.[15]) The removal of not wholly reliable placemen, of course, even further strengthened the Government's almost impregnable position. The weakness of Pitt with no King to keep him in power had been sufficiently demonstrated during the crisis; his strength now reflected not only the King's restored health but the notable soaring of his popularity that accompanied it. He had come through, between the Scylla of sudden death and the Charybdis of permanent insanity. It was a tale whose hero, even if he were not King, would have deserved universal sympathy and congratulation; Parson Woodforde was voicing in his diary a general sentiment: 'May so good a King long live to reign over us.'

But like most dramatic stories, this one had villains too, and high among them, in the public's view, were the Prince of Wales and his brother of York. 'I could have forgiven his [the Duke of York's] wildness,' wrote Lord Cornwallis; 'but the want of feeling that he showed for a father who doated on him, and the meanness of becoming a contemptible runner of a party, and of keeping a [faro] table for fellows he ought to have been ashamed to speak to . . . have made me lament that I ever was acquainted with him.' The cartoonists and popular satirists, never reticent or squeamish, beat about them with venomous joy. The Prince and the Duke – especially the Prince, now weighing over sixteen stone and beginning to qualify for Charles Lamb's description of him as the Prince of Whales – were uncharitably depicted in the unbuttoned enjoyment of their favourite sports and weaknesses, and some of the papers were outspoken in plain abuse. 'Gluttony, drunkenness and gambling,' wrote *The Times*, were 'the only states of happiness looked to' during the visit the brothers undertook on behalf of the Whig cause in Yorkshire. The same journal described the Prince of Wales, not altogether inaccurately, as drinking, wenching, and swearing like one who 'at all times would prefer a girl and a bottle to politics and a sermon'.* A London mob once forced open the door of his carriage and tried, though unsuccessfully, to make him shout 'Pitt for ever!' 'Damn Pitt!' he shouted back at them.

By contrast the King was able to enjoy the experience of receiving nationwide demonstrations of affection. Already, in January, before his recovery, Princess Augusta was reporting to her brother Augustus in the south of France, 'I'm sure it is quite impossible for anybody to be more adored and respected and esteemed than the King is at this moment. It would do your heart good to be witness to it. Well! Thank God he is so much *loved* . . .'[16] Now that he was recovered there was a fine flowering of fêtes, thanksgivings, bands and banners, memorials and triumphal arches, royal salutes, fireworks, illuminations, and other such loyal and joyful celebrations. When on 9th June he drove to the House of Lords to receive and confirm in office the new Speaker of the Commons, it was 'amidst a great crowd and great acclamation', and when on the 25th he began his journey to Weymouth to complete his convalescence,† every mile that he made, every appearance during his two months in Weymouth itself or on his further ventures into Devonshire during August, became the occasion of greeting and felicitation which to a monarch who had in his time borne a heavy load of opprobrium came like sunshine after storm. Winchester, as he passed through, was thronged with welcoming crowds. At Romsey, musicians 'in common brown coarse cloth . . . and even in carters' loose gowns' played *God Save the King* to such hearty acclaim that Miss Burney was almost 'surprised into a sob'. The road through Salisbury was festooned and bemottoed over a sort of triumphal arch – 'it was rapture past description.' To Dorchester folk had come in from all the surrounding villages to give 'the whole scene the air of a rural masquerade'. Every window was full, every balcony occupied. The poor man was at his cottage door and the rich man at his lodge gates all along the road to Weymouth, where the Duke of Gloucester had provided his brother

* It ought to be remembered that John Walter's *Times*, still in its lusty infancy, took £300 a year from Pitt's Government in return for support, and was twice successfully prosecuted for libels on the King's sons. It was one of nine papers receiving an annual governmental subsidy. John Walter served two prison sentences, the second being shortened by the personal intercession of the Prince himself (*History of 'The Times'*, i, 52-60).

† The King had hankered after a sea-voyage to Hanover with the Queen and the three older Princesses, but was dissuaded.

with his house facing the sands, and where the therapeutic quality of the sea-bathing was accounted first-rate – even if, as Fanny Burney faintly lamented, there was really very little at Weymouth *but* the sea.

A King's work never quite ceased; even *en route*, for instance, George had confirmed the death sentence on two prisoners accused of coining, and reduced that on two others to transportation. On 8th August there was a Council of State held at Weymouth. Nevertheless the sojourn by the sea provided novelty and relaxation, and was an undoubted success. It helped restore the King's health; it 'made' Weymouth as a resort; it set a precedent for several subsequent stays. The King, Queen and Princesses promenaded; they took tea in an inner sanctum of the public rooms, with the door left open for patriotic or curious eyes; they drove to visit the 'castles' of Lulworth and Sherborne; they enjoyed the company of the Howes, the Sidneys, the Courtowns, the Chesterfields, 'all our friends and very sincere ones too'; they attended the theatre – unimposing but reinforced for the occasion by the presence of Mrs Siddons and other stars. 'The King bathes,' wrote Fanny Burney, 'and with great success; a machine follows the Royal one into the sea, filled with fiddlers who play "God save the King" as His Majesty takes his plunge!'[17] Queen Charlotte, sending off to Prince Augustus in Göttingen for a copy of 'Monsieur Lesse's lectures upon religion', reported:

> The airings about this place are few and not very good, for excepting the turnpike road to Dorchester* there are no private drives for coaches. Horses may climb up hills with more ease, but that is too slow for the King. Therefore we have begun sailing as a substitute for riding. The King has got the Magnificent, a man of war of 74 guns, and the Southampton frigate of 32 in the Bay . . . and we row frequently in ten-oar cutters. Would our wheather but befriend us we should be merry enough . . .[18]

Towards the end of the Weymouth interlude came a three-week excursion, first to Exeter, where there was again 'one constant mob' to greet the King, and then to Saltram near Plymouth, where the King saw the sights, reviewed the Fleet, and accepted once more tokens of civic and popular welcome. To Saltram also came briefly the Duke of

---

* On a visit to Dorchester Jail the King left a donation to be put towards the discharge of debtors; and three years later, after a new jail had been built, he went there again. Being told there was one specially pitiful and deserving case, of a certain John Pitfield, who had already spent seven years in prison for a debt of £250, the King ordered it to be paid, and the jailer-in-charge wrote: 'Pitfield is liberated. God bless the King!' (Journal of Susan O'Brien, 10.9.1792, and Aspinall, *Later Correspondence*, i, 637).

York, 'low' after his Northern tour on behalf of the Whigs and an attack of what the doctors had decided was measles, and plainly as anxious as the Prince of Wales was at their father's complaints concerning their conduct during his illness, and at 'those appearances of a less gracious disposition' towards them from their mother. Back in Weymouth, the King, still with a kind of stiff kindness ('I have received your letter . . .') dissuaded the Duke from a further visit. As for the family quarrel, he did not

> chuse to enter on the melancholy subject . . . Indeed I have uniformly declined discussing it with everyone, and shall be willing to suppose the P. of Wales's conduct has proceeded from errors of judgement, the moment his public as well as private conduct towards the Queen and myself shall mark that respect and affection, which parents have a right to claim . . .[19]

In mid-September the King drove back to Windsor via Longleat and Tottenham House, Savernake* – 'much stronger,' wrote the Queen, 'and better for the sea-bathing. He began his Levees yesterday [23rd September] and bore it very well . . . so I have hopes that we shall soon come to go on in our old way.'

In one sense, the Kings and Queens of Europe, though they could not yet know it, would never again go on in their old way. While George and Charlotte had been at Weymouth the Bastille had fallen and Louis XVI had been forced at the Hôtel de Ville to wear the tricolour cockade in his hat. By October he and his Queen, forced from Versailles by the Paris mob, were virtually prisoners of the Revolution. In British eyes, however, all the implications, as well as the drama, of these events still belonged comfortably on the other side of the Channel. In domestic politics it was a period, on the whole, of calm. Trade and industry were expanding at an unprecedented rate. The opposition was in the doldrums. Peace seemed secure. Pitt, his reforming tune – to George's relief – already well muted, was confident of his parliamentary majority. For four or five years at least the King and his ministers were more *en rapport* than at any time since the heyday of Lord North. Events in France were turbulent but, since they weakened the ancient enemy, carried comfort more than menace. For George III, the fact that France, the nation which in America had recently stoked the fires

---

* Longleat was the residence of Lord Weymouth, recently created Marquis of Bath by George III. Queen Charlotte found it 'very grand and fine but not comfortable', while Lord Ailesbury's Tottenham House had 'no other beauty but the command of Savernake Forest 17 miles round . . . The house in abominable, built by the late Lrd. Burlington, whose architecture is the very worst one can see'.

of revolution, should now be getting burned was not unsatisfactory. The Bourbon danger was lessened and the Jacobin threat not yet apparent. For a year or two still, in foreign policy, both Pitt and the King were far more exercised over the territorial ambitions of Spain on the North American Pacific coast and of Russia against the Turkish Empire than over any threats posed to Britain by the French Revolution. Pitt looked forward to a France enjoying a constitution akin to the British; and being freer she would be less warlike. Fox saw a still rosier dawn. And when Burke, the new Cassandra, brought out his *Reflections* in October, 1790, his friend Windham lamented that Burke's opinions, far from representing as they ought 'the combined voice of every man' in the country, were those of a man decried, persecuted, and proscribed; not being much valued even by his own party, and by half the nation considered as little better than an ingenious madman'.[20]

By 1791, however, no conservative supporter of law and order, however anti-French, could be happy over what was happening in France in the name of human rights, still less stomach what Tom Paine was beginning to publish on the same subject. Yet *The Rights of Man* was proving a best-seller and, in the larger towns especially, both middle-class intellectuals (many of them Dissenters) and educated artisans were championing the cause, if not of revolution, at least of radical reform of Church and State. In May, Burke left his fellow Whigs; broke, and refused to mend, his long friendship with Fox; and crossed the floor of the House to sit with Pitt and the party of order. In July, the Constitutional Society of Birmingham, with Dissenters well represented, sat down to dinner on Bastille day to celebrate the second anniversary of the event which Fox had in a moment of euphoria once hailed as the greatest and best in the history of the world. According to Colonel de Lancy of the Dragoons, who were soon to be called in to deal with the rioting, 'inflammatory papers' had been passed round for some days previously, 'and on the Church was pasted a paper on which was written "No Church, No King, this barn to lett".' It proved not more difficult in 1791 to raise a mob in the Midlands than it had in London in 1780. Gordon's tinder-sparking part was now played in Birmingham by zealot Anglican clergy and a pair of 'loyal' magistrates; the uglier side of the King's popularity and a new species of 'King's Friends' were now in evidence. For two days, until the Dragoons mustered sufficient force, the patriotic rabble terrorised the streets, Dissenters and reformers taking the brunt of its fire-raising and vandalism. (The following year Manchester's turn came for a similar outbreak.) 'Their cry,' reported the Colonel, 'was Church and King for ever and the inhabitants found no security for their houses but in the strongest expressions of zeal for the King.' Joseph Priestley, who had absented himself from the dinner of the 14th July, nevertheless had both his own house and his meeting-house sacked, and de Lancy, at least, was sure that if the mob could have found the Doctor they would have hanged him. Dephlogisticating air was none of their business, and Priestley might have escaped with the eccentricity of denying the Trinity; but he had repeatedly uttered opinions favourable to the foreign revolutionaries, and he paid a heavy penalty. A touch of *Schadenfreude* in the King was quickly brushed aside in his condemnation of the Birmingham mischief:

> I cannot but feel better pleased that Priestley is the sufferer for the doctrines he and his party have instilled, and the people see them in their true light; yet cannot approve of their having employed such atrocious means of shewing their discontent . . . I approve of the measures proposed of re-enforcing the military corps already ordered to Birmingham. [21]

The King had declared his intention in 1789 of keeping only 'that superintending eye' which could be 'effected without labour or fatigue'; and if he appears over these years to have taken a back seat it is because he continued, in general, to approve of the driver. There were rumours from time to time of recurring ill-health; but these, wrote Lord Auckland, were entirely without foundation. The King had 'never been better'. It was 'impossible to describe', he declared in December, 1791,

> how perfectly well the King is; he is a quite altered man, and not what you knew him even before his illness; his manner is gentle, quiet, and, when he is pleased, quite cordial. He speaks even of those who are opposed to his government with complacency, and without either sneer or acrimony; at the same time he is most steadily attached to his ministers. As long as he remains so well, the tranquillity of this country is on a rock . . . [22]

Such differences as did occur between King and ministers were on minor or personal matters. But these brought some tussles. In May, 1792, Pitt finally indicated his wish to be rid of the Lord Chancellor, Thurlow, ambiguous earlier in his support during the Regency Crisis, intermittently amiable when regaled with Dundas's 'best burgundy and blasphemy', but now outspokenly critical in the Lords of Pitt's Sinking Fund proposals. Awkwardly for Pitt, the rugged and cantankerous Thurlow was one of the ministers closest to the Crown; 'with all his appearance of roughness,' the King once told Pitt, 'he has a feeling heart.' However, it seems that Thurlow now presumed too much on royal friendship and aired his differences with Pitt too publicly and blatantly. Once in 1789 and again in 1790, the King had managed to patch up differences between the two men. Confident in the backing of the rest of the Cabinet, Pitt now threatened to resign himself if Thurlow did not. When the King decided in the only direction possible, despite his 'personal regard, nay affection', Thurlow (refusing an earldom and a pension) sadly admitted 'I did not think the King would have parted with me so easily'.[23]

Another personal matter, occurring in the autumn of the same year, illustrates both the intensity of George's traditionalism and class conservatism, and the subtlety of the contradictions in the master-servant relations between George and Pitt. A Governorship of the Charterhouse, in the King's gift, lay vacant – a very desirable perquisite which the Home Secretary, Dundas, was hoping to put under his belt. The King demurred. This brilliantly successful Scots lawyer, though now one of His Majesty's principal Secretaries of State, was undeniably a commoner with no particular distinction of ancestry, and it was customary, the King told Pitt, for such appointments to go to 'men of rank'. Pitt replied respectfully that it was also customary for them to go to Secretaries of State. Dundas, in considerable dudgeon, unofficially threatened resignation, to which Pitt replied by advising him to lie low and not appear to press. The King's conduct, he agreed, was indeed different from what Dundas had a right to expect. And then followed a significant sentence whose tone by no means suggested the masterful minister riding high both in Parliament and the Closet: 'At the same time I feel with you how impossible it is either for you or me, circumstanced as we are, to indulge any sentiment of discontent.'[24]

Pitt, it is clear, had not the advantage of reading history books that tell how he was continuously prime minister for seventeen years and soon came to dominate the monarch. He never made the mistake of underestimating the King or overestimating the affection in which he was held. In his dealing with his brilliant, industrious, enigmatic first minister, George III was always correct, but it did not go beyond that. Over the years the royal letters to Pitt continue to be introduced soberly with 'Dear Mr Pitt' – never, until once at the hour of his resignation in 1801, 'My dear Pitt.' Even then the actual substance of the letter was strangely curt and business-like. Pitt was not the sort of prime minister to whom one could drop a note – as for instance George did subsequently to Addington – asking him, if the evening proved dry, to drive his family over in his 'sociable', not forgetting 'his lively and engaging youngest daughter', then aged just twelve months. He would never think of Pitt as his *peculiar* minister in the sense that he could address Lord Howe as 'my *peculiar* admiral'. Yet naturally Pitt was conscious enough of the strong cards that lay in his hands. 'The King is supposed to want to get rid of Pitt,' wrote Elliot at the time of the Thurlow showdown, 'but dares not in these times.'[25] It was true that the King, should he wish, might properly and constitutionally dismiss him at any moment, *provided he could find a successor who was capable of commanding a parliamentary majority*; but the proviso was of course Pitt's strong card. There would be occasions after 1794 when Pitt and his ministers would insist on their policy despite the King's known wishes. Even then, there were areas of business – patronage, honours, high clerical, naval, or military appointments – where the King, though sensitive to advice, was always accepted as the ultimate master. The rewards of the Charterhouse were one such matter; and here Pitt's counsel to Dundas to be patient and humble and lie low proved shrewd. Dundas wrote to the King claiming that the last thing he intended was to 'sollicit'. He even wished 'to have it forgot' that his name had ever been mentioned. He had his Governorship in the end,[26] as in the end, by one means or another, Pitt and Dundas became used to getting their way throughout the 'nineties – until Catholic emancipation was to prove a camel the King refused to swallow.

As late as the spring of 1792, Pitt was proposing to cut military and naval expenditure. There still seemed no sign that the French revolution might set fire to Europe or jump the Channel. In Britain, the only rioting had been *against* the reformers. Pitt himself, to George's relief, had abandoned his youthful attachment to parliamentary reform. It gave the King further satisfaction that the two latest attempts to repeal the Test and Corporation Acts had been rejected by substantial majorities. By the summer of 1792, however, and emphatically by the autumn, things were looking differently. There was war between the revolutionaries of France and the *ancien régime* of Germany. In Paris and elsewhere the Jacobins had gained power and massacred their prisoners. The monarchy was eliminated and the royal family imprisoned. The republican armies turned the tide of invasion and were themselves threatening the Low Countries. In England Tom Paine, in his Part Two of *The Rights of Man*, spelt out what these rights ought to mean in practice. Reform clubs began to multiply in the major towns. There was a Society for Promoting Constitutional Information. The largely working-class Corresponding Society, founded in London to demand universal suffrage and annual general elections, spread rapidly inside and beyond the metropolis and soon had 6,000 members. At a different

level of society the young Charles Grey, with Tierney, Erskine, Whitbread, Sheridan, Lauderdale, Mackintosh and others (but not Fox),
came together in The Society of the Friends of the People to promote
similar aims. All three societies repudiated the republicanism of Paine,
but certainly many members of the Corresponding Society approved
of most of the sentiments and proposals of *The Rights of Man*, including
abolition of the monarchy and of the House of Lords.

To George III there was not much to choose between any of these
men, whether they were belted earls like Lauderdale, wealthy brewers
like Whitbread, or humble shoemakers like Hardy of the Corresponding Society. Neither was Fox to be exonerated by not actually being a
member of the Friends of the People. It was more than enough that he
spoke in favour of them. When the Society published its manifesto in
the papers and on the same day the more democratic Whigs – the
epithet 'democratic' was still essentially pejorative – spoke up for it in
the Commons, the King declared the affair

> a most daring outrage . . . and I cannot see any substantial difference
> in their being joined in debate by Mr Fox and his not being a member
> of that Society, but if men are to be found willing to overturn the
> Constitution of this country, it is most providential they so early
> throw off the mask, and I am most happy it has given Mr Pitt so fair
> an opportunity of avowing sentiments that must endear him to all
> lovers of good order and our excellent Constitution.[27]

There was nevertheless talk of Fox joining a strengthened coalition
ministry, and as late as July, 1792, the King declared that he placed no
veto on him, though he would not have him as Foreign Secretary.
Fox's personal ambitions, however, pushed him in the same direction
as his liberal principles; he was strongly disinclined to play second
fiddle to Pitt, and there was no prospect at all of Pitt relinquishing the
premiership. So it was left to the more conservative Whigs gradually
to move towards the ministry as individuals, with their leader Portland
bringing up the rear, while Fox and his small unpopular band were left
out in the cold, mistrusted equally by King and public. Naturally the
King approved of any weakening of faction, any closing of the ranks
by men of goodwill in defence of Constitution, Church, and Property.
'As for Fox and Grey, I wish they would utter treason at once, and
be beheaded or hanged', chattered Lady Malmesbury to Lady Elliot.
Elliot himself felt it his 'duty to give fair and honourable support to
Government in defending the constitution and saving the country';[28]
and he and Malmesbury, with Loughborough, Windham, Spencer,
and Fitzwilliam, were principal candidates for posts in the gradually

maturing coalition. Loughborough was the first to accede, Lord Chancellor from January, 1793. Both Fox and Portland, however, strove to avoid a Whig split. In December Fox wrote to Mrs Armistead:

> The King is at the moment quite master of the country, and every effort one makes for the people and the country only renders one unpopular among them and if possible still more odious at Court, but it does not signify as long as one is satisfied that one is doing right . . . I told you the cry was very great against me and so I fear it continues and will . . . But the cry, be it loud as it will, does not make me feel a tenth part of the uneasiness that I suffer and have suffered from the apprehension of separating from the Duke of Portland and Ld. Fitz[william].[29]

From the end of 1792, Fox and Grey seldom mustered more than forty or fifty members behind them in the Commons, and the King expressed his pleasure that 'the good sense of the majority of the nation' so strongly condemned them. Mr Storer reported to his friend Lord Auckland in the Hague that 'well-dressed ladies' were wearing 'King and Constitution' favours in their hair or their caps, and even the dances at the Opera were to the tune of the national anthem. 'It is astonishing how completely Mr Paine and his adherents are extinguished,' wrote Bland Burges to the same quarter.[30] The Prince of Wales's hatred of the 'damnable doctrines' of the 'hell-begotten Jacobines',[31] and fear of their murderous excesses, cooled him mightily towards Fox, and began to make a ministerialist even of him. He too began to talk of the excellence of the Constitution and to deplore evil and subversive machination against it.

His maiden speech in the Lords in May, 1792, on the address to the King approving the royal proclamation against seditious publications, stressed his unexceptionably loyal 'attachment to our present happy Constitution . . . long the envy and admiration of the world'. The principles of this 'great and sacred fabric' he held to be 'perfect', offering 'the best practicable model of civil government for encreasing the prosperity of the nation and giving the most permanent security of freedom and happiness to the people'. 'I can but feel one principle in my mind,' he wrote to Portland (prudently sending the King a copy of his letter) 'namely, the public good, and wh. I consider will be best effected by being guided by those feelings of duty and affection to my father, wh. will lead me to give every assistance in my power in support of such measures as HE approves.'[32] Reconciled with his mother in March, 1791, he was now writing her effusively affectionate letters, and using her as intermediary to promote better relations with his father. The King, it seems, thinking a prolonged period of deeds more valuable than the Prince's customary avalanche of words, intended to let him work his passage. When in January, 1793, the Queen dropped a hint that the Prince would like to appear again at Levees, she had to report back to her son, 'The King is of oppinion that yr appearance at the Drawing Room will be sufficient, where I am sure everybody will be glad to see you again.'[33]

As for Portland, he remained closely attached to the Prince; delayed a final break with Fox though his supporters were pressing him hard to join Pitt; and 'prayed for unanimity . . . upon all measures respecting the safety of the country, internally and externally'. These patriotic sentiments did not however prevent him, when finally he accompanied his followers Spencer, Fitzwilliam, and Windham into the Government, from making an absolute condition that he must have the dispensation of the Scottish patronage that his predecessor in the Home Office had enjoyed. Dundas grumbled that he was to be asked to 'remain a very responsible minister' – he was to be Third Secretary – 'with a great deal of trouble, and without power or patronage.' Again he threatened to resign; but Pitt persuaded, the King practically commanded,[34] and Dundas, grudgingly agreeing to the new arrangement, earned royal commendation for his 'proper conduct'. The King thought less well of Portland, for whom another black mark followed as he held out for the Garter vacated by the death of the Marquis of Bath. Time had by then run on to July, 1794, and Britain and France had been seventeen months at war. Lord Howe, one of George's particular friends, had just won his victory of the Glorious First of June, and the King, with Pitt's knowledge, had already offered *him* the Garter. Pitt now tried to fob off Howe with a mere marquisate. Howe would not have it, but Pitt did succeed, by appealing to the need for political solidarity, in persuading him voluntarily to forgo the greater honour. George was clearly vexed with Pitt;[35] growled at the behaviour of the Duke of Portland, failing to see why they needed to 'heap favours on his head'; and resolved that Howe should have the next Garter going – which he did in 1797.[36]

These matters were not trifles to George III – nor indeed to Pitt or Portland or Dundas. France and half Europe might be in a state of uproar, and the *ancien régime* fighting for its life. Pitt and George might see such danger of Jacobinism at home that repressive measures of the harshest kind were hurried through Parliament. Steam engines and spinning mules, coal-mines and iron-works, enclosures and canals and turnpikes might be beginning to transform the face of Britain. But politics went on very much as before, and the composition of the

King's government was still liable to depend on who was to have the Scottish patronage or the vacant Blue Riband. In spite of this, the Whig split was made final in 1794, and the absorption of the Portland following into Pitt's government does mark an important political milestone. It was not of course the end of 'factions' and 'connexions'; but if there is any one point in British history at which the beginning of the two-party system may be descried, it must surely be July, 1794, and must be accounted just one more of the consequences of the French Revolution.

The war which was to outlast the King's active reign had finally come in February, 1793. Certainly George III had shown no more desire to rush into it than Pitt. At least until the interception at Varennes in June, 1791, of the French royal family's flight, there was no sort of urgency in his attitude. That event and their ensuing imprisonment in the Temple, did indeed stir him to 'infinite concern'; but a few weeks later he wrote to Louis ('mon cher frère et cousin') expressing the 'exact and perfect neutrality' of his intentions; whatever others did, Britain would take no part whatever in France's affairs. However, as Prussia and Austria moved against the revolutionaries during 1792; as the extreme factions took control in Paris and much of France; as 'more acts of barbarity' were committed 'than by the most savage people'; as wicked or misguided men in his own country seemed to be intent on spreading that poison which in France was 'destroying all religion, law and subordination' – the King's tone changed. In April, 1792, he declared himself very happy that M. de Talleyrand and his fellow-emissary to London had 'no credence' and could therefore be treated by Lord Grenville with 'the contempt their characters entitle them to'. La Fayette's desertion and arrest by the Austrians caused Queen Charlotte (holidaying at Weymouth again) strong if confused feelings: 'Oh had some years ago the English set a price upon that man's head . . . But everything is in the hands of Providence, and we see the very man who wonted to crush England proves the curse to his own country, and I am sure he will meet with his reward. The poor unfortunate Royal Family are well in health but wonting everything . . .' If only, she lamented, the Duke of Brunswick had been able to move faster to their rescue.[37] Then came the September Massacres and the first suggestion that Marie Antoinette was to be put on trial; shocking events, gruesome possibilities – but one should not be surprised, the King wrote, at anything these 'savages' might do, 'cruel wretches who have possessed themselves of power.' When news came at the end of January, 1793, that what had been feared for months was now fact, and Louis XVI had been guillotined, he cancelled that week's Levee as a mark of his horror. 'I trust,' he wrote to Grenville, 'the Privy Council will be immediately ready after the Drawing Room this day for giving the necessary order that Monsieur Chauvelin may instantly leave the kingdom.'[38]

On 1st February France declared war. Few in Britain had wanted it; few until the autumn of 1792 had expected it. Most, now it had come, agreed with Pitt that in view of the shattered French finances it would be short; not, however, Burke, who expected it to be 'long and dangerous'. As for the King, he had been strongly for non-intervention and peace, but now war had arrived he was more of Burke's persuasion than Pitt's. He was never to see the war against France as an up-to-date version of the Seven Years War, with the adoption, suitably modified, of Chatham's tactics, and (as Lord Auckland put it) 'a complete opportunity of annihilating their marine and colonies.'[39] For Pitt, the war was one more war against France, to be entered upon – or later to be abandoned – upon balanced considerations of national profit and loss. For George III, as for Burke and Windham, it more nearly resembled a crusade to overthrow the forces of European anarchy and restore the natural order – which included the Bourbons on the throne of France. It was a war, as George wrote to Pitt on the day following its declaration, 'for the preservation of society . . . Indeed my natural sentiments are so strong for peace, that no event of less moment than the present could have made me decidedly of the opinion that duty as well as interest calls on us to join against that most savage as well as unprincipled nation.'[40] The King, therefore, when in a few years' time things went badly, never had much patience with Pitt's attempts to extricate the country from the struggle. British defeats were setbacks to be endured and remedied; British successes caused him, as he was to reflect upon receiving news of Nelson's victory at Copenhagen, to appreciate indeed the 'honour that must accrue to the British arms', but much more to weigh 'the manifest interposition of Divine Providence in a just cause, and for the destruction of the enemies of his Holy Word and of all civil and domestic happiness'.[41] It was a point of view very close to that of the victor of Copenhagen himself, and one that did not change whether the enemy were the Jacobin 'savages' of 1793 or the 'impious self-created aristocracy' of Bonaparte seven years later.

If Pitt's policy in the war was often to produce royal dissent, his attitude to 'the preservation of society' at home brought him in the closest possible accord with the King, who had no doubt at all of the wisdom of the harsh precautionary acts that the Government passed through Parliament between 1793 and 1795. In May, 1793, when Pitt, in a Commons debate, countered Grey's advocacy of parliamentary reform by trying to pin upon the principles of the moderate British reformers an association with Jacobins, George was prompt to express his 'infinite satisfaction' with the speech. 'The government that adopts such principles,' Pitt had declared, 'ceases to be a government; it unties the bands which knit together society; it forfeits the reverence and obedience of its subjects; it gives up those whom it ought to protect to the daggers of the Marseillese and the assassins of Paris.'[42] The King could not have matched the flow of the rhetoric, but the sentiments were his own: 'I must devoutly pray to Heaven,' he said, 'that this Constitution may remain unimpaired to the latest posterity, as a proof of the wisdom of the nation, and its knowledge of the superior blessings it enjoys.'[43]

Moderate Scottish reformers given savage seven and fourteen year sentences at this time by Lord Justice Braxfield simply for daring to suggest that the *constitution was not perfect* might have been forgiven for underestimating the superiority of their blessings. On the other hand, the blessings of the jury system, which in 1794 secured the triumphant acquittal of thirteen London radical leaders (including Hardy of the Corresponding Society and Horne Tooke, Wilkes's old friend and enemy) must have seemed to Pitt to be not unmixed. Horne Tooke in particular had managed to sustain the impudent tradition of Wilkes and at the same time demonstrate the obstinate reality of British liberties by compelling Pitt to appear as a witness for the *defence* and testify to his own earlier reforming convictions. Those liberties, however, over the next few years took heavy pruning from a Government either honestly panicking before the spectre of Jacobinism or seizing hold of the opportune advantage of popular Francophobia and an enormous parliamentary majority to reduce the reformers to silence. First, a Traitorous Correspondence Act was passed – the only one of the measures meeting significant resistance in Parliament. Then followed a temporary suspension of Habeas Corpus; a very necessary measure, wrote the King. But 'factious and large' assemblies of reformers, which he disliked as much as Pitt or Burke, continued to meet during 1795.

A principal reason for these was the shortage and dearness of bread, following two poorish harvests, some speculation, and very probably the activity of price-rings – though the Duke of Portland, Home Secretary, thought the King ought to beware of 'hastily assenting to the existence of combinations to which too many are always ready to impute the rise in the price'. 'Farmer George' had been demanding weekly reports from Portland on the bread-corn situation, and Portland, while extolling the King's 'parental anxiety' for the people's welfare, plainly thought this anxiety exaggerated. The 1795 harvest would be good, he assured him in his rather defensive reports; Sir Joseph Banks, whose opinion he knew the King respected, was sure the crops would be adequate. Government agents should *not* be employed to lay in stocks; this was the proper field of 'private speculation and adventure'. When by September the King was further reassured of the excellence of the 1795 harvest, he cancelled his demand for weekly reports and accepted the soothing words of Portland, reinforced by Banks. If the King was too easily convinced by the Duke and his Cabinet Committee, at least as a practising farmer he heeded the insistent and more urgent advice of the Board of Agriculture: plant more potatoes, which had already saved lives in 1795, and sow much more wheat for 1796.[44] And as far as the King was concerned the Government was preaching to the converted when it recommended a lower 'quality of bread to be consumed and the abstemious use of flour' in the 'establishments of your Majesty's servants'. The King had already given orders to his Lord Steward, the Duke of Dorset, to see that all the loaves baked at Windsor were of either brown or potato bread.[45]

Despite the fine summer the dearth persisted, and when the King drove in state to open Parliament at the end of October, 1795, he was met by demonstrators shouting for 'Peace and Bread! No War! No King! Down with George!' On the outward journey a stone* broke one of the windows of his coach. Pitt's carriage too, was 'surrounded by a great number of the mobility' on the journey from Downing Street to the Lords, though in his case they hurled execration only. Even though hunger was the principal cause of these mob manifestations, they shocked the King, frightened the upper classes, and were altogether too reminiscent of the Gordon Riots. When there was a further demonstration a fortnight later in Copenhagen Fields, George wrote to Portland that its purpose was

so avowedly to intimidate both Houses of Parliament that I should think it highly proper for them to apply the executive power that all the avenues to Parliament may be kept clear . . . I mention this as the riot of 1780 began with an assemblage before the House of Com-

---

* Or possibly an air-gun pellet. The King thought he had been shot at, and told the Lord Chancellor so, but read his speech calmly and clearly. The following night, when he attended the Opera, the National Anthem had to be twice encored. Once before, in January, 1794, the royal coach, on its way to the opening of Parliament had had a window broken by a stone (Aspinall, *Later Correspondence* . . . , ii, 1324).

mons which, if it had at that period been dispersed, the outrages and mischiefs of the following days would have been prevented.*

Immediately after these events Pitt's Government rushed through a Seditious Meetings Act prohibiting public meetings for the next three years except under magistrate's licence, and a new Treason Act that brought *all* attacks on the constitution within its scope. In fact the sentiments which Pitt himself had voiced in the mid-eighties could by the mid-nineties have taken him to Botany Bay – which was more or less the message Horne Tooke had rubbed home at his trial the year before. The King was of course delighted at the 'handsome majority' these bills inevitably received; the Seditious Meetings Act gave 'the most convincing proof of attachment to our happy Constitution and resolution to continue that blessing to future generations'.[46]

When in May, 1797, Fox (whom the King described in the pre-ceding month as 'an open enemy of his country') moved the repeal of these two acts and was defeated by 260 votes to 52, again George was vocal in expressing to Pitt his joy at the 'decided majority'. 'Every friend of the British Constitution must rejoice . . . and not less to find so many country gentlemen step forward on every occasion to give a support that shews they feel the blessings they enjoy.'[47] He was a little less pleased at the 91 votes that another motion from Grey, with Fox's backing, obtained a week later. It was Fox's 'art', he thought, that had succeeded in keeping his party together, and no doubt he had been joined by some 'speculative men'. But the King need not have winced at the figure of 91. Soon Fox so comprehensively acknowledged ex-asperation and defeat that, for some months, he and his followers seceded altogether from Parliament. Fox went off to his country house near Chertsey to savour the novelties of married life with 'Mrs Armi-stead', which differed from his long-established unmarried life with her only in that they could now share the happy secret which the world was

* Back in April there had been exemplary punishment for looting militiamen in Sussex. Two thousand sacks of flour had been stolen at Newhaven and a quantity of meat at Seaford. For this the four ringleaders were shot. On June 14th, George informed Portland that he had that day had news from the Judge Advocate that two of these men had been executed, 'and the others received 300 of the lashes to which they were condemned, and that the whole had been conducted with perfect military decorum,' i.e., by shooting, 'there being no military man to perform the ignominious office of hangman.' The use of the word *decorum* in this context – ironic, *in*decorous, grotesque even as it might sound to modern sensibilities – is nevertheless very characteristic, as is the whole matter-of-fact tone of the King's note.

still not to be told for another seven years. Being Fox, he could not of course wholly retire. He spasmodically returned to the Commons, and mustered 75 votes against Pitt's new-fangled income tax proposals in January, 1798. And that same month at the annual dinner given to him on his birthday by his supporters of the Whig Club he used a phrase which seemed to the King, if not treason, at least unforgivable *lèse-majesté*. The Duke of Norfolk had set the tone in proposing the toast:

> Not twenty years ago [he said] the illustrious George Washington had not more than two thousand men to rally round him when his country was attacked. America is now free. This day full two thousand men are assembled in this place. I leave you to make the application. I propose the health of Charles James Fox!

Fox's ebullient and probably impromptu share in a toast to the Duke – at a time when invasion threatened, naval mutinies were a recent memory, and Ireland verged on rebellion – was a public repetition of a flamboyant sentiment he had employed several times before in more private circumstances: 'Give me leave, before I sit down, to call on you to drink our Sovereign's health – the Majesty of the People!'[48]

CHAPTER TWENTY-THREE

Family Discord

A CRITICISM of British war strategy from 1793 – and it was more than once made by George himself – was that it was conceived on too many scattered fronts for any one to be effective. Sometimes, tracing the progress of the King's other war, those prolonged campaigns fought inside his own family, one has an impression of theatres similarly widespread, and even of problems akin. Allies were uncertain and liable to treat with hostile forces. Annual allowances, like foreign subsidies, tended to be frittered away. Co-operation and reasonableness, not to mention gratitude, seemed as hard to come by in sons as in continental rulers and generals. In the French war the spread of operations was not always of Britain's choosing; in his domestic campaigns it was deliberate policy on the King's part to keep his sons distanced as safely as possible from the Prince of Wales, so long as he hobnobbed with opposition politicians. Thus if Augustus was in Rome or the south of France, Edward in Geneva or Gibraltar or Canada, Ernest and Adolphus in Germany, and William anywhere but at Carlton House, the King could face his problems with more comfort and confidence. Two of the Princes he did trust more readily than the rest: Adolphus, the youngest and most dependable; and Frederick, who was soon quite rehabilitated in his father's esteem; whose sins were readily diminished into peccadilloes; and whom George was proud to appoint as commander of the British force sent to Flanders on the outbreak of hostilities, even though it was thought prudent to bolster him with senior advisers.

When Prince William at the same time requested a naval command, however, it was only to receive one more of those 'put-downs' that he had so frequently complained of. Neither the Admiralty nor the King showed any enthusiasm whatever for giving this breezy and erratic young man a position of responsibility. And although William's resentment at the favours shown to Frederick had a certain justice in it, his own behaviour, both before the King's illness and after returning home in the middle of it, hardly gave anyone grounds for confidence in him. At first in 1789 he had made common cause with the Prince of Wales and the opposition, and even talked of standing

for the House of Commons unless he was granted his belated Dukedom. When the King, without enthusiasm, created him Duke of
Clarence, thinking it one more vote to the enemy,[1] he at the same time
blackballed some of William's Whig friends among his proposed
household, and when William protested that £12,000 a year would be
inadequate for his needs, his father took the opportunity to suggest
that he might economise by going on foreign service again. As Prince
William he would in any case not have been allowed home leave in
1789, had not the King then been in no condition to forbid it.[2] The
future Sailor King, still insisting that he would never *deserve* the royal
displeasure, and hurt that his father should consider that he 'had
adopted a line of conduct void of kindness' to him,[3] came to anchor at
Petersham House, Richmond, where he became the third and hardest-
wearing of the protectors of Mrs Jordan the actress, supplying her with
status, comfort, domesticity, and ten more bastards to add to those that
had already accrued to her from his predecessors. Nine of these ten
Fitzclarences were named after George III's own sons and daughters.
The Duke was by no means to be outdone in demonstrations of loyal
affection. Fanny Burney recounts how on 4th June, 1791, 'the last
birthday of the good, gracious, and benevolent King I shall ever pass
under his Royal roof,' the Duke dined with his father at St James's, and
afterwards relaxed among the Household, doing his best to get the
company merry by drinking the King's health in champagne; protesting it would do them 'a monstrous deal of good'; telling the redoubt-
able Schwellenberg, fearful for the night's sobriety, to 'hold her potato-
jaw' and then kissing her hand to make amends; and using such
'forcible words' as Miss Burney would not commit to the page, having
'a general objection' to writing them.[4]

'Unless you are a good man,' the King had once written to William,
'you cannot be of utility to your country, nor credit to your family.
This may seem an old-fashioned language, but experience will shew
you that it is most true.' However, though he was saddened by his
son's flouting of the precepts he had laboured so anxiously to instil,
George never had for him the entrenched suspicion he reserved for the
Prince of Wales. The chief trouble with his third son, the King felt (in
common with most), was that he had made himself such 'a trifling
character as it was now become proverbial . . . that anything coming
from William . . . was sufficient for it to merit no further credit'. The
Prince of Wales thought so too; yet 'he is as good natur'd a fellow as
exists; means no harm, but has not the smallest regard for the truth'.[5]
When attempts to pay off the Clarence debts became bogged down, the
King came to William's rescue, upon the death of Lord North's widow,

with the very acceptable rangership of Bushy Park. And once the Duke had promised to soft-pedal his violent criticism of the war and its conduct and to check his uninhibited abuse of Pitt at private functions,[6] he was raised to the strictly nominal rank of Admiral. On the occasions when he visited Windsor, the atmosphere grew to be one of mutual amiability;[7] the King was even prepared to joke with him on the subject of the mistress of Bushy. And the time at last came when the Pittite newspapers tired of comments upon 'bathing in the river Jordan' and 'the actress being brought to bed of a little Admiral'. The Bushy ménage, with its escalating little Fitzclarences, came for fourteen years to be an accepted feature of the royal scene, though the customary ducal debts – despite a loan from the Treasury – necessitated continual assistance from Mrs Jordan's stage earnings. It was not till after George III's mind had finally betrayed him that one day in 1811 a tearful Mrs Jordan was finally given her *congé* and the future William IV began seriously looking for a marriage that would set him up financially and give him an heir who one day might even be King. But as things turned out, William was not to have legitimate children; it was a daughter of the fourth son, Edward, who was in the fullness of time to inherit the throne.

Back in January, 1790, a young man of twenty-two, Prince Edward was finding himself in the hottest of hot water. The King had kept him in Geneva, despite his expressed wish to come home and join the regiment of which he was nominal commander. Like his brothers, he had expensive tastes, was deeply in debt and already well aware of his father's views of him: 'Perhaps,' he granted, 'I have often had the misfortune to meet with your displeasure.' However, the King was 'always so gracious as to forget and forgive'. Not so now. Feeling 'buried alive' at that 'villainous dull place' Geneva, and chafing under the supervision of his governor and military tutor Baron Wangenheim (his 'bear-keeper' as he described him, who had the dispensing of his allowance and kept him short of money for 'those indulgences which not only Princes but private gentlemen expect at a certain age'), he suddenly decided to make a bolt for England, where he gravitated straightway into the company of his two eldest brothers at a time when they were still deeply involved in opposition to the King and the King's Government. George sent for Pitt immediately, asked him to see what frigates were ready for sailing, and whisked his fourth son off in disgrace to Gibraltar, with instructions to the Governor to see that he stayed there, obeyed regulations, and behaved in a manner becoming an officer and a Prince.[8]

Governor O'Hara and his assistant Captain Craufurd did not need to be told that they were handling a hot potato. The Prince, they found, was still very high-spirited, with a 'wild propensity to expense'. Like his brother George, he believed a Prince should be princely, ran a private orchestra, and was soon deep in the toils of moneylenders. O'Hara and Craufurd, however, realised that they must combine firmness with reasonableness 'to prevent his flying off . . . for, however his Majesty may have it in his power to restrain him by coercive measures, yet the exertion of that power must be particularly disagreeable to so good a King and affectionate a father'.[9] Edward was soon writing home to assure the King that he was behaving himself – he was in fact a fanatical disciplinarian where other people were concerned – but not omitting to beg, however apologetically, for the equivalent of his old allowance, plus £2,500 'to clear my first starting here'. It would have been hopelessly inadequate even if he had received it; when after sixteen months he left Gibraltar he was obliged to issue to his creditors five per cent seven-year bonds to the nominal value of £20,000. His health poor and the social amenities of the Rock proving sparse, he begged the King for early release. He dreaded the effect on his health of a second summer there.

In Geneva in 1788, the Prince had himself written to his father of 'a violent rheumatism attended with fever'.[10] Now the Gibraltar surgeon-general diagnosed biliary colic. This was what the King himself was first declared to be suffering from, two years before, and indeed Prince Edward recognised the similarity in his complaint, 'the severity of which is I believe not unknown to your Majesty'.[11] Tall, powerfully-built, and like George III quite healthy for most of his days, Prince Edward nevertheless throughout his life suffered sharp unaccountable attacks of colic, 'rheumatick' pains in the limbs, and affections of the skin.* In May, 1791, the King permitted him to leave Gibraltar, but not to return to home and beauty. Instead he was kept out of political harm's way, in what he described as 'a cruel state of banishment' in Canada, where eventually, in 1799 (by then Duke of Kent) he was appointed Commander-in-Chief. As for beauty, he made his own arrangements, having from Gibraltar sent a confidential emissary on a successful reconnaissance to France. The admirable Mme de St Laurent appeared to the Prince to have 'every qualification'. And 'Edward's French lady' (like Mrs Fitzherbert a Catholic), remained for

---

* Almost certainly his disease was the same as the King's, though never touching his reason. His sudden death in 1820, six days before his father, followed a mysterious sequence of hoarseness, a simple cold, pains in the chest, and high fever. If it *was* porphyria, mercifully he did not transmit it to his daughter Victoria or her descendants.

the next twenty-seven years his wife in the eyes of all but the Church and the law,[12] until that yet distant day in 1818 when the call of dynastic duty and the Duke's ambition to beget a legitimate heir caused him to embark on 'Hymen's war terrific' in the arms of the Duke of Saxe-Coburg's widowed daughter – and necessitated *Madame*'s retirement.

Disappointed of the Irish command that he solicited, he was in 1802 a surprise appointment back in Gibraltar as Governor-General, where he proceeded so radically to interpret his instructions to tighten up discipline and put down drunkenness that he caused a mutiny and was recalled. Breathing very unfraternal fire and brimstone against his Commander-in-Chief the Duke of York, he unsuccessfully demanded a court-martial, and one day at Windsor in 1804 upset the King by calling Frederick a rascal in front of the entire company. A sort of vendetta between the two Dukes continued for many years. And when Edward, feeling both his character and professional reputation besmirched, begged his father to allow him to resume duties in Gibraltar, George curtly refused. Querulous, resentful, under a mountain of debt, the Duke of Kent had to content himself with a Field-Marshal's baton as strictly nominal as Clarence's flag of Admiral.

In 1786, the King had sent his three youngest sons to be educated at Göttingen in Hanover, where Ernest and Adolphus from the beginning set their sights on a military career, which both of them before many years were actively and honourably to pursue with their father's Hanoverian forces. He was paternally proud of them both. Augustus, however, the sixth son, was obliged by a succession of alarming illnesses to abandon any like ambition. He intended instead to enter the Church, an idea to which the King gave his blessing. Travels and sojourns in Italy and southern France failed to bring Augustus health, and in August, 1790, he nearly died. 'Convulsive asthma' was diagnosed, though this hardly seemed to cover such symptoms as 'spasms in the stomach' or 'affection of the bladder' – or what the King in 1792 referred to simply as his son's 'rheumatick fever'.[13] Augustus was in fact, particularly in youth, one of the most harshly afflicted victims of the royal malady.[14] He was an earnest young man, musical and artistic, given to romantic rhapsodising, pious outbursts, and from time to time lacerating self-analyses. A faithful, fluent, but sometimes obscure correspondent, he felt it necessary when he was sixteen to send home separate letters to his mother and father confessing various errors his life had strayed into. Charlotte was obliged to admit that she had no idea what he was talking about: 'therefore I am unable to form any judgment unless it pleases you to clear it up to me, but I am sure

and certain that the King is too good a father and too wise a man as not
to see the difference there is between *a criminal fault* and *an error of
judgment or folly in youth.*' She thought it right however, to add a warning
against 'low company . . . pernicious to everybody but particularly to
Princes'. Augustus, disturbed by his father's failure to reply promptly,
wrote home again in February, 1790, and 'oppressed incessantly by
sorrow and regret . . . guilty but penitent', presumed to lay himself
once more at the King's feet and implore pardon. 'Speak, Sir, and you
shall be obeyed.' In fact the King had already spoken and the letters
had crossed: 'I have received one from you concerning some debts
you have contracted' – it was debts, not low company after all, though
the two were not of course mutually exclusive. 'You seem,' so the King
wrote, 'so sensible of the impropriety of such conduct that it is not
necessary for me to enlarge upon it.' It was as near to reassurance or
endearment as the King ever allowed himself to go in writing.

So unnecessary was it for him to 'enlarge' that by May, 1793,
Augustus was grumbling to the Prince of Wales that their father had
not replied to any of his own fortnightly letters for three years. This
seems to have been at least nearly true – there was one letter from the
King in May, 1791. 'My leaving my country so young must still make
his Majesty think I am a child,' complained Augustus in tones notably
contrasting with those he employed towards his parents.[15] The King's
long silence almost certainly indicates that what he was hearing of
Augustus was displeasing him.* By the beginning of 1793, George and
Charlotte had learned that Augustus was having an affair in Rome with
Lady Augusta Murray, whose age was more than thirty and whose
reputation less than virginal. The susceptible young Prince was indeed
infatuated with his 'Goosy', without whom he protested himself 'half
dead', and he could not rest till he had carried her before the Anglican
priest ministering to the English community in Rome, and married her.
Apprised of his son's act, which he judged equally to flout common
prudence, parliamentary statute, and his own royal and paternal
authority, George wrote to Rome in May, 1793, giving 'permission'
for a return home. Augustus's initial delight was quickly quenched
when he discovered the extent of the King's anger. 'Who can have
dared,' he bemoaned, 'to ruin a son in the opinion of his father, a
father who has constantly been so kind?' He would not, however,
complain, so he declared, but instead – his phraseology was seldom
less than literary – 'feed upon his grief.' As for the Church, he must

---

* This was characteristic of George when he was worried or annoyed by his sons.
William and Ernest both complained that months and *years* went by without their
requests (usually requests to be allowed home) receiving any answer.

abandon his intention to enter it; 'neither my health, nor the present style of life I have observed, permits of it.'[16]

In December of that year, early on a dark morning, a 'Mr Augustus Frederick', dressed 'in a greatcoat like a common shopkeeper', and a heavily pregnant Augusta Murray, accompanied by two witnesses, the bride's aunt and a Mrs Jones, mantua-maker, went through a con-spiratorial second ceremony at St George's Hanover Square, to make the fact of the marriage, at least in the eyes of the bride and the Church, doubly incontestable. A son was born on 13th January, and the follow-ing morning Augustus left the country again for Italy. Publication of the story did nothing to relieve the royal Princes from the burden of public condemnation, and sometimes contempt, that already lay upon them. Augustus had no doubt been foolish, even made himself ridicul-ous; and Lady Augusta was undeniably more than a shade shop-soiled – 'coarse and confident-looking' was one description of her;[17] but given the desperate shortage of potential spouses lying within the King's definition of eligibility, one must feel some sympathy for the Prince, as for all his brothers and sisters. 'Consider,' said Lord Temple, 'what a sad dog a Prince of the Blood is who cannot by law *amuse* him-self with any woman except a d — d German Princess with a nose as long as my arm and as ugly as the Devil. In my opinion a Prince of the Blood is the most miserable being in the world.' However, the Royal Marriages Act, like the supremacy in law of the Church of England, was not a subject on which George III ever experienced doubts or could be expected to budge. The assembled dignity of the Privy Council was soon gathered to examine closely every available witness of the December morning's proceedings, and in July, 1794, His Majesty was pleased upon his Council's advice to order the setting aside of 'the shew or effigy of marriage . . . solemnized, or rather pro-phaned' at St George's.[18]

The King had given an order – 'arbitrary and unconstitutional,' as Augustus complained – that Lady Augusta should not leave the country. However, in 1799, she succeeded in slipping away and join-ing Augustus in Berlin, and for some months the pair did live together. In 1800, Augustus, now twenty-seven, broke his exile and returned home, hoping that the King might relent. He would not, but instead complained of his son's 'coming over without asking my permission', and secretly too, 'like a culprit'. He refused to see him until he was assured that he had abandoned his 'absurd ideas' and admitted the in-validity of his marriage. He would then consent to 'the understanding that a cloud was to be drawn over all passed unpleasant subjects'.[19] Augustus at last, in 1801, accepted his father's terms and threw Lady

Augusta over, just after their second child was born, adopting the doubtful face-saver that he now had 'ocular demonstration' of her 'imprudent conduct'.[20] Only then would the King give him his Dukedom of Sussex and approve the parliamentary grant that went with it. Augustus continued to live abroad, for what was considered to be the good of his health, until 1806, when he came home and took legal action to restrain Lady Augusta from calling herself his Duchess. Three years later he obtained custody of his children, to whom he remained a good and affectionate father; and for the rest of his days (which were many) proved the odd man out among the royal Dukes, being a busy and articulate partisan of reforming and charitable causes, and scandalising his Tory brothers by his association with such radicals as Francis Place and Robert Owen. Upon Lady Augusta Murray's death in 1830, he married again – and again morganatically.

Prince Augustus during his years of virtual exile did not nurse – or at least not unduly advertise – his grievances. If he was sorry for himself, he was also ready to admit sorrow for his past. Prince Ernest, on the other hand, later Duke of Cumberland, was chronically resentful of his fate; of the less than just treatment – or plain neglect – meted out to him by his father; of his failure to get promotion in the Army; and of the unkind conduct towards him both of his commander-in-chief the Duke of York and of the Hanoverian commander, Walmoden.* Even a pair of horses the King sent him as a present were too heavy or rotten-footed and 'not worth a grot . . . However I feel the kindness of his Majesty's intention and therefore beg you won't mention this'.[21] Some at least of his troubles were real and serious enough. In the Netherlands campaigning of 1793-94, he had fought bravely and with distinction and was wounded, first in the face, and then in the arm. After the Battle of Tournai the King, almost as proud of him as Ernest was of himself, celebrated by increasing his allowance – 'fresh proof,' wrote back Ernest, 'that you are satisfied with my conduct . . . Sir, if your Majesty will only have the goodness and enquire of all those who know me, they will tell you that I am a man who can never go round about to do or get anything' – he had of course *asked* for the increase – 'my way is straight forward to the fountain head.'

However, Ernest saw clearly he was 'born to be the most unhappy of men' (the King, though 'very kind' and 'affectionate', had turned down his request to come home), and even before receiving his second wound, he declared to the Prince of Wales that he was 'sick of the war', not for any squeamish reasons, but because he had been given the wrong regiment – a heavy cavalry regiment where most of the officers

* Lady Yarmouth's son by George II.

were 'blackguards'. If the King did not give him the Ninth he would break his heart. With his bad arm and eye, he was allowed home for four months in 1794, and was initially well received. Plainly, however, the King thought he should not hobnob too intimately with the Prince of Wales – despite the fact that by this time as a Portland Whig the Prince was no longer in opposition – and also that Ernest's duty was to return as soon as he was able to the fighting over the Channel. When Ernest would dearly have liked to be with his brother during August at Brighton, the King saw to it that he accompanied the rest of the family to Weymouth. It would 'not be very amusing', in fact 'humdrum' and 'terrible'; but 'notre très cher père thinks sea bathing will comfort him in his old days', and to Weymouth Ernest thought it prudent to go, where he was plainly bored and difficult – complaining in particular of the Queen's sullenness: 'God knows what is the matter with her.' By contrast, in his sardonic letters to the Prince of Wales, he repeatedly emphasised the high spirits of the other 'honoured author of our days' – Weymouth's influence on the King was always tonic.[22]

The measure of his father's feeling was felt in October, 1794, when Ernest, reluctantly returning after his leave, was run into Margate by three French frigates; 'ten minutes later et *me voilà pris*.' Straightway the King sent express orders, first that he was not to move from Margate; then that he was to proceed to Dover till the Admiralty made arrangements for him to be taken back across the Channel. Clearly George would not have him back at Carlton House, and Ernest knew better than to disobey. 'You know how odd his Majesty is,' he wrote to his brother, 'and as I am entirely depending on him, by God I might get into a scrape.' 'God were I but in old England,' he lamented when he arrived at Helvetsluys; and two days later: 'By God, dearest brother, your letter of today moved me to tears. I should be the cursedest rascal if I ever could forget your kindnesses to me.' To his 'dear sisters' he wished to be remembered 'most affectionately'; to his mother and father, just 'respectfully'.[23] For a long time the Prince of Wales remained his 'dearest, dearest brother'.

Prince Adolphus, in command of a Corps in the Netherlands fighting, and mightily approved of by his father, considered that in view of the condition of his wounds, Ernest ought not to have returned to the campaign. However, he not only did, but again distinguished himself in the dismal retreat of late 1794; and he reckoned that he was treated with rank injustice by the Duke of York when he was refused a Corps command. He would never, he vowed, forget the ill-treatment he had received. 'My heart, by God, is ready to burst . . .; how different can *brothers* be.'[24] Fathers, however, appeared only too stubbornly consistent. 'Is it not hard,' complained Ernest, 'to have lost the use of an eye in doing my duty and not to have got as yet an answer from his Majesty though I have wrote four times?' But when Adolphus reported to the King at Christmas, 1795, what his brother was suffering, his arm still 'weack' and painful and his eye needing an operation that ought not to be entrusted to a Göttingen surgeon with a 'shacking' arm, George – who if he was over-authoritarian with his sons was not inhuman – gave permission for Ernest to return home, where the appearance of his shrunken left eye and scarred cheek caused some *frissons* of horror.[25] His disfigured farouche looks were doubly unlucky for him; too readily they enhanced the sinister reputation he later acquired among the public, who were not at all unwilling to believe that such a one-eyed ogre might indeed have begotten the child of his sister Sophia.*

It was in Hanover that Ernest had been educated and it was in the Hanoverian army that he had fought; one day it was to the people of Hanover that he was to return as their King. George III, Elector of Hanover, thought that Ernest should be as willing to stay in the service of the Electorate as Adolphus was, but Ernest's stubbornness matched his father's. In 1798 he refused 'as a matter of honour' to serve under General Walmoden and resigned from the Hanoverian army. Two letters requesting the rank of Lieutenant-General in the *British* army remained unanswered. To George his son's attitude was evidence of further unreliability and of indiscipline – charges which Ernest threatened to challenge by enlisting in the yeomanry as a private: 'by that means I shall shew my anxiety in a glorious cause . . . and shall prove my readiness to come forward in defence of my King and country.' The King presumably thought this a bluff and once again did not reply. 'With sorrow do I perceive,' Ernest wrote, 'that I have met with your disapprobation.' When his father persisted, offering him the rank of Lieutenant-General in the Hanoverian service, he finally and grudgingly accepted, burying his 'private feelings'.[26] Next year, the paternal disapprobation having sensibly lessened, he was given parallel rank in the British army and created Duke of Cumberland. In the House of Lords he was to prove the highest of high Tories and a crusader-in-

* It is at least *almost* certain that he had not. But Creevey, Leigh Hunt's *Examiner*, *The Times*, and the *Morning Chronicle* were among those who thought he had. It is very likely that the rumour originated as one of the Princess of Wales's malicious inventions: 'The Princess of Wales told Lady Sheffield the other day, that there is great reason to suspect the father to be the Duke of Cumberland' (Glenbervie Journals, i, 363).

chief against Catholic Emancipation – which last certainly cannot have displeased the King. He took no further part in the war, though he was present with the Hanoverian contingents at the Battle of Leipzig in 1813; he lived a bachelor* in a suite of apartments in his father's palace of St James's, quarrelled with his 'dearest, dearest brother', and was once all but murdered by his valet. As the valet forthwith committed suicide, public opinion, though not the jury, was more than ready to believe that it was the Duke who had murdered *him*.[27]

Adolphus and Frederick were always George's favourites. Young Adolphus from his earliest days at Kew, especially after the death of the infants Alfred and Octavius in the early 1780's, became the ewe lamb among the King's sons, a lad whose affectionate liveliness was doubly delightful to his father as difficulties mounted with the older boys. At the early age of twelve, Adolphus accompanied his brothers Ernest and Augustus to Göttingen in 1786, and from his 'little colony' there the King was happy to have it reported, and found it easy to believe, that 'Adolphus seems at present the favourite of all'. He was to grow up handsome, sociable, and spirited. Of all the sons of George III he was the only one who contrived to avoid scandal and live within his income. As a Hanoverian officer he proved courageous, energetic, and capable. After the defeat and freezing misery of the Netherlands retreat of 1794-95, he wrote to thank the King for the privilege of serving in the campaign, 'God knows . . . a sad one,' which he would not wish to have missed; 'it is the greatest comfort in the world to have shared all hardships with the men.' These were sentiments to warm his father's heart.[28]

When in 1798, Adolphus asked permission to marry his cousin Frederica of Mecklenburg-Strelitz – the nineteen-year-old widow of Prince Louis of Prussia and eventual Duchess of Cumberland – the King agreed, but considered the marriage should wait for the end of hostilities. Adolphus, however, was very soon noticing 'a great relap on her side'; letters ceased; and in very short time the Princess had married the Prince of Solms-Braunfels, having become pregnant by him.[29] Adolphus, from 1801 Duke of Cambridge, lived on at St James's, the least unpopular of the royal Dukes, much loved by his parents and sisters, and at least respected by his brothers. He returned to Hanover in 1813 and was from the next year Governor-General

---

* Until the month before the Battle of Waterloo. Then he became the third husband of Frederica, the 37-year-old Princess of Solms-Braunfels, sister of Queen Louise of Prussia and Queen Charlotte's niece, who had once jilted Prince Adolphus. The marriage only served to make a black reputation blacker. Queen Charlotte refused to receive the new Duchess at Court.

there. The sudden death of his niece Charlotte, the Prince Regent's heir, was summarily to end his long bachelordom and 'warm' him, like his brothers, 'with desire to be prolific.'[30] Within a fortnight he had been accepted by the young Princess Augusta of Hesse-Cassel, a great-granddaughter of George II, and it was they who won the race to produce the *first* legitimate grandson to King George III and Queen Charlotte, the oldest of whose fifteen children had been born *fifty-seven* years before. The facts are sufficiently remarkable, surely, to qualify for some kind of record.

It certainly seems that George should have striven harder to obtain marriages for his daughters, especially as none of them had the slightest inclination towards spinsterhood. On the contrary, their instincts were healthily normal and, as everyone agreed and Gainsborough consummately demonstrated, they were (the Princess Royal perhaps excepted) far from lacking charms. But objections to potential suitors were depressingly abundant: they might be commoners; alternatively, if of royal or ruling ducal stock, their family history might be physically unhealthy, or mentally unbalanced, or morally suspect; or political considerations might prove a bar; or some satisfactory fish might be all but landed when he would slip the hook.

The Princesses were not by any means confined to a cloistered existence, though they were severely hedged round with etiquette; Queen Charlotte reminded them, for instance, in 1801 that they ought never to visit the apartments of their unmarried brothers without a lady present.* But they moved in society, attended theatres and concerts, enjoyed (or endured) the Windsor and Weymouth routines – or of course for long stretches went on 'much as usual, very quietly, as you know – vegetating'.[31] The theatre was often their escape from boredom, especially at Weymouth during wet Augusts or Septembers. To be obliged to accompany the King twice in one week to the Concerts of Ancient Music the Princess Royal found 'rather a dull piece of business'.† On the other hand the King might wake up to the fact that his daughters were finding life a little tedious: 'The great point is at last decided and we are to have *a Ball* next Monday,' wrote Augusta in May, 1794. 'The King was so good as to name it himself, thinking it would be the amusement we should *prefer* and we all readily accepted of it.'

---

* Possibly in view of some of the brothers' habits and the wagging of some people's tongues, this was not entirely unreasonable. 'Dear Ernest,' for instance, Sophia admitted to be 'rather a little imprudent at times.'

† It should be said, however, that the Princess Royal was the least musical of a generally musical family.

About the annual Weymouth holiday (during most years between 1789 and 1805), in which the King delighted, his wife and daughters had more mixed private feelings, though they never failed to accompany him. Sometimes the attendant society was 'most agreeable and charming', as Augusta found it in 1794. 'We all meet very constantly either at home or on the sands, or driving and walking . . . We cannot improve our set, I am sure.' In other years things went on

> (as the world goes) pretty well: I own though, if I am to give my opinion [it is Princess Mary writing to her 'dearest dear' brother George in 1798] this place is more *dull* and stupid than I can find words to express; a *perfect stand*-still of *every* thing and everybody except every 10 days a very long Review that I am told is very *fine* . . . Mama, I feel, is beginning to feel unwell as she always does whenever she is at Weymouth . . . One thing makes her very happy which is its being *determined* that the *sea* parties are not to take place . . . Whenever the weather will permit we are to row, but *entre nous* mama is so much afraid of *any motion* that I do not think papa will get her to go at all. Augusta and Eliza are both charmingly, they have bathed but Sophia and me do not intend to honour the sea with *our charmes* this year.*

The Queen was no happier in the sea than on it; she was 'not a bather, only a spectator'. Indeed the Prince of Wales put it more flatly; 'I know that Weymouth always disagrees with you.' But the King loved the fine air, the bathing, the yachting and being rowed in the Admiralty barge, the promenading before his loyal subjects, the horse-riding and play-going, the reviewing of the local regiments and staging of manœuvres.[32] 'Ever since the King has been here his spirits and good hewmour have continued. He enjoys his bathing more than anybody and assures us that he never felt better after it than this year,' wrote the Queen. It was all a fine change for the King, but Charlotte did find the routine at times exhausting: 'nothing else but attending reviews and breakfasts and racing the forenoon, and going to the Play at night, and even are returned home so late that we have just had time to pull off one gown in order to put on another and then run downstairs to get into the carriage.'

The King was aware from time to time that he had not done as

---

* Aspinall, *Correspondence of George Prince of Wales*, iii, 1379, 1384. One should remember that sea-bathing was for health, not pleasure, and immersion in the chill of early morning, before the pores of the skin were fully open, was regarded as therapeutically obligatory.

much for his daughters' matrimonial prospects as he might have done, and once offered the lame excuse that it would be heart-rending for him to see them go abroad, which of course a 'settlement' would necessarily involve. Perhaps it is surprising that they did not harbour more resentment against him on this account than they seem to have done. On the contrary, they were unanimous and outspoken in their devotion to him – even Amelia who, however, in some of her private letters did give vent to bitter exasperation. As the years unrolled, and more particularly after 1810, it was their mother whose little tyrannies and censorious grumbling the Princesses found hard to stomach, and whose determination to have her misery *shared* that they rebelled against. All of them craved to be married. Elizabeth, for instance, was constantly writing of her wish to make someone 'a perfect wife', and when at long last her eldest sister did become engaged, she expressed the fervent hope that 'it may open the way for others, for times are much changed and every young woman who has been brought up as we have . . . must look forward to a settlement'. As for Augusta, she intended 'to be very despotic till I have a Lord and Master and then (unless I break the great oaths and promises I shall make) I shall give myself up to his whims.'[33] A few years later she was yearning pathetically to be allowed to marry one of the King's equerries, General Brent Spencer, which was of course out of the question while George III was in command of his faculties. (It is however possible that the Prince Regent sanctioned their private and secret marriage later.)[34] Elizabeth, too, appears to have had an obscure romance, with one George Ramus, though the legend that she also went through some secret wedding ceremony and even had children by him seems to lack hard supporting evidence.[35] Her later desire to marry Louis Philippe of Orleans was frustrated less by her father than by the adamant opposition of Queen Charlotte. At forty she wrote, 'All my bright castles in the air are nearly at an end, if not quite so.' She had to wait for matrimony until the age of almost forty-eight and the proposal of the Landgrave of Hesse-Homburg, with whom, despite the fact that the marriage was 'universally quizzed and condemned' and her moustachioed bridegroom generally written off as an ugly hound, she was to live her eleven happy last years.

Princess Sophia – sweet-tempered, whimsical, 'elfin' Sophia – and Princess Amelia, George's youngest daughter, were two more of the sisterhood who pined for love but were never settled in lawful wedlock. Both of them nevertheless considered themselves married in the eyes of God; Sophia to that courtly equerry and 'fine gentleman' General Garth – old enough to be her father – with whom she went through some secret ceremony and (presumably) by whom at the age of twenty-two she had a son who turned out worthless; and Amelia to another of the royal equerries, General FitzRoy. She wrote to him in 1807, three years before her early death, that she *gloried* in their attachment; and she would dearly have loved to confide the secret of it to her father, as she already had to the mother for whom she had far less affection. At least she wondered if she might earn her father's compassion, for his consent to an official union was, she knew, unthinkable. But Amelia never dared risk telling him.[36] Sophia's persistent ill health outlived her secret love affair, and once during 1813-14 she was confined to her room for a year and a half. From 'the Nunnery', when she was thirty-four, she wrote to her brother and confidant the Prince Regent – her 'dearest G.P.': *'Four old cats* . . . I wonder you do not vote for putting us in a sack and drowning us in *The Thames.'*

Mary, often considered the best-looking of all George's daughters, was forty before she married her cousin the Duke of Gloucester ('Silly Billy'), to whom she had been vaguely 'attached' for twenty years. Her father, then being incapable, was in no state to recall his furious antagonism to the clandestine Gloucester-Waldegrave marriage of the Duke's parents; it was the Prince Regent's consent that was now necessary for this new more humdrum union.

The only one of his daughters for whom George III successfully, if even then belatedly, negotiated an alliance was the eldest, Charlotte the Princess Royal, and she had become almost desperate when every possible match seemed to be slipping from her grasp and she was approaching thirty. Like all her sisters she fled to the Prince of Wales for comfort and practical assistance. As Georgiana Devonshire once said, just after suffering some *'perfect abuse'* from him, he had 'so good a heart *au fond'*. What the Princess Royal had really wanted was to marry the young Duke of Bedford. 'I told her,' wrote the Prince, who could 'hardly forbear laughing' when she ventured this, 'I thought that if I knew my father, wh. I thought I did pretty well, that he would never think of giving his consent.' When her resourceful brother suggested the possible availability of the King of Prussia's son (later Frederick William III – the Duke of York was soon to marry his sister), 'she instantly jump'd at it.' However, she was a good deal older than the Prussian Prince, who eventually married Queen Charlotte's handsome niece Louise instead. That domestic matters at Windsor were often unhappy at this time is plain from several sources. With the Queen herself increasingly plaintive and censorious, and much variety of both son and daughter trouble, tears and tensions were common. Bland Burges in 1794 wrote that there was 'no more unhappy family

in England than that of our good King',* and in April of that year
Adolphus was writing from Flanders: 'Pray in your next letter tell me
how things go on in our family: I hope better than when I left it.' In
Sophia's words, 'Things go on but very *so so*' – running to bury her
head too upon the well-drenched shoulder of the Prince of Wales. But
she would have nothing against her father: 'The dear King is all kindness to me and I cannot say how grateful I feel for it.'[37]

At last, after long negotiation, a settlement for the Princess Royal
was concluded during 1796-97 with the Hereditary Prince (soon to be
Duke) of Württemberg, a middle-aged widower whose first wife
Augusta of Brunswick, George III's own niece, had lived amid such
scandal and died amid such mystery that the King required stringent
investigations before he finally gave consent to his daughter's engagement. At first he had flatly refused to 'bequeath' any daughter of his
upon a prince that he understood to have 'brutal and other unpleasant
qualities'. Charlotte, the least elegant of the King's six daughters, was
already at thirty putting on weight; but her prospective husband – who
was also at this stage Britain's ally in the French war – was so fat that
the wags christened him the Great Belly-gerent, and the cartoonists of
the day, Gillray in particular with his *Bridal Night* and *Baiser à la
Wurtemberg*, had some easy ribaldry at their disposal for a season. It
was not a popular romance; but the Prince proved in no way 'brutal'
and in a personal respect it was to prove a not unsuccessful, though un-
fruitful, marriage.

Until 1805, Charlotte could remain, though cut off from her home-
land, at least an ally if rather a forlorn one; but after Austerlitz, with
Württemberg a not unwilling puppet state of Napoleon and its ruler
promoted to King, Charlotte was obliged to be her own father's enemy.
She even became stepmother-in-law to Napoleon's brother Jerome.
Once as Queen of Württemberg she sent a letter to her mother beginning – '*Ma très chère Mère et Soeur*'; one can guess how that was received.
George III took the trouble to decree that no member of the royal
family might use the expression 'Queen of Württemberg' – much as the
Emperor Napoleon was always to remain General Bonaparte. After
the war Charlotte saw members of her family again from time to time,
though Elizabeth described her appearance as sadly changed, and
Augusta reported in 1819 that she would not have recognised her, she

---

* 'They have lately passed whole hours together in tears . . . The Queen appears
to feel and suffer the least; the King sometimes bursts into tears, rises up and
walks about the room, then kisses his daughters and thanks God for having given
them to him to comfort him; by which the Princesses are variously agitated . . .'
(J. Bland Burges, *Correspondence*, 278).

was so 'large and bulky . . . What strikes the most is, that from not wearing the least bit of corset, her stomach and hips are something quite extraordinary'.[38] Although she became dropsical and had to be carried everywhere, she had the will and courage to pay a last visit to England in 1827. She longed, she said, 'to see Vicky,' who she hoped would 'take a little bit of a fancy' to her.[39] Her own and only child had not survived, and of course she had never seen her father since the day she left England in 1797; but at Royal Lodge she visited that elder brother, now George IV, who had long ago been kind to her, and was very soon to be in as dropsical and moribund a condition as she was herself. She died next year.

CHAPTER TWENTY-FOUR

The King and the Heir Apparent

WHEN war with revolutionary France was seen to be inevitable in January, 1793, and with four of his brothers militarily engaged, the Prince of Wales developed ambitions to become patriotically employed in a command suited to his station; and when his father obliged him by promising him a colonelcy, for a short time his heart overflowed with gratitude. To the Queen, that 'ever dearest mother' whose animus against him he had only a year or two before been so indignant about, he now wrote in terms almost of ecstasy. Indeed he feared that his delight was expressed 'in a tone of insanity'. It was; and with his customary prolixity – but he apologised for that too: '*En vérité je ne me possède plus*'. The King had not only given him *life*, but '*the enjoyment of life*' and was not that 'the greatest of all blessings'? He was prevented from coming to thank his 'good and gracious father' by word of mouth that very evening only by 'the cowardice of the nervous system', but at a more relaxed hour he proposed to throw himself in thankfulness at his Majesty's feet.*

A splendid new uniform and his Dragoons colonelcy did not long satisfy that grateful heart. The Prince, seeing others promoted above him, soon coveted a status more befitting the 'magnificence' of his rank, and involving active service. He even applied to the Duke of Saxe-Coburg for a post in the Austrian Imperial Army, canvassing the Duke of York to support his request. The Duke, however, prudently

---

* The Prince seemed to be well aware of his prodigious talent for overdoing things in the 'effervesient effusions' he poured forth over these years to his mother, that 'confidante of the innermost sentiments' of his heart. Indeed, he wrote, 'I hardly can venture to trust my pen lest you should think I am indulging a vein more calculated for the ear of a mistress than of a mother' (Aspinall, *Correspondence of George Prince of Wales*, iii, 1006). There is no doubt that from the Queen's side there was more warmth for this impulsive, erratic, heart-on-sleeve, incurably self-deceptive firstborn of hers than for any of her other children. As for the 'cowardice of the nervous system' that he refers to, one should take him more seriously than his 'effervesient effusions' seem at first to warrant. He had inherited his father's malady, and strain or excitement did precipitate attacks, always mysterious and debilitating, and sometimes highly alarming. He wrote to Dr John Turton in 1799 that with him 'the disorders of the body' in general owed 'their source to the mind'. If for 'source' we read 'onset', it was a fair self-diagnosis.

stonewalled – all such matters depended 'entirely upon his Majesty's
pleasure'.[1] Repeatedly in the years that followed, Pitt, Dundas, and
the King himself had to point out to the Prince of Wales that his
'magnificence' must lie solely in the fact that he was Heir Apparent, but
he would not take their no for an answer. When the command of the
Horse Guards ('The Blues') fell vacant in 1795 he begged his mother
to put in a word for him to the King. He had 'long wished it . . .
besides which, dearest mama, it is 3000 pretty little shiners every year
. . . I thought it would be more delicate not to put myself too forward,
and if it does come, that it should appear to arrise from the King's own
idea . . .' But while the Queen, by her account, 'laid schemes',

> all was frustrated in five minutes. When the Kg. returned from early
> prayers, Ldy Harrington mentioned to us the sudden death at Park
> Place.* The King put down his tea, went into the next room and
> returned with a letter in his hand, ordered a servant to be sent to the
> Duke of York and said 'after thirty years promise I have given the
> vacant Guards to the Duke of Richmond'.[2]

The Queen attempted consolation: '*Après la pluie il fait beau temps*, I
hope your sunshine days will appear soon.' It is clear, however, that
the Queen could exercise no material influence on the King's decisions.
'My ever dearest and best beloved mother, you might in your good-
humoured way first mention it to the King yourself'; this was the
Prince's method of approach, and the Queen, so she claimed in reply,
was often hoping to catch the fleeting favourable moment. But the
King was either too occupied or too tired, or snatching a quick meal
and a drink of tea between hunting and attending some function; or
he simply was not in an approachable frame of mind. On the question
of the Prince's promotion, the Queen had to write, 'There has not
offered one simple instance even in the King's common talk of business
that could give me an opportunity to touch upon it.'

Despite further repeated solicitations there was never to be any
military sunshine for the Prince. Ministers would not have it. The
Duke of York would not lift a finger. The King flatly rejected it.
When, early in 1797, the Prince was coupling his military demands with
a suggestion that he should be sent as Lord Lieutenant to Ireland,
where chronic disturbance was sliding towards open rebellion, Dundas
at first refused either to see him or to take his requests to the King.
After being much importuned, however, and in the matter of Ireland,
the Prince's insisting that it was not he that was crying out for Ireland,
but suffering Ireland that was 'generally and loudly' crying out for

* Of the commander of the Horse Guards.

him[3] – a hopeful fantasy – Pitt and Dundas did go through the motions of presenting the Prince of Wales's points in the Closet. Nothing, of course, could be expected but blunt refusals. Pitt's reply was icily dismissive:

> His Majesty could not help apprehending that His Royal Highness suffering his name to be mixed in any discussions respecting political questions in that country [Ireland] was not likely to be productive of any beneficial effect.

And on the military request Dundas was as blankly negative:

> His Majesty had only to lament that the Prince of Wales should be induced so repeatedly to urge a point on which he had every ground to know his determination was unalterably taken. His Majesty would resist every idea that bore the semblance of the Prince of Wales being . . . considered as a military man.

When the obstinately persevering Prince made direct application to his father the refusal was polite but no less absolute than it had been two years before:

> I owne I am sorry you have again applied, but I cannot depart from what I have uniformly thought right. My younger sons can have no other situations . . . but what arise from the military lines they have been placed in. You are born to a more difficult one, and which I shall be most happy if I find you seriously turn your thoughts to; the happiness of millions depend on it as well as your own.[4]*

Whatever he was doing, the Prince of Wales never failed to place George III and his governments in quandaries. Even after he had seen the red light of Jacobinism and parted company with Fox, there remained the chronic problem of his ever vaster debts and the personal unpopularity which was always tending – and in very precarious days for European kings – to drag the monarchy downwards with it. At the height of his Mrs Fitzherbert passion, he had several times vowed that he renounced his succession rights in favour of the Duke of York, and although no more such talk now came from *him*, there were plenty of suggestions from others during the nineties that such a man ought never to become King. An anonymous pamphlet of 1792, for instance, had published, together with the hope that the 'wretched farce of

---

* It seems improbable that the King, approaching sixty, remembered at all vividly his own rejected requests for some similar rank befitting *his* station as Prince of Wales in 1759, when George II had grumbled of his young grandson, then twenty-one, '*Il veut monter un pas*'.

royalty' would not last much longer, a virulent attack on the Prince's hypocrisy and vice. The public purse had rescued him once, in 1787, on the understanding that he would retrench; 'but what was the scene which a very few months disclosed? No sooner had Parliament voted this money than decency was set at defiance, public opinion scorned, the turf establishment revived in a more ruinous style than ever, the wide field of dissipation and extravagance enlarged, fresh debts contracted to an enormous amount . . . Had a private individual acted in like manner he would have become the outcast of his family . . .' And in 1796, the *True Briton* (a paper actually founded on Treasury money) outspokenly observed: 'We have long looked upon his conduct as favouring the cause of Jacobinism and democracy in this country more than all the speeches of HORNE TOOKE, or all the labours of the Corresponding Society.' Such sentiments, of course, outraged the King as much as they did the Prince, who several times agitated for prosecutions. Concerning the particular attack in the *True Briton*, the King allowed that it was 'improper' and it would 'be attended to, but you know there is so great a jealousy of any infringement of what is called the liberty of the Press, that it is a chord that must be toutched with great delicacy'; especial delicacy, no doubt, in the case of a pro-Government paper.

Whenever the Prince of Wales complained that the 1787 settlement had been ungenerous, and the funds available for completing Carlton House inadequate, the King's replies were always unpalatable variations on the old theme: the Prince must learn to economise and 'allot a large portion of his income to the discharge of his debts' even if this involved forgoing some of the 'dignity and splendor' due to him.[5] In November, 1792, the Prince announced that he proposed to live solely off his £13,000 from the Duchy of Cornwall; but despite assistance from Coutts the banker, the mortgaging of his diamonds, and liberal professions of resentfully good intentions, his liabilities continued to swell like prize onions and by 1795 exceeded £600,000, or one twenty-fifth of the country's entire annual budget at the outbreak of war. There was again the prospect of the bailiffs executing orders at Carlton House, as they had in 1792.[6]

If he had married, his establishment of £60,000 a year would have been fixed at a higher figure; and his father naturally inquired concerning his matrimonial intentions. In 1791, the reply from the Prince, who was already regarding himself as not quite so irrevocably linked to Mrs Fitzherbert as in the days of first rapture, had been thoughtful but negative. It was at the time when the Duke of York was also considering wedlock, with Princess Frederica of Prussia – similarly as a device for extricating himself from debt. 'As for us Princes,' the Prince of Wales reported telling the King, 'the choice of a wife was indeed a lottery, and one from the wheel of which I did not at least at present intend to draw a ticket. There were very few prizes compared to the number of blanks.' If he *did* marry, he would wish to go abroad personally to view the possibilities. As to the succession, if Frederick's marriage produced children, well and good – 'the inducement then would certainly be less to me to marry, tho' I repeated I did not chuse by any means to bind myself . . .'[7] The Duke of York's marriage, however, proved childless; the Prince of Wales quarrelled more and more frequently with Mrs Fitzherbert, complaining of her bad temper and solacing himself in the company of Lady Jersey; and by 1794, marriage again presented itself to him, as well as to the King, as both a desirable move towards safeguarding the succession and as the only practical escape from insolvency. King, Government, and Parliament might all agree to tie together settlements of marriage and of debt.

Far from travelling in Europe to appraise the market in Protestant princesses, the Prince made his rather casual choice in favour of his cousin Caroline of Brunswick and hurried to obtain his father's consent. There proved no difficulty. When the King was informed by his son that all connection with Mrs Fitzherbert was at an end and that he wished to marry Caroline, paternal approval was immediate: 'Undoubtedly,' he told Pitt, 'she is the person who naturally must be most agreeable to me . . . provided his plan was to lead a life that would make him appear respectable, and consequently render the Princess happy.'[8] The Duke of York's report to his brother was encouraging too: 'She is a very fine girl . . . and a very proper match for you . . . As for what you mention *of one person* not approving of your marrying, all I can say is *je n'y entends rien.*' The *one person* was the Queen, who had heard things about the Princess that no prospective mother-in-law would want to hear: stories of 'indecent conversations with men', 'indecent conduct', a 'pretty tale' generally.[9] Was it perhaps something of all this that Prince Ernest was half-hearing coming through the wall at Weymouth in August, 1794? As he reported to the Prince of Wales:

Something is in agitation, God knows what, but the honoured authors of our days have had yesterday a very long *conversation* tête à tête which seemed to be very boisterous, for though the wind made a horrible noise one could hear them perfectly well talking, but what the subject was exactly I cannot tell, but I suppose *you was*. The King was in remarkable good spirits, but his counterpart the very reverse.[10]

The King preferred to think that Princess Caroline would prove to have those 'amiable qualities' that would divert the Prince 'from objects certainly not so pleasing to the nation' and that he would become so 'engrossed with domestic felicity' that he would be able to achieve both composure of mind and a numerous progeny to ensure the succession of 'these kingdoms and my German dominions', and thus become 'a comfort to me in the decline of my years'.[11]

While the Princess's arrival was delayed for months by bad weather and other frustrations, Cabinet and King concerted the plan of a financial settlement which might expect to prove honourable to the bridegroom, placatory to his creditors, and foolproof to the taxpayer of the future. It was agreed that upon marriage the Prince's annual grant should be raised from £60,000 to £125,000, with safeguards built in to prevent new follies. The whole of the Duchy of Cornwall revenues, plus a fifth of his new allowance – in all £38,000 a year – was to be earmarked for debt discharge. All this the King personally pledged his word to the Prince to support, and he was therefore perturbed when Pitt and Lord Chancellor Loughborough were obliged to come to him in May, 1795, with the opinion that animosity against the Prince was such that if the Government persisted with these proposals, not only might it be defeated on a straight vote, but its 'general strength and credit' might be destroyed. In other words it might be unable to carry on.[12]

This followed immediately upon a period when the Prince of Wales, irked by the cold-shouldering of his military aspirations, had done his own case no service by flirting again with the notion of public opposition. Lord Moira warned him no good would come of it: with the public mind 'soured' against him, it would be prudent to make 'duty and obedience the fashion' by his example. Queen Charlotte begged him to consider: 'I am very anxious, my dear . . . Every opposition to the Crown, headed by a branch of the Royal Famyly, *lessens the power of the Crown!*, and I am sure it cannot be yr. interest to assist in that.'[13] As it happened, too, public discussion of the Prince's affairs coincided with months of economic dislocation, rising taxes, higher food prices, and dearth. It was a time to think of recipes for potato bread rather than make allowances for princely grandeur. The Whigs, once his champions, now spoke with greatly altered voices. Grey was actively hostile. Fox suggested that the Prince might sell the Duchy of Cornwall and raise enough at one blow to pay off his £630,000*; a most

---

* Lord Lonsdale had the even more brilliant notion that the King as 'an act of condescention' might be persuaded to raise £800,000 by selling off to builders a 100-yard strip all round Hyde Park at two guineas a foot.

'insidious and democratical' proposal, declared the King. With him, once again, it was that prized article, his word of honour, that was involved. When Pitt and Loughborough suggested that a total, not of £38,000, but of £78,000 a year should be earmarked for the repayment of debts, George's attitude was that it was they then who must try to persuade the Prince themselves, for 'it is impossible for me, having given my approbation to the Prince of Wales, to take any part in the transaction'.[14] Persuaded of the inevitability of setting aside the larger sum, the Prince, while continuing to complain privately to his mother of Pitt's 'infamous deceit', assured his father of his wish to disembarrass him and only 'to follow such a line of conduct as your Majesty may consider the wisest and properest', thanking him meanwhile for the kindness shown 'through the whole of this very unpleasant business'. 'Mama particularly order'd me to say,' wrote Princess Elizabeth, 'that she would not fail telling the King of all the kind things you say concerning him.'[15]

The marriage of April, 1795, which was the price the Prince paid for his settlement, was of course a catastrophe. Though the original meeting between the couple was ominous,[16] the wedding ceremony itself passed without disaster, despite the Archbishop pausing a painfully long time at 'just cause or impediment' and looking searchingly at both bridegroom and monarch. The Prince of Wales appeared to be moist-eyed and confused, and to show some unsteadiness on his feet, but these symptoms may well have been induced by the brandy he had needed to see him through his ordeal.[17] The King, however, who gave away the bride, seemed to be in excellent spirits both then and four days later when, the Prince not choosing to accompany his new wife to St George's, 'the King made up the deficiency by handing her everywhere himself' and appearing to be delighted with his daughter-in-law.[18] For months after the marriage he seemed to be as unaware of its shipwreck as the rest of the royal family. To some extent at least both the Prince and Princess endeavoured to keep up appearances until the birth of their child – 'an immense girl,' as he reported to the Queen on 7th January, 1796, bowing 'with due defference and resignation to the decrees of Providence' which had neglected to send the preferred boy. The King, however, would not even have it that a boy *was* to be preferred; he had 'always wished' first for a granddaughter, and there was plenty of time for many brothers and sisters to follow. He 'talks of nothing but his grandchild', wrote Elizabeth; 'drank her health at dinner and went into the Equerries room and made them drink it in a bumper.' And the Queen was as full now of 'the little beauty' as she had previously been of advice concerning wet-nurses and childbed linen. ('The youngest milk is always best . . . I hope Lrd Cholmondeley has ordered the cradle.') 'Thank God you are now happy,' wrote Elizabeth; 'long, long may you remain so.'[19]

She could hardly have written in such tones if she and the family had known that the Prince of Wales was then sitting down in an excited turmoil of self-vindication, and *the presence of his Creator*, to make three copies of a long and passionate will (one for his papers, one for his executor Moira, one under seal for the King), denouncing 'the mother of this child, call'd the Princess of Wales'; leaving his possessions to his 'true and real wife' in the eyes of God, Maria Fitzherbert, 'millions of times' dearer to him than life itself; setting down a record of the King's promise (which it is true had recently been given) to guarantee in the event of the Prince's prior death the continuation of Mrs Fitzherbert's settlement of £3,000 a year; and enjoining that the education of his daughter should lie not in the hands of the so-called Princess of Wales but of the King. To his legal wife he left one shilling, and *not* the jewels she wore, which 'are mine, having been bought with my own money'.[20]

Certainly Caroline was a coarse-mouthed, loose-mannered hoyden; flippant, brazen and often maliciously slanderous; even, it is possible, actually crazy at times. Her stories were always inseparable tangles of lies and truth; but even if the Prince did not spend the wedding night dead drunk on the floor, or proceed with his 'constantly drunk and filthy' cronies to behave at Kempshott, their honeymoon residence near Basingstoke, like Falstaff's crew and that other Prince of Wales in Eastcheap,[21] his behaviour to her was to say the least crassly insensitive. He long and unforgivably insisted on the retention of Lady Jersey among her ladies-in-waiting and insisted that the Princess should withdraw the 'indecorous' allegations that this old and respected friend was his *mistress*. The public in general thought Caroline vilely treated, and demonstrated vociferously for her when she appeared at the Opera[22] or in her carriage among the crowd during the Westminster election of 1796. Even Princess Elizabeth, who 'doated' on her brother, told him that 'friends and foes are all of an opinion that a *resignation* [Lady Jersey's] *must* take place for the sake of the country and the whole Royal Family, for if you *fall* all must fall'.

By June, 1796, this last point was very much in the mind of the Prince himself, except that he chose to put it the other way round. Suddenly it was he who was appealing for family solidarity, and especially between him and his father. In this 'aweful crysis', he declared in his egocentric panic, they stood or fell together. Even before he had married Caroline, he told the King (and he cited the Queen as witness), he had diagnosed her evil character; in fact, he wrote – surely a triumph of self-deception – only his 'unalterable devotion' to his father had made him go through with the ceremony at all. Now he threw himself upon the King's 'paternal protection' and begged his approval for a formal act of separation. 'So overpower'd with unhappiness' that he felt 'quite light-headed', he threw off long, excited, self-pitying letters to his mother, wailing indignation at the vile calumnies being spread abroad by Caroline – including her embroidered versions of the love affairs of her sisters-in-law[23] – and pleading for Charlotte's influence on the King to be used to get some strong action from the throne. If so simple a deed as *the taking of his life* would undo the harm, he would of course 'glory in such a sacrifice'. Unhappily, or perhaps happily, that of itself would not do the trick:

> Oh dearest, dearest, dearest mother, if the King does not manage to throw some stigma, and one very strong mark of disapprobation upon the Princess, this worthless wretch will prove the ruin of him, of you, of me, of every one of us. The King must be resolute and firm, or everything is at an end.

He was beside himself with anxiety when he heard the Princess had been to see the King; 'I suppose,' he grumbled, 'she has made the best of her own story and told her lies as usual.' Lord Moira tried to soothe him. From the first, Lord Malmesbury (who had been the diplomat sent to escort Caroline over from Germany and been the first to report on her hygienic, if not moral, deficiencies)* had advised him of the catastrophic effect on public opinion of a separation. And now the King rubbed this in in his own grieved and weighty, but not unfair or unfriendly, manner:

> You seem [he wrote] to look on your disunion with the Princess as merely of a private nature, and totally put out of sight that as Heir Apparent of the Crown your marriage is a public act, wherein the Kingdom is concerned. The public must be informed of the whole business, and being already certainly not prejudiced in your favour, the auspices in the first outset would not be promising ... I am certainly by no means inclined to think the Princess has been happy in the choice of conduct she has adopted, but if you had attempted to guide her, she might have avoided those errors that her uncommon want of experience and perhaps some defects of temper may have given rise to ... I once more call on you to ... have the command

* Briefly, he discovered that she smelt. The Prince, he had warned a Brunswick lady-in-waiting, would require her '*to wash all over*'.

of yourself that shall, by keeping up appearances, by degrees render your home more respectable and at the same time less unpleasant . . . In a contrary line of conduct nothing but evils appear.[24]

It is not altogether true, then, as has often been alleged, that the King throughout was blind to the Princess's faults. On the other hand it *is* true that experience of his son's shortcomings predisposed him towards sympathy with his daughter-in-law, and his determination to see what good in her he could continued for several years to be a factor not only in his quarrel with the Prince, but increasingly in the widening breach between himself and the Queen, who hated and despised Caroline. The extremity of the Prince's loathing and horror of his wife appeared to the King irrational, and at least until he became finally convinced of the full extent of the Princess's 'levity and profligacy' (after the so-called Delicate Investigation in 1806), his considered attitude was that the pair ought in their own, their daughter's, and the public interest, to keep up appearances and try to make the best of a bad business. In this, when at the end of December, 1797, the Prince made another application for a separation, George was supported by the opinion of Lord Chancellor Loughborough, who pointed out that no 'causes of separation' were alleged by the Prince,* and public separation would therefore be 'incompatible with the religion, laws, and government' of the land. It would furthermore be unpopular and held against the Prince of Wales, concerning whom there was already such a 'general indisposition' as not to 'admit at this time of any increase'.[25] Towards the end of 1798, the Prince did make a suggestion that Caroline should take up steady residence at Carlton House for the winter, but the intensity of her distaste for him was no less than his for her, and she declined,[26] preferring to remain, by turns bored and boisterous, in her independent Blackheath establishment, where she held erratic court among her often astonished or bewildered sympathisers, and still at this stage had the custody of her little Charlotte, that lively, promising, and potentially so important child.

* Strictly, in law, Caroline's adultery, as Malmesbury had warned her before she came to England, would have been a capital offence. That pretty soon there *was* adultery, with a various company of uncertain composition, is hardly to be doubted. The Delicate Investigation found, if not quite convincingly, that she had *not* secretly had an illegitimate baby, but that 'other particulars of her conduct had given occasion to very unfavourable interpretations'. The King told Lord Grenville that 'if it had been one attachment, and even a child, he would have screen'd her if he could have done it with safety to the Crown', but in the face of all the evidence by then presented, 'she was not worth the screening' (Granville Correspondence, ii, 203-4).

CHAPTER TWENTY-FIVE

The Conduct of the War
(1793-1801)

THE progress of the war with revolutionary France, and the fortunes in particular of the British and Hanoverian Forces, were followed by the King with the closest attention. The fact that one of his sons commanded the British contingent in the allied army, while two more were seeing active and dangerous service with it, increased the intensity of his involvement. As a commander the Duke of York was a tyro, though the setbacks of 1793-94 ought not to be laid too heavily at his door; as a son he was a reformed character. The mail between Flanders and London was busy for nearly two years with a profuse correspondence between him and his father – from the father's side all approbation and paternal pride, or sometimes latterly commiseration and sympathy; from Frederick's a floridly filial gratitude* for the privilege of leadership granted to him and for the sunshine streaming down upon him from Windsor and Kew – which incidentally brought with it a Civil List loan of £30,000 towards mollification of his dunning creditors – and the most detailed account of every military move.[1] The King obviously expected to have his personal consent sought for anything bigger than day-by-day tactics, since the rest of the allies had their own priorities, and purely British interests, such as the taking if possible of Dunkirk as a base and a bargaining counter, did not necessarily coincide at all with those of the Austrians or Dutch. Austria's principal object in Belgium was to use it as part of a real estate deal in order to acquire Bavaria, while the Prince of Orange's intentions were wholly defensive, to keep the French out of Holland. Coburg, the allied commander and an old-fashioned soldier who believed in proceeding methodically from fortress to fortress, should no doubt have struck boldly for Paris while the French defences were still in confusion; but that he failed to do so was at least partly because the Duke of York, under orders, insisted on first besieging Dunkirk. The Duke sent back to his father enthusiastic praise for his brave Hanoverian contingent

* Gratitude too for the King's 'kind and affectionate conduct' towards the Duchess; 'there is not a letter which I receive from her in which she does not mention it.' The marriage, however, proved barren in every sense.

(Princes Ernest and Adolphus were among their officers) and con-stantly sneered and sniped at the selfishness and cowardice of the Dutch.[2] When the Duke's blow by blow account of the siege of Valenciennes ended in July with his taking the town, George was 'in the deepest manner impressed with gratitude to Divine Providence that my three sons have received no hurt and that an event so glorious to the combined forces in Flanders should have also been entrusted by the Duke of Coburg to my son. My heart is too full at present to add more . . .'[3]

Pardonably, the allies in Flanders did not comprehend that they were beginning to face a new phenomenon in the world's history, and fighting a war which was revolutionary in much more than one sense. For one thing, the enemy was commanded by generals who dis-appeared, including some of the best of them, with confusing rapidity under the blade of the guillotine. The King and his sons could agree that they were fighting 'savages'; but the *levée en masse*, and the emerg-ing revolutionary army, with an *élan* and inexhaustibility that more than compensated for its sudden confusions and panics, soon presented opposition that nobody had bargained for. This puzzlingly novel war was not being fought by the French according to the Coburg rules, or those that the young Duke of York had imbibed in Frederick the Great's Prussia.

It was not only the generals who failed to understand the changes afoot. The politicians were no more perceptive. Pitt, still thinking in terms of a short struggle in which Britain's European rôle would be largely that of paymaster, was quite at sea. Only a few months before the outbreak of war, still confident of peace, he had further reduced Britain's already very small army, and now had no adequate idea of how it might be quickly expanded. Moreover, he and Dundas were soon fatally dividing and sub-dividing such forces as they could muster, some to Flanders, some to the West Indies, some to Toulon when the counter-revolutionaries made an unexpected present of the port to Lord Hood, some to assist other counter-revolutionaries in western France, none numerous or powerful enough to make a de-cisive contribution towards what Burke and Windham – and George III – put highest among their war priorities, the destruction of the French Revolution and all its diabolical works.

Advancing on Dunkirk, the Duke of York was checked at Hond-schoote. Coburg was then defeated at Wattignies and soon the com-bined British-Hanoverian-Dutch army besieging Dunkirk became in-volved in the general retreat. The year 1793, which had begun with the French in disarray and such bright prospects of allied victory, ended dismally not only in the Low Countries but at Toulon. The King wished to keep back some regiments Pitt and Dundas intended for the West Indies, in order to reinforce Hood at Toulon, but being faced by a collective decision of the Cabinet he capitulated, as usual when so confronted. As it was, while more and more unfortunates were being shipped off to the West Indies to encounter, after the early capture of valuable French possessions, unforeseen enemies in the shape of black rebellion and yellow fever, Toulon fell to the revolutionary forces in December. Whether George's few thousand extra troops would have made much difference to the outcome is more than doubtful (Sir Charles Grey had asked for 50,000) and in general it would be wrong to claim better far-sightedness or consistency for him than for his ministers. As earlier in the American war, the one matter upon which he was unfailingly consistent was the necessity of continuing the struggle single-mindedly to the end. But in 1793 he did agree that it would be unwise to commit *too* large a force to the defence of Toulon. The Duke of York's army in Flanders must come first; and again, though he thought that Pitt and Dundas were dispatching disproportionately large forces to the Caribbean, he did agree in October, 1794, when he heard that the French were fitting out a naval expedition to cross the Atlantic, that 'in the present situation the West Indies are the great object to attend to'.* Ultimately he was up against the same brick wall as Dundas and Pitt: Britain simply did not possess an army of sufficient size to undertake decisive operations anywhere, and had neither the political will nor the administrative machinery for creating one. At least it must be granted that in the eventual shaping of something like such an army, which came into its own at last in the Peninsular campaigns and back again in the Low Countries at Waterloo, the unlucky Duke of York was in the long run to play as big a part as anybody.

Not, however, before he had first been subjected to humiliation. The Flanders campaign of 1794 fared worse than that of 1793. Carnot's new French armies began to show now a quality to match their numbers. In May, the Duke was involved in the allied defeat at Tourcoing, and had to do some hard cross-country riding to escape capture. By January, 1795, the Austrians had been forced back over the Rhine and the British over the Waal to extricate themselves as well as might be from potential disaster. The 'cowardly' Dutch, after the French victory at

* What annoyed him beyond measure later was the readiness with which he considered ministers were prepared, having spent so many lives in the conquest of West Indian islands, to bargain them away to secure a peace that he thought 'lowering'.

Fleurus, were left after all to be overrun by the revolutionaries. Spain made her own peace with the French. Prussia, long a sleeping partner in the coalition,* was also about to make a separate treaty and concentrate on the more important business of acquiring further areas of western Poland. The coalition, in fact, had decoalesced.

'Though the Duke of York's retreat was, I believe, perfectly necessary,' Pitt wrote to his brother Chatham in September, 1794, 'there is more and more reason to fear that his general management is what the army has no confidence in, and while that is the case there is little chance of setting things right.'[4] Unhappily not everyone agreed with the King that the Duke of York's conduct was 'beyond praise'. In view of his private and professional disgruntlement, Prince Ernest's hostile view of his brother ought to be somewhat discounted, but there were many other testimonies, not so much to the Duke's incompetence as to his unpopularity among officers junior to him in rank but senior in experience. The most telling of these reports emanated from Windham, at this time the Government's liaison with the troops in the field, who was shocked to hear what he was sure were slanderous accounts of the Duke's behaviour. William Elliot wrote to Sir Gilbert at this time of the fashion among both officers and men to decry the Duke, and (so responsible evidence insisted) unreasonably. General Fox corroborated the stories both of extreme unpopularity and of the lies that circulated concerning the Duke's drinking and riotous behaviour. General Bentinck reported to the King that there was 'a total want of discipline' among the British troops in Flanders, and the Duke of Portland also wrote of a 'mutinous' spirit, even among the Guards.[5] It seems that there were two handicaps the Duke of York could not escape from: he was too young, and he had been involved in a major retreat. In September, 1794, the Cabinet decided that he must be replaced – if possible by Cornwallis, but this never materialised – and in November, Pitt had the unpleasant duty of 'humbly imploring' the King to remove his son from his command. To this request, though it offended and anguished him, George made no active resistance:

Mr Pitt cannot be surprised at my being very much hurt at the contents of his letter. Indeed he seems to expect it, and I am certain that nothing but the thinking it his duty could have instigated him to give me so severe a blow. I am neither in a situation of mind nor from inclination inclined to enter more minutely into every part of

---

* There was an abortive scheme, supported by George and agreed to but never acted on by Pitt's Government, to *hire* 60,000 Prussian troops as mercenaries to assist the Flanders army.

his letter; but I am fully ready to answer the material part, namely, that though loving very much my son, and not forgetting how he saved the Republic of Holland in 1793, and that his endeavours to be of service have never abated, and that to the conduct of Austria, the faithlessness of Prussia, and the cowardice of the Dutch, every failure is easily accounted for without laying blame on him who deserved a better fate, I shall certainly now not think it safe for him to continue in the command on the Continent, when every one seems to conspire to render his situation hazardous by either propagating unfounded complaints against him or giving credit to them. No one will believe that I take this step but reluctantly . . .[6]

Cornwallis, back from his Indian Governorship, was awarded the Blue Riband of the Garter and joined the Cabinet. The Duke of York was consoled with a Field Marshal's baton, and then entered upon his best, reforming, years at the Horse Guards. The King viewed the desire of some of his ministers to escape from the war with the deepest misgivings. The story of British misadventure continued without relief. In the West Indies yellow fever was all-conquering, and the greatest British military disaster of the war accumulated slowly from medical ignorance and neglect. Only Lord Howe brought something to cheer, on the Glorious First of June, 1794, but in that victory too there was in truth an element of failure: the convoy from America did get through to France, even if that could be attributed to fog in the Channel. If Pitt the elder had been the most brilliantly successful of war ministers, Pitt the younger looked by the mid-nineties to be in the running for the wooden spoon.

Only the small band of Fox's followers had been against the war from the beginning; but on the last day of 1794, Wilberforce moved an amendment to the King's Speech advocating an attempt to negotiate 'just and reasonable terms' with France.* This move gained special point because Wilberforce was not only a government supporter but Pitt's most intimate friend from his early days. George thought that while the *cause* of the war was still there, such a move would be folly. If brought off, it could only 'place us in the most unpleasant situation of an armed neutrality', or if Britain began to disarm 'give rise to a fresh war with all the difficulties of again preparing for home defence'. At this stage Pitt appeared to agree with the King, but as the coalition melted away and the Jacobin Terror in France gave way to the reaction of Thermidor and the government of the Directory, Pitt like Wilber-

---

* 'When first I went to the Levee after moving my amendment, the King cut me' (*Life of Wilberforce*, ii, 73).

force began to incline towards the advantages of a negotiated peace. Pitt's whole system, his claim to fame, had been built on the virtues of sound economical administration, peace, retrenchment, and recovery. Now the National Debt that he had laboured to reduce was sky-rocketing with the mounting war expenditure; there were grave economic hardships at home and an unrest necessitating (in the united view of the King, Government, and the propertied classes) the harshest repression. On 27th October, 1795, George Canning was present ('after another turtle dinner at Downing Street') when Pitt discussed with his colleagues the wording of the King's Speech to be delivered two days later – this was to be the occasion when violent 'No War' demonstrations met the state drive to Westminster. 'The tenor of the Speech is peace,' wrote Canning, 'or at least a disposition on our part to *negotiate*,' and in view of the fact that the Austrians had just 'routed' the French, who would, he hoped, be obliged to fall back across the Rhine, all that would remain to be disputed was 'the terms of peace. We feel that we have a right to pretty good ones . . .'[7]

This sort of talk worried the King, who shared neither such optimism nor the belief that a negotiation ought even to be attempted. Nevertheless, Pitt and his Cabinet persisted, and therefore, as so often when driven back on his defences, George sat down to set his thoughts and conclusions on paper in a memorandum, as firmly and lucidly as he could; then he sent copies to Lord Chancellor Loughborough, to the Duke of Portland, and to Dundas and Pitt. Peace overtures, he wrote, though they might mollify some 'overtender friends of Government in the House of Commons', would abort successful operations in both East and West Indies (above all the expected capture of San Domingo); destroy co-operation with Austria and Russia; 'damp the rising in the interior of France . . . and put a stop to the various engines that seem now to threaten the downfall of that horrid fabric, established on the avowed foundation of the dereliction of all religious, moral, and social principles.' Faced by a Cabinet not altogether sharing the uncompromising nature of his ideological principles, the King wrote to Pitt that he did 'not in the least mean . . . to make any obstinate resistance to the measure proposed, though I owne I cannot feel the utility of it'; adding then, in his best vein of moral self-approbation and thereby conveying his judgment upon Pitt's unprincipled opportunism, 'My mind is not of a nature to be guided by obtaining a little applause or staving off some abuse; rectitude of conduct is my sole aim.' Stiff and self-righteous, he was not hypocritical. The issue to him, like the American issue twenty years before, was superficially complicated but basically simple; it should be weighed on a judgment of right and wrong.

Several further attempts were made during 1796 by the Government to escape from the war with France, by a variety of typically eighteenth-century suggestions for horse-trading of provinces and principalities. Belgium at one stage was dangled before Prussia, and Bavaria before Austria, as compensation. George looked critically on these large propositions, in which he could see 'not a shadow of justice', not so much since he objected to the presumptuousness of treating territories as pawns in an international game of chess as because he saw the great powers overriding the rights of smaller ones. Britain was a great power, but Hanover was one of the smaller ones, and George had to remind his ministers that he was its Elector. They appeared to have forgotten, in their broad hypothetical redrawings of the map of Europe, that there were such places as Ansbach and Bayreuth involved, and a 'county of Sayn, which on the death of the present Margrave comes to me'. If he lost the prospect of that, ought he not to be 'indemnified by getting the Bishopric of Hildesheim whenever the present possessor shall die or resign?' His voice was always the voice of the *ancien régime*, and never more so than when he was wearing his Hanoverian hat. What he thought of the way negotiations with the French were going by the end of 1796 is shown in a letter to Dundas on 17th November:

I trust Mr Secretary Dundas, when these dispatches are brought before the Cabinet tomorrow, will enforce the necessity of support-ing Lord Malmesbury in the tone he has held and not allow it in the least to be lowered. I think no question in geometry more fully to be proved than that this is of all moments the worst to make peace, and that if we will but steadily pursue the war, France will soon be obliged to sue for peace . .

When five weeks later the Directory broke off negotiations, the foreign minister, Lord Grenville, and the King both expressed their relief. [8]

Pitt, however, 'the pilot who weathered the storm,' continued for the present to show a preference for sheltering away from it if at all possible. His desire for peace was sharpened during 1797 by months of crisis at home and abroad, mitigated only by the naval victories of Cape St Vincent in February and Camperdown in October. Bonaparte completed his first sensational triumph against the Austrians in Italy. The British fleet abandoned the Mediterranean and then mutinied at Spithead and the Nore. Ireland was on the verge of rebellion; a small French force had already appeared off Bantry Bay in December, 1796, and another invasion force was now assembling in Holland. Weighing perhaps most heavily of all in Pitt's mind was the state of the nation's finances, no longer capable, he judged, of taking the strain of all the actions necessary for victory. This certainly was the point he stressed most emphatically to the King, who seemed, however, not as impressed as he might be. Instead he protested, angrily almost, to Pitt against the way 'this country has taken every humiliating step for seeking peace . . . and . . . met with a conduct from the enemy bordering on contempt . . .' Rushing into a hasty peace would 'for ever close the glory of this country . . . besides fixing the present wicked constitution of France on a solid ground of more extent and preponderancy in the scale of Europe than the most exaggerated ideas of Lewis XIV ever presumed to form'. This rebuke did not deter Pitt or the Cabinet, who stood united against the King. Pitt justified on the grounds of 'public necessity' the sacrifices that might have to be made, and obliquely threatened resignation if the Government's views were not accepted. Lord Grenville, the foreign minister, added his own explanation why his earlier firmness had dwindled: no man could be more deeply sensible than he of the extent of evils arising from a disadvantageous peace, 'but, without resources of finance it is impossible to resist them by war.' Once more the King bowed to his ministers. He could not but acquiesce, he said, in a measure that from the bottom of his heart he deplored, but 'should the evils I foresee not attend the measure, I shall be most happy to avow that I have seen things in a blacker light than the event has proved'.

When the prospect of a joint Anglo-Austrian peace with the French fell through, Pitt again decided to approach the French directly. This time, however, the Cabinet was not unanimous. Windham in particular was strongly for soldiering on until a Government arose in France that would 'grant us terms not utterly destructive'.[9] George of course agreed, and now poured out his feelings to Lord Grenville:

The many humiliating steps I have been advised to take in the last nine months have taken so deep an impression on my mind that I undoubtedly feel this kingdom lowered in its proper estimation . . . I cannot add more on this occasion but that if both Houses of Parliament are in as tame a state of mind as it is pretended, I do not see the hopes that either war can be continued with effect or peace obtained but of the most disgraceful and unsolid tenure.[10]

1798 proved a more fortunate year. The threat of a French invasion of Ireland receded. The Navy returned to the Mediterranean and gave the nation something really substantial to celebrate when Nelson almost annihilated the Toulon fleet in Abukir Bay. When the news came, George was on holiday at Weymouth. He did not shout too loudly. Indeed, approving of the *brevity* of Nelson's dispatch, he would, he wrote to Earl Spencer at the Admiralty,

> certainly so far copy him as not to pretend to express . . . the degree of joy I have felt on the occasion. The beating and destroying of the Brest fleet would be highly glorious and advantageous to this kingdom, but the success of this brave Admiral is of more utility to the cause we are engaged in; if it electrifies Austria and Naples it may save Italy.

At first the King deemed that, Nelson's poverty having made him earlier decline a baronetcy, a peerage was therefore out of the question, though 'a handsome pension' was highly proper. There were conventions to be observed after even so signal a victory; but very little pressure was needed from Earl Spencer and public opinion to bring forth a barony – and 'as the new peer has unfortunately no estate', the proposal that he should become Lord Nelson *of the Nile* possessed a similar happy propriety.[11]

The triumph of Abukir Bay, however, was in the strategic sense a purely defensive victory. It did not 'electrify Austria or save Italy'. Every offensive move made by Britain or her allies in the new coalition that was taking shape came to grief. A second campaign by the Duke of York in the Netherlands, this time in uneasy harness with a Russian force, had no more success than his first. In September, 1799, after there had been a successful attack on the island of Texel and the capture of the Dutch fleet there, the Duke began well by taking Alkmaar. But the hoped-for Dutch desertions were few, and the Dutch people failed disappointingly to recognise as liberators the British or Russian armies. Alkmaar was soon lost again, and within a few weeks the King was signifying to Dundas his approval for the withdrawal of all British forces, and sending 'a few lines of comfort to my son which he richly deserves'. As for the Dutch, he hoped those who had put too much confidence in them would have learned their lesson, and 'Mr Secretary Dundas must do me the justice to remember I was never very sanguine as to the success of the attempt on Holland'.[12] Meanwhile Bonaparte returned from Egypt, brought off the *coup* of Brumaire, and now in his turn made peace proposals, conveyed in general and rather grandiose terms to George III through the two foreign ministers Talleyrand and Grenville. George refused to bandy words with this 'new, impious, self-created aristocracy'. He wrote to Grenville: 'I do not enter on the want of common civility of the conclusion of the Corsican tyrant's letter, as it is much below my attention, and no other answer can be given than by a communication on paper, not a letter, from Lord Grenville to Talleyrand.' Grenville's *paper* to Talleyrand delighted the King; he asked for a copy, so that he could 'with pleasure refer' to it: 'Lord Grenville, I can with truth assert that I never read a paper which so exactly contained the sentiments of my heart . . . and I cannot see the shaddow of reason for altering any expression it contains.' Grenville himself said that 'the universal belief was that we should refuse to treat'.[13]

By now, however, Pitt's Government was rent with dissensions over where and how best to damage the enemy. Dundas had wished to resign as war minister after the failure of the expedition to Holland and devote all his attention to Indian affairs, but both Pitt and the King resisted this. During 1800, Dundas remained at loggerheads with Windham and Spencer, wishing to reinforce General Abercromby's forces in the Mediterranean and showing his disgust when men were diverted to support Windham's project of bolstering the royalists in la Vendée. Dundas also wanted an expedition to Cuba, which Pitt would not countenance; Grenville, on the other hand, wanted one to Italy. It was only reluctantly that George approved Abercromby's expedition to Egypt to eliminate the last remnants of Bonaparte's grand project there, and he felt so strongly opposed to the idea of an expedition to seize Ferrol, and then if things went well Cadiz and the Canaries, that once again Dundas was inclined to hand in his resignation:

> Most of you [he wrote to Grenville] being of the opinion that we ought not to send any force out of Europe . . . and the King and those in whose councils he confides being of opinion that our force is to go nowhere (which is the plain English of all this) my situation is becoming too ridiculous to be longer submitted to.[14]

And to the King he wrote:

> Mr Dundas perceives with great concern that his mode of bringing this business before your Majesty has met with your Majesty's disapprobation . . . Mr Dundas begs leave with the utmost humility, and the most profound respect to state to your Majesty that in his poor judgment the appropriation of the national force must in time of war, like every other resource of the Empire, be subject to the advice and responsibility of your Majesty's confidential servants.[15]

Ministers certainly had reason for suffering from touchy nerves. Bonaparte had just won Marengo and Moreau Hohenlinden, so that the Austrians were on their knees for the second time. The northern powers were re-constituting the old anti-British 'armed neutrality', which Russia was to join in December. The outlook by the second half of 1800 was hardly less bleak than it had been in 1797.

The King would have changed his ministry if he could, and appointed one more in tune with his own ideas of pursuing the war, these in general being nearest to the Burke*-Windham strategy and ideology. While on holiday at Weymouth that summer, he sent for Windham, and also Lord Malmesbury, who later confirmed that the King had been dissatisfied with the 'authoritative manners' of Pitt, and more still of Grenville, towards him, and had intended Windham for prime minister and Malmesbury himself for foreign minister. From the Cabinet side came complaints, also quoted by Malmesbury, that 'of late there has been much opposition in the Closet to all measures proposed by them' and that they could hardly continue 'if the question as to their real power was not distinctly ascertained'. At that time not enough support could be found for any ministry lacking Pitt, but the King's moves show well enough how disenchanted he was with his government and its policies well before Catholic Emancipation forced the issue six months later, when the King found in Addington the man he could not discover in Windham.

---

* Burke had died in 1797. His last three years had been made at least financially tolerable by the royal grant of a pension. The King had agreed to make him a peer – one more of the ironies that never ceased to pursue both men – but the bitter blow of his only son's death at that very moment made Burke decline the honour: 'They who ought to have succeeded me,' he lamented, 'have gone before.' The old man had enough fire left in him nevertheless to blaze forth with *Letters on a Regicide Peace* in 1796 – the final irony, for they largely stated, only so much more eloquently, the King's own position.

CHAPTER TWENTY-SIX

Ireland and the Catholics

THE Irish reforms introduced by North's harassed government from 1778, followed by Rockingham's grant of legislative independence in 1782, had done little to right Ireland's wrongs. Some of the worst abuses of the Penal Code against Catholics had been removed, but vital disabilities remained, and until 1793 Catholics could neither vote nor sit in Parliament. The Anglican oligarchy still ruled the roost, its dominance qualified only by the powers of the Lord Lieutenant and his ministers at Dublin Castle, themselves also of the Anglican ruling class. The Lord Lieutenant, representing the British King and Cabinet, not only wielded executive authority but nominated about one-third of the Dublin Parliament as placemen and needed the support of only a few borough-owners, not too difficult to win or if necessary to purchase, to be master of the legislature.

The French Revolution, and fear of its influence, hastened changes. In Ulster particularly, under the leadership of the Belfast lawyer Wolfe Tone, the 'United Irishmen' pinned their hopes in the early nineties on binding together the two major religious groups, Catholic and Presbyterian, under a revolutionary banner. It was an ill-fated dream. Partly perhaps to meet the Ulster danger by bidding for Catholic support, Pitt in 1793, without significant opposition from the King but having to force his measure through the Dublin Parliament, extended the forty-shilling franchise to Catholics, while still withholding their right to sit in Parliament and to hold the highest civil and military positions. Thus by giving large numbers of humble Catholics the vote, he supplied Catholics of the upper class with what might seem a reasonable grievance. If the relatively poor enjoyed the franchise, why should not rich men of the same faith represent them in Parliament? In such an aristocratic society as theirs, the argument for granting full Catholic Emancipation had been heavily reinforced; but Pitt was not yet prepared to risk travelling the whole distance.

It was the accession of the Portland Whigs to Pitt's government in 1794 that proved a catalyst for Irish developments. Whether as part of his deal with Portland, or to placate Catholic opinion, or a little of both, Pitt, again with the King's full consent, agreed to Earl Fitzwilliam, the heir to Rockingham's vast estates, patrician assumptions, and Whiggish good intentions, being sent out to Dublin as Lord Lieutenant in place of the Earl of Westmorland. There were long delays while attempts were made to find some 'handsome' post for Westmorland, who insisted – and the King agreed – that he must not appear to have been disgraced. Westmorland, who had been Lord Lieutenant since 1789, had carried through governmental policies in Ireland faithfully and efficiently, and he warned Pitt of the consequences of a sell-out to the Duke of Portland's friends; but Fitzwilliam was already before his arrival offering what an indignant Westmorland described as insults and threats to important members of his staff. When he arrived in Dublin at the beginning of January, 1795, he did not wait more than two days before setting about his dismissals of key figures in the Irish Government (the 'Dublin Castle Gang'), including Beresford, head of the revenue department and a kingpin in the old system. This portended war between the old guard and the new. When Grattan indicated that he would introduce a Catholic Emancipation bill in the Dublin Parliament, Fitzwilliam gave him every encouragement short of outright official support. Back in London even Portland was taken aback by his protégé's precipitancy; the Tory establishment wondered what young cuckoo they had fostered; and the King was so alarmed that he began that protracted consultation with his conscience that culminated in the Catholic Emancipation crisis of 1801 and the resignation of Pitt.

George's views on Ireland were as clear-cut and rigid as his views on America had been, and as uncompromisingly conservative. The limit of his horizon was the maintenance of Protestant supremacy and 'the British system'. Religious toleration was one thing, and he approved of it. Religious equality was quite another, and he not only deprecated it, but found solid reasons satisfactory to himself for rationalising his objection. The proposal to admit Catholics to Parliament, he told Pitt, was

> contrary to the conduct of every European government, and I believe to that of every state on the globe. In the states of Germany, the Lutheran, Calvinist, and Roman Catholic religions are universally permitted, yet each respective state has but one church establishment, to which the states of the country and those holding any civil employment must be conformists; Court officials and military commissions may be held also by persons of either of the other persuasions, but the number of such is very small.[1]

This was George's 1795 version of the old German Reformation principle of *cuius regio, eius religio*. He apologised to Pitt for the 'present coarse shape' of his thoughts, but since Portland was putting forward Fitzwilliam's proposals at the following day's Cabinet there had not been time to formulate his notions 'in a more digested shape'. Ireland, he went on, 'varies from most other countries by property residing almost entirely in the hands of the Protestants, whilst the lower classes of the people are chiefly Roman Catholic. The change proposed, therefore, must disoblige the greater number to benefit a few, the inferior orders not being of rank to gain favourably by the change.' To protect *them*, it appeared that Fitzwilliam and Portland were proposing 'a kind of yeomanry which in reality would be Roman Catholic police corps', to 'keep the Protestant interest under awe'. One might think they were 'actuated alone by the peevish inclination of humiliating the old friends of English government in Ireland', and Pitt ought to think very hard before encouraging 'a proposition which cannot fail sooner or later to separate the two kingdoms'. It caused George the 'greatest astonishment' that Fitzwilliam could advocate

> the total change of the principles of government which have been followed by every administration . . . since the abdication of King James the Second, and consequently overturning the fabric that the wisdom of our forefathers esteemed necessary, and which the laws of our country have directed; and thus, after no longer stay than three weeks in Ireland, venturing to condemn the labour of the ages, and wanting an immediate adoption of ideas which every man of property in Ireland and friend to the Protestant religion must feel diametrically contrary to those he has imbibed from his earliest youth . . . I cannot conclude without expressing that the subject is beyond the decision of any Cabinet of Ministers . . . without previous concert with the leading men of every order in the state . . .[2]

This long letter is quintessential George the Third. After receiving it Pitt could hardly in future allege that he was in any doubt of the intensity of royal opinions upon Ireland and the Catholics. Even a little digression towards the letter's conclusion, on the effects of Catholic Emancipation at home, is vintage George:

> It is impossible to see how far it may alienate the minds of this kingdom; for though I fear religion is but little attended by persons of rank, and that the word *toleration*, or rather *indifference*, to that sacred subject has been too much admitted by them, yet the bulk of the nation has not been spoiled by foreign travel and manners, and still feels the blessing of having a fixed principle from whence the

source of every tie to society and government must trace its origin.[3]

Fitzwilliam had obviously exceeded his instructions and raised some dangerously false hopes; but his prompt recall also, by quenching those hopes, made Irish dangers more acute than ever. When he left Dublin his carriage was drawn to the quayside through streets draped in mourning. From 1795 the drift towards rebellion was gradual but unchecked. Catholic 'Defenders' and 'Orange Lodges' wreaked mutual outrage; agrarian crime became general; British troops, dying of fever in the West Indies or thinly scattered in imperial defence posts and futile European expeditions, were not available to intervene; and the ruling oligarchy suffered recurrent fear of a French landing which would add Jacobin horrors to those already rampant. Fitzwilliam's personal protest to the King concerning his 'punishment' and offering an apologia for his political conduct, a long and eloquent document which the King described as 'rather a panegirick on himself', underlined some of the dangers now threatening:

> What time could be more proper for attaching the hearts of your people as when their best blood was to be spilled in the royal cause? What time could be more proper to unite your people to one another, than when it became the duty of your servants to disunite them from the cause and principles of your enemies . . . I would have united all your Kingdom under the Crown. I pray God, Sir, to avert the consequences of proceedings which may tend to unite too many of them under the standard of republicanism.[4]

It was now that the King began formal consultations with the law, the Church, and his private conscience. To Lord Chief Justice Kenyon, to Lord Chancellor Loughborough, and to Dr Moore, Archbishop of Canterbury, he sent copies of an exhaustive set of queries he had conceived concerning the Elizabethan Acts of Supremacy and Uniformity, the Test Act of 1679, the Bill of Rights and Act of Settlement, the 1707 Act of Union, and the 1782 Act governing the existing situation in Ireland. It seemed to him, and he asked for these gentlemen's confirmation, that it required 'very serious investigation how far the King can give his assent to a repeal of any one of these acts without a breach of his coronation oath, and of the articles of union with Scotland'. Furthermore, 'would not the Chancellor of England incur some risk in affixing the Great Seal to a bill for giving the Pope a concurrent ecclesiastical jurisdiction with the King?' To these queries the Archbishop gave the King a wholly satisfactory and compliant set of answers; the Lord Chief Justice (having consulted the Attorney General) one slightly less so; but the Lord Chancellor, while accepting the King's point concerning papal jurisdiction, assured him that the coronation oath would impose no let or hindrance against assent to an act passed by both Houses of Parliament. These learned professional opinions reinforced or at least failed to shake the King in his conviction that Catholic Emancipation would mean a breach of faith with his solemn undertakings and a repudiation of the cause for which his family was invited to mount the throne of Britain.[5]

Despite the breach between Catholics and Presbyterians, the United Irishmen had become a formidable force by 1797, and by 1798 they were perhaps 150,000 strong. The situation was such that Camden,* the Lord Lieutenant who had succeeded Fitzwilliam, decided to disarm and 'pacify' Ulster, which meant in practice flogging and burning rebellion out of the province, and letting loose upon a desperate peasantry regulars, militia, and 50,000 volunteer yeomanry officered by the Anglican gentry. That they confiscated some 50,000 muskets and 70,000 pikes seemed justification enough to the rulers of Ireland for the ruthless methods employed. Grattan and his fellow moderates were now submerged under the rising tide of violence – the double violence of political fear, Government against rebel and potential rebel, and of sectarian hatred, partisan against partisan. Among the ruling circles of both Ireland and England more and more could see no solution except in the union of the two countries; but in Ireland there were some who thought they saw better prospects in a union with France. In exile and now an adjutant-general in the French army, Wolfe Tone was dreaming of a republican Ireland freed alike of the tyranny of English exploitation and the fanaticism of religious hatred.

The first French invasion attempt failed, in December, 1796, to effect a landing. A second missed its chance during the period of the Nore mutiny in 1797. By 1798, those many Irishmen who were straining at the leash could wait no longer, and British forces under General Lake now began applying to the remainder of Ireland the licentious brutality they had earlier employed in Ulster. Inevitably their outrages were matched by counter-outrages. That there should have been a rebellion in Ireland in 1798 is hardly surprising, but that it should have been most vigorously desperate in the wholly Catholic south, where as late as 1796 a majority of the population would have taken sides, if at all, with Protestant King George against atheist Jacobin, is an eloquent commentary on what the English had done and failed to do in Ireland. At Vinegar Hill in June, 1798, the Catholic rebellion was crushed; the

* The second Earl, son of the Chathamite Earl Camden who first gained prominence over Wilkes and general warrants.

Presbyterian risings petered out shortly after. A third French invasion force was too small and arrived too late to make any difference. Wolfe Tone, who came with it and whose request to face the firing squad as a soldier was refused, committed suicide in jail.

A union of Ireland with the rest of Britain had become increasingly an arguable proposition ever since Pitt gave Catholics the vote in 1793. After the rebellion in 1798 it became for the English an imperative necessity. By no other means could the substance of Anglican domination of church and state be maintained. It was from the vested interests of the Dublin Parliament that most hostility to such a union was to be expected, but its venality would render it unlikely to resist the attractions of the bribes, financial and honorific, that Westminster and Dublin Castle could seduce it with. (Buying out the opposition cost eventually about a million and a half, and a score or so of peerages and peerage promotions.) The Government at Dublin Castle was for Union; so was the British Government; so was the King. He called Pitt's Act of Union 'one of the most useful measures that has been effected during my reign, one that will give stability to the whole Empire'. Economically too, it would do little short-term harm in Great Britain, and serve the long-term interests of Ireland, even if these could 'only arise by slow degrees'.[6] Despite the opposition of Fox's supporters the Act of Union became law by July, 1800, to take effect from January, 1801.

There was considerably less solid consensus of opinion however, when Catholic Emancipation was put forward as the corollary of Union. Yet upon this point too, successive Lords Lieutenant of Ireland (Camden and Cornwallis), the Irish Secretary (Lord Castlereagh, Camden's nephew), the British Prime Minister, and a majority of his Cabinet were all agreed. To win over the Catholic majority of Ireland there must be a final removal of their religious disabilities and inferior civic status. Catholic Emancipation, moreover, began to lose its terrors for many of the more thoughtful or calculating members of the Church of England who would earlier have opposed it when they realised that a potential voting majority in a separate Ireland would be converted by Union into a permanent Catholic minority in a united Westminster Parliament.

Why Pitt omitted to broach the Catholic problem to the King before committing himself to Emancipation remains an open question. That he *was* committed is beyond doubt. The Catholic votes that helped the passage of the Act of Union through the Irish Parliament (at the second attempt) were cast only because Catholic hopes had been deliberately flattered, and Cornwallis had gone out of his way to stress to Pitt's Government that no grounds must be afforded for any imputation of trickery. Castlereagh, his Secretary, had attended a British Cabinet meeting where Emancipation was discussed and, so he reported, he 'communicated to Lord Cornwallis that the opinion of the Cabinet was favourable to the principles of the measure . . . and in consequence of this communication the Irish Government omitted no exertion to call forth the Catholics in favour of the Union'.[7] It is conceivable that Pitt did not fully appreciate the depth of the King's disapproval of offering the Church of Rome equality with the Church of England in Parliament and in the holding of public offices. Yet his hostility to the idea had several times been unequivocally put into writing. There was the long statement of his position made at the time of the Fitzwilliam affair. Then in June, 1798, George had written to Pitt, 'No further indulgences must be granted to Roman Catholics, as no country can be governed where there is more than one established religion . . .'[8] and again in a minute of 31st January, 1799, which Pitt must have seen, George wrote 'approving the Lord Lieutenant of Ireland's being directed to use the greatest efforts to prevent an emancipation of the Roman Catholics.'[9] It may well be that Pitt and Dundas were over-confident; they had successfully gone counter to the King's expressed opinion sufficiently often during the preceding decade for them to assume that his opposition would crumble as before. There is no evidence that Pitt ever discussed his Catholic intentions with the King and attempted to win him over, or that he exercised any kind of pressure, such as a tactical threat of resignation. In any case, for such a move to be effective, a united – or at the very least an almost united – Cabinet would have been a necessary card for Pitt to hold; and during the autumn of 1800, once the Act of Union had been passed in both Parliaments, several ministers seemed to be developing doubts.

Loughborough's were the first and the strongest, and by December he had written a memorandum on the Catholic problem which it is certain that the King read,[10] though whether he discussed the matter with Loughborough, as many suspected, is far from certain. By January, 1801, other members of the Government – Westmorland, Chatham, Liverpool,* even the Duke of Portland, were all having second thoughts. Pitt's supporters in his own day, like George Rose, and his subsequent biographers, like Earl Stanhope, heaped obloquy upon Loughborough because it was assumed that he leaked to the King the secrets of Cabinet discussions; that he shifted his legal stance in order to toady to the King's prejudice; and in general schemed to

* Charles Jenkinson, Baron Hawkesbury, 1st Earl of Liverpool. He was now arthritic and frequently absent from Cabinet meetings. He declared his opposition by letter.

sink Pitt and supplant him as prime minister. He may have done, but the case is not fully proven.[11] Others too, who may have seen the King and were certainly suspected of fortifying him against Pitt's proposals were Lord Fitzgibbon, Earl of Clare (the Irish Chancellor); Loughborough's ally and relation Lord Auckland; Auckland's brother-in-law the Archbishop of Canterbury (Dr Moore); and the Primate of Ireland (Dr Stuart). Such suspicions were nothing new; back in 1798, Dundas had been telling Pitt, 'I know not who he is, but I am positive there is somebody about [the King] who does much mischief by agitating his mind and inflaming his prejudices' upon the Catholic issue.[12] As to Loughborough, undoubtedly he was a self-seeker; so too was Auckland. But the King knew their characters perfectly well, and had written them both down as intriguers years before, in Lord North's day when they went by their unennobled names of Wedderburn and Eden. Since, moreover, neither of them profited by the eventual resignation of Pitt (Loughborough in fact lost his Lord Chancellorship) it seems unlikely that George was deceived by their machinations, if any. There seems in fact no need to suppose that George's mind needed fortifying or 'poisoning' at all by anti-Catholic diehards or jealous climbers. On the question of Emancipation it had long been set like concrete. In his coronation oath he had sworn to the utmost of his power to 'maintain the Protestant reformed religion established by law', and he would not forswear that oath to smooth the policy of any minister. He would 'betray his trust and forfeit his crown' by any such perjury, so he told the Duke of Portland, who himself considered that the King would rather suffer martyrdom than yield to Catholic Emancipation.[13]

The story of the Loughborough tale-telling is thrown further in doubt when we find George telling General Budé that his ministers' intentions 'had taken him *quite by surprise, and hurt him much*', and later, writing to Lord Grenville that 'if they had openly, in the beginning, stated their opinions to me, I should have been able to avert it entirely'.[14] George's whole manner at the famous Levee on 28th January, when he suddenly announced to Windham that he would look on anyone who voted for Emancipation as 'personally indisposed' towards him, conveys the impression of someone who had just heard, unofficially and indirectly, of a decision which startled him. From Windham he moved over to Dundas and demanded, 'What is this that this young lord [Castlereagh] has brought over that they are going to throw at my head? I shall reckon any man my personal enemy who proposes any such measure – the most Jacobinical* thing I

* 'Jacobinical' might have seemed to the reformers of the Peterloo era a grotesque

ever heard of.' Dundas, attempting to argue the point, and explaining to the King that there were distinctions to be drawn between the monarch in his personal and constitutional situations, received a smart 'put-down': 'None of your Scotch metaphysics!' And when he ventured to tell the King that ministers would be writing to him on the issue in dispute, he was promptly told that they might spare themselves the trouble.[15] Although George's threat of personal enmity had a striking similarity to the form of words Lord Temple was handed in 1783 in order to rout the Fox-North coalition, the preliminaries and circumstances of the two occasions were markedly different. Pitt and Dundas, though George had often considered their actions wrongheaded, were very far from Fox and North in the royal estimation, and this time there was nothing like a conspiracy to be rid of an intolerable ministry. Certainly Addington was quite unprepared for the high office now to be thrust upon him.

He had been Speaker of the House of Commons since 1789, a likable, pedestrian, unpretentious man of conservative views, the son of that Dr Addington who had been one of the physicians called in to attend the King in 1788. Widely respected as Speaker, he had on occasions in that capacity been asked by Pitt to sit in at Cabinet meetings. He had become the prime minister's close friend, one of those very few intimates in whose company Pitt's stiffly encased private man could escape; who knew him well enough to tell him when he had already drunk more port than was good for him – which was frequently. It was to Addington that Pitt had confided (if that is the right verb for such grey and stilted sentiments) the circumstances of his rejecting the idea of marrying Eleanor Eden, Lord Auckland's daughter and the one woman whose attractions almost persuaded the statesman into committing the indiscretion of becoming a husband. It was among the Addington family that an overworked and overwrought Pitt had stayed as recently as the autumn of 1800 to find seclusion and seek recuperation. 'He wants rest and *consolation*,' the Speaker wrote to his brother Hiley Addington, 'and I trust he will find both here. The feelings towards him, not of myself, for of those I say nothing, but of others under this roof, are really not to be described.'[16]

George naturally thought of Addington, then, as of all men the one most likely to have some chance of pleading successfully with Pitt to

---

epithet to use in connection with Castlereagh. In fact – and ironically in view of the royal outburst – Pitt planned, while repealing the Test Act aimed against Catholics, to introduce what he described as 'a distinct political test, pointed against the doctrine of modern Jacobinism'. (Stanhope, *William Pitt*, iii, Appendix xxv.)

abandon the project of a Catholic Relief Bill. He possessed the further advantages of being liked and respected by the King, and of being doctrinally unshakable. He was as firm an opponent of Emancipation as George himself, if a less excitable one. Hard upon the upset at the Levee, the King wrote to him to communicate his fears. He had proof, he said, that Grenville and Dundas favoured Emancipation, and it was 'suggested by those best informed' that Pitt did too. He therefore asked Addington to go to the prime minister and try persuading him to abandon 'this most mischievous measure'. While Pitt now belatedly sent to the King a long and carefully reasoned explanation and defence of his proposals, Addington made an unsuccessful attempt to dissuade him from them. George then wrote to Pitt, offering, if only the Government would 'stave off' the Catholic question, to 'be silent also; but this restraint I shall put on myself from affection for Mr Pitt, but further I cannot go, for I cannot sacrifice my duty to any consideration.'[17]

The King's earlier consultations with Windham and Malmesbury show that, highly as he valued Pitt's talents and integrity, he did not regard him as indispensable, and now he turned to Addington and earnestly pressed him to undertake 'a new arrangement'. For a few days Addington hovered on the brink of so large an undertaking, and it was only the knowledge that Pitt would not go into opposition, and indeed Pitt's own urgent encouragement, that decided him. 'I see nothing but ruin,' Pitt is reported telling him, 'if you hesitate.'[18] And Addington, modest as he was, was not so self-effacing and unambitious that he could remain unstirred by the prospect before him, in the service of a monarch whom he venerated. On 5th February he accepted office, and five days later, when his prospective ministry was seen to be a practicable proposition, he was perhaps surprised, but one must suppose warmed, to find himself embraced by the King, who declared, 'My dear Addington, you have saved your country.' Pitt put up no resistance on behalf of the Irish Catholics, who were left to feel duped, and had to wait another twenty-eight years before they extracted from Peel and Wellington a less generous measure of emancipation than that envisaged by the 1801 proposals, which besides allowing Catholics to sit in Parliament and hold public office, would have taken in the tithe problem and financial provision for the Catholic priesthood as well. Pitt made no constitutional issue of his differences with the King. Indeed, with a divided Cabinet, a doubtful Commons, and a more than doubtful Lords; with the Primates of England and Ireland, the bench of Bishops, and both the English and Irish Lord Chancellors against him; and behind all these a public opinion as strongly prejudiced against equality for Catholics as the King – it would have been a most dangerous subject to make an issue of. But there is no indication that he ever even contemplated it. He behaved, the King allowed, most honourably, 'like himself'. He stayed on to see his 1801 Budget through, and smoothed Addington's path, at this early stage, in every possible way. When, after seventeen years, he departed – and the King plainly assumed it was the end of his career – he even received, for the first and only time, a note from the Palace beginning 'My dear Pitt', a unique mark of cordiality, and perhaps too, of relief.[19]

Shedding the burdens of office may have given some temporary relief also to Pitt – George Rose the following week reported scarcely ever having seen him in higher spirits, though it was not long before a contrary report came from Lord Malmesbury, who found him 'unwell . . ., shaken, gouty, and nervous'. And increasingly as the months passed, he came to feel what a denial of the natural order it was that an Addington should be in command of the nation's affairs while he, a Pitt, was out of employment. His loyal attachment to the new prime minister was soon to labour under the severest strain.

Suddenly, on 13th February, the King went down with biliousness, a heavy cold, and hoarseness of voice. These preliminary signs seemed ominously like those of the autumn of 1788, and whether mental agitation over the Catholic question had precipitated this new attack must remain surmise. Certainly George himself thought it had. Every day now he was visited by Addington, who found his manner of speech affectionate, but also, unfortunately, 'affected'. 'My bodily health is reasonably good,' George told him; 'I have (I trust) good common sense, and I believe a good heart, but my nerves are weak, I am sensible of that. Your father said twelve years ago that quiet was what I wanted, and that I must have.' On the 17th, Addington observed that the King's 'manner was more hurried and his countenance more heated than usual'; yet he was still perfectly lucid on that day, and on the next too in conversation with the Duke of Portland. Lord Eldon, Loughborough's successor-designate as Chancellor, had several hours' talk with him following his first meeting with his new ministers-to-be, 'and never saw him in a state to talk more rationally.'[20] Deterioration was rapid, however, and when the Rev. Thomas Willis called on 21st February (it appears purely as an acquaintance of the royal family) he noted all the danger signs and found the King pathetically aware of what might be in store for him. He told Willis,

I do feel myself very ill, I am much weaker than I was, and I have prayed to God all night that I might die, or that he would spare my reason . . . If it should be otherwise, for God's sake keep me from your father and a regency.[21]

There was all the old hurry in his conversation as he grabbed hold of Willis's arm and marched him round the room, trying to tell him of the previous day's Privy Council meeting, and quite unable to finish one sentence before the next was begun.

By that night he was wandering about half-undressed, confused and delirious; and it took Thomas Willis and the two doctors in attendance, Gisborne and Reynolds, an hour and a half to get him to bed; where, however, he would not stay but, as in 1788, made for the Queen's bedroom. Princess Elizabeth, writing on behalf of the distracted Queen, 'begged Mr Addington would do what he thought best.' By the following day Willis reinforcements had been brought up, and the Willis régime was in full force once more, directed now entirely by the second generation – the Rev. Thomas, and Drs John and Robert, the three sons of the now octogenarian Dr Francis Willis. The King was so desperately ill that all the professional opinion was that 'there was no room to fear of a lasting derangement of intellect; that he would either recover, or sink under the illness'.[22]

The political situation was peculiarly anomalous, for Addington's government was still neither fully manned nor officially invested with authority, and when, with once again the question arising of a regency, the Prince of Wales sent for Addington, he was cautiously advised to see Pitt also, 'as his father's actual minister.' Fortunately Pitt and Addington were still upon intimate terms and therefore there was nothing like a repetition of the distressing regency contest of twelve years before. The Prince now behaved 'with the greatest civility and propriety', both to Addington and to Pitt, who had no difficulty in getting him to agree not to consort with the opposition, and to accept without demur the restricted regency bill of 1789.[23] None of all this prevented the opposition Whigs from entertaining private hopes, but Fox, Sheridan, and Grey steered rash spirits away from reviving earlier acrimonies.

At Buckingham House, while Drs Gisborne and Reynolds, and Drs John and Robert Willis (with their alarming madhouse attendants) remained in medical supervision of the sickroom, the Rev. Thomas Willis exercised a more general control. He even, quite improperly, procured the royal assent to an Act of Parliament (the repeal of the Brown Bread Act) during an interval of relative calm. Loughborough,

still officially Chancellor, had brought the necessary document, but
was not allowed with it into the King's bedroom. The Rev. Thomas,
therefore, who, unlike his brothers, at this point still enjoyed the
King's confidence, persuaded him 'for the sake of his people' to sign –
even though this meant proceeding in two stages, one for the *George*,
which 'he immediately wrote very well', and one for the R, which required time and patience. 'If it be necessary,' Willis reported him as
declaring, 'I will write as good an R as ever I did.'[24] Since the King
was in no fit state to receive visitors, and not even the Queen or the
Princesses were permitted to go near the sickroom, the Rev. 'Dr'
Willis became briefly a most important person, so much so that George
Rose commented that executive government seemed '*pro tanto*, in the
hands of that gentleman'.[25] All through the last week of February the
King continued gravely ill, though Pitt reported him a little better on
the 27th, and on the 28th Addington told his friend Charles Abbot
(soon to be Speaker Abbot) that the patient had

> slept two and a half hours last night uninterruptedly and that his
> former mode of talking, his 'What, what, what?' returns. He un-
> dresses himself in the usual way, and eats as usual. They now give
> him bark and port wine. Mr Pitt thinks it unnecesary to deliberate
> on modes of Regency, etc. . . . The Willises think the King may
> recover very speedily indeed; at a reasonable allowance within ten
> days, and to a certainty within three weeks.[26]

Within a day or two, however, there was another serious relapse,
with a pulse of 136 and, following an application of hot vinegar and
water to the feet, so great an exhaustion that for a time death was expected. The Prince of Wales, the Duke of York, and the prime minister
were summoned. But once again there was a recovery. For medicines
they gave him musk and 'bark'. Then Mr Addington remembered that
a pillow of warm hops was reckoned a good old remedy for insomnia,
whereupon they made one up and the King slept on it for over eight
hours at a stretch, thus in an original manner demonstrating anew his
faith in Addington personally and traditional doctrine generally. He
awoke to inquire very rationally how long he had been ill, and why he
was in a different bed. When they told him it was Princess Mary's, he
was sorry, he said, to incommode her. Pitt considered the patient's
improvement 'extraordinary', and crowds gathered outside the
Queen's House to rejoice at the good news. But unfortunately it was
only relatively good, for very unpleasant symptoms persisted: 'in-
sensibility and stupor', 'extreme nervous irritability', inability to swallow, retching, clenching of teeth, renewed insomnia. For another week

he was ill enough for a daily bulletin to be posted. Yet though it was erratic, there was now a slow continuing improvement, despite the intervention of tartar emetics and the maintenance of a starvation diet to curb the fever. He was allowed to see the Queen again on 6th March, and played 'three parties of piquet'; and the following day was visited by the Duke of York, of whom he inquired the latest political news. Had there been any resignations? he wanted to know. Frederick putting him off with an evasion, he was told: 'Frederick, you are more nervous than I am. I really feel quite well, and know full well how ill I have been.'[27] The next visitors – still with Thomas Willis present in the room, however – were the Prince of Wales and the Duke of Kent. Everybody, the Prince told his father, had been to the Queen's House to inquire after his progress; and the King was gratified to notice that even Sheridan had been among the callers. Sheridan's stock had already risen after he had so deftly improvised the loyal demonstration from the stage of Drury Lane after the Hadfield assassination attempt a few months before, and now George was inclined to believe that, Prince's man though he was, Sheridan 'had a respect and regard for him'. He did not, he said, notice Fox's name among the others in the visitors' book – though in fact in due course it did appear there. Generally it was conceded that this time the King's sons had behaved well. 'Indeed, everybody has behaved well, even Opposition,' wrote Lady Malmesbury to Lady Minto.[28]

Recovery from gross derangement and acute danger had been swifter in 1801 than 1789, but the King was for many weeks debilitated, irritable, and unaccountable in his behaviour, and showed, according to Drs Macalpine and Hunter, 'what are today recognised as the cardinal signs of organic impairment of the brain.'[29] He could not keep his hands still; 'his state of nerves seemed to compel him to roll up his handkerchiefs,' some days as many as forty or fifty; he frequently, when trying to concentrate, collapsed in puzzlement and perplexity; he would break helplessly into tears. Seeing himself in the mirror, which had been covered with green baize during his illness, he complained of its faulty reflection. He did not recognise the man he saw, and all his visitors noticed his pallor and thinness. His eyes, too, which had suffered from his previous illness, now began to grow much worse. For a long time fever was recurrent; so too were his intestinal attacks. Yet he was officially 'well'; bulletins had ceased; and on 17th March, he even presided at an urgently necessary meeting of the Privy Council. The very incomplete nature of his recovery posed ministers, and Addington in particular, with all kinds of problems. The Government was contemplating, for instance, renewed negotiations for a peace treaty with the French, but Addington dared not go to the King for the authorisation that would normally be required before such a move. In a quandary, he did what Loughborough had sensibly but 'unconstitutionally' done earlier – worked through the lord of the sickroom, Thomas Willis, who procured the requisite approval, if only after a long delay which arose, said Willis, not from 'any disinclination . . . but from a restlessness and an eagerness to talk'.[30]

The slowness of the King's recovery inevitably caused fresh discussion of a possible regency. The Willises, in fact, used this possibility as a weapon in their treatment, as their father had earlier used the threat of a strait-jacket. If the King did not behave, they would recommend a parliamentary inquiry into his condition, and Addington for one was seriously afraid there well might have to be one. All the royal family, however, agreed, as Charles Abbot wrote: 'A regency would overset him for life.'[31] Abbot thought the King's mind and letter-writing 'as good as ever', though there was great physical weakness. Despite this, however, the Willises continued to assault their unlucky patient with emetics and blisters, while feeding Addington with stories of his improvement. It was the Willis triumvirate who were now the arbiters. It was they who persuaded the Queen that the King would be well enough to attend a Drawing Room on 26th March. It was the Willises who intrigued quietly with the Duke of York to prevent the Prince of Wales or the Duke of Kent from getting to hear too much, since they thought it 'unnecessary that His Royal Highness should know everything'. And it had been through Thomas Willis, acting as royal amanuensis, that the notorious message was earlier conveyed to Pitt, who had inquired after the King's condition: 'Tell him I am quite well – quite recovered from my illness; but what has he not to answer for, who is the cause of my being ill at all?' (At the onset of his attack, he had voiced a very similar sentiment to Lord Chatham: 'As to my cold, that is well enough; but what else I have I owe to your brother.')

Such reproofs as this could hardly fail to shake Pitt, who in the presence of Addington authorised Willis to return to the King the message that he would never again during the reign 'agitate the Catholic question, that is, whether *in* office or *out* of office'. From this pledge, of which Pitt made no secret, he never retreated.[32]

CHAPTER TWENTY-SEVEN

Public Postures and Private Distresses

(1801-1804)

THE Queen's Drawing Room of 26th March, intended to show the world that the patient had recovered, proved more like a funeral wake, for the King after all was prevented by the Willises from attending, suffering two painful blisterings on the morning of the event. Everybody present could see there had been a family crisis. The Queen, Lady Malmesbury noted, 'looked like death,' and all the Princesses were 'crying and the picture of despair'. Approaching sixty, querulous and difficult and ill, Charlotte, who had been manœuvred into holding the function, was quite unjustly criticised for allowing it at all,[1] and it was either naïve or disingenuous of Thomas Willis later to express surprise that she 'imbibed a prejudice' against his two brothers and himself. Princess Elizabeth plainly did not share any such prejudice. Signing herself 'your friend', she assured him, 'We are not a little thankful to you for all the trouble you take for us,' and she only hoped that God would grant her father's 'eyes may soon open, and that he may see his real and true friends in their true colours!'[2] The Willises were more philosophical about the *King*'s hating them, since, with his mental condition still uncertain, he was in the irksome state of being 'too well to be confined yet not well enough to be wholly at liberty'. He was, however, well enough to make a very strong complaint concerning them to Addington, who encouraged him to take a firm stand and send them away. What he needed most, Addington thought, was plenty of asses' milk, whose excellent restorative virtues were universally attested. The Willises' services were accordingly dispensed with. On 16th April, the King slept once more in the Queen's bedroom, and two days later took an early morning fancy to ride over to Blackheath to visit a surprised Princess of Wales and her little daughter, 'never telling anyone where he was going till he turned up at the Princess's door,' arriving before she was up and dressed. She had been on his mind, he told her, throughout his illness;[3] and indeed over the succeeding months he did harp constantly on the Princess and her situation, to the distress of the Queen, who was an uncompromising partisan for the Prince of Wales

against his wife, and had 'the most fervent wish' that her husband
might 'do nothing to form a breach' between himself and his heir.[4]

The Willises, however, who took their responsibilities and family
reputation very seriously, were not yet finished with. Left with her
daughters, and with a still unpredictable charge, the Queen took fright,
and Princess Elizabeth wrote to Thomas Willis asking him and his
brothers to come back. But before they could take control, the King
had slipped off to Kew, where he planned to stay till he could go to
Weymouth for the summer. In hot and conscientious pursuit therefore
to Kew the three Willises, their four assistants, and Dr Gisborne re-
paired, and in the Dutch ('Prince of Wales's') House adjoining the
Palace waylaid their truant monarch by stratagem and took possession
of his person. 'The King sat down,' runs Thomas Willis's narrative,
'turning very pale and . . . exclaimed, "Sir, I will never forgive you
whilst I live".'[5] For another month or so George performed his kingly
duties by messenger, wrote as lucidly as usual to his ministers, signed
documents as required, took the air in the Gardens, read books, played
cards and chess – but always under the surveillance of one of the
Willises or their men. At last on 19th May, he told Lord Eldon that
'as a gentleman and a king', he absolutely refused 'to sign his name to
any paper or to do one act of government whatever' unless he were
allowed to exist as a free man; a determination which he forthwith
celebrated by walking across the lawn to pay his compliments to the
Queen on her birthday.[6] Two days later he presided at a Privy Council
meeting, and on 31st May, wrote to his valued old friend Dr Hurd,
Bishop of Worcester:

> I have most wonderfully escaped the jaws of death . . . I can now
> assure you that my health is daily improving, though I cannot boast
> of the same strength and spirits I enjoyed before. Still, with quiet
> and sea-bathing, I trust they will soon be regained. Public events in
> every part of the globe appear more favourable, and the hand of
> Divine Providence seems stretched forth to protect this favoured
> island, which alone has stood forth constantly in opposition to our
> wicked neighbours. I flatter myself, the fact of having a ministry
> composed of men of religion and great probity will tend to the
> restoration of more decorum . . .[7]

Sometimes now, pleasing himself when and where and to whom he
rode out ('his Majesty still talks much of his prudence, but shows
none . . . he is not so right as he should be,' wrote Willis), he would go
the few miles into Richmond Park, where he enjoyed overseeing the
repairs and improvements being undertaken at George I's old hunting

lodge, known as the Stone Lodge or White Lodge, which he now presented as a gift to the head of this decorous new ministry. He wished Addington to take it with sixty acres of park and gardens, but Addington protested he would be happier with five.* [8] The prime minister was being favoured in these early days of his administration, not only by the King who was genuinely attached to him, but by good fortune too in the war. The 'favourable public events in every part of the globe', ascribed to the divine hand in the King's letter to Dr Hurd, included the assassination of the Tsar Paul, Nelson's victory at Copenhagen, the collapse of the armed neutrality of the northern powers, and Abercromby's defeat of the French in Egypt. Addington could perhaps claim little personal share in these strokes, but it may be that mediocre men deserve a little luck.

By the end of June the King was ready to set off for his holiday convalescence at Weymouth, with the Queen, the Princesses, and Prince Adolphus, on his way making a short break at Cuffnells with George Rose, another of the politicians whose company he enjoyed. Before he left Kew he had to fight one more battle to remain free of the Willises. The Lord Chancellor had been persuaded to write to him that one of them, 'at least for the present,' should travel with the royal party. George rebelled. He would have Dr Gisborne or Sir Francis Milman if necessary, but the idea of Dr Robert Willis he would 'in the strongest manner decline'. [9] It was at Cuffnells that George Rose, who like Canning was a devout Pittite, informed the King of Pitt's calamitous personal finances – he had managed the nation's so infinitely better than his own – whereupon George immediately offered to rescue him from debt as he had once rescued Lord North. Wisely perhaps, Pitt declined royal assistance, though he was relieved enough (as Fox had been in a like predicament) to accept that of his friends. At Lymington the King, to the alarm of George Rose, who was feeling his responsibilities, got wet through in a heavy shower, 'and no entreaties could prevail with him to put on a great coat'; but no ill results ensued and, arrived at Weymouth, George wrote to Eldon and Addington that he was sleeping perfectly, had done with medicines, and so long as he avoided

* Canning, who idolised Pitt and despised Addington with the smart man's contempt for the plodder, christened White Lodge *Villa Medici*, from Addington's nickname of 'The Doctor', which arose either by association with his father's profession or since his well-publicised suggestion for promoting the King's sleep by using a hop-pillow. It was of course Canning too who perpetrated the all-too-memorable little rhyme about Addington and Paddington. For a prime minister to be a mere doctor's son was regarded by some of the bluer-blooded as itself a subject for mirth – much as Canning himself was never quite allowed to live down being the son of an actress.

'hurry' remained well. As usual, he persuaded himself that the effects of sea-bathing were beneficial. Even after he had returned to Windsor, however, he confessed to Dr Hurd that he still suffered 'many unpleasant sensations', tired quickly, and was 'forced to be very careful'.[10] The diplomat, Lord Malmesbury, seeing him at the end of November, noticed that he stooped rather more than before and seemed less firm on his legs, but found no 'marks of sickness or decline in his countenance and manner'. The King, Malmesbury recalled from his thirty years' acquaintance, had always been an attentive listener, 'full as ready to hear as to give an opinion, though perhaps not always disposed to adopt it and forsake his own,' but now he seemed to be less hurried and more 'conversable'; he allowed 'the person to whom he addressed himself more time to answer and talk than he used to do'.[11]

On this visit Malmesbury made one of the Queen's cribbage party; was taken by the charm of Princess Mary; and also stood two full hours talking alone with the King. Addington's Government had just agreed the preliminaries of peace (which emerged as the Treaty of Amiens the following March), and Malmesbury found the King speaking 'friendly of Pitt', who supported the terms, but expressing 'strong resentment against Lord Grenville', who like Windham was attacking them as a surrender to Bonaparte. In fact George's own views on the Peace were not very dissimilar from Grenville's or Windham's, but he always tended to equate opposition with faction, and while lacking any faith in the durability of the settlement, had approved Addington's efforts to achieve it. 'Do you know what I call the Peace?' he asked Malmesbury ' – an *experimental* Peace, for it is nothing else. But it was unavoidable. I was abandoned by everybody, allies and *all*. I have done, I conscientiously believe, for the best, because I could not do otherwise.' The use of the first person emphasises how little, still, George was inclined to regard himself as a cipher; and his next words – with their implied criticism of Pitt and Dundas – Malmesbury, that old hand in the business of diplomacy and European negotiation, would have well understood: 'Had I found more opinion like mine, better might have been done.' The King did not add, though he perhaps should have done, that public opinion had played at least as large a part as the dereliction of allies in making imperative some attempt to reach peace, for food scarcity and high prices had hit the poor severely; taxes were high, frustration and war weariness general. The Peace of Amiens briefly succeeded in uniting behind it such opposites as Addington and Sheridan, Pitt and Fox. Nobody but Fox threw his hat in the air, since it left France formidably strong; but in 1801 a bad peace was felt to be better than a bad war. George accepted it with resigned scepticism and doubted

> whether any confidence can be placed in any agreement made with that country [France] till it has a settled Government . . . [The King] will not oppose the concluding peace though he cannot place any reliance on its duration but trusts such a peace establishment will be kept up as may keep this country on a respectable footing without which our situation would be most deplorable.[12]

Addington enjoyed one relatively calm and unharassed year, 1802, with the comfort of support from Pitt, from the King, and from a public glad to be freed from the unpropitious war. It was not long, however, before the 'experiment' of the Peace was seen to be as fragile as the King had reckoned it. When Britain protested at new French aggressions against Piedmont, Holland, and Switzerland, Bonaparte reminded her that she had by the Treaty specifically renounced Continental interests outside Naples and Portugal. Addington's Government nevertheless took these new evidences of French intentions as a good enough reason for not evacuating Malta, as promised under the Treaty, and by the close of 1802 was again asking Parliament for funds to increase the establishment of the army and navy. Addington and Hawkesbury,* generally written off as second-rate men, proved unexpectedly anxious to show that they could take as tough a line as any; as tough, in fact, as the King expected of them. They presented Bonaparte with new demands, which as far as Malta was concerned proposed treating the Peace of Amiens as a dead letter; and when these were rejected, declared war in May, 1803. One of its immediate consequences was the loss of Hanover, which George seemed to accept with a surprising degree of equanimity.

From the middle of 1803 to the middle of 1804, England was once more threatened with invasion, more ominously than before in view of the strength of the Grand Army across the Channel, less ominously only in the much improved strength and morale of the Navy as compared with 1779 or 1797. And if the nation had lost its taste for war by 1801, by 1803 after two good harvests and a breather, with a growing awareness of the megalomaniac insatiability of Bonaparte's ambitions, and above all quickened by the spur of national danger, it had rediscovered a fighting spirit. Volunteer and Yeomanry corps sprouted universally, with 380,000 men enrolled by early December, 1803, marching and drilling with conscientious fervour.[13] Pitt might no longer

---

* Robert Banks Jenkinson, Baron Hawkesbury, later second Earl of Liverpool; heir of Charles Jenkinson, first Earl; prime minister, 1812-27.

be prime minister (convinced though he now was that the time for his
return was overdue), yet still as Lord Warden of the Cinque Ports he
could put his stiff unmartial figure at the head of three thousand local
defenders of the national soil. Wordsworth, far removed now from the
radical enthusiast who had thought it very heaven to be young in the
Revolution's dawn, was exhorting his countrymen to show their
mettle:

> *Vanguard of Liberty! Ye men of Kent,*
> *Ye children of a soil that doth advance*
> *Its haughty brow against the coast of France,*
> *Now is the time to prove your hardiment.*

Coastal defences were busily prepared; the new Martello towers sprang
up in large numbers along the shores of the southern and eastern
counties, despite the blue-water opinion of such as Thomas Campbell,
who sang that Britannia and the mariners of England needed no such
bulwarks, 'no towers along the steep.' The King held a contrary view.
Martello towers were 'capital things', he pronounced; they ought to
have some at Weymouth. He was now of course in his element, as he
had been in 1779, visiting Volunteer camps, viewing and inspecting
Yeomanry parades, stimulating the enthusiasm and encouraging the
defiance of a nation which in general felt much as he did about 'the
Corsican usurper'. The climax of all these warlike civilian preparations
came in October with a grand parade in Hyde Park where George,
attended by his seven sons on horseback and his womenfolk in carriages, reviewed the City of London Volunteers, and 'on quitting the
ground was followed to the Queen's Palace by a vast multitude of
people, who rent the air with their cheers and huzzas'.[14] Two days later
there was a not less numerous turn-out for the combined Westminster,
Lambeth, and Southwark review.

Even Fox no longer whitewashed Bonaparte in quite his old uncritical manner, but moved on to less shaky and more orthodox
opposition ground, condemning the inadequacy of Addington's military preparations. He continued to attack as 'detestable hypocrisy'
the ideological view of the war associated with Windham, and of
course with the King too: 'I do sincerely hope, sir,' he declared in the
Commons, 'that we shall hear nothing more of wars undertaken for
religion, or of the blessings of social order . . . while we were all along
fighting for ends of a nature totally opposite.' The Prince of Wales, to
whom the ship of Fox's fortunes had once been moored, and was soon
to be so again ('the worst anchoring ground in Europe,' it was observed), now renewed his old request, so many times rejected by King

and ministers, for high military rank. What would the country think of him, he asked, if he was not allowed to stand forth, and play his part in 'exciting the loyal energies of the nation?' – and in the Commons, Fox and some of his supporters backed the Prince's request. On 6th August, he wrote direct to his father: 'I ask to be allowed to display the best energies of my character; to shed the last drop of my blood in support of your Majesty's person, crown, and dignity.' The King's dusty answer came straight back:

> Though I applaud your zeal and spirit, of which, I trust, no one can suppose any of my family wanting, yet, considering the repeated declarations I have made of my determination on your former applications to the same purpose, I had flattered myself to have heard no further on the subject. Should the implacable enemy so far succeed as to land, you will have the opportunity of showing your zeal at the head of your regiment. It will be the duty of every man to stand forth on such an occasion; and I shall certainly think it mine to set an example in defence of everything that is dear to me and to my people.[15]

Not willing to take this further rejection for a final answer, the Prince of Wales expostulated on the injustice of a situation where his younger brothers were at least Generals or Lieutenant Generals,* while he remained a mere Colonel of Dragoons. Up against the same unyielding wall, eternally resentful on this subject, and anxious to prove his loyalty to the public, the Prince caused the exchange of letters to be published in the *Morning Chronicle* of 7th December, 1803. The King never forgave him for it – 'the publisher of *my* letters' – and the breach between the monarch and his heir, which Queen Charlotte and the Princesses had done their best to lessen, was once more as gaping and as public as ever.

If Bonaparte should invade, the King had made his dispositions. He would put himself 'at the head of his troops', either at Dartford if the landing were to come in Kent, or at Chelmsford if in Essex, and from there endeavour to 'repel the usurper's forces'.† Lord Cornwallis was 'to take command of the central army, being the real reserve of the Volunteers and all the producible force of the kingdom, in case the French made any impression on the coast'. However, as George wrote to his esteemed old Bishop of Worcester,

---

* He overlooked the Duke of Clarence, who was simultaneously a sort of Admiral and a sort of private with the Teddington Volunteers (*Annual Register* of 1803, 422).

† 'The King certainly has his camp equipage and accoutrements quite ready for

Should the enemy approach too near to Windsor, I shall think it right the Queen and my daughters should cross the Severn, and shall send them to your Episcopal Palace at Worcester. By this hint I do not in the least mean they shall be any inconvenience to you, and shall send a proper servant and furniture for their accommodation. Should such an event arise, I certainly would rather that what I value most in life should remain during the conflict in your diocese and under your roof, than in any other place in the island.[16]

Less than seven weeks after writing this letter, the King showed the early signs of what was to prove the third major attack of porphyria to affect his reason. By mid-January, 1804, the preliminary symptoms were there again – a cold, 'a slight attack of gout in the foot,' lameness, and 'hurry'. The physician in attendance at Buckingham House told Lord Eldon that while the King needed the exercise of his walks in the garden, his family were afraid of going with him – in itself an ominous straw in the wind – and that if he, the doctor, did so, the two of them were unpleasantly conscious of being overlooked from the windows of Grosvenor Place, from where malicious and false reports of the King's eccentric and violent behaviour were being fed to the Press. Lord Eldon therefore volunteered to accompany him round the grounds himself, if his Majesty were pleased to allow it.

'With all my heart,' I overheard the King say, and he called for his hat and cane. We walked two or three times round Buckingham House Gardens. There was at first a momentary hurry and incoherence in his Majesty's talk, but this did not endure two minutes. During the rest of the walk there was not the slightest aberration . . . and he gave me the history of every administration in the reign. When we returned into the house, his Majesty, laying down his hat and cane, placed his head upon my shoulder and burst into tears.[17]

In mid-February he suddenly became much worse. 'Yesterday,' recorded Abbot on the 14th, 'the fever was very high. He talked for five hours incessantly last night. His head at times much affected.' And three days later Abbot wrote:

The King had foreseen his illness coming on, and had made arrangements in case of his death. For a short time he suffered a sort of

---

joining the army if the enemy should land, and he is quite keen on the subject and angry if any suggests that the attempt may not be made . . . God forbid he should have the fate of Harold . . .' (Glenbervie Journals, i, 361).

paralysis, which created great apprehensions for his life; but there soon appeared no ground for that alarm. The disorder has now taken the decided character of a complete mental derangement. His health, however, is better now than it was at the commencement of his illness in 1801. The Willises have not yet been introduced; that remains to be done. Mr Addington desired me to contradict absolutely the assertion in the public papers that he, Mr Addington, has been averse to the Willises being introduced. On the contrary, he had from the first said that, so soon as it was said to be proper, he would take them in his own carriage. The Queen and family had put themselves entirely in the hands of the Minister . . . The Willises were now waiting in his (Mr Addington's) house.[18]

However, as Abbot added a few hours later, 'the going of the Willises to the Queen's House was postponed unavoidably.' There had in fact, from the 13th to the 17th February, been a protracted confrontation between, on the one side, Addington's Cabinet and the Willises, and on the other the Dukes of Kent and Cumberland, supported by the physicians Sir Francis Milman and William Heberden, junior. Kent firmly informed Addington that the King, when fully sane after his illness of 1801, had solemnly engaged his brother and himself, if another attack were to present itself, to prevent *any and every* member of the Willis family from being placed about him. Perhaps the view jointly expressed by Milman and Heberden that seeing the Willises might well cause the King's death finally decided the Cabinet. Dr Samuel Simmons, of St Luke's Hospital for Lunaticks, was called in instead.

His administrations, though the King seems at first to have suffered them rather more philosophically than those of the Willises, were hardly less rigorous. Speaker Abbot, and presumably his friend the prime minister, thought the King 'perfectly contented' under his management; but George himself was soon referring to him as 'that horrible' Doctor Simmons. He can hardly be expected to have shown much enthusiasm for a man who, attended by strong-arm assistants, regularly forced him into a strait-jacket.[19]

A somewhat odd feature of this attack of the royal malady was that its earlier stages coincided with a serious illness at Brighton of the Prince of Wales, whose troubles very probably arose from the self-same biochemical abnormality. It is indeed a remarkable fact that not only on this occasion, but also early in 1811 when his father's collapse enforced a regency, and again early in 1820, during the weeks of his father's impending death, the Prince of Wales was alarmingly ill – in

1820, so desperately that many expected a double funeral; one might say a triple funeral, for the Duke of Kent died only six days before his father. It may of course have been coincidence merely, for the Prince of Wales was ill on very many occasions, more than once dangerously so; he was moreover frequently thought by those near him to be going, or even at last to have gone, mad; but it seems to be at least possible that the Prince's illness of January, 1804, may have arisen from the same condition of vexation and stress as his father's, and from the same cause of that condition – the quarrel over military rank and the publication of the royal correspondence in December. Sheridan even declared that 'his life was despair'd of for two days'.[20] By the latter part of February, however, he was sufficiently recovered to consult Addington repeatedly concerning his father's afflictions – though 'nothing has passed on political subjects', Abbot wrote, 'and the Prince has professedly abstained from them.'[21] The key word here is 'professedly'.

As in 1801, although the King was soon pronounced out of danger, his progress was disappointingly erratic; and especially in private, among his own family, he long proved desperately difficult to live with. By the beginning of March, however, the physicians having been formally examined by the Cabinet, he was declared competent both to sign documents and transact business with his Parliament 'by commission and message'. In public life he was soon back in the swim of affairs, where the Prince of Wales's supporters, having had the prospect of a regency dangled once more before them, were now aiming at a ministry headed by the chief of them, Lord Moira. The other three main groups outside the Government party – Foxites, Grenvilles, and Pittites – were agreed at least on one thing: Addington was not the man to lead his country in a life and death struggle with Bonaparte. Pitt's own nominee for the man who *was* fit was not difficult to discover. As he wrote to Dundas* – and he had earlier delivered much the same message to a rather wounded Addington – 'You will not I think wonder at my saying that I do not see how, under any circumstances, I can creditably or usefully consent to take part in any Government without being the head of it; and I should be very sorry that either Lord Moira, or through him the Prince, should suppose that there is any chance of my changing my opinion on this point.'[22] That was the authentic Pitt voice; and studded with calamity as his earlier war record had been, most politicians were again ready to take him at something approaching his own valuation and agree that he must resume as prime minister.

* Raised to the peerage in 1802 as Viscount Melville.

The King was personally on the best of terms with Addington still, and would have liked to retain him in office. He may not have impressed in the House; his speeches ranged from the insipid to the pompous; but he had not been incompetent. 'Can I do nothing to reconcile you and Mr Pitt?' George asked him. But he recognised the strength of the demand for Pitt, not least from Pitt himself who, when he wrote to the King in April, 1804, made it clear that he would insist on Addington's removal. Addington, his majorities dwindling, had in any case determined to resign. If the King were to have Pitt back again, however, it was only to be on well understood terms; and Pitt, somewhat to mollify the still unpredictable King and remembering 1801, promised to avoid committing himself 'to any engagement the effects of which would be likely to occasion, in any contingency, a sentiment of dissatisfaction or uneasiness in your Majesty's mind'.[23] This was to be understood to mean certainly no Catholic proposals, and perhaps no Fox, though it was known that Pitt was ready to head a grand coalition of parties, not excluding even Fox.

Lord Eldon handed the King Pitt's suggestions for a new administration on 27th April. On the 29th, Abbot quoted Addington as saying, 'The King dreads a defeat of his ministry in Parliament as the forerunner of a Regency. To keep his health safe is the cause of the country.' George's reply to Pitt, however, does not read like the letter of a man on the brink of mental incapacity. Obdurate on the expected issues, it was still measured, rational, and tough. He lamented that Pitt had taken 'so rooted a dislike' to Addington, who had 'handsomely come forward to support his King and country when the most ill-digested and dangerous proposition was brought forward by the enemies of the Established Church'. He would therefore demand 'strong assurances' from Mr Pitt against any attack on 'the palladium of our Church Establishment'. As for Fox, he could only express 'astonishment' that Pitt could even bring such a man before his royal notice; and if he pressed Fox's claims (which Pitt had not the slightest intention of doing) the King would have to look elsewhere, and 'call for the assistance of such men as are truly attached to our happy constitution'. Pitt replied in a masterly letter of tactful self-exculpation, lamenting in his turn 'the unfavourable impression which your Majesty seems to entertain respecting parts of my conduct'; but when he went to the Queen's House for an audience on 7th May, he was delighted – though as he confessed baffled – to find the King all graciousness and willingness to accept his suggestions. He would accept Grenville and his followers; he would accept the Foxites; he would even accept Fox *as an ambassador* – as a minister he was of course unthinkable. When Pitt remarked how much better the King looked than after his recovery in 1801, he received the perfect retort courteous: 'That was not to be wondered at, as he was then on the point of *parting* with an old friend, and he was now about to *regain* one.'[24] In the event Lord Grenville and his supporters did not accept Pitt's invitation to join him, and the Foxites stayed out because their leader was blackballed. The project, therefore, of a 'ministry of all the talents' had to wait. What appeared to concern the King, however, more than these groups remaining in opposition was the fact that to come to their decision the followers of Fox held their meeting at *Carlton House*.

His continuing illness seemed by no means either to have deprived the King of his appreciation of political niceties or to have weakened his determination to hold on to what he considered essential royal rights. His political behaviour during 1804 was not that of an irremediably enfeebled man. Yet in many respects that was what he now was, physically and mentally; and the effects of that deterioration, masked somewhat to the public and the politicians, bore sadly upon his personal life and domestic relationships.

The King's first derangement in 1788-89, with all its attendant family and political bitterness, had brought the Queen near to breakdown. She had taken time to recover. Perhaps indeed she never did fully recover, even after that first attack. The Court had been a battlefield. The King had been violent, and might become violent again if the illness struck again. When it did in 1801, she was clearly frightened, mentally and perhaps physically too. Plainly there was no great outflow of protective tenderness towards her husband – and there is indeed considerable agreement in the testimony of her sons and daughters during the last twenty years of her life that tenderness and affection did not by then rank highest among her qualities. Such love as she retained for the King – and this is true also for the Princesses, who loved him dearly – had always during the months when George's faculties were impaired to be set against their desire to adhere to what they were advised was medically correct; to stand by the prescribed regimens of treatment, however severe and even brutal.

When the King was acutely ill, the royal household was miserable and apprehensive enough, but at least then he was under supervision and restraint. It was when he was half-better that tensions became almost impossible to bear. During most of the year 1804, George continued to suffer occasional fevers and flurries; he was afflicted by a variety of unaccountable pains and swellings; his sight and hearing were both affected. So on many occasions were his behaviour and judgment. At Weymouth for instance in September 'he would absolutely have rode on horseback into church' (so at least reported the Duke of Clarence) if one of his equerries had not stopped him. Not unnaturally, he was often moody and irritable, partly because of the nature of his disease, partly because, despite his protests, he was still kept under surveillance and treated as potentially dangerous long after he had resumed his full political functions. (These, following the negotiation with Pitt, included coming down to prorogue Parliament and reading the King's Speech 'with great animation' on 31st July.) Pitt, only two days after his puzzlingly gracious reception by the King, had a second interview in which he noticed a 'hurry of spirits and an excessive love of talking', though he would not say there was 'anything positively wrong'. However, as Lord Malmesbury wrote:

> His manners and conversation were far from steady – fanciful, suspicious, etc. . . . He dismissed and turned away, and made capricious changes everywhere, from the Lord Chamberlain to the grooms and footmen. He had turned away the Queen's favourite coachman, made footmen grooms, and *vice versa* and . . . had removed lords of the bedchamber without a shadow of reason . . . The Queen was ill and *cross*; the Princesses low, depressed, and quite sinking under it. [25]

No doubt, in this condition, he was most difficult to live with; and certainly the Queen had for some years in her own manner been difficult too; her despotic treatment of her daughters was eventually to lead, in 1812, to a grand if belated revolt by the sisterhood, discreetly backed by their eldest brother.

It is Dr Heberden who seems to go closest to the heart of the 1804 family situation when we read of him telling Lord Camden after having visited Weymouth, that

> on the part of the Queen and the Princesses there is an impression that the King is not as well as he really is, that on that account there is a suspicion which is discernable to the King in their manner to him, that he is hurt and irritated by their behaviour . . . [Dr Heberden] has endeavoured and trusts he has made some impression to convince the Queen that his Majesty is really well except that his nerves have not yet recovered their former tone and he is therefore subject to irritation and hurry, and that he takes too little sleep, and that the way to make him quite well now is to show him that they think him so. [26]

In May, the Duke of Kent had reported 'a great coolness towards our mother', and on her side Charlotte had absolutely refused to share a bedroom with her husband, even when formally requested to do so by Addington's Cabinet. Every night two or three of the Princesses would remain with their mother until they had seen the King safely away, and then they would bid her good night and she would lock herself in. 'I have never been able to ascertain the cause of the Queen's disgust for the King since his last illness,' wrote Sir Robert Wilson,[27] 'for disgust it amounts to, but no doubt she must have very good reason to resist nature, her duty, the advice of her physicians, and the entreaties of the ministers.' It seems probable that some additional mistrust between King and Queen arose from his suspicion of her closeness to the Prince of Wales, who by July was endeavouring to enlist his mother's support for having his father declared incapable, and calling the Lord Chancellor's attention to the extraordinary circumstance of a King of England, while exercising his regal powers, being kept under personal restraint.[28] The King never mentioned the Queen with disrespect, wrote Lord Auckland, 'but he marks unequivocally . . . that he is dissatisfied with her, and is come to a decided system of checking her knowledge of what is going forward, and her interference between him and his heir, etc., etc.'[29]

In response to family attempts to close the breach between the King and the Prince of Wales, George consented before he went on his Weymouth holiday that a meeting should take place, with the Queen, the Princesses, and Adolphus present – a family gathering. But he stipulated that 'no explanation or excuses' should be made by the Prince '. . . as any retrospect could but oblige the King to utter truths which, instead of healing, must widen the present breach'. On receiving this unforgiving overture, and then, worse still, finding that his father had invited the Princess of Wales to Windsor and had a private and friendly interview with her, the Prince discovered that he was suffering from an indisposition which would, after all, prevent his attending. However, after the Weymouth holiday and another stay with George Rose at Cuffnells, an encounter was effected; according to the King, 'in every way *decent*, and as both parties avoided all subjects except of the most trifling kind, certainly it has done no harm.' The Prince of Wales's version, as retailed to Fox and others of his acquaintance, was that the King's talk was 'very idle and foolish in manner, and running wildly from topic to topic'. Apparently the Prince rallied his friends (so Pitt heard and reported) with the opinion that his father was 'much broken in all respects'.[30]

One family problem on whose solution the King and his son did come eventually to agree, concerned the education of the now eight-year-old Princess Charlotte. After a long struggle the Prince had, in 1804, finally succeeded in wresting full custody of his child from his detested wife, and he now took the advice of Mrs Fitzherbert and Lord Moira that the King himself should be offered the guardianship of the child. George undertook the charge of this his only granddaughter with the utmost seriousness, supervising the preparation of quarters for her at Windsor and formulating a plan of upbringing suitable for an heir presumptive, with 'a bishop to superintend . . . a proper clergy-man to instruct the young Princess in religion and Latin, and daily to read prayers', another instructor for 'history, geography, belles lettres and French', masters for 'writing, music, and dancing', and (since night and day she must be 'under the care of responsible persons') a governess, sub-governess, and assistant sub-governess.[31] His original idea that it would be proper and pleasant for her to see not only her father but to continue also visiting her mother – which the Prince wished at all costs to avoid – was banished when the findings (however muted) of the 'Delicate Investigation' made it at last clear to the King that there were grounds, as he himself put it mildly enough in a letter to her, for 'serious concern' at her conduct.

The King never came to a public breach with his wife, which would have offended against ideas of propriety held by both of them. They continued to attend functions together when occasion demanded, but when George was at Windsor, Frogmore became the Queen's retreat in a very literal sense. When at Buckingham House, as Malmesbury wrote, she 'locks the door of her *white room* – her *boudoir* – against him.' She would never receive him 'without one of the Princesses being present; never says in reply a word. Piques herself on this discreet silence'. The two of them, Speaker Abbot noted sadly, lived 'on ill terms . . . They never sleep or dine together' – though apparently the King, who dined early himself, sometimes appeared at the table of the Queen and the Princesses with the dessert. It was melancholy, said Lord Hobart, 'to see a family that had lived so well together for such a number of years completely broken up.'[32]

CHAPTER TWENTY-EIGHT

Last Active Years
(1805-1810)

AFTER this painful year, 1804, the King, hardly surprisingly, was never quite the same man again. Even after some balance was restored in his metabolism and steadiness returned to his nerves and judgment, he never fully regained his vigour. He was sixty-six, and his constitution had withstood the buffetings of recent years only at a heavy price. When he wrote again now to Bishop Hurd of the plans to send his wife and daughters beyond the Severn in case of invasion, there was no more talk of putting himself at the head of the defending troops. At Weymouth that summer he grudgingly consented to take tepid sea-water baths instead of his customary early morning plunges into the Channel. His eyes too, suddenly grew much worse and, at Cuffnells on his way back from Weymouth to Windsor, he confessed to George Rose that he was nearly blind. He could see nothing at all with one eye, he said, and only with difficulty could he decipher print with the other by candlelight. In January, 1805, he nevertheless managed to read the Speech from the Throne, according to Speaker Abbot, 'with un-common spirit and distinctness,' but it had to be printed for him specially and it proved the last such occasion. Just after his sixty-seventh birthday he was obliged for the first time to employ a secretary, and from November, 1805, he had to dictate all his correspondence.

There was 'spirit and distinctness' too, and certainly a distinctive-ness of tone, in George's comment to Pitt on the Cabinet's rejection of Napoleon's rather spurious peace offer of December, 1804. This had been made for the first time from monarch to monarch, from the newly self-crowned Emperor to his fellow-sovereign King George ('Monsieur mon frère'), who expressed himself as

> rather astonished that the French usurper had addressed himself to him; and, if he judged it necessary, that he could not find a less objectionable manner. Mr Pitt has put the mode of answering it in the only possible shape that could with any propriety be devised; and, as such, the King approves of the proposed unsigned answer. No time ought to be lost in transmitting a copy of it to the Court of

Russia, to whom also the Convention with Sweden should be communicated. On the French proposal it might be right to express to
the Emperor of Russia that this proposal ought to stimulate the
entering into a thorough concert to attack France with vigour.[1]

Attack was again a key word, the Addington war policy of concentrat-
ing on insular defence having given way to planning for Pitt's third
major attempt to build a grand European alliance against France,
which by enlisting a combination of Russia, Austria, Prussia, Sweden,
and Naples, would at worst draw Napoleon off from his invasion plans
and at best compass his defeat and downfall. All this was more in tune
with the King's general inclinations than the earlier defensive posture,
however rewardingly the stress then laid upon home defence – with its
atmosphere of the British lion defending its lair, and all the patriotic
busyness of Yeomanry and Volunteers and 'bang-up locals' – had
unified the nation behind the shelter of the Navy and under the banner
of the Throne.

Addington, who had earlier rejected the King's offer of a peerage on
the grounds that he had not the means to support it, was now temporarily reconciled with Pitt, joined his ministry, and was persuaded to
become Lord Sidmouth. He brought with him forty or fifty Commons
votes that Pitt was badly in need of; and the King was delighted to
have been the agent, or so he persuaded himself, of bringing about this
restoration of friendship. Pitt's parliamentary position over the last
months of his life remained nevertheless very frail; and it was as
severely shaken as Pitt was personally – he was in tears in the Commons
– when the House voted in favour of a criminal prosecution of Melville (Dundas) for having connived when Navy Treasurer at the mal-
versation of public funds. Melville escaped impeachment but was
forced to resign. To avoid having his name struck off the list of Privy
Councillors at the Commons' request, he and Pitt were obliged to ask
the King to remove it by consent. George had never had overmuch
liking for him, but was now 'much hurt at the virulence' against him,
'which is unbecoming the character of Englishmen.' He did not con-
done the offence, but hoped that after the name was struck off the
subject would be 'buried in oblivion'. The Commons in general, and
in particular Mr Whitbread the brewer radical who had been the
leading terrier of the pack, had shown, he considered, 'an unnecessary
severity'.[2]

Quarrels over this affair led in turn to the renewed resignation of
Sidmouth, whose supporters had been among the most vindictive

against Lord Melville. Sidmouth and Pitt were now full of mutual grudges, and it would have taken much more than George's good intentions to hold them together. With his majority by the late summer of 1805 in some danger, Pitt turned again towards the project of a junction with the Grenvilles and Foxites, but once more the King brushed aside any such notion. Indeed, when Pitt and George Rose saw him at Weymouth in September, 1805 – the month before Trafalgar – they found him even more intractable on the subject than he had been the previous year.

> He was persuaded [Rose wrote] there existed no necessity whatever for such a junction; that we did very well in the last session, and he was confident we should not be worse in the ensuing one . . . I observed . . . if Mr Pitt should be confined by the gout, or any other complaint, for only two or three weeks, there would be an end of us . . . I had not the good fortune, however, to make any impression whatever on his Majesty.[3]

Between the spring and autumn of 1805, Pitt secured the alliance of Russia, Austria, Sweden, and Naples. Only the Prussians wavered, trying to play off Britain against France and vice versa, and eventually signing a provisional alliance with Russia, which did not commit them to immediate hostilities and had, written into it, a secret agreement by which, once Napoleon was defeated, Hanover would be transferred to Prussia. Pitt, banking on Prussian assistance, had sent the main weight of British forces to the Weser, aiming primarily at a reconquest of Hanover. When he discovered the secret article, in which he dared not concur, even to buy Prussian support – it would, he said, either kill the King or drive him mad – it was too late to transfer the British troops to southern Italy, where they might have had better success. Napoleon eventually agreed (though like all Napoleonic agreements it was essentially temporary) to buy off Prussia with the offer of Hanover. Pitt's European coalition certainly had the effect of dispersing the Grand Army encamped at Boulogne; but there was little to cheer in that, when it swept across Europe to engulf the Austrians and Russians at Ulm and Austerlitz. Faced with these renewed disasters, and with the alarming and worsening illness of Pitt, the British Cabinet once again decided to withdraw its expeditionary force from Europe – a move, though it meant the abandonment of Hanover, which George had no option but to accept. Only Trafalgar offered any consolation, and the joy even at that massive victory was muted by mourning for Nelson. The last of Pitt's years as war minister had proved more disastrous than those before 1801, which had been nerve-wracking enough. As Holland Rose wrote,

> England had sent forth some 60,000 troops in order to bring them back again. She had paid a million sterling to Austria, and the results were Ulm and Austerlitz. Nearly as much had gone to Russia, and the outcome was the armistice. A British subsidy had been claimed by Prussia, and in return she was about to take Hanover as a gift from Napoleon.[4]

Pitt's death in January, 1806, old and exhausted at forty-six, might have been thought likely to prove a blow to the King. In the words engraved on the Guildhall monument, it was he who had 'rallied the loyal, the sober-minded, and the good around the venerable structure of the British monarchy', and now a buttress would seem to have been removed. George himself, however, had never viewed Pitt exactly as a buttress, except perhaps in the minister's earliest days; nor, in latter days, as indispensable. In any case his death could scarcely have come as a shock; he had been ill for months, and sinking for some weeks. The King had had time to take stock of a future bereft of this political giant. He no longer had the will, the strength, or even as it proved the need, to fight the political battles of the early 1780's over again. Though Fox still talked of 'giving a good stout blow to the influence of the Crown', he also was a different man from the Fox of 1782; or from the Fox of 1792, defiant in praise of the French Revolution; or even of 1802, the uncritical champion of Bonaparte. Since then Fox had actually become a member of the Chertsey Volunteers. He was truer to his principles than most, but *tempora mutantur, nos et mutamur in illis.* Besides, ambition was always hungry in him, and the long years of frustration had not dulled it.

By January, 1806, the King's mind must have been to some extent prepared for what at any previous time he would have considered *the worst*. There were none of the meaningless heroics he had indulged in, a short time before, with George Rose, about 'risking a civil war' rather than accepting Fox as minister; no mention of threatened abdication; not a hint of a menace to his health. After Pitt died, and when it was clear that his colleagues had no intention of trying to carry on as a team, George sent almost immediately for Lord Grenville. He did initially once more resist employing Fox, but when Grenville insisted on his inclusion, the King is reported to have given a reply the general sense of which, even if it was not *quite* accurately recounted, would at any previous time have been thought incredible: 'I thought so, and I meant it so.' The sooner Grenville could make his arrangements the better; 'I will come to town and stay till it is done. There are to be no exclusions.' Grenville's new ministry not only had Fox himself as its foreign (and in fact principal) minister, but was composed predominantly of Fox's friends and followers. The others who completed the coalition belonged to three groups: the Grenvilles; Sidmouth* and his following; and the 'Prince of Wales's friends' in the persons of Lord Moira and Sheridan. Far from being 'a ministry of all the talents' (as it somehow came to be called), it included no Pittites. Canning, Castlereagh, Hawkesbury and the rest who, now that their leader was dead, came increasingly to accept being spoken of as Tories, went into opposition.[5]

Fox knew well enough that Pitt and the King – and no doubt also the unpopularity of his own opinions – had kept him waiting too long; power had come too late. He was only fifty-seven, and by no means proposing to 'give the thing up', which he said his father had done; but he was aware that it might not be long before he 'made a pair with Pitt'. He knew too, that many of the causes he had once championed, parliamentary reform and religious equality, for example, were not practical politics in 1806, though he cherished hopes that he might achieve the abolition of the slave trade and a peace with Napoleon. Because of his ill health it was suggested he might be attracted by the offer of a peerage, and perhaps allow his nephew Lord Holland ('the young one') to take over the Foreign Office. 'Don't think me selfish, young one,' he said, 'the slave trade and peace are two such glorious things, I can't give them up, even to you. If I can manage *them*, I will then retire.'

There seemed no prospect of his putting the King's sanity at risk. 'When Mr Fox came into the Closet for the first time, his Majesty purposely made a short pause and then said, "Mr Fox, I little thought you and I should ever meet again in this place. But I have no desire to look back upon old grievances, and you may rest assured I shall never remind you of them." Mr Fox replied, "My deeds, and not my words, shall commend me to your Majesty".' So at least affirmed a memorandum written by no less a one than Princess Augusta, and subsequently the basis of a narrative in the *Quarterly Review*.[6] Fox was in no mood to 'strike stout blows' against the influence of this amiable, almost blind, and apparently appreciative sovereign. The dispatch and efficiency with which he conducted Foreign Office business pleased the King; so too did his personal manner, which was equally courteous and proper; it contrasted remarkably, the King observed, 'with that of another of his

---

* His inclusion elicited a typical Canning *mot*: 'The Doctor is like measles. Everybody has him once.'

Whig Ministers, who, when he came into office, walked up to him in the way he should have expected from Buonaparte after the battle of Austerlitz.'[7] The anti-slave-trade legislation was put in hand; the negotiations with France were begun, though they soon fell into a bog; and then in June, less than six months after Fox's appointment, the doctors took over, with their poultices, plasters, leeches, purges – all the punishing palliatives and killing cures of Georgian medicine. While his face and upper trunk wasted rapidly away, the fatal dropsy took possession of his abdomen and legs. They twice drew from him a formidable quantity of fluid, and for a time he rallied. They drove him out to the Duke of Devonshire's, and when he could no longer read, his niece and his nephew Lord Holland read to him from Swift and Crabbe and the eighth book of the *Aeneid*. All the time he was tended and consoled by Mrs Fox, to whom on 13th September, he spoke his farewell, after some earlier muttered messages had failed to get through to her: 'It don't signify, my dearest dearest Liz.' As last words they do not have quite the ring of Pitt's, but somehow they seem equally in tune with the man and his qualities. According to Sidmouth, whom it is reasonable to believe, the King said, 'Little did I think I should ever live to regret Mr Fox's death.'[8] According to the third Lord Holland, with whom denigration of George III was by way of being a family obligation, he 'could hardly suppress his indecent exultation' when he heard the news. It does not sound on the face of it a likely story, however long and passionately George had detested this most significant of his enemies.

Now that Fox was dead, the King had one more blow to deal to the reforming Whigs. He had accepted the abolition of the slave trade with no enthusiasm but no active opposition. Grenville and Grey knew that full Catholic emancipation, the King being the King, was not possible, yet they wished to make some gesture at least in that direction. By Pitt's act of 1793, Roman Catholics in Ireland had been allowed to hold army commissions up to colonel's and parallel naval rank; it was now proposed that such permission be extended to the rest of the British Isles. Persuaded by Sidmouth that no dangerous new principle was involved, but that this new measure was a mere corollary of the Irish Act of 1793, George grudgingly consented to let it go forward. However, when the draft of the bill eventually emerged (after some pressure from Irish members), it appeared that *all* military and naval appointments, up to the highest, were to be opened to Catholics. Grenville claimed, and Sidmouth denied, that the King understood the significance of what was being proposed; he had returned the draft, said Grenville, with no comment. (The King was of course blind now

though he had a secretary, and was not usually slow to pick up details.)
When he came to realise, however, what he was supposed to have
approved, George was wideawake enough. If this was the thin end of the
Catholic wedge, he was having none of it. He required Sidmouth,
instead of resigning (as Sidmouth had intended), to stay in office and
resist his own Cabinet's measure in Parliament. Grenville tried to out-
manœuvre the King by bringing Canning into the Government and
enlisting such Pittite support as would follow his lead, but he found
himself in a cleft stick. He could not have both the Doctor *and* Canning;
they were oil and water. Win one, he must lose the other. Once more,
in his stubborn resolve to maintain the supremacy of the Protestant
religion, the King appeared to hold the better cards; and again his
views (or prejudices) coincided with those of a majority of Englishmen. 'No popery!' was as popular a cry as ever.

Grenville's Cabinet acknowledged at least a partial defeat, and
offered to withdraw the bill, but only with a proposed public declaration that they disapproved of the policy that had been forced upon
them. This gesture of defiance George met with a counter-request,
which he must have realised was tantamount to a demand for capitula-
tion or resignation. (He had been further fortified by receiving a letter
of support from the Duke of Portland, now a very conservative Whig
indeed – together with what amounted to an offer to form an alternative administration.) What the King now required – with very doubtful constitutional propriety – was a written undertaking that Grenville
and his colleagues would never raise the Catholic issue again. When
Grenville refused, then, replied the King, 'I must look about me.'[9] At
least he parted with the son more civilly than he had with the father
over forty years before. Grenville went so far as to declare that he had
'experienced much personal kindness during this business from the
King', and when his colleagues attended to surrender their offices they
were individually assured that *on every matter but this* the King much
appreciated their services. But as Sheridan wrote, not relishing his
removal from the Navy Treasurership, 'I have known many men knock
their heads against a wall; but I never before heard of a man collecting
bricks and building a wall for the express purpose of knocking out his
own brains against it.'[10]

This departure from power of Grenville and the friends and heirs
of Fox marked in effect the end of the last chapter in the long story of
King George and the Whigs. After Grenville resigned in March, 1807,
there were no more Whig ministries either in the reign of George III
or of George IV, who was to discover with middle age that he was a
Tory after all. Yet it was not, of course, in any permanent sense a

struggle that the King won. Like Napoleon, the British monarchy won many battles but (in the political sense) lost the war. The posthumous victors were rather to be George's old enemies: Burke, with his championship of the party principle; Fox, with his claims for the supremacy of the House of Commons; and even Wilkes in his one-time rôle as hero of the middling and lower orders. Royal power and prerogative were to be steadily whittled away over the coming century, regardless of whether the monarch were popular or unpopular. The process was hastened over George III's remaining years by his increasing physical and mental helplessness, and during the reigns of his two successor sons by their lack of his will to fight. But more important pressures came from the rise of a new middle class and an immense broadening of what either Burke or George III would have understood by the term 'the public'; and, above all, from the emergence of a basically two-party system which could provide a strong and simple mechanism for changing ministries without recourse to the Crown and its prerogative of choice. George III had always seen party as the prime enemy of his system of government. He proved to be right, but not for the reason he would himself have offered – indeed, for a diametrically opposite reason. He had regarded party, or 'faction', as a fissiparous force, a cause of disunity and instability. In the long run the party principle dissolved the political strength of the monarchy just because it provided a guarantee of stability and continuity as important as that given by the monarchy itself. It removed from the Crown the necessity, and hence the right, of choosing its executive ministers. 'The Government is dead, long live the Government.'

Little of this could have been perceived in 1807, with the King quite confident that the Duke of Portland's new ministry would avoid undesirable domestic innovation and pursue the marathon war with adequate spirit. In the new Cabinet George missed one of his most trusted ministers in Sidmouth, resigning for the third time, but gained another in Eldon, a Chancellor constructed of reassuringly conservative granite. Of the Duke of Portland himself, once execrated as 'my son's minister', the man who presided over the 'infamous coalition', but by 1807 grown old and infirm, and for a long time now the enemy of 'democratical' or pro-Catholic reform, George could not speak too kindly. Canning expressed the view to the King that 'nothing like a substitute *can* be found for the Duke of Portland . . . the last of his species . . . His rank, his age, his relation of friendship with your Majesty, the prescriptive veneration which he enjoys from having been so many years of his life at the head of political parties', made him unique; and noted how 'the King here entered into a warm and vehement panegyric' upon him, 'his honesty, his disinterestedness, his affectionate attachment to him, etc.' Times had indeed changed since 1783.[11]

George was altogether very satisfied with his new Government – of which Portland was, of course, no more than the dignified figurehead, each department, under the Crown, being in effect a law unto itself. When Eldon's predecessor Lord Erskine, during an audience, warned the King that he 'stood on the brink of a precipice' by turning out his late ministers, he replied amiably, 'Sir, you are a very honest man, and I am very much obliged to you,' and showed him out. Soon the King, the Established Church, and the new Government had strengthened their position even further by holding an election largely on the issue of 'No Popery'. Even the City of London, whose communications to the King throughout the reign had seldom been other than hostile, voted an address of thanks to his Majesty for protecting the Protestant religion as by law established. Always seeking to ensure and reinsure this protection, George, when at last Portland resigned – just before his death in 1809 – still wished to have a written pledge from his successor Spencer Perceval that he would never raise the Catholic question. Perceval succeeded in persuading him, however, that the known convictions of a majority of the Government's members provided a sufficient guarantee.

Apart from his defective eyesight, the King's health had recovered to a tolerable extent during the years after 1804. Out of doors he could still enjoy his after-breakfast ride, usually in the company of one or two of his daughters; and indoors there was music, and chess, and conversation. On summer evenings he still made appearances on the Terrace at Windsor, again usually with a Princess on each arm to guide him and introduce visitors to him. For intimate company and cheer, it was mostly his daughters now that he depended on, though he was probably on as good terms with his sons as at any time since they were children. With the Queen his relations were correct but distant. They kept up appearances and little more. When in 1810 Charlotte's finances became overstrained and the tradesmen were getting restive, she did not feel able personally to apply to the King for relief except by letter, while her Under-Treasurer made simultaneous application to the prime minister. Perceval with the King's immediate approval found means of satisfaction. 'I have desired Elyza to read you my letter,' Charlotte wrote to her husband, 'as it is out of my power to speak for myself, and tho' I have the highest opinion of C[olonel] Taylor [the King's secretary], I thought anything between yr. M. and me was better to remain among ourselves. I will not detain yr. M. any longer with such an unpleasant epistle, but throw myself entirely upon yr. goodness, being convinced that you will always be just and kind.'[12]

In January, 1808, Charles Abbot, after a long talk with him, noted that he looked 'remarkably clear and well, rather grown large within the last twelvemonth; very cheerful'; and almost exactly a year later he was writing of the King's 'usual cheerfulness . . . good health and countenance'.[13] Even so, his correspondence, though his attention to business was as unfailing as ever, marks the decline of his vigour and faculties. The stiff formal phrases that in the old days might have prefaced a packet of detailed suggestions, a pungent personal observation, or a throwaway fragment of self-revelation, now in these years of almost total blindness constituted the complete dictated letter. An event of such stirring significance as Sir John Moore's death at Corunna, and the successful evacuation of his forces, did elicit rather more expansive comment: he wrote of his 'sincere satisfaction from Lord Castlereagh's communication of the dispatches'; and of his approval of the Parliamentary recommendation to erect a monument to the memory of Moore, 'the sense of whose valuable and distinguished services cannot be too strongly marked.'[14] But it was not until a major scandal was laid bare affecting the reputation of a member of the royal family that the King's official letters resumed anything like their former length and character.

That an actress should have accepted very large sums of money from military gentlemen was not of itself unusual. That the same actress should also happen to have been a mistress of one of the King's sons was equally unremarkable; a large number of ladies at one time or another had been thus honoured. When the officers, however, were alleged to have paid the money as bribes to obtain promotion; when the King's son was Frederick Duke of York, Commander-in-Chief; and when it was declared that he himself had taken his share from the payments made to his mistress, the suspicion of corruption in high places was too rank for the Government to ignore and too sweet for some of the more ill-disposed of the opposition to miss making the most of. For nearly two months the House of Commons examined witnesses – among them, conscious of her stardom, the still very dashing Mrs Clarke, who was only too anxious to implicate her ex-lover to the fullest extent, and not only expose his sexual morals in some detail to a fascinated public,* but to accuse him of complicity in the financial improprieties. George remained convinced that his son was being traduced and that he was innocent at least in the essential matter of corruption. He wrote:

> The King heartily concurs with the [Lord] Chancellor in deploring that the Duke of York should ever have formed any connection with so abandoned a woman as Mrs Clarke, but his Majesty never will allow himself to doubt for one moment the Duke of York's perfect integrity and his conscientious attention to his public duty, or to believe that in the discharge of it he has ever submitted to undue influence ... His Majesty derives much relief from Mr Perceval's opinion that if justice is done to the Duke of York there is no evidence which ought to convince any fair and unbiased mind that the Duke of York knew anything of Mrs Clarke's nefarious practices.[15]

Nevertheless, Perceval could not conceal from the King the unpleasant facts of the situation. The general impression of the House was that the evidence showed Mrs Clarke *had* exercised undue influence on the making of appointments and 'the sentiment expressed by Mr Windham of the necessity that H.R.H. should retire, at least for a time, is so general . . . that Mr Perceval does not think it will be possible to resist a vote to that effect'.[16] Although insisting that the Duke's exoneration ought to be unconditional, the King was of course unable to prevent his best-loved son for a second time being disgraced. The House acquitted him of knowledge of corruption, but his resignation was inescapable.† The King, in his letter to Perceval of 18th March, 1809, officially informing him that he had agreed to his son's stepping down, could not

> forbear adding . . . that he must ever regret any circumstances that have deprived him of the services of the Duke of York in a situation in which his able, zealous, and impartial conduct during so many years have secured to him his Majesty's entire approbation; and have appeared to him not less conspicuous than his strict integrity, all tending to confirm the King's sincere affection for the Duke of York and to convince him of the benefits which have resulted to the King

---

* Not only to the public. 'What a scene we are exhibiting to the world!' lamented Wilberforce; '. . . the reception which every *double entendre* meets in the House must injure our character greatly with all religious minds' (*Life of Wilberforce*, iii. 402).

† He was reinstated in 1811.

and the country from his honourable administration of the Army . . .[17]

It was a testimonial far from being undeserved. The Duke's behaviour had been careless and foolish, but over the preceding fourteen years he had done a good deal to reduce the amount of political jobbery in army appointments, and had taken a praiseworthy share, with Moore and Abercromby, in building an army which only now, in Portugal and Spain, was on the point of proving itself.

Frederick, of course, was an old favourite with his father, a prodigal son always readily forgiven. Between his daughters, who unlike his sons were his daily companions, the King's affection was more evenly spread, but of Amelia, the youngest, he was probably fondest of all. It was not the whole Amelia that he knew and loved, for there were things about her that it was not considered prudent for the King to be advised of – as indeed there were about others of his daughters. And as also with those others – Augusta, Elizabeth, Sophia – it was the Prince of Wales to whom the secrets might be confided. Amelia referred to herself in letters to him as 'your *own child*' (he was twenty years her senior). She *felt* and *suffered* for him, she wrote, and longed for him to be happy and for his quarrel with the King to be composed. It was the Prince of Wales, that expert in affairs of the heart, who could be relied on to understand her passion for General FitzRoy, to whom she considered herself married in the eyes of God; it was in writing to the Prince that she could take pride in signing herself 'A.F.R.'. The Queen knew of the connection, and allowed (so she wrote) for Amelia's youth, ignorance of the world, and ill-health, but thought at twenty-three she should see how necessary it was to subdue a passion which must make her disgraced and miserable. 'Add to this the melancholy situation of the King at this present moment [April, 1807], who, could he be acquainted of what has passed, would be rendered miserable for all his life, and I fear it would create a breach in the whole family.' The sad fact was that there were times when Princess Amelia was in her own mind waiting – even guiltily half hoping – for her father's death so that with her eldest brother's approval she might be openly and officially married. She even drafted tentative letters intended for the Privy Council, referring to 'the late King'.[18]

The ill-health the Queen referred to, which had earlier included a tuberculous knee-joint and 'Saint Anthony's fire' in the face (erysipelas), had by Amelia's mid-twenties taken a serious turn. She had a relentless cough, and a persistent pain in her side, which by 1806 the surgeons were attempting to relieve – though succeeding only in aggravating – by the insertion of 'seatons' to drain away fluid. There followed three years of worsening health, until by 1809 it was being discussed whether moving her down to Weymouth might not give her a better chance. Weymouth meant separation from FitzRoy; but everything, the doctors declared, depended 'on her being kept as *quiet* as possible'; she 'must be worried about nothing, which *entre nous*', wrote Princess Mary to the Prince of Wales, 'in our house is very difficult.'[19] The Queen opposed her going, but the King, that champion of Weymouth, thought it a capital suggestion and, said Amelia, 'not only consented to my request to have Miny [Mary] but said he was *determined she should go*.' In August, therefore, the two Princesses set off for the sea. 'A good deal tired,' Amelia wrote to her father from Hartford Bridge, *en route*: 'Once more allow me to express my thanks for your *never ceasing* but *increasing kindness* to me . . . All I felt at leaving Windsor I will not attempt to say anything about, but assure you my heart is left behind . . . Dearest Miny is all goodness . . .' Arrived at Weymouth, she continued: '. . . Long has it been out of my power to express what my heart feels for your affection . . . God bless you, my dear papa, and excuse this long dull letter, but I wished to give you an account of myself, knowing how kind you are on this subject.'[20]

To these and many more such letters, both from Amelia and from Mary, the King dictated his punctual, faithful, but stiff-sounding replies that might conceal from an unperceptive eye the depth of his concern. George, with a lifetime spent in reading and writing communications devoted to official and political business, seldom (and then only clumsily) managed to unbend in a private letter, even to those close to him. 'Of my affection for you and my anxiety for your welfare,' he wrote to Amelia in September, 1809, 'you are too well assured not to believe how sincerely I grieve that you should continue to suffer so much from the pain in the side and be forced to submit to remedies so painful and distressing' – that was a subject he was well acquainted with – 'while you bear them with a degree of patience and resignation which cannot be sufficiently commended.'[21] Mary wrote of the 'tortures' caused by the continuing 'seatons'. About this time (October, 1809), the King made one brave effort to write to his daughter in his own hand. 'My dear Amelia, I attempt a few lines to accompany the book . . .' What followed, apart from the phrase, 'I am most happy', was undecipherable. For a time letters passed each way daily, with accounts of gruelling little experimental rides in a specially fitted-up carriage designed to permit the Princesses' return to Windsor – an ordeal suffered early in November, with the jolting of the carriage causing Amelia agonies of pain. She wished to go not to Windsor but to Kew, but this the Queen objected to, as she also objected to the way Amelia was 'selfishly' monopolising Mary's attentions. When Mary wrote to her father to tell him that if *that* was said to Amelia it would 'half kill her', the King wrote back, 'I have taken care to have it understood that you are not to be separated from her.'[22] The two Princesses were finally settled at Augusta Lodge, Windsor, which had formerly been Dr Heberden's; and now the King was able to pay daily visits, which Amelia told him were the greatest comforts of her life. However, as for the Queen, her attitude, wrote Amelia, 'was the strongest contrast to the dear King possible, but I am much too used to it to feel hurt by it . . . I certainly am no better and going on so was absurd.'[23] Erysipelas now returned to add to her sufferings, which were to last nearly another sad year. By the time the anniversary had come round of the King's accession, on 25th October (the royal family were meticulous observers of anniversaries), it was plain to almost everybody that Amelia was dying of consumption. Yet the King would not, could not, believe it. He had recently been demanding bulletins on her condition from Sir Henry Halford three times a day. She was so ill that the time even he was allowed to spend with her on his visits had had to be severely limited. He would sometimes, perhaps alarmingly to the patient, peer closely down upon her with his almost sightless eyes in an attempt to reassure himself that she was not as desperately ill as they were all telling him. It was on one of these last visits that she, knowing well that she was dying, gave him a diamond ring she had had specially made, set with a lock of her hair under crystal.

At the anniversary celebration all his sons were present, and all his daughters except the oldest, who was in Württemberg, and the youngest, who had a week to live. The King's agitation was alarmingly clear as he moved from guest to guest. He said to Miss Cornelia Knight, the Queen's companion, 'You are not uneasy, I am sure, about Amelia,' and squeezed her hand so tightly that she almost shouted out loud. He called each of his sons over to him in turn and 'said things to them equally sublime and instructive, but very unlike what he would have said before so many people' if he had been in full command of himself.[24] On the very day that Amelia died, 2nd November, Canning gave it as his opinion that *if* she were to die it would probably, once he was over the shock, hasten the King's recovery; 'it is the lingering suspense and daily leave-taking that have worked upon his feelings and irritated him into madness.' For, as Canning unfeelingly put it, the truth was 'poor old Knobbs' was once more 'just as mad as ever he was in his life'.[25]

CHAPTER TWENTY-NINE

The Final Decade

THE old patterns of the royal malady were soon being repeated. This time, however, the physicians were at first hopeful that the King, now seventy-two, would not have the strength to be violent, and therefore that the strait-jacket might be unnecessary. They had underestimated the staying power of the King's physique. On 31st October, he again became very difficult to manage, and Dr Simmons, the mad-doctor that had attended him in 1804, was sent for. At this the Queen protested to Perceval and the Cabinet, but Simmons promptly arrived with his formidable paraphernalia and alarming assistants. When the King had felt the approach of his old symptoms, however, he had extracted a promise from his doctors that 'he should never be left entirely alone with any medical person specially engaged in the department of insanity'.[1] When, therefore, Simmons demanded unhampered authority, this was refused him, and he departed.

After a week of intense disturbance, during which the King's life was again in danger, he became less fevered and more lucid, and by 11th November, was judged collected enough to bear being told of his daughter's death. The remission of symptoms, however, lasted only a few days before another severe attack began; and so for many weeks the illness continued its fluctuating course. On Christmas Eve he was seized with such violent abdominal pain and so high a fever that the Prince of Wales was sent for, and drove post-haste to Windsor; but once again there was an improvement, and on the King's better days he was calm and reasonable, playing when he felt inclined on the harpsichord. On two days in January he even walked on the Terrace, being particularly anxious that members of the public should see him and know beyond a doubt that he was alive.

Again, as on the three previous occasions of derangement, the question of a regency arose. The physicians – Halford, Reynolds, Heberden the younger, and Robert Willis, who had again been called in, on Perceval's initiative, despite protests from the other doctors and from the royal Dukes – were severally examined by the Privy Council, and offered their differing judgments and prognoses, though '*all* spoke with confidence of the King's ultimate recovery'.[2] On presenting the Privy Council's report to Parliament, the Government announced that it would introduce a bill assigning to the Prince of Wales a restricted regency on the lines of Pitt's bill of 1789, to be effective for one year. Again as proposed in 1789, care of the King's person was to be vested in the Queen, who would be advised by the Archbishop of Canterbury and six other Privy Councillors. On 29th January, Perceval attended the King, hoping to find him sufficiently well and sufficiently convinced of his need for prolonged rest to be ready to give his personal assent to the bill which was then approaching its final stages in Parliament. The patient conversed very rationally for half an hour, though seeming 'rather impatient of any pressure on the subject of resigning his power'; after that his attention began to wander. Lord Eldon, the Chancellor, visited him a week later, when the bill had passed through all its parliamentary stages, and he, too, found the royal conversation sensible enough to be embarrassing to one who was about to have the duty and responsibility of affixing the Great Seal to the commission for giving the monarch's 'consent' to a regency.

The new Regent did not, after all, dismiss his father's ministers. Ever since he took fright at the 'hell-begotten Jacobines' nearly twenty years previously, the Prince of Wales's Whig convictions had been largely nominal, and such small sympathy as he proffered for Foxite doctrines (in Irish affairs for instance)* had been purely opportunist; yet many of his old contacts had survived his being in and out of opposition, and it was generally thought to be in accord with the laws of nature that he must turn out his father's ministers. When, with the solid support of all his brothers, he wished solemnly to record his objections to the limitations to be imposed on his regency – the inability, for example, to create peers – it was to the Whig leaders Grenville and Grey that he first turned to indite his protest. These two, however (whom the Prince personally disliked) were incensed when he rejected their draft in favour of a more vigorous version by Sheridan. (Grenville's scope for effective protest was under the severe handicap of his having been a leading member of Pitt's ministry that had framed the original 1789 restrictions.) There was, all in all, little love lost either between the various Whig groups or between the Prince and the Whigs in general. When, therefore, both the Queen and Sir Henry Halford put it very strongly to the Regent that a change of ministers might well worsen the King's condition and perhaps kill him, they were pushing against a partly open door. Even so, Perceval was pre-

* Even here he had retreated to a neutral position after 1807, ostensibly out of respect for his father's convictions and fears for his health if they were flouted.

sumably surprised to hear on 4th February of the Regent's 'irresistible impulse of filial duty and affection to his beloved and afflicted father' that had led him to eschew any act 'which might, in the smallest degree, have the effect of interfering with the progress of his sovereign's recovery'. In other words, the Whigs were still *out*. For another year they cherished some hope that things would change when the restrictions lapsed or the King died; but they were to find, to their chagrin, that the Regent's Toryism only intensified as the years passed. As Byron wrote:

Nought's true among the human race
Except the Whigs not getting into place.

Thus the reign of George III effectively ended on 6th February, 1811, when the Prince Regent took his oath of office. The strain of events, however, took their usual toll of the Prince too, and later that month he was so ill with fainting fits, 'sickness, swelled legs, etc.,' that humorists suggested that his father, who seemed better again, might be made vice-Regent to the Regent. The King was at times so confident that he was soon going to recover that he grew impatient and irritable when members of the Queen's Council did not come to consult him about future arrangements. The Queen herself saw him on 9th February, for the first time in three and a half months, and indicated to her Council that she now wished Sir Henry Halford to take over from Robert Willis 'the general direction of his Majesty's cure', at the same time warning that the royal attendants must be instructed not to take seriously orders given them by the King who, as in 1804, now that he was feeling rather better, was conceiving wild and extravagant schemes for rebuilding and expanding the royal residences, Kensington in particular. As always, the doctors were in conflict over the best methods of treating their patient, Willis being the chief protagonist of restraint, seclusion, and when necessary coercion, while Heberden was the champion of an altogether more modern approach, to 'call forth the energies of [the King's] mind, and divert the wanderings of fancy, not by vain expostulation, but by objects of natural interest'.[3] For a time Heberden's treatment was adopted, at least to the extent of allowing the King to see his family, to have his chaplain read prayers in the sickroom, and even at one point during May, 1811, to go riding in Windsor, amid the premature rejoicing of the town's inhabitants. That the King was on occasions pitiably, even embarrassingly, aware of the true nature of his situation had been demonstrated when a concert was held in the Castle on 'the Duke of Cambridge's night' in

March, the King being invited to choose the programme. He selected from his capacious store of Handel memories a complete concert of arias and extracts descriptive of madness and blindness, 'particularly of those in the opera *Samson*; there was one also upon madness from love, and the lamentation of Jephtha upon the loss of his daughter; and it closed with "God Save the King" to make sure of the application of all that went before.'[4]

It was the kind and practical Princess Mary who for some time had the self-imposed duty of keeping the Prince Regent informed day by day of his father's condition. The King being lodged on the ground floor giving on to the North Terrace, a visit to see him she would simply term 'going down'. When he was severely ill or under coercion, the family was always kept at a distance, but after a visit on one of his not quite so bad days, she wrote to her brother: 'I went down with the Queen, and it was shocking to hear the poor dear King run on so, and her unfortunate manner makes things so much worse.' The Princess considered this unhappy behaviour in her mother to arise partly from her 'extreme timidity' – undoubtedly she must have been terrified earlier by fear of physical violence – and partly from a deficiency of 'warmth, tenderness, affec' '. The Duke of Kent, writing to Sir Henry Halford, was another who referred to his mother's 'natural want of warmth'.[5] It was many years now since she had had any power, or perhaps even any compelling inclination, to comfort and console her stricken and in so many ways impossible husband. Compassion was lacking. His condition was a matter of abhorrence to her. As far as possible she attempted to shut herself off from it, while remaining very ready to accuse her daughters of failing in duty to the King if they should seek respite or relaxation from the shadow overhanging Windsor.

The Queen I am sure [wrote Princess Mary to the Regent] will never do *but her duty*; it is in trifles that she always contrives to *fail*, not only by the King but, if I may say so, by us all. It therefore strikes me that if the *power* was given us either by the phy[sic]ians or proposed by the Council, that we might go down two at a time we might do both the K. and the Q. good, save the Q. much fatigue, and it would enable us to speak kindly of her to the K. and agreeably so of the K. to the Q., repeating all that could do good and give comfort to both.

I fear we can never make them a *real comfort* to each other again, as all confidence has long gone, but I am sure they have a *great respect* for each other, and that the Q. loves him as much as she can love anything *in this world*, but I am clear it is in the power of their daughters, if they are allowed to act, to keep them tolerably together . . .[6]

This last was for several reasons a forlorn hope, but while Halford was in control of the King's room he did agree to the Princesses in pairs making visits to their father. The Queen went down to see him for a quarter of an hour in June, 1812, but it seems likely that during the six and a half years she still had to live she never saw him again.

Halford was not to remain unchallenged in authority. When a relapse occurred at the end of May, 1811, it was blamed on the more liberal régime strongly favoured by Heberden and at least tolerated by Halford. The Queen and her Council now proceeded to reinstate Willis in general control, and the old restrictions and punishments, including frequent use of the strait-jacket, were reimposed. Worse followed in July, when again the King's paroxysms proved so violent that it was thought he could not live; and although there were frequent remissions, the disease continued very active for the succeeding twelve months. In November, John Willis arrived to join his brother – when he first entered the sickroom, wrote Halford, 'His M[ajesty] was enraged'[7] – and between them the brothers succeeded in down-grading the rôle of the three physicians Halford, Heberden and Baillie to such a degree that together these signed a strong but fruitless memorandum of protest to the Queen's Council. They were forced, they said, 'to bear the humiliation and indignity of being made mute spectators of His Majesty's condition without the power of contributing our services either to his recovery or to his comfort.'[8]

Many of the delusions which the King had suffered from on the three previous occasions of derangement reappeared during these months. 'Is it not a strange thing,' he demanded of the Duke of Cambridge, 'that they still refuse to let me go to Lady Pembroke, although everybody knows I am married to her; but what is worst of all is that that infamous scoundrel, Halford, was by at the marriage, and has now the effrontery to deny it to my face.'[9] He often spoke of himself in the third person as of one already dead – 'the late King.' Sometimes, too, it was his sons whom he fancied dead as well, 'or sent away to a distant part of the globe.' As before, his waking nightmares were, on occasions, of an all-submerging flood. The whole country was being inundated, and he was busy with preparations for escaping to Denmark. Often he wept, and then as suddenly would change to unnatural laughter. 'There has been,' wrote Princess Augusta to the Regent, 'a great deal of unpleasant laughing very early this morning,' and in March, 1812, Heberden was reporting him 'more than usually subject to laugh, which always carries some appearance of imbecillity'. Sometimes, when abstracted in his manner, he would sit or lie 'arranging, tying and untying his handkerchiefs and nightcaps, buttoning and unbuttoning his waistcoat'. On the other hand he would suddenly make 'very sensible observations relative to the Treaty of Amiens', or discourse 'with exact memory of the Seven Years War', or speak 'in a rational and correct manner, upon the amusements his Majesty took in his recovery from the illness of 1801'.[10]

In February, 1812, the Regency was made permanent, and in the following month the Prince sent a message to Parliament through the Chancellor of the Exchequer requesting funds to enable his sisters to enjoy establishments of their own. If they were thus made independent, and at the same time appeared more frequently with him on public occasions, they might serve to reduce his unpopularity, while performing something of the rôle that a presentable Princess of Wales might otherwise have played. The Prince also honestly wished to help emancipate his sisters, women in their forties or late thirties, from the chains that still bound them to their mother. Then in April, 1812, there began a grand revolt of the sisterhood against the domination of the Queen, who one morning, after breakfast, was handed four letters by her Keeper of the Robes, one signed jointly by all four daughters, and another three individually by Elizabeth, Mary, and Sophia; and for the rest of that year, 1812, while the King downstairs was settling into the routine of his melancholy situation, and Napoleon's Grand Army was marching to Moscow and leaving its frozen bones on the road of retreat, and the Americans for the second time went to war with King George's England – upstairs at Windsor battle continued intermittently for the liberation of the Princesses. In view of the King's condition, the Queen wrote on receiving their April manifestoes, 'Going to public amusements except where duty calls could be the highest mark of indecency possible . . . I beg to see none of you today. If I can bring myself to see you tomorrow, I shall appear at breakfast – for I do not think I ever felt so shattered in my life.' After the Princesses Mary and Elizabeth accompanied their niece Princess Charlotte to the ceremony of opening Parliament in November, 1812, against the expressed wish of the Queen, 'a dreadfull scene' took place, during the course of which the Queen accused Elizabeth of not caring for the King's feelings – which brought on in the Princess a fit of hysterics. 'I own,' she wrote later, 'the blow of being thought unfeeling and wanting in duty to the King haunts me.'

None of these family disturbances can have penetrated into the

private world of the patient imprisoned downstairs. Nor can the great
events deciding the destiny of Europe have made any impact upon it.
Armies fighting in the name of this slowly disintegrating man drove the
French from Spain and over the Pyrenees as far as Toulouse. His
European allies meanwhile rid the German states – including of course
his own dominion of Hanover – of their French and French-dominated
régimes, and fought on to Paris. 'The Corsican usurper' was overthrown once and banished, and overthrown a second time to live out
his last years in the remoteness of his South Atlantic exile. Napoleon's
isolation from the European scene, however, was nothing compared
with that of the King at Windsor. George III's confused and shifting
world was peopled by the living and the dead, attendants ministering
to his wants or denying them, and figures no less real to him, whom he
would engage in long and frequently cheerful discussion. He arranged
solemn ceremonies; prepared the programmes of imagined concerts;
reviewed ghostly regiments; capriciously promoted or demoted
servants high and low, present or visionary; conversed 'with some of
his ideal friends' (Fanny d'Arblay was informed that they were angels);
and 'was disposed to laugh and then to shed tears upon very slight
suggestions of persons or things which presented themselves to his
imagination'. When he lay torpid on his bed, as he often did for long
periods, nothing might alert him. At other times, though weak on his
legs, he would put on his violet-coloured dressing gown and walk a
little way, bearded now and with sunken cheeks, and settle to pass some
time by playing on one of his harpsichords or on the flute. Handel was
possibly the last of his friends to desert him; and sometimes, when he
had played a passage, he would stop and remark that that was a favourite piece of *the King, when he was alive*. The Willises continued in control,
and guarded their empire against every encroachment; even the
physicians were required to make application if they wished to see the
royal patient. As the months passed, however, and senility increasingly
took hold of him even during his better spells, the need for coercion
grew less, though the means of applying it always remained ready if he
were to be seized by another of the feverish paroxysms that on occasions
tormented him.

The time came, from 1817, when he could hear less and less of what
was said to him, or of what he himself was playing on his instruments,
for deafness was added to his many other afflictions; and after 1818 he
was no longer able to walk. Sometimes he was then carried in a chair
from his bed to another room, and placed near an old harpsichord of
Queen Anne's, on which he would play for hours. He could under-

stand nothing, of course, of the marriage of his granddaughter Charlotte to Prince Leopold, or of her death in 1817 following the birth of her still-born child, and nothing of the consequent marriages the next year of the Dukes of Clarence, Kent, and Cambridge, in the pursuit of legitimate offspring. He is unlikely to have known of the wedding, at last, of Princess Elizabeth (in her forty-eighth year), or even of the death of Queen Charlotte, which occurred in November of this same year, 1818, after she had braced herself, already in failing health, to attend the marriages of her middle-aged children. She died in the Dutch House at Kew, attended by Princesses Augusta and Mary, sitting up in her arm-chair and holding the hand of her eldest and favourite son. 'I wish to God I could see your brothers,' she had said to Augusta; 'tell them I love them . . . I pray from night till morning and from morning till night . . . I wish I was near the dear King.' 'She cried,' wrote Augusta, 'very much indeed.'[11] Upon her death the Duke of York assumed the headship of the Council supervising matters that affected the King.

At least the King could not, in his sad state, be accounted responsible for the country's woes, which in these years after Waterloo were indeed heavy. George could be pitied as the 'poor old King', but also remain the 'good old King', while Cobbett damned the wretched corrupt system, and the distressed poor of the industrial districts petitioned the Regent and cursed his Government, in which the once mild and feeble-seeming Sidmouth was now transmogrified into the ogre of Peterloo and the Six Acts. Many had almost forgotten that George the Third was still their monarch, and Lord Byron at this time stated his opinion that the King would live to be two hundred. From time to time an official inquiry would be conducted in the Windsor sickroom to report on how the patient was faring. Having first obtained the Willises' authority, Sir Henry Halford in January, 1819, undertook one of these expeditions at the Council's request, and

> address'd the King as soon as His Majesty had dined – and having stated his humble desire to ask His Majesty how he did, and given his name, the King appeared forcibly impress'd – collected himself – used the manner of a solemn, enthusiastic, silent, appeal by lifting up his eyes and his hands – but returned no answer – and precluded all further address by striking rapidly the keys of his harpsichord . . . His Majesty went to sleep very soon afterwards.[12]

Eight months later, when the Duke of York visited in person, he found his father 'amusing himself with playing on the harpsichord and singing with as strong and firm a voice as ever I heard'. But he was very emaciated and the Duke thought he saw a look of death about him. He was right. At Christmas the King suffered the last violent onset of his malady, talking restlessly for a period of fifty-eight consecutive hours without sleep. He faded gradually over the next few weeks, and died, aged eighty-one years and seven months, on 29th January.

CHAPTER THIRTY

Postscript

THE best that Byron's *Vision of Judgment* could manage to say for George III on his death was that he had been a faithful husband and 'decent' father, a good farmer, and a moderate spender.

> *A better farmer ne'er brushed dew from lawn,*
> *A worse king never left a realm undone.*

Agriculture and domestic fidelity apart, all that Byron could find to approve was

> *. . . his household abstinence; I grant*
> *His neutral virtues, which most monarchs want.*

Now such virtues as George III possessed were no more neutral than Byron's own; and the same might be said of his failings. His character was in fact remarkably unneutral. Right or wrong, his views were never less than strong. His pugnacity was as firm as his conviction of the propriety of his own actions, his dogged tenacity in the face of setbacks and disasters as unwavering and unneutral as his conservatism. There is paradox and irony in such a man as George III reigning over Britain during the first half-century of our era of runaway industrial and social transformation, the first great age of modern revolutions. Few could have been less well-fitted to move with the times. All his life he believed in what he had been brought up to think right: conventional morality; correctness of behaviour; love of family and of country; the Established Church; the British constitution undistorted by 'faction' and uncorrupted by 'democracy'; a proper social hierarchy, with due subordination of the inferior sort and due responsibility and humanity in their betters. He had a powerful feeling for the status and dignity of the monarchy, but as a man he was unaffected, modest, and courteous. He became after painful experience a shrewd and capable politician. In his private interests he ranged widely, from horology to music, from book-collecting to astronomy and the making of mathematical instruments, from the Royal Academy to the *Annals of Agriculture*. The idea that he was a dunce dies harder than the old notion that he wished to be a despot. His conscientiousness was almost painful, and his industry tireless until ill-health and failing sight defeated it at last. No one more strongly disliked humbug and sophistry. Most of his detractors even did not deny him courage, which happened to be the virtue he himself prized highest.

That he was obdurate and bigoted, and intent on staying the march of progress, historians of the century that followed his death were not in doubt. 'He invariably declared himself upon the wrong side in a controversy,' wrote Sir George Otto Trevelyan. And Lecky wrote him down as 'a sovereign of whom it may be said without exaggeration that he inflicted more profound and enduring injuries upon his country than any other modern English king'. Verdicts such as this cause one to wonder what an *exaggerated* estimate of George III might amount to, and also to question what major reforms, if any, might have been enacted by the British Parliament between 1760 and 1820 if another than he had occupied the throne. It seems likely that even Catholic Emancipation, the one obvious possibility, would have had a hard struggle to get through the House of Lords. And even on this Catholic question that loomed so large in the King's later years, it must be granted that his objections, even if by 1800 they were unrealistic and backward-looking, had conscience behind them and their own logic. The House of Hanover *had* been called to the British throne to protect Protestant supremacy. The ageing monarch, like Waldegrave's young prince, proved to have 'too correct a memory'.

George III's greatest strength was his greatest weakness – he could never abandon his ingrained notions of what the world should be, and come to terms with it as it lamentably was. 'I cannot depart,' he once wrote to the Prince of Wales, 'from what I have uniformly thought right.' It was not strictly true, for he was often forced to, but being coerced into acting contrary to his judgment and principles caused him the most destructive upheavals, and sometimes there came a sticking point when he would not budge because he could not. On Catholic Emancipation he spoke to Pitt of 'the blessing of having a fixed principle'. Such a blessing often enough proved, too, a curse and an affliction. A man of more elastic principles would have had an easier life of it.

From his earliest days George had been encouraged to look for snakes in the grass. His mother's narrow world, inside which he was so long confined, had always breathed an atmosphere of suspicion. Politicians were untrustworthy or vicious men. His uncle might plot to rob him of the throne. Beyond the fences that enclosed and pro-

tected him lurked wickedness and treachery. He was never altogether
to escape from the influence of this early ambience. He never ceased to
bemoan the profligacy of the age he lived in. As a young man he trusted
none but Bute, of the orotund homily and spurious 'loftiness'. As a
father, he proved almost obsessively anxious to shield his sons from
folly and vice; and the chasms here between his overwhelming desire
to form his children so that they might 'be useful examples and worthy
of imitation', and the unhappy facts as they turned out, proved traumatic and embittering to him in the extreme. Never did he sound more
forlorn and all but broken than in 1780, when he expostulated to his
son and heir, 'Where am I therefore to turn, if not into the bosom of
my own family?'

The breach with the Prince of Wales – a son any father might have
found heart-breaking – was of course a prime cause of the bedevilment
of the King's relationship with his other sons. He proved always too
emphatically the arbiter of their destiny to receive the spontaneous
affection that he craved; too consciously and conscientiously responsible a King to be a happy parent. Among his many sterling
qualities imagination and empathy were not to be found. The insistent
pressures of his own problems and crises left no room for a proper
comprehension of those of others. The ability to see the world, or the
consequences of his own actions, through different eyes was denied
him. He simply failed to understand how any sons of his could depart
from their filial or public duty, just as his imagination never managed
to grasp that his dearly loved daughters might wish for a life of their
own away from the frustrations of the 'Nunnery'. Yet he would have
been hurt beyond measure to have been thought a negligent father,
cried out at the injustice of being thought tyrannical. George had himself come nearest to reacting against authority when he was still a
rather difficult and sometimes sullen small boy. By the time he had
arrived at youth's natural age of rebellion his attitudes and opinions
were formed and obedient, and when his own sons began to conform
to more normal patterns of adolescent behaviour he was all the more
unable to understand or sympathise with them, never having himself
kicked over the traces.

Imbued from his youth with a powerful conviction of the responsibilities and prerogatives of royalty, and endowed as he was with
outstanding will-power and tenacity, he might be expected to be pug-
nacious for his royal rights and regal dignities, but it was for his sons
and daughters a wretched misfortune that he was led to conceive of
royalty as a superior caste. In this, however, he was himself a victim of
the preconceptions of the European *ancien régime* of which he was a

part. It may be idle to speculate how differently matters might have turned out if he had allowed himself, or had been allowed, to marry his Lady Sarah, that delightful girl who became so charming and intelligent a woman. Certainly some domestic crisis and misery might have been avoided if his sons and daughters had been permitted to marry outside those rigid royal limits. King and Queen, Princes and Princesses, were all slaves, willing or unwilling, to this exalted idea of the monarchy. Yet of all George III's achievements, the most significant must surely remain this, that in an era when thrones were disintegrating and ancient monarchies tumbling in the dust, the British monarchy not only survived, but survived with its standing strengthened and its popularity enhanced. As long as the King remained well, wrote Lord Auckland at the height of the French Revolution, 'the tranquillity of this country is on a rock'. Again it may be idle, but it is nevertheless of interest, to consider what might have happened to British history if George had succumbed to his desperate illness in 1788, and George IV and the French Revolution had come in together.

In another respect his weakness was also his strength. His lack of imagination permitted him unfailing confidence in the rightness of his judgment and that rectitude of conduct which he so often and tiresomely proclaimed. This certainty, allied to a never-to-be-questioned belief in the support of Divine Providence, gave him a measure of impregnability that such waverers as Bute and North might well have envied. The nation *cannot* desert me, he insisted at the height of his struggle with the Rockinghams. Failing to see how he *could* be wrong, how the Deity *could* desert so honest a cause, enabled him on many occasions to add a cubit to his stature, and even to subtract (as in 1779) a dozen or more battleships from the numbers in the enemy's line. In any case he did not doubt that one Englishman must in the nature of things be worth two Frenchmen. He had not a few of Nelson's qualities, and the ability at a critical moment to find a blind eye for his telescope was one of them.

The only greatness he could have was that which birth had thrust upon him. It was more ordinary qualities – but not so common as to be easily taken for granted – that enabled him, well before he began to be defeated under the weight of his physical and mental afflictions, to win through to general respect, and become the 'good old King'. He had a certain recognisable 'decency'. Although he protested it too much, he was in fact a man of honour and integrity. His views, and more especially his prejudices, were very much in tune with the views and prejudices of other ordinary Englishmen of his day, probably a majority of them. Though he sometimes appreciated 'improvement,' he never of course believe in 'progress.' He had no view of the future, and if by some miracle he could have foreseen it, he would have been more than ever convinced that it was 'highly necessary to avoid all novelties. We know that all wise nations have stuck scrupulously to their antient customs'.

REFERENCES
BIBLIOGRAPHY
INDEX

REFERENCES
(Notes, and a List of Abbreviations)

The following abbreviations have been used:

Add. MSS.	Additional Manuscripts in the British Museum.
*Aspinall LC	ed. A. Aspinall: Later Correspondence of George III.
*Aspinall PW	ed. A. Aspinall: Correspondence of George Prince of Wales.
Auckland	ed. R. J. Eden: Journal and Correspondence of William Eden, first Lord Auckland.
Buckingham	Memoirs of the Courts and Cabinets of George III.
Colchester	Diary and Correspondence of Charles Abbot, Lord Colchester.
D'Arblay	ed. C. F. Barrett: Diary and Letters of Madame D'Arblay.
Dobrée	ed. B. Dobrée: Letters of King George the Third.
Dodington	ed. H. P. Wyndham: Diary of G. Bubb Dodington.
Dropmore	The MSS. of J. B. Fortescue, preserved at Dropmore.
*Fortescue	ed. Sir J. Fortescue: Correspondence of King George III (1760-1783).
Fox Corr.	ed. Lord J. Russell: Memorials and Correspondence of Charles James Fox.
Grafton	Autobiography of Augustus Fitzroy, third Duke of Grafton.
Grenville	ed. W. J. Smith: The Grenville Papers.
Hervey	ed. R. Sedgwick: Some Materials for the Memoirs of the Reign of George II by Lord Hervey.
H.M.C.	Historical Manuscripts Commission.
Huish	R. Huish: Public and Private Life of George III.
Jesse	J. H. Jesse: Memoirs of the Life and Reign of George III.
Lennox	ed. Lady Ilchester and Lord Stavordale: Life and Letters of Lady Sarah Lennox.
Macalpine and Hunter	I. Macalpine and R. Hunter: George III and the Mad-Business.
Malmesbury	Diaries and Correspondence of James Harris, first Earl of Malmesbury.
Minto	ed. Lady Minto: Life and Letters of Sir Gilbert Elliot, first Earl of Minto.
Namier, EAAR	Sir L. Namier: England in the Age of the American Revolution (2nd edition).
Papendiek	ed. V. D. Broughton: Court and Private Life in the Time of Queen Charlotte.
Parl. Hist.	The Parliamentary History of England.
Rose	Diaries and Correspondence of George Rose.
*Sedgwick	ed. R. Sedgwick: Letters from George III to Lord Bute.

* In these collections the number of a letter, not of a page, is referred to, unless otherwise stated.

Stanhope   Earl Stanhope: Life of William Pitt.
Stuart   D. M. Stuart: The Daughters of George III.
Walpole G3   Horace Walpole: Memoirs of the Reign of George III.
Wraxall   Sir N. Wraxall: Historical and Posthumous Memoirs.
Yorke   .   ed. P. C. Yorke: Life and Correspondence of the first Earl of
                      Hardwicke.

CHAPTER 1: FREDERICK PRINCE OF WALES

1. Hervey, 626
2. Ibid., *passim* for years 1736-37
3. Ibid., 371
4. Ibid., 628
5. Ibid., 486
6. Ibid., 487
7. Ibid., 552-53
8. Egmont, *Diary*, ii. 436
9. Doran, *Lives of the Queens of England of the House of Hanover*, i. 426
10. Prince of Wales to Sir Thomas Bootle, June, 1747
11. Chesterfield to S. Dayrolles, 25.4.1749

CHAPTER 2: THE EDUCATION OF A PRINCE

1. Lady Hervey, *Letters*, 139
2. *Gentleman's Magazine*, Jan., 1749
3. Jesse, i. 11
4. Jesse, i. 11
5. Rose, ii. 188
6. Dodington, 15.10.1752
7. Rose, ii. 188
8. See Ilchester, *Henry Fox*, Appendix A
9. Rose, ii. 188
10. Dodington, e.g., 15.10.1752 and 18.12.1753
11. Ibid., 6.8.1755
12. Ibid., 18.12.1753
13. Waldegrave, *Memoirs*, 63
14. Sedgwick, xx-xxi
15. Dodington, 25.2.1753
16. Ibid., 6.8.1755
17. Waldegrave, *Memoirs*, 40
18. Dodington, 6.8.1755
19. Sedgwick, 30
20. Jesse, i. 11
21. Dodington, 6.8.1755
22. Walpole, *Memoirs . . . of the Reign of George II*, ii. 36

CHAPTER 3: THE RISE OF BUTE

1. Waldegrave, *Memoirs*, 38-39

2. Wraxall, i. 327
3. Murray to Newcastle, 10.7.1756
4. Sedgwick, Intro., lii-liv
5. Ibid., 14
6. Ibid., 2
7. Walpole, *Memoirs . . . of the Reign of George II*, ii. 259
8. Newcastle to Hardwicke, 4.2.1758
9. Sedgwick, 3
10. Ibid., 4
11. Ibid., 18
12. Namier, EAAR, 133-4
13. Sedgwick, 25
14. Bute to Dr Campbell, quoted in Sedgwick, Intro., lxii
15. Sedgwick, 60
16. Ibid., 34
17. Lennox, ii. 171
18. Walpole G3, i. 49
19. Sedgwick, 47
20. Ibid., 46-49

CHAPTER 4: THE WHIGS AND THE MONARCHY

1. Walpole, *Memoirs . . . of the Reign of George II*, iii. 302-3
2. Wesley, *Journal*, 25.10.1760
3. Hardwicke to Newcastle, 18.4.1761
4. Sedgwick, Intro., xvi
5. Butterfield, *George III and the Historians*, 216-18

CHAPTER 5: THE NEW REIGN

1. Sedgwick, 61
2. Ibid., 62
3. Lennox, 4
4. Newcastle to Hardwicke, 26.10.1760
5. H. V. Jones to Duchess of Newcastle; Yorke, iii. 306
6. Walpole G3, i. 9
7. Lennox, 8
8. Yorke, iii. 308
9. Minto Papers, quoted in Namier EAAR, 121
10. Sedgwick, p. 49
11. Ibid., 63
12. Newcastle to Hardwicke, 7.11.1760; Yorke, iii. 310
13. Walpole to Montagu, 13.11.1760
14. Montagu, *Letters*, iv. 355
15. Sedgwick, 64
16. Lennox, 33
17. Annual Register (1760), 241
18. Lennox, 13
19. Lecky, *History of England in the 18th Century*, iii. 190
20. See in particular Namier, EAAR Chapter 2, and *Structure of Politics . . .* Chapter 3

21. C. G. Robertson, *England under the Hanoverians* (1911) 218
22. Namier, EAAR, 158-61
23. Lennox, 76-77
24. Namier, *Personalities and Powers*, 42
25. Pares, *George III and the Politicians*, 100
26. Butterfield, *George III and the Historians*, 256-9
27. Fryer, in *Renaissance and Modern Studies* (University of Nottingham) 82-4 and n.
28. Christie, *Myth and Reality* . . . 32n.
29. Walpole, *Collected Works*, ii. 365
30. Namier, EAAR, 167-70
31. Ibid.

CHAPTER 6: SARAH LENNOX AND CHARLOTTE OF MECKLENBURG

1. Sedgwick, 66-73
2. Lennox, i. 99
3. Ibid., ii. 288
4. Ibid., i. 27, 90, ii. 287
5. Ibid., ii. 91
6. Walpole G3, i. 51
7. Lennox, 91-92
8. Ibid., 26-27 and 51
9. Ibid.. ii. 288
10. Ibid., i, 110-11
11. Ibid., ii. 171
12. Ibid., ii. 180
13. Sedgwick, 85
14. Walpole to Conway, 9.9.1761
15. Lennox, ii. 315
16. Papendiek, i. 15-17
17. Walpole G3, i. 125
18. Buckingham, *Works*, ii. 310 (1753 ed.)
19. Sedgwick, 86

CHAPTER 7: THE PEACE AND THE POLITICIANS

1. Adolphus, *History of England from the Accession of George III* . . ., i. 19-21
2. Sedgwick, 87
3. Albemarle, *Rockingham Memoirs*, i. 44
4. Walpole G3, i. 70
5. Sedgwick, 108 and 112
6. Lennox, 64
7. Sedgwick, 148
8. Lennox, 65
9. Sedgwick, 177. See also Lecky, *op. cit.*, iii. 44
10. Grenville, i. 483
11. Sedgwick, 184-9
12. Ibid., 194
13. Ibid., 195
14. *Bedford Correspondence*, iii. 133-4

15. Grenville, i. 452
16. Bute to Rigby, 30.10.1762
17. Sedgwick, 215
18. Ibid., 217
19. Ibid., 228
20. Ibid., 205
21. Yorke, iii. 439-43
22. Sedgwick, 215
23. Walpole G3, i. 184
24. Ibid., i. 140-1
25. Temple to Wilkes, 20.6.1762; Grenville, i. 459
26. Walpole G3, i. 186
27. Ibid., i. 135
28. Walpole to Montagu, 8.4.1763
29. Bute MSS., printed in Sedgwick, Intro., lxii
30. Chesterfield, *Letters*, ii. 482
31. Sedgwick, 231
32. Ibid.
33. Ibid., 324
34. Ibid., 291
35. Ibid., 281
36. Ibid., 274
37. Ibid., 309
38. Yorke, iii. 508
39. Sedgwick, 329

CHAPTER 8: GRENVILLE, WILKES, AND AMERICA

1. Sedgwick, 284
2. Ibid.
3. Grenville, ii. 191; Yorke, iii. 495-6
4. *Chatham Correspondence*, ii. 237-41
5. Walpole G3, i. 229
6. D. A. Winstanley, *Personal and Party Government* 1760-66, 181-2
7. Grenville, ii. 105
8. Yorke, iii. 526
9. Grenville, ii. 196-7
10. Ibid., ii. 207, 211-12, 222, 486
11. Fortescue, i. 140
12. Yorke, iii. 528-29
13. Grenville, ii. 210
14. Ibid., iii. 220
15. Albemarle, *Rockingham Memoirs*, i. 176
16. Ibid., i. 175
17. Sedgwick, 328
18. Grenville, ii. 73
19. Fortescue, i. 32-7
20. Grenville, ii. 165
21. Fortescue, i. 37
22. Grenville, ii. 162 and 166

23. Walpole to Thomas Pitt, 5.6.1764
24. Fortescue, i. 140
25. Grenville, ii. 535
26. G. F. S. Elliot, *The Border Elliots*, 393
27. Walpole G3, i.
28. Lennox, 76
29. Grenville, ii. 517-20; Sedgwick, 335

CHAPTER 9 : THE KING'S ILLNESS AND THE FALL OF GRENVILLE

1. J. Brooke, *The Chatham Administration*, xii
2. Macalpine and Hunter, xii
3. Lennox, 67
4. Walpole to Mann, 20.6.1762
5. Grenville, ii. 118-24
6. Grenville, iii. 152
7. Fortescue, i. 139
8. Walpole G3, ii. 105 and 108
9. Grenville, iii. 175-7
10. Fortescue, i. 75
11. Grenville, iii. 187
12. Fortescue, i. 82
13. Grenville, iii. 188-9
14. *Bedford Correspondence*, iii. 284
15. Sedgwick, 336
16. Grenville, iii. 190-3; Fortescue, i. 139
17. Fortescue, i. 85
18. Ibid., i. 141
19. Ibid., i. 88
20. Ibid., i. 92 and 100
21. Ibid., i. 143
22. Ibid.
23. Grenville, iii. 212-13

CHAPTER 10 : THE ROCKINGHAMS AND THE BREAK WITH BUTE

1. Fortescue, i. 79
2. Ibid., i. 175
3. Ibid., i. 177 and 186
4. Albemarle, *Rockingham Memoirs*, i. 267; Fortescue, i. 183
5. Hardwicke to Rockingham, Albemarle, i. 307
6. Walpole G3, ii. 204
7. Macaulay, *Chatham*
8. Walpole G3, ii. 210
9. Albemarle, *op. cit.*, i. 284-8
10. Sedgwick, 337
11. Albemarle, *op. cit.*, i. 301-2; Fortescue, i. 247-8
12. Sedgwick, 337
13. Fortescue, i. 342
14. Ibid., i. 319

15. Ibid., i. 334
16. Sedgwick, 338
17. Fortescue, i. 355
18. Sedgwick, 339
19. Fortescue, i. 176
20. Ibid., i. 372
21. Sedgwick, pp. 255-58
22. Albemarle, *op. cit.*, i. 360-61
23. Ibid., i. 359-60
24. H. Home, *Works*, i. 148 and 150
25. Rose, ii. 189

CHAPTER 11 : THE CHATHAM FIASCO

1. Walpole G3, ii. 256
2. Fortescue, i. 430
3. Selwyn Correspondence, ii. 60
4. Fortescue, i. 459
5. Ibid., i. 462
6. Ibid., i. 475
7. Ibid., 521
8. Camden MSS., quoted in Brooke, *The Chatham Administration*, 311-12
9. Grafton, 215
10. Fortescue, ii. 667, 669, 671
11. Ibid., ii. 670
12. Grafton, 229-34
13. Junius, *Letters*, 30.5.1769
14. Fortescue, ii. 598
15. Ibid., ii. 701, 701A
16. Grafton, 234

CHAPTER 12 : 'WHEREON ALMOST MY CROWN DEPENDS'

1. Fortescue, ii. 600
2. Walpole G3, iii. 131
3. Fortescue, ii. 616
4. These letters of the King to Weymouth, omitted in Fortescue, are printed in Jesse, i. 426-38 and 508-9 (Bath MSS.)
5. Jesse, i. 437
6. Rockingham to Newcastle, 10.5.1768
7. Jesse, i. 438
8. Fortescue, ii. 613
9. Ibid., ii. 630
10. Grafton, 199-201
11. J. Almon, *Letters of John Wilkes*, iii. 297; W. Rough, *Letters of Wilkes*, i. 86
12. Fortescue, ii. 693
13. Annual Register (1769), 84
14. Malmesbury, i. 176-9
15. Fortescue, ii. 706-7
16. Grafton, 195-6

17. Fortescue, ii. 711
18. Grafton, 234
19. Huish, 332
20. *Bedford Correspondence*, iii. 414
21. Walpole G3, iii. 266
22. Junius, Letter No. 35, 19.12.1769
23. *Chatham Correspondence*, iii. 370-6
24. Grafton, 246n.
25. Ibid., 250
26. Ibid., 241
27. Fortescue, ii. 913
28. Ibid., ii. 933
29. G. Rudé, *Wilkes and Liberty*, 159
30. Fortescue, ii. 938
31. Ibid., ii. 939

CHAPTER 13: MAN AND MONARCH

1. Fortescue, ii. 1008
2. Ibid., ii. 977
3. Huish, 352; Aspinall PW, i. 26
4. Thackeray, *The Four Georges*, 373-4 (Everyman ed.)
5. Wraxall, i. 293
6. Brougham, *Historical Sketches of Statesmen . . .*, i. 11-14
7. Bessborough, *Georgiana*, 289
8. Malmesbury, iv. 317-18
9. R. F. Greville, *Diaries*, 86
10. Twiss, *Eldon*, ii. 358
11. Watson, *Anecdotes of My Own Life*, i. 242
12. Aspinall, LC, i. 648
13. Ibid., i. 659
14. Ibid., i. 576
15. Rose, ii. 193-4
16. Fortescue, iv. 2717, 2719
17. Ibid., iv. 2434
18. Ibid., v. 3044; Brougham, i. 147
19. *Reminiscences of Michael Kelly*, quoted in Jesse, iii. 235
20. D'Arblay, ii. 373
21. Wraxall, i. 282
22. Huish, 350
23. D'Arblay, iii. 67-8
24. Papendiek, i. 246
25. Auckland, ii. 225-6
26. Wraxall, i. 139-41
27. Aspinall LC, i. 380-1
28. Pellew, *Sidmouth*, ii. 342
29. Huish, 350
30. Annual Register (1775)
31. Aspinall PW, iii. 1012
32. Wraxall, ii. 20-1

33. Malmesbury, iv. 383
34. Aspinall LC, i. 655
35. Fortescue, v. 2991
36. Ibid., ii. 1061
37. Ibid., ii. 1048
38. Jesse, ii. 58
39. Althorp MSS., quoted in Aspinall LC, ii. 1229n.
40. Fortescue, iii. 1837
41. Aspinall PW, i. 269

CHAPTER 14: PATRON AND AMATEUR

1. Papendiek, i. 272
2. D'Arblay, ii. 343-4
3. Boswell, *Johnson*, i. 334-9 (Everyman ed.)
4. Dobrée, 139
5. D'Arblay, ii. 344
6. Ibid., iii. 403
7. Burney, *General History of Music* (ed. Mercer), ii. 865
8. H. C. Robbins Landon, *Haydn*, 122-4 and 147n.
9. Burney, *op. cit.*, ii. 1022-3
10. Aspinall LC, i. 570 and n.
11. Papendiek, i. 275
12. H. C. Smith, *Buckingham Palace*, 80-3
13. Lady M. Coke, *Letters and Journals*, ii. 180
14. H. C. Smith, *op. cit.*, 67-9
15. Aspinall LC, i. 563
16. A. Young, *Annals*, vii. 65 and 332
17. A. Young to Mrs Oakes, quoted in Edwards, *Fanny Burney*, 105-6
18. Rose, ii. 183
19. Dobrée, 206

CHAPTER 15: PATERFAMILIAS (1762-1788)

1. The King to Weymouth, 8.6.1768; Jesse, i. 450-4
2. Lennox, i. 152
3. Ibid., i. 189
4. Jesse, ii. 2
5. The King to North; Jesse, ii. 3
6. Walpole to Mann, 7.11.1771
7. Macalpine and Hunter, 223-8
8. Walpole G3, iv. 355
9. Cumberland to Croker, Jesse, i. 365 and n.
10. Fortescue, ii. 1012, 1013
11. Ibid., ii. 1024, 1034, 1036, 1044
12. Ibid., iii. 1574
13. Ibid., 2087
14. Aspinall PW, i. 38
15. D'Arblay, ii. 338

16. Ibid., iii. 57-8
17. Macalpine and Hunter, 255-66; Stuart, 141, 269
18. Papendiek, i. 93-4
19. Ibid., i. 77
20. Ibid., i. 77-8
21. Ibid., i. 50
22. Hurd MSS., quoted in Richardson, *George IV*, 10
23. Papendiek, i. 94
24. Angelo, *Reminiscences*, i. 191
25. Stuart, 193-4
26. Aspinall LC, i. xiv
27. Papendiek, i. 91
28. Ibid., i. 159
29. Aspinall PW, i. 26
30. Ibid., i. 31
31. Ibid., i. 35
32. Ibid., i. 31
33. Ibid.
34. Ibid., i. 41 and nn.
35. Ibid., i. 51, 54
36. Ibid., i. 51
37. Prince Frederick to Prince of Wales, 25.8.1783, Aspinall PW, i. 97
38. Aspinall LC, i. 90
39. Ibid., i. 77 and 107
40. Aspinall PW, i. 140
41. Ibid., i. 118
42. Ibid., 116
43. Prince William to Prince of Wales, Aspinall PW, i. 157
44. Aspinall LC, i. 475
45. Aspinall PW, i. 247, 250, 254, 262
46. Ibid., i. 266
47. Aspinall LC, i. 48, 63, 88
48. D'Arblay, iii. 297
49. Minto Papers, 1788
50. Wraxall, v. 394-5
51. Aspinall PW, i. 47, 50
52. Lennox, ii. 36
53. Ibid., 76
54. Walpole, *Last Journals*, ii. 628
55. See Chapter 19, *passim*.
56. Aspinall PW, i. 71
57. Walpole, *Last Journals*, ii. 496-7
58. Aspinall PW, i. 79 (revised draft)
59. Ibid.
60. Ibid., i. 80
61. Ibid., i. 87
62. Ibid., i. 95
63. Aspinall PW, i. 119
64. Aspinall LC, i. 114
65. Ibid., 114, 181

66. Minute of a conversation between Lord Southampton and Fox, 28.3.1785, Aspinall LC, i. 193
67. Aspinall PW, i. 225
68. Malmesbury, ii. 124-30

CHAPTER 16: 'BLOWS MUST DECIDE'

1. Walpole, *Memoirs G3*, iv. 50-3; Walpole to Mann, 30.1.1770
2. Fortescue, ii. p. 251; Valentine, *Lord North*, i. 238-9
3. Fortescue, iii. 1405
4. Ibid., 1525, 1537, 1543, 1554-5
5. Laprade, *Parliamentary Papers of John Robinson*, 24-5
6. Fortescue, iii. 1379
7. Ibid., 1424, 1486
8. Burke, *Correspondence* (gen. ed. Copeland), ii. 528
9. Undated memorandum, headed '1773?' in Fortescue, iii. 1361, probably 1774
10. Fortescue, iii. 1398
11. Mumby, *George III and the American Revolution*, 211; Parl. Hist., xvii. 1316
12. Fortescue, iii. 1692
13. Ibid., 1508
14. Ibid., 1557, 1563, 1595
15. Ibid., 1556
16. Ibid., 1630, 1670, 1689, 1702, 1737
17. Wedderburn Papers, quoted in Valentine, *Lord North*, i. 375
18. Miller, *Triumph of Freedom*, 168, 170
19. Gen. Harvey to Gen. Irwin, Fortescue, *History of the British Army*, II, iii. 167
20. Fortescue, iii. 1702
21. Ibid., 1570
22. Dobrée, 110
23. Valentine, *Lord George Germain*, 146
24. Fortescue, iii. 1724
25. Stevens, *Facsimiles*, XXV. 2038
26. Fortescue, iii. 1810
27. Ibid., 1849
28. Ibid., 1964
29. Ibid.
30. Ibid., 1743-4
31. Ibid., 1874-89
32. Ibid., 1890
33. H. M. C. Abergavenny MSS., 17; Add. MSS. 33823, f. 208; Fortescue, iii. 2057-60
34. Fortescue, iii. 1938
35. Ibid., 2010

CHAPTER 17: AFTER SARATOGA

1. e.g. in Fortescue, iv. 2847
2. Ibid., 2226
3. Ibid., 2179
4. Ibid., 2257

5. Ibid., 2309
6. Ibid., 2328
7. Ibid., 2219-2234
8. Ibid., 2239-42
9. Ibid., 2247
10. Ibid., 2251
11. Ibid., 2212, 2251
12. Ibid., 2518
13. Ibid., 2405, 2449, 2451
14. Ibid., 2223-30
15. Ibid., 2534, 2538, 2540, 2549-51; Walpole, *Last Journals*, ii. 343
16. Fortescue, iv. 2146
17. Ibid., 2158, 2202
18. Ibid., 2626
19. Ibid., 2346, 2347, 2355, 2358
20. Ibid., 2615, v. 3099
21. Ibid., iv. 2543
22. Ibid., 2536
23. Add. MSS., 37834, f. 93
24. Fortescue, iv. 2494
25. Ibid., 2686
26. Ibid., 2649
27. Ibid.
28. Ibid., 2449
29. Ibid., 2715, 2813
30. Ibid., 2726-8
31. See Butterfield, *George III, Lord North and the People*, 138-61
32. Butterfield, *op. cit.*, 160n.
33. Fortescue, iv. 2840
34. Ibid., 2209. Fortescue assigns this letter to 9th March, 1778, and the original in the Windsor Archives is dated so, in the King's hand. Sandwich's letter (No. 2233), which seems to relate to it, is also dated March, 1778 (the 18th), and endorsed so by the King. The sequence of the known facts, however, seems to demand a much later date, nearer to March, 1779. I have not been able to fathom this mystery.
35. Ibid., 2654
36. Ibid., 2682
37. Add. MSS. 37834, f.90; Fortescue, iv. 2670, 2674, 2683; Knox MSS., quoted in Butterfield, *op. cit.*, 43-4
38. Fortescue, iv. 2722
39. e.g. in ibid., 2687, 2752
40. Ibid., 2686, 2756
41. Butterfield, *op. cit.*, 57-8
42. Fortescue, iv. 2722, 2734
43. Round MSS., quoted in Butterfield, *op. cit.*, 66n.
44. Fortescue, iv. 2764
45. Ibid., 2774
46. Ibid., 2840-1
47. Ibid., 2773
48. Ibid., 2845

49. Ibid., 2849, 2857
50. Ibid., 2850
51. Dobrée, 133-4
52. Butterfield, *op. cit.*, 174n.
53. Parl. Hist. xx. 1116-28
54. Burke, *Correspondence* (gen. ed. Copeland), ii. 435
55. Fortescue, iv. 2823, 2830, 2852, 2858; v. 3556
56. Ibid., iv. 2829, 2838, 2895; v. 3543
57. Ibid., v. 3504

CHAPTER 18: TOWARDS YORKTOWN

1. Bessborough, *Georgiana*, 32
2. Fortescue, v. 3261
3. Ibid., 3080
4. Ibid., 2987, 2991
5. Ibid., 3015
6. Ibid., 3019
7. H.M.C., Abergavenny MSS., 29
8. Sandwich to Robinson, 1.8.1780, quoted in Christie, *End of North's Ministry*, 30-1
9. Quoted in Christie, *op. cit.*, 44-5
10. Fortescue, v. 3156
11. Ibid., 3357
12. Stanhope, i. 61
13. Camden to T. Walpole, 8.11.1781; Rockingham to Portland, 19.11.1781
14. Fortescue, v. 3462, 3470
15. Ibid., 3449-50
16. Parl. Hist. xxii. 705
17. Fortescue, v. 3566, 3568
18. Dobrée, 152-3, 156

CHAPTER 19: 'THE CONTEST IS BECOME PERSONAL'

1. Fox Corr. i. 292
2. Christie, *Myth and Reality . . .*, Chapter 14; *End of North's Ministry*, 102
3. Grafton, 338
4. Fortescue, vi. 3758-9
5. Ibid., 3825
6. Ibid., 3677, 3759, 3761-2, 3765
7. Ibid., 3778, 3808, 3841, 3878
8. Ibid., 3871-2
9. Ibid., 3978
10. Lee Papers, quoted in Reid, *Charles James Fox*
11. Lord North to Earl of Guildford, 18.2.1783
12. Cannon, *The Fox-North Coalition*, 61
13. Fortescue, vi. 4125
14. Ibid., 4213
15. King to Thurlow, Fortescue, vi. 4133
16. Ibid., 4169, 4261

17. Ibid., 4231-39, 4242, 4268
18. Ibid., 4247
19. Ibid., 4272
20. Ibid.
21. Ibid., 4272, 4289, 4302
22. Ibid., 4308, 4316
23. Ibid., 4336
24. Add. MSS., 47570, f.153
25. Minto MSS., quoted in Cannon, *op. cit.*, 112
26. Aspinall LC, i. Intro. xxv
27. H.M.C., Abergavenny MSS., 61
28. Buckingham, i. 285
29. Fortescue, vi. 4546; Lennox, ii. 43-4

CHAPTER 20: RECOVERY AND RETRENCHMENT

1. Fox Corr., ii. 221
2. Stanhope, i. 22
3. Wilberforce, *Life*, i. 38; Stanhope, i. 22
4. Stanhope, i. Appendix, iv
5. Bessborough, *Georgiana*, 72
6. Parl. Hist. xxiv. 597
7. Aspinall LC, i. 14
8. J. H. Rose, *Pitt and Napoleon*, 203
9. Stanhope, i. Appendix, iv-v
10. Ibid.
11. J. H. Rose, *Pitt and Napoleon*, 204
12. Parl. Hist., xxiv. 677-8
13. Stanhope, i. Appendix x
14. Malmesbury, ii. 61
15. B. Connell, *A Whig Peer*, 152
16. Parl. Hist., xxiv. 745-6
17. Dobrée, 184-5; Stanhope, i. Appendix x
18. M. D. George, *Transactions of Royal Hist. Soc., 4th Series*, xxi
19. Wraxall, iii. 3
20. Aspinall LC, i. 226
21. Ibid., 312
22. Farington *Diary*, 22.11.1793
23. Aspinall PW, ii. 600n.
24. D'Arblay, ii. 406
25. Ibid.
26. Stanhope, i. Appendix xii
27. Aspinall LC, i. 274
28. Stanhope, i. Appendix xxii
29. Dobrée, 193-4
30. Stanhope, i. Appendix xvii
31. Ibid.
32. Ibid., Appendix xix-xx
33. Aspinall LC, i. 89
34. Wyvill, *Political Papers*, iv. 119

35. Aspinall LC, i. 159
36. Ibid., i. 182
37. Ibid., i. 183
38. Stanhope, i. Appendix xv-xvi
39. Aspinall LC, i. 283
40. Ibid., xii
41. Ibid., 309, 325
42. Ibid., 190
43. Stanhope, i. Appendix xix
44. Aspinall LC, i. 95
45. Stanhope, i. Appendix xx
46. Fox Corr., ii. 140
47. John Adams, *Works* (ed. C. F. Adams), viii. 255-7
48. Aspinall LC, i. 274
49. J. H. Rose, *Pitt and Napoleon*, 214
50. Stanhope, ii. Appendix iii-iv; Aspinall LC, i. 485

CHAPTER 21: THE ROYAL MALADY AND THE REGENCY CRISIS

1. Baker MSS., quoted in Macalpine and Hunter, 7-8
2. D'Arblay, iv. 1-88; Wraxall, iii. 139-41; Aspinall LC, i. 474, 476
3. D'Arblay, iv. 120
4. Ailesbury *Diary*, 297
5. D'Arblay, iv. 131 and n.
6. Ibid., 135-6
7. Ibid., 152
8. Ailesbury *Diary*, ii. 297
9. Buckingham, i. 433-6; ii. 3
10. Aspinall PW, i. 293
11. Sheffield to Eden, 22.11.1788, Auckland, ii. 244
12. Buckingham, ii. 6-7
13. Minto, i. 238
14. Ibid., i. 240
15. R. F. Greville, *Diaries*, 105
16. D'Arblay, iv. 194
17. R. F. Greville, *Diaries*, 117
18. *Political Memoranda of the Duke of Leeds*, 133
19. Add. MSS., 47570, ff. 180-1
20. Aspinall PW, i. 339, 360
21. Buckingham, ii. 68
22. Auckland, ii. 277n., 279-80
23. Macalpine and Hunter, 54
24. D'Arblay, iv. 215
25. Buckingham, ii. 47
26. R. F. Greville, *Diaries*, 133
27. Sichel, *Sheridan*, ii. 424-5
28. R. F. Greville, *Diaries*, 139-40, 161
29. Macalpine and Hunter, 281-2
30. D'Arblay, iv. 253
31. Macalpine and Hunter, 80

32. Auckland, ii. 286
33. Derry, *Regency Crisis and the Whigs*, Chapters 4 and 5

CHAPTER 22: 'GOOD ORDER AND OUR EXCELLENT CONSTITUTION'

1. Dobrée, 200
2. Buckingham, ii. 125
3. Mrs Harcourt, *Diary*, 25-6; Wraxall, v. 255-8
4. Aspinall LC, i. 489, 490
5. Jesse, iii. 111-12
6. Add. MSS., 47570, f.180
7. Cornwallis, *Correspondence*, i. 408
8. Aspinall PW, ii. 448, 462
9. Storer to Eden, Auckland, ii. 318
10. Sidney Smith, to Eden, Ibid.
11. Buckingham, ii. 149, 152
12. Minto, i. 275
13. Stanhope, iii. Appendix vii
14. Auckland, ii. 318; Aspinall LC, i. 516; Stanhope, ii. Appendix viii-ix
15. Jesse, iii. 128-31
16. Aspinall LC, i. xi
17. D'Arblay, iv. 289-309
18. Aspinall LC, i. 541
19. Ibid., 535, 547, 550; D'Arblay, iv. 310-23
20. Windham, *Diary*, 213
21. King to Dundas, 16.7.1791
22. Auckland, ii. 391, 396
23. Stanhope, ii. 149-51 and Appendix xv; Gore-Browne, *Chancellor Thurlow*, 279-99
24. Pitt to Dundas, 14.10,1792
25. Minto, ii. 29
26. Aspinall LC, i. 793, 795, 797
27. Ibid., 751
28. Minto, ii. 96
29. Add. MSS., 47570
30. Auckland, ii. 423, 498
31. Aspinall PW, ii. 694
32. Ibid., 720
33. Ibid., 718
34. Stanhope, ii. 253-4
35. Ibid., Appendix xx
36. Aspinall LC, ii. 1090 and n., 1091, 1093, 1095
37. Aspinall PW, ii. 686
38. Dobrée, 212-16; Aspinall LC, i. 829
29. Auckland, ii. 458
40. Stanhope, ii. Appendix xvii
41. Dobrée, 256
42. Parl. Hist., xxx.901
43. Dobrée, 226
44. Aspinall LC, ii. 1297, 1299, 1306, 1311

45. Aspinall PW, iii. 1012
46. Dobrée, 227
47. J. H. Rose, *Pitt and Napoleon*, 241
48. Annual Register, 1798, ii. 6

CHAPTER 23 : FAMILY DISCORD

1. Wraxall, v. 171
2. Dobrée, 201-4
3. Aspinall LC, i. 520
4. D'Arblay, iv. 469-76
5. Aspinall PW, ii. 599
6. Glenbervie Diaries, i. 59
7. Aspinall PW, iii. 1042
8. Aspinall LC, i. 512, 572-4; Dropmore, i. 558
9. Aspinall LC, i. 581
10. Ibid., 464
11. Ibid., 643
12. See M. Gillen, *The Prince and His Lady*
13. Aspinall LC, i. 745
14. Macalpine and Hunter, 258-61
15. Aspinall PW, ii. 747
16. Aspinall LC, ii. 906
17. Farington Diaries, 27.11.1793 and 11.8.1804
18. Aspinall LC, ii. 1009-10
19. Aspinall LC, iii. 2145, 2149
20. Ibid., 2565
21. Aspinall PW, ii. 820
22. Ibid., 836, 852, 858, 863, 871
23. Ibid., 877, 881; Aspinall LC, ii. 1146
24. Aspinall PW, ii. 896, 904
25. Aspinall LC, ii. 1240, 1348; Aspinall PW, iii. 963, 976, 1051, 1079
26. Aspinall LC, iii. 1669, 1718, 1737
27. Fulford, *Royal Dukes*, 206-10
28. Aspinall LC, ii. 1220
29. Ibid., iii. 1905 and n.
30. 'Peter Pindar,' *Poems*
31. Princess Elizabeth to Prince of Wales, Sept., 1808
32. Aspinall PW, ii. 686; iii. 1277, 1381, 1389
33. Ibid., ii. 762
34. Stuart, 109-20; M. Marples, *Six Royal Sisters*, 113-17
35. Stuart, 142
36. Ibid., 335; Marples, *op. cit.*, Chapter 13
37. Ibid., 782, 819
38. Stuart, 63
39. Windsor Archives, quoted in Stuart, 65

CHAPTER 24 : THE KING AND THE HEIR APPARENT

1. Aspinall PW, ii. 775

2. Ibid., iii. 1012
3. Ibid., iii. 1245
4. Ibid., iii. 980n., 1250, 1347 and n., 1353, 1357-8, 1361
5. King's Memorandum, Oct., 1792 (Aspinall LC, i. 798)
6. Malmesbury, ii. 450
7. Aspinall PW, ii. 599
8. Stanhope, ii. Appendix xx
9. Aspinall PW, ii. 859; iii. pp. 8-10
10. Prince Ernest to Prince of Wales, 28.8.1794
11. Aspinall PW, iii. 980n.
12. Aspinall LC, ii. 1250-1, 1253
13. Aspinall PW, iii. 970
14. Aspinall LC, ii. 1253, 1255
15. Aspinall PW, iii. 1002, 1006, 1044, 1082
16. Malmesbury, iii. 210
17. Ibid., 212-13
18. Aylesford MSS., quoted in Aspinall PW, iii. 986n.
19. Aspinall PW, iii. 1044, 1059-60, 1065; Aspinall LC, ii. 1356
20. Aspinall PW, iii. 1067
21. Minto, iii. 14
22. *Political Memoranda of the Duke of Leeds*, 221-2; Aspinall PW, iii. 1153
23. Aspinall PW, iii. 1124
24. Ibid., 1117
25. Ibid., 1314; Aspinall LC, iii. 1667
26. Lord to Lady Minto, 12.12.1798, Minto, iii. 36

CHAPTER 25 : THE CONDUCT OF THE WAR (1793-1801)

1. Aspinall LC, ii. 840-1071, *passim.*
2. Ibid., 868, 882, 891, 926, 939
3. Ibid., 913
4. Stanhope, ii. 259
5. Aspinall LC, ii. Intro. xxxiv-xxxv
6. Stanhope, ii. Appendix xxi-xxii
7. Harewood MSS., quoted in Aspinall LC, ii. p. 414n.
8. Dropmore, iii. 227-8, 290; Aspinall LC, ii. 1467, 1484
9. Windham Papers, ii. 61
10. Dropmore, iii. 327
11. Aspinall LC, ii. 1844, 1846
12. Ibid., iii. 2060, 2066
13. Ibid., 2095, 2097; Buckingham, iii. 4
14. Dundas to Grenville, 25.7.1800, quoted in Aspinall iii. Intro. xv
15. Quoted in Barnes, *George III and William Pitt*, 300-1

CHAPTER 26 : IRELAND AND THE CATHOLICS

1. Stanhope, ii. Appendix xxiii-xxv
2. Ibid.
3. Ibid.
4. Aspinall LC, ii. 1243

5. H.M.C., Kenyon MSS., 542-3; Stanhope, iii. Appendix xxiii-xxv; Aspinall LC, ii. 1219, 1221; Barnes, *op. cit.*, 348-51
6. Stanhope, iii. Appendix xx
7. Castlereagh, *Memoirs*, iv. 8-11
8. J. H. Rose, *Pitt and Napoleon*, 243-44
9. Barnes, *op. cit.*, 362
10. Pellew, *Sidmouth*, ii. 500-12
11. Barnes, *op. cit.*, 369-70
12. Aspinall LC, iii. Intro. xvii
13. Malmesbury, iv. 46
14. Ibid., 8-9; Pellew, *op. cit.*, i. 298
15. Colchester, i. 232
16. Sidmouth MSS., quoted in P. Ziegler, *Addington*, 89
17. Stanhope, iii. Appendix xxviii-xxx
18. Pellew, *op. cit.*, i. 288
19. Dobrée, 244
20. Colchester, i. 242-4
21. Willis MSS., quoted in Macalpine and Hunter, 113
22. Macalpine and Hunter, 114
23. Stanhope, iii. 294-7; Rose, ii. 320-1
24. Macalpine and Hunter, 116
25. Rose, i. 319
26. Colchester, i. 247-8
27. Malmesbury, iv. 33-4
28. Minto, iii. 204-5
29. Macalpine and Hunter, 119
30. Ibid., 122
31. Colchester, i. 263
32. Stanhope, iii. 302-5; Colchester, i. 245

CHAPTER 27: PUBLIC POSTURES AND PRIVATE DISTRESSES (1801-1804)

1. Minto, iii. 205; Malmesbury, iv. 54
2. Jesse, iii. 281-2
3. Minto, iii. 217
4. Princess Elizabeth to Thomas Willis, 6.6.1801
5. Macalpine and Hunter, 126-7
6. Rose, i. 354; Macalpine and Hunter, 125-8
7. Jesse, iii. 278-9
8. Pellew, *Sidmouth*, i. 408-9
9. Macalpine and Hunter, 129
10. Jesse, iii. 288-9; Macalpine and Hunter, 130
11. Malmesbury, iv. 64-6
12. King to Lord Hawkesbury, 30.9.1801
13. Colchester, i. 468
14. Jesse, iii. 338
15. Ibid., 333
16. Ibid., 330
17. Twiss, *Eldon*, i. 422-3

18. Colchester, i. 479-80
19. Ibid., 481; Macalpine and Hunter, 133-5
20. Macalpine and Hunter, 233
21. Colchester, i. 481
22. Barnes, *George III and William Pitt*, 426
23. Stanhope, iv. Appendix ii-iii
24. Rose, ii. 121
25. Malmesbury, iv. 317, 326-7
26. Dacres Adams MSS., quoted in Macalpine and Hunter, 137
27. Aspinall PW, v. 1958; a memorandum, very belittling to the King, which Professor Aspinall presumes was written by Sir Robert Wilson. The extant copy is in the handwriting of Colonel MacMahon, the Prince of Wales's secretary.
28. Ibid., 1896
29. Auckland, iv. 212-13
30. Twiss, *Eldon*, i. 473; King to Eldon, 13.11.1804; Pitt to Eldon, 12.11.1804
31. Jesse, iii. 406
32. Malmesbury, iv. 344; Colchester, i. 528, 531; C. Knight, *Autobiography*, 83

CHAPTER 28: LAST ACTIVE YEARS (1805-1810)

1. J. H. Rose, *Pitt and Napoleon*, 247
2. Ibid., 248; Stanhope, iv. Appendix xxv
3. Rose, ii. 199-200
4. Barnes, *op. cit.*, 467
5. J. H. Rose, *William Pitt*, ii. 556
6. Jesse, iii. 473-4
7. Twiss, *Eldon*, i. 510
8. Pellew, *Sidmouth*, ii. 435
9. Wilberforce, *Life*, iii. 307
10. Auckland, iv. 294; Malmesbury, iv. 379-81
11. Aspinall LC, v. 3960
12. Ibid., 4208-9
13. Colchester, ii. 136, 162
14. Aspinall LC, v. 3795
15. Ibid., 3820
16. Ibid., 3820-1
17. Ibid., 3836
18. Stuart, 345-50
19. Ibid., 352
20. Aspinall LC, v. 3949
21. Ibid., 3965
22. Stuart, 363
23. Ibid., 366
24. C. Knight, *Autobiography*, 85
25. Aspinall LC, v. 4238n.

CHAPTER 29: THE FINAL DECADE

1. Macalpine and Hunter, 145
2. Colchester, ii. 293-4; Buckingham, iv. 459-60

3. Macalpine and Hunter, 156-8
4. Buckingham, *Memoirs of the Court of England during the Regency*, i. 57-8
5. Stuart, 215, 219
6. Ibid., 214-16
7. Macalpine and Hunter, 162
8. Ibid., 164
9. Buckingham, *Memoirs of the . . . Regency*, i. 411
10. Stuart, 94; Macalpine and Hunter, 166-8
11. Stuart, 124-5
12. Macalpine and Hunter, 170

BIBLIOGRAPHY

CONTEMPORARY SOURCES

ABERGAVENNY MSS.: (Historical MSS. Commission, 1887).

ADOLPHUS, J.: History of England from the Accession of George III (2nd ed. 1803, 3rd ed. 1840).

AIKIN, J.: Annals of the Reign of George III 1760-1815 (1816, 2 vols.).

ALBEMARLE, DUKE OF: Memoirs of the Marquis of Rockingham (1852, 2 vols.).

ANGELO, H.: Reminiscences (1828-30).

ASPINALL, A. (ed.): Correspondence of George, Prince of Wales, 1770-1812 (8 vols.).
  Later Correspondence of George III, 1783-1810 (5 vols).

ASPINALL, A. and SMITH, E. A. (eds.): English Historical Documents 1783-1832.

AUCKLAND, WILLIAM EDEN, LORD: Journal and Correspondence (ed. R. J. Eden) (1861-62, 4 vols).

BARRINGTON PAPERS: (ed. D. Bonner-Smith) (1937-41, 2 vols).

BEDFORD, DUKE OF: Correspondence (ed. Lord J. Russell) (1842-46, 3 vols).

BELSHAM, W.: Memories of the Reign of George the Third to . . . 1793 (1802, 3 vols).

BESSBOROUGH, EARL OF: Georgiana, Extracts from the Correspondence of the Duchess of Devonshire (1955).

BISSET, R.: History of the Reign of George III (1803).

BLACKSTONE, SIR WILLIAM: Commentaries on the Laws of England (1791, 4 vols).

BOADEN, J.: Memoirs of Mrs Siddons (1893).

BOSWELL, J.: Life of Dr Johnson (Everyman ed.) (1920).

BROUGHAM, LORD: Historical Sketches of Statesmen who flourished in the Reign of George III (1845, 3 vols).

BUCKINGHAM AND CHANDOS, DUKE OF: Memoirs of the Courts and Cabinets of George III (1853-55, 4 vols).

BURGES, SIR J. BLAND: Letters and Correspondence (ed. J. Hutton) (1885).

BURKE, E.: Correspondence (ed. T. W. Copeland and others) (1958, in progress).
  Thoughts on the Cause of the Present Discontents (1770).
  Works and Correspondence (ed. Earl Fitzwilliam and Sir R. Bourke) (1852, 8 vols; 1894, 4 vols).

BURNEY, C.: General History of Music (ed. Mercer) (1957 ed.).

BURNEY, F.: see D'Arblay.

BYRON, LORD: The Vision of Judgment (1820).

CASTLEREAGH, VISCOUNT: Memoirs and Correspondence, vol 4 (ed. Lord Londonderry) (1849).

CHATHAM, EARL OF: Correspondence (ed. W. H. Taylor and J. H. Pringle) (1838-40, 4 vols).

CHESTERFIELD, P. D. STANHOPE, EARL OF: Letters (ed. Stanhope) (1845-53, 5 vols) (ed. B. Dobrée) (1932, 6 vols).

COLCHESTER, C. ABBOT, LORD: Diary and Correspondence (1861, 3 vols).

CORNWALLIS, MARQUIS: Correspondence (ed. C. Ross) (1859, 3 vols).

CROKER, J. W.: Correspondence and Diaries (ed. L. V. Jennings) (1885).

D'ARBLAY, F.: Diary and Letters (ed. C. F. Barrett) (1904 ed., 6 vols).

DELANY, MRS: Autobiography and Correspondence (ed. Lady Llanover) (1862, 3 vols).

DEVONSHIRE, DUCHESS OF: Georgiana's Diary, in Sichel's *Sheridan* (q.v.).

DOBRÉE, B. (ed.): The Letters of King George III (1935).

DODINGTON, G. BUBB: Diary, and Memorial to the Prince (ed. H. P. Wyndham((1809).

DONNE, W. B.: Correspondence of George III with Lord North 1768-83 (1867).

DROPMORE PAPERS: (Historical MSS. Commission, the MSS. of J. B. Fortescue, Esq., preserved at Dropmore) (1892-1927, 10 vols).

EGMONT, LORD: Diaries (Historical MSS. Commission) (1920-24, 3 vols).

FARINGTON, J.: The Farington Diary (ed. J. Greig) (1922-28, 8 vols).

FITZMAURICE, LORD E.: Life of William Earl of Shelburne (1875-76, 3 vols).

FORTESCUE, J. B.: *see* Dropmore Papers.

FORTESCUE, SIR JOHN (ed.): Correspondence of King George III from 1760 to December, 1783 (1927-28, 6 vols).

FOX, C. J.: Memorials and Correspondence (ed. Lord J. Russell) (1853-57, 4 vols).

FOX MSS. IN B.M. Add. MSS. 47449-47597.

FRANKLIN, B.: Works (ed. J. Sparks) (1882, 10 vols).

FULFORD, R. (ed.): The Autobiography of Miss Knight . . . (1960).

GALT, J.: George III, his Court and Family (1824, 2 vols).

GIBBON, E.: Letters (ed. J. E. Norton) (1956, 3 vols).

GLENBERVIE, SYLVESTER DOUGLAS, LORD: Diaries (ed. F. Bickley) (1928, 2 vols).

GRANVILLE (Lord Granville Leveson-Gower) Private Correspondence 1781-1821 (ed. Lady Granville) (1916).

GRENVILLE PAPERS (ed. W. J. Smith) (1852-53, 4 vols).

GREVILLE, R. F.: Diaries (ed. F. McK. Bladon) (1930).

HARCOURT, COUNTESS OF: Memoirs of the Years 1788-1789, ed. E. W. Harcourt, in *Harcourt Papers*, vol 4 (1895).

HARCOURT, MRS.: Diary of the Court of King George III (in Miscellanies of the Philobiblon Society 1871, vol. 13).

HERVEY, LORD: Some Materials for the Memoirs of the Reign of George II (ed. R. Sedgwick) (1931, 3 vols).

HERVEY, MARY LEPEL, LADY: Letters (1821).

HOLLAND, HENRY FOX, LORD: Memoir, printed in Life and Letters of Lady Sarah Lennox (q.v.).

HOLLAND, (THIRD) LORD: Memoirs of the Whig Party during my Time (ed. Lord Henry Holland) (1852).

HOLT, E.: Public and Domestic Life of George III (1820).

HORN, D. B. and RANSOME, M.: English Historical Documents 1714-1783 (1957).

JENKINSON, C.: The Jenkinson Papers 1760-1766 (ed. N. S. Jucker) (1949).

JERNINGHAM LETTERS (ed. E. Castle) (2 vols, 1896).

JOHNSON, S.: Taxation No Tyranny (1775).

'JUNIUS': Letters (ed. C. W. Everett).

KENYON, LORD: The MSS. of Lord Kenyon (Historical MSS. Commission) (1894).

LANDON, H. C. ROBBINS: Collected Correspondence and London Notebooks of Joseph Haydn (1959).

LEEDS, DUKE OF: Political Memoranda (ed. O. Browning) (1884).

LENNOX, LADY S.: Life and Letters (ed. Lady Ilchester and Lord Stavordale) (1901, 2 vols).

MALMESBURY, J. HARRIS, EARL OF: Diaries and Correspondence (1844, 4 vols) Letters to his Family and Friends (1870, 2 vols).

MINTO, SIR G. ELLIOT, EARL OF: Life and Letters (1874, 3 vols).

MORISON, S. E. (ed.): Sources and Documents Illustrating the American Revolution (1929).

MUMBY, F. A. (ed.): George III and the American Revolution (1924).

NEWCASTLE, DUKE OF: A Narrative . . . 1765-1767 (ed. M. Bateson) (1898).

NEWSPAPERS AND JOURNALS: Annual Register, Gentleman's Magazine, Morning Herald, The Times, The True Briton, The London Chronicle, The Oracle, The Auditor, The North Briton, The Monitor, The Briton . . .

PAINE, T.: The Rights of Man (1791-92).

PAPENDIEK, C.: Court and Private Life of the Time of Queen Charlotte (ed. V. D. Broughton) (1886, 2 vols).

PARKE, W. T.: Musical Memoirs 1784-1830 (1830).

PARLIAMENTARY HISTORY OF ENGLAND (1806-20, 36 vols).

PELLEW, G.: Life and Correspondence of Henry Addington, First Viscount Sidmouth (1847, 3 vols).

POLE, J. R. (ed.): The Revolution in America 1758-1788 (1970).

PYNE, W. H.: The History of the Royal Residences (1819, 3 vols).

ROBINSON, J.: Letters to Charles Jenkinson B.M. Add. MSS. 38206-23 Letters to George III B.M. Add. MSS. 37833-36, 38567. Parliamentary Papers 1774-1784 (ed. W. T. Laprade) (1922).

ROMILLY, SIR S.: Memoirs of the Life of Sir Samuel Romilly, written by himself (1840, 3 vols).

ROSE, G.: Diaries and Correspondence (ed. L. V. Harcourt) (1860, 2 vols).

RUSSELL, LORD J.: The Life and Times of Charles Fox (1859-66, 3 vols).

RUTLAND, DUKE OF: Correspondence between William Pitt and Charles, Duke of Rutland 1781-87 (1890).

SANDWICH, JOHN, 4TH EARL OF: Private Papers (Navy Records Society ed. G. R. Barnes and J. H. Owen) (1932-38).

SEDGWICK, R.: Letters from George III to Lord Bute (1940).

STEPHENS, A.: Memoirs of John Horne Tooke (1813, 2 vols).

STEVENS, B. F.: Facsimile of MSS. in European Archives relating to America 1773-1785 (1889-95, 25 vols).

TAYLOR, SIR H.: The Taylor Papers (1913).

TOMLINSON, J.: (ed.) Additional Grenville Papers, 1763-1765 (1962).

TWISS, H.: The Public and Private Life of Lord Chancellor Eldon (1844, 3 vols).

WALDEGRAVE, EARL: Memoirs (1821).

WALPOLE, H.: Collected Works (1798-1825, 9 vols). Last Journals (ed. F. Steuart) (1910). Letters (ed. P. Toynbee) (1918-25, 19 vols).

WALPOLE, H.: Memoirs of the Last Ten Years of the Reign of George II (ed. Lord Holland) (1846). Memoirs of the Reign of George III (ed. G. F. R. Barker) (1894, 4 vols).

WILBERFORCE, R., I., AND S.: Life of William Wilberforce (1838, 5 vols).

WINDHAM, W.: Diary (ed. H. Baring) (1866).
   The Windham Papers (1913, 2 vols).
WRAXALL, SIR N. W.: Historical and Posthumous Memoirs (ed. H. B. Wheatley) (1884, 5 vols).
   A Short Review of the Political State of Great Britain (pub. anon. 1787).
YORKE, P. C.: Life and Correspondence of Lord Chancellor Hardwicke (1913, 3 vols).
YOUNG, A.: Autobiography (ed. M. Betham-Edwards) (1898).

SECONDARY SOURCES

ASPINALL, A.: Politics and the Press 1780-1850 (1949).
BARNES, D. G.: George III and William Pitt, 1783-1806 (1939).
BELOFF, M. (ed.): The Debate on the American Revolution 1761-1783 (1949).
BLEACKLEY, H.: Life of John Wilkes (1917).
BOULTON, W. B.: Thomas Gainsborough, his Life, Works, Friends, and Sitters (1905).
BROOKE, J.: The Chatham Administration of 1766-68 (1956).
BROWN, P.: The Chathamites (1967).
BRYANT, SIR A.: Years of Endurance (1942).
   Years of Victory (1944).
BUTTERFIELD, SIR H.: George III, Lord North, and the People (1949).
   George III and the Historians (1957).
CAMERON, H. C.: Sir Joseph Banks (1952).
CAMPBELL, J. C.: Lives of the Lord Chancellors, vol. 5 (1846).
CANNON, J.: The Fox-North Coalition: Crisis of the Constitution 1782-84 (1969).
CHAPMAN, H. W.: Caroline Matilda Queen of Denmark (1971).
CHENEVIX-TRENCH, C.: The Royal Malady (1964).
CHILDE-PEMBERTON, W. S.: The Romance of Princess Amelia (1910).
CHRISTIE, I. R.: Crisis of Empire: Great Britain and the American Colonies, 1754-1783 (1966).
   The End of Lord North's Ministry 1780-82 (1958).
   Myth and Reality in Late 18th-century British Politics . . . (1970).
   Wilkes, Wyvill, and Reform (1962).
CONNELL. B.: Portrait of a Whig Peer (1957).
COPELAND, T. W.: Edmund Burke (1950).
DALE, A.: James Wyatt, Architect (1936).
DAVIES, J. D. G.: George the Third (1936).
DERRY, J. W.: The Regency Crisis and the Whigs (1963).
   William Pitt (1962).
DICKERSON, O. M.: The Navigation Acts and the American Revolution (1951).
DICTIONARY OF NATIONAL BIOGRAPHY
DONOUGHUE, B.: British Politics and the American Revolution: the Path to War 1773-75 (1964).
DORAN, J.: Lives of the Queens of England under the House of Hanover (1855, 2 vols).
EDWARDS, A.: Fanny Burney (1948).
   Frederick Louis, Prince of Wales (1947).
EHRMAN, J.: The Younger Pitt: the Years of Acclaim (1969).

ELLIOT, G. F. S.: The Border Elliots and the Family of Minto (1897).

EYCK, E.: Pitt versus Fox, Father and Son (1950).

FEILING, SIR K.: The Second Tory Party 1714-1832 (1938).

FITZGERALD, P.: Royal Dukes and Princesses of the Family of George III (1882).

FOORD, A. S.: His Majesty's Opposition, 1714-1830 (1964).

FOTHERGILL, B.: Mrs Jordan (1965).

FRYER, W. R.: King George III, his Political Character and Conduct 1760-1784; a new Whig interpretation (Renaissance and Modern Studies 1962. University of Nottingham).

FULFORD, R.: George the Fourth (1935).
Royal Dukes (1933).

FURBER, H.: Henry Dundas, 1st Viscount Melville (1931).

GEORGE, M. D.: English Political Caricature (1959, 2 vols).
'Fox's Martyrs: The General Election of 1784' Transactions of the Royal Historical Society, 4th series XXI, 136-68 (1939).

GILLEN, M.: The Prince and His Lady (1970).

GORE-BROWNE, R.: Chancellor Thurlow (1953).

GRAY, D.: Spencer Perceval (1963).

GUTTMACHER, M.: America's Last King, an Interpretation of the Madness of George III (New York, 1941).

HARDY, T.: The Dynasts (1904-08).

HARRIS, J. and others: Buckingham Palace (1968).

HARWOOD, T. E.: Windsor Old and New (1929).

HIBBERT, C.: King Mob, the Story of Lord George Gordon and the Riots of 1780 (1958).

HOBHOUSE, C.: Fox (1934).

ILCHESTER, LORD: Henry Fox, First Lord Holland (1920, 2 vols).

JESSE, J. H.: George Selwyn and his Contemporaries (1843-44, 4 vols).
Memoirs of the Life and Reign of George III (1867, 3 vols).

KEMP, B.: Crewe's Act, 1782. English Historical Review vol. 68 King and Commons 1660-1837 (1957).

KNOLLENBERG, B.: Origin of the American Revolution (New York, 1960).
Washington and the Revolution, a Reappraisal (New York, 1940).

LECKY, W. E. H.: History of England in the Eighteenth Century, vols 3-8 (1879-90).

LUCAS, R.: Lord North (1913, 2 vols).

LYTE, SIR H.: A History of Eton College 1490-1910 (1911, 4th ed.).

MACALPINE, I., and HUNTER, R.: George III and the Mad-Business (1969).

MACALPINE, I., HUNTER, R., and others: Porphyria, a Royal Malady (1968).

MACAULAY, LORD: Essay on Chatham (1844).

MACCOBY, S.: English Radicalism 1762-1785 (1935).
English Radicalism 1786-1832 (1955).

MACKESY, P.: The War for America 1775-1783 (1964).

MAGNUS, SIR P.: Edmund Burke (1939).

MARPLES, M.: Poor Fred and the Butcher (1970).
Six Royal Sisters: the Daughters of George III (1969).

MARSHALL, D.: Eighteenth-century England (1962).

MARTELLI, G.: Jemmy Twitcher (1962).

MELVILLE, L.: Farmer George (1907, 2 vols).

METEYARD, E.: Life of Wedgwood (1865-66, 2 vols, republished 1971).

MILLAR, O.: Tudor, Stuart and Early Georgian Pictures in the Royal Collection (1963, 2 vols).
   Later Georgian Pictures in the Royal Collection (1969, 2 vols).
MILLER, J. C.: Origins of the American Revolution (New York, 1945, 1959).
   The Triumph of Freedom 1775-1783 (Boston, 1948).
MORSHEAD, SIR O.: Windsor Castle (1957).
NAMIER, SIR L.: Additions and Corrections to Sir John Fortescue's Edition of the Correspondence of George III (1937).
   Crossroads of Power (1962).
   England in the Age of the American Revolution (1961, 2nd ed.).
   Personalities and Powers (1955).
   The Structure of Politics at the Accession of George III (1957, 2nd ed.)
NAMIER, SIR L., BROOKE, J. and others: The History of Parliament; The Commons 1754-1790 (1964, 3 vols).
NAPIER, P.: The Sword Dance: Lady Sarah Lennox and the Napiers (1971).
NATAN, A. (ed.): Silver Renaissance (1961).
NORRIS, J.: Shelburne and Reform (1963).
OWEN, J. B.: The Rise of the Pelhams (1957).
PARES, R.: King George III and the Politicians (1953).
   Limited Monarchy in Great Britain in the Eighteenth Century (Historical Association Pamphlet, 1957).
PARES, R. and TAYLOR, A. J. P.: Essays Presented to Sir Lewis Namier (1956).
PEMBERTON, W. B.: Lord North (1938).
PLUMB, J. H.: The First Four Georges (1956).
POSTGATE, R.: That Devil Wilkes (1956 ed.).
REID, L.: Charles James Fox, a Man for the People (1969).
RICHARDSON, J.: The Disastrous Marriage (1960).
   George IV (1966).
RITCHESON, C. R.: British Politics and the American Revolution (1954).
ROSCOE, E. S. and CLERGUE, H.: George Selwyn, his Letters and his Life (1889).
ROSE, J. H.: Life of William Pitt (1911, 2 vols).
   Pitt and Napoleon (1912).
RUDÉ, G. F. E.: The Gordon Riots (Transactions of the Royal Historical Society, 5th series, vi) (1956).
   Wilkes and Liberty (1962).
RUVILLE, A. VON: William Pitt Earl of Chatham (1907, transl. 3 vols).
SHERRARD, O. A.: Life of Lord Chatham (1952-58, 3 vols).
SICHEL, W. S.: Sheridan (1909, 2 vols).
SIME, J.: William Herschel and his Work (1900).
SMITH, E.: Life of Sir Joseph Banks (1911).
SMITH, H. C.: Buckingham Palace (1931).
STANHOPE, EARL: Life of William Pitt (1861-62, 4 vols).
STUART, D. M.: The Daughters of George III (1939).
SUTHERLAND, L.: The East India Company in 18th-Century Politics (1952).
TERRY, C. S.: John Christian Bach (1929).
THOMAS, P. D. G.: The House of Commons in the 18th Century (1971).
TUNSTALL, W. C. B.: William Pitt, Earl of Chatham (1938).
TURBERVILLE, A. S.: The House of Lords in the 18th Century (1927).
   The House of Lords in the Age of Reform (1958).
TURBERVILLE, A. S. (ed.): Johnson's England (1933, 2 vols).

TURNER, E. S.: The Court of St James's (1959).
VALENTINE, A. C.: Lord George Germain (1962).
  Lord North (1967, 2 vols).
VAN DOREN, C. C.: Benjamin Franklin (1939).
VEITCH, G. S.: The Genesis of Parliamentary Reform (1965, 2nd ed.).
VULLIAMY, C. E.: Royal George (1937).
WATSON, J. S.: The Reign of George III 1760-1815 (1960).
WHITE, R. J.: The Age of George III (1968).
WILKINS, W. H.: Mrs Fitzherbert and George IV (1905, 2 vols).
WILLIAMS, B.: Life of William Pitt, Earl of Chatham (1913, 2 vols).
WILLIAMS, E. N.: The Eighteenth Century Constitution 1688-1815 . . . (1960).
WILLIAMS, N. J.: The Royal Residences of Great Britain (1960).
WILLIS, G. M.: Ernest Augustus, Duke of Cumberland and King of Hanover
  (1954).
WILLSON, B.: George III as Man, Monarch, and Statesman (1907).
WINSTANLEY, D. A.: Lord Chatham and the Whig Opposition (1912).
  Personal and Party Government in the Reign of George III (1910).
YOUNG, SIR G.: Poor Fred, the People's Prince (1937).
ZIEGLER, P.: Addington (1965).

INDEX

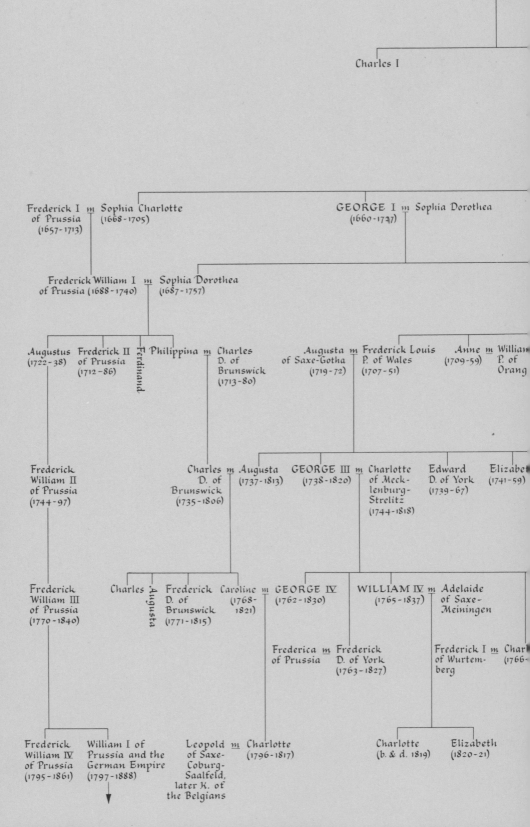